MW01064447

Professional Responsibility In Focus

Focus Casebook Series

PROFESSIONAL RESPONSIBILITY IN FOCUS

John P. Sahl

Joseph G. Miller Professor of Law and Director of
The Joseph G. Miller and William C. Becker Center for Professional Responsibility
University of Akron School of Law

R. Michael Cassidy

Professor of Law and Faculty Director, Rappaport Center for Law and Public Policy
Boston College Law School

Benjamin P. Cooper

Senior Associate Dean and Associate Professor of Law
Frank Montague, Jr. Professor of Legal Studies and Professionalism
University of Mississippi School of Law

Margaret C. Tarkington

Professor of Law
Indiana University Robert H. McKinney School of Law

Published by Wolters Kluwer in New York.

Wolters Kluwer Legal & Regulatory U.S. serves customers worldwide with CCH, Aspen Publishers, and Kluwer Law International products. (www.WKLegaledu.com)

To contact Customer Service, e-mail customer.service@wolterskluwer.com, call 1-800-234-1660, fax 1-800-901-9075, or mail correspondence to:

Wolters Kluwer
Attn: Order Department
PO Box 990
Frederick, MD 21705

Printed in the United States of America.

2 3 4 5 6 7 8 9 0

ISBN 978-1-4548-7758-5

Library of Congress Cataloging-in-Publication Data

Names: Sahl, John P., author.
Title: Professional responsibility in focus / John P. Sahl, Joseph G. Miller Professor of Law and Director of The Joseph G. Miller and William C. Becker Center for Professional Responsibility, University of Akron School of Law, R. Michael Cassidy, Professor of Law and Faculty Director, Rappaport Center for Law and Public Policy, Boston College Law School, Benjamin P. Cooper, Senior Associate Dean and Associate Professor of Law, Frank Montague, Jr. Professor of Legal Studies and Professionalism, University of Mississippi School of Law, Margaret C. Tarkington, Professor of Law, Indiana University Robert H. McKinney School of Law.
Description: New York: Wolters Kluwer, 2017. | Series: Focus casebook series
Identifiers: LCCN 2017034087 | ISBN 9781454877585
Subjects: LCSH: Legal ethics — United States. | Legal ethics — United States — Cases. | LCGFT: Casebooks.
Classification: LCC KF306.P77 2017 | DDC 174/.30973 — dc23
LC record available at https://lccn.loc.gov/2017034087

About Wolters Kluwer Legal & Regulatory U.S.

Wolters Kluwer Legal & Regulatory U.S. delivers expert content and solutions in the areas of law, corporate compliance, health compliance, reimbursement, and legal education. Its practical solutions help customers successfully navigate the demands of a changing environment to drive their daily activities, enhance decision quality and inspire confident outcomes.

Serving customers worldwide, its legal and regulatory solutions portfolio includes products under the Aspen Publishers, CCH Incorporated, Kluwer Law International, ftwilliam.com and MediRegs names. They are regarded as exceptional and trusted resources for general legal and practice-specific knowledge, compliance and risk management, dynamic workflow solutions, and expert commentary.

To Joann, and our two children, Mandakini and Anish, for their constant love, patience and support while I was "busy with the book."—JS

I dedicate this book to my family, with deep gratitude for their love and support. You bring joy and meaning to all of my pursuits.—MC

To Michelle, Noah, Nathaniel, and Adam: Thank you for loving and supporting me on my professional path. I wouldn't be here without you.—BC

I would like to dedicate this book to my son Gabriel Isaac Tarkington.—MT

Summary of Contents

Table of Contents

Chapter 6: Conflicts of Interest 301

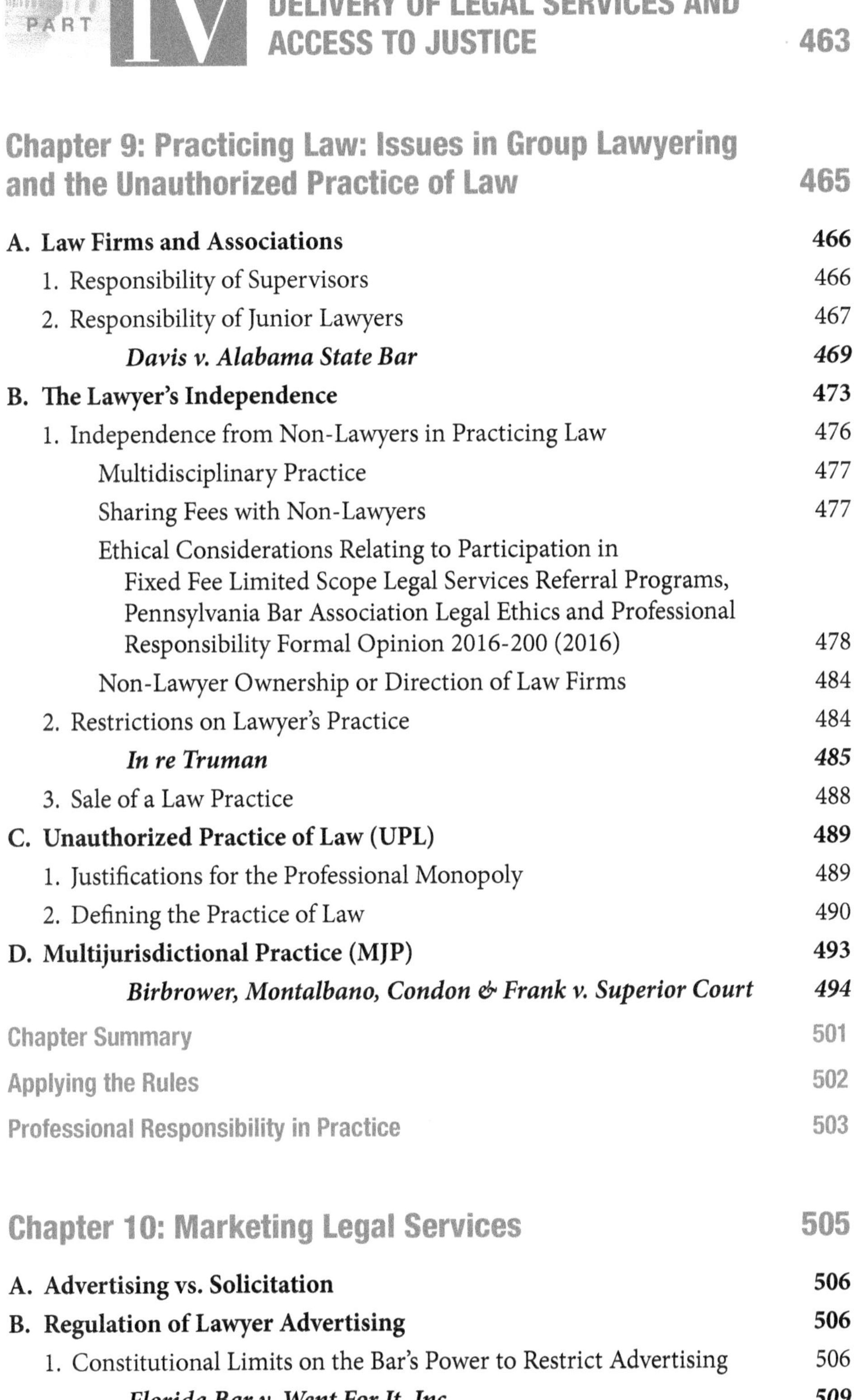

PART IV DELIVERY OF LEGAL SERVICES AND ACCESS TO JUSTICE 463

The Focus Casebook Series

Help students reach their full potential with the fresh approach of the **Focus Casebook Series**. Instead of using the "hide the ball" approach, selected cases illustrate key developments in the law and show how courts develop and apply doctrine. The approachable manner of this series provides a comfortable experiential environment that is instrumental to student success.

Students perform best when applying concepts to real-world scenarios. With assessment features, such as Real Life Applications and Applying the Concepts, the **Focus Casebook Series** offers many opportunities for students to apply their knowledge.

Focus Casebook Features Include:

Case Previews and Post-Case Follow-Ups — To succeed, law students must know how to deconstruct and analyze cases. Case Previews highlight the legal concepts in a case before the student reads it. Post-Case Follow-Ups summarize the important points.

Case Preview

Brady v. Maryland

The petitioner in this case, Brady, and his companion, Boblit, were separately convicted of first degree murder and sentenced to death. At his trial, Brady did not deny playing a role in the murder but, seeking to avoid the death penalty, testified that Boblit did the actual killing. While on death row, Brady moved for a new trial after discovering statements made by Boblit — in which Boblit admitted to doing the actual killing — that had previously been withheld by the prosecutor.

As you read the *Brady* decision, ask yourself:

1. Is the withholding of e
sentation of perjured t

Attorney Francis Belge, the attorney who was the subject of this formal opinion, was also criminally charged under two sections of the New York Public Health statute making it a misdemeanor to fail to report the death of someone who died without medical assistance. Although Belge was subsequently exonerated by the trial judge in that criminal matter, the public outcry over the choices he made in the Dead Bodies case undercut his standing in the small-town community and ultimately his law practice. His life was ruined in many ways for "stepping up" to take on a difficult case, and then making a very courageous and unpopular decision within the context of that case.

Defendant Garrow in the Dead Bodies case was actually represented by two attorneys — Francis Belge and Frank Armani. Armani was not present when Belge observed and photographed one of the bodies, so he escaped indictment. In interviews after the Garrow prosecution, both attorneys explained that one of their motivations for checking to see if the bodies were located where the client said they would be was that they thought their client had mental health issues and might be fabricating the other crimes. Is this the sort of "preparation" contemplated by Rule 1.1?

The Focus Casebook Series

Real Life Applications — Every case in a chapter is followed by Real Life Applications, which present a series of questions based on a scenario similar to the facts in the case. Real Life Applications challenge students to apply what they have learned in order to prepare them for real-world practice. Use Real Life Applications to spark class discussions or provide them as individual short-answer assignments.

Republican Party of Minnesota v. White: Real Life Applications

1. The *White* majority did not address the constitutionality of the "pledges and promises" clause of the Minnesota rules (which is substantially similar to Rule 4.1 of the current Model Code). What are the arguments for and against the constitutionality of this provision?
2. Willie Singletary was a candidate for traffic court judge in Philadelphia. While campaigning for the primary election, he spoke to a gathering of a motorcycle club. During the meeting, he asked attendees to donate to his campaign and stated, "You're going to need me in traffic court, am I right about that? . . . Now you all want me to get there, you're all going to want my hook-up, right?" Is Judge Singletary subject to discipline?
3. As noted earlier, Model Rule 4.1 prohibits judges from "act[ing] as a leader in, or hold[ing] an office in, a political organization," "mak[ing] speeches on behalf of a political organization," "mak[ing] a contribution to a political organization or a candidate," and "publicly endors[ing] . . . a candidate for any public office."

Applying the Concepts/Rules and Professional Responsibility in Practice
These end-of-chapter exercises encourage students to synthesize the chapter material and apply relevant legal doctrine and code to real-world scenarios. Students can use these exercises for self-assessment or the professor can use them to promote class interaction.

Applying the Rules

1. In its opinion above, the California Bar determined that examples 2, 3, and 4 constitute advertising within the meaning of the rules of professional conduct. Do those statements violate the Model Rules?
2. Your law firm has been hired to represent two personal injury lawyers.
   a. The first created a television commercial in which he called himself "The Hammer
   b. The seco
   ing as "T

Professional Responsibility in Practice

1. Eli comes to you asking you to represent him in slip and fall case against his neighbor, Cyrus, for an incident that occurred ten months ago. You meet with him for a half hour, but decide you do not want to take his case. Draft an appropriate declination letter to Eli.
2. Same facts as above, only this time you decide to take Eli's case and want to charge a one-third contingency fee. Draft a contingency fee agreement that complies with Rule 1.5.
3. Research whether an in-house attorney has a cause of action for wrongful discharge when fired for complying with mandatory rules of professional conduct in the state where you plan to practice or are attending law school.
4. Select a state that has decided to legalize marijuana. Research the ethics opinions in that state to see how that state approaches the problem of compliance

Preface

Ensure student success with the Focus Casebook Series.

THE FOCUS APPROACH

In a law office, when a new associate attorney is being asked to assist a supervising attorney with a legal matter in which the associate has no prior experience, it is common for the supervising attorney to provide the associate with a recently closed case file involving the same legal issues so that the associate can see and learn from the closed file to assist more effectively with the new matter. This experiential approach is at the heart of the ***Focus Casebook Series***.

Additional hands-on features, such as Real Life Applications, Applying the Rules, and Professional Responsibility in Practice provide more opportunities for critical analysis and application of concepts covered in the chapters. Professors can assign problem-solving questions as well as exercises on drafting documents and preparing appropriate filings.

CONTENT SNAPSHOT

Professional Responsibility in Focus offers a comprehensive, practice-oriented approach to the legal and ethical rules governing lawyers and judges. By providing real world scenarios throughout the text, this casebook gives students numerous opportunities to apply what they learn and solidify their understanding of important concepts. Clear explanatory text, case previews, and case follow-ups further clarify the rules and aid in student understanding. The casebook begins with an introduction to the legal profession, and follows with concise, well-written chapters on the attorney-client relationship, covering competence, confidentiality, and conflicts of interest; discussion of the lawyer as advocate; special issues in criminal practice; coverage of delivery of legal services and access to justice, and a final chapter on judicial ethics. The first chapter on moral responsibility of lawyers helps situate and contextualize the rule-centric discussion of legal ethics that follows, by inviting students to appreciate the various roles that lawyers play in the legal system, their responsibilities to multiple stakeholders, and competing values at play in professional regulation.

RESOURCES

Casebook: The casebook is structured around text, cases, and application exercises. The *Key Concepts* section at the beginning of each chapter alerts students to fundamental principles and provides a helpful benchmark for understanding the chapter. Highlighted cases are introduced with a *Case Preview*, which sets up the issue and identifies key questions. *Post-Case Follow-Ups* expand on the holding in the case.

Real Life Applications present opportunities to challenge students to apply concepts covered in the case to realistic hypothetical cases.

There are several features at the end of each chapter to help students better understand the material. The *Applying the Rules* feature offers opportunities for students to apply the Ethical Rules and better prepare them to actually handle cases. The *Summary Section* underscores and expands upon some of the key concepts noted in the beginning—nicely bringing the chapter to a full circle. The *Professional Responsibility in Practice* feature provides further hypotheticals for critical analysis and application of concepts covered in the chapter, often asking students to research their jurisdiction's law and to discuss points related to the delivery of legal services. This unique feature allows students to be more practice ready in the jurisdiction they intend to practice.

Other resources to enrich your class include: Practice Skills Exercises, or supplementary material such as *Examples & Explanations for Professional Responsibility, Fifth Edition* by W. Bradley Wendel. Ask your Wolters Kluwer sales representative or go to WKLegaledu.com to learn more about building the product package that's right for you.

Acknowledgments

My special thanks to my research assistants, Dakota Perez, Tristan Serri, Patricia Ochman, and Cynthia Menta, for their valuable help with my chapters. Likewise, Susan Altmeyer and Kyle Passmore of the University of Akron Law Library provided significant research and support. Yale Law School Law Librarian Teresa Miguel-Stearns and her colleagues, Michael VanderHeijden and Jordan Jefferson, provided noteworthy assistance; and I am indebted to Art Garwin, the former Director of the ABA Center for Professional Responsibility, for his valuable suggestions and guidance. JS

I am enormously grateful for the advice and guidance of Mary Ann Neary of the Boston College Law Library, and for the research and editing assistance of Mitchell Perne (BC Law '18) and Matthew Sawyer (BC Law '19). MC

Thank you to Abigail Abide (University of Mississippi School of Law '17) for outstanding research assistance. I am also grateful to the Legal Profession students I have taught over my 10 years as a professor — your insightful comments and class participation helped shape this book. BC

A special thanks to my father, Jim Robertson, for reviewing and making insightful comments on the drafts of my chapters, and also thanks to my children, Joseph, Eli, Maisy, Cy, and Hal, for their patience and support during my work on this book. MT

We would like to thank the following for permission to reprint the identified material:

The American Bar Association (ABA) for:

ABA Model Rules of Professional Conduct and related materials (e.g., comments, articles)

I Did Not Sleep with that Vice President, Professional Lawyer, ©2004 by the American Bar Association.

William Bergmann, Julianne M. Hartzell, Elizabeth Ann Morgan, and Preston K. Ratliff for the *Sample Joint Defense and Common Interest Agreement*, from Best Practices in Multi-Defendant Litigation, 2010 IPO [Intellectual Property Owners Association] Annual Meeting, reprinted by permission.

Martin Cole, *The Hardiest Perennials*, 64 Bench and Bar of Minnesota 12 (2007).

District of Columbia Bar Association Legal Ethics Committee, for excerpts of Formal Opinion 79 (1979), reprinted by permission.

Food Fight Films, LLC.

Georgetown Journal of Legal Ethics, for excerpts from Fred Zacharias, *Structuring the Ethics of Trial Advocacy*, 44 Vand. L. Rev. 45 (1991), reprinted by permission.

Neil Hamilton, *Professionalism Clearly Defined*, 18 The Professional Lawyer 4 (2007).

Alexander Meiklejohn, excerpt from pp 73-77 from *Free Speech and Its Relation to Self-Government*. Copyright © 1948 by Harper & Brothers, renewed © 1976 by Helen E. Meiklejohn. Reprinted by permission of HarperCollins Publishers.

Alexander M. Meiklejohn and D. Stuart Meiklejohn, for the photo of Alexander Meiklejohn.

New York Times, for "Doubting Case, A Prosecutor Helped the Defense" (June 23, 2008), reprinted by permission.

Ohio State Bar Associations, Informal Advisory Opinion 2013-03.

Pennsylvania Bar Association Legal Ethics and Professional Responsibility Committee, Formal Opinion 2016-200.

Lucian T. Pera and the ABA for the *Joint Representation Checklist* from *The Ethics of Joint Representation*, at 40 Litig. 1 (Fall 2013); ABA © 2013, reprinted by permission.

The State Bar of California's Committee on Professional Responsibility and Conduct, Formal Opinion No. 2012-186 © 2017 The State Bar of California. All rights reserved. Reprinted with permission. No part of this work may be reproduced, stored in a retrieval system, or transmitted in any medium without prior written permission of The State Bar of California. The following is the complete text of The State Bar of California's Committee on Professional Responsibility and Conduct, Formal Opinion No. 2012-186. The full text is also available on the State Bar's website at: *http://ethics.calbar.ca.gov/Ethics/Opinions.aspx.*

Utah Bar Journal — Discipline Corner, April 27, 2007.

Vanderbilt Law Review, for excerpts from John Mitchell, *Reasonable Doubts are Where You Find Them: A Response to Professor Subin's Position on the Criminal Lawyer's "Different Mission," 1 Geo. J. Legal Ethics* 339 (1987), reprinted by permission.

W. Bradley Wendel and the Nebraska Law Review, for an excerpt of *Conflicts of Interest Under the Revised Model Rules*, 81 Neb. Law Rev. 1363 (2003), reprinted by permission.

Staci Zaretsky, The Struggle: Will Alcoholism Treatment Affect Your Character and Fitness Review?, Above the Law, August 22, 2016.

Professional Responsibility In Focus

PART I

Introduction to the Legal Profession

1

The Role and Responsibility of Lawyers

Lawyers play an important role in the United States justice system. It is through lawyers that individuals are able to gain access to government power in the protection of their lives, liberty, and property. This primary, and constitutional, role of lawyers in our justice system carries with it significant responsibilities. The lawyer has a responsibility to her client to protect life, liberty, and property. The lawyer has a responsibility to the integrity of the justice system, constitutional guarantees, and the rule of law. The lawyer has a responsibility to those affected by her actions. And the lawyer has a responsibility to herself — to her own integrity and moral identity.

A. THE ROLE OF THE LAWYER IN THE SYSTEM OF JUSTICE

Lawyers play a significant role in the administration of justice in the United States. A license to practice law renders the lawyer an instrument of government power — the lawyer's actions directly affect the extent of government power to be imposed in favor of or against people and their property. Despite this significant power over people's lives, lawyers are largely self-regulated with substantial autonomy from outside control. Yet self-regulation necessitates the undertaking of correlative duties to protect public goods, particularly justice and due process.

Key Concepts

- The role of the lawyer in the United States justice system
- The lawyer's social contract with the public
- Lawyer and client moral responsibility
- Moral dialogue and ascertaining client purposes
- Understanding and cultivating professionalism
- The differing responsibilities of lawyers as litigators, advisors, and transactional planners

1. Guardians of Due Process

Unlike other professions, the lawyer's work is directly tied to individual access to and protection from government power. Lawyers alone provide individuals meaningful access to an entire branch of government — the judiciary, which itself is composed almost entirely of lawyers. In addition, lawyers constitute a major component of the executive branch through the prosecutorial function. For those facing criminal charges, defense lawyers are constitutionally guaranteed to help protect the life, liberty, and property of the accused from government deprivation and overreaching.

Lawyers also provide meaningful access to law itself. Through litigation and other processes, lawyers enable people to enforce their rights against government and societal actors. Lawyers correlatively enable individuals, governments, and corporate or associative actors to mitigate and avoid purported liability. Notably, in transactional and non-litigation settings, lawyers assist people in creating legally binding contracts, business associations and structures, wills, trusts, and a manifold of other agreements and arrangements. If executed correctly, these agreements will have the force of law — meaning that the agreement will be backed by the full weight of government power should a breaching party be brought to court to enforce it. This access to the force of law is made available to individuals primarily through legal counsel. Even in the advice context, lawyers assist individuals in understanding what the law requires. This advice allows individuals to structure their conduct to avoid or invoke government power in the protection of life, liberty, and property.

Thus, in our justice system, lawyers should recognize their principal professional responsibility as guardians of due process.[1] It is through lawyers' actions that individuals are able to avoid or invoke government power to protect their lives, liberty, and property. This is true in civil, criminal, transactional, and advice contexts. Correspondingly, lawyers are also the primary mechanism through which law is enforced against individuals both civilly and criminally, thus depriving people of life, liberty, and/or property. Through lawyers' actions people may be sentenced to death or imprisonment; may be convicted of a crime and with that conviction face a host of legal and social consequences; may lose custody of their children; may have their property seized and sold, their wages garnished, their homes foreclosed on, or their savings and assets depleted — to name a few examples. Lawyers are instruments of state power. And attorneys who abuse their powers, act unethically, and work to deprive people unjustly of life, liberty, and property become instruments of state oppression.

A potent example is found in prosecutors who hide exculpatory evidence, resulting in the conviction of an innocent person. In Connick v. Thompson, 563 U.S. 51 (2011), several prosecutors colluded in hiding multiple pieces of exculpatory evidence that proved the accused defendant was innocent. Lab testing revealed that the perpetrator's blood was type B, yet Thompson, who was charged with the

---

1. *See* Geoffrey C. Hazard, Jr., *The Future of Legal Ethics*, 100 Yale L.J. 1239, 1246 (1991) ("The legal profession's basic narrative is a defense of due process. The lawyer's work consists of resistance to government intervention in the lives, liberty, or property of private parties.").

crime, had type O blood. Prosecutors failed to disclose the existence of the evidence or the lab results to the defense. Thompson was imprisoned for crimes he did not commit for 18 years, 14 of them on death row. His execution was stayed when an "eleventh-hour" effort by a private investigator uncovered a microfiche copy of the lab report identifying the perpetrator's blood type.[2] These prosecutors were instruments of state oppression, using their license to practice law to deprive Thompson of his liberty and Thompson's children (aged 4 and 6 at the time of his arrest) of being raised by their father.[3] No one can restore the 18 years of lost time and lost experiences to Thompson or his family.

As the instrument through which law is accessed and enforced, lawyers owe special duties to the integrity of the system of justice, the rule of law, and the rights and obligations of individuals. In the American adversary system, it is important that lawyers are committed to "a core of basic rights that recognize and protect the dignity of the individual in a free society."[4] As Monroe Freedman and Abbe Smith have noted, these rights include "personal autonomy, the effective assistance of counsel, equal protection of the laws, trial by jury, the rights to call and to confront witnesses, the right against involuntary self-incrimination, the right to require the government to prove guilt beyond a reasonable doubt, [] the right to petition the government for redress of grievances . . . and other rights [that] are also included in the broad and fundamental concept that no person may be deprived of life, liberty, or property without due process of law."[5] Lawyers thus exhibit an amplified devotion to professional duties associated with the protection of these rights, including confidentiality, loyalty, competence, communication, and complete knowledge.

Lawyers also understand the importance to any system of justice of creating and maintaining procedures that allow individuals to vindicate their rights. Lawyers thus often possess a strong commitment to adherence to procedures, especially those procedures that are created specifically to preserve a client's rights, such as the rights to call and confront witnesses. Nevertheless, complicated procedural requirements can also frustrate access to justice, resulting in a default of client rights and creating a trap for the unwary or the unrepresented.

By protecting the rights of their clients, lawyers in theory protect the overall adversary system and thus the rights of society as a whole. Behind the recognition of every major constitutional right is a lawyer whose ingenuity and perseverance on behalf of a specific client made it possible for the court to formally recognize the right. Indeed, the Supreme Court has indicated that the right to a lawyer is perhaps the most important right because it is essential to the protection of every other right.[6] However, the theory that society is protected by partisan lawyering is only accurate to the extent that both sides to a controversy have access to competent and ethical legal counsel. There are many people in the United States who have little or no access to legal counsel, and generally the divide between those with access and those without is attributable to the relative wealth or poverty of the

---

2. Connick v. Thompson, 563 U.S. 51, 87 (2011) (Ginsburg, J., dissenting).
3. *See* John Thompson, *The Prosecution Rests, But I Can't*, N.Y. Times, Apr. 9, 2011, Op-Ed.
4. Monroe H. Freedman & Abbe Smith, Understanding Lawyers' Ethics 15 (4th ed. 2010).
5. *Id.* at 15-16.
6. *Id.* at 16 (quoting United States v. Cronic, 466 U.S. 648, 654 (1984)).

individuals. This wealth-based allocation of access to legal counsel—and of one's ability thereby to invoke or avoid government power—undermines the basic fairness that should exist in a system of justice.

2. Self-Regulation and the Protection of Our Public Good

The legal profession is generally considered a self-regulated profession. The notion that attorneys are self-regulated is overstated: lawyers are indeed subject to external regulation, including any regulations imposed by federal and state legislatures or administrative agencies, or applicable to attorneys through constitutional law or international treaties. Indeed, the United States Supreme Court has made clear that traditional self-regulation is not a shield from valid external regulation—lawyers can be and are regulated by Congress and other external entities.[7]

Nevertheless, in large part, lawyers' rules of professional conduct can be viewed as a form of self-regulation. Generally, the legal profession in each state is governed by that state's judiciary—with the state's supreme court acting as the ultimate authority for professional governance. Judiciaries are primarily made up of attorneys, so regulation of lawyers by the judiciary can be considered a form of self-regulation. State supreme courts in turn delegate professional governance duties to the state bar and/or other state agencies—although retaining their status as the final authority governing the profession. Further, nearly all states, through their supreme courts and their state bar designees, have adopted some form of the Model Rules of Professional Conduct as the primary codified law governing lawyers in that jurisdiction. The **Model Rules of Professional Conduct** (Model Rules) are drafted by the American Bar Association (ABA), which is also composed of lawyers. Thus, the rules governing the profession are proposed by lawyers and adopted and enforced by lawyers (state supreme courts, state bars, and their designees)—which is why lawyers can be viewed as a self-governing profession.

But self-regulation comes with some responsibilities. Like other traditional self-regulating professions, lawyers have a social contract with the public. Neil Hamilton has explained that "[t]he public grants a profession autonomy to regulate itself through peer review, expecting the profession's members to control entry into and continued membership in the profession, to set standards for how individual professionals perform their work so that it serves the public good in the area of the profession's responsibility, and to foster the core values and ideals of the profession."[8]

As Hamilton explains, the public good committed to the care of the legal profession is justice.[9] If the legal profession safeguards that public good and polices its members, then the public will continue to allow the legal profession to largely govern itself, as outlined above. If, however, the legal profession fails to demonstrate its commitment to its public good or fails to punish erring members, then

7. Milavetz, Gallop & Milavetz v. United States, 559 U.S. 229, 237 (2010).
8. Neil Hamilton, *Professionalism Clearly Defined*, 18 Prof. Law. 1, 4-5 (2008).
9. *Id.* at 8.

the public can revoke the social contract, which it does by enacting legislation that regulates lawyers externally. For example, in the fallout of the Enron and Worldcom corporate scandals, it became clear that lawyers played a major role in the lawbreaking and cover-up of massive fraud that adversely affected the entire United States economy. Consequently, Congress enacted the Sarbanes-Oxley Act, which required attorneys to "report up" regarding potential violations of the securities laws and directed the SEC to create "minimum standards of professional conduct for attorneys appearing and practicing" before the SEC.[10] Congress and the SEC appropriated the task of professional governance of lawyers when it became clear that lawyers were not doing it themselves. When lawyers fail to fulfill their duty to safeguard justice—when they act unethically and undermine public confidence that they can be trusted to regulate themselves—legislatures and other governmental entities can and will supplant the profession's traditional self-regulation.

So how does the legal profession fulfill its public duty to safeguard justice? Hamilton explains that in return for the ability to self-regulate, "each member of the profession and the profession as a whole agree to meet certain correlative duties to the public." Lawyers are obliged to maintain "high standards of minimum competence and ethical conduct, to serve [justice,] the public purpose of the profession, and to discipline those who fail to meet these standards."[11] As will be covered in Chapter 4, incompetent attorneys impair and even nullify their clients' legal rights. It is imperative that the legal profession in performing self-government insist on minimum levels of competence and ethical conduct so that clients and third parties are not unjustly deprived of their life, liberty, and property through lawyers acting as agents of state power. Protecting the public good of justice is precisely compatible with lawyers acting as guardians of due process.

Oliver Wendell Holmes
Library of Congress, Prints & Photographs Division, [reproduction numberLC-DIG-npcc-26413]

B. LAW AND MORAL RESPONSIBILITY

In the *Path of the Law*, Oliver Wendell Holmes forged the path of the legal realists with an audacious analytical device for understanding law. This device, often referred to as the "bad man perspective," boldly proposed the separation of law from morality. Holmes's hypothetical client, "the bad man," does not care at all about doing what is morally good—yet he still cares about avoiding government-enforced consequences for breaking laws. Holmes invites lawyers to take the view of this hypothetical "bad man." Under Holmes's view, the practice of law is concerned with predicting the actual monetary and

10. 15 U.S.C. §7245 (2002).
11. Hamilton, *supra* note 8, at 5.

physical consequences for breaking the law, and, correspondingly, the practice of law is not concerned with the moral implications of those laws or with the morality of the client's or the lawyer's actions.

Oliver Wendell Holmes, The Path of the Law

10 Harv. L. Rev. 457 (1897)

When we study law we are not studying a mystery but a well known profession. We are studying what we shall want in order to appear before judges, or to advise people in such a way as to keep them out of court. The reason why it is a profession, why people will pay lawyers to argue for them or to advise them, is that in societies like ours the command of the public force is intrusted [sic] to the judges in certain cases, and the whole power of the state will be put forth, if necessary, to carry out their judgments and decrees. People want to know under what circumstances and how far they will run the risk of coming against what is so much stronger than themselves, and hence it becomes a business to find out when this danger is to be feared. The object of our study, then, is prediction, the prediction of the incidence of the public force through the instrumentality of the courts.

. . .

The primary rights and duties with which jurisprudence busies itself again are nothing but prophecies. One of the many evil effects of the confusion between legal and moral ideas, about which I shall have something to say in a moment, is that theory is apt to get the cart before the horse, and to consider the right or the duty as something existing apart from and independent of the consequences of its breach, to which certain sanctions are added afterward. But, as I shall try to show, a legal duty so called is nothing but a prediction that if a man does or omits certain things he will be made to suffer in this or that way by judgment of the court;—and so of a legal right.

. . .

I take it for granted that no hearer of mine will misinterpret what I have to say as the language of cynicism. The law is the witness and external deposit of our moral life. Its history is the history of the moral development of the race. The practice of it, in spite of popular jests, tends to make good citizens and good men. When I emphasize the difference between law and morals I do so with reference to a single end, that of learning and understanding the law. For that purpose you must definitely master its specific marks, and it is for that that I ask you for the moment to imagine yourselves indifferent to other and greater things.

. . . If you want to know the law and nothing else, you must look at it as a bad man, who cares only for the material consequences which such knowledge enables him to predict, not as a good one, who finds his reasons for conduct, whether inside the law or outside of it, in the vaguer sanctions of conscience. The theoretical importance of the distinction is no less, if you would reason on your subject aright. The law is full of phraseology drawn from morals, and by the mere force of language continually invites us to pass from one domain to the other without perceiving it, as we are

sure to do unless we have the boundary constantly before our minds. The law talks about rights, and duties, and malice, and intent, and negligence, and so forth, and nothing is easier, or, I may say, more common in legal reasoning, than to take these words in their moral sense, at some stage of the argument, and so to drop into fallacy.

. . .

Take the fundamental question, What constitutes the law? You will find some text writers telling you that it is something different from what is decided by the courts of Massachusetts or England, that it is a system of reason, that it is a deduction from principles of ethics or admitted axioms or what not, which may or may not coincide with the decisions. But if we take the view of our friend the bad man we shall find that he does not care two straws for the axioms or deductions, but that he does want to know what the Massachusetts or English courts are likely to do in fact. I am much of his mind. The prophecies of what the courts will do in fact, and nothing more pretentious, are what I mean by the law.

Take again a notion which as popularly understood is the widest conception which the law contains;—the notion of legal duty, to which already I have referred. We fill the word with all the content which we draw from morals. But what does it mean to a bad man? Mainly, and in the first place, a prophecy that if he does certain things he will be subjected to disagreeable consequences by way of imprisonment or compulsory payment of money. . . . You see how the vague circumference of the notion of duty shrinks and at the same time grows more precise when we wash it with cynical acid and expel everything except the object of our study, the operations of the law.

. . .

I hope that my illustrations have shown the danger, both to speculation and to practice, of confounding morality with law, and the trap which legal language lays for us on that side of our way. For my own part, I often doubt whether it would not be a gain if every word of moral significance could be banished from the law altogether, and other words adopted which should convey legal ideas uncolored by anything outside the law. We should lose the fossil records of a good deal of history and the majesty got from ethical associations, but by ridding ourselves of an unnecessary confusion we should gain very much in the clearness of our thought.

1. Impact and Critique of the Bad Man Perspective

Holmes's view in fact redefined the path of the law. His article became one of the defining statements of both legal realism and positivism. Even today, although lawyers may not recognize that their legal perspectives trace back to Holmes, the fact is that much of the teaching and practice of law adopts Holmes's view. Students and lawyers are trained and expected to decipher what the operation of law is or will be upon their clients and to lessen any negative impacts—without much, or perhaps any, attention to the morality of the actions of the client and the effect of those actions on others. Even the Model Rules are primarily stated in ways that avoid wording containing moral implications; instead, the rules are written as purely law with defined consequences. Thus, the Rules of Professional Conduct themselves are written to be disassociated from morality—precisely what Holmes proposed and desired in order to grasp his, and the bad man's, "clear" picture of the law.

William Simon critiqued the bad man perspective, noting that many lawyers adopt the perspective by imputing certain basic ends—the ends of the hypothetical bad man—to their clients at the outset of a representation. In other words, lawyers work from the assumption that their clients are Holmes's bad man; they impute to their clients the selfish ends of the bad man and then work to achieve those ends. "The specific ends most often imputed are the maximization of freedom of movement and the accumulation of wealth." Simon says: "Of course, in practice lawyers often do not even go through the motion of presenting critical questions to the client as occasions for choice. They decide the questions unilaterally in terms of the imputed ends of selfishness."[12] Roger Cramton similarly explains: "Lawyers have a terrible habit of fitting client objectives into a simplified framework—an assumed world in which clients are governed only by selfish concerns—and then deciding matters for them as if the clients were moral ciphers."[13] Further, Simon argues that many clients, particularly those unfamiliar with the legal system, acquiesce in this redefinition of themselves:

> Confronted with the need to act in this strange situation, the client must make sense of it as best he can. The lawyer puts himself forth quite plausibly as the client's best hope of mastering his predicament. If he is to avoid being overwhelmed by chaos, he must acquiesce in his lawyer's definition of the situation. He must think in a manner which gives coherence of the advice he is giving. He may begin to do this quite unconsciously. If he is at all aware of the change, he is likely to see it as a defensive posture forced on him by the hostile intentions of opposing parties . . . . His only strategy of survival requires that he see himself as the lawyers and the officials see him, as an abstraction, a hypothetical person with only a few crude, discrete ends. He must assume that his subtler ends, his long-range plans, and his social relationships are irrelevant to the situation at hand. . . .
>
> The role of the bad man, conceived [by Holmes] as an analytical device for the lawyer becomes, under pressure of circumstances, a psychological reality for the client.[14]

Importantly, and as Simon reiterates, the "vague, crudely drawn psychological assumption" of the bad man "cannot begin to do justice to the specific complexity" of actual clients and their actual ends. Unlike "hypothetical" people, actual clients do not have "just a few, discrete ends, but rather many ends which are interrelated in a complex fashion . . . and are set in a social context in which the individual's fulfillment depends on his relations with others."[15]

It is not surprising that lawyers often see their clients in terms of the Holmesian bad man. Their bread-and-butter training in law school teaches them to view the law through the lens of the bad man—to see law sanitized of morality and often of

---

12. William H. Simon, *The Ideology of Advocacy: Procedural Justice and Professional Ethics*, 1978 Wis. L. Rev. 29, 56-57.
13. Roger C. Cramton, Spaulding v. Zimmerman *Revisited: Confidentiality and Its Exceptions*, *in* Legal Ethics: Law Stories 182 (Deborah L. Rhode & David J. Luban eds., 2006).
14. Simon, *supra* note 12, at 55-56.
15. *Id.* at 54-55.

societal ends. Law students are taught to think of law through hypothetical situations and borderline cases where making creative arguments to better a client's individual position is prized and rewarded. As Eli Wald and Russell Pearce have lamented regarding legal education, "the law itself is taught as a morally-free zone, a body of abstract principles subject to manipulation, in which the public interest is nothing more than an aggregate of clients' private interests, and in which a lawyer's role is to pursue aggressively her client's autonomous self-interest."[16] Moreover, imputing clear-cut ends is easier than taking the time and effort to know one's individually complex client. As Roger Cramton has explained, "[i]mputing selfish goal[s] simplifies the lawyer's work by allowing her to shirk the hard work of client counseling" because counseling requires that a lawyer "tak[e] the client seriously as a person, communicating with and advising the real client, not a client stereotype, and engaging in a moral dialogue in which lawyer and client can learn from each other."[17]

Indeed, Wald and Pearce argue that the Holmesian bad man ideal has carried over into the formation of professional identity because students are taught in law school to adopt an "autonomous self-interest professional ideolog[y]."[18] **Autonomous self-interest** "views clients as individualistic and atomistic entities whose goal is to pursue and maximize their self-interest aggressively without regard to others." In contrast, Wald and Pearce promote focusing student and lawyer professional ideology on "**relational self-interest**." They explain: "Relationally self-interested professionalism understands clients as attempting to pursue and maximize their self-interest in relation to others."[19] Both the attorney and the client have self-interests that are dependent upon their relationships with others, the long-term stability of such relationships, and the success of the overall economy and society in which they live. In fact, no one is solely autonomously self-interested. Everyone has relational self-interests precisely because we are human beings; and humans are social creatures,[20] whose happiness and success are often dependent upon the happiness and success of others. Thus, even the most selfish and materialistic individuals will still care about certain relationships with others, both personal and business, and about a stable economy and government because such are essential to their own personal success. Neither attorneys nor clients have to be altruistic, selfless people to recognize that considering their own relational self-interests is wise and likely to lead to better results for all affected in a circumstance warranting legal advice or action.

Wald and Pearce urge students and lawyers to help clients perceive their relational self-interests in dealing with a legal or ethical problem. Unfortunately, as Wald and Pearce thoroughly reveal, law students are generally taught "to understand their clients as autonomously self-interested, and to pursue their clients' autonomous self-interest *at the expense* of their clients' relational self-interest in considering the interests of opposing parties, third parties, the public good, and the spirit of the law."[21] Good lawyers when advising clients — whether in litigation or

16. Eli Wald & Russell G. Pearce, *Making Lawyers Good*, 9 U. St. Thomas L.J. 403, 415 (2011).
17. Cramton, *supra* note 13, at 182, 183.
18. Wald & Pearce, *supra* note 16, at 411.
19. *Id.*
20. Aristotle, Politics ("Man is by nature a social animal.").
21. Wald & Pearce, *supra* note 16, at 415.

transactions — will assist their clients in recognizing and then taking into account the client's relational self-interests. It disserves clients when lawyers fail to consider interests that in the long term are important to the client and to the client's success.

But above and beyond the fact that everyone has relational self-interests that a competent lawyer should take into account, what about the client who simply does not fit into the self-centered Holmesian bad man mold? There are good people in the world. There are people who care deeply about helping others and about the welfare of society or of a specific community. How should a lawyer proceed for such a client? Imputing bad man ends to such a client is unwarranted and may entirely undermine the client's actual goals and desires.

Irrespective of the client, if the lawyer perceives law from the point of view of the Holmesian bad man, is that a desirable or accurate picture of what the law and justice system are, of what they should be, and of the appropriate role of the lawyer in the United States justice system? Alexander Meiklejohn criticized the bad man perspective as distorting the purposes of law and of our justice system. Taking his vantage from constitutional theory, Meiklejohn explored the democratic social contract created by the Constitution whereby "We, the People of the United States" established a government through which we could govern ourselves. Meiklejohn explained that under our system of government, all citizens have the privilege and responsibility of participating in government and all agree to abide by the laws thus created. Our governmental structure has "one basic purpose that the citizens of this nation shall make and shall obey their own laws, shall be at once their own subjects and their own masters."[22] Meiklejohn contended that Holmes's bad man construction of law — while a useful analytical device — is inconsistent with these basic constitutional purposes and social ends, "upon which the legal procedure depends for life and meaning." Meiklejohn viewed the Constitution and the democratic theory underlying our government as "an expression of human goodness" — an indication of faith in humanity to be able to govern themselves, to do so justly on the whole, and to choose what is best for society.[23] For Meiklejohn, law in the United States should be understood and interpreted through the lens of this democratic theory.

Alexander Meiklejohn
Courtesy of Alexander M. Meiklejohn and D. Stuart Meiklejohn

22. ALEXANDER MEIKLEJOHN, FREE SPEECH AND ITS RELATION TO SELF-GOVERNMENT 15-16 (1948).
23. *Id.* at 74-79.

Alexander Meiklejohn, What of the Good Man?

Free Speech and Its Relation to Self-Government 73-77 (1948)

As a student of philosophy, Mr. Holmes was, of course, deeply interested in the relation between the machinery of the law and the moral purpose of justice. His reflections upon that relation, though partial, were keen and incisive. With the zest of a good craftsman, he was, in legal theory, a mechanist. The activities of legislatures and courts he sees, from this point of view, simply as a play of forces which are in conflict. And he delights in the technical game of the manipulation of those forces. He follows the ups and downs of the contests of the law with lively interest and, at times, it must be said, with ironical glee. Human living is, he tells us, "a roar of bargain and battle." And though, as a dispassionate spectator, he is convinced that there is little, if anything, to be gained by the fighting except the fun of the fighting itself, Mr. Holmes, as a good soldier, plunges gloriously into the conflict.

That Mr. Holmes is a mechanist in legal theory is shown by his fascinating description of "The Path of the Law," in a speech given at the Boston University School of Law in 1897. "If you want to know the law and nothing else," he said, "you must look at it as a bad man, who cares only for the material consequences which such knowledge enables him to predict, not as a good one, who finds his reasons for conduct, whether inside the law or outside of it, in the vaguer sanctions of conscience." And again, "But, as I shall try to show, a legal duty so-called is nothing but a prediction that if a man does or omits certain things he will be made to suffer in this way or that by judgment of the court — and so of a legal right." And still again, "People want to know under what circumstances and how far they will run the risk of coming against what is so much stronger than themselves, and hence it becomes a business to find out when this danger is to be feared. The object of our study, then, is prediction, the prediction of the incidence of the public force through the instrumentality of the courts."

With the exception of the phrase, "the vaguer sanctions of conscience," these statements are impressive, both in their audacity and in their validity. As a technician, Mr. Holmes strips "the business of the law" of all "moral" implications. Legal battles he finds to be fought in terms of the conflict of interests, individual and social. Their results are the victories and defeats of forces and counterforces. And they are, for the technician, nothing else, except, it may be, a source of revenue. This is magnificent, clearheaded legal technology.

But there is a philosophic weakness in this mechanistic theory which can be stated in two different ways. First, being partial, it gives no adequate account of the deeper social ends and ideas upon which the legal procedure depends for life and meaning. These battles of which Mr. Holmes speaks are not fought in a jungle, in a moral vacuum. They are fought in the legislatures and courts which have been established by a self-governing society. They are not mere conflicts of interest. They are conflicts under laws which define a public interest. They are, therefore, fought by agreement as well as by difference — an agreement which is accepted by both sides. That agreement provides judges and juries whose duty it is to determine not merely what is going to happen, but what, under our plan of life, should happen. The fighting goes on under a Constitution in which We, the People, have formulated and made authoritative our deepest convictions concerning the welfare of men and of society. And Mr. Holmes' description of the legal machinery, valid as it is technologically, provided these deeper and wider meanings be given assured control, is utterly invalid if it be taken as an account of the total legal process. On this basis it seems fair to say that, as he interprets the freedom of speech which the Constitution protects, the one thing to which Mr. Holmes, the mechanist, does not pay attention is the Constitution itself. One finds in his arguing little reference to the fact that we of the United States have decided to be a self-governing community. There is not much said about a fundamental agreement among us to which we have pledged "our Lives, our Fortunes, and our sacred Honor." We are for the argument merely a horde of fighting individuals, restrained or supported by laws which "happen" to be on the books.

The same conclusion will be reached if we examine carefully what Mr. Homes says about "the vaguer sanctions of conscience," the demands and principles of morality. As we read his words about law and morality we must recognize that it is not strictly accurate to say that he takes no account whatever of the moral factor. It would be more true to say that he is troubled by it, that he does not know where to place it. As he studies legislation and litigation, morality constantly thrusts itself forward as a disturbing influence which threatens to clog the legal machinery. Mr. Holmes has told us that one cannot understand the law unless one looks at it as a bad man. But meanwhile, he is aware that men are, in some respects, good, even when they are dealing with the law. In the very midst of the conflicting forces of interest Mr. Homes finds "other things" such as "a good man's reason for conduct," revealing themselves and claiming relevance. In his statement of the mechanistic theory he says, ". . . I ask you for the moment to imagine yourselves indifferent to other and greater things." But the account of those other things when Mr. Holmes, in other moments, comes back to them, is vague, unclear, and shifting. As contrasted with the sharp and skillful phrases which describe the battles of the courts, the descriptions of morality are neither sharp nor skillful. The mind of Mr. Holmes deals easily, and even merrily, with the "bad man." But the "good man," as an object of philosophical inquiry, mystifies and confuses him. The bad man is clear—too clear to be true. He wants to know what he can get away with. He wants a prediction of the differing consequences of law-breaking, and of law-observance, so that he may have a ground for choosing between them. He hires a lawyer to tell him. The lawyer does what he is paid to do. And Mr. Holmes delights in beating them both at their own game. But meanwhile, what of the good man? What does he want? What is he trying to find out when, if ever, he goes to his lawyer? To those questions Mr. Holmes has no ready answer. His thought has very great difficulty in piercing through the legal machinery to discover those elements of human fellowship and virtue for the sake of which good men [and women] have established and maintained, against the assaults of bad men and their legal advisers, the laws and the Constitution of the United States. As against the dogma of Mr. Holmes, I would venture to assert the counterdogma that one cannot understand the basic purposes of our Constitution as a judge or a citizen should understand them, unless one sees them as a good man, a man who, in his political activities, is not merely fighting for what, under the law, he can get, but is eagerly and generously serving the common welfare.

2. Communication, Moral Dialogue, and Role Morality

How are attorneys to ascertain their clients' moral ends? Is a particular client Holmes's bad man or Meiklejohn's good man — or a complex mix of various desires, moral experiences, and ends? Robert Vischer has emphasized the importance of engaging in **moral dialogue** with the client to determine the client's actual desires and moral ends. He contends that "lawyers should openly discuss with their clients moral considerations, including their own moral views, that bear on the representation."[24]

Model Rule 2.1 expressly permits (but does not require) a lawyer to refer "not only to law, but to other considerations such as moral, economic, social and political factors, that may be relevant to the client's situation." Comment 2 explains that "it is proper for a lawyer to refer to moral and ethical considerations" precisely because "moral and ethical considerations impinge upon most legal questions and may decisively influence how the law will be applied."

Moral dialogue with the client should not interfere with the autonomy of the client. As will be explored in Chapter 3, Model Rule 1.2 explains that "a lawyer shall abide by a client's decisions concerning the objectives of representation." Thus, the attorney takes on a **role morality** where the lawyer acts as an agent for the client's purposes. Indeed, Rule 1.2(b) emphasizes that the "lawyer's representation of a client . . . does not constitute an endorsement of the client's political, economic, social or moral views or activities." This role morality of the lawyer is important in the system of justice precisely because lawyers are the guardians of due process and it is lawyers who provide individuals with access to government power. Such access to government power "should not be denied to people . . . whose cause is controversial or the subject of popular disapproval."[25] The United States bar has a long and honored tradition of lawyers who represented people despite their disagreement with their clients' causes or actions. At the inception of our country, John Adams agreed to represent the British soldiers involved in the Boston Massacre, thus ensuring that these unpopular clients were afforded a fair process. As Margaret Tarkington has explained:

> Adams the revolutionary aligned himself with British soldiers for legal representation precisely to preserve the legitimacy of the United States' emerging justice system. He did not agree with the British soldiers' actions or beliefs, but he did understand the need for due process, for the fair administration of the law, and for exertion of government power to be based on evidence (which he found wanting in this prosecution) — rather than being based on "[s]uspicions and prejudices," a hallmark of tyrannical legal systems. Attorneys today continue to recognize that the legitimacy of our justice system is not based solely on what process and protection is provided to the clearly innocent, deserving, or popular, but especially to the accused and to the unpopular. Consequently, despite their client's alleged bad acts, attorneys associate with

24. Robert K. Vischer, *Legal Advice as Moral Perspective*, 19 Geo. J. Legal Ethics 225, 272 (2006).
25. Model Rule 1.2 cmt. 5.

> clients to provide legal advice, assistance, and representation to lawfully protect life, liberty, and property—and thereby promote the legitimacy of our justice system.[26]

The comments to Model Rule 6.2 remind lawyers of this responsibility to the integrity of the justice system to accept "a fair share of unpopular matters or indigent or unpopular clients."

Thus, as comment 1 to Model Rule 1.2 expounds, the client has "the ultimate authority to determine the purposes to be served by legal representation." Nevertheless, there are limits to the lawyer's role morality: the client's purposes must be "within the limits imposed by law and the lawyer's professional obligations." The lawyer cannot advise or assist a client in conduct "the lawyer knows is criminal or fraudulent." *See* Model Rule 1.2(d). Further, lawyers have moral and professional obligations to the system of justice, the rule of law, and ultimately to their own moral identity. The Model Rules allow a lawyer to withdraw from a representation on the basis that "the client insists on taking action that the lawyer considers repugnant or with which the lawyer has a fundamental disagreement." *See* Model Rule 1.16(b)(4). Further, lawyers "ordinarily" are "not obliged to accept a client whose character or cause the lawyer regards as repugnant." *See* Model Rule 6.2 cmt. 1. Such provisions recognize that lawyers have their own moral moorings on which they can rely in fulfilling their obligations as agents for individuals who seek access to or avoidance of government power.

By engaging in moral dialogue—by discussing the moral issues that are relevant to a representation—the attorney can ascertain the client's actual ends and moral interests rather than working from the lawyer's assumption or guess at those interests and ends. Most often this will allow for greater client input into the representation. Further, where the lawyer and client disagree as to the morality of a situation, that disagreement will be known and considered rather than obscured. When lawyers ignore moral issues or impute bad man ends to clients, the lawyers avoid moral responsibility by relying on their role morality as agents and placing any moral blame with the client, whose assumed (but actually unascertained) interests the lawyer claims to be protecting. At the same time, without moral dialogue, clients may acquiesce in the lawyer's amoral framing of the issues, assuming that the lawyer's legalistic recommendations indicate a moral permissibility to the course of conduct. Thus, neither the lawyer nor the client are taking moral responsibility for the ensuing conduct or legal strategy. This dual shifting of moral accountability creates latitude for moral failure. Moral dialogue between the attorney and client—discussing relevant moral issues, including any negative effects on third parties, public interests, or society—results in the identification of the moral stakes pertinent to a representation and requires the attorney and client to consider their own moral moorings and responsibilities.

The crux of the matter is that even considering the role morality inherent in lawyering, the lawyer cannot escape being a moral agent.[27] It is part of what it means

---

26. Margaret Tarkington, *Freedom of Attorney-Client Association*, 2012 Utah L. Rev. 1071, 1116.
27. "The fact of [moral] pluralism, without more, cannot be used to squeeze out freestanding moral advice from the attorney-client relationship because an attorney remains a moral agent when acting in a professional capacity."

to be a human being and to live in society.[28] Thus, "the autonomy of the client is not some kind of moral trump card over the lawyer's own moral agency."[29] Lawyers' advice and actions have consequences that affect their clients, opposing parties, third parties, the larger community, the system of justice, and their own personal and professional identity. As Deborah Rhode puts it, "[l]awyers must assume personal moral responsibility for the consequences of their professional actions."[30] She contends that "the critical question is not by what right do lawyers impose their [moral] views, but by what right do they evade the responsibility of all individuals to evaluate the normative implications of their acts?"[31]

Case Preview

Spaulding v. Zimmerman

The *Spaulding* case presents a poignant framework for understanding the concepts discussed above. It revolves around the tragic story of 20-year-old David Spaulding, who was seriously injured as a passenger in a car wreck—he was unconscious for three days, suffered a severe brain concussion, broke both clavicles and multiple ribs, and had a "crushed chest." David was from a poor family who could not afford the "staggering" medical bills. The Spaulding family decided to sue the drivers and owners of the two cars, the Zimmerman and Ledermann families, in hopes of being able to obtain compensation from the car insurance policies. Both the Zimmerman and Ledermann families had lost a child in the same wreck. David worked for the Zimmermans, who ran a small road construction business, and had been getting a ride home from work with the Zimmermans at the time of the wreck. The Zimmermans' attorney, Norman Arveson, hired a medical expert to examine David's injuries. The defense medical expert, Dr. Hewitt Hannah, discovered something that none of the doctors treating and examining David had previously seen: in addition to his other serious injuries, the wreck had caused an aneurysm in David's aorta, which could rupture at any moment and cause David's immediate death unless surgically repaired. Dr. Hannah's report detailing this fact was given to Arveson, who shared it with the defense attorney for the Ledermanns, Chester Rosengren. David's attorney (negligently) failed to request the defense expert medical report. And neither of the defense attorneys nor Doctor Hannah told David about the fatal condition affecting him. The case was settled and, because David was still a minor, the trial court approved the settlement—without David (or the court) ever learning of the aneurysm. Over the next two and a half years David experienced severe chest pains; fortunately, he then had a physical examination as part of his army reserve status that revealed the aneurysm. He was sent to Minneapolis for immediate surgery, which

W. Bradley Wendel, *Legal Ethics and the Separation of Law and Morals*, 91 CORNELL L. REV. 67, 111 (2005).
28. Vischer, *supra* note 24, at 273 ("Moral claims are part of human understanding, regardless of what attorneys would like to believe about the appropriate limit of their professional role.").
29. W. Bradley Wendel, *Professionalism as Interpretation*, 99 NW. U. L. REV. 1167, 1181 (2005).
30. Deborah L. Rhode, *Ethical Perspectives on Legal Practice*, 37 STAN. L. REV. 589, 643 (1985).
31. *Id.* at 623.

took ten hours. The aneurysm had grown significantly over the two years such that the doctors had to sacrifice the recurrent laryngeal nerve to save David's life. David lost most of his speaking voice as a direct consequence of the delay in treatment.[32]

As you read *Spaulding v. Zimmerman*, look for the following:

1. Did the Minnesota Supreme Court view the law surrounding professional responsibility as informed by morality or, as Holmes recommended, as separated from ordinary morality?
2. Why didn't the defense lawyers or the Zimmermans/Ledermanns tell David Spaulding about the aneurysm? Were the attorneys required by their duty of confidentiality to keep the information secret?
3. What approach did the defense lawyers take in this case? Did they impute bad man ends to their clients? Did they consider the relational self-interests of their clients (whether the Zimmermans/Ledermanns or the insurance companies)?
4. What did the defense risk by not telling Spaulding or the court about the aneurysm?

Spaulding v. Zimmerman

116 N.W.2d 704 (Minn. 1962)

Appeal from an order of the District Court of Douglas County vacating and setting aside a prior order of such court dated May 8, 1957, approving a settlement made on behalf of David Spaulding on March 5, 1957, at which time he was a minor of the age of 20 years; and in connection therewith, vacating and setting aside releases executed by him and his parents, a stipulation of dismissal, an order for dismissal with prejudice, and a judgment entered pursuant thereto.

The prior action was brought against defendants by Theodore Spaulding, as father and natural guardian of David Spaulding, for injuries sustained by David in an automobile accident, arising out of a collision which occurred August 24, 1956, between an automobile driven by John Zimmerman, in which David was a passenger, and one owned by John Ledermann and driven by Florian Ledermann.

On appeal defendants contend that the court was without jurisdiction to vacate the settlement solely because their counsel then possessed information, unknown to plaintiff herein, that at the time he was suffering from an aorta aneurysm which may have resulted from the accident, because (1) no mutual mistake of fact was involved; [and] (2) no duty rested upon them to disclose information to plaintiff which they could assume had been disclosed to him by his own physicians . . . .

After the accident, David's injuries were diagnosed by his family physician, Dr. James H. Cain, as a severe crushing injury of the chest with multiple rib fractures; a severe cerebral concussion, probably with petechial hemorrhages of the brain; and bilateral fractures of the clavicles. At Dr. Cain's suggestion, on January 3, 1957, David

32. *See* Timothy W. Floyd & John Gallagher, *Legal Ethics, Narrative, and Professional Identity: The Story of David Spaulding*, 59 MERCER L. REV. 941, 944-52 (2008); Roger Cramton, *supra* note 13, at 175-76, 179-81.

was examined by Dr. John F. Pohl, an orthopedic specialist, who made X-ray studies of his chest. Dr. Pohl's detailed report of this examination included the following:

> ". . . The lung fields are clear. The heart and aorta are normal."

Nothing in such report indicated the aorta aneurysm with which David was then suffering. On March 1, 1957, at the suggestion of Dr. Pohl, David was examined from a neurological viewpoint by Dr. Paul S. Blake, and in the report of this examination there was no finding of the aorta aneurysm.

In the meantime, on February 22, 1957, at defendants' request, David was examined by Dr. Hewitt Hannah, a neurologist. On February 26, 1957, the latter reported to Messrs. Field, Arveson, & Donoho, attorneys for defendant John Zimmerman, as follows:

> "The one feature of the case which bothers me more than any other part of the case is the fact that this boy of 20 years of age has an aneurysm, which means a dilatation of the aorta and the arch of the aorta. Whether this came out of this accident I cannot say with any degree of certainty and I have discussed it with the Roentgenologist and a couple of Internists. . . . Of course an aneurysm or dilatation of the aorta in a boy of this age is a serious matter as far as his life. This aneurysm may dilate further and it might rupture with further dilatation and this would cause his death.
>
> "It would be interesting also to know whether the X-ray of his lungs, taken immediately following the accident, shows this dilatation or not. If it was not present immediately following the accident and is now present, then we could be sure that it came out of the accident."

Prior to the negotiations for settlement, the contents of the above report were made known to counsel for defendants Florian and John Ledermann.

The case was called for trial on March 4, 1957, at which time the respective parties and their counsel possessed such information as to David's physical condition as was revealed to them by their respective medical examiners as above described. It is thus apparent that neither David nor his father, the nominal plaintiff in the prior action, was then aware that David was suffering the aorta aneurysm but on the contrary believed that he was recovering from the injuries sustained in the accident.

On the following day an agreement for settlement was reached wherein, in consideration of the payment of $6,500, David and his father agreed to settle in full for all claims arising out of the accident.

Richard S. Roberts, counsel for David, thereafter presented to the court a petition for approval of the settlement, wherein David's injuries were described as:

> ". . . severe crushing of the chest, with multiple rib fractures, severe cerebral concussion, with petechial hemorrhages of the brain, bilateral fractures of the clavicles."

Attached to the petition were affidavits of David's physicians, Drs. James H. Cain and Paul S. Blake, wherein they set forth the same diagnoses they had made upon completion of their respective examinations of David as above described. At no time was there information disclosed to the court that David was then suffering from an aorta aneurysm which may have been the result of the accident. Based upon the petition for settlement and such affidavits of Drs. Cain and Blake, the court on May 8, 1957, made its order approving the settlement.

Early in 1959, David was required by the army reserve, of which he was a member, to have a physical checkup. For this, he again engaged the services of Dr. Cain. In this checkup, the latter discovered the aorta aneurysm. He then reexamined the X rays which had been taken shortly after the accident and at this time discovered that they disclosed the beginning of the process which produced the aneurysm. He promptly sent David to Dr. Jerome Grismer for an examination and opinion. The latter confirmed the finding of the aorta aneurysm and recommended immediate surgery therefor. This was performed by him at Mount Sinai Hospital in Minneapolis on March 10, 1959.

Shortly thereafter, David, having attained his majority, instituted the present action for additional damages due to the more serious injuries including the aorta aneurysm which he alleges proximately resulted from the accident. As indicated above, the prior order for settlement was vacated. In a memorandum made a part of the order vacating the settlement, the court stated:

> "The facts material to a determination of the motion are without substantial dispute. The only disputed facts appear to be whether . . . Mr. Roberts, former counsel for plaintiff, discussed plaintiff's injuries with Mr. Arvesen, counsel for defendant Zimmerman, immediately before the settlement agreement, and, further, whether or not there is a causal relationship between the accident and the aneurysm.
>
> "Contrary to the . . . suggestion in the affidavit of Mr. Roberts that he discussed the minor's injuries with Mr. Arvesen, the Court finds that no such discussion of the specific injuries claimed occurred prior to the settlement agreement on March 5, 1957.
>
> ". . . the Court finds that [] the aneurysm now existing is causally related to the accident . . . , which, so far as the Court can find from the numerous affidavits and statements of fact by counsel, stands without dispute.
>
> "The mistake concerning the existence of the aneurysm was not mutual. For reasons which do not appear, plaintiff's doctor failed to ascertain its existence. By reason of the failure of plaintiff's counsel to use available rules of discovery, plaintiff's doctor and all his representatives did not learn that defendants and their agents knew of its existence and possible serious consequences. Except for the character of the concealment in the light of plaintiff's minority, the Court would, I believe, be justified in denying plaintiff's motion to vacate, leaving him to whatever questionable remedy he may have against his doctor and against his lawyer.
>
> "That defendants' counsel concealed the knowledge they had is not disputed. The essence of the application of the above rule is the character of the concealment. Was it done under circumstances that defendants must be charged with knowledge that plaintiff did not know of the injury? If so, an enriching advantage was gained for defendants at plaintiff's expense. There is no doubt of the good faith of both defendants' counsel. There is no doubt that during the course of the negotiations, when the parties were in an adversary relationship, no rule required or duty rested upon defendants or their representatives to disclose this knowledge. However, once the agreement to settle was reached, it is difficult to characterize the parties' relationship as adverse. At this point all parties were interested in securing Court approval. . . .
>
> "When the adversary nature of the negotiations concluded in a settlement, the procedure took on the posture of a joint application to the Court, at least so far as the facts upon which the Court could and must approve settlement is concerned. It is here that the true nature of the concealment appears, and defendants' failure to

act affirmatively, after having been given a copy of the application for approval, can only be defendants' decision to take a calculated risk that the settlement would be final. . . .

"To hold that the concealment was not of such character as to result in an unconscionable advantage over plaintiff's ignorance or mistake, would be to penalize innocence and incompetence and reward less than full performance of an officer of the Court's duty to make full disclosure to the Court when applying for approval in minor settlement proceedings."

1. The princip[le]s applicable to the court's authority to vacate settlements made on behalf of minors and approved by it appear well established. With reference thereto, we have held that the court in its discretion may vacate such a settlement, even though it is not induced by fraud or bad faith, where it is shown that in the accident the minor sustained separate and distinct injuries which were not known or considered by the court at the time settlement was approved; and even though the releases furnished therein purported to cover both known and unknown injuries resulting from the accident. The court may vacate such a settlement for mistake . . . as to the nature and extent of the minor's injuries, [] where it is shown that one of the parties had additional knowledge with respect thereto and was aware that neither the court nor the adversary party possessed such knowledge when the settlement was approved. . . . "Equity will prevent one party from taking an unconscionable advantage of another's mistake for the purpose of enriching himself at the other's expense."

2. From the foregoing it is clear that in the instant case the court did not abuse its discretion in setting aside the settlement which it had approved on plaintiff's behalf while he was still a minor. It is undisputed that neither he nor his counsel nor his medical attendants were aware that at the time settlement was made he was suffering from an aorta aneurysm which may have resulted from the accident. The seriousness of this disability is indicated by Dr. Hannah's report indicating the imminent danger of death therefrom. This was known by counsel for both defendants but was not disclosed to the court at the time it was petitioned to approve the settlement. While no canon of ethics or legal obligation may have required them to inform plaintiff or his counsel with respect thereto, or to advise the court therein, it did become obvious to them at the time, that the settlement then made did not contemplate or take into consideration the disability described. This fact opened the way for the court to later exercise its discretion in vacating the settlement and under the circumstances described we cannot say that there was any abuse of discretion on the part of the court in so doing under Rule 60.02(6) of Rules of Civil Procedure.

. . .

4. It is also suggested that the settlement made on behalf of the minor was in part at least dependent upon insurance limitations relating to plaintiff's injuries; and that these having been a factor should constitute a bar to the court's exercise of its discretion in vacating such settlement. No decisions are cited in support of this contention. There are, however, numerous decisions holding that insurance limitations have no part in the trial of actions relating to personal injuries or property damage; and it would seem fairly clear that the principles governing this rule would be equally applicable here. . . .

Affirmed.

Post-Case Follow-Up

Spaulding is a striking example of professional and moral failure in a Holmesian framework where law and morality are entirely separated. The incompetence and amorality of those in the legal profession risked David's life — and actually caused him two and a half years of severe pain and the permanent loss of his natural speaking voice. Who failed David? David's lawyer was incompetent in failing to request the defense medical report. But what of the defense lawyers and their hired expert? What of the Minnesota trial court and supreme court? Note the extreme legalistic tone of both court opinions. Both courts skirt the high-stakes moral issue raised in the case by relying on the letter of the professional responsibility rule regarding confidentiality that existed at that time. According to the court, defense counsel acted in "good faith" because "no rule required or duty rested upon defendants or their representatives to disclose this knowledge." The rules of professional conduct appear to be the beginning and end of the court's moral discussion — without even acknowledging the life-or-death drama at issue.

But did the defense lawyers act in "good faith" — did they fulfill their professional responsibilities to their clients, to the justice system, to third parties, and to themselves? As will be discussed in a later chapter, a lawyer's duty of confidentiality is nearly sacrosanct with only a few limited exceptions; and while the Model Rules today would permit a lawyer to disclose confidences to "prevent reasonably certain death," the rule existing at the time of the *Spaulding* case only permitted disclosure where the lawyer was "accused by his client" or to protect others from "[t]he announced attention of a client to commit a crime."[33]

Nevertheless, the defense lawyers utterly failed in their duties to communicate to and counsel with their own clients. Neither the Zimmermans nor the Ledermanns were informed of David's aneurysm, and it appears that the Zimmermans' insurance company was also left uninformed.[34] Apparently, the lawyers imputed bad man ends to their clients, assuming that their clients wanted the least liability at all costs — even the cost of David's life. But is that actually what their clients wanted? The defense lawyers failed to treat their clients as human beings with their own moral moorings; and they failed to consider that their clients had relational self-interests and may care about third parties in the community in which they lived. What is the likelihood that the Zimmermans, who employed and knew David personally, would want to let him die of an aneurysm caused by the car wreck? The Zimmermans and Ledermanns both lost a family member in the car wreck and personally knew the pain of such loss — would they want to inflict that pain on a neighbor in their community? If the defense lawyers were only considering the interests of the insurance company, then they were acting under a conflict of interest, as they owed loyalty to the individual clients.[35] But even to the extent that it was proper to protect the interests of the insurance companies, would the insurance

---

33. ABA, Canon of Professional Ethics 37.
34. *See* Cramton, *supra* note 13, at 180.
35. *See id.* at 179.

companies (made up of actual people) want to risk David's life to save a few thousand dollars on the payout of a policy?[36] If David had died, could the individual defendants or the insurance companies have been held liable for an even larger amount? If it came out that the insurance companies had let David die to save them part of a policy payout, could that affect the insurance company's public relations and corporate value? The defense lawyers did not even discuss these issues with their clients. Similarly, Dr. Hannah, the medical expert, was so loyal to his role as a defense witness that he didn't tell David. What happened to his Hippocratic Oath?

The defense lawyers also failed in their responsibility to the trial court—to inform the court of the aneurysm when making a joint application to the court regarding the extent of David's injuries for settlement. Lawyers have a duty of candor to the court and cannot present false statements of fact or law to the court. This misstep by defense counsel is the only one acknowledged by the court. The court says the defense lawyers thereby took an unjustified "calculated risk" that the settlement would be invalidated—yet the court makes no mention of the "calculated risk" taken as to David's life.

What about the defense lawyers' responsibility to themselves and their own moral identity? If you let a person die of something curable by withholding information from that person, could you look yourself in the mirror? Do not forget to ask yourself who you are becoming and whether that is the person you want to be. Richard Pemberton argued the *Spaulding* case on behalf of the defense to the Minnesota Supreme Court. He was a new lawyer and believed he was asked to do it because the senior lawyers were concerned about facing the justices in light of their actions. In hindsight, Pemberton has this to say about the case:

> When I briefed and argued the *Spaulding* case in the Supreme Court, I was within the first few months of legal practice and was attempting to defend a senior partner's handling of the matter in the trial court. After twenty years of practice, I would like to think that I would have disclosed the aneurysm of the aorta as an act of humanity and without regard to the legalities involved, just as I surely would now. You might suggest to your students in the course on professional responsibility that a pretty good rule for them to practice respecting professional conduct is to do the decent thing.[37]

David's Voice

In 2000, Timothy Floyd and John Gallagher located and interviewed David Spaulding.[38] David was in college studying to be a teacher at the time of the 1956 accident. He received a teaching certificate after the surgery to fix the aneurysm. However, as a direct result of the delay in treatment, he explained, "I didn't have much of a voice for teaching. I talked in a very high pitch." He was unable to find work as a permanent teacher, although he worked for three years as a regular substitute. With a "thin and reedy" voice, "I just couldn't survive in the classroom." He used the last money from the settlement to get a master's degree in school psychology and "was a school psychologist for about thirty-one years." As he explained,

36. *See id.* at 182 ("Most people do the right thing under such circumstances and insurance personnel who adjust and settle liability claims are ordinary people doing ordinary work. Why do law students and lawyers assume that corporate actors are only interested in company profits and are totally lacking in moral sensitivity?").
37. *See id.* at 201.
38. *See* Floyd & Gallagher, *supra* note 32, at 933 & nn. 8 & 15.

"[w]ith this psychology business, it is just one-to-one." He ultimately had Teflon put on his left larynx, which lowered his vocal range to an appropriate pitch. Even so, Floyd and Gallagher note that "[o]nly when he speaks very quietly, emotionlessly, and with a steady control, can he say what is on his mind." In David's words, "People do not know what it is like to go through a life without a voice. If I try to shout, nothing comes out. If I talk like this [quiet, emotionlessly, and controlled], then I can talk. But if I try to increase my volume, it just comes out in a squeal. You know, we are in a coffee klatch, and the thing is, I'll start talking, and somebody else will take over the conversation. And there is nothing I can do. So I back away. Even when I am with four or five of my men friends and I will feel it's my turn to come in and start talking, I'll start to talk and then somebody just takes over." Floyd and Gallagher summarize: "It seemed to David Spaulding that all those people who might have saved him from more than two-and-a-half years of severe pain and the permanent loss of his natural voice had betrayed him. All of his assumptions about how decent people behave and how the system might support people's welfare had been dashed."[39]

Spaulding v. Zimmerman: Real Life Applications

1. What if the aneurysm had ruptured and David Spaulding had died? Who, if anyone, could have been held liable?
2. You work for Down & Out, a personal injury plaintiffs' law firm. Jane slips and falls in Leah's driveway. Jane and Leah are neighbors. Jane comes to you and asks about filing suit against Leah, but Jane believes that Leah's homeowners' insurance will actually be paying any sums in the lawsuit. You file suit against Leah on Jane's behalf. Not long thereafter, the homeowners' insurance company denies coverage for the slip and fall under Leah's policy, saying that the incident does not fall within the policy Leah purchased. As filed, Jane's lawsuit will proceed against Leah without insurance. What do you need to do?
3. You are hired to represent Zyg Bikes Inc. in a dispute with Tubular Co., the component manufacturer of the tubes that are incorporated into Zyg bicycles. You examine the documents in the matter, which show that Tubular failed to ship 10,000 tire tubes to Zyg in breach of their contract. In correspondence, Tubular claims that it shipped the tubes, and that Zyg must bear the loss if for some reason they did not arrive. Zyg disagrees. Assume that Tubular makes the best tire tubes in the industry, which is important to Zyg for the types of bikes it sells. In representing Zyg and deciding how to proceed, what interests are at stake that you should identify and discuss with your client?

3. Cultivating Moral and Professional Judgment

One of the lessons of *Spaulding* is that rules are not the beginning and end of the lawyer's moral and professional responsibilities. In this course and casebook, you will learn — and you must know — the rules of professional conduct. But the rules are the floor — the point below which you cannot go without risking discipline.

39. *See id.* at 951-52.

Moreover, as every lawyer knows, there is always some level of ambiguity in written rules—whether because of the language itself, the scope of application to particular facts, or the state's exercise of discretion in enforcing the rule. Lawyers are trained to see such ambiguity in written codes, and can use those skills to game and manipulate the Model Rules themselves to excuse unethical conduct. Many of the Model Rules are underenforced.[40] Moreover, the Model Rules are largely stripped of moral directives. Marianne M. Jennings criticizes lawyers for having "shaped a profession governed by rules and devoid of morality."[41] Whenever "the code, rules, or an opinion sanction an activity," or can be construed to sanction an activity, "we separate our own consciences from the behavior, label the behavior ethical and march forward with [] full confidence."[42] The situation is perhaps worse when the rules are silent on a matter. She quips: "If it ain't written down, it can and will be done."[43] If the rules fail to expressly prohibit an activity, does that make the activity ethical?

While knowing the rules is essential to becoming a lawyer and to avoiding discipline, compliance with the rules does not make one an exemplar of professionalism. Good lawyers aspire beyond the floor of the rules and the risk of discipline. As Floyd and Gallagher posit in their article telling David Spaulding's story, "[e]thics is more than rules, principles, and obligations, it's about how we live our lives and the kind of persons we are."[44] So what is professionalism, and how can one start down the path of cultivating moral and professional judgment?

The American Bar Association (ABA) and the Conference of Chief Justices (CCJ) have commissioned reports and plans to increase attorney professionalism. Synthesizing these reports and building on moral psychology, Neil Hamilton has offered the following five principles of professionalism.

Neil Hamilton, Professionalism Clearly Defined

18 Prof. Law. 4 (2007)

A. FIVE PRINCIPLES OF PROFESSIONALISM

[P]rofessionalism means that each lawyer:

1. **Continues to grow in personal conscience over his or her career;**
2. **Agrees to comply with the ethics of duty—the minimum standards for the lawyer's professional skills and ethical conduct set by the Rules;**

---

40. *See* Fred C. Zacharias, *The Future Structure and Regulation of Law Practice: Confronting Lies, Fiction, and False Paradigms in Legal Ethics Regulation*, 44 Ariz. L. Rev. 829, 861 ("many rules simply go unenforced or are patently underenforced").
41. Marianne M. Jennings, *The Model Rules and the Code of Professional Responsibility Have Absolutely Nothing to Do with Ethics: The Wally Cleaver Proposition as an Alternative*, 1996 Wis. L. Rev. 1223, 1238.
42. *Id.* at 1226.
43. *Id.* at 1238.
44. *See* Floyd & Gallagher, *supra* note 32, at 943.

3. Strives to realize, over a career, the ethics of aspiration—the core values and ideals of the profession including internalizing the highest standards for the lawyer's professional skills and ethical conduct;
4. Agrees both to hold other lawyers accountable for meeting the minimum standards set forth in the Rules and to encourage them to realize core values and ideals of the profession; and
5. Agrees to act as a fiduciary where his or her self-interest is overbalanced by devotion to serving the client and the public good in the profession's area of responsibility: justice.
   a. Devotes professional time to serve the public good, particularly by representing pro bono clients; and
   b. Undertakes a continuing reflective engagement, over a career, on the relative importance of income and wealth in light of the other principles of professionalism.

B. FURTHER ANALYSIS OF THE PRINCIPLES

1. *Personal Conscience*

Personal conscience, the first principle of professionalism, is an awareness of the moral goodness or blameworthiness of one's own intentions and conduct together with a feeling of obligation to be and to do what is morally good. Personal conscience in this definition includes (1) awareness that the person's conduct is having an effect on others, (2) a reasoning process to determine the moral goodness or blameworthiness of the person's intentions or conduct, and (3) a sense of obligation to be and to do what is morally good.

Personal conscience is the foundation on which a law student or practicing lawyer builds an ethical professional identity. Without this foundation, the remaining four principles of professionalism will collapse into a calculus of simple self-interest, including gaming the Rules of Professional Conduct themselves for self-advantage.

a. The Importance of Self-Scrutiny and Feedback from Others

The [ABA's] MacCrate and the Haynsworth Reports and the CCJ National Action Plan note the importance over a career of self-scrutiny along with feedback from and moral dialogue with others to contribute to a lawyer's professional growth. . . .

b. The Four Component Model and Personal Conscience

Moral psychology also offers a useful analytical framework with which to explore and understand personal conscience. Personal conscience involves awareness of a moral issue, a reasoning process to determine the moral goodness or blameworthiness of alternative courses of conduct, and a sense of obligation to do what is morally good. Similarly the moral psychology literature starts with the question, "what must we suppose happens psychologically in order for moral behavior to take place?" Morality in this meaning focuses on the social condition that humans live in groups and what one person does can affect others. In light of our understanding that what one person does can affect others, morality asks what do we owe others?

What are our duties to them? What rights can they claim? Scholars posit that four distinct capacities, called the Four Component Model, are necessary in order for moral behavior to occur:

1. Moral Sensitivity. "Moral sensitivity is the awareness of how an individual's actions affect other people. It involves being aware of different possible lines of action and how each line of action could affect the parties concerned. It involves imaginatively constructing possible scenarios and knowing cause-consequence chains of events in the real world; it involves empathy and role-taking skills."[66] Moral sensitivity requires the understanding of one's own intuitions and emotional reactions.

2. Moral Judgment. "Once the person is aware of possible lines of action and how people would be affected by each line of action (Component 1), then Component 2 judges which line of action is more morally justifiable—which alternative is just, or right."[68] It involves deliberation regarding the various considerations relevant to different courses of action and making a judgment regarding which of the available actions would be most morally justifiable. It entails integrating both shared moral norms and individual moral principles.

Shared moral norms and an individual's moral principles—what philosophy calls normative ethics—flow from one of two general sources. A rational approach uses analysis and logic in any situation to reason out right conduct from a set of first ethical principles. This "ethics of principle" approach can be derived from (1) faith or religious teachings, (2) cultural norms, or (3) moral philosophy like Kant's categorical imperative or Mills's utilitarianism. A second general source emphasizes the virtues and good habits of character in any situation and is more intuitive about the right conduct that a virtue or habit of character demands in the situation. Some people using this "ethics of character" approach find the relevant virtues or habits of character in faith or religious teachings. Others look to moral philosophy or cultural norms.

3. Moral Motivation and Commitment. Moral motivation and commitment have "to do with the importance given to moral values in competition with other values. Deficiencies in Component 3 occur when a person is not sufficiently motivated to put moral values higher than other values—when other values such as self-actualization or protecting one's organization replace concern for doing what is right."[72]

It is not only competing values that can halt moral action at this point, but competing drives and emotional states. For example, if someone must choose between having a steady paycheck to ensure her family has food on the table, with acting on her moral values, the drive to care for basic needs may override all else. . . .

4. Moral Character and Implementation. "This component involves ego strength, perseverance, backbone, toughness, strength of conviction, and courage. A person may be morally sensitive, may make good moral judgments, and may place a high priority on moral values, but if the person wilts under pressure, is easily distracted or discouraged, is a wimp and weak-willed, then moral failure occurs because of

66. James Rest & Darcia Narvaez, Moral Development in the Professions 23 (1994).
68. *Id.* at 23-24.
72. *Id.* at 24.

deficiency in Component 4 (weak character)."[74] Problem-solving skills including figuring out the necessary sequence of concrete actions and working around impediments and unexpected difficulties as well as interpersonal skills are important. Component 4 includes the knowledge, skills and abilities to manage conflicts, communicate effectively and minimize polarization.

Lawrence Walker notes that, "Moral failure can be a consequence of a deficiency in any component: being blind to the moral issues in a situation, being unable to formulate a morally defensible position, failing to accord priority to moral concerns, or being unable or unwilling to implement action."[76] It is important therefore to attend to development of all four components. . . .

. . .

The greatest concern about "personal conscience in a professional context" as the foundation of professionalism is the fear that a lawyer's personal conscience will limit client autonomy and client equal access to justice. The lawyer's personal conscience will trump client choices that are lawful. The central point of "personal conscience in a professional context" is that the lawyer's personal conscience is now informed and guided also by the role morality of the lawyer's function in the justice system. That role morality calls on the lawyer who accepts a representation to honor principles of client autonomy and equal access to justice. In the counseling role, for example, the lawyer's duty is to help the client think through the client's best interests in the situation *from the client's shoes including the client's morality*. The lawyer is not to impose the lawyer's morality on the client. This duty includes fairly and completely presenting the law applicable to the client's situation. However a lawyer who develops over a career in any of the capacities of the Four Component Model should be a better counselor for all clients and should better understand adversaries. For example, a lawyer whose own moral reasoning is at an early stage of development will be limited in his or her ability to counsel a client who is at a more developed stage of moral reasoning. The lawyer simply will not understand the client well. If the reverse is true, the lawyer will understand the moral reasoning of the client and can help the client think through the client's best interests from the client's shoes.

2. *The Ethics of Duty*

. . . The ethics of duty—the obligatory and disciplinary elements of the Rules—state the minimum floor of competence and ethical conduct below which the profession will impose discipline. An ethical professional identity requires each law student and practicing lawyer to understand and internalize the ethics of duty.

3. *The Ethics of Aspiration—The Core Values and Ideals of the Profession*

The ethics of aspiration call on each law student and practicing lawyer, over the course of a career, both to internalize and to strive to realize the core values and

74. Muriel Bebeau & Verna Monson, *Guided by Theory, Grounded in Evidence: A Way Forward for Professional Ethics Education*, *in* HANDBOOK ON MORAL AND CHARACTER EDUCATION (D. Narvaez & L. Nucci eds., in press).
76. Lawrence J. Walker, *The Model and the Measure: An Appraisal of the Minnesota Approach to Moral Development*, 31 J. OF MORAL EDUC. 353, 355 (2002).

ideals of the profession [as taken from the Model Rules of Professional Conduct and the ABA Reports and CCJ Action Plan on professionalism].

a. The Core Values of the Profession

- Competent Representation Including Reasonable Diligence and Reasonable Communication with the Client
- Loyalty to the Client
- Confidentiality of Client Information
- Zealous Advocacy on Behalf of the Client Constrained by the Officer of the Legal System Role
- Independent Professional Judgment
- Public Service to Improve the Quality of Justice, Particularly to Maintain and Improve the Quality of the Legal Profession and to Ensure Equal Access to the Justice System
- Respect for the Legal System and All Persons Involved in the Legal System

b. Ideals of the Profession

- Commitment to Seek and Realize Excellence at the Principles of Professionalism and the Core Values and Ideals of the Profession
- Integrity
- Honesty
- Fairness

4. The Duty of Peer-Review

. . . The Model Rules and the ABA Reports tend to focus on the requirement that peers report misconduct below the floor of the Rules. This is important, but the creation of strong ethical cultures emphasizing excellence at the skills, core values, and ideals of the profession is even more important. As the recent corporate scandals in corporations with well-drafted written ethics codes but corrupt cultures demonstrated, unethical culture will trump rules.

. . .

5. The Duty to Restrain Self-Interest to Some Degree to Serve the Client and the Public Purpose of the Profession

. . . The public good served by the legal profession is justice. The peer-review professions have always been about making a satisfactory living in addition to serving the client's interest and the public good. . . . A lawyer owes a client the fiduciary duties of safeguarding confidences and property, avoiding impermissible conflicts of interest, dealing honestly with the client, adequately informing the client, following the instructions of the client, and not employing adversely to the client powers arising from the attorney-client relationship. . . .

[In addition,] a lawyer is an agent and fiduciary not just for the client, but also for the legal system, the purpose of which is justice. The first sentence of the Preamble to the Model Rules in effect states this concept by providing that a lawyer is "a representative of clients, an officer of the legal system and a public citizen having special responsibility for the quality of justice." . . .

a. The Duty to Give Professional Time to Serve the Public Good, Particularly Pro Bono Assistance to the Disadvantaged

. . . [The] duty to provide pro bono or low fee assistance to the disadvantaged is uniquely compelling for the legal profession in comparison with the other peer-review professions. The moral justification for the work of the other peer-review professions depends to a much lesser degree on the proper functioning of the system within which the work is done than is the case with the moral justification for the work of the legal profession. A physician for example can serve the major public purpose of the profession, the health of individual patients, without significant concern that others will be negatively affected . . . . However a lawyer in litigation will serve the major public purpose of the profession, justice, only when the adversary system is working properly. The adversary system is the society's best approximation of justice only with (1) a competent neutral decision maker and (2) competent representation for all affected persons. . . .

b. The Duty to Reflect on How Much Is Enough

A common failing of all the definitions of professionalism is that they do not address adequately on the business aspects of the profession that may create tension between a lawyer's personal goals of income and wealth and the correlative duties, core values and ideals of the profession. The Stanley Commission Report states "All segments of the bar should . . . resist the temptation to make the acquisition of wealth a primary goal of law practice." . . .

While two ABA professionalism reports and the Preamble raise the question how much is a satisfactory living, that question is actually part of a larger question posed by the steadily increasing time demands of professional life in our culture. The larger question is how much life energy should be devoted to meeting professional duties (including making a satisfactory living) in comparison with the life energy devoted to other duties as a parent, spouse, adult child in support of elderly parents, friend, contributing member of non-professional communities and a whole person with dimensions other than work? . . .

C. PROFESSIONAL RESPONSIBILITIES IN LITIGATING, ADVISING, AND TRANSACTIONAL PLANNING

A major critique of the traditional law school curriculum is that it is primarily focused on training students for litigation as opposed to training them for transactional planning or for advising and counseling clients as to prospective client conduct. Indeed, to some extent this critique can be made of the Model Rules themselves. The Model Rules do not address transactional planning or counseling work to the same extent that they address litigation issues. Yet there are some major differences between these contexts that should be recognized and that should shape the lawyer's professional responsibilities in these roles.

Unfortunately, lawyers in practice often do not appreciate these differences — thus the issue is not solely one of training that will be completed upon graduation from law school. Many lawyers in practice approach transactional planning and providing legal advice about prospective client conduct in precisely the same way as they would approach legal analysis in litigation. So what are the differences between these contexts and how do those differences call for a correspondingly different approach to one's professional responsibilities?

1. Shaping Client Conduct

The first major difference — and one that almost cannot be overstated — is that in the advising and transactional planning scenarios, often the client has not yet acted. In the litigation context, the client has usually already acted and the question is how to mitigate liability or maximize compensation in light of those completed actions. But when a lawyer is asked to advise a client about prospective conduct or to perform transactional work, the client has yet to act. Thus, the attorney's interpretation of the law will most likely shape client conduct, which in turn will shape the consequences for all affected by that conduct, including both third parties and the client's own long-term interests and exposure to civil or criminal liability for those actions. In the transactional context, the lawyer's assistance is often needed to make the client's actions legally effective. Thus, lawyers are needed for bona fide, true sale, nonconsolidation, and other legal certifications in order for transactions to close and take legal effect. Consequently, the lawyer is not solely advising the client, but is assisting the client in effectuating whatever conduct the client is engaged in.

Importantly, Model Rule 1.2(d) prohibits a lawyer from either counseling a client to engage or assisting clients "in conduct that the lawyer knows is criminal or fraudulent." The rule refers to conduct that the lawyer "knows" is criminal or fraudulent, and the rules in turn define knowledge to require "actual knowledge," but such knowledge "may be inferred from the circumstances," as stated in Model Rule 1.0(f). Lawyers who provide certifications that they know are false in order to close a deal are assisting their clients in fraud, and in some cases, in criminal conduct.

For example, in the fallout of the Enron and Worldcom scandals, it became evident that the lawyers assisted in the fraud. As Susan Koniak has described, lawyers showed corporate executives and constituents how to break the law by "structuring bogus deals, vouching for nonexistent 'sales,' writing whitewash reports to keep the sheriff fooled and away."[45] Koniak claims that "lawyers were central, even more central than accountants to the corporate fraud at Enron." She notes that one major aspect of Enron's fraud was in "money-go-round" deals where "Enron made money and other assets go round in circles to inflate its profits." Koniak explains that "[a]ccountants cannot book such circles as 'sales'" — which is how they were

45. Susan P. Koniak, *When the Hurlyburly's Done: The Bar's Struggle with the SEC*, 103 Colum. L. Rev. 1236, 1237 (2003).

booked—"instead of 'loans' without two legal opinions, a 'true sale' opinion and a 'nonconsolidation' opinion." Thus, the accountants "could not act without the lawyers vouching for these deals." She states:

> Vinson [& Elkins] apparently issued "true sales" opinions in a number of these transactions, although it was surely not the only [law] firm to do so. More importantly, each of the banks [who made these deals with Enron] had their [own] lawyers who helped the banks with their part of the sham. The banks' lawyers set up puppet SPEs [special purpose entities] to allow the banks to funnel loans to Enron disguised as trades or sales. The lawyers also helped the banks to protect themselves from the prospect that Enron would go belly-up from the weight of all this undisclosed debt. . . . How many major law firms were helping banks in what appear to be fraudulent transactions? The Texas court denied motions to dismiss charges of securities fraud in connection with Enron's shady deals against Citigroup, J.P. Morgan, Credit Suisse First Boston, and Merrill Lynch. I have no doubt that those banks were represented by the "best" legal talent in this country—law firms considered to be of the highest caliber. And none of those lawyers noticed anything amiss? . . . Are we [] to believe that all the lawyers who worked on these deals were incapable of grasping just what it was they were doing? I rest my case.[46]

Why does the law require that lawyers be part of closing such transactions—that lawyers must issue true sale, bona fide, nonconsolidation, and other legal opinions for transactions to close? Because the lawyers, even as advocates, are supposed to maintain some level of gatekeeping for the rule of law. W. Bradley Wendel posits that lawyers have a moral obligation to the law itself when engaged in legal counseling and planning. Wendel notes that "citizens are obligated to treat the law as legitimate," and so too must lawyers, who are acting as agents of those citizens in their dealings with society; consequently, "lawyers are prohibited from manipulating legal norms to defeat the substantive meaning of these norms."[47] If lawyers engage in such instrumental manipulation, they "can commit a moral wrong vis-à-vis their obligation to serve as custodians or trustees of the law." Wendel recognizes the relational self-interests at issue in transactional planning:

> [The lawyer] must be concerned about the effective functioning of the law, because without it, neither she nor her client could realize their own interests. The market economy presupposes a background of stable law, custom, and enforcement that enforces private ordering. Even if a lawyer and client were concerned only with pursuing their own narrow interests, paradoxically it is only possible to behave self-interestedly within a framework of other-regarding obligations. A lawyer might evade regulatory requirements by aggressive structuring of transactions in one case, but cause long-run damage by eroding the capability of the legal system to facilitate the functioning of financial markets.[48]

46. *Id.* at 1242-43.
47. Wendel, *supra* note 27, at 72.
48. Wendel, *supra* note 29, at 1209.

Under Model Rule 1.2, lawyers are allowed to advise a client regarding "the legal consequences of any proposed course of conduct" and "the validity, scope, meaning or application of the law." This generally allows attorneys to advise clients to walk up to the edge of what is legal, but the rule expressly prohibits lawyers from advising or assisting clients to cross that line into what is illegal, false, and fraudulent. The Enron lawyers crossed that line. If we didn't need someone to vouch for the legal validity of transactions, we simply wouldn't need lawyer involvement. With that in mind, what if Enron's lawyers at Vinson & Elkins or the lawyers for the banks had refused to issue true sales opinions, had refused to structure the deals that hid Enron's debt, had told their client, "No, we cannot do that for you, it's a violation of securities laws and a fraud upon shareholders"? If the lawyers had refused, the transactions would not have closed, Enron (once a stable company) may not have gone bankrupt, the public would not have been duped into buying Enron's inflated stock (which sold at $90.75 in August 2000 and reduced to $0.67 in January 2002),[49] thousands of people would not have lost their jobs, and thousands more would not have lost billions of dollars in their life savings and 401k accounts.

And what of the executives who apparently wanted the lawyers to structure these deals and hide Enron's actual debt to inflate share prices? Many of the executives — Jeffrey Skilling, Kenneth Lay, Andrew Fastow, Richard Causey, Lea Fastow — were convicted of crimes for their roles in the massive fraud, serving various prison sentences, and J. Clifford Baxter, former Enron vice chairman, committed suicide.[50] The lawyers certainly did not serve their corporate client — Enron and its shareholders — well. But did they even provide good service to the non-client executives? How much of a favor is it to those executives to help them do something that ended up putting them in prison? The lawyers' actions shaped client conduct — had they said "No," things might very well have gone differently. Had they refused to issue fraudulent opinions and refused to structure bogus deals — which they were professionally required to refuse to do under Rule 1.2(d) — the drastic consequences for their client, their client's employees and shareholders, the executives, and the U.S. economy may have been avoided. The transactions could not have closed without lawyer help. Lawyers shaped the conduct and the resultant consequences.

Another striking example of shaping client conduct is found in the advising context. In the wake of the events of September 11, 2001, the Bush administration sought advice regarding legal restraints on the use of coercive interrogation techniques against detainees captured in Afghanistan. The Office of Legal Counsel (OLC) issued memos (now universally dubbed the "Torture Memos") narrowly construing the definition of "torture" as prohibited in the 1984 Convention Against Torture and the implementing federal statute, 18 U.S.C. §2340(A), which makes it a federal crime to engage in torture. As Wendel details:

> Lawyers in the OLC [] sought to construe the operative term, torture, as narrowly as possible. Torture is defined in the [federal] statute as an "act . . . specifically intended

49. CNN, *Enron Fast Facts*, *available at* http://www.cnn.com/2013/07/02/us/enron-fast-facts/.

50. The sentences ranged from one year to 14 years. Kenneth Lay was convicted of conspiracy and fraud, but died of a heart attack in Aspen, Colorado less than two months after his conviction. *See id.*

> to inflict severe physical or mental pain or suffering," and severe pain and suffering is further defined as the prolonged harm caused by one of several enumerated acts. By focusing on the specific intent requirement and the element of severe pain or suffering, the lawyers created an implausibly restrictive definition of torture: "[T]he victim must experience intense pain or suffering of the kind that is equivalent to the pain that would be associated with serious physical injury *so severe that death, organ failure or permanent damage resulting in a loss of significant body function will likely result*." Despite the plain meaning of the statutory language to the contrary, burning detainees with cigarettes, administering electric shocks to their genitals, hanging them by the wrists, submerging them in water to simulate drowning, beating them, and sexually humiliating them would not be deemed "torture" under this definition.[51]

Further, the lawyers in the OLC advised the administration that they could rely on "[s]tandard criminal law defenses of necessity and self-defense" to avoid liability for engaging in torture. As Milan Markovic explains, "[t]here is nothing 'standard' about this argument" because the statute "mentions no defenses, and the Convention Against Torture specifically states, 'No exceptional circumstances whatsoever, whether a state of war or a threat of war, internal political instability or any other public emergency, may be invoked as a justification of torture.'"[52] Thus, the advice regarding defenses was patently erroneous.

Importantly, the administration's purpose in seeking this advice—and the effect of the lawyers giving it—was to insulate the interrogators engaging in such techniques from prosecution for violating the laws against torture. Jack Goldsmith, who subsequently headed the OLC, characterized advice in the memos as a "golden shield," "get-out-of-jail-free card," or an "advance pardon" in order to "immunize officials from prosecutions for wrongdoing."[53] Daniel Pines explains that "in virtually every situation, government employees who rely on an [OLC] opinion in taking action will likely be absolved from any legal sanction."[54] Thus, as Markovic concludes, "[t]he Torture Memo's impact cannot be overstated. It was the basis for coercive techniques used against several high-ranking detainees" and ultimately led to "a list of aggressive interrogation procedures to be used at Guantanamo Bay that eventually migrated to Iraq."[55]

Why are executive employees who rely on OLC opinions immune from prosecution? Is it so that the executive branch can successfully avoid the purposes, restraints, and punishments created by law—as happened with the Torture Memos? Exactly the opposite. The purpose behind providing such immunity is to enable the proper functioning of law and government—specifically, to encourage the executive branch to seek legal advice so that the rule of law can be upheld, even when complex or unclear, and to encourage government officials to fulfill their government duties without being hindered by the prospect of prosecution or

---

51. Wendel, *supra* note 27, at 80-81.
52. Milan Markovic, *Can Lawyers Be War Criminals?*, 20 Geo. J. Legal Ethics 347, 352 (2007).
53. Office of Professional Responsibility Final Report, *available at* http://nsarchive.gwu.edu/news/20100312/OPR-FinalReport090729.pdf.
54. Daniel L. Pines, *Are Even Torturers Immune from Suit? How Attorney General Opinions Shield Government Employees from Civil Litigation and Criminal Prosecution*, 43 Wake Forest L. Rev. 93, 97 (2008).
55. Markovic, *supra* note 52, at 348.

liability.[56] But in order for these purposes to be realized, lawyers as advisors (especially government advisors) must not construe and stretch the law to mean that anything a government actor wants to do is "legal." Otherwise the constraints and public purposes of law are eviscerated. Lawyers as advisors are to be gatekeepers and must show fidelity, not only to their clients, but also to the existence, meaning, and rule of law.

As in the transactional context, the Torture Memos were integral to the client's ultimate conduct. Had the lawyers refused to give them the green light, so to speak—had they advised their client that the activities the client wanted to engage in were likely torture under the Convention Against Torture and the implementing federal statute and that the Convention had a clear non-derogation rule that prohibited reliance on criminal law defenses or the extent of the national emergency—then the administration could not have engaged in the extreme interrogation techniques without risking prosecution. The interrogators likely would have decided not to engage in such conduct and, consequently, detainees wouldn't have been tortured. Again, the attorneys' advice shaped both the client's conduct and the resultant consequences for third parties—in this case being tortured.

2. Providing Advice Outside of the Checks of the Adversary System

In law school, students are taught how to make creative arguments regarding the meaning of law or application to a given fact pattern; indeed, students are rewarded for their ability to recognize and make creative arguments. Such creativity, and the ability to see the malleability of law, is an essential skill of lawyering. But do legal advising and planning require a more tempered approach to creativity and legal interpretation than what is appropriate in litigation?

In the litigation context, lawyers can exercise significant creativity in proffering interpretations of the law because that creative interpretation will always be challenged by checks inherent in the adversary system. First, the opposing party will provide a competing interpretation of the law. Second, the judge—as the authority constitutionally established to do so—will determine the actual meaning of the law given the circumstances at hand, and a jury or judge will determine any questions of fact. Further, lawyers in litigation have duties of candor to the court; they are required to disclose controlling adverse authority and cannot make false statements of law or fact.[57] Similarly, in alternative dispute resolution processes, an arbitrator or other third-party neutral will make a decision about what should happen after hearing from both sides.

Thus, even if a lawyer advocates a farfetched interpretation of the law, that interpretation will be countered and then can only be accepted if the judge or third-party neutral agrees with it. Notably, the existence of an opposing party and

56. Pines, *supra* note 54, at 152-53.
57. Model Rule 3.3(a); Wendel, *supra* note 29, at 1172-73.

a third-party neutral can in fact cabin lawyer creativity in the first place. Litigators take into account the fact of opposition and the need to create an interpretation that the judge will be able to select as the authoritative interpretation of the law; they are wary of proffering arguments that the opposing party can mock as laughable or that will elicit the derision of the judge. Moreover, the opposing party and the judge will consider the effects of the client's actions on others and on the system of justice, as well as the meaning or public purpose behind the law. Thus, good litigators will also take such countervailing and relational interests into account in framing their arguments — even while advocating zealously for their clients — because doing so represents the most promising chance of success.

Much of lawyer training focuses on how to make creative arguments when these safeguards of the adversary system are in place, but when lawyers are acting in an advisory or transactional role, there are no such safeguards. Indeed, the attorney will often provide the only point of view to the client as to what the law means and what third-party and public interests are at stake before the client acts.[58] Wendel explains that advising and transactional planning "are distinctive precisely because there is no impartial referee to resist the lawyer's client-centered construction of the law." As "the sole legal interpreter," the "lawyer has the power to shape the law for good or for ill."[59]

Model Rule 2.1 requires lawyers as advisors to "exercise independent professional judgment" and "render candid advice." Comment 1 elaborates that "[a] client is entitled to straightforward advice expressing the lawyer's honest assessment," which may include "unpleasant facts and alternatives that a client may be disinclined to confront." Wendel argues that a good measure for evaluating whether advice and transactional planning is candid is whether the lawyers' interpretations of the law "could be publicly justified to other members of the relevant community."[60]

Both the Enron and the Torture Memos debacles provide potent examples of problematic advising. One Enron employee infamously reported:

> Say you have a dog, but you need to create a duck on the financial statements. Fortunately, there are specific accounting rules for what constitutes a duck: yellow feet, white covering, orange beak. So you take the dog and paint its feet yellow and its fur white and you paste an orange plastic beak on its nose, and then you say to your accountants, "This is a duck! Don't you agree that it's a duck?" And the accountants say, "Yes, according to the rules this is a duck." Everyone knows that it is a dog, not a duck, but that does not matter because you have met the rules for calling it a duck.[61]

The lawyers at Enron were the ones who actually structured the deals and wrote legal opinions vouching for their bona fide and legally compliant nature — essentially they were dressing up the dog and then verifying that it was in fact a duck. As Koniak reports, transactional lawyers, like those involved in the Enron scandal,

58. *See* Wendel, *supra* note 29, at 1173 ("In counseling and transactional representation, the only constraint on the assistance the lawyer may provide to the client is provided by the law itself, as interpreted by the lawyer on whose client the law is expected to act as a constraint.").

59. *Id.* at 1199.

60. *Id.* at 1210.

61. *Id.* at 1171.

don't need "to discover what the client is up to; they know, because they are drafting the scripts, structuring the transactions. They are in, if you will, on the ground floor. The problem is not so much knowing what the client is doing; it is respecting that the law has limits that apply to one's client."[62]

Similarly, with the Torture Memos, the lawyers came up with their implausibly narrow definition of torture[63] by relying on and misconstruing an unrelated health care benefits statute that contained the term "severe pain." The statute had absolutely nothing to do with defining torture, but dealt with what constitutes an "emergency condition" for health care benefits. As Wendel summarizes:

> The statute is plainly not setting out a definition of severe pain in terms of organ failure or dysfunction, but using severe pain as one symptom among many — including organ failure or dysfunction — which might reasonably lead a prudent layperson to conclude that a person is in need of immediate medical attention. A lawyer conscientiously applying the plain meaning rule could not in good faith conclude that severe pain is limited to cases threatening organ failure or dysfunction. The lawyers also downplayed cases arising under statutes in more closely analogous contexts, such as the Torture Victim Protection Act.[64]

Further, the OLC lawyers advised their clients of the availability of common law defenses such as necessity and self-defense, despite the fact that the Convention Against Torture has a clear non-derogation principle disavowing the availability of such defenses. The likely explanation for this shoddy work from "some of the ablest lawyers in government" is that the OLC lawyers were reverse engineering their legal advice: starting with the legal conclusion that their clients wanted them to reach and then working backwards to concoct a legal interpretation to support it — "in effect adopting the attitude that they would make the law say what they wanted it to say."[65]

Lawyers understand the indeterminacy of many laws; law is often malleable and can be shaped through interpretation and application. Yet, unlike the judiciary, lawyers simply lack the constitutional power to make authoritative determinations as to "what the law is" and how it will be applied in a given case.[66] At best, lawyers' creative interpretations of the law are mere predictions of what the law may be once a judge has ruled in that regard.[67] And at worst, their creative interpretations are one-sided manipulations calculated to excuse or mitigate client bad acts — and such "interpretations" have zero chance of representing or ever becoming law. Consequently, as David Luban reminds us, the lawyer's duty under Model Rule 2.1 is "to provide 'independent' and 'candid' advice about what the law requires, not advice

62. Koniak, *supra* note 45, at 1280.
63. Again, the OLC lawyers defined torture thus: "[T]he victim must experience intense pain or suffering of the kind that is equivalent to the pain that would be associated with serious physical injury so severe that death, organ failure, or permanent damage resulting in a loss of significant body function will likely result." *See* Wendel, *supra* note 27, at 81.
64. *Id.* at 81-82.
65. Wendel, *supra* note 29, at 1172.
66. Marbury v. Madison, 5 U.S. 137, 177 (1803).
67. Oliver Wendell Holmes, *The Path of the Law*, 10 HARV. L. REV. 457 (1897) ("The object of our study, then, is prediction, the prediction of the incidence of the public force through the instrumentality of the courts.").

spun to say whatever the client wants."[68] Even if the client doesn't want to hear it, the lawyer's duty is clear. As comment 1 to Model Rule 2.1 states, "a lawyer should not be deterred from giving candid advice by the prospect that the advice will be unpalatable to the client."

Importantly, lawyers often disserve their clients when they act as yes-men and provide unqualified approvals of prospective client conduct based on creative and aggressive interpretations of the law. Clients need an "honest assessment" of the law—one that will notify them of nontrivial chances of liability, prosecution, or sanctions. As Wendel explains, "[t]here is nothing necessarily wrong with advancing creative arguments as long as they are clearly identified as such, with weaknesses and counterarguments candidly noted," but "a lawyer who does not flag creative and aggressive arguments as such violates her fiduciary duty to her client by providing purportedly neutral advice without the caveat that the lawyer's interpretation may not accurately represent the applicable law."[69] Further, in the fallout of any deal or advice gone bad that results in litigation or criminal prosecution, the opposing party and the judge, jury, or other third-party neutral will consider the countervailing interpretations of the law as well as the effects of the client's actions on others. It is absolutely in the client's best interest to have been informed of such considerations before the client has acted on the attorney's advice.

In addition to these duties to their clients, lawyers acting as advisors and transactional planners serve "as custodians or trustees of the law."[70] In examining the Enron scandal, Koniak criticized "lawyers [who] believe it is their duty to contort all law to meet the client's ends. And here is the crux of the matter. In such a world, law is no longer possible. Law, in such a world, does not affect behavior at all, it just recharacterizes it. If lawyers tear down all our laws, where shall we stand? What will protect us then?"[71] If the Enron and OLC lawyers had provided their clients with candid advice, an "honest assessment" of what the law means,[72] the laws and the public interests underlying them—including a stable economy and international norms prohibiting torture and inhumane treatment of people—may have been upheld.

Chapter Summary

- Lawyers play a significant role in the administration of justice in the United States. A license to practice law makes the lawyer an instrument of government power and a guardian of due process—the lawyer's actions directly affect the

68. David Luban, *Torture and the Professions*, 26 Crim. Just. Ethics 2, 60 (2007).
69. Wendel, *supra* note 27, at 85; *see also* Milan Markovic, *Advising Clients After Critical Legal Studies and the Torture Memos*, 114 W. Va. L. Rev. 109, 157 (2011) ("[A]n attorney cannot fulfill his or her duty qua advisor by offering only his or her own view of what the law is"—rather, "lawyers should convey not only their own views of the law but also countervailing considerations because the law does not dictate any one outcome.").
70. Wendel, *supra* note 27, at 72-73.
71. Koniak, *supra* note 45, at 1280.
72. Model Rule 2.1 cmt. 1.

extent of government power to be imposed in favor of or against people and their property.

- Lawyers owe professional responsibilities to their clients, to the system of justice and the rule of law, to third parties, and to their own integrity and moral identity.
- The legal profession is generally considered a self-regulated profession because lawyers create and enforce the rules of professional conduct. Self-regulation implies a social contract with the public whereby the legal profession agrees to police its members, maintain high standards of conduct, and to safeguard its public good: justice.
- As an agent for their clients' purposes, lawyers engage in role morality, which is important to preserve equal access to government power for people who are unpopular or have limited means.
- Lawyers should engage in moral dialogue with their clients to determine their clients' actual ends and desires instead of imputing bad man ends to them. Lawyers should recognize that their clients are complex human beings with varying desires and ends and that they have relational self-interests that can be negatively affected and should be taken into account in any legal representation.
- Lawyers cannot escape being moral agents and must assume moral responsibility for their actions. Lawyers should introspectively examine the person they are becoming and strive to cultivate moral and professional judgment.
- Lawyers' professional responsibilities are different when they are acting in an advising or planning role, as opposed to as a litigator in the adversary system. In the advising and planning role, the lawyer's legal advice will shape client conduct and must be candid, providing an honest assessment of the law.

Applying the Rules

1. Hal practices family law and is assisting Gary in a divorce from his wife, Ann. The court issues a custody order giving Ann full custody of their minor son, James, and giving Gary biweekly visitation. Gary learns that a police report has been filed against Ann alleging that she punched James. Gary picks up James for visitation. He asks Hal whether he can disregard the custody order and not return James in light of the allegations of abuse by Ann. Hal advises Gary to not return James, and files an application for emergency custody with the court. The court denies the application, reaffirming custody with Ann. Nevertheless, Gary believes that Ann is abusive. Can Hal advise or assist Gary in continuing to keep James with him? What should Hal do?

2. Makayla is a transactional lawyer. She becomes aware that the financial statements for her client, Toys Inc., are inaccurate as they fail to properly disclose all of Toys Inc.'s debt. Makayla confronts Toys Inc.'s chief financial officer (CFO) about the inaccuracies. The CFO responds that he is aware of the inaccuracies, and that he will be sure to fix them by the next reporting period. Toys Inc. is in

the process of merging with Wild Child Inc. At the closing, Makayla checks the financial statements and realizes the inaccuracies have not been fixed or disclosed to Wild Child Inc. Can Makayla close the deal? What actions might she take?

3. Paulina works for the law firm Hunter & Shell. John Hunter, the senior partner, asks Paulina to write a letter for a client, Food Corp, advising it regarding whether it can unilaterally revoke accrued paid vacation of its employees with no compensation. Hunter stresses to Paulina that Food Corp is planning on taking this action and wants her to write a letter advising Food Corp that it legally can revoke the accrued paid vacation, so that it can show the letter to employees who object. Paulina researches the issue and determines that in the relevant state accrued paid vacation is considered wages and cannot be revoked without compensation; indeed, should Food Corp take such action it could be liable for treble damages and may be sanctioned by the Department of Labor. How should Paulina advise Food Corp? What should she tell John Hunter?

4. Johanna is in-house lawyer for Car Co. Xavier brings a personal injury case against Car Co., alleging that he was seriously injured because of faulty brakes in his car. When Johanna investigates the claim, it becomes evident that the faulty brakes are not solely a problem for Xavier's car, but derive from a design defect that affects hundreds of thousands of cars that Car Co. has already sold and/or are on the market. Car Co. asks Johanna for advice on whether to recall the car—which it believes will be somewhat more expensive than settlement payouts for injuries, even serious injuries, to consumers. How might Johanna advise Car Co.? Think about relational self-interests, as well as moral, economic, and legal concerns.

Professional Responsibility in Practice

1. What are your responsibilities as a member of the legal profession? Articulate your personal understanding of your professional obligations to your clients, the system of justice, third parties, and yourself.

2. In the Four Component Model for Personal Conscience discussed by Neil Hamilton, the first component is Moral Sensitivity—the awareness that one's actions affect others and the ability to trace through the consequences for different possible courses of action. Assume that you are Zimmerman's lawyer and decide to meet with Zimmerman to discuss the existence of Spaulding's aneurysm. Outline the possible different courses of action and the potential consequences of each.

3. Consider the OLC's expansive definition of torture. If you were representing someone who was being prosecuted for allegedly violating the federal statute implementing the Convention Against Torture by engaging in enhanced interrogation techniques, could you ethically argue that the OLC's interpretation is correct and should be adopted by the court? Is there any reason you might not do so?

2

The Regulation of the Legal Profession

The law governing lawyers is increasingly fragmented and no longer neatly accessible in one source.[1] The "traditional duo of courts and bar associations" historically provided the source of law governing lawyers, and it was primarily contained in professional ethics or conduct codes.[2] This duo of courts and bar associations and their conduct codes still play a leading role in the regulation of lawyers but today state and federal legislators, administrators, and others increasingly create additional duties for lawyers.[3] As we noted in Chapter 1, for example, Congress authorized the Securities and Exchange Commission (SEC) to create standards governing lawyer conduct in the securities field. The SEC has expanded lawyers' reporting duties beyond ABA Model Rule 1.13 to require lawyers to report any material breach of securities law to an organization's general counsel or CEO, whereas

Key Concepts

- Each state's highest court generally has inherent authority to regulate the legal profession
- Many federal courts adopt lawyer conduct rules patterned after state rules
- Government organizations may also regulate lawyers
- Applicants must show good character and fitness for bar admission
- Each state's highest court generally disciplines lawyers; federal courts usually adopt the state court's discipline
- Lawyers and clients have an agency relationship creating fiduciary duties
- Lawyers are professionally liable for breach of contract, breach of fiduciary duties, and negligent representation

1. John Leubsdorf, *Legal Ethics Falls Apart*, 57 Buff. L. Rev. 959 (2009) ("Nowadays, a lawyer's duties . . . are likely to vary with the lawyer's specialty, the tribunal or agency before which the lawyer practices, the state or states in which the lawyer is acting, and other factors.").
2. *See* Jack P. Sahl, *Cracks in the Profession's Monopoly Power*, 82 Fordham L. Rev. 2635-37 (2014) (quoting Leubsdorf, *supra* note 1, at 961).
3. *See* Leubsdorf, *supra* note 1, at 959-62; James M. Fischer, *External Control over the American Bar*, 19 Geo. J. Legal Ethics 59, 108 (2006).

Rule 1.13 requires reporting to higher authority in the organization only if the violation will result in substantial injury to the organization.[4]

In addition to the increasing fragmentation of the law governing lawyers, dramatic changes in the legal services market promise new challenges for lawyer regulation.[5] For example, the increasing cross-border practice of lawyers to meet client needs that traverse state and national boundaries and involve different legal systems, major law firm consolidations and closures, and the development of new technologies that promote a quick-paced and often stressful practice all potentially enhance the risk of lawyer mistakes and abuses. As a result of this changing landscape, lawyer regulation will continue to be an important concern of the profession. Regulators will need to be proactive and creative in this changing landscape to protect the public and the courts from lawyer misconduct and to maintain the integrity of the legal profession — the traditional goals of lawyer regulation.

A. LAWYER REGULATION

1. Regulatory Powers of State Courts

In general, each state's high court, usually its supreme court, possesses the authority to regulate the legal profession.[6] Some state constitutions expressly provide this regulatory authority to the courts, but in most states the supreme courts assert inherent and exclusive regulatory power based on the separation of powers doctrine.[7] In some states, the legislature and the courts share authority to establish rules regulating the profession with the courts having the ultimate authority over regulation.[8] This means there are at least 50 different regulatory regimes governing the legal profession and the delivery of legal services in the United States, presenting a regulatory compliance challenge for lawyers given the increase in cross-border practice.

The state supreme courts adopt professional conduct codes and regulate many aspects of practice ranging from bar admission and defining the practice of law to establishing continuing legal education and professional discipline standards. The state ethics codes and related rules generally track in whole or in part ABA model codes and standards, such as the ABA Model Rules of Professional Conduct for lawyers and the **ABA Standards for Imposing Lawyer Sanctions**. These courts rely on a

---

4. 17 C.F.R. §205.3(d)(2). Sarbanes-Oxley also established minimum practice standards for lawyers appearing before the SEC. 15 U.S.C. §7245 (2006). Leubsdorf, *supra* note 1, at 1018.

5. Elizabeth Olson, *Law Firms Cull Partner Ranks in Face of Market Changes*, N.Y. TIMES, Nov. 22, 2016, at B1 (reporting firms are de-equitizing partners, demoting them from firm ownership, because of limited growth in the legal services market; stating "22 percent of the 93,000 lawyers in the top 100 firms are equity partners, . . . compared with 35 percent in 1996").

6. The idiosyncratic nature of lawyer regulation in the United States is reflected, in part, in New York, where the state legislature has vested regulatory control of the bar with four appellate divisions of the state supreme courts instead of with its high court, the New York Court of Appeals. *See* ABA/BNA LAW. MAN. ON PROF. CONDUCT at 201:101-02 (1996) (citing N.Y. Jud. Law §90 (2013)) [hereinafter ABA/BNA MAN.].

7. *See id.* at 201:102. *But see* N.Y. Jud. Law §90 (2013) (where legislature authorized regulatory authority).

8. In re Garcia, 315 P.3d 117, 124 (Cal. 2014) (acknowledging the legislature and the California Supreme Court possess authority to create rules regulating admission to the bar but that the court "bears the ultimate responsibility" to determine admission and regulate law practice under its inherent powers).

system of administrative offices, such as a professional conduct board or a **continuing legal education** (CLE) office, to handle the actual regulatory work. Annual lawyer registration fees, reinstatement fees, and other funds, such as cost reimbursements from disciplined lawyers and civil penalties, help fund this regulatory framework.

State bar associations often provide valuable assistance to state supreme courts concerning lawyer and judicial regulation, for example, by recommending changes to ethics or conduct standards, issuing advisory opinions interpreting ethics rules, establishing task forces to examine the role of lawyers, and staffing fee dispute and discipline panels. Such assistance occurs irrespective of whether the bar is an "**integrated**" or "unified" state bar association (where the high court requires bar membership to practice law) or a "**non-integrated**" or "non-unified" bar, where bar association membership is voluntary.[9]

In addition to adopting lawyer and judicial ethics codes, each state's high court promulgates related rules for the internal governance of the bar and courts, such as rules concerning admission, CLE, lawyer discipline, and certification as a specialist. For example, the Florida Supreme Court adopted two amendments to the Rules Regulating the Florida Bar, making it the first state to require technology-related CLE courses for lawyers.[10]

2. Bar Associations and Lawyer Ethics (Conduct) Codes

Bar associations arose in the American colonial period as a result of lawyers' social gatherings and eating clubs, where lawyers shared professional concerns.[11] Although the significance of bar associations declined in the early nineteenth century, by the 1870s they spearheaded an effort to professionalize the legal community and enhance its reputation by increasing training and admission standards while highlighting the profession's goal of promoting the administration of justice and upholding the honor of the profession.[12] In 1870, the landmark founding of the City Bar of New York was soon followed by the creation of other local bar associations, and ultimately, the establishment of a national bar association in 1878, the American Bar Association.[13] These bar associations promoted their members'

9. Charles W. Wolfram, Modern Legal Ethics 37-39 (1986) (noting integrated bars existed in 33 states and the District of Columbia by the 1980s and that they do not violate the First Amendment's freedom of speech or association principles (discussing Lathrop v. Donohue, 367 U.S. 820 (1961)). The Supreme Court held in Keller v. State Bar of California, 496 U.S. 1 (1990), that the integrated bar's mandatory dues may support matters that benefit all members of the bar, for example, supporting the lawyer disciplinary process or CLE. However, bar dues may not be used to support unrelated political or ideological issues that do not benefit the general membership, such as lobbying for legislation to ban armor-piercing ammunition. *Id.* at 15.

10. ABA/BNA Man., *supra* note 6, at 620-21. The Amendment to Rule 6-10.3 (Minimum Continuing Legal Education Standards) increased Florida's CLE requirement beginning in 2017 from 30 to 33 hours over a three-year period with the additional three hours being in technologically related CLE.

11. Wolfram, *supra* note 9, at 34.

12. Allison Marston, *Guiding the Profession: The 1887 Code of Ethics of the Alabama State Bar Association*, 49 Ala. L. Rev. 471, 473-75 (1998).

13. Mary M. Devlin, *The Development of Lawyer Disciplinary Procedures in the United States*, 17 J. Prof. Law. 364-66 (1994) (reporting that "Jacksonian democracy's anti-elitist ethos, combined with the elimination of formal training requirements made admission to the bar relatively easy" causing, in part, the creation of local bar associations by the 1870s to establish professional control).

economic and social status, in part, by controlling admission to the profession and assisting in the regulation of the practice of law.[14]

In 1887, the Alabama State Bar Association promulgated the first code of ethics for lawyers in the United States and it became the basis for the ABA's first ethics code in 1908, the Canons of Legal Ethics.[15] There were originally 32 canons that provided general guidance for lawyer behavior in hope of promoting public "confidence in the integrity and impartiality" of the administration of justice. For example, Canon 1, The Duty of the Lawyer to the Courts, provided, in part: "[i]t is the duty of the lawyer to maintain towards the Courts a respectful attitude, not for the sake of the temporary incumbent of the judicial office but for the maintenance of its supreme importance."[16] Other canons addressed different aspects of practice in general terms such as directing lawyers to avoid abusing a client's trust for personal gain and to be candid and fair when dealing with the courts and other lawyers.[17] Twenty-two states adopted the canons by 1910, and the ABA ultimately issued 47 canons.[18]

In 1969, the ABA issued a new ethics code, the **Model Code of Professional Responsibility**. It consisted of nine canons that addressed broad principles of lawyer behavior with each canon followed by multiple ethical considerations (ECs) or aspirational statements that discussed those principles in greater detail. ECs were followed by Disciplinary Rules (DRs) that identified minimum standards of lawyer behavior. To illustrate, Canon 6 stated, "A Lawyer Should Represent a Client Competently," and EC 6-5 added the aspirational statement "[a] lawyer should have pride in his professional endeavors." DR 6-101, titled "Failing to Act Competently," warned that "[a] lawyer shall not: . . . [n]eglect a legal matter entrusted to him." A lawyer was subject to professional discipline for violating a DR but not for violating a canon or an EC.

In the summer of 1977, the ABA appointed the **Commission on the Evaluation of Professional Standards**, commonly known as the Kutak Commission in honor of its chair, Robert J. Kutak. It was charged with "evaluating whether existing standards of professional conduct provided comprehensive and consistent guidance for resolving the increasingly complex ethical problems in the practice of law."[19] As a result of the Kutak Commission's work, the ABA created a new ethics code, the Model Rules of Professional Conduct, adopted on August 2, 1983.

The Model Rules adopted a new format, consisting of rules and comments. The Model Rules' preamble explains that some rules are partly obligatory and disciplinary in nature, usually stated as imperatives—"a lawyer shall or must" act a certain way or be subject to discipline. Some rules, however, are more permissive, stating "a lawyer may or should" act a certain way, giving the lawyer some discretion over

---

14. Wolfram, *supra* note 9, at 34.
15. Marston, *supra* note 12, at 471.
16. ABA Canons of Professional Ethics, Canon 1.
17. *Id.* Canons 11 & 22, at 426 & 429.
18. M. Louise Rutherford, The Influence of the American Bar Association on Public Opinion and Legislation 89 (1937).
19. Commission on Evaluation of the Rules of Professional Conduct, Chair's Intro. ("Ethics 2000"), ABA Model Rules of Professional Conduct, ABA Compendium of Professional Responsibility Rules and Standards 11 (2015) [hereinafter ABA Rules Compendium].

his conduct. Yet other rules simply describe the relationship between the lawyer and the client or others.

The comments provide explanations and illustrations for each rule, and help guide lawyers and regulators in interpreting the rules. Failure to comply with a comment does not subject the lawyer to potential discipline, whereas noncompliance with a rule does create the risk of discipline.

Review of the Model Rules is a continual process and is part of the charge of the ABA Standing Committee on Ethics and Professionalism. As a result, the Model Rules have been amended periodically. In 1997, the ABA established an **Ethics 2000 Commission** to conduct the first comprehensive review of the Model Rules since its creation in 1983.[20] A primary impetus for Ethics 2000 involved the desire to better understand the reasons for the lack of uniformity among the states' ethics codes based on the ABA Model Rules. Although 42 states and Washington, D.C. had adopted versions of the ABA Model Rules, there was "an undesirable lack of uniformity" among the versions.[21] A few states, like Ohio, still followed the old 1969 Code of Professional Responsibility, and California retained a separate regulatory system. Another impetus that would resurface in future ABA ethics reviews concerned the impact of technological developments on the delivery of legal services. The ABA House of Delegates, its legislative body, adopted the Ethics 2000 Commission's Report in August 2002 after some earlier modifications. Some of the Ethics 2000 changes included strengthening the lawyer's duty to communicate with a client and clarifying the lawyer's obligations to the tribunal and justice system.[22]

After Ethics 2000, the ABA conducted two more studies to determine what, if any, possible changes were necessary to the Model Rules or the regulation of the profession in general given developments in the legal services market. In 2009, the ABA appointed the **Ethics 20/20 Commission** to examine the impact of globalization and technology on the legal profession. The 20/20 Commission ultimately submitted ten resolutions to the ABA House of Delegates in 2012 and 2013 and all were adopted, albeit with some changes.[23]

Ethics 20/20 provided some new ethics duties and concepts for lawyers, for example, requiring lawyers to keep abreast of technological changes, mandating an affirmative duty to communicate with clients, and clarifying which jurisdiction's conflict of interest rules apply to lawyers who are engaged in cross-border

---

20. The ABA has traditionally created commissions to consider possible reforms to its ethics code. They include the Kutak Commission (1977), the **Multidisciplinary Commission** (2000), and the **Multijurisdictional Commission** (2002). These commissions have met with varying degrees of success. *See* James E. Moliterno, *Ethics 20/20 Protected, Preserved, and Maintained*, 47 Akron L. Rev. 151, 158-50 (2014) (arguing that various ABA commissions' reform proposals fail due to the ABA's self-interest in protecting and maintaining the status quo, or fending off outside challengers and cultural change).

21. ABA Rules Compendium, *supra* note 19, at 15.

22. *Id.* at 17.

23. The resolutions covered such topics as Technology and Confidentiality; Technology and Client Development; Outsourcing; Practice Pending Admission (easing the burden on lawyers moving to a new jurisdiction by permitting practice after applying for admission and awaiting final approval); Admission by Motion (reducing the recommended years in practice prerequisite for motion admission); and Model Rule 1.6, Detection of Conflicts of Interest (permitting some disclosure of client information when a lawyer changes firms to avoid a conflict of interests). Laurel S. Terry, *Globalization and the ABA Commission on Ethics 20/20: Reflections on Missed Opportunities and Roads Not Taken*, 45 Hofstra L. Rev. 95, 98-100 (2014).

practice.[24] Two of the final four resolutions addressed the ability of foreign lawyers to practice in the United States as in-house counsel; a third resolution added foreign lawyers to the ABA's Model Rules on **Pro Hac Vice Admission**, and the final one addressed the "predominant effects" test for resolving which jurisdiction's conflict of interests rules apply in the transnational context.[25]

In 2014, the ABA created the **Commission on the Future of the Legal Services** (Futures Commission) in hope of improving both the delivery of and access to legal services. The Futures Commission Report issued 12 recommendations, with many containing multiple subsections or comments. For example, Recommendation 2 urged courts to consider regulatory innovations to promote greater access to legal services, such as authorizing new service providers like Washington's Triple LTs (Limited Licensed Legal Technicians) and alternative business structures (ABS) that might allow non-lawyers to own entities delivering legal services. Recommendation 5 also encouraged courts to be accessible and user-friendly to all litigants by providing forms in plain English, multilingual written materials, and physical and virtual access to everyone. Recommendation 6 called for the establishment of an innovation center to develop new and creative ways to address critical needs in the legal sector.

While there have been many changes to the Model Rules, they continue to highlight the fundamental notion that "lawyers play a vital role in the preservation of society" because of their training and special privilege to deliver legal services.[26] They assist clients and others in resolving their problems and obtaining access to justice. Lawyers are also officers of the court and owe it special duties, for example, to avoid unnecessary delay and misrepresentations. In short, lawyers occupy a unique place in our society and government, functioning as gatekeepers in the administration of justice with a special responsibility to promote access to justice.

B. ADMISSION TO THE BAR

Like other professions, the legal profession has historically cited its members' specialized training and their obligation to follow a code of ethics that highlights their commitment to deliver high quality service to the public as reasons to exercise strict control over entry into the profession and the delivery of legal services. However, some observers contend the profession's "behavioral norms and implementation of discipline are self-serving."[27] As you proceed in this chapter, you should consider whether the current regulatory regime effectively promotes the public interest in access to legal services and justice.

The United States Supreme Court has rejected some bar admission decisions and regulations as violative of the United States Constitution. For example, in Supreme Court of New Hampshire v. Piper, 470 U.S. 274 (1985), the Court held a New

24. Rule 1.1 cmt. [8]; Rule 1.4 cmt. [3]; Rule 8.5 cmt. [5].
25. Terry, *supra* note 23, at 98-99.
26. ABA Rules Compendium, *supra* note 19, at 21.
27. *See, e.g.*, Fred C. Zacharias, *The Myth of Self-Regulations*, 93 Minn. L. Rev. 1147, 1150-51 (1999).

Hampshire court rule limiting bar admission to only state residents violated the **Privileges and Immunities Clause** of Article IV of the United States Constitution.[28] The New Hampshire Supreme Court defended its rule by arguing that nonresident lawyers will be less likely to become familiar with local rules and procedures, to behave ethically, to be available for court proceedings, and to do pro bono work. The Court found no evidence to support the belief that nonresident lawyers will not keep abreast of rules and procedures, behave ethically, and attempt to perform pro bono work. The Court acknowledged that a nonresident might find it more difficult to attend meetings on short notice but that this reason was insufficient to justify the exclusion of nonresidents. Also, the state could protect its interests with less restrictive means by requiring the distant, nonresident lawyer to retain a local lawyer to be available for unscheduled meetings.[29]

1. Educational Requirements

In most states, admission to the practice of law requires applicants to complete a special course of study at law school and then to pass a multiday bar examination. Seven states still permit students to take the bar examination after completing a period of apprenticeship instead of attending law school.[30] Wisconsin is the only "diploma privilege" state where graduates of Wisconsin law schools are admitted to the bar without taking Wisconsin's bar examination.[31] Graduates of ABA-accredited law schools are eligible to take the bar examination in any state. Graduates of non-ABA or state-only accredited law schools are limited to taking the bar examination in the state where the school is accredited. For example, California has a significant number of state-only accredited law schools and graduates of these schools are eligible to take only the California bar examination. The different treatment concerning bar examination eligibility may stem, in part, from the belief that ABA accreditation standards are sufficiently

In most states, admission to the bar requires applicants to pass a multiday bar examination.
bibiphoto/Shutterstock.com

28. *See also* Supreme Court of Virginia v. Friedman, 487 U.S. 59, 67 (1988) (declaring unconstitutional under the Privileges and Immunities Clause a rule requiring experienced lawyers waiving into Virginia to maintain a residence in the state).
29. Supreme Court of New Hampshire v. Piper, 470 U.S. at 279-80.
30. Comprehensive Guide to Bar Admission Requirements 2016, Nat'l Conf. of Bar Exam. & ABA Sec. of Legal Ed. & Admission to the Bar 8-9 (identifying the seven "apprenticeship" states as California, Vermont, Virginia, Washington, Maine, New York, and West Virginia, the last three requiring a combination of apprenticeship and law school); Sean Patrick Farrell, *The Lincoln Lawyers*, N.Y. Times, Aug. 3, 2014, at 22 (reporting that only 60 of the 83,986 people who took the bar examination in 2014 were "law office readers" or apprentices).
31. Wiesmueller v. Kosobucki, 571 F.3d 699 (7th Cir. 2009).

rigorous to promote any state's interest in protecting the public from unqualified persons practicing law.[32]

Many states permit "admission on motion." This approach permanently admits experienced lawyers in good standing in another state bar without requiring them to take a bar examination or only requiring a partial examination. States may limit admission on motion to those lawyers applying from states that offer a similar policy. To illustrate, state A waives its bar examination requirement and admits experienced lawyers from state B if state B reciprocates or similarly waives its bar examination requirement and admits experienced lawyers from state A. Courts have upheld these "reciprocity agreements."[33]

Section 2 of the Restatement (Third) of the Law Governing Lawyers (Restatement) notes that each federal district court, court of appeals, specialized federal court, and the Supreme Court have separate bars that require a separate admission and ongoing registration compliance to remain in good standing for each. It further notes admission to these bars is routine on application and may require lawyers to be admitted to a local bar. Section 2 reports some federal administrative agencies also have bars; admission to a state bar generally "suffices . . . to practice before almost all federal agencies."

2. Character and Fitness

The lawyer-client relationship is a fiduciary one with the lawyer acting as the agent for the benefit of the client-principal. Clients repose great trust in their lawyers to help them resolve their problems. The lawyer's knowledge and training gives the professional significant power in the lawyer-client relationship and provides corrupt lawyers with the opportunity to harm clients and diminish public confidence in the justice system.

Given this potential for harm, bar admission applicants must typically demonstrate by clear and convincing evidence that they possess the requisite character, fitness, and moral qualifications to practice law. Some states only require the applicant to show the requisite **good character and fitness** by a preponderance of the evidence.

Section 2 of the Restatement provides guidance in construing the "good moral character and fitness" requirement: "[t]he central inquiry concerns the present ability and disposition of the applicant to practice competently and honestly." United States Supreme Court Justice Felix Frankfurter believed good moral character

32. ABA Accreditation Standard 301(a) provides that "[a] law school shall maintain a rigorous program of legal education that prepares its students, upon graduation, for admission to the bar and for effective, ethical, and responsible participation as members of the legal profession." A recent, controversial provision requires law schools to also publish "learning outcomes designed to achieve these objectives." Standard 301(b). ABA Section on Legal Education and Admissions, 2016-2017 Standards and Rules of Procedure for Approval of Law School, http://www.americanbar.org/groups/legal_education/resources/standards.html. These outcomes should reflect knowledge of the substantive law, and the acquisition of skills and ethical judgment necessary to competently represent clients. *Id.* at Standard 302.

33. National Ass'n for Advancement of Multijurisdictional Practice v. Berch, 973 F. Supp. 2d 1082 (Ariz. 2013); *aff'd sub nom.* 773 F.2d 1037 (9th Cir. 2014).

involves "qualities of truth-speaking, of a high sense of honor, of granite discretion, [and] of the strictest observance of fiduciary responsibility."[34] Fitness also encompasses the principle that the bar candidate be free of chemical addiction or emotional stability problems that would prevent the lawyer from competently implementing the client's objectives.

Although the good moral character and fitness standard is broad and open to many interpretations, bar applicants must fully answer all the questions on the bar application, which requires an extensive personal history.[35] Applicants will be notified of any concerns based on the application or any other source, perhaps something regarding the applicant's criminal history or a record that lacks honesty, trustworthiness, or reliability. Possible factors affecting an applicant's character and fitness assessment include a violation of the honor code at the applicant's undergraduate or law school; a pattern of disregard for the law; failure to provide complete and accurate information concerning the applicant's past; evidence of psychological disorder that if left untreated would affect the person's ability to practice law; evidence of an existing and untreated chemical dependency; false statements; and acts involving dishonesty, fraud, deceit, misrepresentation, or neglect.[36]

In hope of promoting the integrity of the profession through a careful and thorough bar admission process, ABA Model Rule 8.1(a) prohibits the applicant, or a lawyer recommending the applicant, from knowingly making a false statement of a material fact in connection with a bar admission application. When the lawyer has knowledge of a falsehood and what constitutes a material fact is sometimes unclear, presenting difficult and debatable questions of fact.

Rule 8.1(b) imposes the affirmative duty on the applicant or a lawyer recommending the applicant to disclose facts necessary to correct any misapprehensions about the applicant to help provide admission authorities with a more complete picture of the applicant. Rule 8.1(b) also directs applicants and lawyers to cooperate with a demand for information from admissions or disciplinary authorities, unless the information is protected by Rule 1.6. For example, if a lawyer represents the bar applicant in a matter separate from her application and learns unflattering information about the applicant, the lawyer would not have to volunteer that information to bar admission authorities under Rule 1.6.

A local bar committee, commonly called the character and fitness or admissions committee, often meets with the applicant to further investigate any concerns that are flagged on the application. In some states, these committees will interview each candidate for the bar, irrespective of any red flags, to obtain additional information about a candidate's character.[37] If there is an adverse determination after the character and fitness committee's review, then the applicant generally may appeal to another administrative level of review and ultimately to the state's high court, which

---

34. Schware v. Board of Bar Examiners, 353 U.S. 232, 247 (1957).

35. *See* Konigsberg v. California, 366 U.S. 36 (1960) (upholding the denial of admission when the applicant failed to answer questions during a character investigation concerning his membership in the Communist party because it interfered with the character investigation).

36. Ohio Gov. Bar Rule I, §11(D)(3(a)-(o).

37. *Id.* §11(C)(2) (also requiring the report of the National Conference of Bar Examiners that conducts a separate examination of the candidate's bar questionnaire).

makes the final decision. Applicants must fully cooperate during the investigation and the entire process; the failure to cooperate can trigger adverse consequences. The United States Supreme Court held in Schware v. Board of Bar Examiners, 353 U.S. 232, 239 (1957), that states can require "high standards of qualifications, such as good moral character or proficiency in the law" for bar admission but such "qualifications must have a rational connection with the applicant's fitness or capacity to practice law." In *Schware*, the Court concluded the applicant's prior membership in the Communist party, several arrests without convictions that occurred many years ago, and his use of aliases to avoid anti-Semitism and to obtain work and be an effective labor activist did not show a lack of the requisite good character and fitness for bar admission. As a practical matter, relatively few applicants are denied admission for lack of good character and fitness, but a more substantial "number [are] deterred, delayed or harassed" in gaining admission.[38]

For example, in In re McKinney, 134 Ohio St. 3d 260 (2012), McKinney first wrote on the bar application that she left a former job because it conflicted with her school schedule. McKinney also wrote on the application that she was fired from the job for using the firm's email for personal reasons. In fact, she was fired for violating firm policy by using its email for personal reasons *and* creating fictitious letters on firm letterhead indicating McKinney was being transferred to another location for work. The work transfer scheme allowed McKinney to terminate her apartment lease without liability. McKinney also changed the voicemail on her sister's telephone to help the sister impersonate a fictitious human resource person at the firm in case the landlord called to verify McKinney's transfer.

Before conducting McKinney's character and fitness interview, the local admissions committee contacted the employer and learned of McKinney's scheme to defraud the landlord. The interviewers gave her open-ended questions to allow her to fully disclose the circumstances of her termination. Instead, she gave evasive answers, causing the committee to recommend disapproval of her application. McKinney appealed to a three-person panel of the Board of Commissioners on Character and Fitness, which noted her various volunteer work, including assistance at a domestic violence and sexual assault center and for a law student society. She also had five character reference letters, three of them from professors and one from a current lawyer-employer who testified he believed her to be honest and would retain her after bar admission. The panel also recommended disapproval of her application with an opportunity to reapply for the July 2014 bar exam. The full board adopted the panel's findings but decided McKinney could never establish her character and fitness to practice law, noting she was a 30-year-old law student at the time of her deceptive scheme and was evasive throughout the entire process.

The Ohio Supreme Court agreed McKinney had continued her deceitful scheme from her first year of law school through the admissions process and thus failed to show by clear and convincing evidence the requisite character and fitness to practice law. The court also noted McKinney had applied herself in law school, had good references, including a lawyer who planned to hire her after the bar exam,

38. ABA/BNA Man., *supra* note 6, at 21:705 (Aug. 31, 2010) (citing Deborah Rhode, *Moral Character as Professional Credential*, 94 Yale L.J. 491, 493-94 (1985)).

and she appeared genuinely remorseful. The court rejected the full board's permanent ban on McKinney taking the exam, ruling McKinney could rehabilitate her character and reapply for the July 2014 bar examination subject to a full character and fitness investigation.

As reflected in *McKinney*, an applicant's deceitful conduct generally prompts serious concerns about the applicant's character and fitness to practice law. In addition to the blatant deceit in *McKinney*, there are other forms of conduct that pose difficult questions for bar regulators in assessing an applicant's character. For example, what role, if any, do you think an applicant's immigration status should play in assessing whether the applicant has the requisite good character and fitness for bar admission?

In 2014, the California Supreme Court admitted an undocumented immigrant, Sergio C. Garcia, to the California bar following a newly enacted California law that authorized the court to admit "an applicant [to the bar] who is not lawfully present in the United States [but who] has fulfilled the requirements for admission to practice law."[39] The California Supreme Court held the new law complied with an exception in the federal law that prohibited states from granting professional licenses to undocumented immigrants, thus avoiding any conflict with federal law that would create a preemption issue under the Supremacy Clause. The state high court emphasized that although the Committee of Bar Examiners makes the initial determination on a case-by-case basis about whether the applicant has demonstrated the requisite good character, the California Supreme Court makes the final decision. It noted that "'[g]ood moral character' has been traditionally defined as the absence of conduct imbued with elements of 'moral turpitude.' It includes 'qualities of honesty, fairness, candor, and trustworthiness, observance of fiduciary responsibility, respect for and obedience to the laws of the state and the nation and respect for the rights of others and for the judicial process.'" The California Supreme Court decided an undocumented immigrant's unlawful presence in the United States does not itself demonstrate unfitness to be admitted to the bar. Reviewing Garcia's entire background, including "one or two problematical incidents" and the numerous strong references attesting to his good character, the court held Garcia had demonstrated that "he possesses the requisite good character to qualify for a law license."

In another controversial case, Hale v. Committee on Character and Fitness to Practice for the State of Illinois, 335 F.3d 678 (7th Cir. 2003), the appeals court affirmed a dismissal of the applicant's §1983 claim that the state's Committee on Character and Fitness (Committee) had violated his First Amendment rights. Hale was denied admission to the Illinois bar because the committee found him unfit to practice law. Hale's life mission was to further the hegemony of the white race, to abolish

Professional Licenses for Undocumented Immigrants: Sergio Garcia

Sergio Garcia, the first undocumented lawyer to be granted a law license, began practicing law in California in 2014 after his successful legal battle to obtain his law license. After his acceptance into the California bar, in June of 2015 Garcia received a green card, which allows him to live and work on a permanent basis in the United States. *Immigrant California Lawyer Finally Gets Green Card*, The San Mateo Daily J. (Cal.), June 5, 2015.

39. In re Garcia, 315 P.3d 117, 124 (Cal. 2014).

equal protection, and to deport non-white Americans by nonviolent means. The committee believed that Hale was likely to engage in conduct inconsistent with bar membership and stated: "Hale's active commitment to bigotry . . . demonstrated a 'gross deficiency in moral character, particularly for lawyers who have a special responsibility to uphold the rule of law for all persons.'" A hearing panel affirmed this determination, and the Illinois Supreme Court refused to hear the appeal.

An applicant's financial situation is also a relevant factor in the character and fitness review. For example, in In re Anonymous, 889 N.Y.S.2d 713 (N.Y. App. Div. 2009), the applicant had passed the 2008 bar examination but was denied admission after reporting $430,000 in delinquent student loans covering a 20-year period without making any substantial payments. The applicant said the economic downturn and bad faith negotiations by some of the lenders caused the nonpayment. The court concluded: "His application demonstrates a course of action amounting to neglect of financial responsibilities"—the loans with interest now totaling $480,000. "His recalcitrance in dealing with lenders [was] incompatible with a lawyer's duties and responsibilities. . . ."

Case Preview

In re Glass

The *Glass* case was decided the same year as *In re Garcia*, discussed above. But in *Glass*, the California Supreme Court reached a result adverse to the applicant, denying Mr. Glass bar admission after he had passed the 2004 bar examination. The court did not believe Mr. Glass was sincere in contending he had rehabilitated his dishonest character.

In reading this case, consider the following:

1. As noted in *Glass*, applicants generally get the "benefit of the doubt" where there are "conflicting equally reasonable inferences" about one's fitness for the bar. Why did the court reject that approach here?
2. What facts led the court to conclude Glass's conduct was "reprehensible"?
3. What was the court's response to the witnesses who supported Glass's bar admission because they believed in his personal redemption?
4. Does the court suggest that its denial of Glass's admission was simply a case of an applicant seeking bar admission too soon after a serious infraction?

In re Glass

316 P.3d 1199 (Cal. 2014)

THE COURT:

Stephen Randall Glass made himself infamous as a dishonest journalist by fabricating material for more than 40 articles for The New Republic magazine and other publications. He also carefully fabricated supporting materials to delude The New

Republic's fact checkers. The articles appeared between June 1996 and May 1998, and included falsehoods that reflected negatively on individuals, political groups, and ethnic minorities. During the same period, starting in September 1997, he was also an evening law student at Georgetown University's law school. Glass made every effort to avoid detection once suspicions were aroused, lobbied strenuously to keep his job at The New Republic, and, in the aftermath of his exposure, did not fully cooperate with the publications to identify his fabrications.

Glass applied to become a member of the New York bar in 2002, but withdrew his application after he was informally notified in 2004 that his moral character application would be rejected. In the New York bar application materials, he exaggerated his cooperation with the journals that had published his work and failed to supply a complete list of the fabricated articles that had injured others.

Glass passed the California Bar examination in 2006 and filed an application for determination of moral character in 2007. It was not until the California State Bar moral character proceedings that Glass reviewed all of his articles, as well as the editorials The New Republic and other journals published to identify his fabrications, and ultimately identified fabrications that he previously had denied or failed to disclose. In the California proceedings, Glass was not forthright in acknowledging the defects in his New York bar application.

I. FACTS

A. Committee of Bar Examiners' Evidence

In September 1995 Glass accepted a position at The New Republic magazine. In early June 1996 he began fabricating material for publication. The fabrications continued and became bolder and more comprehensive until he was exposed and fired in May 1998.

Glass testified at the State Bar Court hearing that he "wrote nasty, mean-spirited, horrible" things about people: "My articles hurt, and they were cruel. . . ." He testified that the fabrications gave him "A-plus" stories that afforded him status in staff meetings and also gave particular enjoyment to his colleagues. He said: "Overwhelmingly, what everyone remembers about my pieces are the fake things."

. . .

In [an] article, entitled *Deliverance*, published in November 1996, Glass recounted receiving unsatisfactory service from a named computer company, and claimed that his complaints to a telephone customer service representative were met with an anti-Semitic slur. In truth, no such slur ever was uttered. Glass also wrote a letter to the president of the company, repeating the accusation, and sent a copy to the Anti-Defamation League.

Glass also engaged in fabrications in freelance articles published by other magazines. [For example], Glass wrote an article entitled *The Vernon Question* for George magazine. The lengthy article, published in April 1998, concerned Vernon Jordan, an advisor to then President Clinton during the then emerging Monica Lewinsky scandal. In two paragraphs, Glass used nonexistent sources to describe Jordan's supposed reputation as a "boor" and attributed various fictitious statements to "political operatives," "socialites," "political hostesses" and officials. These persons assertedly stated that Jordan was well known for sexually explicit comments, unwanted sexual advances, and crude stares, and added that he was known in their circles as "Vern the Worm" or "Pussyman," and that young women needed protection against him. Another paragraph attributed to a fictional "watchdog" group contained certain claims about Jordan's asserted conflicts of interest and questionable corporate ethics . . . . These were all fabrications.

Charles Lane, who was the editor of The New Republic at the time of Glass's exposure, testified for the Committee of Bar Examiners (hereafter sometimes Committee) that he had received an early complaint about Glass concerning an article entitled *Boys on the Bus*, depicting the actor Alec Baldwin and his brother as silly celebrities whose efforts during a bus tour to campaign on the issue of campaign finance reform were based on ignorance. A representative of Baldwin's disputed the assertion in the article that the actor had been giving out autographs during the bus tour, but Glass repudiated the accusation in print in The New Republic.

Although at the time, the *Boys on the Bus* incident seemingly was resolved in Glass's favor, Lane's suspicions were aroused in May 1998 when a journalist employed by Forbes Digital Tool telephoned to warn him that factual assertions in Glass's recent article for George magazine, *Hack Heaven*, did not seem to be true. The article had described a teenager hacking a California software company and extorting money to stop the intrusion. The article described a convention in Bethesda, Maryland, where some of the events occurred, and when Lane challenged Glass, the latter journeyed with Lane to Bethesda, purporting to identify the building where the convention had been held. A person working in the building denied such a convention had occurred, and Lane became persuaded that Glass was lying. Lane pressed Glass about the factual basis for the article, and although Glass was evasive, he insisted the article was accurate. Glass spent the night at home fabricating what he would assert were his reporter's notes from interviews, fake business cards, a voicemail box, a Web site, and newsletters. He also induced his brother to impersonate a source.

[At one point while in the home office in Bethesda, Lane] . . . confronted Glass with evidence that Glass had used his brother as a false source in the *Hack Heaven* piece. Ultimately, during this exchange Glass admitted the article was fabricated, and Lane fired him.

Lane reviewed all of Glass's articles over the course of the following three or four weeks. He received a letter from Glass apologizing and saying he had instructed his lawyers to cooperate with The New Republic. Lane compiled a summary of the material in Glass's articles that he found suspicious and submitted the summary to Glass's counsel, who it was agreed would stipulate to those findings of Lane's that Glass believed to be correct. At the time, Lane concluded that 27 of the 42 articles Glass had written for the magazine contained fabrications, and Lane wrote two editorial articles informing the magazine's readership to this effect.

. . .

Glass graduated from law school in 2000, when he also took and passed the New York bar examination. He applied to become a member of the New York bar in 2002. After an evidentiary hearing before a subcommittee of a committee on character and fitness, and pursuant to apparent custom, in September 2004, a representative of that committee informed Glass informally that his application would be rejected, so he withdrew it. The record does not disclose the reason for the tentative decision.

In his application to the New York bar, Glass described his misconduct and firing. His application and supporting materials included only 20 articles containing fabrications. Glass wrote that he had apologized to the editor of The New Republic, saying, "I also worked with all three magazines [(referring to The New Republic, Harper's, and George magazines)] and other publications where I had written free-lance articles to identify which facts were true and which were false in all of my stories, so they could publish clarifications for their readers."

At the hearing, Lane challenged the quoted statement as untrue. Lane believed that Glass had failed to come forward to actively assist The New Republic in identifying his fabrications, and instead had placed the entire burden of identifying his errors on Lane.

B. Applicant's Evidence

Once he was fired from The New Republic, Glass was distraught, suicidal, and unable to focus, almost immediately entering therapy. He nonetheless hired counsel whom he directed to "work with The New Republic." Glass testified that he believed that The New Republic wanted to conduct its own investigation because it did not trust him and testified that "I came to understand that they were going to provide me with a list of [fabricated] articles, and that I was to affirm whether or not the article was fabricated that they showed me or that they listed." He had fabricated more than The New Republic had discovered in its investigation, although he testified that due to his distress he did not realize this when he reviewed the list . . . . Glass testified that he had "no information" indicating that his lawyers had failed to convey information to The New Republic.

Members of Georgetown University's law school faculty testified on his behalf at the hearing, finding him to be bright, honest, trustworthy, and having learned from his wrongdoing. In addition, California attorney Paul Zuckerman testified that he decided to give Glass a chance as a law clerk. After initially assigning Glass minor projects and exercising close oversight, Zuckerman became convinced that Glass was one of the best employees in the firm, with a fine intellect, a good work ethic, and reliable commitment to honesty.

Also offered in support of Glass's application were affidavits that had been submitted in support of his New York bar application from the judges for whom Glass had worked during and immediately after completing law school. Both found him highly competent and honest at that time. Additional declarations from attorneys and friends that had been submitted with the New York bar application were offered in support.

. . .

II. DISCUSSION

A. Applicable Law

. . . "Persons of good character . . . do not commit acts or crimes involving moral turpitude — a concept that embraces a wide range of deceitful and depraved behavior." A lawyer's good moral character is essential for the protection of clients and for the proper functioning of the judicial system itself.

When the applicant has presented evidence that is sufficient to establish a prima facie case of his or her good moral character, the burden shifts to the State Bar to rebut that case with evidence of poor moral character. Once the State Bar has presented evidence of moral turpitude, the burden "falls squarely upon the applicant to demonstrate his [or her] rehabilitation."

Of particular significance for the present case is the principle that "the more serious the misconduct and the bad character evidence, the stronger the applicant's showing of rehabilitation must be." "Cases authorizing admission on the basis of rehabilitation commonly involve a substantial period of *exemplary* conduct following the applicant's misdeeds." (*Ibid.*, italics added.) Moreover, "truly exemplary" conduct ordinarily includes service to the community.

. . .

B. Analysis

Although an applicant ordinarily receives the benefit of the doubt as to "conflicting equally reasonable inferences" concerning moral fitness the State Bar Court majority failed to recognize that this rule does not materially assist applicants who have engaged in serious misconduct. This is because "[w]here serious or criminal misconduct is involved, positive inferences about the applicant's moral character are more difficult to draw, and negative character inferences are stronger and *more reasonable.*" When there have been very serious acts of moral turpitude, we must be convinced that the applicant "is no longer the same person who behaved so poorly in the past," and will find moral fitness "only if he [or she] has since behaved in exemplary fashion over a meaningful period of time."

. . .

Glass's conduct as a journalist exhibited moral turpitude sustained over an extended period. As the Review Department dissent emphasized, he engaged in "fraud of staggering proportions" and he "use[d] . . . his exceptional writing skills to publicly and falsely malign people and organizations for actions they did not do and faults they did not have." As the dissent further commented, for two years he "engaged in a multi-layered, complex, and harmful course of public dishonesty." Glass's journalistic dishonesty was not a single lapse of judgment, which we have sometimes excused, but involved significant deceit sustained unremittingly for a period of years. Glass's deceit also was motivated by professional ambition, betrayed a vicious, mean spirit and a complete lack of compassion for others, along with arrogance and prejudice against various ethnic groups. In all these respects, his misconduct bore directly on his character in matters that are critical to the practice of law.

Glass not only spent two years producing damaging articles containing or entirely made up of fabrications, thereby deluding the public, maligning individuals, and disparaging ethnic minorities, he also routinely expended considerable efforts to fabricate background materials to dupe the fact checkers assigned to vet his work. When exposure threatened, he redoubled his efforts to hide his misconduct, going so far as to create a phony Web site and business cards and to recruit his brother to pose as a source. In addition, to retain his position, he engaged in a spirited campaign among the leadership at The New Republic to characterize Lane's obviously well-founded concerns as unfair and to retain his position.

Glass's conduct during this two-year period violated ethical strictures governing his profession [of journalism]. [T]he Code of Ethics of the Society of Professional Journalists provides that "[t]he duty of the journalist is to further those ends by seeking truth and providing a fair and comprehensive account of events and issues . . . . Glass's behavior fell so far short of this standard . . . .

Glass's misconduct was also reprehensible because it took place while he was pursuing a law degree and license to practice law, when the importance of honesty should have gained new meaning and significance for him.

. . .

The record also discloses instances of dishonesty and disingenuousness occurring after Glass's exposure, up to and including the State Bar evidentiary hearing in 2010. In the New York bar proceedings that ended in 2004, as even the State Bar Court majority acknowledged, he made misrepresentations concerning his cooperation with The New Republic and other publications and efforts to aid them identify all of his fabrications. He also submitted an incomplete list of articles that injured others. We have previously said about omissions on bar applications: "Whether it is caused by intentional concealment, reckless disregard for the truth, or an *unreasonable refusal to perceive the need for disclosure*, such an omission is itself strong evidence that the applicant lacks the 'integrity' and/or 'intellectual discernment' required to be an attorney."

Our review of the record indicates hypocrisy and evasiveness in Glass's testimony at the California State Bar hearing, as well. We find it particularly disturbing that at the hearing Glass persisted in claiming that he had made a good faith effort to work with the magazines that published his works. He went through many verbal twists and turns at the hearing to avoid acknowledging the obvious fact that in his New York bar application he exaggerated his level of assistance to the magazines that had published his fabrications, and that he omitted from his New York bar list of fabrications some that actually could have injured real persons. . . . He has "not acted with the 'high degree of *frankness* and truthfulness' and the 'high standard of integrity' required by this process."

. . .

We also observe that instead of directing his efforts at serving others in the community, much of Glass's energy since the end of his journalistic career seems to have been directed at advancing his own career and financial and emotional well-being.

. . .

The Review Department majority relied heavily on the testimony of Glass's character witnesses, but the testimony of character witnesses will not suffice by itself to establish rehabilitation. Moreover, stressing that Glass's reputation as a journalist had been exploded and that so many years had passed, some of the character witnesses did not sufficiently focus on the seriousness of the misconduct, incorrectly viewing it as of little current significance despite its lingering impact on its victims and on public perceptions concerning issues of race and politics. They also did not take into account, as we do, that the misconduct reflected poorly on the particular commitment to honesty that Glass might have been expected to have had as a law student. For these reasons we believe the Review Department majority accorded too much probative value to the testimony of Glass's character witnesses.

Glass emphasized the remorse he expressed through his letters to victims, and characterized his novel and his appearance on *60 Minutes* as efforts to make amends. Remorse does not establish rehabilitation, however, and in any event, the weight of this evidence is diminished because the letters were not written near the time of his misconduct and exposure, when they might have been most meaningful to the victims, but rather seemed timed to coincide with his effort to become a member of the New York bar. The novel served Glass's own purposes, producing notoriety and a fee of $175,000, and the appearance on *60 Minutes* was timed to coincide with the release of the novel. . . .

The record of Glass's therapy does not represent "truly exemplary conduct in the sense of returning something to the community." To be sure, through therapy he seems to have gained a deep understanding of the psychological sources of his misconduct, as well as tools to help him avoid succumbing to the same pressures again. His treating psychiatrists are plainly highly competent and well regarded in their field, and they are convinced that he has no remaining psychological flaws tending to cause him to act dishonestly. Glass believed that he could best make amends by changing himself. But his 12 years of therapy primarily conferred a personal benefit on Glass himself. . . .

Glass points to the pro bono legal work he does for clients of his firm as evidence of sustained efforts on behalf of the community, but we observe that pro bono work is not truly *exemplary* for attorneys, but rather is expected of them.

Glass and the witnesses who supported his application stress his talent in the law and his commitment to the profession, and they argue that he has already paid a high enough price for his misdeeds to warrant admission to the bar. They emphasize his personal redemption, but we must recall that what is at stake is not compassion for Glass, who wishes to advance from being a supervised law clerk to enjoying a license to engage in the practice of law on an independent basis. Given our duty to protect the public and maintain the integrity and high standards of the profession, our focus is on the applicant's moral fitness to practice law. On this record, the applicant failed to carry his heavy burden of establishing his rehabilitation and current fitness.

III. CONCLUSION

For the foregoing reasons, we reject the State Bar Court majority's recommendation and decline to admit Glass to the practice of law.

Post-Case Follow-Up

The *Glass* decision produced significant discussion about the bar admission process. Some critics believed that Glass had sufficiently demonstrated present fitness and good character to warrant admission to the bar or that the character review process is, at best, questionable when it comes to predicting how someone will act once admitted.[40] This may be related to the burden of proof. Should the courts apply a different stan-

40. *See* W. Bradley Wendel, *Steven Glass, Situational Forces, and the Fundamental Attribution Error*, 4 J.L.: Periodical Laboratory of Legal Scholarship 99, 104-05 (2014) (raising questions about the basis for the decision).

dard of review for candidates seeking *admission* from those seeking *readmission*? For example, should first-time bar applicants be required to offer only "substantial," instead of "clear and convincing," evidence of their good character and fitness since they have not violated the profession's conduct code? What additional evidence could Glass have offered to meet his burden of showing by clear and convincing evidence that he possessed the requisite good character for admission?

Although the concept of rehabilitation is often discussed in the context of discipline and lawyers seeking readmission, *Glass* highlights the important role it plays in the admission process itself. The seriousness of some offenses appears to require a longer probationary period than others to reassure the courts that an applicant is truly rehabilitated and deserving of a license to practice law. Should there be some instances of misconduct, for example, the applicant murdering his wife and children, committing a series of rapes, failing to file income tax forms for seven years, or being a scofflaw driver (e.g., not paying 12 university parking tickets over a three-year period in law school), that should permanently disqualify one from admission to practice law?

In re Glass: After the Decision

In 2003, Stephen Glass wrote a self-serving novel entitled *The Fabulist* (Simon & Schuster 2003). This novel, an explanation piece, shows Glass's process through his turmoil and tribulations following the 1998 revelation of his scandalous behavior at *The New Republic* and how this led to his being denied bar admission in New York and California. Glass's story received even more attention when a made-for-TV movie, *Shattered Glass*, was released on the USA Network (Shattered Glass, http://www.imdb.com/title/tt0323944/ (last visited Mar. 29, 2017)). This movie portrayed Glass's rise to fame and dramatic fall.

Shortly after Glass's last failed attempt to gain admission to the California bar, Hanna Rosin, a former colleague, conducted an interview with Glass in late 2013. Hanna Rosin, *Hello, My Name Is Stephen Glass, and I'm Sorry*, New Republic, Mar. 29, 2017, https://newrepublic.com/article/120145/stephen-glass-new-republic-scandal-still-haunts-his-law-career. During this interview, Glass reflected on a variety of events in his life, including the challenges of obtaining a position as a paralegal. As of February 2017, Glass worked as the director of special projects at two firms, where he prepares the firms' clients for trial and helps them "discover their stories." Grant Rodgers, *Infamous Journalist Glass Works for Iowa Law Firm; Career Undone After Fabrications Found*, Des Moines Register, Feb. 6, 2017.

In re Glass: Real Life Applications

1. Harold is 45 years old. In his mid-20s, he became involved in smuggling marijuana. Harold was indicted for his involvement and fled the country to escape prosecution. On return, Harold took responsibility for his actions and pleaded guilty to all charges. As part of his probation, Harold provided care for terminally ill AIDS patients. Harold attended the University of Maine law school, where he served on the law review and graduated summa cum laude. After graduation, he clerked for the Maine Supreme Court and recently applied for admission to the New Hampshire bar.

   As a member of the character and fitness committee, you have been asked to review Harold's application, which contains the information set out above. Do you feel comfortable recommending Harold as having the requisite character and fitness for bar admission? What additional questions might you ask Harold? What, if any, additional materials would you like to review?

2. Petitioner M.C. filed an application for admission to the Florida bar. The Board of Bar Examiners investigated M.C. because of inconsistencies in his application and determined M.C. did not disclose on his application several financial debts and delinquent payments regarding outstanding student loans totaling $80,000. The board also found that M.C. owed roughly $17,000 dollars in child support and that M.C. failed to file state and federal income tax returns for five years. During a board interview, M.C. expressed deep remorse for his past financial "issues" and promised to follow Florida's lawyer conduct rules. M.C. also submitted five letters in support of his good character, including two from college professors, two from employers, and one from a prominent local church pastor.

   Should the board recommend a denial of M.C.'s application for bar admission? Should the board recommend a permanent ban on his admission? Would you change your decision to deny M.C.'s application if he had satisfied all of his outstanding debts two months prior to taking the bar examination?

C. LAWYER DISCIPLINE

1. Misconduct Defined

Each state has a lawyer disciplinary system to protect clients, the public, the legal system, and the profession from lawyer misconduct. Given these important goals, there is no statute of limitations in most jurisdictions for filing lawyer discipline actions. As you continue reading this section, and at the risk of oversimplification, the following brief admonition might prove useful in avoiding the lawyer discipline system: "don't lie, steal, or cheat."

Under Rule 8.4 ("Misconduct"), lawyers commit professional misconduct and are subject to discipline when they violate or attempt to violate any Model Rule of Professional Conduct or knowingly induce or assist others to do so. The specific disciplinary rules that can result in sanctions are discussed in Chapters 3-10. But Rule 8.4 also contains several important "catchall" provisions that can result in lawyer discipline. Rule 8.4 defines misconduct to include criminal acts that adversely reflect on the lawyer's honesty, trustworthiness, or fitness to practice law, for example, income tax fraud, perjury, or money laundering. Misconduct also includes dishonesty, fraud, deceit, misrepresentation, or any conduct that is prejudicial to the administration of justice. For example, it is dishonest and unethical conduct for a lawyer to use web bugs to track email communications with opposing counsel to learn how much time they devoted to reviewing the bugged email and whether and to whom it was forwarded.[41] Finally, Rule 8.4 specifically prohibits lawyers from suggesting they are able to improperly influence a government agency or official

---

41. ABA/BNA MAN. *supra* note 6, at 638-39 (2016) (citing Alaska Bar Ass'n Ethics Comm. Op. 2016-1 as the second ethics opinion to ban web bugs for providing unfair advantage to the sender and stating that "[s]eeking to invade [the attorney-client relationship] through the use of tracking devices (whether disclosed or not) is dishonest and unethical").

and knowingly assisting a judge or judicial officer in violating judicial conduct rules.

In August 2016, the ABA added subsection (g) to Rule 8.4's list of misconduct. Under it, a lawyer shall not

> engage in conduct that the lawyer knows or reasonably should know is harassment or discrimination on the basis of race, sex, religion, national origin, ethnicity, disability, age, sexual orientation, gender identity, marital status or socioeconomic status in conduct related to the practice of law. This paragraph does not limit the ability of a lawyer to accept, decline or withdraw from a representation in accordance with Rule 1.16. This paragraph does not preclude legitimate advice or advocacy consistent with these Rules.

Rule 8.4(g) generated concern that its broad ban on conduct might deter constitutionally protected speech. For example, the Texas Attorney General advised the state legislature that the adoption of Rule 8.4(g) "is unnecessary to protect against prohibited discrimination . . . and were it to be adopted, a court would likely invalidate it as unconstitutional" because it infringes on First Amendment free speech rights.[42] Other commentators believe the ABA's new **antidiscrimination provision** in Rule 8.4(g) does not necessarily infringe on the First Amendment. *See* Claudia E. Haupt, *Antidiscrimination in the Legal Profession and the First Amendment: A Partial Defense of Model Rule 8.4(g)*, 19 U. Pa. J. Const. L. Online (forthcoming 2017), *available at* SSRN: https://ssrn.com/abstract=2911219.

Rule 8.4's catchall provisions are broad and capture a wide variety of miscreant activity. The following subsections provide some common categories of misconduct that may result in discipline under Rule 8.4, with some representative cases.

Drug and Alcohol Abuse

Substance abuse affects a significant percentage of law students and lawyers and is reported to be higher than in other populations. Not surprisingly, substance abuse is a root cause for a significant amount of lawyer discipline. In Office of Disciplinary Counsel v. Alderman, 734 S.E.2d 737 (2012), Alderman began taking prescription medication following a surgical procedure and eventually became addicted to OxyContin. Alderman later struggled with illegal drug use, for which he pled guilty to two misdemeanor charges. Although he sought treatment, Alderman relapsed and voluntarily ceased the practice of law for 16 months while continuing to undergo treatment for drug addiction. During this sabbatical, he was charged with possession of a controlled substance and incarcerated for five days.

The court held Alderman violated Rules 8.4(b), (c), and (d), compromising his professional duty to his clients, the public, the legal system, and the profession. Although the court found his efforts at rehabilitation to be mitigating factors, the court nevertheless suspended him for two years (one year retroactively). *See also* In

42. Texas Att'y Gen. Op. KP-0123 (2016), https://www.texasattorneygeneral.gov/opinions/opinions/51paxton/op/2016/kp0123.pdf.

re Minter, 367 P.3d 1238 (Kan. 2016) (holding indefinite suspension was appropriate because evidence established the attorney's possession of a controlled substance with intent to distribute warranted a severe sanction).

Financial Misconduct

Attending law school; starting and maintaining a practice; and additional personal obligations, such as purchasing a home or raising a family, demand substantial time and financial resources. Thus, another common cause of lawyer discipline involves financial misconduct. In Iowa Supreme Court Att'y Disciplinary Board v. Taylor, 2016 BL 375312, Iowa No. 16-0130 (Nov. 10, 2016), a lawyer was suspended for 6 months for failing to file income taxes for 11 years. The dissent sought a one-year suspension, writing that "[w]e would not hesitate to revoke the license of a lawyer who stole money from a client. Taylor, in effect stole money from all Iowans for many years." The Iowa Supreme Court Disciplinary Board recommended an 18-month suspension for violation of Rule 8.4(b) and (c) after the Iowa Grievance Commission had recommended a suspension for no more than 30 days. The court majority found that mitigating factors such as the lawyer's pro bono work, acceptance of responsibility, and efforts to pay back taxes warranted a lesser sanction. How do you explain the wide disparity in recommended sanctions? What sanction do you think is appropriate?

In In re Brost, 850 N.W.2d 699 (Minn. 2014), a lawyer was indefinitely suspended in 2009 for using the expired notary stamp of a deceased notary to fraudulently notarize the lawyer's own signature on a certificate of trust prepared for a client. The lawyer submitted the fraudulent document to a bank to steal funds. The court held Brost's theft of $43,000 from her client's annuity payments stemmed directly from Brost's fiduciary relationship with her client and constituted misconduct under Rule 8.4(b) and (c) warranting disbarment. In addition, Brost failed to cooperate in the investigation and had a prior disciplinary record, including being currently under indefinite suspension for similar dishonest and fraudulent misconduct.

Falsehoods and Other Deceptions

Another common category of misconduct under Rule 8.4 concerns lawyer deception. While representing a trustee, the respondent, Rokahr, backdated an easement to correct a mistake Rokahr made while drafting the trusts. State ex rel. Counsel for Discipline v. Rokahr, 675 N.W.2d 117 (Neb. 2004). Through the backdating, Rokahr assisted her client in breaching his fiduciary duties. In addition, when she filed the easement with the county register of deeds, Rokahr knew it to be backdated and false. The referee found Rokahr's deceitful conduct violated DR 1-102(A) and DR 7-102(A) of the Nebraska Code of Professional Responsibility, conduct standards that are consistent with Rule 8.4(a) and (c).

The court ruled that colluding with the client to backdate the easement and then filing the false document was serious misconduct. The court rejected the referee's recommendation for a six-month suspension, ultimately deciding Rokahr's conduct deserved a one-year suspension. *See also* Neal v. Clinton, No. CIV 2000-5677, https://courts.arkansas.gov/sites/default/files/opc_opinions_59 (Ark. 5th Div. 2001) (suspending President William Jefferson Clinton from the practice of law in Arkansas for five years for violating Rule 8.4(d) by engaging in conduct prejudicial to the administration of justice when he knowingly gave evasive and misleading answers concerning his relationship with Monica Lewinsky in the Paula Jones case).

2. The Disciplinary Process

Clients may initiate the lawyer discipline process by complaining about their lawyer to statewide or local disciplinary counsel operating under the authority of that jurisdiction's highest court. A judge or opposing counsel may also initiate the process by alleging misconduct, and sometimes disciplinary counsel starts the process after learning of lawyer misconduct, perhaps through the media.

Although states' disciplinary processes differ, many share some common attributes. The following discussion in this subsection is based, in part, on the ABA Disciplinary Enforcement Processes that provides a useful model for better understanding the disciplinary process. MODEL RULES FOR LAWYER DISCIPLINARY ENFORCEMENT (AM. BAR ASS'N 2002). In general, the disciplinary authority or counsel evaluates the client's grievance at the intake stage of the disciplinary process to determine if sufficient facts are alleged, that if true, constitute a violation of a professional conduct rule.

Assuming the alleged facts, if true, would violate a professional conduct rule, the disciplinary counsel further investigates the matter. Counsel contacts the lawyer who is the subject of the grievance to obtain the lawyer's version of the facts and to obtain other possible evidence.

Lawyers who are the subject of investigations are well advised to spend time explaining their version of the facts and answering disciplinary counsel's questions in hope of having the grievance dismissed at intake. They may wish to confer with a lawyer specializing in professional responsibility matters even at this investigation phase of the process to help present their version of events concerning the client grievance in hope of facilitating a quick resolution.

Lawyers need to maintain good communications with their clients to avoid misunderstandings that might lead to the filing of a disciplinary or malpractice action. *Shutterstock.com*

Lawyers have an ethical duty under Rule 8.1 to cooperate with the disciplinary investigation, and their failure to cooperate is a separate chargeable disciplinary offense. For example, in In re Disciplinary Action Against Hansen, 868 N.W.2d 55 (Minn. 2015), the Minnesota Supreme Court ruled that an indefinite suspension with a 90-day minimum and a requirement that the respondent, Hansen, take the professional responsibility portion of the state bar exam before petitioning for reinstatement were appropriate sanctions given several acts of misconduct. This included improperly violating trust account requirements for almost a year and also a separate count for failing to cooperate with disciplinary counsel's investigations of the underlying trust problem and other matters.

Disciplinary counsel asked Hansen for a retainer agreement multiple times but he never produced it, saying he was waiting for his client to sign a release. After months of delay, Hansen admitted there was no retainer; he then failed to respond to an ethics committee report and two follow-up letters. In the trust account matter, Hansen failed to respond to multiple requests for a written explanation of overdrafts. He sometimes said he would send all the documents but never did. Hansen finally admitted in a meeting several months later that he never kept any records. The court emphasized that failing to cooperate with an investigation "is serious misconduct and in itself generally warrants suspension." The cumulative effect of both the nature and the multiple instances of misconduct over a long period warranted a more severe sanction. Hansen's misconduct was also aggravated because he was already on disciplinary probation.

Lawyers or respondents are sometimes cleared of the underlying disciplinary charge but nevertheless disciplined for not cooperating during the investigation with disciplinary counsel or the relator.[43] Lawyers cannot be disbarred, however, for asserting their Fifth Amendment right not to testify in the discipline process, but the assertion can be considered "together with other evidence to substantiate a charge of other misconduct."[44]

After the investigation is completed, disciplinary counsel may dismiss the grievance; refer the respondent if involved in lesser misconduct to an **Alternative Discipline Program** (ADP); recommend probation or an admonition (i.e., a public or private reprimand depending on the jurisdiction's rules); file formal charges; or petition for a transfer to disability inactive status or for a stay. ADP occurs before disciplinary counsel files formal charges, and depending on the jurisdiction, might include arbitration, mediation, law office management assistance, lawyer assistance programs, psychological counseling, and continuing legal education.

If disciplinary counsel files formal charges or a complaint against the lawyer with the disciplinary board, the respondent-lawyer gets a copy of the complaint and files a written answer. There is usually a board committee or panel that first hears the matter. The initial hearing panel consists of lawyers and sometimes nonlawyers; it is a formal trial process. The complainant gets to make a statement at the hearing, and the respondent can be represented by counsel at the hearing, cross-examine witnesses, and present evidence and arguments. The panel makes findings of fact and recommends a disposition in a report that is forwarded to the full board that approves, modifies, or disapproves the panel report.

---

43. *See* In re Disciplinary Action Against Cowan, 540 N.W.2d 825, 827 (Minn. 1995) (noting that the court has held that an "attorney's failure to cooperate can lead to indefinite suspension from the practice of law").

44. Wolfram, *supra* note 9, at 104-05 (discussing Spevak v. Klein, 385 U.S. 511 (1967)). If a lawyer is granted immunity from future prosecution to testify in a case, any statements made under that immunity grant is admissible in a subsequent discipline proceeding because it is not a criminal prosecution. *Id.* (citing In re Daley, 549 F.2d 469 (7th Cir.), *cert. denied*, 434 U.S. 829 (1977)).

The respondent or disciplinary counsel may file objections with the board concerning the panel's report. The full board conducts another hearing in which the parties can submit briefs and oral arguments but it cannot consider any new evidence by the parties unless the opponent has an opportunity to respond. In this model, the panel is the trier of fact and the board provides the appellate review. The decision by the full board is then sent to the state's supreme court.

The state supreme court may review a matter on its own discretion or if the respondent or disciplinary counsel files objections to the board's report. If objections are filed, the parties may file briefs and present oral arguments in accordance with the rules governing civil appeals. Most state courts acting on bar disciplinary matters will apply a highly deferential standard of review to the board's finding of fact (clearly erroneous) but review *de novo* its application of law to facts, conclusions of law, and sanctions.

3. Sanctions—Aggravating and Mitigating Factors

What form of and how much discipline should be imposed? The ABA Standards for Imposing Lawyer Sanctions identify four factors that courts should consider in imposing appropriate discipline involving the following concerns: (1) the duty violated; (2) the lawyer's mental state (intentional or negligent); (3) the seriousness of the actual or potential injury; and (4) the existence of aggravating and mitigating factors.[45] Although the terms vary among jurisdictions, sanctions generally include **disbarment** (a permanent separation from the bar and with no chance of reinstatement in some jurisdictions); suspension (a removal from the bar for a set period, often ranging between 6 to 24 months, that permits the lawyer upon satisfactorily completing the suspension to automatically apply for reinstatement); public reprimand (a type of public censure with no removal from practice); and a private reprimand (a non-public admonition also without removal from practice). The court may also order the respondent to make full restitution to the complainant and attend and pay for a substance abuse or other treatment program.

Each disciplinary case involves unique circumstances and warrants consideration by the disciplinary authority of the particular misconduct and case precedent in hope of reaching a fair result. What qualifies as an aggravating or mitigating factor may vary among jurisdictions, although some factors are well established and common in many jurisdictions. These

Insurance Policies and the Cost of Defense

Lawyers should make sure their errors and omissions insurance policies, commonly referred to as malpractice insurance, cover the cost of defense in a disciplinary action. Some malpractice policies cover only the expenses of defense and civil judgment for actions in damages stemming from the lawyer's negligence or unintentional errors and omissions in delivering legal services. A discipline action is not a personal claim for damages resulting from the negligent delivery of legal services. It is instead an action by disciplinary counsel to protect the public's interest by seeking a sanction for a lawyer who violated professional conduct rules.

45. *See II Theoretical Framework*, ABA Standards for Imposing Lawyer Sanctions 48 (1986, amended in 1992).

factors can play a decisive role regarding the severity of the sanction following the establishment of misconduct. The following lists provide a good overview of both aggravating and mitigating factors and are based on factors adopted by Ohio.[46]

After the establishment of misconduct, **aggravating factors** calling for a more serious sanction include (1) prior disciplinary offenses; (2) a dishonest or selfish motive; (3) a pattern of misconduct; (4) multiple offenses; (5) a lack of cooperation; (6) the submission of false evidence, false statements, or other deceptive conduct during the disciplinary process; (7) a refusal to acknowledge wrongdoing; (8) the failure to make restitution; and (9) the vulnerability of and resulting harm to victims of the misconduct.

Some **mitigating factors** favoring a lesser sanction are (1) the lack of a prior disciplinary record; (2) the absence of a dishonest or selfish motive; (3) a timely, good faith effort to make restitution or rectify the consequences of misconduct; (4) full disclosure; (5) cooperation during the process; (6) imposition of other penalties (e.g., loss of employment); (7) good character or reputation; and (8) existence of a medical disorder. Another common mitigating factor is the lawyer's remorse for the misconduct.

Many of these factors leave room for interpretation and application in any given disciplinary proceeding.[47] For example, should a recommendation for discipline that is before the state's high court but not yet decided count as a "prior offense"? How similar must the acts be and how close in time must they occur to constitute a "pattern"? Should all clients who are unsophisticated and are inexperienced with the court system be considered "vulnerable clients"? Should restitution or rectification of misconduct that is made reluctantly under the pressure of a disciplinary or criminal investigation or proceeding count as a "timely, good faith effort to make restitution or rectify consequences of misconduct"?

4. Disciplinary Authority; Choice of Law

One consequence of the increase in cross-border practice by lawyers is the potential risk of being less familiar with another jurisdiction's professional conduct rules that differ from the lawyer's home jurisdiction or place of licensure. Rule 8.5 guides practitioners and disciplinary authorities concerning which jurisdiction's conduct rules will govern a lawyer's actions and possibly place the lawyer at risk of discipline. It states that any jurisdiction in which the lawyer is admitted retains authority to discipline the lawyer for misconduct occurring within or outside the jurisdiction.

For example, assume Roberta Gomez is a lawyer licensed in Maine who represents a Maine client in purchasing a home in Florida. Gomez negotiates the terms of the purchase contract in Florida, executes the contract there, and later returns to do the closing. During the closing, Gomez violates a Florida ethics rule. Maine retains authority to discipline its licensed lawyer, Gomez, even though the

46. Ohio Gov. Bar Rule I, §13(A)-(C).
47. *See Evidence Required to Establish Aggravating and Mitigating Factors—Differing Views and Perspectives*, Miller-Becker Ctr. for Prof. Responsibility Annual Disciplinary Program Panel (Oct. 21, 2016).

violation involves a Florida rule. Under Rule 8.5(a), Florida also can discipline Gomez because she is providing legal services within its jurisdiction even though Gomez is only licensed in Maine. Thus, both jurisdictions have authority to discipline Gomez.

If Maine elects to discipline Gomez for her work in Florida, Maine must decide whether it will apply its rules or Florida's in reviewing Gomez's conduct. Rule 8.5(b)(2) provides that the jurisdiction's rule where the conduct occurred or where the predominant effect of the conduct will occur determines which jurisdiction's rule applies to Gomez's conduct. Given the facts above, Maine should apply Florida's rule in the discipline proceeding since the terms of the purchase, the signing of the contract, and the closing occurred in Florida. Both the conduct and the predominant effect happened in Florida.

The "**predominant effects**" standard could change the result with different facts. For example, if the negotiation for the purchase, the financing, and the signing of the deal occur in Maine as well as the alleged misconduct, then arguably Maine should apply its rules because the conduct occurred in Maine. However, Gomez or Florida could also argue that Florida's rules should govern Gomez's conduct because the predominant effect of the conduct occurred in Florida where the closing took place and the property is located. In this scenario, Maine has to decide which rules, Maine's or Florida's, to apply in assessing Gomez's alleged misconduct. However, Rule 8.5(b)(2) provides a safe harbor for lawyers by not subjecting them to discipline for following the professional conduct rules of a state where the lawyer "reasonably believes" the predominant effects of his legal services occur.

The choice of law question in the disciplinary context is more straightforward when the lawyer is involved in litigation. In that context, the rules of the jurisdiction where the tribunal is located govern the disciplinary proceeding. To illustrate, if Gomez's work in Florida on behalf of a Maine client involved litigation before a Florida court or administrative agency, then Florida's rules would govern Gomez's conduct.

5. Reciprocal Discipline

Given the need for the lawyer discipline system to protect the public and the administration of justice from miscreant lawyers, courts commonly impose the same disciplinary sanction both in terms of length of time and severity as that which was issued by the other jurisdiction. After providing notice of the imposition of **reciprocal discipline**, the respondent bears the burden of showing that the predicate discipline was not appropriate, perhaps because of important procedural or substantive deficiencies, such as a lack of notice or proof. This is not an easy burden to meet. The following cases illustrate the concept of reciprocal discipline.

In Kentucky Bar Association v. Clifton, 504 S.W. 3d 690 (Ky. 2016), the Ohio Supreme Court found Clifton knowingly made false statements of fact or law to a tribunal that warranted a public reprimand. Due to Clifton being a member of the Kentucky and Ohio bars, the Kentucky Bar Association initiated this proceeding against Clifton under Kentucky Supreme Court Rule 3.435(4), which states: "a lawyer shall be subject to identical discipline in the Commonwealth of Kentucky unless [he] proves by substantial evidence: (a) a lack of jurisdiction or fraud in the out-of-state disciplinary proceeding, or (b) that the misconduct established warrants substantially different discipline in this State." Because the Kentucky Bar Association found Clifton did violate Ohio's Rules of Professional Conduct, Kentucky also publicly reprimanded Clifton for the violations or imposed reciprocal discipline.

Midlen, the respondent in Attorney Grievance Commission of Maryland v. Midlen, 911 A.2d 852 (2008), represented the Jimmy Swaggart Ministries (JSM) in the royalty distribution process. Midlen would deduct his fees from JSM royalties and then remit the balance despite being asked numerous times by JSM to cease doing this. Further, Midlen failed to provide an accounting of the legal fees and deductions. The D.C. Court of Appeals found that Midlen violated the D.C. Rules of Professional Conduct and suspended him for 18 months for negligently misappropriating funds.

The Maryland Court of Appeals agreed that based on the findings of the D.C. court, Midlen's conduct also violated several Maryland Rules of Professional Conduct. The Maryland court rejected Midlen's claims that his due process rights were violated when the D.C. board did not adhere to the findings of the hearing panel because the board and the court were not strictly bound by its findings. Also, the Maryland court rejected Midlen's claims that the D.C. sanction was more severe than what Maryland normally imposed for similar conduct. The Maryland Court of Appeals disagreed and said it might have imposed a more severe sanction than D.C. but for the Maryland Bar Counsel's recommendation. The court also said that although the norm for reciprocal discipline is to have sanctions run concurrently, it was not doing so in this case because there was no evidence of when Midlen notified the bar counsel of the D.C. suspension or whether he continued to practice in Maryland after the D.C. suspension. *Compare* In re Peters, 2016 D.C. App. LEXIS 423 (D.C. 2016) (attorney's conduct warranted substantially different discipline in D.C. because reciprocal seven-year suspension was inappropriate as it exceeded D.C's disbarment rule that provided for five years with an opportunity to seek reinstatement, and is far longer than the three years that D.C. allows for suspensions under D.C. Bar R. XI, §§3(a)(2), 16(a)).

6. Lawyers' Duty to Report Misconduct

The legal profession has a strong tradition of self-regulation, although its effectiveness in protecting the public from incompetent and miscreant lawyers is subject to criticism. The Model Rules' Preamble recognizes that preserving self-regulation for the profession requires lawyers to ensure that other lawyers observe the Model Rules, including reporting lawyer misconduct.

Rule 8.3(a) requires a lawyer who knows about another lawyer's violation of a Model Rule to report it to the appropriate professional authority if the violations raise a "substantial question" about the lawyer's "honesty, trustworthiness or fitness to practice law." Rule 8.3(b) similarly obligates a lawyer who knows that a judge has violated the judicial ethics code in a way that raises a substantial question about the judge's honesty, trustworthiness, or fitness to serve as a judge. These obligations are sometimes derisively referred to as the "snitch" rules. When a lawyer "knows" that conduct violates a disciplinary rule and what kind of misconduct qualifies for reporting are fact-sensitive and often debatable questions.

A lawyer is not obliged to report every rule violation, only violations raising a "substantial question" about the lawyer's honesty and character fitness to practice law. Thus, according to Texas Ethics Opinion 632 (2013), a lawyer does not have to report another lawyer who impermissibly uses a trade name in Texas, without additional misconduct, because this does not raise a substantial question of honesty or trustworthiness under Rule 8.3. Other examples of misconduct that have not raised a substantial question of honesty or fitness involved dilatoriness, ineffective assistance, and "technical" violations.[48]

Some states, like Ohio, have a version of Rule 8.3(a) and (b) that imposes a greater duty of reporting. This version mandates the reporting of another lawyer's or judge's rule violation if it raises any "question," and not a "substantial question," about the lawyer's or judge's character and fitness. Thus, a lawyer might have to report a lawyer in Ohio for misconduct that raises a "question" about that lawyer's fitness to practice law while a lawyer would not have to report a lawyer for the same misconduct in another jurisdiction that requires reporting only if the misconduct raises a "substantial" question about the lawyer's fitness.

ABA Formal Opinion 94-383 prohibits a lawyer from threatening to file a disciplinary complaint against another lawyer under Rule 8.3 in order to gain an advantage in a matter, such as civil litigation. Rule 8.3 clearly requires the lawyer to report — not merely to *threaten* to report — conduct raising a substantial question about the lawyer's honesty and fitness to practice. Of course, it is not always clear when conduct constitutes a substantial question. The lawyer's failure to report under Rule 8.3(a) also constitutes a separate violation of Rule 8.4(a)'s duty not to violate, attempt to violate, or assist another to violate a rule. It is important to know what your jurisdiction's rules provide. Several states, including California, Texas, Illinois, Florida, Ohio, and the District of Columbia, have rules expressly banning threats to file disciplinary complaints.

Some state versions of Rule 8.3 identify the "appropriate professional authority" to receive reports of violations. The phrase likely includes statewide and local disciplinary counsel's offices or similar authorities that are better suited than the courts to initiate the disciplinary investigation described in Comment 1 of Rule 8.3. For example, in Ohio, a lawyer who needs to report another lawyer under Rule 8.3 can no longer discharge that obligation by informing the local court. Instead, the matter must be reported to the Office of Disciplinary Counsel or local certified grievance committee.[49]

Subsection (c) provides two exceptions to Rule 8.3's general reporting obligations. First, one does not have to report if knowledge of the violation is considered

---

48. *See* ABA/BNA Man., *supra* note 6, at 101:203.
49. Ohio Supreme Court Ethics Op. 2007-1.23 (concluding that a tribunal is not a "disciplinary authority" empowered to investigate or act upon misconduct under Ohio's Rule 8.3(a)).

confidential and protected from disclosure under Rule 1.6. For example, if lawyer A seeks lawyer B's legal assistance concerning A's misconduct that raises a substantial question of A's honesty and fitness to practice law, B is not required under 8.3(c) to report A's misconduct to the appropriate disciplinary authorities. Second, the lawyer does not have to report misconduct learned in an approved lawyer assistance program. Thus, when a disabled lawyer joins a lawyer's assistance program and tells the program's lawyer that he has overcharged his clients, the program lawyer does not have to report the disabled lawyer's misconduct under 8.3(a). Another common scenario involves a lawyer representing a client who reveals the misconduct of his prior counsel. The lawyer would not have to report this misconduct because it is protected as confidential under Rule 1.6, but comment 2 to Rule 8.3 recommends the lawyer seek the client's permission to disclose the prior counsel's misconduct.

In In re Riehlmann, 891 So. 2d 1239 (La. 2005), the Louisiana Supreme Court addressed the question of when a lawyer has to report another lawyer's misconduct. It held Rule 8.3(a) requires a lawyer to promptly report another lawyer's misconduct whenever the evidence would permit "a reasonable lawyer under the circumstances" to form a firm belief that the conduct in question had "more likely than not occurred." Riehlmann and his friend, Deegan, were former prosecutors. While dying of cancer, Deegan told Riehlmann he had suppressed exculpatory blood evidence in an unnamed case; Deegan also rejected Riehlmann's suggestion to report his misconduct. Approximately five years after Deegan's passing, Riehlmann learned of a case where the crime lab found the perpetrator of the crime had a different blood type than the person on death row for the crime. Riehlmann spoke to the defendant's lawyer about his discussion with Deegan. Riehlmann then executed an affidavit to the Disciplinary Counsel's Office reporting his discussion with Deegan. Riehlmann was charged with a Rule 8.3(a) violation for failing to promptly report Deegan's misconduct. The Louisiana Supreme Court decided a lawyer must promptly report misconduct to facilitate a timely investigation of the matter and to protect the public and the profession from the lawyer's possible future misconduct. The court reprimanded Riehlmann and held a reasonable lawyer would have formed a firm belief at the time of Deegan's confession that the misconduct likely occurred.

Case Preview

In re Himmel

In a disciplinary proceeding, Justice Stamos of the Illinois Supreme Court held that Attorney Himmel's failure to report the misconduct of another attorney who had formerly represented Himmel's client warranted a one-year suspension, not merely a private reprimand. The former attorney violated Illinois ethics rules when he converted the client's settlement funds from an insurance company. The client retained Himmel to help recover the stolen funds, and he managed to recover some of the funds. *In re Himmel* sent shock waves through the profession by underscoring the potentially significant consequences lawyers face when they breach their ethical duty to report other lawyers who violate the profession's ethics rules.

As you read *Himmel*, ask yourself the following questions:

1. What was the basis for the Illinois Supreme Court concluding that Himmel's information about the miscreant lawyer, Casey, was not protected from disclosure by the attorney-client privilege?
2. How does the court respond to Himmel's contention that he did not report Casey because his client told him not to report Casey?
3. At what point should Himmel have reported Casey?
4. What aggravating and mitigating factors did the court consider in determining the quantum of discipline to impose on Himmel?

In re Himmel

533 N.E.2d 790 (1988)

. . .

In October 1978, Tammy Forsberg was injured in a motorcycle accident. In June 1980, she retained John R. Casey to represent her in any personal injury or property damage claim resulting from the accident. Sometime in 1981, Casey negotiated a settlement of $35,000 on Forsberg's behalf. Pursuant to an agreement between Forsberg and Casey, one-third of any monies received would be paid to Casey as his attorney fee.

In March 1981, Casey received the $35,000 settlement check, endorsed it, and deposited the check into his client trust fund account. Subsequently, Casey converted the funds.

Between 1981 and 1983, Forsberg unsuccessfully attempted to collect her $23,233.34 share of the settlement proceeds. In March 1983, Forsberg retained respondent to collect her money and agreed to pay him one-third of any funds recovered above $23,233.34.

Respondent investigated the matter and discovered that Casey had misappropriated the settlement funds. In April 1983, respondent drafted an agreement in which Casey would pay Forsberg $75,000 in settlement of any claim she might have against him for the misappropriated funds. By the terms of the agreement, Forsberg agreed not to initiate any criminal, civil, or attorney disciplinary action against Casey. This agreement was executed on April 11, 1983. Respondent stood to gain $17,000 or more if Casey honored the agreement. In February 1985, respondent filed suit against Casey for breaching the agreement, and a $100,000 judgment was entered against Casey. If Casey had satisfied the judgment, respondent's share would have been approximately $25,588.

The [Illinois Attorney Registration and Disciplinary Commission (Commission)] complaint stated that at no time did respondent inform the Commission of Casey's misconduct. According to the [Commission's] Administrator, respondent's first contact with the Commission was in response to the Commission's inquiry regarding the lawsuit against Casey.

A hearing on the complaint against the present respondent was held before the Hearing Board of the Commission on June 3, 1986 [and] . . . provided [the] additional facts.

Before retaining respondent, Forsberg collected $5,000 from Casey. . . . Forsberg told respondent that she simply wanted her money back and specifically instructed respondent to take no other action. Because of respondent's efforts, Forsberg collected another $10,400 from Casey. Respondent received no fee in this case.

The Hearing Board found that respondent received unprivileged information that Casey converted Forsberg's funds, and that respondent failed to relate the information to the Commission in violation of Rule 1-103(a) of the Code. The Hearing Board noted, however, that respondent had been practicing law for 11 years, had no prior record of any complaints, obtained as good a result as could be expected in the case, and requested no fee for recovering the $23,233.34. Accordingly, the Hearing Board recommended a private reprimand.

Upon the Administrator's exceptions to the Hearing Board's recommendation, the Review Board reviewed the matter. The Review Board's report stated that the client had contacted the Commission prior to retaining respondent and, therefore, the Commission did have knowledge of the alleged misconduct. Further, the Review Board noted that respondent respected the client's wishes regarding not pursuing a claim with the Commission. Accordingly, the Review Board recommended that the complaint be dismissed.

The Administrator now raises three issues for review: (1) whether the Review Board erred in concluding that respondent's client had informed the Commission of misconduct by her former attorney; (2) whether the Review Board erred in concluding that respondent had not violated Rule 1-103(a); and (3) whether the proven misconduct warrants at least a censure.

As to the first issue, the Administrator contends . . . that even if Forsberg had reported Casey's misconduct to the Commission, such an action would not have relieved respondent of his duty to report under Rule 1-103(a). Additionally, the Administrator argues that no evidence exists to prove that respondent failed to report because he assumed that Forsberg had already reported the matter.

Respondent argues . . . that the record is not clear that Forsberg failed to disclose Casey's name to the Commission. Respondent also argues that Forsberg directed respondent not to pursue the claim against Casey, a claim she had already begun to pursue.

We begin our analysis by examining whether a client's complaint of attorney misconduct to the Commission can be a defense to an attorney's failure to report the same misconduct. Respondent offers no authority for such a defense and our research has disclosed none. Common sense would dictate that if a lawyer has a duty under the Code, the actions of a client would not relieve the attorney of his own duty. Accordingly, while the parties dispute whether or not respondent's client informed the Commission, that question is irrelevant to our inquiry in this case. We have held that the canons of ethics in the Code constitute a safe guide for professional conduct, and attorneys may be disciplined for not observing them. The question is, then, whether or not respondent violated the Code, not whether Forsberg informed the Commission of Casey's misconduct.

As to respondent's argument that he did not report Casey's misconduct because his client directed him not to do so, we again note respondent's failure to suggest any legal support for such a defense. A lawyer, as an officer of the court, is duty-bound to uphold the rules in the Code. The title of Canon 1 reflects this obligation: "A lawyer should assist in maintaining the integrity and competence of the legal profession." A lawyer may not choose to circumvent the rules by simply asserting that his client asked him to do so.

As to the second issue, the Administrator argues that . . . respondent had unprivileged knowledge of Casey's conversion of client funds, and that respondent failed to disclose that information to the Commission. The Administrator states that respondent's knowledge of Casey's conversion of client funds was knowledge of illegal conduct involving moral turpitude [and] . . . that the information respondent received was not privileged under the definition of privileged information. Therefore, . . . respondent violated his ethical duty to report misconduct under Rule 1-103(a).

. . .

Our analysis of this issue begins with a reading of the applicable disciplinary rules. Rule 1-103(a) of the Code states:

> "(a) A lawyer possessing unprivileged knowledge of a violation of Rule 1-102(a)(3) or (4) shall report such knowledge to a tribunal or other authority empowered to investigate or act upon such violation."

Rule 1-102 of the Code states:

> "(a) A lawyer shall not
>
> (1) violate a disciplinary rule;
>
> (2) circumvent a disciplinary rule through actions of another;
>
> (3) engage in illegal conduct involving moral turpitude;
>
> (4) engage in conduct involving dishonesty, fraud, deceit, or misrepresentation; or
>
> (5) engage in conduct that is prejudicial to the administration of justice."

. . .

This court has also emphasized the importance of a lawyer's duty to report misconduct. We stated, "Under Disciplinary Rule 1-103 a lawyer has the duty to report the misconduct of other lawyers." Thus, if the present respondent's conduct did violate the rule on reporting misconduct, imposition of discipline for such a breach of duty is mandated.

The question whether the information that respondent possessed was protected by the attorney-client privilege, and thus exempt from the reporting rule, requires application of this court's definition of the privilege. We have stated that "'(1) [w]here legal advice of any kind is sought (2) from a professional legal adviser in his capacity as such, (3) the communications relating to that purpose, (4) made in confidence (5) by the client, (6) are at his instance permanently protected (7) from disclosure by himself or by the legal adviser, (8) except the protection be waived.'" . . . In this case, Forsberg discussed the matter with respondent at various times while her mother and her fiancé were present. Consequently, unless the mother and fiancé were agents of respondent's client, the information communicated was not privileged. Moreover, we have also stated that matters intended by a client for disclosure by the client's attorney to third parties, who are not agents of either the client or the attorney, are not privileged. The record shows that respondent, with Forsberg's consent, discussed Casey's conversion of her funds with the insurance company involved, . . . [and] with Casey himself. Thus, the information was not privileged.

Though respondent repeatedly asserts that his failure to report was motivated not by financial gain but by the request of his client, we do not deem such an argument relevant in this case. This court has stated that discipline may be appropriate even if no dishonest motive for the misconduct exists. In addition, we have held that client approval of an attorney's action does not immunize an attorney from disciplinary action. We have already dealt with, and dismissed, respondent's assertion that his conduct is acceptable because he was acting pursuant to his client's directions.

Respondent does not argue that Casey's conversion of Forsberg's funds was not illegal conduct involving moral turpitude under Rule 1-102(a)(3) or conduct involving dishonesty, fraud, deceit, or misrepresentation under Rule 1-102(a)(4). It is clear that conversion of client funds is, indeed, conduct involving moral turpitude. We conclude, then, that respondent possessed unprivileged knowledge of Casey's conversion of client funds, which is illegal conduct involving moral turpitude, and that respondent failed in his duty to report such misconduct to the Commission. Because no defense exists, we agree with the Hearing Board's finding that respondent has violated Rule 1-103(a) and must be disciplined.

The third issue concerns the appropriate quantum of discipline to be imposed in this case. The Administrator contends that respondent's misconduct warrants at least a censure, although the Hearing Board recommended a private reprimand and the Review Board recommended dismissal of the matter entirely. In support of the request for a greater quantum of discipline, the Administrator cites to the purposes of attorney discipline, which include maintaining the integrity of the legal profession and safeguarding the administration of justice. The Administrator argues that these purposes will not be served unless respondent is publicly disciplined so that the profession will be on notice that a violation of Rule 1-103(a) will not be tolerated. The Administrator argues that a more severe sanction is necessary because respondent deprived the Commission of evidence of another attorney's conversion and thereby interfered with the Commission's investigative function under Supreme Court Rule 752. Citing to the Rule 774 petition filed against Casey, the Administrator notes that Casey converted many clients' funds after respondent's duty to report Casey arose. The Administrator also argues that both respondent and his client behaved in contravention of the Criminal Code's prohibition against compounding a crime by agreeing with Casey not to report him, in exchange for settlement funds.

In his defense, respondent reiterates his arguments that he was not motivated by desire for financial gain. He also states that Forsberg was pleased with his performance on her behalf. According to respondent, his failure to report was a "judgment call" which resulted positively in Forsberg's regaining some of her funds from Casey.

We have stated that while recommendations of the Boards are to be considered, this court ultimately bears responsibility for deciding an appropriate sanction. We reiterate our statement that "'[w]hen determining the nature and extent of discipline to be imposed, the respondent's actions must be viewed in relationship "to the underlying purposes of our disciplinary process, which purposes are to maintain the integrity of the legal profession, to protect the administration of justice from reproach, and to safeguard the public." ' "

Bearing these principles in mind, we agree with the Administrator that public discipline is necessary in this case to carry out the purposes of attorney discipline. While we have considered the Board's recommendations in this matter, we cannot agree with the Review Board that respondent's conduct served to rectify a wrong and did not injure the bar, the public, or the administration of justice. Though we agree with the Hearing Board's assessment that respondent violated Rule 1-103 of the Code, we do not agree that the facts warrant only a private reprimand.

. . .

This failure to report resulted in interference with the Commission's investigation of Casey, and thus with the administration of justice. Perhaps some members of the public would have been spared from Casey's misconduct had respondent reported the information as soon as he knew of Casey's conversions of client funds. We are particularly disturbed by the fact that respondent chose to draft a settlement agreement with Casey rather than report his misconduct.

Both respondent and his client stood to gain financially by agreeing not to prosecute or report Casey for conversion. According to the settlement agreement, respondent would have received $17,000 or more as his fee. If Casey had satisfied the judgment entered against him for failure to honor the settlement agreement, respondent would have collected approximately $25,588.

We have held that fairness dictates consideration of mitigating factors in disciplinary cases, therefore, we do consider the fact that Forsberg recovered $10,400 through respondent's services, that respondent has practiced law for 11 years with no record of complaints, and that he requested no fee for minimum collection of Forsberg's funds. However, these considerations do not outweigh the serious nature of respondent's failure to report Casey, the resulting interference with the Commission's investigation of Casey, and respondent's ill-advised choice to settle with Casey rather than report his misconduct.

Accordingly, it is ordered that respondent be suspended from the practice of law for one year.

Post-Case Follow-Up

Himmel represents the uncommon case in which a lawyer is sanctioned for the sole violation of not reporting another lawyer's misconduct. Often the lawyer who fails to report is involved in additional misconduct. Following *Himmel*, lawyers became more sensitive about the potential costs of not reporting another lawyer's misconduct under Rule 8.3. For example, the rate of lawyer reporting jumped in Illinois during the period of 1992-1995 to 8.9 percent of all complaints received, with 18.2 percent of them resulting in formal disciplinary charges. *See* Laura Gaitland, *"Snitch Rule" Remains Controversial But Effective Especially in Illinois*, A.B.A. J. 24 (Apr. 1997). In *Himmel*'s wake, there was a call for other states to sanction lawyers for nonreporting in the belief that lawyer reporting was particularly effective because of lawyers' familiarity with conduct rules and their contact with other lawyers. Lawyer reporting would help cleanse the profession of miscreant lawyers and support the profession's interest in self-regulation — both important goals. Whether imposing a mandatory lawyer reporting requirement is necessary to achieve these goals remains at least an open question. There is some evidence that lawyers will also report other lawyer misconduct even when such reporting is not mandatory. *See* Arthur F. Greenbaum, *The Attorney's Duty to Report Professional Misconduct: A Roadmap for Reform*, 16 GEO. J. LEGAL ETHICS 259 (2003). What do you think? Is it fair, or even efficient to expect lawyers to report the misconduct of fellow lawyers? Also, what should lawyers do when they suspect, but are not certain, that a fellow lawyer violated an ethics rule? Should the violation of any ethics rule trigger the lawyer's duty to report another lawyer?

In re Himmel: Real Life Applications

An exotic dancer alleged that she was raped by three men at an early morning party hosted by members of the lacrosse team at a university in Vermont. Prosecutor Nitro oversaw the investigation and made several extrajudicial statements to the media. For example, he told CBS News that the "lacrosse team has not been fully cooperative," and implied that the men were uncooperative: "[i]f it's not the way it's been reported, then why are they so unwilling to tell us what, in their own words, did take place that night?" In fact, Nitro knew the three men were cooperative, including making voluntary statements and submitting DNA samples.

Nitro relied on Dr. Meehan, president of DNA Security Inc. (DSI), to conduct DNA tests. He informed Nitro that the DNA tests excluded the three defendants as possible contributors of the multiple male DNA from the rape kit. Nitro and Meehan orally agreed they would not include all of the DNA results in the DSI Report and instead would only include the positive results, effectively shielding potentially exculpatory evidence from the defendants. Nitro failed to memorialize his oral communications with Dr. Meehan as required by law. The DNA test from a vaginal swab also showed a sperm fraction from the victim's boyfriend.

Nitro did not tell the defendants that the statements from the other exotic dancer at the party that night were inconsistent with the victim's statements. Nitro also filed written documents with the court stating that "the State is not aware of any additional material or information which may be exculpatory in nature with respect to the defendants."

a. Assume a confidential source informs the lawyer for one of the three defendants about all of the above information related to the alleged rapes and Nitro's conduct. She would prefer not to report the information because the report may reveal the identity of the confidential source who is at risk of harm. Must the defense lawyer report this information to the disciplinary authorities?
b. Assume the defense lawyer contacts you, the Vermont statewide disciplinary counsel, and discloses all of the above information about the alleged rape and

the related conduct of Nitro. What possible ethics standards did Nitro violate? What disciplinary sanctions, if any, would you recommend to the court? What aggravating factors might you argue support a more serious sanction?

D. LEGAL MALPRACTICE

1. Background

Lawyer self-regulation protects the public, the profession, and the courts from miscreant lawyers. The disciplinary system is not designed to compensate individuals for injuries caused by their lawyers' wrongful conduct, although clients may obtain some recompense by filing claims with state client protection funds that are supported by mandatory contributions from the bar. Instead, clients can file a civil action for damages, commonly known as a legal malpractice lawsuit, for injuries suffered because of their lawyers' wrongful conduct.

Legal malpractice cases generally involve claims of negligence, breach of fiduciary duty, or breach of contract against a lawyer and are often pled in the alternative. All three claims may be asserted in a single case. There is significant overlap in the application of these three claims as they all hinge on the lawyer breaching a standard of reasonable or ordinary care. The Restatement notes the similarities between legal malpractice actions based in negligence and breach of contract, stating the reasonable care element is viewed as an implied contract term. RESTATEMENT (THIRD) OF THE LAW GOVERNING LAWYERS §48 cmt. c, §55 cmt. c. That is why in legal malpractice cases involving a claim for breach of contract sometimes authorities note that "the contract claim sounds in tort." Thus, when the lawyer signs a written retention agreement to represent the plaintiff in an automobile collision case, an implied term of that agreement is the lawyer's duty to exercise reasonable or ordinary care in litigating the plaintiff's case. In this scenario, the lawyer arguably violates the duty of reasonable care when she fails to interview the only eyewitness to the accident and may find herself sued for legal malpractice.

In Volume 1, §1:2 of his treatise, LEGAL MALPRACTICE (2016), Ronald E. Mallen similarly recognizes the close relationship between negligence and breach of fiduciary duty:

> Often, the same conduct may be characterized as negligence and alternatively as a fiduciary breach. Although the terminology usually makes no substantive or procedural difference, the prevailing and better view is that legal malpractice encompasses any professional misconduct whether attributable to a breach of a standard of care or of the fiduciary obligations[, or of contract].

One practical difference concerning the three theories of legal malpractice is that the statute of limitations may vary for each claim, allowing the legal malpractice case to go forward based on one claim but not another. Some jurisdictions have one statute of limitation for the general category of legal malpractice lawsuits.[50]

2. Lawyer Negligence and Legal Malpractice

Traditional principles of negligence apply to **legal malpractice** actions.[51] Thus, in a negligence action for legal malpractice the plaintiff must prove the following elements by a preponderance of evidence: (1) the existence of an attorney-client relationship that establishes a duty on the part of the attorney; (2) a negligent act or omission constituting a breach of that duty; (3) the proximate cause (or legal cause) of the injury; and (4) the actual damages suffered by the plaintiff.

The threshold for establishing the professional relationship is not a high one: it is the client's reasonable belief that the lawyer is the client's legal advisor. The client can form a reasonable belief in the lawyer's office as well as during a brief contact in an informal setting. Ideally, a retention agreement memorializes the creation of the professional relationship after an initial client interview in the office.

The lawyer owes a client a duty of reasonable care in rendering legal services following the creation of a professional relationship. Lawyers who hold themselves out as specialists are generally held to a stricter or higher standard of care; they are expected to practice with the care ordinarily used by lawyers in that specialty.[52]

Sometimes lawyers owe a duty of reasonable care to non-clients or third parties with whom they have no direct contact. Traditionally, the lawyer's duty and liability to third parties was limited by the doctrine of privity of contract. This restricted the lawyer's duty of care and liability to only persons with whom he had some contact. "The traditional privity defense has remained most effective in situations where the non-client is a clear adversary of the lawyer's client."[53]

Today, however, there are many exceptions to the privity defense to lawyer malpractice. Lawyers may owe a duty of reasonable care to third parties with whom the lawyer has never had any contact. This third-party duty of care and potential liability arises when the lawyer knows that his work is intended to benefit others or he is inviting others to rely on his opinion.[54] The classic example of third-party or non-client liability is when the client asks the lawyer to draft a trust for the benefit of a third party or to draft an opinion letter about the client's financial status to facilitate a bank loan for the client. The lawyer should know that these documents are benefitting the trust beneficiary or are inviting the bank's reliance. Restatement §51 identifies four circumstances in which a lawyer might be liable to a non-client: (1) where the non-client is a prospective client; (2) where the lawyer invites the non-client's reliance on the lawyer's work and the non-client is not too remote to be entitled to protection; (3) where the lawyer knows that his services are intended by

50. Restatement (Third) of the Law Governing Lawyers §48 cmt. c.
51. *Id.* §§48 & 53.
52. Ronald Mallen, with Allison Martin Rhodes, 2 Legal Malpractice §20:4 (2016).
53. *See* ABA/BNA Man., *supra* note 6, at 301:602.
54. *See id.* at 301: 608-09.

the client to primarily benefit a non-client;[55] and (4) where the client acts as trustee, guardian, or fiduciary and the lawyer knowingly assists the client in breaching his obligations.[56]

After establishing a professional relationship or some other basis for the lawyer owing a duty of care, the parties usually offer expert testimony to define the applicable standard of reasonable care. Sometimes courts reject the use of expert testimony as unnecessary for establishing the duty of care and the breach of it when both are readily apparent to the judge and jury. In many states, experts cite professional conduct rules as some evidence of what constitutes a reasonable standard of care. Restatement §52 reports that some authorities hold that professional conduct rules alone define the standard of care. Other authorities take a more limited view of the conduct rules in establishing the duty of care, as in Hizey v. Carpenter, 830 P.2d 646 (Wash. 1992), where the court prohibited the use of the language of the rule in a jury instruction. *See* Rios v. McDermott, Will and Emery, 613 So. 2d 544 (Fla. Dist. Ct. App. 1993) ("an alleged [ethics rule violation] does not state a cause of action for malpractice"). The Scope Section of the Model Rules notes that a rule violation "should not give rise to a cause of action against a lawyer nor should it create any presumption in such a case that a legal duty has been breached . . . nor warrant any other nondisciplinary remedy, such as disqualification of a lawyer in a pending proceeding. [The rules] are not designed to be a basis for civil liability." Even with the Scope Section's caveats, the rules often play a role in establishing the appropriate duty of care in legal malpractice cases. *See* Desimini v. Durkin, 2015 U.S. Dist. LEXIS 68266 (D.N.H. May 27, 2015) (ethics rules are relevant in most jurisdictions for establishing standard of care in malpractice cases, and reporting *Hizey* is a minority view if it excludes opinions of ethics rule violations).

Once the plaintiff shows the lawyer owed a duty and breached it, the party must prove causation and damages. Where the defendant-lawyer's error or omission in a previous case caused an adverse judgment against the plaintiff in litigation, the plaintiff must show that he would have obtained a different result in the previous case but for the lawyer's negligence. This is commonly known as the "trial within a trial" or a "case within a case" requirement. For example, the plaintiff must show that he would have obtained a better damages award or settlement in the first case if the defendant-lawyer had exercised reasonable care in litigation. The same principle applies in the non-litigation context. The legal malpractice plaintiff has to show in the transactional setting that he would have obtained a different result but for the lawyer's negligence. For example, assume a former client retained a lawyer to negotiate a real estate lease that the client now claims is deficient. The former client must show that but for the lawyer's errors and omissions, the client would have obtained a different result, presumably a better lease.

---

55. For example, in Bullis v. Downes, 612 N.W.2d 435 (Mich. Ct. App. 2000), the court held that the daughter of the decedent had standing to bring suit against the attorney who drafted the decedent's will and trust. The daughter was promised two specific real properties via the will; however, the properties were deeded to the trust, which contained no provision for the distribution of real property. As a result, she was deprived of one of the properties. The court of appeals concluded a third-party beneficiary has standing to sue for legal malpractice if the party was named as a beneficiary in the decedent's overall estate plan.

56. *See id.* at 608-09.

In many jurisdictions, a criminal defendant may also sue for legal malpractice but only after the underlying conviction is set aside. The defendant must also show that, but for the lawyer's misconduct, the result in the previous criminal case would have been different. Other jurisdictions impose a stricter standard for relief. They require the criminal defendant to prove his actual innocence in addition to having the conviction set aside and showing that a different result would have occurred but for the lawyer's misconduct.

Case Preview

West Bend Mutual Insurance Co. v. Schumacher

In *West Bend Mutual Insurance Co. v. Schumacher*, the court of appeals ultimately affirmed the district court's dismissal of the plaintiff's legal malpractice case.

While reading the case, ask yourself the following questions:

1. What are the elements for legal malpractice under Illinois law?
2. Was Attorney Schumacher's conduct in representing West Bend consistent with the lawyer's duty to exercise reasonable care in providing professional services?
3. Why did the court find Schumacher's allegations concerning causation and damages to be deficient?
4. Finally, did the lawyer who represented West Bend in the instant legal malpractice case commit malpractice in not offering sufficient evidence to the satisfy the "case within a case" requirement that is necessary for litigating a negligence claim in Illinois?

West Bend Mutual Insurance Co. v. Schumacher

844 F.3d 670 (7th Cir. 2016)

I. BACKGROUND

A

In December 2005, West Bend retained RLGZ to provide legal representation with respect to a workers' compensation claim filed by John Marzano against West Bend's insured, Nelson Insulation. Mr. Schumacher was the attorney with principal responsibility for defending against the Marzano claim.

. . .

According to the complaint, West Bend alleged that Mr. Schumacher breached duties to West Bend by virtue of "(a) his unauthorized stipulation concerning compensability; (b) his failure to adequately investigate the claim or claimant's preexi[s] ting medical condition; (c) his subsequent representations to [West Bend] regarding their litigation options[;] and (d) his failure to adequately advise [West Bend]

of material facts and legal options prior to hearing." The specific allegations also concerned Mr. Schumacher's failure to depose Dr. Nelson [Marzano's independent medical expert whose testimony would be favorable to West Bend], his disclosure to Marzano's counsel of information beneficial to West Bend, and his failure to discover and remedy the unavailability of a relevant witness for the hearing.

All of these, West Bend alleged, resulted in its being "forced to accept a disadvantageous position which greatly compromised its ability to defend the claim." It also was "forced to pay additional sums and eventually chose to reach a disputed settlement in order to mitigate its exposure" . . . .

B

The district court determined that, with respect to the bulk of West Bend's allegations about Mr. Schumacher's performance—including the failure to depose Dr. Nelson, the failure to contact witnesses prior to the hearing, and the disclosure of certain facts to Marzano's counsel—West Bend's complaint "does not . . . explain how any of these alleged acts and omissions harmed its defense." With respect to the allegation that Mr. Schumacher had represented that West Bend would accept liability, the district court stated:

> [P]laintiff admits that it could have contested the claim, despite the representation. In short, because plaintiff does not and cannot allege that defendants' representation was the cause of any damages it may have suffered, the representation cannot support a malpractice claim.

The court . . . concluded that West Bend had failed to state a claim in three successive complaints, [and] it terminated the case. West Bend now appeals.

II. DISCUSSION

A

2

The parties agree that Illinois law governs the elements of this legal malpractice action. The Supreme Court of Illinois has stated succinctly that a cause of action for legal malpractice includes the following elements: (1) the existence of an attorney-client relationship that establishes a duty on the part of the attorney, (2) a negligent act or omission constituting a breach of that duty, (3) proximate cause of injury, and (4) actual damages. Illinois courts have described the State's legal malpractice cause of action as following a case-within-a-case model:

> A legal malpractice suit is by its nature dependent upon a predicate lawsuit. Thus, a legal malpractice claim presents a case within a case. *[N]o* malpractice exists unless counsel's negligence has resulted in the loss of an underlying cause of action, or the loss of a meritorious defense if the attorney was defending in the underlying suit.

Therefore, in assessing the sufficiency of a complaint of legal malpractice we must focus on the underlying claim. The plaintiff must set forth a plausible statement not only that a breach of duty occurred but that the breach caused the plaintiff to lose a valid claim or defense in the underlying action and that, absent that loss, the underlying claim "would have been successful." "These elements effectively demand that the malpractice plaintiff present two cases, one showing that her attorney performed negligently, and a second or predicate 'case within a case' showing that she had a meritorious claim [or defense] that she lost due to her attorney's negligence." Mihailovich v. Laatsch, 359 F.3d 892, 904-05 (7th Cir. 2004).

B

There is no dispute that West Bend has described adequately the duty element in its malpractice claim. Nor is there any disagreement about the adequacy of West Bend's narrative with respect to the alleged attorney conduct constituting a breach of that duty. In that respect, West Bend alleges that Mr. Schumacher, having assumed responsibility for the defense of the claim, failed to prepare adequately for the hearing, revealed inappropriately the defense theory of the case to Marzano's counsel, and then, without authorization, conceded liability for Marzano's workers' compensation claim.

The allegations with respect to causation and damages present, however, significant concerns. . . . While the complaint describes the conduct in some detail, it describes the underlying workers' compensation claim in rather summary fashion. Specifically, while the complaint identifies the injured party as John Marzano, it tells us nothing about his claimed injury or his claim against his employer. Instead, it summarily states that "[p]rior to August 2006, there existed *certain factual defenses and a medical causation defense* to the Marzano claim."

West Bend's brief on appeal invites our attention to paragraph 25 of the Second Amended Complaint as "set[ting] forth [its] factual allegations concerning defendants' breach of duty, proximate cause and damages." That paragraph of the complaint contains an abbreviated description of Mr. Schumacher's claimed errors, but, with respect to the crucial elements of causation and damages, says only that West Bend "was forced to accept *a disadvantageous position* which *greatly compromised* its ability to defend the claim." This same sort of general language appears in paragraph 28; there West Bend refers to a loss of "*valuable factual and legal defenses* that would have eliminated or substantially reduced any liability of [West Bend] to the claimant." These allegations are conclusory assertions and certainly do not set forth a plausible description of a lost defense that, absent Mr. Schumacher's alleged neglect, would have assured West Bend's success on the underlying claim.

West Bend has not invited our attention to any other factual allegations which detail the "valuable factual and legal defenses" lost because of Mr. Schumacher's litigation conduct.

With respect to the allegation that Mr. Schumacher had stipulated improperly to the compensability of the claim, West Bend at least makes the allegation that it was required to pay substantial amounts of money because of the stipulation. But it makes no concrete allegation that its final liability in this matter would have been any different if the stipulation had not occurred.

The . . . Complaint therefore leaves us to speculate as to whether and how West Bend would have prevailed on the underlying claim in the absence of the missteps of which it now accuses its former attorney. But, as our colleague in the district court

recognized throughout West Bend's several attempts to improve the complaint, a plaintiff "must plead some facts that suggest a right to relief that is beyond the speculative level." The district court correctly concluded that the allegations that deal with the substance of the underlying compensation claim and defense fall short of that standard because they provide no plausible description as to how the attorney's negligence, if it occurred, was the cause of harm to West Bend. Even when evaluated as a whole, the complaint fails to describe, in even the most rudimentary of ways, "that but for [Mr. Schumacher's] negligence, the plaintiff would have been successful in th[e] underlying" workers' compensation action. . . .

Post-Case Follow-Up

The *Schumacher* case highlights the need to be careful in pleading legal malpractice cases, especially in proving the lawyer's breach of a duty of reasonable care and that it caused the client's harm. Plaintiffs' lawyers may rely on multiple experts to establish these elements. For example, an ethics professor may testify about the defendant-lawyer's general duty of care under the jurisdiction's professional conduct rules, whether the defendant-lawyer's conduct breached that standard of care, and whether the breach caused the plaintiff's injury. A second expert who may be an experienced practitioner in the same or similar type of work giving rise to the instant legal malpractice claim may testify about how lawyers customarily act, whether the defendant-lawyer's conduct comported with the custom, and whether the breach caused the client's harm in the underlying case. Legal malpractice and the "trial within a trial" principle promise to remain a significant part of the litigation landscape. Based on West Bend's allegations of misconduct, what would you advise Schumacher to do differently in his next defense of a workers' compensation case? Would you hire Schumacher to represent you in light of his conduct in the West Bend case?

West Bend Mutual Insurance Co. v. Schumacher: Real Life Applications

1. After being eliminated from the Miss Universe beauty pageant, Monin took to social media and television to claim that the competition was rigged. The Miss Universe Organization filed an arbitration demand for $10 million alleging breach of contract and defamation. Her attorney in the matter, Klineburger, advised Monin that the arbitration agreement did not apply because her copy of the agreement was unsigned. Klineburger notified the arbitrator that they were not obligated to participate in arbitration and refused to comply with discovery requests. Klineburger also demanded that the arbitrator communicate only with him as counsel for Monin, but he then did not relay information regarding the proceedings or hearing date to her. The arbitration proceeding that neither he nor Monin attended resulted in a $5 million award for the Miss Universe

Organization as the arbitration clause was found applicable to Monin. The arbitrator noted that Monin's absence resulted in his drawing an adverse inference against her. It was at this time that Klineburger informed Monin of the proceedings and adverse judgment, but stated that he could no longer represent her because he was not licensed in New York.

Monin retains you to file a legal malpractice action against Klineburger to hopefully cover the $5 million judgment against her.

a. What malpractice claims may you raise on her behalf?
b. What ethics rules, if any, did Klineburger violate, and what is the significance of such violations in a legal malpractice action?
c. Must you also report Klineburger to the statewide disciplinary counsel's office?
d. Should you contact Klineburger before reporting him to the proper disciplinary authority?
e. If Klineburger acted in good faith when he incorrectly advised Monin about the applicability of the arbitration clause, should the court in the discipline system be more forgiving of Klineburger's conduct?

2. A finance company sued attorney Ida Forti for legal malpractice for making a negligent misrepresentation in connection with loans made to Forti's brother-in-law, Dave King, a longtime and trusted client. King offered to secure the loan with farm machinery and asked Forti to prepare a letter stating there were no prior liens on the machinery. Relying on King's representation, Forti promptly prepared the letter without knowing that most of the farm machinery had already been pledged to other lenders. King obtained the loan, and a year later defaulted, then committed suicide.

   The finance company asks you, a local real estate lawyer who has done work for the company, if it can sue Forti for legal malpractice and what you think is its likelihood of success.

   a. Advise the company about any possible claims it might have against Forti for legal malpractice and the company's likelihood of success.
   b. In addition, the company believes Forti when she says she had no knowledge of the liens. The company's CEO feels sorry for her and does not want to jeopardize Forti's law license. The CEO asks you if there is any way to protect Forti's license.
   c. Should the fact that Forti relied on the representation of her "longtime and trusted" client insulate her from liability for either a legal malpractice claim or potential disciplinary action against her? Please discuss.

---

3. Legal Malpractice and Breach of Fiduciary Duty

The cornerstone of the fiduciary relationship is trust. This is reflected in traditional agency law, which is often used to characterize the lawyer-client professional relationship. The agent-lawyer owes a fiduciary duty to the principal-client to be trustworthy, including being loyal, competent, and protective of client confidences.

Case Preview

Burnett v. Sharp

Burnett identifies the core values of the fiduciary relationship as "integrity and fidelity." The case also demonstrates the close connection between the rules of professional conduct and the establishment of a fiduciary relationship. Plaintiffs often claim that a lawyer's violation of a duty contained in professional conduct rules is significant evidence that the lawyer breached his fiduciary responsibility to protect and promote the client's interests.

In reviewing *Burnett*, consider the following questions:

1. Did the court think there was a plausible justification for the lawyer believing he did not have to return the client's funds?
2. How does the court justify its holding that the lawyer's fiduciary duty to the client extends, even after the lawyer's discharge, until the lawyer returns funds belonging to the client?
3. What test does the court use to determine whether Burnett's claims have an arguable basis in the law?
4. Does the court provide for a change in its analysis if Burnett's decision to discharge his attorney was made in "bad faith"?

Burnett v. Sharp

328 S.W.3d 594 (Tex. App. 14th Dist. 2010)

[W]e construe the trial court's determination that Burnett "failed to state a cause of action as a matter of law" to be a determination that Burnett's claims have "no arguable basis in law." . . .

B. What Claims Did Burnett Plead?

. . .

Under a liberal construction of the petition, Burnett alleges the following:

- **In June 2006, Burnett retained Sharp, a lawyer, to represent him in a criminal matter.**
- **Burnett gave Sharp a $3,000 retainer.**
- **Sharp had Burnett's case reset five times but did not provide any other legal services before Burnett replaced Sharp with another lawyer.**
- **Burnett called Sharp's office once, and Burnett's family called Sharp many times on behalf of Burnett, requesting a refund of the unearned portion of the retainer.**
- **Burnett served Sharp with a written demand for the return of the unearned portion of the retainer. Sharp did not respond to this demand, nor did Sharp return any part of the unearned retainer to Burnett.**
- **Sharp breached his fiduciary duty to Burnett by refusing to return the unearned part of Burnett's retainer.**

- Sharp committed legal malpractice, negligence, and "deception."
- Burnett is seeking compensatory damages in the amount of $10,000.

Under a liberal construction of his petition, Burnett has pleaded claims for breach of fiduciary duty, money had and received, [and] conversion . . . . Avila v. Havana Painting Co. (Tex. App.-Houston [14th Dist.] 1988, writ denied) (holding that lawyer breached his fiduciary duty by refusing to return to former client funds in his possession which the former client was entitled to receive). The next question is whether the trial court erred in concluding that these claims have no arguable basis in law.

C. Do Burnett's Claims Have an Arguable Basis in Law?

Whether a claim has an arguable basis in law is a legal question to be reviewed de novo. A claim has no arguable basis in law only if it is based on (1) wholly incredible or irrational factual allegations; or (2) an indisputably meritless legal theory. An inmate's claim may not be dismissed merely because the court considers the allegations "unlikely." If Burnett's claims have an arguable basis in law, then the trial court erred in dismissing them as frivolous. Burnett's claims are not based on wholly incredible or irrational factual allegations. Therefore, the main issue on appeal is whether each of Burnett's claims is based on an indisputably meritless legal theory.

1. Breach-of-Fiduciary-Duty Claim

This court noted in *Avila* that, under a provision of the former Code of Professional Responsibility, a lawyer was required to promptly pay or deliver to the client all funds in the possession of the lawyer which the client was entitled to receive. The *Avila* court concluded that a lawyer's failure to promptly pay or deliver such funds constitutes a breach of fiduciary duty. In *Avila*, this court held that a lawyer breached his fiduciary duty by refusing to tender funds recovered for the client in a collection suit until after the client sued the lawyer for return of the funds. By the time the client sued the lawyer, the lawyer's representation must have been terminated. Therefore, the Avila court concluded that the lawyer had a fiduciary duty even after the lawyer's representation of the client in the collection suit had ended. A lawyer who refuses to pay or deliver funds belonging to his former client upon termination of the representation has breached a fiduciary duty owed to the former client.

The word fiduciary " 'refers to integrity and fidelity.' " A breach of fiduciary duty occurs when a lawyer benefits improperly from his representation of the client by, among other things, a "failure to deliver funds belonging to the client." This court repeatedly has affirmed that a lawyer breaches his fiduciary duty if he refuses to give a client funds belonging to the client, and this court has never stated that this duty ceases if the client discharges the lawyer. Indeed, given that a client may be discharging his lawyer for good cause based on prior breaches by the lawyer of his fiduciary duty to the client, there are compelling reasons why this fiduciary duty should continue until the lawyer returns the client funds in his possession.

. . .

. . . Under Texas Disciplinary Rule of Professional Conduct 1.15(d), entitled "Declining or Terminating Representation," upon termination of a representation, the attorney shall, to the extent reasonably practical, surrender property that the client is entitled to receive to the client and shall refund any advance payment of attorney's fees that has not been earned. Given that, upon termination of the representation, a lawyer has a duty to return any unearned part of the retainer and any other client property to which the client is entitled, the return of such property to the client would appear to be one of the purposes of the representation and therefore would be part of the attorney-client relationship . . . .

For the reasons stated above, if, as alleged, Sharp refused to return unearned retainer belonging to Burnett, then Sharp breached his fiduciary duty. Therefore, Burnett's breach-of-fiduciary duty claim is not based on an indisputably meritless legal theory, and the trial court erred in dismissing this claim as frivolous . . . .

. . .

III. CONCLUSION

Burnett's petition, liberally construed, contains claims for breach of fiduciary duty, money had and received, [and] conversion . . . . The first three claims are not based on (1) wholly incredible or irrational factual allegations; or (2) indisputably meritless legal theories. Therefore, the trial court erred in dismissing these three claims as frivolous . . . . However, Burnett's negligence and intentional-misrepresentation claims are based on indisputably meritless legal theories, and the trial court did not err in dismissing these claims as frivolous. Accordingly, . . . the judgment is . . . reversed, and remanded for further proceedings consistent with this opinion. . . .

Post-Case Follow-Up

Burnett highlights why plaintiffs allege more than one legal theory or claim when possible in a legal malpractice case. The *Burnett* court reversed the trial court's dismissal of the plaintiff's breach of fiduciary duty claim while affirming the dismissal of other claims, including the claim that Sharp was negligent. Burnett had not alleged a necessary element in his negligence claim, "that Sharp had exercised less care, skill or diligence than would be exercised by lawyers of ordinary skill and knowledge." Instead, Burnett's lawyer simply alleged in conclusory manner that Sharp was negligent. Lawyers must be careful to allege some factual basis to support each element of a negligence or fiduciary claim. In addition to the malpractice action, should Burnett's conduct also subject him to potential discipline? What sanction would you recommend? What strategies might you recommend to Burnett to help defend him in a discipline action?

Other courts have similarly held that the lawyer's failure to return client funds or property supports a breach of fiduciary duty claim. For example, in Hickey v. Scott, 738 F. Supp. 2d 55 (D.C. 2010), the parties signed a contract providing Scott would pay Hickey $225 per hour for legal services. In return, Hickey "will render [to Scott] a short summary statement of fees and disbursements for each month containing only the hours and fees spent on these matters along with a summary of disbursements spent during that month along with a reconciliation amount." After Scott won her Title VII action, a dispute arose concerning the amount owed to Hickey.

Hickey sued Scott for breach of contract and she counterclaimed contending Hickey failed to provide competent legal services, violated D.C. Rule of Professional Conduct 1.5, and breached his fiduciary duty due to "a significant portion of hours which appear to have been excessive or inadequately documented." Both parties moved for summary judgment. The court held a jury could find on the record that Hickey violated the rules of professional conduct, and under the law such a finding would be sufficient to establish a breach of fiduciary duty, making summary judgment inappropriate.

Hickey highlights a common scenario. When a lawyer sues for legal fees, the client may respond by alleging the lawyer is not entitled to any fees because he committed malpractice and instead the lawyer owes the client damages. Professional conduct rules do not bar lawyers from suing clients for legal fees, but it should be a last resort strategy given the potential costs and adverse publicity associated with the effort.

Burnett v. Sharp: Real Life Applications

The Isley Brothers, a music group, sued singer Coty Perez for copyright infringement, alleging Perez's 1991 hit "Love Is a Wonderful Thing" infringed on the Isley Brothers' copyright of their 1964 song with the same name. Mark Harris of Jones Night LLP jointly defended Perez; his record company, Sony Music Entertainment, Inc.; and Perez's music publishing company, Warner/Chappell, Inc. TIG, Warner/Chappell's insurance company, paid Jones Night for its joint representation. No one at Jones Night discussed the disadvantages of joint representation.

The Isley Brothers offered to settle the case for $700,000, but Harris never informed Perez of the offer. Nor did Harris inform Perez that an indemnification provision in his publishing contract would make him liable for damages if there was a final adverse judgment in the case. The case ended with a $5.4 million judgment against Perez and the other defendants. Perez believes there was a secret agenda between his lawyers and the publisher's insurance company to push the case to a final judgment instead of reaching a settlement, thereby triggering the indemnification provision in Perez's publishing contract and allowing TIG to recover from Perez.

He consults with you about suing Harris and his firm for $30 million for breach of fiduciary duty. Advise Perez.

---

4. Minimizing Liability for Legal Malpractice

Lawyers can minimize their exposure to legal malpractice claims by listening to their client's concerns and objectives, and establishing a good rapport to enhance client trust. This requires spending time with the client and promptly returning client calls and emails. Even if the lawyer cannot personally contact the client, someone in the lawyer's office should contact the client and provide an update, although non-lawyers have to be careful not to offer legal advice and commit the unauthorized practice of law. Also, lawyers can attend CLEs, periodically review office protocol, use a reliable calendaring and client intake process to safeguard against possible conflicts of interest, and conduct a peer review of firm forms or documents.

Another effective way for lawyers to minimize exposure to malpractice claims is to limit the scope of representation. Rule 1.2(c) permits this limitation "if the limitation is reasonable and the client gives informed consent." The rule assumes that the lawyer's legal services can be limited or compartmentalized without harming the client's overall legal objective. The lawyer is still obligated to provide competent representation even if the scope is limited. For example, a lawyer could agree to represent the author of a book for the limited purpose of only negotiating the publishing agreement once the author finds a publisher. This is unlike a situation where the lawyer undertakes the general representation of the author and is arguably responsible for a variety of related services, such as creating a corporation, tax planning, and marketing the book. The lawyer's obligation to negotiate the book can be neatly unbundled from the author's other related legal needs. Switch the matter to a contested divorce case and the result likely changes. A lawyer should not be permitted to agree to handle only the husband's property division in a contested divorce but not be responsible for the tax consequences of such a division or its effect on the custody battle over the children. These services are arguably inextricably bound together; it would be hard to competently negotiate a property division without taking into consideration its tax consequences and likely effect on custody.[57]

Another common method of limiting liability exposure among individual members in the firm is the creation of **limited liability partnerships** (LLPs) or **limited liability companies** (LLCs). General partnership doctrine holds partners jointly and individually liable for the misconduct of fellow partners. Following successful suits based on this doctrine, lawyers and other professional service providers advocated for these new limited liability structures. Under the structure, the firm still remains vicariously liable for a partner's, associate's, or part-time lawyer's malpractice, but individual partners' assets cannot be reached to satisfy a judgment beyond the LLP or firm insurance policy. In short, the LLP business form permits lawyers to be only personally liable for their own individual misfeasance should the firm's policy not cover a malpractice settlement or judgment.

Professional liability insurance policies are technically labeled "errors and omissions" (E & O) policies, generally insuring the firm or individual lawyers for errors and omissions or negligent mistakes. E & O policies do not cover damages caused by a lawyer's intentional or criminal act, such as stealing client fees. Lawyers

57. *See* Colo. Bar Ass'n, New Ethics Op. 101 (May 21, 2016), http://www.cobar.org/Portals/COBAR/repository/ethicsOpinions/FormalEthicsOpinion_101.pdf; Stephanie L. Kimbro, *The Ethics of Unbundling*, 1 GPSolo eReport 3 (Oct. 2011), http://www.americanbar.org/publications/gpsolo_ereport/2011/october_2011/ethics_unbundling.html.

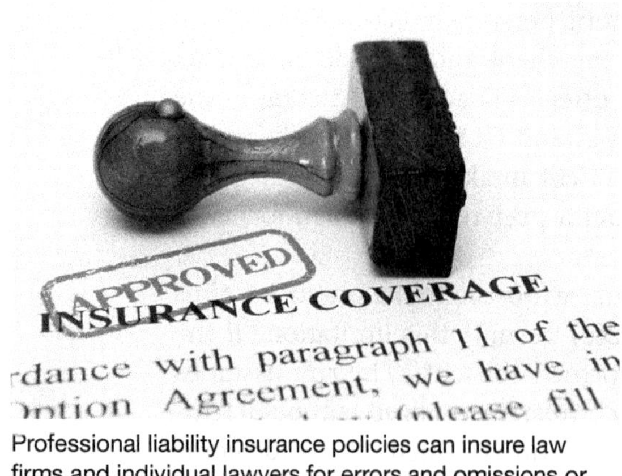

Professional liability insurance policies can insure law firms and individual lawyers for errors and omissions or negligent mistakes.
Shutterstock.com

should also check their policy to see if it contains a "burning limit" provision that deducts the cost of defense from the policy coverage. Defense costs can be expensive, and this might expose the lawyer to financial risk if the damages exceed the policy cap. In addition, the lawyer needs to examine the policy's definition of legal services to ensure that the lawyer's work is covered. For example, will the policy cover advice to clients about where to invest the proceeds of a settlement?

Strong public policy reasons bar lawyers from contracting with clients to expressly limit their malpractice liability for professional work. It is unfair to force clients to waive future malpractice claims against their lawyers as the price for obtaining legal services and access to justice. The policy barring such contracts promotes public confidence in the profession because it precludes lawyers from contracting around liability for their misconduct, in effect discouraging shoddy services. Rule 1.8(h)(1) bars a lawyer from "mak[ing] an agreement prospectively limiting the lawyer's liability to a client for malpractice unless the client is independently represented in making the agreement." *See* Joann C. Rogers, *Mid-Representation Covered Future Malpractice*, 32 Law. Man. on Prof. Conduct (ABA/BNA) 655 (2016) (discussing an Indiana case that permitted the firm to prospectively limit malpractice liability where client consulted independent counsel). In contrast, Restatement §54(4)(a) unconditionally prohibits a lawyer from prospectively limiting malpractice liability, a minority approach followed by a substantial number of states. Rule 1.8(h)(2) also bars lawyers from settling a claim or potential claim of malpractice without advising the client in writing of the desirability of seeking independent legal counsel in the matter. The lawyer must give the client adequate time to contact independent counsel. It is important to remember this rule as no one is perfect and the instinctive reaction for many lawyers is to reimburse the client as soon as possible for harm. Any ultimate settlement under this rule must be reasonable.

Chapter Summary

- Each state's high court has inherent authority to regulate the practice of law; federal courts and many government organizations (e.g., administrative agencies) also regulate the practice of law in their respective jurisdictions.
- Given the fiduciary nature of the lawyer-client relationship, courts generally require bar applicants to prove by clear and convincing evidence that they possess the requisite good character and fitness for bar admission.

- The legal profession is self-regulating, requiring lawyers to report misconduct that raises a substantial question about another lawyer's good character and fitness to practice law.
- Each state's high court normally disciplines lawyers for conduct code violations. Federal courts often adopt state disciplinary findings and sanctions.
- Lawyer regulation is critical for protecting the public interest in access to justice, maintaining the integrity of the profession, and facilitating the administration of justice by the courts. The aim of the lawyer discipline system is to protect the public from miscreant lawyers through regulation; the purpose of legal malpractice lawsuits is to compensate clients and other private parties for harm caused by lawyers.
- Lawyers may be civilly liable to clients and to some third parties for legal malpractice. Typical legal malpractice claims include breach of an express or implied contract, breach of fiduciary duty, and a breach of a duty of ordinary care or negligent representation.

Applying the Rules

1. John Burney applied for admission to the Massachusetts bar. In his application, Burney disclosed that he had been "wrongfully terminated" by two employers, and that he had brought multiple lawsuits involving separate incidents against former employers, attorneys, police officers, and a media outlet. These lawsuits alleged, in part, wrongful termination, violation of civil rights, defamation, breach of contract, malicious prosecution, and abuse of process.

   Due to inconsistencies with Burney's application, the board further investigated his litigation background and discovered information that Burney had failed to disclose in his application. During this investigation, it was determined that Burney represented himself *pro se*, and was reprimanded for various litigation misconduct, which resulted in Burney being sanctioned and held liable for costs and fees. Does Burney's personal history of litigation in his application alone suggest a lack of good character for bar admission? What, if any, effect do the board's investigation and findings have on your assessment of Burney's character and fitness for bar admission? If you were on the board, would you recommend that Burney reapply in a year?

2. Attorney Jupiter pled guilty in 2013 to one of four counts of making false, fictitious, or fraudulent claims to the IRS arising out of his ill-advised scheme to claim $9.7 million in tax refunds. He served 18 months in prison. At his disciplinary hearing in 2013, Jupiter testified that he was at an "all-time low" in his life when he committed the crime because of years of physical and emotional abuse by his wife, making him depressed and anxious. Jupiter was also going through a divorce and maintaining two households, and receiving counseling and taking antidepressant medication. Jupiter testified he never intended to obtain the tax refunds.

According to his doctor, Jupiter suffered from a depressive disorder with psychotic features but because of subsequent treatment it was "highly unlikely that he would repeat the misconduct." His law partner for 25 years testified that Jupiter went "above and beyond the call of duty" to help his clients and that Jupiter appeared to be the victim of physical abuse on several occasions. Two of Jupiter's former clients also testified to his good character, with one being a friend who joined Jupiter on religious retreats.

In 2002, Jupiter was suspended for 6 months and again in 2010 for 18 months. The offenses included failing to communicate with a client and returning client files, neglecting a legal matter, failing to disburse settlement proceeds for more than a year, and maintaining an insufficient trust account balance. All but 30 days of the suspension time was stayed. You are part of the disciplinary board given the task of possibly disciplining Jupiter. What conduct rules has Jupiter violated? After considering possible aggravating and mitigating factors, what sanction would you recommend?

3. Attorney Rivera represented Jim Jones, the plaintiff in a medical malpractice case. Jones believed the surgeon committed malpractice during a routine "hip adjustment" at Mercy Hospital that left him unable to walk without a cane. Rivera had never handled a medical malpractice action, and before consulting anyone, including five other medical personnel in the operating room, Rivera sent a hasty demand letter to the surgeon and hospital seeking a $300,000 settlement. They both agreed to settle for that amount if Jones and Rivera kept the settlement confidential. Jones accepted the settlement based on Rivera's strong recommendation. Jones later learned from a nurse in the operating room that the surgeon was intoxicated during Jones's surgery and that the hospital had known about the surgeon's substance abuse problem for two years.

   Jones contacts you to see if he has a potential malpractice claim against Rivera. Jones also tells you that Rivera reluctantly offered him $50,000 if Jones promised not to sue him for malpractice or file a disciplinary complaint. Advise Jones about the possibility of a legal malpractice lawsuit. Also, what, if any, ethics rules did Rivera violate?

Professional Responsibility in Practice

1. Should law schools play a greater gatekeeper role in screening graduates for good character and fitness for bar admission? How would schools assume a greater role? Outline your reasons why law schools should, or should not, assume a greater gatekeeper role and possible ways for law schools to implement such a role.

2. Explain the responsibility that individual lawyers have in the regulation of the profession. What are some of the practical problems associated with lawyers reporting the misconduct of other lawyers?

3. Research your state's law to learn if law firms, as well as individual lawyers, are subject to professional discipline. Is it a good idea to discipline law firms and not just individual lawyers? Articulate the reasons why law firms should, or should not, be required to adopt proactive, management-based polices to ensure that their lawyers comply with ethics rules.

4. Should bar association websites post a lawyer's disciplinary history to protect the public? Should any posting include all grievances filed against a lawyer or only those resulting in discipline?

5. Identify the measures a lawyer can undertake in your state, consistent with professional conduct rules, to limit her exposure to a malpractice or disciplinary action.

6. There is recent literature discussing the benefits of doctors apologizing to their patients for their mistakes. Discuss the possible benefits and detriments of having lawyers or law firms apologize to their clients for their mistakes. Should an apology from a lawyer or law firm to a client for misconduct play any role in the lawyer disciplinary process?

PART III

The Attorney-Client Relationship

3

The Attorney-Client Relationship

The defining attribute of nearly all lawyering is the relationship between attorney and client. Lawyers work as agents for a client-principal — they work in a representative capacity, acting on behalf of other people or entities. This agency relationship entails fiduciary duties of the lawyer on behalf of the client. The lawyer owes the client core duties of loyalty, confidentiality, competence, communication, and conflict avoidance. The lawyer must protect the client's interests and must pursue the objectives of the client. The lawyer must fully disclose the nature of the engagement and any limitations on the lawyer's representation. The lawyer should undertake representation with the expectation that the lawyer will pursue it until completion. In addition, lawyers must not take advantage of their client-principal. They can only charge a reasonable fee and must safeguard client property. If the lawyer decides or is required to withdraw from a representation, the lawyer should work to mitigate any harm to the client flowing from that withdrawal. The lawyer is the client's loyal agent and must act as such in forming and dissolving the attorney-client relationship.

Key Concepts

- Express and implied attorney-client relationships
- Duties owed to clients and prospective clients
- Allocation of authority between attorney and client
- Client identity: responsibilities to entity and government clients
- Charging and collecting attorneys' fees
- Handling client funds and property
- Terminating the attorney-client relationship

A. FORMING AN ATTORNEY-CLIENT RELATIONSHIP

As Susan Martyn summarizes, whenever an attorney-client relationship is created, either expressly or impliedly, "the law governing lawyers recognizes that the lawyer has assumed four core fiduciary obligations (the '4 C's'): Competence, Communication, Confidentiality, [and] Conflict of interest resolution."[1] The lawyer can be disqualified or subject to discipline or liability for breach of these core duties to her client. In a typical situation, the formation of the attorney-client relationship is done expressly—the attorney is formally hired by her client or appointed by a court and both the attorney and client are aware of the contours of the relationship and the obligations undertaken. Best and prudent practices commend an engagement letter or contract that clearly—in plain language that the client can understand—sets forth the terms of the relationship.

But best practices are not always possible. For example, on Friday, January 27, 2017, at 4:42 P.M. EST, President Donald Trump signed an executive order creating a three-month ban on entry into the United States by immigrants and nonimmigrants from seven countries—Iraq, Syria, Sudan, Iran, Somalia, Libya, and Yemen. Federal officials from the Department of Homeland Security detained travelers—including those with valid green cards and visas—who arrived on flights beginning Friday evening and throughout Saturday and Sunday. Over that weekend, hundreds of lawyers throughout the United States went to international airports and offered to represent people who were being detained. Some lawyers had been recruited by the International Rescue Committee via email. Others were recruited through social media campaigns, and some lawyers saw news reports and just showed up at an airport. Lawyers held signs written in multiple languages offering free legal services and asked travelers who were disembarking if they knew of anyone who had been detained and then followed such leads.[2] Lawyers then filed petitions for writs of habeas corpus on behalf of these spur-of-the-moment clients, ultimately leading to several federal court preliminary injunctions as to certain classes of travelers.[3] Attorney Simon Sandoval-Moshenberg reported that he "reached out on Facebook trying to find potential plaintiffs and his inbox filled quickly. 'I was getting messages from people all over the world,' he said, 'including people who were writing in using the Wi-Fi from their planes. These are people who were lawfully boarding their flights, but as soon as the wheels hit the ground, they were covered by the executive order.' "[4] The exigency of the circumstances prescribed what would otherwise be very hastily made attorney-client relationships.

1. Implied Attorney-Client Relationships

An attorney-client relationship can also be implied—that is, the relationship is created without an express agreement. Courts have found an **implied attorney-client**

---

1. Susan R. Martyn, *Accidental Clients*, 33 HOFSTRA L. REV. 913, 914 (2005).
2. *See, e.g.*, Jennifer Peltz & Frank Eltman, *Volunteer Lawyers Have Descended on Major Airports After Trump's Immigration Order*, TIME, Jan. 31, 2017, *available at* http://time.com/4656131/trump-immigration-lawyers-airports/; Jonah Engel Bromwich, *Lawyers Mobilize at Nation's Airports After Trump's Order*, N.Y. TIMES, Jan. 29, 2017, *available at* https://www.nytimes.com/2017/01/29/us/lawyers-trump-muslim-ban-immigration.html.
3. *See* Orin Kerr, *Four Federal Judges Issue Orders Blocking Parts of Trump's Executive Order on Immigration*, WASH. POST, Jan. 29, 2017, https://www.washingtonpost.com/news/volokh-conspiracy/wp/2017/01/29/four-federal-judges-issue-orders-blocking-parts-of-trumps-executive-order-on-immigration/?utm_term=.aa7baf87c657.
4. Dahlia Lithwich, *The Travelers Trapped in Horrific Limbo by Trump's Immigration Order*, SLATE, Jan. 29, 2017, *available at* http://www.slate.com/articles/news_and_politics/jurisprudence/2017/01/court_rulings_couldn_t_protect_everyone_detained_because_of_trump_s_immigration.html.

relationship where attorneys received confidential information from a person and then provided legal advice. The relationships are found even though the attorney did not execute a formal contract or engagement agreement, did not receive a fee, and did not think that an attorney-client relationship had been formed. In certain situations courts can and do infer—for purposes of malpractice, conflicts, confidentiality, and other duties—the existence of implied professional relationships between attorneys and clients.

Case Preview

Togstad v. Vesely, Otto, Miller & Keefe

In *Togstad v. Vesely, Otto, Miller & Keefe*, attorney Jerre Miller was held liable for malpractice to the tune of $650,000 as to a client with whom Miller met for only 45 minutes and with whom he had no contract or engagement agreement. Indeed, Miller did not believe that he had undertaken an attorney-client relationship with the Togstads at all.

As you read *Togstad*, look for the following:

1. What actions did Miller undertake that led the court to find an implied professional relationship despite Miller's belief that no such relationship had been formed?
2. What are the two theories for finding an implied professional relationship set out by the court?
3. What could Miller have done to protect himself from malpractice in this case?

Togstad v. Vesely, Otto, Miller & Keefe

291 N.W.2d 686 (Minn. 1980)

This is an appeal by the defendants. . . . The jury found that the defendant attorney Jerre Miller was negligent and that, as a direct result of such negligence, plaintiff John Togstad sustained damages in the amount of $610,500 and his wife, plaintiff Joan Togstad, in the amount of $39,000. Defendants (Miller and his law firm) appeal to this court from the denial of their motion for judgment notwithstanding the verdict or, alternatively, for a new trial. We affirm.

In August 1971, John Togstad began to experience severe headaches and on August 16, 1971, was admitted to Methodist Hospital where tests disclosed that the headaches were caused by a large aneurism on the left internal carotid artery. The attending physician, Dr. Paul Blake, a neurological surgeon, treated the problem by applying a Selverstone clamp to the left common carotid artery. The clamp was surgically implanted on August 27, 1971, in Togstad's neck to allow the gradual closure of the artery over a period of days. . . . In the early morning hours of August 29, 1971, a nurse observed that Togstad was unable to speak or move. At the time, the clamp

was one-half (50%) closed. Upon discovering Togstad's condition, the nurse called a resident physician, who did not adjust the clamp. Dr. Blake was also immediately informed of Togstad's condition and arrived about an hour later, at which time he opened the clamp. Togstad is now severely paralyzed in his right arm and leg, and is unable to speak.

Plaintiffs' expert, Dr. Ward Woods, testified that Togstad's paralysis and loss of speech was due to a lack of blood supply to his brain. Dr. Woods stated that the inadequate blood flow resulted from the clamp being 50% closed and that the negligence of Dr. Blake and the hospital precluded the clamp's being opened in time to avoid permanent brain damage. . . .

About 14 months after her husband's hospitalization began, plaintiff Joan Togstad met with attorney Jerre Miller regarding her husband's condition. . . .

Mrs. Togstad had become suspicious of the circumstances surrounding her husband's tragic condition due to the conduct and statements of the hospital nurses shortly after the paralysis occurred. . . .

Mrs. Togstad testified that she told Miller "everything that happened at the hospital," including the nurses' statements and conduct which had raised a question in her mind. She stated that she "believed" she had told Miller "about the procedure and what was undertaken, what was done, and what happened." She brought no records with her. Miller took notes and asked questions during the meeting, which lasted 45 minutes to an hour. At its conclusion, according to Mrs. Togstad, Miller said that "he did not think we had a legal case, however, he was going to discuss this with his partner." She understood that if Miller changed his mind after talking to his partner, he would call her. Mrs. Togstad "gave it" a few days and, since she did not hear from Miller, decided "that they had come to the conclusion that there wasn't a case." No fee arrangements were discussed, no medical authorizations were requested, nor was Mrs. Togstad billed for the interview.

Mrs. Togstad denied that Miller had told her his firm did not have expertise in the medical malpractice field, urged her to see another attorney, or related to her that the statute of limitations for medical malpractice actions was two years. She did not consult another attorney until one year after she talked to Miller. Mrs. Togstad indicated that she did not confer with another attorney earlier because of her reliance on Miller's "legal advice" that they "did not have a case." . . .

Miller's testimony was different in some respects from that of Mrs. Togstad. Like Mrs. Togstad, Miller testified that . . . the meeting [] lasted about 45 minutes. According to Miller, Mrs. Togstad described the hospital incident, including the conduct of the nurses. He asked her questions, to which she responded. Miller testified that "(t)he only thing I told her (Mrs. Togstad) after we had pretty much finished the conversation was that there was nothing related in her factual circumstances that told me that she had a case that our firm would be interested in undertaking."

Miller also claimed he related to Mrs. Togstad "that because of the grievous nature of the injuries sustained by her husband, that this was only my opinion and she was encouraged to ask another attorney if she wished for another opinion" and "she ought to do so promptly." He testified that he informed Mrs. Togstad that his firm "was not engaged as experts" in the area of medical malpractice, and that they associated with the Charles Hvass firm in cases of that nature. Miller stated that at the end of the conference he told Mrs. Togstad that he would consult with Charles Hvass and if Hvass's opinion differed from his, Miller would so inform her. Miller recollected that he called Hvass a "couple days" later and discussed the case with him. It was Miller's impression that Hvass thought there was no liability for malpractice in the case. Consequently, Miller did not communicate with Mrs. Togstad further.

. . .

Hvass stated that he had no recollection of Miller's calling him in October 1972 relative to the Togstad matter. He testified that: "when a person comes in to me about a medical malpractice action . . . I have to make a decision as to whether or not there probably is or probably is not . . . medical malpractice. . . . Hvass stated, however, that he would never render a "categorical" opinion. In addition, Hvass acknowledged that if he were consulted for a "legal opinion" regarding medical malpractice and 14 months had expired since the incident in question, "ordinary care and diligence" would require him to inform the party of the two-year statute of limitations applicable to that type of action.

. . . The jury found that Dr. Blake and the hospital were negligent and that Dr. Blake's negligence (but not the hospital's) was a direct cause of the injuries sustained by John Togstad; that there was an attorney-client contractual relationship between Mrs. Togstad and Miller; that Miller was negligent in rendering advice regarding the possible claims of Mr. and Mrs. Togstad; that, but for Miller's negligence, plaintiffs would have been successful in the prosecution of a legal action against Dr. Blake; and that neither Mr. nor Mrs. Togstad was negligent in pursuing their claims against Dr. Blake. The jury awarded damages to Mr. Togstad of $610,500 and to Mrs. Togstad of $39,000.

. . .

In a legal malpractice action of the type involved here, four elements must be shown: (1) that an attorney-client relationship existed; (2) that defendant acted negligently or in breach of contract; (3) that such acts were the proximate cause of the plaintiffs' damages; (4) that but for defendant's conduct the plaintiffs would have been successful in the prosecution of their medical malpractice claim.

This court first dealt with the element of lawyer-client relationship in the decision of Ryan v. Long, 35 Minn. 394, 29 N.W. 51 (1886). The *Ryan* case involved a claim of legal malpractice and on appeal it was argued that no attorney-client relation existed. This court, without stating whether its conclusion was based on contract principles or a tort theory, disagreed:

> (I)t sufficiently appears that plaintiff, for himself, called upon defendant, as an attorney at law, for "legal advice," and that defendant assumed to give him a professional opinion in reference to the matter as to which plaintiff consulted him. Upon this state of facts the defendant must be taken to have acted as plaintiff's legal adviser, at plaintiff's request, and so as to establish between them the relation of attorney and client.

Id. More recent opinions of this court, although not involving a detailed discussion, have analyzed the attorney-client consideration in contractual terms. . . . The trial court here . . . applied a contract analysis in ruling on the attorney-client relationship question. . . .

We believe it is unnecessary to decide whether a tort or contract theory is preferable for resolving the attorney-client relationship question raised by this appeal. The tort and contract analyses are very similar in a case such as the instant one,[4] and we conclude that under either theory the evidence shows that a lawyer-client relationship is present here. The thrust of Mrs. Togstad's testimony is that she went to Miller for legal advice, was told there wasn't a case, and relied upon this advice in failing to pursue the claim for medical malpractice. In addition, according to Mrs. Togstad, Miller did not qualify his legal opinion by urging her to seek advice from another attorney, nor did Miller inform her that he lacked expertise in the medical malpractice area. Assuming this testimony is true, as this court must do, we believe a jury could properly find that Mrs. Togstad sought and received legal advice from Miller under circumstances which made it reasonably foreseeable to Miller that Mrs. Togstad would be injured if the advice were negligently given. Thus, under either a tort or contract analysis, there is sufficient evidence in the record to support the existence of an attorney-client relationship.

Defendants argue that even if an attorney-client relationship was established the evidence fails to show that Miller acted negligently in assessing the merits of the Togstads' case. They appear to contend that, at most, Miller was guilty of an error in judgment which does not give rise to legal malpractice. However, this case does not involve a mere error of judgment. The gist of plaintiffs' claim is that Miller failed to perform the minimal research that an ordinarily prudent attorney would do before rendering legal advice in a case of this nature. The record, through [expert testimony], contains sufficient evidence to support plaintiffs' position.

In a related contention, defendants assert that a new trial should be awarded on the ground that the trial court erred by refusing to instruct the jury that Miller's failure to inform Mrs. Togstad of the two-year statute of limitations for medical malpractice could not constitute negligence. . . .

The defect in defendants' reasoning is that there is adequate evidence supporting the claim that Miller was also negligent in failing to advise Mrs. Togstad of the two-year medical malpractice limitations period and thus the trial court acted properly in refusing to instruct the jury in the manner urged by defendants. One of defendants' expert witnesses, Charles Hvass, testified:

Q: Now, Mr. Hvass, . . . wouldn't ordinary care and diligence require that you inform them that there is a two-year statute of limitations within which they have to act or lose their rights?

A: Yes. I believe I would have advised someone of the two-year period of limitation, yes.

---

4. Under a negligence approach it must essentially be shown that defendant rendered legal advice (not necessarily at someone's request) under circumstances which made it reasonably foreseeable to the attorney that if such advice was rendered negligently, the individual receiving the advice might be injured thereby. *See, e.g.*, Palsgraf v. Long Island R. Co., 248 N.Y. 339 (1928). Or, stated another way, under a tort theory, "(a)n attorney-client relationship is created whenever an individual seeks and receives legal advice from an attorney in circumstances in which a reasonable person would rely on such advice." 63 Minn. L. Rev. 751, 759 (1979). A contract analysis requires the rendering of legal advice pursuant to another's request and the reliance factor, in this case, where the advice was not paid for, need be shown in the form of promissory estoppel. *See*, 7 C.J.S., Attorney and Client, § 65; *Restatement (Second) of Contracts*, § 90.

Consequently, . . . we must reject the defendants' contention, as it was reasonable for a jury to determine that Miller acted negligently in failing to inform Mrs. Togstad of the applicable limitations period.

. . .

Affirmed.

Post-Case Follow-Up

Mrs. Togstad and Miller report somewhat conflicting accounts of their meeting. When a client is under the impression that an attorney is representing her and testifies as much, is a jury likely to find more credible the testimony of the client or a conflicting account by the lawyer? Moreover, consider whether a judge is likely to place responsibility on the attorney to communicate clearly with a prospective client regarding whether or not the attorney is undertaking a representation.

In Westinghouse Elec. Corp. v. Kerr-McGee Corp., 580 F.2d 1311 (7th Cir. 1978), the United States Court of Appeals for the Seventh Circuit explained that an implied professional relationship arises "when the lay party submits confidential information to the [lawyer] with reasonable belief that the latter is acting as the former's attorney." Thus, in *Togstad*, the fact that Mrs. Togstad conveyed confidential information to Miller and reasonably believed he was acting as her attorney created an attorney-client relationship for purposes of malpractice. The onus is on the attorney to clarify the absence of a relationship whenever there is reasonable ambiguity. A common and prudent method to avoid such misunderstandings is by using a written declination letter memorializing that the attorney is not undertaking a representation or establishing an attorney-client relationship and advising the putative client of any statute of limitations or other deadlines and of the need to seek other legal counsel should she wish to pursue the matter.

Togstad v. Miller: Real Life Applications

1. Tamara is an attorney who is asked to speak at a local Chamber of Commerce event in her hometown about basic issues regarding small business operation and contracts. After the meeting, one of the attendees, Behzad, comes up and asks Tamara about the enforceability of a contract that he had entered into to perform contractor work, where the homeowner is obnoxious and has made it difficult for him to complete the work. He tells her he really wishes he didn't have to complete it. Tamara responds, "Don't we all wish that about our jobs! But it sounds to me like the owner maybe already breached the contract by making your work difficult — which would mean you wouldn't be obligated to finish." Assume that Behzad decides, based on this conversation, to stop working on the project and is successfully sued for $25,000 for breach of contract. Analyze whether Behzad had an attorney-client relationship with Tamara and whether he can sue her for legal malpractice.

2. Charles hired Joel to file a personal injury lawsuit on his behalf. Joel realized that the statute of limitations was running soon and that a complaint needed to be filed immediately. He was about to file the complaint when he realized that he had failed to pay his yearly bar dues and his license had lapsed for that failure. Joel called his friend, Thomas, and asked Thomas if he would just sign the complaint and file it for him, promising that Joel would then take care of serving the complaint, pay his dues and get his license reinstated, and take over the matter — Thomas need do nothing further. Thomas agreed, then affixed his name, signature, and attorney number on the complaint and had it filed. Unbeknownst to Thomas, Joel failed to timely serve the complaint. Charles's case was dismissed for failing to serve the complaint, and the statute of limitations had meanwhile run. Did Thomas have an attorney-client relationship with Charles, and can he be sued for malpractice or disciplined for incompetence in handling the case?

---

2. Prospective Clients

Model Rule 1.18 was added by the Ethics 2000 Commission and defines when someone is a "**prospective client**" and what duties are owed to those who fall within that category. The duties created by Rule 1.18 exist regardless of whether an express or implied attorney-client relationship is formed. Thus, even if an attorney makes it absolutely clear that he is not taking on a representation, the attorney will still owe the "prospective client" the duties set out in Rule 1.18. Yet the duties established in Rule 1.18 are watered down from the duties owed to a client under a normal express or implied attorney-client relationship. Under the rule, a prospective client is defined as "[a] person who consults with a lawyer about the possibility of forming a client-lawyer relationship with respect to a matter." The key term in this definition is "consult." If an attorney has consulted with a person, then that person is a prospective client.

How much communication is required for there to be a consultation triggering the application of Rule 1.18? Comment 2 to Rule 1.18 explains that it "depends on the circumstances," yet "a consultation is likely to have occurred if a lawyer, either in person or through the lawyer's advertising in any medium, specifically requests or invites the submission of information about a potential representation," "and a person provides information in response." On the other hand, the comment makes clear that where "a person communicates information unilaterally to a lawyer, without any reasonable expectation that the lawyer is willing to discuss the possibility of forming a client-lawyer relationship," the person is not a prospective client and the requirements of Rule 1.18 do not apply.

Could a prospective client seek a consultation with an attorney for the very purpose of creating a conflict so that the attorney cannot represent the opposing side? Indeed, couldn't a scheming person arrange to have initial consultations with all the best attorneys in a locality, purposefully disclose information, and then argue that the opposing side is conflicted out from using any of those attorneys?

Comment 2 to Model Rule 1.18 directly addresses this kind of **conflict shopping**, stating that "a person who communicates with a lawyer for the purpose of disqualifying the lawyer is not a 'prospective client'" under the rule and thus the duties imposed by Rule 1.18 do not apply. Nevertheless, it is not always easy to demonstrate that a party was engaged in conflict shopping rather than honestly seeking an excellent attorney.

Case Preview

In re Marriage of Perry

In January 2008, Karen Perry called Gail Goheen's law office to discuss potentially filing for divorce from Karen's husband, Terance Perry. Karen spoke with Goheen's assistant and later with Goheen herself, but ultimately hired a different attorney. In 2009, Terance, himself an attorney, filed for divorce. He went through three different attorneys and even briefly represented himself. Then in February 2011—three years after Karen had called Goheen's office and spoken with her—Terance hired Goheen to represent him in the divorce. Karen moved to disqualify Goheen, arguing both (1) that she had an implied professional relationship with Goheen; and (2) that she was Goheen's prospective client and thus Goheen was prohibited from representing Terance under Montana Rule 1.20—which is nearly identical to Model Rule 1.18, although numbered differently.

As you read *Perry*, look for the following:

1. What is the standard for finding a disqualifying conflict of interest under Rule 1.18?
2. Did Goheen receive confidential information from Karen in the initial consultation? Was the information significantly harmful to Karen?
3. Did Goheen use or reveal confidential information she received from Karen? How does the court determine this issue?

In re Marriage of Perry

293 P.3d 170 (Mont. 2013)

On December 4, 2009, Terance filed for dissolution of his marriage to Karen in Missoula County. . . . [On February 25, 2011, Terance filed a substitution of counsel] naming Goheen as his counsel of record.

In January 2008, before any dissolution proceedings were filed, Karen contacted Goheen's office in Hamilton seeking legal advice concerning the potential filing of a dissolution action. Karen spoke with Goheen's assistant, Kailah Van Note (Van Note), and later Goheen herself.

Karen filed a motion to disqualify Goheen and an application for a preliminary injunction on March 1, 2011. Terance opposed the motion and filed two office

memorandums and affidavits from Goheen and Van Note regarding their telephone conversations with Karen. A disqualification hearing was held on November 7, 2011. . . .

At the hearing, Karen testified that she provided personal information about herself and Terance during one telephone conversation with Van Note and two telephone conversations with Goheen. Karen said the conversations with Goheen lasted 45 minutes and 3 minutes, respectively. She said that she gave information about the marriage, including domestic abuse [which Terrance denied occurred] and finances, and that she asked for legal advice on her "position," which she described as: "[w]here I wanted to end up. If I could end up at a certain place. What would happen if I stayed here. What [would] happen if I left here. Goals of settlement. My weaknesses and fears." Karen testified that she identified individuals who were present during domestic disputes. She said Goheen quoted her a "ridiculously enormous" retainer, but conceded that she was never sent a retainer agreement and that Goheen had "denied representation." . . . Karen testified that she thought the information she gave to Goheen's office would be confidential. . . .

When asked "[h]ow does Gail Goheen's representation of your husband now, in this dissolution of marriage that he brought three years later, harm you," Karen responded:

> [P]sychologically, it's like getting beat up again by him. It's like I can't trust anybody. There's nobody I can turn to. He took away everything and everybody I could trust. And now he's done it again with somebody who I confided in, who's now on the opposite side of the table. And it — I — I'm betrayed again. It's another form of abuse and control . . . .

[T]he District Court permitted Goheen to offer testimony about the length of the telephone conversations, her office procedures, and background information established in the court file. Goheen testified without another attorney questioning her. Goheen admitted to having one conversation with Karen in January 2008, which she said lasted less than 12 minutes because the time entry information on the record was left blank and it is her office policy that time information is left blank when a conversation lasts 12 minutes or less. Goheen denied having a second conversation with Karen. Explaining her office procedures for new clients, Goheen stated:

> Whenever I meet with a client, Your Honor, I don't do it over the phone, in the sense of getting information. I sit down and I meet with the client for a half a day, usually, is my first meeting with a client on a divorce action. . . .
>
> It's at that time that I go over everything I can think of . . . . All details.
>
> I'm not interested in it, information, in terms of any details prior to that time. And my policy is that I never give anybody a retainer quote until I get all that information.
>
> So I can state unequivocably [sic] that I would not have given a retainer quote to Karen Perry, or any other client under these circumstances.

Goheen said she was aware that Karen's husband was an attorney at Datsopoulos, MacDonald & Lind and that she does not represent someone against an attorney in Ravalli or Missoula County when the opposing attorney is from a firm that she regularly faces in divorce cases. Goheen said she did not remember the details of a conversation with Karen, relying on the office memorandums created from her and Van Note's conversations with Karen. Goheen said that a 45 minute telephone conversation did not occur, and that her telephone records indicate she made a two or three minute telephone call to refuse the case and refer Karen to someone else. Goheen said she was notified by Karen's current attorney that Karen had contacted Goheen's office in September 2009 and in January 2010 but that her telephone records revealed only two telephone conversations with Karen in January 2008. Van Note also testified about Goheen's office procedures.

[T]he District Court denied Karen's motion to disqualify and application for a preliminary injunction....

DISCUSSION

1. Did the District Court err by denying Karen's motion to disqualify Goheen as counsel for Terance pursuant to Rule 1.20 of the Montana Rules of Professional Conduct?

Karen claims that the District Court erred by not disqualifying Goheen because an implied attorney-client relationship was formed between Karen and Goheen when Karen gave Goheen information that was "confidential" in nature.... Karen [argues] that she is "psychologically harmed" by the fact that Terance has hired Goheen and "[t]he district court did not properly address the correct standard or pertinent issue relative to Rule 1.20(c) with respect to the harm to Karen in determining Goheen's conflict of interest."

We have not yet addressed a lawyer's duty to prospective clients under the Montana Rules of Professional Conduct as amended in 2004. We considered this relationship under prior rules in *Pro-Hand Services*, stating:

> An implied attorney-client relationship may result when a prospective client divulges confidential information during a consultation with an attorney for the purpose of retaining the attorney, even if actual employment does not result.... In determining whether an implied attorney-client relationship exists, we will examine whether the alleged client reasonably believed that such relationship was formed.

... [At that time,] [i]f confidential information was not disclosed [by the client], then an attorney-client relationship did not exist. [Moreover,] "[i]f an attorney-client relationship was not formed, there is no conflict of interest," and an attorney could then represent a client in a matter that was adverse to the former prospective client.

In 2004, Rule 1.20 [the same as Model Rule 1.18], entitled "Duties to Prospective Clients" was adopted. Rule 1.20 defines and addresses a lawyer's relationship with a prospective client. It provides ...:

> **(a) A person who consults with or has had consultations with a lawyer about the possibility of forming a client-lawyer relationship with respect to a matter is a prospective client.**
>
> **(b) Even when no client-lawyer relationship ensues, a lawyer who has had consultations with a prospective client shall not use or reveal information learned in the consultation(s), except as Rule 1.9 would permit with respect to information of a former client.**

(c) A lawyer subject to paragraph (b) shall not represent a client with interests materially adverse to those of a prospective client in the same or a substantially related matter if the lawyer received information from the prospective client that could be significantly harmful to that person in the matter, except as provided in paragraph (d). If a lawyer is disqualified from representation under this paragraph, no lawyer in a firm with which that lawyer is associated may knowingly undertake or continue representation in such a matter, except as provided in paragraph (d). . . .

Instead of determining whether an attorney-client relationship was created by disclosure of confidential information, Rule 1.20 creates duties to the prospective client "[e]ven when no client-lawyer relationship ensues." Mont. R. Pro. C. 1.20(b). Generally, and subject to exceptions discussed herein, a lawyer may not "use or reveal information learned in the consultation(s)" with a prospective client. Pertinent to the present issue, Rule 1.20 also prohibits a lawyer from representing a party with "interests materially adverse" to the prospective client in the same or substantially related proceeding "if the lawyer received information from the prospective client that could be significantly harmful to that person in the matter." Mont. R. Pro. C. 1.20(c). Thus, Rule 1.20 does not merely consider whether information was divulged by the prospective client but whether such information could be significantly harmful to that person in that or a related matter. Rule 1.18 of the American Bar Association's Model Rules of Professional Conduct (Model Rules) is nearly identical to Montana Rule 1.20. The Committee Comments to Model Rule 1.18 state "the lawyer is not prohibited from representing a client with interests adverse to those of the prospective client in the same or a substantially related matter unless the lawyer has received from the prospective client information that could be significantly harmful if used in the matter." Model R. Prof. Conduct 1.18 cmt. 6 (ABA 2012).

. . . Karen is a "prospective client" as defined by Rule 1.20(a) ("A person who consults with or has had consultations with a lawyer about the possibility of forming a client-lawyer relationship with respect to a matter is a prospective client."). Karen called Goheen's office more than once and spoke with Van Note and Goheen concerning representation. The question here does not depend on whether an attorney-client relationship was established or whether Karen reasonably believed such a relationship was formed, as in *Pro-Hand Services*. Rather, under Rule 1.20, the question [relevant to disqualification] is whether the information conveyed in Karen's conversations could be significantly harmful to Karen in this dissolution proceeding.

After hearing the testimony, the District Court found that the information conveyed by Karen to Goheen was not harmful to Karen. The court found that Goheen's office documentation of Karen's phone calls and the testimony of Goheen and Van Note were credible and that "there was nothing disclosed by Karen to Ms. Goheen or her staff 'that could be significantly harmful' to Karen in this matter." Karen claims a personal or psychological victimization by Goheen's representation of Terance. While we do not minimize the significance of such an effect, Rule 1.20 requires that the lawyer receive "information" that is "significantly harmful" to Karen in the proceeding. Karen did not establish that any information she divulged to Goheen in the telephone calls several years earlier could have any impact on the proceeding, particularly since, as discussed [], Goheen was not associated as counsel until three years into the proceeding, by which time substantially more information had been disclosed than the information Karen claims to have shared during those phone calls. We therefore conclude that the District Court did not abuse its discretion in denying Karen's motion to disqualify under Rule 1.20.

. . . Karen also argues that Goheen violated Rule 1.9 by using or disclosing information Karen had divulged to her. Because the provisions of Rule 1.9 regarding use of former client information are incorporated by Rule 1.20, governing the duties to prospective clients, we take up Karen's argument in that regard.

Rule 1.20(b) provides that "a lawyer who has had consultations with a prospective client shall not use or reveal information learned in the consultation(s), except as Rule 1.9 would permit with respect to information of a former client." Mont. R. Pro. C. 1.20(b). In turn, Rule 1.9 states, in pertinent part:

> (c) A lawyer who has formerly represented a client in a matter or whose present or former firm has formerly represented a client in a matter shall not thereafter: (1) use information relating to the representation to the disadvantage of the former client except as these Rules would permit or require with respect to a client, or when the information has become generally known; or (2) reveal information relating to the representation except as these Rules would permit or require with respect to a client.

Mont. R. Pro. C. 1.9(c).

. . . As established under Issue 1, Karen has not demonstrated that Goheen received information that could be significantly harmful to her in this proceeding. . . . The parties had previously filed information detailing Karen's and Terance's personal information, the parties' financial situations, and Karen's affidavits alleging spousal abuse. In its order, the District Court found that "any information regarding Terance's alleged abuse of Karen is now moot given what Karen herself subsequently disclosed early on in this case." The District Court permitted Goheen to testify concerning the background information in the court file, then permitted Goheen to testify as to the length of the telephone conversations with Karen, and Goheen's office procedures. It was permissible under the Rules for Goheen to use this information about her previous contact with Karen "to respond to allegations in any proceeding concerning the lawyer's representation of the client." Mont. R. Pro. C. 1.6(b)(3). The District Court properly limited Goheen's testimony to prevent disclosure of Karen's confidences, if any.

Karen's allegations against Goheen are generalized and vague. Goheen's limited use of Karen's information was permitted under Rules 1.6(b) and 1.9(c), and Goheen did not violate a duty to Karen.

Post-Case Follow-Up

In *Perry*, even though Karen had given Goheen confidential information, the court did not find a disqualifying conflict under Rule 1.18 because Goheen had not obtained "information from the prospective client that could be significantly harmful" to Karen. Karen argued that the information was "significantly harmful" because it was psychologically harmful to have someone she had confided in turn around and represent her husband. For Karen, it was the feeling of betrayal that was "significantly harmful" to her. What language from the rule did the court rely on in rejecting Karen's interpretation?

When is information "significantly harmful" to the prospective client such that a disqualification is appropriate? A Wisconsin ethics opinion surveys cases where information has been found to be significantly harmful within the meaning of Rule 1.18. The opinion synthesizes the cases to "fashion a loose definition of 'significantly harmful information.'" The opinion states:

> Information may be "significantly harmful" if it is sensitive or privileged information that the lawyer would not have received in the ordinary course of due diligence; or if it is information that has long-term significance or continuing relevance to the matter, such as motives, litigation strategies, or potential weaknesses. "Significantly harmful" may also be the premature possession of information that could have a substantial impact on settlement proposals and trial strategy; the personal thoughts and impressions about the facts of the case; or information that is extensive, critical, or of significant use.[5]

What happens when a consulting attorney receives information that is "significantly harmful" to the prospective client? Under Model Rule 1.18(c), the consulting attorney is prohibited from representing a client in the same or a substantially related matter adversely to the prospective client, and the disqualification is imputed to the entire firm. However, the lawyer and law firm can avoid imputation through a screening and notice procedure outlined in Model Rule 1.18(d). The screening and notice option is only available if the consulting lawyer "took reasonable measures to avoid exposure to more disqualifying information than was reasonably necessary to determine whether to represent the prospective client." If so, then the conflict is not imputed to the firm as long as the consulting lawyer is "timely screened" from the matter and "apportioned no part of the fee therefrom," and "written notice is promptly given to the prospective client."

In re Marriage of Perry: Real Life Applications

1. Kelly has just been injured in a car accident. She searches online for personal injury lawyers, opening the website of Jarret & Maine, a personal injury law firm. As soon as she opens the site, a chatbox pops up with the words, "Can we help you?" Kelly types in the facts of what happened in the lawsuit and submits it. She gets a response that Jarret & Maine will get back to her shortly. Kelly decides not to wait and closes the page. A couple months later, Kelly is sued by the other driver involved in the wreck, Jason. Jason is represented by Jarret & Maine. Consider whether Kelly is a prospective client of Jarret & Maine. Can the firm represent Jason against her?

---

5. Wisconsin State Bar Professional Ethics Committee, Wisconsin Ethics Op. EI-10-03: *Avoid Conflicts When Consulting with Prospective Clients.*

2. Attorney Carpenter has a friend, Thompson, who is an oil and gas landman. Thompson learns that a deceased person owned the mineral rights to a large portion of land. Thompson spent 300 hours researching the decedent's heirs. He discovers that part of the mineral rights were bequeathed to a local church. Thompson meets with Carpenter about potentially helping him lease the mineral rights from the church. Thompson shows Carpenter all of the documents that he has found pertaining to the mineral interests, including a prior notice from the surface owners that the mineral rights have lapsed. The next day Carpenter sends Thompson a letter stating that he cannot represent Thompson because he previously represented the church. Can someone else in Carpenter's firm represent Thompson? Can Carpenter represent the church? Can Carpenter notify the church of its rights and the potential lapse discovered by Thompson?

B. ALLOCATION OF ATTORNEY AND CLIENT AUTHORITY

Once an attorney-client relationship is formed, how should this agent-principal relationship work? Does the principal-client get to call the shots while the agent-lawyer simply takes orders? For example, imagine that a client comes to you and tells you about a situation where the client feels she has been wronged and wants to sue immediately on a whole panoply of claims. The area of law is one with which you are familiar and you know that some of the things for which your client wants to sue are not legally cognizable wrongs — although your client has one or two possible causes of action. Who makes the decision to sue or not? Who decides what claims and legal theories should be asserted? Who decides how much discovery should be done and how much should be spent on discovery? If the case goes to trial, who decides which witnesses to call? Who decides what the scope of cross-examination will be? Who decides whether to appeal an adverse judgment?

1. Basic Allocation of Authority

Model Rule 1.2 addresses the basic allocation of authority between the attorney and client. The rule explains that, in general, "a lawyer shall abide by a client's decisions concerning the objectives of the representation." In other words, it is the client who has the ultimate authority to decide the objectives, or as comment 1 puts it, "the purposes to be served," by the representation. Nevertheless, there are limits on the client's ability to determine the objectives of a representation — as indicated by Rule 1.2(d) and comment 1, the client's objectives must fall "within the limits imposed by law and the lawyer's professional obligations." Thus, a lawyer is prohibited under Rule 1.2(d) from counseling or assisting a client in knowingly criminal or fraudulent conduct — even (and perhaps especially) if that's what the client wants the lawyer to do.

While the client determines the objectives of the representation, the attorney is given more control over "the means by which [those objectives] are pursued."

Importantly, the attorney is required to "consult with the client" regarding those means as set forth in Rule 1.4. In addition, the attorney is permitted to "take such action on behalf of the client as is impliedly authorized to carry out the representation." *See* Model Rule 1.2(a). When there is a dispute between the attorney and client as to the means to be used, comment 2 provides a basic methodology for resolution:

> Clients normally defer to the special knowledge and skill of their lawyer with respect to the means to be used to accomplish their objectives, particularly with respect to technical legal and tactical matters. Conversely, lawyers usually defer to the client regarding such questions as the expense to be incurred and concern for third persons who might be adversely affected.

The comment explains that this basic dichotomy does not specify how all potential disputes should be resolved. If a lawyer and client disagree about whether to depose a certain person, for example, both interests are called into play—on the one hand, deposing someone is a tactical and technical matter for a case, yet it is also expensive and can adversely affect third persons (the person being deposed). Ultimately, comment 2 indicates that if a conflict cannot be resolved, the lawyer may withdraw on the basis of "a fundamental disagreement with the client" or the client can fire the attorney.

Attorneys should work with clients to resolve differences in an amicable and supportive manner. Badgering a client or being obnoxious or abusive will likely lead to being fired and may even lead to discipline. In *Sallee v. Tennessee Board of Professional Responsibility* (excerpted later in this chapter), attorney Yarboro Sallee wrote the following to her client when seeking additional fees:

> Your back seat driving will destroy [the case] . . . I will not brook [sic] anymore second guessing. . . . The cases need what they need Fran[,] and you don't know anything about it. . . . I will send you a proposal and you can agree to find someone else, but I will have the right to file against any funds recovered in the future by any other lawyer. . . . You are not the lawyer, I am. You don't know enough to know what I need. I do.

As we will see below, Sallee was charging her client a clearly excessive fee, and ultimately was fired and suspended from the practice of law.[6]

Case Preview

Red Dog v. Delaware

James Allen Red Dog, a Native American of the Lakota tribe of the Sioux, was sentenced to death for murder, kidnapping, and rape. He was executed by lethal injection on March 3, 1993.[7] A week before his execution, attorneys from the public defender's office representing him filed a motion for a stay of

6. Sallee v. Tennessee Board of Professional Responsibility, 469 S.W.3d 18, 24 (Tenn. 2015).
7. *See States Execute Two Murderers*, N.Y. Times, Mar. 4, 1993, *available at* http://www.nytimes.com/1993/03/04/us/states-execute-two-murderers.html.

execution. When the stay was denied, the attorneys filed an appeal. As the Supreme Court of Delaware explained, both the motion for the stay and the appeal were filed "without Red Dog's authorization and despite his express oral and written directions to the contrary."[8] Indeed, Red Dog had stated in a handwritten note: "I desire no appeals or any motions for stay of execution, scheduled for March 3, 1993 to be filed on my behalf." And when Red Dog learned about the motion for the stay of execution, "he personally advised the Superior Court in writing, on February 25, 1993, that the motion was 'against my wishes.'"[9] Red Dog asserted that disputing his death sentence "would violate his warrior's code."[10]

As you read *Red Dog*, consider the following:

1. Were the attorneys required to abide by Red Dog's desire to accept the death penalty and his instructions not take any appeals?
2. What could the attorneys have done if they were strongly morally opposed to the death penalty?
3. Should a lawyer take actions (such as asserting a client's mental incompetence) that absolutely undermine the client's autonomy in order to pursue what the lawyer believes is in the client's "best interest" (here, the value of Red Dog's life)? Is it necessarily irrational for a client to prefer death over, say, life imprisonment?
4. If his attorneys truly believed that Red Dog was mentally incompetent to make decisions, what should they have done?

Red Dog v. Delaware

625 A.2d 245 (Del. 1993)

In Red Dog v. State, 620 A.2d 848 (1993), this Court affirmed a decision of the Superior Court which denied a stay of execution in a capital case. Therein, we held "that in the absence of a genuine issue of material fact as to Red Dog's present mental competency, the public defenders had no standing to file . . . a motion to stay his execution in derogation of his express directions to the contrary." ***Id.*** **at 853. On independent and alternative grounds, we affirmed Red Dog's competency as well as the lack of standing of the Public Defender.**

. . . Thereafter, Rules to Show Cause were directed to Lawrence M. Sullivan, the Public Defender of the State of Delaware, and Brian J. Bartley, Bernard J. O'Donnell, Edward C. Pankowski, and Nancy J. Perillo, all Assistant Public Defenders (collectively "Respondents"), directing responses as to why sanctions should not be imposed upon them for certain aspects of their representation of the defendant.

The Respondents filed written responses defending their actions as within the bounds of professional responsibility and required by the exigencies of representation of a defendant facing execution. . . .

---

8. *See* Red Dog v. State, 620 A.2d 848, 848 (Del. 1993).
9. *See id.* at 848-49.
10. *See States Execute Two Murderers, supra* note 7.

Respondents' efforts in pursuing an eleventh hour attempt to raise the question of the defendant's competency to forego further appeals or postconviction relief, despite the defendant's clearly expressed, longstanding and consistent desires to that effect, implicate conflicting ethical considerations. A defendant's wish to forego further appeals and accept the death penalty, like other decisions relating to the objectives of litigation, is essentially that of the client, whose decision the attorney must respect. Delaware Lawyers' Rules of Professional Conduct ("DLRPC") Rule 1.2(a). The means to be employed to achieve such objectives are "a matter on which the attorney is to consult with the client [and over which] the lawyer retains the ultimate prerogative to act." Modern Legal Ethics §4.3, p. 157. The deliberate decision of a defendant to accept the death penalty to avoid other penal alternatives is not, in itself, an irrational act. An attorney who is unable in good conscience to represent a client intent upon achieving such an objective, or to whom the death penalty is "repugnant," may seek leave to withdraw from the representation if the client's interests would not be prejudiced thereby. DLRPC Rule 1.16(b)(3).

If an attorney has a reasonable and objective basis to doubt a client's competency to make a decision foregoing further appeals, the attorney must, in a timely fashion, so inform the trial court and request the court to make a judicial determination of the defendant's competency. *See* DLRPC Rule 1.14(b). Where the lawyer's actions appear contrary to the client's stated decision, the lawyer who so moves, presumably in good faith, must, at a minimum, demonstrate an objective and reasonable basis for believing that the client cannot act in his own interest.

After full consideration of the circumstances surrounding the actions of Respondents in this matter, we find no basis for concluding that any of them acted in bad faith or were motivated by other than the best interests of their client. . . .

The Court recognizes the professional and personal demands which counsel experience in the defense of a capital case. A defendant facing execution is entitled to a vigorous and energetic defense, but a conscientious defense as well. A lawyer who renders such service is not free to fashion his or her own code of ethics. For members of the Bar of this Court those standards have already been established and they afford sufficient flexibility to accommodate proper zealous advocacy.

. . . Under such circumstances, we find no basis for the imposition of sanctions . . . .

Post-Case Follow-Up

Red Dog illustrates that lawyers are required to abide by their client's lawful decisions regarding the objectives of the representation—even when the lawyer does not think that such a decision is in the best interest of the client or the decision conflicts with the lawyer's personal views. Rule 1.2 makes clear that a representation of a client "does not constitute an endorsement of the client's political, economic, social, or moral views or activities."

In addition to having the ultimate authority regarding the objectives of the representation, clients also have the ultimate authority in deciding whether to settle a case in a civil matter. In criminal matters, the client has the ultimate authority as to the "plea to be entered, whether to waive jury trial, and whether the client will testify." *See* Model Rule 1.2(a). Importantly, Rule 1.2 confers the authority to the criminal defendant to make these decisions "after consultation with the lawyer." The lawyer must first consult with the accused about the legal effects and consequences of those decisions. As discussed in Chapter 4, it may constitute a denial of the defendant's Sixth Amendment right to effective assistance of counsel for an attorney to fail to inform a client about significant consequences attendant to pleading guilty (such as deportation if the accused is not a citizen). Such consultation is also an integral part of the lawyer's duty to communicate with his client. Comment 2 to Rule 1.4 explains that if any of the rules require the client to make a particular decision, then Rule 1.4 in turn requires that the attorney "promptly consult" with the client about that decision and "secure the client's consent prior to taking action unless prior discussions with the client have resolved what action the client wants the lawyer to take."

Red Dog v. Delaware: Real Life Applications

1. You represent Kim in a medical malpractice case. You receive a phone call from opposing counsel, who makes a settlement offer of $25,000. You reasonably believe that a jury would give Kim at least $300,000. Further, you know that Kim needs at least $75,000 just to cover outstanding medical bills, so you are sure that Kim would not even consider — indeed, she would likely be insulted by — the offer. Can you decline the offer on her behalf?

2. Molly represents Joaquin in a criminal matter for transporting marijuana. Joaquin is a non-citizen, but has lived in the United States for 40 years and served in the U.S. armed forces. Molly tells Joaquin he does not need to worry about deportation because he has been in the United States so long. Relying on this advice, Joaquin accepts a deal and pleads guilty to a criminal charge that (unbeknownst to him at the time) mandates his deportation. Has Molly violated Rule 1.2? Does Joaquin have any recourse?

---

2. Counseling or Assisting the Client in Crime or Fraud

A very significant limit on the client's ultimate authority over the objectives of the representation is that a lawyer is prohibited from either counseling a client to engage or assisting clients "in conduct that the lawyer knows is criminal or fraudulent." Rule 1.2(d) refers to conduct that the lawyer "knows" is criminal or fraudulent, and the rules in turn define knowledge to require "actual knowledge," but such knowledge "may be inferred from the circumstances," as stated in Rule 1.0(f). Nevertheless, Rule 1.2 allows a lawyer to discuss with the client "the legal consequences of any proposed course of conduct" and to "counsel or assist a client to make a good faith effort to determine the validity, scope, meaning or application of the law."

For example, in People v. Chappell, 927 P.2d 829 (Colo. 1996), the Colorado Supreme Court disbarred attorney Lorraine Chappell for assisting her client in violating a child custody order. Chappell represented a mother who was pregnant with her second child in a child custody dispute. After learning from the court-ordered custody evaluator that she would recommend sole custody of both children to the father, Chappell told her client that "as an attorney" she would advise the client to stay in Colorado and comply with court orders, but "as a mother" she would advise her "to run." Chappell then undertook elaborate efforts to assist her client to evade the court's orders and jurisdiction. Chappell "informed her client about a network of safehouses for people in her situation," "helped her to liquidate her assets and empty her bank accounts," arranged for a friend of the client to pack the belongings out of the marital home, and paid the friend moving and storage fees. Chappell kept the key to the storage unit where the belongings were kept. At the upcoming custody hearing, when the judge realized that Chappell's client likely had fled the jurisdiction with the children, the court ordered sole custody to the father. Ultimately, Chappell's client returned to Colorado, was convicted with a felony charge for violating a child custody order, and lost custody of her children — and Chappell was consequently disbarred.

A lawyer need not provide assistance to a client's crime or fraud to violate Rule 1.2(d). In In re Scionti, 630 N.E.2d 1358 (Ind. 1994), an attorney merely advised his client to violate a child custody order and not return his son to the mother (whom the client believed was abusive). The attorney was disciplined, and the client was convicted for contempt and incarcerated for 90 days. As a lawyer and an "officer of the court," advising or assisting a client to violate a court order will nearly always get you in serious trouble with the bar; it can also have substantial negative consequences for your client, as it did in *Chappell* and *Scionti.*

Transactional lawyers should take especial care to comply with Rule 1.2(d). A lawyer's knowing assistance in preparing for, closing, or otherwise effectuating a fraudulent transaction will violate Rule 1.2(d). Lawyers cannot issue bona fide, true sales, nonconsolidation, or other legal certifications if they know they are not true or are otherwise fraudulent. As explained in Chapter 1, the law requires that lawyers issue such legal opinions to effectuate legal transactions precisely because the lawyers — even as advocates — are supposed to maintain a level of gatekeeping for the rule of law.

Case Preview

Iowa Supreme Court Attorney Disciplinary Board v. Engelmann

Marc Engelmann had practiced law, with a focus in real estate transactions, since 1976. As the Iowa Supreme Court summarized, prior to this case Engelmann "had practiced law for three decades with an unblemished record and had closed thousands of real estate transactions for his clients." Engelmann's legal career and exceptional reputation came to a tragic end after he closed nine real estate transactions for three swindlers. Engelmann was convicted of conspiracy, wire fraud, and bank fraud; he was sentenced to three years in prison and ordered to pay $392,937.73 in restitution to the defrauded lenders. Such charges, of course, also led to professional discipline.

As you read *Engelmann*, consider the following:

1. Did Engelmann profit financially from the ill-gotten gains obtained through the fraud?
2. What should Engelmann have done once he realized that his clients wanted him to create HUD forms that misrepresented the actual price paid for the homes?

Iowa Supreme Court Attorney Disciplinary Board v. Engelmann

840 N.W.2d 156 (Iowa 2013)

Engelmann was among the many casualties of the market crash in 2008, after purchasers of real estate sold by his clients defaulted on nine mortgage loans he helped obtain through fraud. On May 17, 2011, federal prosecutors filed a nine-count felony criminal indictment against him [for conspiracy, bank fraud, and wire fraud] . . . .

The transactions involved Laures as seller and Robert Herdrich (Herdrich) and Darryl Hanneken (Hanneken) as buyers. The parties agreed upon the purchase price for each property, but also agreed to list on the loan documents an inflated price of between $30,000 and $35,000 more than the actual purchase price for each property. The various lenders then loaned Herdrich and Hanneken money for the transaction based on the inflated price listed on the loan documents. Laures received the inflated price for each sale and then returned approximately $30,000 for each property to Herdrich and Hanneken after each closing as a "kickback."

Defendant admits he knew about the two different prices and that Laures returned money to the buyers. Defendant also knew that the inflated price was not being listed on the HUD-1 forms that were submitted to the lenders. Government witnesses testified that Defendant never disclosed the inflated price or the kickbacks to the lenders or the closing company, Excel Title. . . .

Engelmann charged a $350 fee for each of the nine closings, a volume discount from his standard $400 fee. There is no evidence or claim he otherwise personally benefited financially from these transactions. . . .

Rule 32:1.2(d) prohibits a lawyer from assisting a client "in conduct that the lawyer knows is criminal or fraudulent." Iowa R. Prof'l Conduct 32:1.2(d). Rule 32:1.16(a)(1) provides guidance to a lawyer confronted with a situation in which the lawyer's assistance will facilitate illegality. It states that "a lawyer shall not represent a client or, where representation has commenced, shall withdraw from the representation of a client if . . . the representation will result in violation of the Iowa Rules of Professional Conduct or other law."

Engelmann testified at trial that Laures had signed a contract to sell his properties to Herdrich and Hanneken before retaining Engelmann on the matter. This does not change the fact that Engelmann assisted the parties in executing their fraudulent contract by preparing the inaccurate forms and representing Laures at the closings. Comment 10 to rule 32:1.2(d) addresses this situation:

> When the client's course of action has already begun and is continuing, the lawyer's responsibility is especially delicate. The lawyer is required to avoid assisting the client, for example, by drafting or delivering documents that the lawyer knows are fraudulent or by suggesting how the wrongdoing might be concealed. A lawyer may not continue assisting a client in conduct that the lawyer originally supposed was legally proper but then discovers is criminal or fraudulent. The lawyer must, therefore, withdraw from the representation of the client in the matter.

Engelmann knew the true sales prices of the properties were less than stated on the HUD-1 forms. He also knew the buyers were receiving loans that exceeded the actual sales prices. As an experienced real estate lawyer, Engelmann knew or should have known that such a contract was not aboveboard. He helped the parties complete their fraudulent transaction by preparing documents that misrepresented the facts of the transaction, deceiving the lenders. The jury's finding that Engelmann was guilty of bank fraud and wire fraud establishes that he "knowingly did one or more overt acts for the purpose of carrying out" the fraud. We apply issue preclusion to find that Engelmann knowingly assisted his client in defrauding the buyers' lender, in violation of rule 32:1.2(d).

Engelmann should have declined to represent Laures in the transactions in the first instance. And, he should have withdrawn his representation before making misrepresentations. Engelmann had ample opportunity to withdraw. In fact, he had nine opportunities. But, instead of withdrawing, Engelmann continued to represent Laures in nine separate closings, misrepresenting the true price of the property in each transaction. We find Engelmann violated rule 32:1.16(a)(1).

. . .

For the reasons stated in this opinion, the license of the respondent, Marc R. Engelmann, is revoked. We assess costs to the respondent . . . .

Post-Case Follow-Up

Engelmann charged a discounted rate of $350 per transaction to close these fraudulent deals. Thus, in total, Engelmann obtained $3,150 in fees for the nine closings. He paid dearly for those three thousand dollars—it cost him his license to practice law, three years in jail, and nearly $400,000 in restitution. It is certainly likely that some lawyers have closed deals containing fraudulent misrepresentations and were not caught. But it is absolutely never worth the risk. Assisting with client crime or fraud is not just a violation of Rule 1.2; it can easily lead to disbarment, civil liability, criminal indictment, and even imprisonment.

Iowa Supreme Court Attorney Disciplinary Board v. Engelmann: Real Life Applications

1. You work in a state that has legalized marijuana for medicinal and/or recreational use. Marijuana continues to be a Schedule I controlled substance under federal law, and thus it is a crime under federal law to use (for any purpose), manufacture, or distribute marijuana. A client comes to you and wants you to help him organize a business that distributes marijuana. Can you assist the client in organizing this business without violating Rule 1.2(d)?

2. Chen runs Sunrider, Inc., a business manufacturing health care products that Chen imports into the United States. Chen hires you to assist him in making disclosures and paying tariffs to U.S. Customs. You begin examining Sunrider's documents and discover that Chen is reporting different prices to Customs than he is reporting on his taxes to the IRS. Indeed, Chen has two sets of invoices for each product—a high one and a low one. Chen has been reporting the higher prices to the IRS (resulting in lower profits and thus lower taxes) while reporting lower prices to Customs (resulting in lower tariffs). You aren't sure which invoices are fake (the ones for taxes or the ones for tariffs), but are confident one set of invoices is fraudulent. Can you assist in making the disclosures to U.S. Customs if you don't know whether the invoices you are using are fraudulent? If you determine that the invoices used for U.S. Customs are genuine, but the ones used for the IRS are fraudulent, can you continue assisting Chen as long as you don't assist with the taxes?

C. UNDERSTANDING THE IDENTITY OF THE CLIENT

When an attorney creates an attorney-client relationship with an individual person, there generally is no question as to the identity of the attorney's client. Thus, the attorney's duties of loyalty, confidentiality, competence, communication, and conflict avoidance clearly run to that individual client. But what happens when the client is an organization? To whom do the attorney's duties and loyalties run? For a corporate client, does the attorney represent just the corporation, or does she also represent the officers of the corporation with whom the attorney deals directly? What about attorneys for the government? Do they represent their immediate supervisor? Their branch of government? The entire body politic? What happens when an attorney works for an insurance company and represents an insured? Where an attorney's client has diminished mental capacity, should the attorney turn to others to make decisions for the client? In these and other situations, properly identifying the client and the duties owed to that client is critical.

1. Organizational Clients

When a lawyer represents an organization—be that a business association, a government entity, a union, or other association—the client is the organization itself and not any of the organization's individual constituents (such as officers, directors, employees, or shareholders). The rule holds even though the organization is a fictitious person — a creature of law — and can only operate through the actions of its human constituents. This **entity theory of organizational representation**, as Darian M. Ibrahim explains, "is based on two ideas: that an organization is a distinct legal entity; and that under the laws of agency, a lawyer, as agent of the entity-principal, owes her duties to the principal and not its other agents."[11] Although other theories for organizational representation have been proffered,[12] the entity theory of representation dominates American law. Model Rule 1.13(a) adopts the "entity theory" — although using the term "organization" rather than "entity" — and addresses a lawyer's duties to an organizational client.[13]

Case Preview

Yablonski v. United Mine Workers of America

Yablonski provides an example of attorneys whose loyalties were misplaced in favor of constituents and to the detriment of their actual organizational client. In 1969, Joseph Yablonski ran against incumbent Tony Boyle for the presidency of the union, United Mine Workers of America (UMWA). Boyle ended up winning the election, but Yablonski and other UMWA members filed several lawsuits contesting the election and the conduct of Boyle and the UMWA.[14] One of those lawsuits was a cause of action under §501 of the Labor Management Reporting and Disclosure Act brought against the UMWA, Boyle, and two other officers of the union. The §501 claim sought an accounting of UMWA funds and sought restitution for any misappropriated funds. Although the lawsuit was filed against both the UMWA and the individual officers, the cause of action was similar to a shareholder's derivative suit — the Yablonski group was arguing that the officers had violated their duties to the UMWA by misappropriating union funds. Any recovery of misappropriated funds from the individual officers in the lawsuit would go to the UMWA.

The UMWA was represented by its regular outside counsel, Williams and Connolly. When the case was initially filed, Williams and Connolly also represented Boyle and the individual officers. After six months of joint representation, Williams and Connolly withdrew from its representation of the individual defendants in the §501 case, but continued to represent Boyle individually in the other related election cases. The Yablonski group moved to disqualify Williams and Connelly from representing the UMWA in the §501 case.

---

11. Darian M. Ibrahim, *Solving the Everyday Problem of Client Identity in the Context of Closely Held Businesses*, 56 Ala. L. Rev. 181, 188 (2004).
12. *See id.* at 181-218 (identifying and analyzing various theories and proffering a new theory for representation of closely held businesses).
13. See *id.* at 187 ("The entity theory — that the lawyer represents the entity itself and not its individual constituents — is the most widely accepted theory of entity representation . . . [and is] adopted by both the Model Rules and the Model Code . . . .").
14. *See* Yablonski v. UMWA, 466 F.2d 424 (D.C. Cir. 1972).

As you read *Yablonski*, consider the following:

1. Was it appropriate for Williams and Connolly to represent the UMWA and the individual defendants at the outset of the suit? Why? Were the interests of Boyle and the UMWA aligned?
2. What is the role of the entity's counsel in a §501 claim against a union or in a shareholder's derivative suit against a corporation?
3. Why did the UMWA need separate, independent counsel?

Yablonski v. United Mine Workers of America

448 F.2d 1175 (D.C. Cir. 1971)

This is an action under §501 of the Labor-Management Reporting and Disclosure Act brought by the late Joseph A. Yablonski and 48 other members of the United Mine Workers of America against the UMWA and three named officers—Boyle, President; Titler, Vice President; Owens, Secretary-Treasurer—asking for an accounting of UMWA funds disbursed by them and for restitution of funds allegedly misappropriated and misspent.

... At the outset of the lawsuit, [Williams and Connolly], the then counsel for all defendants set about with commendable diligence to delineate the real issues of the lawsuit, filing in behalf of the UMWA and the three individual defendants answers setting forth all customary general defenses, and filing 34 pages of interrogatories to develop more fully the scope of the case.

The appellants argue that this period of six months' prior representation in this same suit disqualifies the regular union outside counsel to continue its representation of the UMWA, even after its withdrawal as counsel for the three individual officer-defendants. With this we do not agree. It has been inferentially held that one lawyer can properly represent all defendants if a suit appears groundless, and that separate counsel is required only in a situation where there is a potential conflict between the interests of the union and those of its officers. We regard the actions of the regular UMWA counsel during its six-month representation of both the union and its officers as an effort to ascertain the exact nature of the lawsuit and protect the interests of all defendants, and by our ruling herein do not imply any censure of counsel's action during this period of joint representation. But there does exist in our judgment a more serious barrier to the continued representation of the UMWA by its regular outside counsel in this particular lawsuit.

... Of far more concern is the existence of other litigation in which the regular UMWA counsel is representing Boyle, sometimes in conjunction with representation of the union, at other times not....

Each of these [other cases where Williams and Connolly represents Boyle individually] has been minutely examined by appellees' counsel to demonstrate that in no instance is the representation of Boyle individually in conflict with the good faith representation of the UMWA in this case; in effect, that the interests of the UMWA and of Boyle individually are the same. We are assured that if any conflict should arise appellees' counsel would be prompt to withdraw as counsel to the UMWA in this case.

While the issues involved in each of the individual cases, and the past or present existence or nonexistence of any conflict, are relevant to the propriety of the regular UMWA counsel continuing its representation of the union in the case at bar, yet we do not think that this analysis is determinative of the real problem here. It is undeniable that the regular UMWA counsel have undertaken the representation of Boyle individually in many facets of his activities as a UMWA official, as a Trustee of the Fund, as a Director of the Bank owned 74% by the union. With strict fidelity to this client, such counsel could not undertake action on behalf of another client which would undermine his position personally. Yet, in this particular litigation, counsel for the UMWA should be diligent in analyzing objectively the true interests of the UMWA as an institution without being hindered by allegiance to any individual concerned.[7]

We are not required to accept at this point the charge of the appellants that the "true interest" of the union is aligned with those of the individual appellants here; this may or may not turn out to be the fact. But in the exploration and the determination of the truth or falsity of the charges brought by these individual appellants against the incumbent officers of the union and the union itself as a defendant, the UMWA needs the most objective counsel obtainable. Even if we assume the accuracy of the appellee's position at the present time that there is no visible conflict of interest, yet we cannot be sure that such will not arise in the future.

. . . We think that the objectives of the Labor-Management Reporting and Disclosure Act[8] would be much better served by having an unquestionably independent new counsel in this particular case. The public interest requires that the validity of appellants' charges against the UMWA management of breach of its fiduciary responsibilities be determined in a context which is as free as possible from the appearance of any potential for conflict of interest in the representation of the union itself.

---

7. "Where, as here, union officials are charged with breach of fiduciary duty, the organization is entitled to an evaluation and representation of its institutional interests by independent counsel, unencumbered by potentially conflicting obligations to any defendant officer." Int'l Bhd. of Teamsters etc. v. Hoffa, 242 F. Supp. 246, 256 (D.D.C. 1965). . . .

8. 29 U.S.C. §401 (1964) sets forth the congressional declaration of findings, purposes and policy of the LMRDA, including inter alia the statement that "in order to accomplish the objective of a free flow of commerce it is essential that labor organizations, employers, and their officials adhere to the highest standards of responsibility and ethical conduct in administering the affairs of their organizations . . . ." The legislative history of the Act makes plain that a major congressional objective was to provide union members, as well as the Government in the public interest, with a variety of means to ensure that officials of labor organizations perform their duties in accordance with fiduciary standards. Both the Senate and House reports relating to the Act stressed the importance of such standards, the Senate Committee noting that:

> Labor organizations are creations of their members; union funds belong to the members and should be expended only in furtherance of their common interest. A union treasury should not be managed as the private property of union officers, however well intentioned, but as a fund governed by fiduciary standards appropriate to this type of organization. The members who are the real owners of the money and property of the organization are entitled to a full accounting of all transactions involving their property. (S. Rep. No. 187, 86th Cong. 1st Sess. 8 (1959)). . . .

II. OBJECTIVE DETERMINATION OF THE UMWA'S INSTITUTIONAL INTEREST

Counsel for the appellees here have stressed the "institutional interest" of the UMWA in all of the issues raised, and particularly the institutional interest of the union in "repose." Counsel's interpretation of the "institutional interest" of the union appears to have been broad enough to authorize UMWA counsel to undertake practically everything worthwhile in the defense of this lawsuit. After the withdrawal of the regular union counsel from representation of Boyle individually in this case, the individual practitioner selected to represent Boyle has apparently contributed little to the defense.

By far the strongest laboring oar has been stroked by the regular UMWA counsel on behalf of the union. On oral argument appellees' counsel stated that it had prepared 94 pages of answers to interrogatories, that the individual practitioner representing Boyle had agreed they should do this, as the UMWA had a definite interest that all questions as to the conduct of union affairs previously were accurately answered and that the accurate answers were to be found in the union records. We can see the UMWA interest in having such interrogatories answered accurately, but we would think that since it is the individual defendants who are charged with the misconduct, their counsel would be the one to initiate and to carry the burden. It appears that, since the division of work between the UMWA counsel and counsel for the individual defendants in July 1970, until 15 March 1971 approximately 250 pages of pleadings, motions, memoranda, exhibits, affidavits and papers relating to discovery were filed by the regular UMWA counsel, while the individual defendants' counsel contributed only about 50 pages of similar documents.

In the crucial area of discovery matters, clearly representing the vast bulk of the effort expended by the parties defendant at this stage of the litigation, UMWA counsel have prepared 174 pages of answers to plaintiffs' initial interrogatories which were directed to all defendants, while counsel for the individual defendants, until 2 April 1971, some 7 ½ months after the interrogatories were originally served, had contented himself with filing 2 pages of answers for each individual defendant, a total of 6 pages. On 2 April 1971 counsel finally filed additional answers on behalf of defendant Boyle; however, as of the date of argument of this appeal, answers on behalf of the other individual defendants had not been filed. . . .

This points up the difficulty of defining an "institutional interest" such as that of the union. In trying to achieve a valid definition of an institution's interest, it would seem that counsel charged with this responsibility should be as independent as possible. It appears that in 18 months of representation (6 months for both the UMWA and Boyle individually, and 12 months for the UMWA alone), the regular UMWA counsel has not brought forth a single issue on which the UMWA and the Boyle individual interest have diverged.

We think the analogy of the position of a corporation and its individual officers when confronted by a stockholder derivative suit is illuminating here. We believe it is well established that when one group of stockholders brings a derivative suit, with the corporation as the nominal defendant and the individual officers accused of malfeasance of one sort or another, the role of both the corporate house counsel and the regular outside counsel for the corporation becomes usually a passive one. Certainly no corporate counsel purports to represent the individual officers involved, neither in the particular derivative suit nor in other litigation by virtue of which counsel necessarily must create ties of loyalty and confidentiality to the individual officers, which might preclude counsel from the most effective representation of the corporation itself. The corporation has certain definite institutional interests to be protected, and the counsel charged with this responsibility should have ties on a personal basis with neither the dissident stockholders nor the incumbent officeholders.

Purportedly a stockholder derivative suit is for the benefit of the corporation, even though the corporation is a nominal defendant, just as the appellants here assert (yet to be proved) that their action is for the benefit of the UMWA and that the individual incumbent officers are liable to the union itself for their alleged misdeeds. And, under established corporate law, if the individual officers are successful in the defense of a suit arising out of the performance of their duties as corporate officers, then they may justifiably seek reimbursement from the corporation for the costs of their successful defense.

In the ordinary case the action taken here by the regular UMWA counsel in the District Court might well have been the proper one, i.e., after establishing the nature of the lawsuit by interrogatories and filing answers on behalf of both the union and the individual officers in order fully to protect the position of all parties, then to step aside as counsel for the individual defendants and continue the representation of the union. But this particular case is a derivative action for the benefit of the union, and furthermore must be viewed in its relationship to this entire complex of numerous cases already pending or decided in this and the District Courts in which the regular UMWA counsel has already undertaken the representation of Boyle individually. Each and every one of these cases either directly arises out of or is directly connected with the struggle for power in the UMWA being waged by the Yablonski group on one side and the incumbent officers headed by President Boyle on the other. In this situation, the best interests of the UMWA and the purposes of the Labor-Management Reporting and Disclosure Act will be much better served by the disqualification of the regular union counsel in this particular suit and its continued representation of the individual Boyle in the other lawsuits.

We are cognizant that any counsel to represent the UMWA selected by President Boyle will be to some degree under his control. But such counsel will still only have one client — the UMWA — to represent in matters growing out of the union's affairs. Such counsel would never be professionally obligated to consider Boyle's personal interests, because they would not be representing him individually in related matters. And the extent of their labors would be gauged by the need to protect the UMWA position in this litigation.

Therefore, the Order of the District Court denying the appellants' motion to disqualify the regular UMWA outside counsel from representing the UMWA in this particular action is vacated . . . .

Post-Case Follow-Up

Consider whether Boyle's interests and the union's were the same. What indicators did Williams and Connolly have that their interests actually diverged dramatically? (As it turned out, Boyle was in fact misappropriating union funds and would ultimately be convicted of embezzlement.[15])

The *Yablonski* court indicated that it was proper for Williams and Connolly to initially represent both the UMWA and the individual defendants while determining whether or not the union needed separate counsel. Model Rule 1.13(g) seems to be in accord, stating: "A lawyer representing an organization may also represent any of its directors, officers, employees, members, shareholders or other constituents, subject to the provisions of Rule 1.7." As you will see in Chapter 6, covering conflicts of interest, Rule 1.7 only allows a joint representation where the attorney reasonably believes that she can "provide competent and diligent representation to each affected client" and each affected client gives written informed consent — among other requirements. If an entity attorney does in fact represent both the entity and the individual officers, then pursuant to Rule 1.13(g) the necessary informed written consent must come from an entity official "*other than* the individual who is to be represented."

Comment 14 to Model Rule 1.13 goes even further by indicating that generally the entity attorney may represent the individual officers even in a shareholder's derivative suit — as such suits are "are a normal incident of an organization's affairs, to be defended by the organization's lawyer like any other suit." The comment contains the caveat that such representation may produce a conflict prohibiting representation where "the claim involves serious charges of wrongdoing by those in control of the organization." Notably, the Model Rule's allowance of joint representation in derivative actions conflicts with the holding of several courts and the Restatement (Third) of the Law Governing Lawyers. As stated by the Third Circuit: "We have no

Power Struggle in the UMWA: The Murder of the Yablonski Family

Joseph A. "Jock" Yablonski
AP Photo/Henry Burroughs

Joseph A. "Jock" Yablonski ran for president of the UMWA against decade-long incumbent William Anthony "Tony" Boyle in 1969. Boyle won by a 2-to-1 margin — results that Yablonski formally protested, giving rise to an investigation of the election by the Secretary of Labor. In addition, during the election and after his defeat, Yablonski filed several lawsuits against Boyle and the UMWA objecting to unlawful actions taken by the union against Yablonski during the election (including demoting Yablonski, using the union's official journal to promote Boyle's campaign, refusing

William Anthony "Tony" Boyle
AP Photo/Bill Ingraham

15. *See* Wolfgang Saxon, *W.A. Boyle Dies*, N.Y. Times, June 1, 1985, *available at* http://www.nytimes.com/1985/06/01/us/wa-boyle-dies-led-miners-union.html.

to distribute Yablonski's campaign materials, and using unfair election processes).[18] In 1972, a federal court voided the 1969 election and ordered a new election. Arnold R. Miller defeated Boyle in the 1972 election. Tragically, Jock Yablonksi could not run against Boyle in 1972 because he, his wife Margaret, and his 25-year-old daughter Charlotte had been murdered on New Year's Eve 1969 — not long after Yablonski had objected to the election results. Yablonski and his family were shot and killed by three men — Paul Gilly, Claude Vealey, and Aubran Martin — who invaded the Yablonski farmhouse while the family slept. Ultimately, it was uncovered that these hitmen were hired by Boyle, who had paid them $20,000 in UMWA funds. In 1974, Boyle was convicted of three counts of first-degree murder and sentenced to life imprisonment. He died in 1985. Recall that the §501 lawsuit excerpted above alleged that Boyle was misappropriating union funds. Yet no one at that time realized that union funds had been used to finance the killing of Yablonski and his wife and daughter.[19]

hesitation in holding that — except in patently frivolous cases — allegations of directors' fraud, intentional misconduct, or self-dealing require separate counsel."[16] The Restatement asserts that in a derivative action, "[e]ven with informed consent of all affected clients, the lawyer for the organization ordinarily may not represent an individual defendant as well." Indeed, according to the Restatement, joint representation of the officers and the organization in a derivative suit is only allowed if "the *disinterested* directors conclude that *no basis exists* for the claim that the defending officers and directors have acted against the interests of the organization" and there is "effective consent of all clients."[17]

Yablonski v. United Mine Workers of America: Real Life Applications

1. Oliver is the attorney for the city of Springfield. He works very closely with the mayor, whom Oliver discovers has been taking municipal property for his personal use. The mayor comes to Oliver and asks for his assistance in the face of ethics charges being brought against him by the state. Whom does Oliver represent? Can he represent the mayor in this matter?

2. Newman represented 25 doctors who wanted to form a business entity for the limited purpose of buying a magnetic resonance imaging (MRI) machine. Newman meets with the individual doctors to discuss their goals and then organizes an appropriate entity, serving as the corporate counsel for that entity. Later, Dr. Danforth, one of the 25 physicians who met with Newman, is sued for medical malpractice, and Jacob, the attorney who represents the plaintiff in the med mal matter, is a partner at the same law firm as Newman. Dr. Danforth moves to disqualify Jacob on the theory that Danforth had a personal attorney-client relationship with Newman. Danforth argues that prior to the creation of the entity, Newman represented each of the doctors individually. Did Newman represent each of the individual doctors prior to the creation of the corporate entity?

---

16. Bell Atlantic Corp. v. Bolger, 2 F.3d 1304, 1317 (3d Cir. 1998).
17. *See* Restatement (Third) of the Law Governing Lawyers §131(g) (emphasis added).
18. *See Yablonski*, 466 F.2d at 425-27 & n.2.
19. *See generally* Wolfgang Saxon, *W.A. Boyle Dies*, N.Y. Times, June 1, 1985, *available at* http://www.nytimes.com/1985/06/01/us/wa-boyle-dies-led-miners-union.html; *W.A. "Tony" Boyle, Ex-Union President Convicted of Murder*, United Press International, Chi. Trib., June 1, 1985, *available at* http://articles.chicagotribune.com/1985-06-01/sports/8502040215_1_joseph-jock-yablonski-umw-district-mr-boyle.

"Mirandizing" the Organization's Constituents

An individual constituent (such as an officer, director, employee, shareholder, member) of an organization may not understand that the entity's lawyers do not represent the constituent. The constituent may believe, erroneously, that the attorney represents the constituent individually in addition to the organization. Consequently, Model Rule 1.13(f) requires the organization's attorney to clarify her role and "explain the identity of the client" to an organization's constituents "when the lawyer knows or reasonably should know that the organization's interests are adverse to those of the constituents with whom the lawyer is dealing." The Ninth Circuit has called this a "corporate *Miranda* warning."[20] Because the warning is required regarding representation of any entity or organization (not just corporations), we will call it the **entity warning**.

The requisite content of the entity warning is spelled out in Model Rule 1.13 and comment 10 thereto, which instruct attorneys to explain four basic points to constituents with interests potentially adverse to the organization: (1) that the lawyer represents the organization; (2) "that the lawyer cannot represent such constituent"; (3) "that such person may wish to obtain independent representation"; and (4) "that discussions between the lawyer for the organization and the individual may not be privileged." Despite the fact that comment 10 says that the "discussions . . . may not be privileged," in jurisdictions that follow the *Upjohn* rule (discussed in Chapter 5) most of the discussions between the attorney and organizational constituents will be covered by the attorney-client privilege — but it will be the *organization's* attorney-client privilege and not the constituent's. The comment is accurate in that there will not be an *individual* attorney-client privilege between the constituent and the attorney; thus, the individual constituent will not be able to invoke the privilege on her own behalf. Further, because the organization holds any privilege created by the communication, the organization can choose to waive the privilege and disclose the contents of the discussion to the detriment of the constituent. The Ninth Circuit presents an entity warning that explains this nuance:

> Such warnings [should] make clear that the corporate lawyers do not represent the individual employee; that anything said by the employee to the lawyers will be protected by the company's attorney-client privilege subject to waiver of the privilege in the sole discretion of the company; and that the individual may wish to consult with his own attorney if he has any concerns about his own potential legal exposure.[21]

In a similar vein, information shared by the constituent with the entity attorney is also covered by the attorney's duty of confidentiality — but again, the confidentiality is owed to the organization and not to the individual constituent. As the D.C. bar clarified in Ethics Opinion 269, "communications between the lawyer and the [constituent] being interviewed are protected by Rule 1.6 (Confidentiality of Information), but the protection accorded is for the benefit of the client corporation,

20. *See* United States v. Ruehle, 583 F.3d 600, 604 n.3 (9th Cir. 2009). Chapter 5 examines Upjohn Co. v. United States, 449 U.S. 383 (1981), and covers the scope of an entity's attorney-client privilege.
21. *See Ruehle*, 583 F.3d at 604 n.3.

not the interviewee."[22] The D.C. bar further explained that "the interviewee has no right to expect that disclosure or use of the information provided by him or her to the lawyer will be subject to his/her control under Rule 1.6, as the corporation will have the right to use the information to serve its purposes."[23]

If no entity warning or other clarification is provided to the individual constituent, can the constituent claim to have a personal attorney-client relationship with the entity attorney? In *Meehan v. Hopps*, 301 P.2d 10 (Cal. Ct. App. 1956), the California Court of Appeal held that Hopps, who had been a director and chairman of the board, could not claim an implied individual attorney-client relationship with corporate counsel. Hopps had given information to corporate counsel that implicated himself, and apparently he believed that corporate counsel would keep it confidential. The court held that because of Hopps's position in the company, Hopps had a fiduciary obligation to turn that information over to the entity attorneys. The court further explained:

> The attorney for a corporation represents it, its stockholders and its officers in their representative capacity. He in nowise represents the officers personally. It would be a sorry state of affairs if when a controversy arises between an attorney's corporate client and one of its officers he could not use on behalf of his client information which that officer was required by reason of his position with the corporation to give to the attorney.

In other words, the corporation was free to use against Hopps the information that Hopps provided to the corporation's attorneys.

However, some recent cases indicate that if no entity warning is given and the constituent reasonably believes that the entity attorney is acting on behalf of the constituent, then an implied attorney-client relationship may exist between the entity attorney and the individual constituent. But where adversity between the entity and the constituent exist, the finding of an implied individual attorney-client relationship with a constituent creates a conflict of interest with the attorney's representation of the organization, requiring the withdrawal or disqualification of the attorney from representing the entity.[24]

Individual constituents have been subjected to liability or even criminal prosecution based on statements made to the entity attorney. In *United States v. Ruehle*, the chief financial officer of Broadcom Corporation, William Ruehle, provided information in interviews with the entity attorneys regarding backdating company stock options. The backdating allegedly inflated the financial portfolio of the corporation by $2.2 billion. The information Ruehle conveyed to Broadcom's attorneys was initially provided to outside auditors and ultimately conveyed to the Securities and Exchange Commission (SEC) and the United States Attorney's Office. Ruehle

---

22. D.C. Bar Ethics Op. 269, *Obligation of Lawyer for Corporation to Clarify Role in Internal Corporate Investigation, available at* https://www.dcbar.org/bar-resources/legal-ethics/opinions/opinion269.cfm.

23. *Id.*

24. For example, in Home Care Industries Inc. v. Murray, 154 F. Supp. 2d 861 (D.N.J. 2001), the court found that the entity attorneys—who had not given an entity warning—had created an implied attorney-client relationship with the former chief executive officer (CEO) of the entity. Consequently, the court granted a motion to disqualify the entity attorneys from representing the entity against the CEO.

was then indicted for securities and wire fraud. Ruehle argued that the information he had conveyed in interviews to Broadcom's attorneys was protected by an individual attorney-client privilege. While the district court agreed, the Ninth Circuit reversed and held that even if the Broadcom attorneys had failed to give an appropriate warning (the attorneys claimed they did warn him; Ruehle said they did not), Ruehle was not only aware that the information would be given to outside auditors, but provided the information for that very purpose. The court therefore held that Ruehle failed to show that the communications were intended to be confidential, and even if so, he waived any claim to privilege by the disclosure to the outside auditors. In a vein similar to *Meehan*, the court noted that Ruehle knew of his corporate duty to disclose the information, and that the information had to be provided to outside auditors and the SEC.[25]

Reporting Up and Out

In the wake of Enron and other corporate scandals, Congress enacted the Sarbanes-Oxley Act, which required the SEC to create "minimum standards of professional conduct for attorneys appearing" before the SEC, and mandated that such standards include a requirement that attorneys report up to the chief legal officer any evidence the attorney received regarding a "material violation of securities law or breach of fiduciary duty" by the company or any constituent thereof. It further mandated that attorneys be required to report up to the board of directors, should the chief legal officer fail to appropriately respond (through remedial measures) to the violation. *See* 15 U.S.C. §7245 (2002). The SEC has promulgated such standards. *See* 17 C.F.R. §205.3.

The ABA followed suit and amended Model Rule 1.13(b) in 2003 to require attorneys to report up the corporate chain when the attorney knows that a constituent of an organizational client is violating or intends to violate "a legal obligation to the organization" or a violation of law that could be imputed to the organization and "is likely to result in substantial injury to the organization." Importantly, unlike the SEC regulations, a jurisdiction's version of Model Rule 1.13(b) does not just

---

25. The Ninth Circuit stated:

> Ruehle was no ordinary Broadcom employee. He served as the public company's CFO—the senior corporate executive charged with primary responsibility for Broadcom's financial affairs. This was a sophisticated corporate enterprise with billions of dollars in sales worldwide, aided by accountants, lawyers, and advisors entrusted with meeting a multitude of regulatory obligations. The duties undertaken by Ruehle broadly encompassed not only accurately and completely reporting the company's historical and current stock option granting practices, but also Broadcom's strict compliance with reporting and record keeping requirements imposed through the Securities Exchange Act of 1934 and the Sarbanes-Oxley Act of 2002, among many other federal and state rules and regulations. As the head of finance, Ruehle cannot now credibly claim ignorance of the general disclosure requirements imposed on a publicly traded company with respect to its outside auditors or the need to truthfully report corporate information to the SEC.

Ruehle, 583 F.3d at 610. In an unusual twist, Ruehle was ultimately acquitted when the district court dismissed the charges rather than submitting the case to the jury because of prosecutorial misconduct involving intimidation of Ruehle's witnesses. *See generally* Peter J. Henning, *How the Broadcom Backdating Case Has Gone Awry*, N.Y. TIMES, Dec. 14, 2009, *available at* https://dealbook.nytimes.com/2009/12/14/how-the-broadcom-backdating-case-has-gone-awry/?_r=0; *Charges Dismissed Against 2 Broadcom Executives*, N.Y. TIMES, Dec. 15, 2009, *available at* http://dealbook.blogs.nytimes.com/2009/12/15/charges-dismissed-against-2-broadcom-executives/.

apply to attorneys practicing before the SEC, but to all attorneys in their representation of any kind of organizational client, including government clients.[26]

However, not all jurisdictions have adopted the 2003 amendments to Rule 1.13(b). As of September 2016, only 19 jurisdictions had adopted the 2003 amendments in toto, with another 9 jurisdictions adopting part or a modified version thereof.[27] A number of jurisdictions still have in place the prior version of Rule 1.13(b) or a variation thereof, in which the attorney who knows of illegality by an organizational constituent is required to "proceed as is reasonably necessary in the best interest of the organization" and then is given discretion as to what measures to take. The appropriate measures may (or may not) include reporting up the corporate ladder.[28]

Under the 2003 Model Rule approach, if an attorney has completed the mandatory report up to the highest authority that can act on behalf of an organization (usually the board of directors for corporate entities), and the highest authority has failed to fix or timely address the law violation, then the lawyer is permitted (but not required) to report outside the organization—regardless of whether an exception to confidentiality under Rule 1.6 would allow the disclosure. Notably, this *permissive* outside disclosure found in Rule 1.13(c) is allowed "only if and to the extent the lawyer reasonably believes necessary to prevent substantial injury to the organization." Further, Rule 1.13(c) does not apply to (and thus outside disclosure is not allowed by) attorneys who are hired by an organization to investigate or defend the organization as to allegations or claims of law violation. As comment 7 explains, this limitation on reporting out "is necessary in order to enable organizational clients to enjoy the full benefits of legal counsel in conducting an investigation or defending against a claim."

Not surprisingly, clients often are not particularly happy with attorneys who report their misdeeds. Lawyers should expect that taking such action may get them fired. If a lawyer is fired for disclosing information as required or permitted by Rule 1.13(b) and (c), the lawyer still owes duties to the organization. Of course, the lawyer owes duties of confidentiality and conflict of interest avoidance—the same as with all former clients. But Model Rule 1.13(e) additionally requires the attorney who is fired as a consequence of reporting information—or who withdraws under circumstances where the rule would require or permit reporting—to "proceed as the lawyer reasonably believes necessary to assure that the organization's highest

---

26. *See, e.g.*, In re Harding, 223 P.3d 303 (Kan. 2010) (city); In re DeMers, 901 N.Y.S.2d 858 (N.Y. App. Div. 2010) (zoning board).

27. *See* ABA, CPR Policy Implementation Committee, *Variations of the ABA Model Rules of Professional Conduct, Rule 1.13: Organization as Client* (Sept. 15, 2016), *available at* http://www.americanbar.org/content/dam/aba/administrative/professional_responsibility/mrpc_1_13.authcheckdam.pdf.

28. *See, e.g.*, Michigan Rule of Professional Conduct 1.13(b), which states:

> Any measures taken shall be designed to minimize disruption of the organization and the risk of revealing information relating to the representation to persons outside the organization. Such measures may include among others:
>
> (1) asking reconsideration of the matter;
> (2) advising that a separate legal opinion on the matter be sought for presentation to appropriate authority in the organization; and
> (3) referring the matter to higher authority in the organization, including, if warranted by the seriousness of the matter, referral to the highest authority that can act in behalf of the organization as determined by applicable law.

authority is informed of the lawyer's discharge or withdrawal." For example, if an attorney for a corporation is fired by the CEO for reporting up illegalities, then the attorney needs to inform the board of directors of the situation and of the fact of being fired. This rule should preclude the ability of officers with firing authority from being able to fire the attorney to effectively stop the attorney's reporting up to the board of directors. It similarly eliminates the option for attorneys to withdraw as a method of avoiding their report up duties. If an attorney is obligated by Rule 1.13(b) to report up, the attorney cannot just withdraw from the representation to avoid that obligation. Rule 1.13(e) requires the attorney to notify the highest authority for the organization of the withdrawal.

Case Preview

Pang v. International Document Services

If an attorney is fired for complying with Rule 1.13(b) or (c) by reporting up or out, can the attorney then sue the organization for wrongful discharge? In *Pang v. International Document Services*, the Utah Supreme Court addressed this issue.

As you read *Pang*, consider the following:

1. Should it be against public policy to allow organizations to freely fire attorneys for complying with the applicable rules of professional conduct?
2. Why might it be important to allow clients to freely fire their attorneys?
3. Do the report up requirements of Rule 1.13 protect public interests or only the private interests of the attorney and the client organization?
4. Will attorneys comply with duties to report up if the attorney cannot obtain any recourse in the event that the attorney is fired for that compliance?

Pang v. International Document Services

356 P.3d 1190 (Utah 2015)

This case requires us to determine whether rule 1.13(b) of the Utah Rules of Professional Conduct reflects a clear and substantial public policy of the kind sufficient to prevent companies from terminating in-house legal counsel for reporting illegal activity to management. David K. Pang, an attorney, filed a complaint against his employer alleging that he was terminated for refusing to ignore the company's violation of several states' usury laws. He asserted that the company had effectively asked him to violate the Utah Rules of Professional Conduct in order to keep his job. The district court dismissed his complaint, concluding that Mr. Pang was an at-will employee and that his firing did not violate a clear and substantial public policy of the State of Utah. We affirm the district court's decision. Rule 1.13(b) does not constitute a clear and substantial public policy that prevents the termination of an at-will employee. And even if it did, other rules of professional conduct evince strong policy choices that favor allowing clients to terminate the attorney-client relationship at

any time, including firing an in-house lawyer with whom an organizational client disagrees.

. . .

Beginning in September 2011, Mr. Pang became concerned that the Company was violating "usury laws in numerous states by charging an interest rate above statutory limits and not registering as a loan institution." He warned the Company's owners "repeatedly" that these oversights "rendered their out of state practice illegal." Mr. Pang "made a final attempt to convince" the Company of its "illegal lending practices" in May 2012. He "printed, and took home, loan contracts from different states in order to develop a spreadsheet report to show the specific number of . . . usury violations." Two weeks later, the Company fired Mr. Pang "for taking home documents," citing a provision of the employee handbook that prohibited such conduct. "[A]t the time of his termination," Mr. Pang learned "for the first time" that "the owners were aware of the problems but did not plan to correct" them. And he "was told to ignore" the Company's "non-compliance."

According to Mr. Pang, the "real reason" for his termination was "the fear that [he] would expose [the Company's] illegal activities, and to punish and intimidate him into silence." He sued the Company for wrongful termination . . . .

. . . In Utah, all employment relationships are presumed to be at-will, meaning that the employer can terminate the relationship at any time for any reason, or no reason at all. There are several exceptions to the at-will employment doctrine. . . .

A. MR. PANG'S COMPLAINT DOES NOT IMPLICATE A STATE PUBLIC POLICY OF SUFFICIENT MAGNITUDE TO QUALIFY AS AN EXCEPTION TO AT-WILL EMPLOYMENT

On appeal, Mr. Pang has conceded that he was an at-will employee. But he argues that his firing falls within an exception to the at-will employment doctrine because he was terminated in "violation of a clear and substantial public policy." . . . [T]o support a wrongful discharge claim under the public policy exception, Mr. Pang's complaint must identify a public policy "so clear and weighty," and as to which "the public interest is so strong" that the policy should be "place[d] . . . beyond the reach of contract."

To make this determination, we consider a number of factors: (1) whether the policy at issue is reflected in authoritative sources of state public policy, (2) whether the policy affects the public generally as opposed to the private interests of the employee and employer, and (3) whether countervailing policies outweigh the policy at issue. Below, we discuss each factor and conclude that rule 1.13 does not reflect a public policy of sufficient magnitude to qualify as an exception to the at-will employment doctrine.

1. Mr. Pang has not raised a policy that is adequately reflected in the kind of sources we have recognized previously as authoritative expressions of Utah public policy

. . . [A] policy cannot be clear and substantial unless it is recognized by an authoritative source of Utah public policy. In other words, the policy must be "plainly defined" by authoritative sources of state law, such as "legislative enactments, constitutional standards, or judicial decisions." Rule 1.13 directs an in-house counsel to "refer" any "matter to higher authority in the organization" that "is a violation of a legal obligation to the organization, or a violation of law that reasonably might be imputed to the organization, and that is likely to result in substantial injury to the organization." . . .

We do not decide whether the rules of professional conduct qualify as "judicial decisions" that could independently establish an exception to at-will employment. This is because even if some of the rules may reflect a public policy of sufficient magnitude to override at-will employment, rule 1.13, upon which Mr. Pang exclusively relies, clearly does not. . . .

2. Rule 1.13 regulates private attorney-client conduct, not matters of broad public importance

In addition to being defined by an authoritative source, clear and substantial public policies must be "of overarching importance to the public as opposed to the parties only." . . . Policies that "inure[ ] solely to the benefit of the employer and employee" are accordingly "insufficient to give rise to a substantial and important public policy." Mr. Pang has not shown that the policy he identifies in rule 1.13 meets this standard . . . . [W]hile rule 1.13, like many of the rules of professional conduct, indirectly benefits the public, its primary purpose is to regulate private conduct between a lawyer and his or her client. . . . Accordingly, rule 1.13 does not reflect a policy of sufficient public importance to qualify as an exception to at-will employment.

It is true that when in-house attorneys report illegal conduct to their superiors, the public reaps incidental benefits from corrective action the company might undertake to comply with the law. But rule 1.13 regulates conduct that is, at its core, a private matter between attorneys and their clients, not one of broad public concern. And in similar contexts, we have explicitly characterized an employee's duty to disclose information to an employer as "serv[ing] the private interest of the employer, not the public interest."

For instance, our caselaw has established that even though the public may reap incidental benefits when a company polices its own activity through hiring compliance officers, the principal benefits flow to the employer by minimizing its risk of liability. . . .

. . . [Mr. Pang] does not allege that he reported the Company's illegal activity to anyone outside the organization or that rule 1.13 required him to contact public authorities. And the fact that Mr. Pang had an ethical obligation as an attorney under rule 1.13 to take the action he did does not distinguish his case from [our prior cases where employees] acted on similar legal obligations to disclose information to their employers.

Moreover, rule 1.13's plain terms characterize the attorney's duty to "report up" as serving the employer's private interest, not an obligation to the public. The rule requires attorneys who suspect that their employer may be involved in illegal activity "that is likely to result in substantial injury to the organization " to "refer the matter to higher authority in the organization, including, if warranted by the circumstances, to the highest authority that can act on behalf of the organization." Other provisions in the rule allow disclosure of confidential information "to the extent the lawyer reasonably believes necessary to prevent substantial injury to the organization." And it instructs lawyers representing the employer to inform "directors, officers, [and] employees" within the organization that the lawyer represents the employer when its "interests are adverse to those of the constituents with whom the lawyer is dealing." Consequently, the duty to "report up" under the rule is like the regular duty an employee might have to "disclose information concerning the employer's business to [his or her] employer," a duty we characterized in [our prior cases] as distinctly private. Accordingly, we conclude that an in-house counsel's duty to "report up" illegal activity to his or her superiors is not the type of clear and substantial public policy that qualifies as an exception to the at-will employment doctrine.

This conclusion is buttressed by the significant weight and overarching importance of other clear and substantial public policies we have recognized previously, which contrast sharply with the private nature of the policy Mr. Pang has raised in this case. As we have already discussed, Utah public policy does not allow an employer to fire someone for refusing to commit a crime or for reporting illegal activity to law enforcement. This is because of the substantial benefits such policies confer on the public at large. . . . We have also held that an employer cannot terminate anyone for attempting to exercise his or her workers' compensation rights or for pressuring an employee to ignore state reporting requirements that "ensure [] the safety of financial institutions in the state."

These examples share a common feature — they involve overarching statutory frameworks designed by the legislature to protect the public from bodily injury and financial harm. Mr. Pang's claim, by contrast, involves an internal report he was required to make as in-house counsel to minimize the regulatory risks of his employer's out-of-state lending practices. It would be one thing if Mr. Pang's complaint invoked other rules of professional conduct — like rule 1.6 — that are designed to protect others from death, substantial bodily injury, and serious financial harm. That might be a different case. But here, the policy Mr. Pang asks us to recognize is a distinctly private matter of attorney-client relations, an issue that is qualitatively different than other public policies we have recognized previously.

3. Any policy reflected in rule 1.13 is outweighed by other countervailing interests

. . . [E]ven if an in-house counsel's duty to "report up" was clear and substantial, we are persuaded that other provisions of the ethical rules express countervailing policy interests that outweigh any Mr. Pang has raised in this case.

Two such policies are protecting a client's right to choose representation and deterring illegal conduct. And the rules strike a delicate balance between allowing clients to secure the representation of their choice and guarding against a client's use of an attorney's services to engage in criminal activity. For example, rule 1.2(a) provides that lawyers must "abide by a client's decisions concerning the objectives of representation" but cannot "assist a client[] in conduct that the lawyer knows is criminal or fraudulent." Other provisions give these directives some teeth — rule 1.16 requires an attorney to "withdraw from the representation of a client" if "the representation will result in violation of the rules of professional conduct or other law." And the lawyer must also withdraw if "the lawyer is discharged" by the client. Comment 4 to that rule further emphasizes that the client "has a right to discharge a lawyer at any time, with or without cause."

Accepting Mr. Pang's argument would upset this careful weighing of two important public policies — deterring crime and protecting a client's right to choose a lawyer. If organizational clients faced a potential wrongful termination suit every time they terminate an in-house lawyer with whom they disagreed, it would be more difficult for such clients to secure the representation of their choice — and there is no doubt that a client's right to choose a lawyer occupies a position of paramount importance throughout the rules of professional conduct. Accordingly, we conclude that countervailing policies outweigh the public policy Mr. Pang has raised in this case — that an in-house counsel who "reports up" illegal activity under rule 1.13 should be shielded from the consequences of the at-will employment doctrine.

In so concluding, we recognize that in-house attorneys are situated differently than those at law firms who can withdraw from a case without becoming unemployed. That may well cause attorneys who suspect their employer is engaged in harmful, illegal conduct trepidation. We emphasize, however, the narrow scope of our decision today — we do not hold that in-house attorneys may never raise a wrongful termination claim, nor do we foreclose the possibility that an attorney fired for complying with an ethical rule, such as reporting criminal activity to public authorities under rule 1.6, could ever make out such a claim. We hold only that an attorney's duty to "report up" illegal activity to an organizational client's highest authority is not founded in the type of clear and substantial public policy that qualifies as an exception to the at-will employment doctrine. We leave these broader issues to a future case that squarely presents them.

Post-Case Follow-Up

Some states have followed *Pang's* reasoning and similarly refused to provide a cause of action for wrongful discharge for attorneys — including in-house attorneys — who are fired because of compliance with rules that require an attorney to report up or report out. In Balla v. Gambro, Inc., 584 N.E.2d 104 (Ill. 1991), the Illinois Supreme Court held that former in-house counsel Roger Balla did not have an action for wrongful discharge against Gambro, Inc., for firing Balla when Balla disclosed to the U.S. Food and Drug Administration (FDA) that Gambro was selling defective kidney dialyzers, the use of which could cause serious injury or death. The FDA seized the dialyzers, prohibiting their distribution. Under the Illinois Rules of Professional Conduct, Balla was required to make this disclosure.[29] Nevertheless, citing the client's right to choose and fire counsel, the Illinois Supreme Court held that Balla could not sue for wrongful discharge. Balla argued that the lack of such a cause of action forces attorneys into a Scylla and Charybdis dilemma — either obey the rules but lose their job *or* keep their job but violate the rules and expose people to harm. The Illinois Supreme Court responded in strident terms:

29. Unlike Model Rule 1.6(b)(1), which only permits disclosure to prevent death or serious bodily injury, the Illinois Rules of Professional Conduct require attorneys to disclose confidential information in such situations. *See Balla*, 584 N.E.2d at 108 ("A lawyer *shall* reveal information about a client to the extent it appears necessary to prevent the client from committing an act that would result in death or serious bodily injury.").

> [I]n-house counsel plainly are not confronted with such a dilemma. In-house counsel do not have a choice of whether to follow their ethical obligations as attorneys licensed to practice law, or follow the illegal and unethical demands of their clients. In-house counsel must abide by the Rules of Professional Conduct. Appellee had no choice but to report to the FDA Gambro's intention to sell or distribute these dialyzers . . . . [30]

Not all courts agree with the approach taken in *Pang* and *Balla*. For example, the Supreme Court of California in *General Dynamics Corp. v. Superior Court*, 876 P.2d 487 (1994), held that in-house counsel can sue for retaliatory discharge if "terminated for refusing to violate a mandatory ethical duty embodied in the Rules of Professional Conduct" or if discharged under circumstances where a non-attorney would have a claim for retaliatory discharge. Other states are in agreement with California.[31] In Van Asdale v. International Game Technology, 577 F.3d 989 (9th Cir. 2009), the Ninth Circuit held that in-house counsel who is fired for reporting up pursuant to obligations created by the Sarbanes-Oxley Act could bring claims under Nevada wrongful discharge laws and under Sarbanes-Oxley itself, which expressly provides a federal cause of action for retaliatory discharge. *See* 18 U.S.C. §1514A. Nevertheless, maintaining a successful cause of action for retaliatory discharge under Sarbanes-Oxley is quite difficult.[32]

Pang v. International Document Services: Real Life Applications

1. Lyle represents Ratchet, Inc. While working on a deal that requires certification of compliance with federal and state safety standards, Lyle discovers that Ratchet, Inc.'s tools do not comply with safety standards. Lyle meets with Ursula, who is in charge of safety and compliance. Ursula assures Lyle that while she has made mistakes in the past that have allowed noncompliant tools to be sold, that going forward Ratchet's products will be compliant with all safety standards. Under these circumstances, does Lyle need to report up regarding Ursula's past failures and noncompliance?

2. You are in-house counsel for Home Chefs, Inc., which makes high-quality kitchen utensils and appliances for home use. In preparing for a retail deal, you discover that the Home Chefs documents substantially misstate the financial status of the company. You decide to talk to the CFO about the problems. The CFO is evasive regarding your questions. You then go to the CEO who, upon

---

30. *See Balla*, 584 N.E.2d at 109.
31. *See, e.g.*, Crews v. Buckman Laboratories Int'l, Inc., 78 S.W.3d 852 (Tenn. 2002) (discussing split in authority); GTE Products Corp. v. Stewart, 653 N.E.2d 161, 167 (1995) (allowing narrow right to retaliatory discharge where attorney is fired for refusing to violate "(1) explicit and unequivocal statutory or ethical norms (2) which embody policies of importance to the public at large in the circumstances of the particular case, and (3) the claim can be proved without any violation of the attorney's obligation to respect client confidences and secrets").
32. *See* Megan E. Mowrey, L. Stephen Cash & Thomas L. Dickens, *Does Sarbanes-Oxley Protect Whistleblowers? The Recent Experience of Companies and Whistleblowing Workers Under SOX*, 1 Wm. & Mary Bus. L. Rev. 431 (2010).

hearing your concerns, fires you effective immediately. Are you really fired? What, if any, duties do you still owe to the company? How should you proceed? Can you sue for wrongful termination?

---

2. Government Clients

Rule 1.13 applies to government clients as a specific type of organizational client. Thus, government lawyers are required to report up under Rule 1.13(b), to report to the highest authority regarding being fired for reporting up or out, and to provide entity warnings to their government client constituents whom the attorney does not represent. But who is the ultimate client of a government attorney and who is the "highest authority" that can act on behalf of the government client under Rule 1.13(b) and (c)?

Comment 9 explains that, although Rule 1.13 applies to government attorneys, "[d]efining precisely the identity of the client and prescribing the resulting obligations of such lawyers may be more difficult in the government context and is a matter beyond the scope of these Rules." Properly identifying the appropriate client is not only important for the obligations under Rule 1.13, but also for lawyers to fulfill their duties of competence, communication, confidentiality, and loyalty. For government attorneys, there is a wide range of possible ultimate clients. As Roger Cramton explains:

> The possibilities include: (1) the public (2) the government as a whole (3) the branch of government in which the lawyer is employed (4) the particular agency or department in which the lawyer works and (5) the responsible officers who make decisions for the agency. Although a scattering of support can be found for each possibility, the dispute has been primarily between a broader loyalty to "the public interest" or the government as a whole, on the one hand, and a more restricted vision of the government lawyer as the employee of a particular agency, on the other.[33]

Moreover, attorneys for the government perform nearly the whole range of legal activity—counseling, drafting, planning, negotiating, litigating—and they work in a manifold of legal specialties.[34] The vast range of government lawyer roles complicates defining a government client.

Kathleen Clark has argued that a universal definition of the government client is not attainable in light of the wide range of lawyer roles; rather, she argues that "one can determine a particular government lawyer's client by examining the particular context and the precise structure of governmental authority."[35] Thus, for example, Clark notes that some government attorneys, such as Judge Advocate General military defense lawyers, represent individual clients and have a typical individual attorney-client relationship with them. Similarly, she argues that most congressional

---

33. Roger C. Cramton, *The Lawyer as Whistleblower: Confidentiality and Government Lawyer*, 5 Geo. J. Legal Ethics 291, 296 (1991).
34. *See id.* at 292.
35. Kathleen Clark, *Government Lawyers and Confidentiality Norms*, 85 Wash. U. L. Rev. 1033, 1056 (2007).

lawyers represent individual legislators; however, some congressional lawyers represent a larger slice of the legislative branch, such as "the Senate Legal Counsel, [which] represents the Senate as an institution." As to the executive branch, Clark takes issue with the "unitary-executive view" that claims "that all executive-branch lawyers have as their client the entire executive branch, with the President ultimately responsible for defining client interests." She notes that some agencies are independent from the President. Thus, for example, lawyers for the SEC and the FCC should be seen as representing the agency rather than the executive branch as a whole. Nevertheless, Clark argues that the Justice Department and federal prosecutors represent the executive branch as a whole.[36] Significantly, Clark notes that while some government lawyers serve and answer to a specific government client or entity, others "serve both as the lawyer and essentially as a trustee, entrusted to make decisions that clients normally make."[37] For example, prosecutors make the decision whether to bring charges, appeal, or accept a plea deal—decisions usually allocated to the client in a traditional attorney-client relationship. Clark posits:

> While some have asserted that, for these lawyers, the "public interest" is their client, it makes more sense to conceive of these lawyers as trustees of the client (such as the state government) who can consider the public interest in making their decisions. . . .
>
> If a government lawyer has the authority to make client-like decisions (such as whether to bring or settle cases), then she also has the responsibility to act not just like any client, but in a way this particular client—a sovereign—should act. In our legal tradition, the sovereign is not free to act in the same way as any private litigant but is expected to act fairly and impartially.[38]

Because government lawyers ultimately represent a sovereign, "whose obligation to govern impartially is as compelling as its obligation to govern at all"—government lawyers may have a greater duty to ensure that their client is acting justly and in accordance with law.[39] Indeed, comment 9 to Rule 1.13 explains that "a government lawyer may have authority under applicable law to question" the conduct of government officials for whom the lawyer works "more extensively than that of a lawyer for a private organization in similar circumstances." This is so because where government is acting and is employing the weight and legitimacy of state power, "a different balance may be appropriate between maintaining confidentiality and assuring that the wrongful act is prevented or rectified."

3. Insureds

Insurance agreements generate another area with client identity complications. Insurers hire attorneys to represent an insured person in accordance with a policy

---

36. *Id.* at 1052-68.
37. *Id.* at 1062.
38. *Id.* at 1069.
39. Berger v. United States, 295 U.S. 78, 88 (1935).

between the insurer and the insured. In such a situation, does the attorney represent the insurer (who is paying for the attorney) or the insured? The relationship between the insured, the insurer, and the attorney hired by the insurer has been termed a **tripartite relationship.**[40] The Restatement (Third) of the Law Governing Lawyers maintains that the "lawyer designated to defend the insured has a client-lawyer relationship with the insured." Moreover, "[t]he insurer is not, simply by the fact that it designates the lawyer, a client of the lawyer."[41] The insurer may also have an attorney-client relationship with the attorney — in which case the attorney is representing the insured and the insurer as joint clients. Ellen Pryor and Charles Silver contend that the identity of the insurance defense lawyer depends entirely "on the agreement that actually is reached at the time the defense lawyer is engaged to handle the case."[42]

In many insurance contracts, the insured will have agreed to allow the insurer to control the defense, including whether or not to settle the claim. Given that the insured is either the sole or the joint client of the attorney, and that the decision to settle is given to the ultimate authority of the client, is such an arrangement permissible? Model Rule 1.2(c) generally allows an attorney to limit the scope of a representation with a client, as long as "the limitation is reasonable under the circumstances and the client gives informed consent." Read the following opinion, and consider what steps a lawyer has to take to successfully limit the scope of her relationship with an insured client to allow the insurer to control the defense and settlement of the claims.

Obligations of a Lawyer Representing an Insured Who Objects to a Proposed Settlement Within Policy Limits

ABA Formal Opinion 96-403 (1996)

. . . The Model Rules of Professional Conduct offer virtually no guidance as to whether a lawyer retained and paid by an insurer to defend its insured represents the insured, the insurer, or both. . . . The Model Rules assume a client-lawyer relationship established in accordance with state law, and prescribe the ethical obligations of the lawyer that flow from that relationship.

The insurer, the insured, and the lawyer may agree on the identity of the client or clients the lawyer is to represent at the outset. For example, the parties might agree that the lawyer will represent (1) the insured alone, (2) the insured and the insurer, or (3) the insured and the insurer for all purposes except settlement, and with respect to settlement the lawyer will represent the insurer alone. Provided there is appropriate disclosure, consultation, and consent, any of these arrangements would be permissible. Absent an express agreement specifying the identity of the lawyer's client or

40. Charles Silver, *The Professional Responsibilities of Insurance Defense Lawyers*, 45 Duke L.J. 255, 264 (1995).
41. Restatement (Third) of the Law Governing Lawyers §134 cmt. f.
42. Ellen S. Pryor & Charles Silver, *Defense Lawyers' Professional Responsibilities: Part I — Excess Exposure Cases*, 78 Tex. L. Rev. 599, 607 (2000).

clients, however, a lawyer hired by an insurer to defend its insured may be held to have a client-lawyer relationship with the insured alone or with both the insured and the insurer.

We have no reason to enter the debate as to whom the lawyer represents in this context absent an express agreement as to the identity of the client. For purposes of this opinion, nothing fundamental turns on whether the lawyer represents the insured alone or both the insurer and the insured. If a lawyer hired and paid by an insurer to defend a claim against an insured represents the insured—whether alone or jointly with the insurer, whether by virtue of a provision in an engagement letter or otherwise—the Rules of Professional Conduct govern the lawyer's obligations to the insured, and "[t]he essential point of ethics involved is that the lawyer so employed shall represent the insured as his client with undivided fidelity. . . ." ABA Committee on Professional Ethics, Formal Opinion 282 (1950) (construing the 1908 Canons of Professional Ethics). Whatever the rights and duties of the insurer and the insured under the insurance contract, that contract does not define the ethical responsibilities of the lawyer to his client.

If the lawyer is to proceed with the representation of the insured at the direction of the insurer, the lawyer must make appropriate disclosure sufficient to apprise the insured of the limited nature of his representation as well as the insurer's right to control the defense in accordance with the terms of the insurance contract. Generally a lawyer must abide [by] his client's decisions as to the objectives of the litigation and specifically as to whether to accept a settlement. . . .

Rule 1.2(c) provides that a "lawyer may limit the objectives of the representation," but only if "the client consents after consultation" with the lawyer. "Consultation" "denotes communication of information reasonably sufficient to permit the client to appreciate the significance of the matter in question." Model Rules of Professional Conduct, Terminology. . . .

We presume that in the vast majority of cases the insured will have no objection to proceeding in accordance with the terms of his insurance contract. Nonetheless, communication between the lawyer and the insured is required. Rule 1.2 explicitly requires the lawyer to communicate with the client, and convey information "sufficient to permit the client to appreciate the significance of the matter in question." We cannot assume that the insured understands or remembers, if he ever read, the insurance policy, or that the insured understands that his lawyer will be acting on his behalf, but at the direction of the insurer without further consultation with the insured.

A short letter clearly stating that the lawyer intends to proceed at the direction of the insurer in accordance with the terms of the insurance contract and what this means to the insured is sufficient to satisfy the requirements of Rule 1.2 in this context. We do not believe extended discussion is required or, indeed, that any oral communication is necessary. As long as the insured is clearly apprised of the limitations on the representation being offered by the insurer and that the lawyer intends to proceed in accordance with the directions of the insurer, the insured has sufficient information to decide whether to accept the defense offered by the insurer or to assume responsibility for his own defense at his own expense. No formal acceptance or written consent is necessary. The insured manifests consent to the limited representation

by accepting the defense offered by the insurer after being advised of the terms of the representation being offered.

4. Diminished Capacity Clients

Lawyers may represent clients who have diminished mental capacity. This diminished capacity may exist because of the client's age (whether due to youth or old age) or other mental impairments. For example, if a lawyer represents a 13-year-old boy in a juvenile proceeding, should the lawyer follow the instructions of the 13-year-old, even when the lawyer believes such action is not in her client's interest? Jurisdictions differ on the precise answer to that question.[43] For example, in some states the attorney is to consider the juvenile client's wishes, yet the lawyer is not required to follow the juvenile's instructions if it does not appear to be in the client's best interests.[44] In stark contrast, other jurisdictions maintain that the attorney must comply with the juvenile's instructions — even when it does not appear to be in the client's best interests.[45] Attorneys representing juvenile clients, or other clients with potential diminished capacities, should take care to examine the approach of the pertinent jurisdiction.

Model Rule 1.14 sets out the basic principle that the attorney should — whenever possible — treat the client as a normal client in an attorney-client relationship, with the client making decisions for the representation. Only in exigent circumstances — situations where the client "is at risk of substantial physical, financial or other harm unless action is taken" and "cannot adequately act in the client's own interest" — should the lawyer take "reasonably necessary protective action." *See* Model Rule 1.14(b). Moreover, attorneys should undertake protective measures that are the least intrusive to client autonomy as possible given the circumstances. Again, comment 5 counsels that in taking protective measures:

> the lawyer should be guided by such factors as [1] the wishes and values of the client . . . , [2] the client's best interests . . . , [3] the goals of intruding into the client's decisionmaking autonomy to the least extent feasible, [4] maximizing client capacities and [5] respecting the client's family and social connections.

Guardianship should be sought only when absolutely necessary, as a guardianship eviscerates the decision-making autonomy of the client. Often, even with a diminished capacity, a client will have "the ability to understand, deliberate upon, and reach conclusions about matters affecting the client's own well-being." *See* Model Rule 1.14 cmt. 1. And even when protective measures are appropriate, there are many options far less intrusive to the client than guardianship. As comment 5 points out, "[s]uch measures could include consulting with family members, using

---

43. *See* Annotated Model Rules of Prof'l Conduct, Rule 1.14, Representation of a Minor.
44. *See id.*; *see, e.g.*, In re Christina W., 639 S.E.2d 770 (W. Va. 2006).
45. *See, e.g.*, Mass. Ethics Op. 93-6 (1993).

a reconsideration period to permit clarification or improvement of circumstances, using voluntary surrogate decisionmaking tools such as durable powers of attorney or consulting with support groups, professional services, adult-protective agencies" and the like. Importantly, wherever possible, the attorney must keep in mind the identity of his client, to whom the attorney owes duties of communication, confidentiality, and loyalty. Thus, for example, when the client needs the assistance of family to communicate with the attorney or make decisions, the lawyer must do his best to ensure that the client's family is not interfering with the attorney's duties to his actual client.

D. ATTORNEY AS FIDUCIARY

Attorneys are supposed to be the champion of their client's interests (within the bounds of the law), yet there are aspects of the attorney-client relationship where the lawyer's interest and the client's interest inevitably diverge—most notably in the charging and payment of attorneys' fees. In such situations where the lawyer's and client's interests actually or potentially diverge, lawyers cannot take advantage of their clients. The lawyer owes the client the duties of a fiduciary—the client trusts the lawyer to safeguard the client's interests in charging a fee, handling client funds and property, and withdrawing from the case.

1. Fees

Fees create an inherent adversity of interest between the attorney and client. It is in the client's financial interest to pay a lower fee, while it is in the lawyer's financial interest to charge a higher one. Further, when a fee must be collected, the lawyer and client enter into an adverse relationship as creditor and debtor. Yet the lawyer is still the fiduciary of the client—even in the charging or collecting of a fee; the client trusts and the rules require that the lawyer will protect the client's interests.

Communicating the Fee to the Client

Clients, especially those who are unfamiliar with legal services, may not appreciate (or have the slightest concept of) the cost of legal representation in a matter. Thus, the first obstacle in the charging of a fee is effectively communicating to the client what the basis or rate of the fee will be. The Model Rules require attorneys to "communicate[] to the client" the basis or rate of both the fee and the expenses that the client will be responsible to pay. The lawyer is also required to communicate "the scope of the representation" to the client, meaning that the lawyer must communicate what legal actions the lawyer is agreeing to undertake and/or any limitations on the scope of the lawyer's services. *See* Model Rule 1.5(b). This requirement goes hand in hand with communicating the fee so that the client understands what it is she is (and is not) purchasing when hiring the attorney. Notably, Model Rule 1.2

allows an attorney to limit the scope of a representation, as long as the "limitation is reasonable under the circumstances and the client gives informed consent."

The Model Rules themselves do not require that non-contingent fee agreements be in writing; rather, Rule 1.5 only requires communication to the client, while stating that a writing is preferable. However, any marginally prudent lawyer will put the fee agreement in writing. Moreover, a number of jurisdictions require a written communication outlining the basis and rate whenever a fee is charged.

Contingent Fees

The Model Rules generally allow an attorney to charge a contingent fee, with a couple of important exceptions. Under Rule 1.5, attorneys cannot charge a contingent fee in a criminal matter or if the contingent fee is prohibited by other law. In addition, attorneys are prohibited in domestic relations cases from charging a fee that "is contingent upon the securing of a divorce or upon the amount of alimony or support or property settlement in lieu thereof."

Further, Model Rule 1.5(c) requires that two writings accompany any contingent fee agreement with a client. First, at the outset of the representation, the contingent fee agreement must be made in writing and be signed by the client. This first writing must contain several components: (1) "the method by which the fee is to be determined," which itself must include "the percentages that shall accrue to the lawyer in the event of settlement, trial or appeal"; (2) "litigation and other expenses to be deducted from the recovery"; (3) "whether such expenses are to be deducted before or after the contingent fee is calculated"; and (4) a statement of any expenses that the client must pay whether or not the client prevails. The second required writing comes at the conclusion of the contingency case. The lawyer is required to prepare "a written statement" that informs the client both of the final disposition of the action and of the "remittance to the client and the method of its determination" as to any recovery.

A Reasonable Fee

Model Rule 1.15(a) expressly prohibits a lawyer from agreeing to, charging, or collecting "an unreasonable fee or an unreasonable amount for expenses." The requirement of reasonableness applies whether the fee is calculated on an hourly or a contingent basis. The rule sets out a list of eight factors to consider in determining the reasonableness of a fee, which will be discussed in the *Sallee* case below. Importantly, there is not a safe harbor where a fee will be deemed reasonable if the fee is calculated by multiplying the hours actually and honestly worked by the agreed-upon hourly rate.[46] In Board of Professional Responsibility, Wyoming State Bar v. Casper, 318 P.3d 790 (2014), the Wyoming Supreme Court held that a lodestar determination ("reasonable hours times a reasonable rate") is only a first

46. In re Fordham, 668 N.E.2d 816, 821, 824 (Mass. 1996) (rejecting "safe harbor" that a fee is reasonable "as long as an agreement existed between a client and an attorney to bill a reasonable rate multiplied by the number of hours actually worked").

step to examining reasonableness. The second step requires considering other factors to "adjust the fee either upward or downward." The Wyoming Supreme Court explained:

> The second step requires the application of "billing judgment," which usually is demonstrated by the attorney writing off unproductive, excessive, or redundant hours. Billing for legal services . . . should not be a merely mechanical exercise. . . . A reasonable fee can only be fixed by the exercise of judgment, using the mechanical computations simply as a starting point. . . . [47]

Thus, in In re Fordham, 668 N.E.2d 816 (Mass. 1996), the Massachusetts Supreme Judicial Court held that a $50,000 fee for defending an accused for operating a motor vehicle under the influence of alcohol (OUI) was unreasonable where the standard fee in the locality was between $1,500 and $5,000. One of the most significant factors set out in Rule 1.5 for measuring the reasonableness of a fee is "the fee customarily charged in the locality for similar legal services." Fordham's fee was ten times the customary fee for the location. Thus, the fee was unreasonable even though the attorney honestly and diligently worked each of the hours billed, secured an excellent result (acquittal), and the client agreed to the hourly rate. The court noted that Fordham, who had not previously performed criminal work, had charged for the time spent to educate himself regarding criminal defense. The court explained that Fordham could not charge for his education, stating: "It cannot be that an inexperienced lawyer is entitled to charge three or four times as much as an experienced lawyer for the same service."[48] Importantly, the first factor for determining reasonableness in Model Rule 1.5(a) is not the time actually *spent* by the attorney, but "the time and labor *required*" — that is, the time that would be taken by a reasonably proficient attorney.

In a similar vein, the Utah Supreme Court held that an attorney could not charge fees that were generated by the attorney's own incompetence and attempts to fix that incompetence. In Dahl v. Dahl, 2015 UT 79, excerpted in Chapter 4, Christensen sought an award of attorneys' fees for his representation in a divorce. Christensen made numerous procedural errors that led to nearly all of his exhibits being excluded at trial, the exclusion of expert witness testimony on behalf of his client, and the exclusion of evidence regarding his client's financial need. Consequently, his client was not awarded either temporary or permanent alimony and the client's ex-husband was awarded sole custody of their children. Nevertheless, Christensen sought an award of fees and expenses of over $2.1 million, including $327,000 related to experts that were largely excluded from trial (because Christensen did not prepare proper expert reports). The court noted that many of the hours billed were for review of the file with "huge, almost impossible hours recorded during the trial months" that were billed "to gain an understanding of evidence and facts that should have been mastered months earlier."[49] In addition,

---

47. *Casper*, 318 P.3d at 796 (internal citations omitted).
48. *Fordham*, 668 N.E.2d at 822-23.
49. *Dahl*, 2015 UT 79, ¶179.

many of the hours billed were for motions to reconsider rulings that resulted from Christensen's poor handling of the case. In sum, the court held that Christensen's fee was "unreasonable as a matter of law" and that "most of the fees and expenses seem to have been driven by Mr. Christensen's inability to effectively manage basic discovery and pretrial disclosure procedures."[50] The court admonished:

> When an attorney proceeds competently, but nonetheless is unsuccessful for his client, we ascribe no error. But when an attorney consistently fails to perform basic skills in a competent manner, and the client is harmed as a result, we will not allow that attorney to collect [what has become] patently unreasonable fees.[51]

Just as in *Fordham*, where an inexperienced attorney cannot charge more than an experienced attorney, so too an incompetent attorney cannot charge more than a competent attorney despite actually spending significant time engaged in or seeking to undo wasteful or even counterproductive measures.

Case Preview

Sallee v. Tennessee Board of Professional Responsibility

Attorney Yarboro Sallee was suspended from the practice of law for one year for charging an unreasonable fee in a wrongful death case, failing to communicate the rate and basis of the fee to the client, and failing to protect her client's interests once her client fired her.

As you read *Sallee*, consider the following:

1. What made Sallee's fees unreasonable? Which of the factors outlined in Rule 1.5(a) indicated an unreasonable fee? What types of activities did Sallee charge for that the court found inappropriate?
2. Was Sallee's failure to communicate her rate and basis of fee the primary problem? If Sallee had employed the "preferable" path of a written fee agreement fully explaining her rate and basis of fee (including the charges for time and a half) and provided clear billing statements, would Sallee's fee have been reasonable?

---

50. *Id.* ¶211, ¶205.

51. *Id.* ¶206. The court was also concerned that Christensen devoted so much of his presentation to the court to secure his own fees rather than to protect his client's interests. The court noted:

> Ms. Dahl's counsel devoted nearly seventeen pages of her appellate brief to her request for attorney fees while devoting less than two pages to Ms. Dahl's request for joint custody of her children. While counsel is certainly entitled to pursue an award of fees on his client's behalf, the focus on the attorney fees issue to the exclusion of issues such as custody raises serious concerns.

See id. ¶210.

Sallee v. Tennessee Board of Professional Responsibility

469 S.W.3d 18 (Tenn. 2015)

The case that prompted this disciplinary complaint arose from a tragic occurrence. On October 15, 2009, Lori Noll fell down steps in her home. She died five days later. Ms. Noll was a wife, mother of two children, and the daughter of the claimants in this case, Frances Rodgers and Vearl Bible (collectively, the "Claimants"). Despite a medical examiner's finding that the death was accidental, the Claimants suspected that their daughter's husband, Adam Noll, was responsible for her death, motivated by a one-million dollar insurance policy on Ms. Noll's life. A close friend of the Claimants recommended Attorney Sallee to advise them on their legal options.

On September 18, 2010, the Claimants had an initial meeting with Attorney Sallee, to discuss the feasibility of a wrongful death action on behalf of their deceased daughter. . . . At this initial meeting, Attorney Sallee did not discuss her compensation with the Claimants . . . .

A few days later, on September 21, 2010, Attorney Sallee met with the Claimants to discuss the 911 call Mr. Noll made regarding their daughter's death. In the 911 call, Mr. Noll gave the dispatcher a questionable explanation for Ms. Noll's fall and his subsequent actions. After Attorney Sallee conveyed her preliminary thoughts, the Claimants agreed to retain Attorney Sallee and wrote her a check for $5,000. In this meeting, the Claimants orally agreed to pay Attorney Sallee $250 per hour for her services.

. . . Even though she had only an oral representation agreement, in light of the looming expiration of the limitations period, Attorney Sallee launched into intensive work on the case. . . . [O]n October 13, 2010, Attorney Sallee told the Claimants that, in order to continue representing them, she would need a $20,000 retainer. Despite the absence of a written representation agreement, Ms. Rodgers wrote Attorney Sallee a check for an additional $15,000. . . . During this time, Attorney Sallee did not provide the Claimants with any sort of billing statement.

On October 15, 2010, Attorney Sallee filed a timely wrongful death complaint against Mr. Noll in the Circuit Court of Knox County, Tennessee. Attorney Sallee's agreement was to represent only the Claimants. Despite this, the complaint drafted by Attorney Sallee was filed on behalf of not only the Claimants, but also on behalf of Ms. Noll's children and the estate of Ms. Noll. The complaint did not plead the claim by the grandparents as "next friend" of the grandchildren.

On October 19, 2010, Attorney Sallee sent another email to Ms. Rodgers. . . . That same day, Ms. Rodgers received a visit at her home from the friend who had initially recommended Attorney Sallee to the Claimants. The friend admonished Ms. Rodgers that the Claimants had not given Attorney Sallee enough money for her retainer. This prompted Ms. Rodgers to immediately write Attorney Sallee an additional check, in the amount of $10,000. The friend then delivered Ms. Rodgers' check to Attorney Sallee.

. . . Finally, in early December 2010, the Claimants asked Attorney Sallee for a written contract addressing her representation of them. In response, Attorney Sallee gave the Claimants several confusing draft agreements that included "a conglomeration of hourly charges, plus contingency [fees]." The inclusion of contingency fees in the draft agreements came as a surprise to the Claimants; they had been under the impression that Attorney Sallee was to receive only hourly fees, not contingency fees. In view of this discrepancy, the Claimants declined to sign the proposed agreements. . . .

In an apparent attempt to pressure the Claimants into executing her proposed fee agreement, in early January 2011, Attorney Sallee threatened to "drop [the Claimants] from the case." Finally fed up, the Claimants instead "decided it was time to drop her." The Claimants sent Attorney Sallee a formal letter terminating her representation of them in all matters.

. . . When the Claimants requested their file, Attorney Sallee refused to provide them the entire file. As justification, Attorney Sallee asserted that the Claimants owed her "eighty-plus thousand dollars, in addition to what [they had] already paid her." She mailed the Claimants a letter to this effect on January 5, 2011.

In mid-January 2011, Mr. Bible and Ms. Rodgers each sent a complaint letter to the Tennessee Board of Professional Responsibility ("BPR" or "the Board"), outlining some of the difficulties with Attorney Sallee's representation of them. . . .

In early February 2011, Attorney Sallee sent the BPR her initial response to the Claimants' complaints: a 21-page letter, single-spaced. Although she had never given the Claimants an itemization of her time spent on their cases, Attorney Sallee attached to her BPR response an itemized "billing statement" with detailed time entries on the work she claimed to have done for the Claimants.[4]

Despite the Claimants' complaint to the BPR, Attorney Sallee continued to refuse to turn over to the Claimants items from their files. This forced the Claimants to hire another attorney, Larry Vaughan, to obtain the withheld items. To that end, in early March 2011, Attorney Vaughan filed an action on behalf of the Claimants against Attorney Sallee in the Knox County Chancery Court. The lawsuit specifically sought medical records on Ms. Noll that Attorney Sallee had retrieved from the hospital, as well as brain tissue slides from Ms. Noll's autopsy that were in Attorney Sallee's possession.

The filing of the chancery court complaint did not persuade Attorney Sallee to turn over the disputed items to the Claimants. . . . In early April 2011, the chancellor ordered Attorney Sallee to turn over the remaining items to the Claimants. . . .

. . .

Attorney Sallee contends that the record does not contain substantial and material evidence to support the Panel's finding that the fee she charged to the Claimants was excessive. She argues strenuously that her fee was "on average per hour less tha[n] the average hourly fee of attorney[s] in Knoxville" and that "the record is replete with hundreds of e-mails and proof of calls every day" demonstrating her constant communication with the Claimants.

4. . . . The "billing statement" has time entries for the time period of September 16, 2010 (the date of the initial meeting) to December 3, 2010, totaling 493.5 hours. Of this total, 135 hours were shown at a rate of $375 per hour, and the remaining 358.5 hours were shown at the agreed rate of $250 per hour. According to Attorney Sallee's "billing statement," in a time span of less than three months, the accrued hourly charges on the Claimants' legal matters came to over $140,000. Subtracting the $54,000 the Claimants had already paid, Attorney Sallee maintained that the Claimants still owed her over $86,000. The "billing statement" provided to the BPR did not include the contingency fees Attorney Sallee sought in addition to the hourly charges.

. . . Rule 1.5 of the Tennessee Rules of Professional Conduct at [the time of the misconduct] required that "[a] lawyer's fee and charges for expenses shall be reasonable" and mandated that "the basis or rate of the fee shall be communicated to the client, preferably in writing, before or within a reasonable time after commencing the representation." Tenn. Sup. Ct. R. 8, RPC 1.5(a) and (b) (2010). In determining whether an attorney fee is reasonable, courts examine the following factors:

(1) The time and labor required, the novelty and difficulty of the questions involved, and the skill requisite to perform the legal service properly;
(2) The likelihood, if apparent to the client, that the acceptance of the particular employment will preclude other employment by the lawyer;
(3) The fee customarily charged in the locality for similar legal services;
(4) The amount involved and the results obtained;
(5) The time limitations imposed by the client or by the circumstances;
(6) The nature and length of the professional relationship with the client;
(7) The experience, reputation, and ability of the lawyer or lawyers performing the services;
(8) Whether the fee is fixed or contingent;
(9) Prior advertisements or statements by the lawyer with respect to the fees the lawyer charges; and
(10) Whether the fee agreement is in writing.

Tenn. Sup. Ct. R. 8, RPC 1.5(a) (2010). The Panel's written decision demonstrates that it properly considered these factors in reaching its decision. . . . We consider them as well.

Initially, we confess a certain amount of skepticism about Attorney Sallee's claim that she in fact worked well over 493.5 hours on the Claimants' matters in a span of three months, while also continuing to service the 28 to 30 other clients she claimed she had during that time period.[24] Nevertheless, we assume, for purposes of this appeal, that she actually worked those hours. Attorney Sallee's arguments are considered in light of this assumption.

. . .

The record indicates that Attorney Sallee initially represented to the Claimants that she had considerable experience relevant to their legal concerns. She told the Claimants that her legal qualifications were such that she normally commanded $500 per hour for her time but, in this instance, she was willing to give them a "discounted" rate of $250 per hour. She estimated that the contemplated wrongful death lawsuit would cost the Claimants no more than $100,000. A mere three months later, Attorney Sallee claims, she had amassed charges totaling over $140,000.[25] For this fee, in the wrongful death case, she had accomplished only the filing of a basic wrongful death complaint—which was pled incorrectly—and the gathering of the

24. Asked about time entries on the "billing statement" indicating that she worked up to 19 or even 23 hours in a single day, Attorney Sallee insisted that she actually worked those hours, but added vaguely that certain columns on the so-called "billing statement" may not have lined up correctly.

25. This total comes from the so-called "billing statement" that Attorney Sallee gave to the BPR. The entries on the document are confusing and disorganized, with time spent on each of the Claimants' matters combined. The entries are generally billed at a minimum increment of 0.5 hours. While the document has been referred to in these proceedings as a "billing statement," it is in fact no such thing, since it was never given to the Claimants until they filed complaints with the Board. We consider it instead to be an exhibit created by Attorney Sallee for the purpose of defending the BPR complaint.

recording of the 911 call and a few pertinent documents and medical records. She had taken no witness statements, prepared no expert statements, taken no depositions, propounded no discovery requests. She had, however, engaged in a prodigious amount of wheel-spinning, spending countless hours, charged at a lawyer rate, in activities such as watching *48 Hours* television episodes, waiting in hospitals for medical records, and doing internet research on strangulation. Her communications with the Claimants referred to the hours she had worked only in general terms, and only in the context of badgering them for more money. At no point did she tell them that her original estimate had quickly proven unrealistic, that she was charging them a "time-and-a-half" $375 per hour rate for tasks performed after business hours, or that she intended to charge them lawyer rates for administrative tasks and watching television. At no point did she give them an itemized statement of her charges. As the final straw, toward the end of the three-month period, she insisted that the Claimants sign a representation agreement that would entitle her to charge contingency fees in addition to the high hourly rates she was already charging them.

The Rules governing lawyers require transparency and candor with clients. Many a lawyer has been asked by a prospective client to estimate how much a contemplated legal matter will cost. If the lawyer has sufficient experience, such an estimate can be given. However, under most circumstances, once it becomes reasonably clear to the lawyer that the estimate is inaccurate, this fact should be communicated to the client, so the client can make an informed decision about going forward with the case. In this case, if Attorney Sallee's "billing statement" is to be believed, her fees reached the $100,000 level of her original estimate for the entire wrongful death litigation only two months after her engagement, at a time when the litigation was just getting started. Yet, she said nothing to the Claimants about the inaccuracy of her estimate. Thus, the Panel did not err in considering the fact that Attorney Sallee did not tell the Claimants that her original estimate of $100,000 for the entire wrongful death action had proven inaccurate.

Clients who are being charged hourly rates should be kept reasonably informed about the amount of work being done by the lawyer, the type of work being done, and the rates being charged for the hours worked. Here, the Claimants had no way to know the enormous number of total hours Attorney Sallee was claiming to have worked. They were not told that Attorney Sallee sought to change the oral representation agreement to charge them "time and a half" for time spent working after regular business hours, or that she intended to charge them contingency fees in addition to hourly fees. They were not told that she intended to charge them lawyer rates, either $250 per hour or $375 per hour depending on the time of day, for tasks such as sitting at a hospital to wait for medical records. . . .

Assuming *arguendo* that the hourly rate of $250 per hour is reasonable for Attorney Sallee's experience and ability,[26] it is important under the Rules that the lawyer ensure that the work for which he or she seeks to charge the client is "reasonable." For example, a lawyer who represents criminal clients may be interested in watching *Perry Mason* or *Breaking Bad* on television, and may even pick up a useful tidbit or

26. Our review of the time entries on the "billing statement" Attorney Sallee furnished to the BPR shows she spent many hours on activities for which an attorney with sufficient experience in wrongful death actions to command $250 per hour would not have spent his or her billable time. This indicates that the rate Attorney Sallee sought to charge the Claimants was not commensurate with her experience and ability.

two from doing so. The lawyer may not, however, equate that to research for which he or she may charge a client. In this case, the Panel did not err in considering the many hours Attorney Sallee sought to charge the Claimants for watching television shows such as *48 Hours.* In addition, the Panel considered the explanations offered by Attorney Sallee for charging the Claimants a lawyer's rate for many, many hours spent on essentially administrative tasks, and it found that she did not have adequate justification under the facts of this case for such charges. The Panel did not err in considering either of these factors in reaching the conclusion that Attorney Sallee sought to charge the Claimants for work that was not reasonable. RPC 1.5 cmt. 5 (2010) ("A lawyer should not exploit a fee arrangement based primarily on hourly charges by using wasteful procedures.").

In assessing the reasonableness of the charges, the lawyer must also take into account the "results obtained." At the time her representation of the Claimants was terminated, the legal matters for which Attorney Sallee was hired were far from resolved, so the ultimate result was not yet known. However, as outlined above, after three months' work, she had achieved little more than filing the wrongful death complaint and gathering obvious documents and records. Attorney Sallee was obliged to recognize that the $140,000 she sought to charge the Claimants at that juncture was outlandish in light of how little had been accomplished, and reduce her fee to a level commensurate with the very modest results she had obtained for the Claimants at that point. The Panel did not err in concluding that the fee Attorney Sallee sought to charge the Claimants was not reasonable in light of the minimal results accomplished for the Claimants at the time of the termination.

Based on our careful review of the record, and considering all of Attorney's Sallee's conduct with regard to the fees she sought to charge the Claimants, we find material and substantial evidence to support the Panel's determination that Attorney Sallee violated Rules 1.4 [Communication] and 1.5 [Fees] of the Tennessee Rules of Professional Conduct . . . .

Post-Case Follow-Up

Notice that Tennessee's Rule 1.5 contains two additional factors beyond the eight found in Model Rule 1.5(a). Several other jurisdictions have either added factors or modified the eight standard factors listed in Rule 1.5(a). Although the court gave Sallee the benefit of the doubt, the court expressed skepticism as to whether Sallee in fact worked all of the hours she billed. As noted below, if Sallee did not work those hours, she is charging a fraudulent fee and is engaged in theft.

The court noted in footnote 25 that the smallest increment in Sallee's bills was 0.5 hours. Would that alone render the fee unreasonable? In Board of Professional Responsibility, Wyoming State Bar v. Casper, 318 P.3d 790 (Wyo. 2014), the attorney, Stacy Casper, billed her client in increments of 15 minutes (.25 hours). The court noted that of the 106 entries in the billing record, "few if any of those tasks would reasonably require a quarter hour of her time." Indeed, Casper "routinely billed .25 hours each to sign such documents as subpoenas, stipulated orders and pleadings." The court ultimately found Casper had charged an unreasonable fee and expounded:

> Use of billing with minimum time increments does not necessarily result in an unreasonable fee. The Court recognizes that use of minimum billing increments is a useful tool which is not, in and of itself, unethical. The Task Force on Lawyer Business Ethics has explained:
>
>> For convenience, lawyers generally keep track of the time spent using standard increments of time, commonly six minutes (0.1 hour), ten minutes (1/6 hour) or fifteen minutes (1/4 hour). This approach is essential and should not be objectionable unless the increments are unreasonably large or are used in an abusive manner. It would not be practical to keep track of time in constantly varying measurements, and minimum increments serve the practical needs of both lawyers and clients. On the other hand, the practice should not be abused. Legitimate use of a minimum time increment may depend on how the lawyer records the balance of the increment. Two fifteen-minute charges for two five-minute calls within the same fifteen-minute period seem inappropriate; some balancing should be used.

Sallee v. Tennessee Board of Professional Responsibility: Real Life Applications

1. Josh is an attorney who has consistently had low billable hours compared with others in his firm. He decides to perform extra work to make up the difference. For example, he makes his own copies of motions and briefs for filing, rather than having his secretary do it. He also personally delivers discovery requests to the office of opposing counsel and files documents rather than having the courier perform those tasks. Making these changes in his habits has allowed Josh to work an extra 30 hours a month. Are there any problems with Josh billing this time to his clients?

2. Michelle practices law at a New York City law firm, where she charges, as a new partner, $780 an hour. She decides to move her practice to Boise, Idaho, where she grew up. The going rate in Boise is $250 an hour for partners. Michelle believes that she should be able to charge for her "big city" experience, and decides to charge a middle-ground rate of $450 an hour. Under Rule 1.5, what hourly rate can Michelle charge in Boise?

Fraudulent Fees

The charging of a fraudulent fee is *per se* unreasonable under Rule 1.5—it additionally can lead to criminal charges or civil liability for the lawyer. Many lawyers have gone to prison for fraudulent billing.[52]

---

52. *See, e.g.*, Lisa G. Lerman, *Blue-Chip Bilking: Regulation of Billing and Expense Fraud by Lawyers*, 12 GEO. J. LEGAL ETHICS 205 (1999). Lerman examines the cases of 16 lawyers who were indicted for fraudulent billing—some of them sentenced to multiple years in prison. *See id.* at 211-15.

Observance of a few basic principles will protect a lawyer from the pitfall of fraudulent billing. First, only charge your client for time you actually work. As noted in ABA Formal Opinion 93-379, "a lawyer who has undertaken to bill on an hourly basis is never justified in charging a client for hours not actually expended." Padding a bill by adding or increasing time that was not actually spent working is not only unethical, it is theft. While it is generally permissible to bill clients in agreed-upon increments of time (typically tenths of an hour), lawyers cannot fraudulently inflate the bill with time they did not work. Lisa Lerman provides a few examples of fraudulent billing:

- Some lawyers are just sloppy about keeping time records.
- Some systematically "pad" timesheets, or bill one client for work done for another.
- Some create entirely fictitious timesheets.
- Some record hours based on work done by other lawyers, paralegals or secretaries, representing that they did the work. This may result in nonbillable time being billed, or in work being billed at a rate higher than that of the person who actually did the work.
- Some lawyers bill for time that their clients might not regard as legitimately billable—for schmoozing with other lawyers, chatting with clients about sports or families, for doing administrative work that could be done by a non-lawyer, or for thinking about a case while mowing the lawn or watching television.[53]

Second, do not bill an impossible number of hours. Many lawyers have gotten into serious trouble when they have billed for hours that they could not possibly have worked. An Ohio attorney, Kristen Stahlbush, received a two-year suspension for billing "more than 24 hours per day on at least three occasions" with numerous other days billed at "14 to 24 hours." Indeed, "[i]n one 96-hour period [she] billed 90.3 hours, and in a separate 144-hour period, she billed 139.5 hours."[54] Similarly, Jerome Berg was disbarred for repeatedly billing an insurance company more than 24 hours per day—and on some days he billed 100 hours.[55]

Third, do not **double bill** or otherwise charge for the same hour of work more than once. If you work for one hour, you can only charge for one hour—even if you are representing multiple clients, acting in multiple capacities (such as trustee and attorney), or want to use the same work product in another case. Double billing occurs when a lawyer charges multiple clients each for the same block of time spent. Billing recycled work product means billing a subsequent client for the time spent for (and already billed to) a prior client for reusing the work product. In ABA Formal Opinion 93-379, the ABA condemned these practices as unethical:

> A lawyer who spends four hours of time on behalf of three clients has not earned twelve billable hours. A lawyer, who flies for six hours for one client, while working for five hours on behalf of another, has not earned eleven billable hours. A lawyer who is able to reuse old work product has not re-earned the hours previously billed and compensated

53. *See id.* at 208.
54. Toledo Bar Association v. Stahlbush, 933 N.E.2d 1091 (Ohio 2010).
55. In re Berg, 3 Cal. State Bar Ct. Rptr. 725 (1997).

> when the work product was first generated. Rather than looking to profit . . . , the lawyer who has agreed to bill solely on the basis of time spent is obliged to pass the benefits of these economies on to the client. The practice of billing several clients for the same time or work product, since it results in the earning of an unreasonable fee, therefore is contrary to the mandate of the Model Rules.

Thus, for example, if you travel for one client and work for another client while on the airplane, you are going to have to reasonably apportion the travel hours between the two.

Fourth, do not churn the bill. **Churning** — unnecessarily overstaffing a case or performing duplicative or unnecessary work to drive up a bill — is a form of fraudulent billing. David Segal relates the story of Sporicidin Co., which wanted to hire a couple of high-end lawyers, and ended up with "53 attorneys and paralegals" working on the case, billing $830,000 in less than a year and a half.[56] Adam Victor hired DLA Piper to assist with a bankruptcy, but then objected to the bill as being excessive. DLA Piper sued Victor for the $675,000 bill. During the lawsuit, emails were uncovered from firm lawyers, one reading, "I hear we are already 200k over our estimate — that's Team DLA Piper!" and another noting that "random people" were being added to work "full time on random research projects in standard 'churn that bill, baby!' mode."[57] DLA Piper released a statement that "the emails were in fact an offensive and inexcusable effort at humor, but in no way reflect actual excessive billing"[58] — yet, whether made in jest or for other purposes, the statements were revelatory.[59] Victor amended his counterclaim in light of these emails, adding a claim for fraud and seeking $22.5 million in punitive damages — a claim that DLA Piper settled in 2013.[60] The pressure to produce billable hours may result in churning. While some of these examples are extreme, any time a lawyer performs duplicative or unnecessary work — such as unnecessarily rereading or reviewing a document or filing — in order to drive up one's billable hours, that constitutes a violation of Rule 1.5.

There are other problematic billing practices — such as charging for firm overhead or having an attorney perform and charge for work that should be done by a less-expensive worker, such as a paralegal, secretary, or courier. Always remember

---

56. David Segal, *In the Business of Billing? The Ethics Squeeze*, WASH. POST, Mar. 22, 1998, *available at* http://www.washingtonpost.com/wp-srv/business/longterm/ethics/ethics2.htm.

57. *See* Martha Neil, *"Churn That Bill, Baby!" Email Surfaces in Fee Dispute with DLA Piper*, A.B.A. J., Mar. 25, 2013, *available at* http://www.abajournal.com/news/article/sued_by_dla_piper_for_675k_ex-client_discovers_lighthearted_churn_that_bill/.

58. *Id.*

59. In 2016, one of the lawyers involved in the emails, Erich Eisenegger, sued the firm that represented DLA Piper in the fee dispute for turning over the emails. Eisenegger said he lost his job (he had left DLA Piper prior to the publicizing of the email) and suffered reputational damage because of the publicity surrounding the emails. He also contended that the email statements were taken out of context and were "part of a much more thoughtful and serious discussion amongst associates and a DLA partner about DLA's billing habits." *See* Martha Neil, *Ex-DLA Piper Partner Caught in "Churn That Bill, Baby!" Crossfire Sues Firm's Counsel*, A.B.A. J., Mar. 24, 2016, *available at* http://www.abajournal.com/news/article/ex_dla_piper_partner_caught_in_churn_that_bill_baby_crossfire_sues_law_firm.

60. *See* Neil, *Churn That Bill, Baby!*, *supra* note 57. The lawsuit was settled in April 2013. *See DLA Piper Settles $22.5M Suit over "Churn That Bill" Emails*, LAW360, Apr. 17, 2013, *available at* https://www.law360.com/articles/433837/dla-piper-settles-22-5m-suit-over-churn-that-bill-emails.

that the lawyer is the client's fiduciary. Any billing practices that take advantage of or otherwise defraud the client will violate the lawyer's duties.

2. Safeguarding Client Funds and Property

An attorney, as the fiduciary of the client, holds client funds and property in sacred trust. As an attorney, you will be responsible to hold client funds and property. If you cannot be trusted (whether due to malfeasance or negligence) to safeguard client money and property, then you cannot be an attorney. The seriousness of mishandling client funds cannot be overstated. The presumptive sanction in most jurisdictions for misappropriating client funds is disbarment. In the words of the Colorado Supreme Court, "lawyers are almost invariably disbarred for knowing misappropriation of client funds."[61]

Despite the extreme potential sanction, many lawyers steal or misappropriate client funds. States take measures to prevent misappropriation and partially reimburse victimized clients. Nearly all states have adopted laws requiring banks to notify the bar of overdrafts in any client trust account.[62] Further, all states administer client protection fund programs whereby monies collected from licensed attorneys through state bar fees are used to partially reimburse clients whose lawyers misappropriate funds. A survey performed from 2008 to 2010 of client protection funds found that on average, each state received requests for reimbursements of approximately 4 to 5 million dollars per year (that's about 200 to 250 million dollars per year nationwide).[63] Most states reimburse victimized clients at a fraction of what they lost through attorney malfeasance.[64]

Attorneys have five basic fiduciary duties relating to handling client funds and property: (1) **segregation**; (2) **record keeping**; (3) **notification**; (4) **delivery**; and (5) **accounting**. The first two are set out in Model Rule 1.15(a) to (c), while the last three are described in 1.15(d).

Segregation

As noted in Rule 1.15(a), a lawyer is required to keep a client's funds or property "separate from the lawyer's own property." Client money must be placed in a client trust account. The lawyer is absolutely forbidden from commingling her own funds

61. People v. Rhodes, 107 P.3d 1177, 1185 (2005).

62. *See* ABA, Standing Committee on Client Protection, *State by State Adoption of ABA Client Protection Programs* (December 2015), *available at* http://www.americanbar.org/content/dam/aba/administrative/professional_responsibility/state_by_state_cp_programs.authcheckdam.pdf.

63. *See* ABA, Standing Committee on Client Protection, *2008-2010 Survey of Lawyers' Funds for Client Protection*, *available at* http://www.americanbar.org/content/dam/aba/administrative/professional_responsibility/29th_forum_2008_2010_survey_of_lawyers_funds_for_client_protection.authcheckdam.pdf.

64. *See id.* at 32 (noting that in the same years where per state reimbursement requests were approximately 4 to 5 million dollars on average, the average total of awards approved during the year were approximately $550,000 to $660,000). *See also* Harriet L. Turney & John A. Holtaway, *Client Protection Funds — Lawyers Put Their Money Where Their Mouths Are*, 9 No. 2 Prof. Law. 18 (1998) (noting that because of the number and size of claims, most client protection funds cap the reimbursement an aggrieved client can receive).

with those of the client. Thus, a lawyer cannot put her own money in the client trust account. Rule 1.15(b) allows a limited exception in that an attorney can deposit the attorney's own money in a client trust account "for the sole purpose of paying bank service charges on that account." But even for this exception, the attorney is allowed to deposit only the requisite amount to cover bank service charges.

If a lawyer is holding funds for several clients, the lawyer generally is permitted to deposit the funds of multiple clients into the same client trust account. If an attorney is holding a substantial amount for a specific client for an extended time, or is holding estate or trust monies, then the attorney should place the funds in their own interest-bearing account, which interest belongs to the client. *See* Model Rule 1.15 cmt. 1. Because attorneys often hold the funds of multiple clients in one pooled client trust account, with each client's funds only being held for short periods of time, individual clients do not recover interest on their funds. Before the 1980s, lawyers simply held such funds in a non-interest bearing trust account (as it was unethical for the lawyer to profit from handling client funds by collecting the interest from the pooled client monies).[65] Today, states instead require attorneys to participate in the state's IOLTA program. **IOLTA (Interest On Lawyers' Trust Accounts)** is a program where the interest earned on the pooled client funds in attorneys' general client trust accounts escheats to the state to pay for charitable programs, primarily the state's legal aid services for people with low incomes. The U.S. Supreme Court upheld the constitutionality of IOLTA programs against a challenge that they constituted an unconstitutional taking of property. The Court noted that the client's pecuniary loss under IOLTA is zero[66] — because without IOLTA, clients received no interest from funds placed in lawyer trust accounts. All states have IOLTA programs, and attorney participation is mandatory in all but five states.[67]

Non-monetary property of the client that is given to the attorney during a representation must be "identified" as client property and "appropriately safeguarded."[68] Comment 1 to Rule 1.15 directs lawyers to keep securities in a safe deposit box absent "special circumstances" that warrant different arrangements.

Case Preview

In re Sather

What happens when a client pays a retainer or flat fee to an attorney at the outset of a representation? Does the money belong to the client until it is earned (in which case it should be placed in the client trust account) or does the money belong to the attorney? In *Sather*, Frank Perez hired attorney

65. *See* ABA, Commission on Interest On Lawyer Trust Accounts, *Overview, available at* http://www.americanbar.org/groups/interest_lawyers_trust_accounts/overview.html.
66. *See* Brown v. Legal Found. of Wash, 538 U.S. 216, 240 (2003).
67. Four states allow lawyers to opt out of IOLTA (Alaska, Kansas, Nebraska, Virginia) and one makes participation voluntary (South Dakota). *See* ABA, Commission on Interest on Lawyer Trust Accounts, *Status of IOLTA Programs, available at* http://www.americanbar.org/groups/interest_lawyers_trust_accounts/resources/status_of_iolta_programs.html.
68. Model Rule 1.15(a).

Larry D. Sather to represent Perez in a civil rights lawsuit. Sather charged Perez a "non-refundable" flat fee of $20,000 for the representation, and Sather filed the lawsuit. A few months later, Sather was suspended from the practice of law due to a separate disciplinary proceeding, and, consequently, Perez fired him. Perez asked for a refund of any unearned fees. Sather agreed that he had not earned approximately $13,000 of the fee, but could not immediately make a refund because he had spent the entire $20,000.

As you read *Sather*, consider the following:

1. According to the court, what are the underlying interests served by requiring attorneys to keep client funds separated from an attorney's personal funds?
2. What should Sather have done with the $20,000 when he received it? Had he earned any of the fee at that time? According to the court, when has an attorney "earned" a fee?
3. The court divides retainers into two basic categories. What are those categories?
4. When, if ever, can an attorney charge a retainer at the outset of a case that is earned upon receipt and can immediately be placed in the attorney's account as property of the attorney? Even then, is the fee completely nonrefundable?

In re Sather

3 P.3d 403 (Colo. 2000)

Sather agreed to represent Franklin Perez in a lawsuit against the Colorado State Patrol and certain individual troopers [for allegedly] violat[ing] his civil rights during a traffic stop. . . . [O]n November 15, 1996, Sather and Perez entered into a written agreement for legal services, captioned "Minimum Fee Contract." Sather drafted the agreement, the terms of which required Perez to pay Sather $20,000 plus costs to represent Perez in the case against the State Patrol. . . .

The contract stated that Perez understood his obligation to pay this fee "regardless of the number of hours attorneys devote to [his] legal matter" and that no portion of the fee would be refunded "regardless of the time or effort involved or the result obtained." The contract acknowledged Perez's right to discharge Sather as his attorney, but the contract informed Perez that in no circumstance would any of the funds paid be refunded:

> IN ALL EVENTS, NO REFUND SHALL BE MADE OF ANY PORTION OF THE MINIMUM FEE PAID, REGARDLESS OF THE AMOUNT OF TIME EXPENDED BY THE FIRM. . . .

Perez paid Sather $5,000 of the minimum fee on November 17, 1996. He paid the remaining $15,000 on December 16th. Sather spent the $5,000 soon after receiving the money. Sather kept the second payment of $15,000 for approximately one month before spending these funds. Sather did not place any of these funds in his trust account before spending them . . . because he believed he earned the fees upon receipt. . . .

. . . [O]n December 6, 1996, Sather filed suit in Denver District Court on behalf of Perez against the State Patrol and three troopers. . . .

On April 21, 1997, in a matter unrelated to the Perez case, this court suspended Sather from the practice of law for thirty days, effective May 21, 1997. As required, Sather notified Perez of his suspension and Perez responded on May 23, requesting an accounting of the hours Sather worked on his case. . . . [O]n June 4, 1997, Perez faxed Sather notice discharging him from his case because of the suspension. . . . [Perez, acting *pro se*, settled the lawsuit for $6,000.]

Sather provided the accounting requested by Perez on June 27, 1997. Sather claimed that his fees, his paralegal assistant's fees, costs and expenses in Perez's case as of the date of discharge totaled $6,923.64. . . .

Despite acknowledging his duty to return the unearned $13,076.36 to Perez, Sather did not refund any money to Perez because at the time of discharge he had spent Perez's funds. On September 3, 1997 — three months after Perez discharged him — Sather paid Perez $3,000. Sather paid the remaining $10,076.36 on November 2, 1997. The hearing board found that this delay prejudiced Perez because he did not have access to his funds for almost five months. . . .

III. DISCUSSION

Sather contends that under Colorado law it is unclear whether an attorney must deposit all advance fees — including flat fees — into a trust account until the fees are earned. Sather further argues that an attorney earns flat fees upon receipt and the fees are thus the attorney's property and not subject to the trust requirements of Colo. RPC 1.15. Sather's fee agreement also raises the issue of "non-refundable" fees.

In order to address the issues raised in this case, we examine first Colo. RPC 1.15's requirement that attorneys segregate their property and funds from their clients'. Second, we discuss when and under what circumstances a client's property or funds are earned by an attorney and may therefore be treated as the attorney's property. Thirdly, we address whether an attorney may charge a "non-refundable" fee.

A. *Colo. RPC 1.15 Requires Segregation of Attorney and Client Property*

Initially, we address Colo. RPC 1.15(a), which requires that an attorney keep client funds separate from the attorney's own property:

> In connection with representation, *an attorney shall hold property of clients or third persons that is in an attorney's possession separate from the attorney's own property. Funds shall be kept in a separate account* maintained in the state where the attorney's office is situated, or elsewhere with the consent of the client or third person. . . . Complete records of such account funds and other property shall be kept by the attorney and shall be preserved for a period of seven years after termination of representation.

(Emphasis added.) In addition to this subsection of the rule, Colo. RPC 1.15(f)(1)[9] requires that an attorney maintain client funds submitted to the attorney as advance fees in a separate trust account until the attorney earns the fees . . . .

9. We note that Colo. RPC 1.15(f)(1) became effective July 1, 1999, after Sather's conduct in this case. However, we include Colo. RPC 1.15(f)(1) in our discussion because it helps clarify the current state of the rules.

... Thus, Colo. RPC 1.15(a) and (f) indicate that an attorney has an obligation to keep clients' funds separate from his own, and that advance fees remain the property of the client until such time as the fees are "earned." ...

The rule requiring that an attorney segregate funds advanced by the client from the attorney's own funds serves important interests. As a fiduciary to the client, one of an attorney's primary responsibilities is to safeguard the interests and property of the client over which the attorney has control. Requiring the attorney to segregate all client funds — including advance fees — from the attorney's own accounts unless and until the funds become the attorney's property protects the client's property from the attorney's creditors and from misuse by the attorney. Thus, Colo. RPC 1.15(a) and (f) further the attorney's fiduciary obligation to protect client property.

In addition to protecting client property, requiring an attorney to keep advance fees in trust until they are earned protects the client's right to discharge an attorney. ... Upon discharge, the attorney must return all unearned fees in a timely manner, even though the attorney may be entitled to quantum meruit recovery for the services that the attorney rendered and for costs incurred on behalf of the client.

If an attorney suggests to a client that any pre-paid or advance funds are "non-refundable" or constitute the attorney's property regardless of how much or how little work the attorney performs for the client, then the client may fear loss of the funds and may refrain from exercising his right to discharge the attorney. Because the unearned portion of the advance fees must be kept in trust and cannot be treated as the attorney's property until earned, the client will not risk forfeiting fees for work to be performed in the future if the client chooses to discharge his attorney. Thus, the requirement that the attorney place advance fees in trust protects the client's right to discharge his attorney.

B. An Attorney Earns Fees by Conferring a Benefit on or Providing a Service for the Client

As we discussed, rule 1.15's requirement that an attorney hold in trust all unearned fees furthers important interests central to the attorney-client relationship. When a client pays an attorney before the attorney provides legal services, the crucial issue becomes whether funds are "earned on receipt" and may be treated as the attorney's property, or whether the fees are unearned, in which case the funds must be segregated in a trust account under Colo. RPC 1.15. As one publication aptly framed this dilemma:

> The basic question is, Whose money is it? If it's the client's money in whole or in part, it is subject to the trust account requirements. If it is the lawyer's money, placing it into a trust account would violate the anti-commingling rule.

ABA/BNA Lawyers' Manual on Professional Conduct 45:109 (1993). We hold that an attorney earns fees only by conferring a benefit on or performing a legal service for the client. Unless the attorney provides some benefit or service in exchange for the fee, the attorney has not earned any fees and, with a possible exception in very limited circumstances, the attorney cannot treat advance fees as her property.

Funds given by clients to attorneys as advance fees or retainers benefit attorneys and clients. Some forms of advance fees or retainers appropriately compensate an attorney when the fee is paid because the attorney makes commitments to the client that benefit the client immediately. Such an arrangement is termed a "general retainer" or "engagement retainer," and these retainers typically compensate an attorney for agreeing to take a case, which requires the attorney to commit his time to the client's case and causes the attorney to forego other potential employment opportunities as a result of time commitments or conflicts. Although an attorney usually earns an engagement retainer by agreeing to take the client's case, an attorney can also earn a fee charged as an engagement retainer by placing the client's work at the top of the attorney's priority list. Or the client may pay an engagement retainer merely to prevent the attorney from being available to represent an opposing party. In all of these instances, the attorney is providing some benefit to the client in exchange for the engagement retainer fee.

In contrast to engagement retainers, a client may advance funds — often referred to as "advance fees," "special retainers," "lump sum fees," or "flat fees" — to pay for specified legal services to be performed by the attorney and to cover future costs. We note that unless the fee agreement expressly states that a fee is an engagement retainer and explains how the fee is earned upon receipt, we will presume that any advance fee is a deposit from which an attorney will be paid for specified legal services. *See* Draft Restatement §50 cmt. (g) ("A fee payment that does not cover services already rendered and that is not otherwise identified is presumed to be a deposit against future services.").

Advance fees present an attractive option for both the client and the attorney. Like engagement retainers, advance fees allow clients to secure their choice of counsel. Additionally, some forms of advance fees, e.g., "lump sums" or "flat fees," benefit the client by establishing before representation the maximum amount of fees that the client must pay. In these instances, the client knows how much the total cost for legal fees will be in advance, permitting the client to budget based on a fixed sum rather than face potentially escalating hourly fees that may exceed the client's ability to pay. So long as the fees are reasonable, such arrangements do not violate ethical rules governing attorney fees.

Advance fees benefit the attorney because the attorney can secure payment for future legal services, eliminating the risk of non-payment after the attorney does the work. Often, attorneys collect a certain amount from the client in advance of any work and deduct from that amount according to the hours worked or mutually agreed-upon "milestones" reached during representation (e.g., investigation, pretrial work and motions, negotiations, filings, handling a company's initial public offering, etc.). Attorneys often deduct costs from advance payments as they incur the costs, similar to the manner in which they deduct their fees as they are earned. Advance fees represent an alternative method of obtaining legal assistance that accommodates legitimate needs of both clients and attorneys, and by this opinion we do not intend to discourage these fee arrangements provided the fee agreements comply with the ethical principles discussed in this case.

In the case of both advance fees and engagement retainers, the attorney performs a service or provides a benefit to the client in exchange for the fee. We recognize that we have not previously explained the ethical principle that determines when an attorney may treat funds paid as engagement retainers or advance fees as property of the attorney. Because this principle is a crucial element of the attorney-client relationship, we make our interpretation of the underlying ethical principle explicit: an attorney earns a fee only when the attorney provides a benefit or service to the client. Under Colo. RPC 1.15(a) and (f), all client funds — including engagement retainers, advance fees, flat fees, lump sum fees, etc. — must be held in trust until there is a basis on which to conclude that the attorney "earned" the fee; otherwise, the funds must remain in the client's trust account because they are not the attorney's property.

With respect to fees mutually agreed to be "earned on receipt," an attorney must describe in writing the nature of the benefit being provided to a specific client in order to claim some portion or all of an engagement retainer as earned when paid. . . . That is, an attorney cannot treat a fee as "earned" simply by labeling the fee "earned on receipt" or referring to the fee as an "engagement retainer." Rather, the attorney must explain in detail the nature of the benefit being conferred on the client, whether it is the attorney's guarantee of availability, prioritization of the client's work, or some other appropriate consideration.

. . .

C. *"Non-refundable" Fees*

. . . [W]e [now] address Sather's characterization of his fee as "non-refundable." Because fees are always subject to refund under certain conditions, labeling a fee "non-refundable" misleads the client and may deter a client from exercising their rights to refunds of unearned fees under Colo. 1.16(d). Thus, we hold that attorneys cannot enter into "non-refundable" retainer or fee agreements. . . .

A fee labeled "non-refundable" misinforms the client about the nature of the fee and interferes with the client's basic rights in the attorney-client relationship. Attorney fees are always subject to refund if they are excessive or unearned. A fee agreement that suggests that advance fees are "non-refundable" undermines the client's understanding of her rights and may discourage a client from seeking refunds to which the client may be entitled.

In addition to misinforming the client, "non-refundable fees" may discourage the client from discharging his attorney for fear that the client will not be able to recover advance fees for which the attorney has yet to perform any work. Because the label is inaccurate and misleading, and discourages a client from exercising the right to discharge an attorney, we hold that attorneys may not enter into "non-refundable fee" agreements or otherwise communicate to their clients that the fees are "non-refundable."

We acknowledge that in some instances a client may agree with an attorney to allow the attorney to treat funds paid in advance of legal services or other consideration as property of the attorney and thus not subject to the trust account requirements. Although we do not address the exact contours of such an arrangement in this opinion and recognize that narrow exceptions to this rule may exist, we caution that at minimum such arrangements will be construed against the attorney and in favor of the client. Furthermore, the attorney must expressly communicate to the client verbally and in writing that the attorney will treat the advance fee as the attorney's property upon receipt; that the client must understand the attorney can keep the fee

only by providing a benefit or providing a service for which the client has contracted; that the fee agreement must spell out the terms of the benefit to be conferred upon the client; and that the client must be aware of the attorney's obligation to refund any amount of advance funds to the extent they are unreasonable or unearned if the representation is terminated by the client. Further, any arrangement that allows the attorney to treat unearned advance fees as his own property must protect the client's property interests in the funds and the client's right to discharge the attorney at any time without being penalized by "non-refundable" fees or retainers.

In the limited circumstances in which an attorney earns fees before performing any legal services (i.e., engagement retainers) or where an attorney and client agree that the attorney can treat advance fees as the attorney's property before the attorney earns the fees by supplying a benefit or performing a service, the fee agreement must clearly explain the basis for this arrangement and explain how the client's rights are protected by the arrangement. In either of these situations, however, an attorney's fees are always subject to refund if excessive or unearned, and an attorney cannot communicate otherwise to a client.

. . .

Because we have not previously made clear an attorney's obligation to deposit all forms of advance fees into trust accounts or explained the prohibition against "non-refundable" fees, we do not sanction Sather for violating these rules. . . . Because Sather knowingly failed to return unearned fees and knowingly misrepresented the nature of the fees paid by a client, and in light of his disciplinary history, we hold that Sather be suspended for six months.

Post-Case Follow-Up

Retainers are typically split into two overarching categories: the general retainer and the special retainer. The court in *Sather* adopted this dichotomy, but tried to clarify the types by calling general retainers "engagement retainers" and calling special retainers "advance fees." Using the *Sather* court's terminology, a general or an engagement retainer is a fee that is earned upon receipt. But notice the very limited circumstances under which the court will allow an engagement retainer — the attorney must provide some benefit to the client in return for that retainer and must explain as much in writing to the client. Further, the engagement retainer cannot be truly nonrefundable despite being the attorney's property upon receipt because, according to the court, all fees are subject to refund if found to be unreasonably excessive or unearned. What possible benefits to the client does the court list as potentially justifying an engagement retainer?

The other type of retainer is the special retainer or advance fee. This type of retainer is the standard type of retainer used by attorneys — and if there is any question as to which type of retainer is created, it will be presumed to be an advance fee. An advance fee or special retainer is the client's upon receipt by the attorney. Thus, the attorney must place the advance fee in a client trust account. The attorney can withdraw funds from the advance fee only as she earns them. As the *Sather* court noted, even flat fees paid upfront are still advance fees or special retainers. Thus, the attorney must put the flat fee in a client trust account and can only make withdrawals as they are earned. Model Rule 1.15(c) endorses this view, requiring attorneys to deposit "legal fees and expenses that have been paid in advance" into a client trust account and allowing the lawyer to make withdrawals "only as fees are earned or expenses incurred."

In re Sather: Real Life Applications

1. New Alliance Bank is reorganizing and is selling stock to patrons in priority of those who hold certain amounts of money in their accounts. Larry has a client trust account with New Alliance Bank. He would like to purchase stock, but to obtain priority, he needs the client trust account to maintain a higher balance. Larry deposits some of his own money in the client trust account in order to obtain the priority to buy the stock. Larry decides that he will "forgo" ownership of any money that he placed into the client trust account in order to avoid commingling. Has Larry violated the rules?
2. Mason handles complex business disputes and wants to start charging an engagement retainer of $2,500 that is his upon receipt. What must Mason do to successfully charge an engagement retainer?

Record Keeping

Rule 1.15(a) requires that attorneys keep "[c]omplete records of such account funds and other property." As noted in comment 1, such records must be kept current and must be kept in accordance with generally accepted accounting practices (GAAP) in addition to "any recordkeeping rules established by law or court order." The rule further requires that such records be preserved by the attorney for a period of years following the end of the representation. The Model Rule recommends a record preservation period of five years, but many states have selected a longer preservation period, ranging from six to eight years.[69]

Notification, Delivery, and Accounting

Rule 1.15(d) covers three fiduciary duties owed as to client property and funds. First, if the lawyer receives funds or other property (commonly a settlement check) as to which the client or another person has an interest, the lawyer must "promptly notify the client or third person." Second, the attorney is then required to "promptly deliver" the funds or property to the client or third person with the ownership

---

69. *See* ABA, CPR Policy Implementation Committee, *Variations of the ABA Model Rules of Professional Conduct, Rule 1.15: Safekeeping Property* (Dec. 12, 2016), *available at* http://www.americanbar.org/content/dam/aba/administrative/professional_responsibility/mrpc_1_15.authcheckdam.pdf.

interest. Finally, if a client or a third person claiming an interest in property or funds held by the attorney makes a request for an accounting, the lawyer is required to "promptly render a full accounting regarding such property."

Disputes over Property Held by the Attorney

Model Rule 1.15(e) sets out how an attorney is to handle disputes over ownership of property, especially money. Third parties, including creditors of the client, may have enforceable claims against client funds held by the attorney.[70] Yet, not too surprisingly, the most common situation in which there is a dispute over ownership of money held by the attorney involves disputes between the attorney and client. For example, the attorney will deposit an advance fee into the client trust account. The attorney then bills the client, who objects to the attorney's bill as being excessive. Or, the attorney receives a settlement check for the client, but the attorney is owed fees or expenses — and then the client objects to the attorney taking as much as the attorney asserts he is owed under a contingent or other fee agreement. So how much, if anything, can an attorney withdraw in such cases (and in other cases where a third party may assert an interest in client funds)?

Model Rule 1.15(e) states that "the property shall be kept separate by the lawyer until the dispute is resolved," but also that "the lawyer shall promptly distribute all portions of the property as to which the interests are not in dispute." Thus, the attorney is required to distribute any undisputed portions, but must keep any disputed portions in the client trust account. So if an attorney bills a client for $2,000, and the client thinks the attorney has only earned $1,000, then the attorney must withdraw the $1,000 that both agree the attorney has earned — but the attorney must also keep the disputed $1,000 in the client trust account until the dispute is resolved.

There is a split in authority as to whether an attorney must return funds to the client trust account if the attorney makes a disbursement prior to learning of a dispute, but thereafter becomes aware that the disbursement is disputed. In *In re Martin*, the D.C. Court of Appeals held that where an attorney disbursed settlement funds to himself from the trust account, but learned shortly thereafter that the client disputed the disbursement, the attorney was required to return the disputed portion to the client trust account. However, the court noted the existence of conflicting authority, citing both courts that agreed with its holding and courts that held that once an attorney has disbursed funds, she need not return disputed portions to the client trust account.[71]

3. Terminating the Representation

An attorney should undertake a representation only if it appears that he can carry it through to completion. *See* Model Rule 1.16 cmt. 1. Completion occurs when the

70. For example, comment 4 to Rule 1.15(a) notes that a creditor of the client may have "a lien on funds recovered in a personal injury action."
71. *See In re Martin*, 67 A.3d 1032, 1045-46 & n.14 (D.C. Ct. App. 2013) (collecting conflicting authority).

attorney has performed the assistance for which the client hired him. *See id.* Certainly, as long as the limitation is reasonable, an attorney and client can agree at the outset to narrow the scope of the representation so that an attorney is hired only to undertake limited or preliminary tasks as to a legal matter.[72] But attorneys, as fiduciaries of their clients, cannot willy-nilly abandon a client's matter. As noted in the *Pang* and *Sather* cases above, clients have a right to discharge their lawyer at any time with or without cause,[73] but an attorney lacks a similar right and cannot always withdraw from a representation with which the attorney is dissatisfied. At the same time, the rules require attorneys to withdraw under certain circumstances. But even then, the attorney's withdrawal may require permission from a tribunal. The bottom line is that attorneys cannot count on being able to easily withdraw from a matter—especially if withdrawing will prejudice the client or interfere with a court's adjudication of a case.

Model Rule 1.16 divides attorney withdrawal into two basic categories: mandatory withdrawal and permissive withdrawal. Model Rule 1.16(a) covers mandatory withdrawal—situations in which the attorney is required to withdraw; while 1.16(b) covers permissive withdrawal—situations in which an attorney is allowed to withdraw. If an attorney wishes to withdraw and cannot fit the withdrawal into one of the categories outlined in 1.16(a) and (b), the attorney cannot withdraw. Moreover, under Rule 1.16(c), a lawyer will have to obtain permission from the tribunal, in accordance with local law, in order to effectuate withdrawal in a case involving an adjudicative proceeding. If the court denies the attorney's petition to withdraw, the attorney must continue with the representation even if Rule 1.16(a) or (b) would have permitted or required the attorney to withdraw.[74]

Case Preview

In re Kiley

Michael McGibbon hired Thomas M. Kiley and Associates to assert a medical malpractice claim on his behalf. McGibbon entered a contingency fee contract with the firm, and Pamela Swift, an attorney for the firm, filed suit and entered an appearance on McGibbon's behalf. Swift decided to take a "sabbatical from the practice of law." She notified McGibbon that he needed to seek successor counsel. McGibbon's search for successor counsel was unsuccessful. Nevertheless, Swift moved to withdraw from the case, which motion the court denied because no successor counsel had appeared. Swift moved to reconsider, and after a hearing, the court allowed Swift to withdraw, but ordered that Kiley, the named partner of the Kiley firm, represent McGibbon. The court explained that McGibbon had a valid contract to have the Kiley firm represent him

72. Model Rule 1.2(c) allows an attorney, with client informed consent, to undertake representations that are limited in scope, as long as "the limitation is reasonable under the circumstances."
73. *See also* Model Rule 1.16 cmt. 4.
74. *See* Model Rule 1.16(c) (explaining that when a court so orders, "a lawyer shall continue representation notwithstanding good cause for terminating the representation").

and that the case was "falling behind" the court-ordered schedule for its disposition. Nevertheless, Kiley informed McGibbon by letter that their contingency contract had been terminated; however, the judge would not let Kiley out of the case. Kiley filed an interlocutory appeal, which is excerpted here.

As you read *In re Kiley*, consider the following:

1. Under the Massachusetts rules, which follow the Model Rules, when is an attorney required to withdraw? When is an attorney permitted to withdraw?
2. When an attorney seeks court permission to withdraw, what factors do the Massachusetts courts consider in deciding whether to allow the attorney to withdraw?
3. When an attorney who practices with a law firm enters an appearance, is the law firm also bound to continue that appearance if the individual attorney is unable to complete the representation?
4. If a lawyer undertakes a case on contingency, but comes to realize after filing the case that it will not be profitable for the lawyer, is the lawyer free to withdraw on that basis?

In re Kiley

459 Mass. 645 (2011)

An attorney who has entered an appearance in a case filed in court may not withdraw from the representation of the client without complying with two rules: Mass. R. Prof. C. 1.16, which identifies the limited circumstances under which an attorney must or may withdraw; and Mass. R. Civ. P. 11(c), which identifies the limited circumstances where withdrawal may be done without leave of court and otherwise requires leave of court.

Under rule 1.16(a), an attorney "shall" withdraw from representation where the client discharges the lawyer, where continued representation will result in violation of the rules of professional conduct or other law, or where the lawyer's physical or mental condition materially impairs the lawyer's ability to represent the client. Under rule 1.16(b), a lawyer "may" withdraw from representation where the withdrawal can be accomplished "without material adverse effect on the interests of the client." Where withdrawal will have a material adverse effect on the client's interests, a lawyer may withdraw only if at least one of the following circumstances is present:

(1) the client persists in a course of action involving the lawyer's services that the lawyer reasonably believes is criminal or fraudulent;
(2) the client has used the lawyer's services to perpetrate a crime or fraud;
(3) a client insists upon pursuing an objective that the lawyer considers repugnant or imprudent;
(4) the client fails substantially to fulfil an obligation to the lawyer regarding the lawyer's services and has been given reasonable warning that the lawyer will withdraw unless the obligation is fulfilled;

(5) the representation will result in an unreasonable financial burden on the lawyer or has been rendered unreasonably difficult by the client; or
(6) other good cause for withdrawal exists.

Mass. R. Prof. C. 1.16(b). Regardless whether a lawyer must or may withdraw in these circumstances, where the lawyer has entered an appearance on behalf of the client and "the rules of a tribunal" require approval of the withdrawal by the tribunal, the lawyer shall not withdraw the appearance without the tribunal's permission. Mass. R. Prof. C. 1.16(c).

Where an attorney has entered an appearance in a civil proceeding in a Massachusetts court, the "rules of [the] tribunal" require the attorney to obtain leave of court before withdrawing from a case unless three conditions are met: the notice of withdrawal is accompanied by the entry of appearance of successor counsel, no motions are pending, and no trial date has been set. Mass. R. Civ. P. 11(c). Where at least one of these conditions is not met, the decision whether to allow an attorney's withdrawal is left to the sound discretion of the judge and will be reversed only for an abuse of discretion.

As reflected in these two rules, an attorney may not terminate an agreement to represent a client simply because the attorney no longer wishes to continue the representation. *See* Rusinow v. Kamara, 920 F. Supp. 69, 72 (D.N.J. 1996) ("Sudden disenchantment with a client or a cause is no basis for withdrawal. Those who cannot live with risk, doubt and ingratitude should not be trial lawyers"). Even if an attorney has not entered an appearance on behalf of the client, the attorney may withdraw in accordance with rule 1.16 only if the withdrawal will not have a material adverse effect on the client's interests or if at least one of the circumstances requiring or permitting withdrawal is present. . . .

Where, as here, the client enters into a representation agreement with a law firm rather than a sole practitioner, the law firm may not terminate the agreement simply because the attorney who had been handling the case has died, left the practice of law, or moved to a different firm. While the departure of the responsible attorney may cause the client to leave the firm, it may not cause the firm to leave the client if withdrawal will have a material adverse effect on the client's interests and none of the circumstances requiring [or] permitting withdrawal is present.

Because McGibbon was unable to retain successor counsel to prosecute his medical malpractice case, the Kiley firm's withdrawal would have had a material adverse effect on the client's interest in prevailing at trial or obtaining a reasonable settlement. Apart from conclusory assertions of "irreconcilable differences" with the client, neither Swift nor Kiley had identified any justification under rule 1.16(b) or (c) to terminate representation . . . . While McGibbon was willing to discharge Swift in light of her intention to leave the practice of law, he wanted the Kiley firm to continue to represent him in the case. Kiley's letter to the client on June 21, 2010, in which he declared that his law firm was "unilaterally terminating" the agreement to represent the client in the medical malpractice case, effective immediately, demonstrates his apparent disregard of the dictates of rule 1.16 and rule 11(c), as well as the judge's order, because it suggests that an attorney has the authority unilaterally to terminate an agreement to represent a client even where the attorney has filed a complaint on behalf of the client and entered an appearance in the case.

Even if there had been a permissible basis under rule 1.16 for the Kiley firm to move to withdraw from the case, the judge did not abuse his discretion by allowing Swift's motion to withdraw but requiring the Kiley firm to continue the representation and file an appearance. "[An] attorney who agrees to represent a client in a court proceeding assumes a responsibility to the court as well as to the client." V.H. v. J.P.H., *supra*. In deciding whether to allow the withdrawal of an attorney or the attorney's law firm, a judge may consider the impact of a withdrawal on the timely and fair adjudication of the case and the "reasonable expectation of the opposing party to have a case efficiently adjudicated." Zabin v. Picciotto, 73 Mass. App. Ct. 141, 165 (2008). The judge noted in his findings that he had been informed by defense counsel that the dispute over McGibbon's representation had "severely retarded discovery progress" in the case, and that the case was already three years old and was "falling behind" in its compliance with time standards. In view of all these circumstances, we conclude that the judge did not abuse his discretion in denying what was, in effect, the Kiley firm's motion to withdraw. . . .

The judge also did not abuse his discretion in refusing to allow withdrawal of the Kiley firm after Kiley, in his motion to vacate or reconsider the June 16 findings and order, provided the judge with documents that McGibbon had sent to opposing counsel. . . .

Kiley contends that, as a result of the production of these documents to opposing counsel, continued representation "has been rendered unreasonably difficult by the client" and justified termination of the representation under rule 1.16(b)(5). The judge did not address this issue in denying the motion for reconsideration, but the record provides ample basis for us to conclude that the denial of the motion was within his discretion. There is nothing in the record to suggest that McGibbon provided these documents to opposing counsel to sabotage his own case or otherwise acted in bad faith. Kiley cannot improperly abandon his client and then, when the client injures his position during settlement negotiations because the Kiley firm was no longer advising him, argue that the client's error now justifies his firm's withdrawal from the case. Moreover, even if McGibbon's conduct provided a ground for the Kiley firm to withdraw from the representation under rule 1.16(b)(5), the judge did not abuse his discretion in refusing to release the Kiley firm from the representation where the case was already three years old, discovery was delayed, and no successor counsel could be found.

The judge erred however, in requiring Kiley himself to file an appearance . . . . The language of the agreement is clear that the agreement is between McGibbon and Kiley's law firm, not Kiley individually.

When an attorney who is a partner, shareholder, or employee of a law firm enters an appearance in a civil case, the appearance binds both the individual attorney and that law firm to appear on behalf of the client. . . . Where an attorney leaves a law firm and moves to withdraw, and where successor counsel from another law firm does not file an appearance, a judge is entitled to expect that another attorney from the law firm will enter an appearance and continue to represent the client. In such circumstances, unless specified in the order, the allowance by a judge of a departing attorney's motion to withdraw does not also permit the law firm to withdraw its representation in the case. A judge may allow the attorney's motion but require the law

firm to select another attorney to enter an appearance and continue the representation. A judge may not, however, select the attorney in the law firm who will enter the appearance; the law firm may select the appropriate attorney.

On remand, the single justice is to affirm the judge's order only to the extent that it denies the Kiley law firm's motion to withdraw from the representation and requires another attorney affiliated with the Kiley firm to file an appearance on behalf of McGibbon. . . .

We address briefly the argument raised in one of the amicus briefs that motions to withdraw filed by attorneys who are retained on a contingency fee should be more generously allowed to prevent claims that are meritless from being brought to trial, "at no cost to the client, but at great cost to all others involved." Nothing in the record suggests that McGibbon's claim is without merit. . . .

A law firm, after agreeing to represent a client for a contingent fee and filing a complaint that presumably complies with the requirement of a good faith basis under Mass. R. Civ. P. 11(a) may not withdraw from a case simply because it recognizes belatedly that the case will not be profitable for the law firm. A lawyer's miscalculation of the time or resources necessary to represent a client, the likelihood of success, or the amount of damages "is usually a dubious ground" for withdrawal, because lawyers are better able than clients to forecast these matters. . . . Attorneys who agree to represent clients on a contingent fee basis must choose their cases carefully, because the law does not allow them easily to jettison their mistakes, especially after the complaint has been filed.

Post-Case Follow-Up

Kiley illustrates the reality that attorneys cannot abandon their clients should the representation prove less profitable than initially thought — the lawyer's circumstance must fall within one of the provisions of Rule 1.16 to allow appropriate withdrawal. Further, where attorneys are associated in a firm, the fact that one lawyer must withdraw due to personal reasons does not give license to the entire firm to withdraw from the client.

In re Kiley: Real Life Applications

1. Peter works for the law firm Price and French. Peter personally represents Mike in a civil rights lawsuit that's been filed in federal district court. Peter is diagnosed with cancer and is required to take a leave of absence. He tells Mike that he is going to have to withdraw because his physical condition completely impairs his ability to continue the representation. Assume no one else at Price and French wants to take on Mike's case. What should Peter do? What should Price and French do?

2. Heather, an attorney, learns that opposing counsel previously represented her client in a different matter years before the case. Heather's client is not interested

in a quick resolution of the case because the client will likely be held liable. The client recommends that Heather move to disqualify opposing counsel, but wants to wait until close to trial in order to delay the proceedings. Is this a good idea? Is such a plan likely to be successful?

Mandatory Withdrawal

As noted in *Kiley* and Model Rule 1.16(a), a lawyer is required to withdraw under three circumstances. First, the lawyer must withdraw when "the representation *will result* in violation" of the jurisdiction's professional conduct rules or other law. Often this occurs when a lawyer is faced with an unconsented to or nonconsentable conflict of interest. But it may also include other situations where continued representation will result in a violation of the rules, for example, the prohibition in Rule 1.2(d) from assisting a client in crime or fraud. Withdrawal is also required when the lawyer is too sick to handle a case. Be it a physical or mental impairment, the lawyer is required to withdraw if the ailment "materially impairs the lawyer's ability to represent the client." *See* Model Rule 1.16(a)(2). Finally, a lawyer must withdraw when the client fires the lawyer. The client has the right to fire the lawyer "at any time, with or without cause." *See* Model Rule 1.16 cmt. 4. However, if the situation involves appointed counsel of a criminal defendant—particularly if this is not the first time that a defendant has fired an appointed attorney in the matter—negative consequences may follow the defendant's firing and the attorney should inform the defendant of such. Specifically, the appointing authority may determine "that appointment of successor counsel is unjustified, thus requiring self-representation by the client." *See* Model Rule 1.16 cmt. 5. Again, even with mandatory withdrawal, the lawyer will have to obtain permission to withdraw if a proceeding has been filed. While courts are likely to grant permission in such situations, the court may deny permission if withdrawal is unduly prejudicial. Courts have denied petitions for mandatory withdrawal, for example, where the withdrawal is sought on the eve of trial.[75]

Permissive Withdrawal

Permissive withdrawal can also be categorized into three basic types: (1) lack of harm to the client; (2) the client's bad or otherwise repugnant acts; and (3) the client's failure to pay or otherwise fulfill an obligation to the attorney. In addition, Rule 1.16(b)(7) is a catchall provision allowing for withdrawal when "other good cause for withdrawal exists."

As the *Kiley* court explained, an attorney is permitted to withdraw under Rule 1.16(b)(1) whenever withdrawal can be accomplished "without material adverse

---

75. *See, e.g.*, Georgia Baptist Health Care System, Inc. v. Hanafi, 559 S.E.2d 746, 747-49 (Ga. Ct. App. 2002) (denying motion to disqualify made at conclusion of discovery and initially raised 17 months after learning of the conflict); Velazquez-Velez v. Molina-Rodriguez, 2017 WL 395105, at *2 (D.P.R. 2017) (noting that the "great majority of cases where motions to disqualify were denied as untimely involved motions filed on the eve of trial").

effect on the interests of the client." The attorney needs no other reason to withdraw if it will not harm his client. This basis for withdrawal indicates that in the other forms of permissive withdrawal, the withdrawal may adversely affect the client's interests.

Several of the bases for permissive withdrawal center around a client's bad or otherwise repugnant actions. Thus, under Rule 1.16(b)(2) and (b)(3), a lawyer is permitted to withdraw (1) if the client is using the lawyer's services to engage in conduct that the lawyer "reasonably believes is criminal or fraudulent" or (2) if the client has previously "used the lawyer's services to perpetrate a crime or fraud." In both of these situations, the client is not currently using the lawyer's services to perpetrate a known crime or fraud, which would trigger mandatory withdrawal. Nevertheless, the lawyer is not required to maintain a relationship with a client who is using or has used the lawyer's services in potentially criminal or fraudulent ways that are just shy of triggering mandatory withdrawal. Similarly, Rule 1.16(b)(4) allows an attorney to withdraw from representing a client who "insists upon taking action that the lawyer considers repugnant" or fundamentally disagrees with. Notably, if an attorney decides to continue a representation, despite personally disagreeing with the client's views or ends, the attorney is not thereby endorsing the client's views.[76]

The final bases under which a lawyer can permissively withdraw revolve around a client's failure to pay fees or comply with other obligations to the attorney, or a representation that will create an unreasonable financial burden on the attorney. As noted in ABA Formal Opinion 476, courts have generally held under Rule 16(b)(5) and (b)(6) that "if a client fails over time to pay a lawyer's fees, and that failure continues after a lawyer provides a reasonable warning to the client, the lawyer may be permitted to withdraw."

Comment 3 to Rule 1.16 instructs lawyers to carefully guard their duty of confidentiality, covered in Chapter 5, in moving to withdraw from a court proceeding. The comment explains that if a court seeks an explanation, the lawyer may be prohibited by the duty of confidentiality from disclosing facts constituting the explanation. However, in such instances, the attorney is to provide the court with the following explanation as the reason for withdrawal: "professional considerations require termination of the representation." Comment 3 indicates that normally this explanation should suffice.[77]

---

76. *See* Model Rule 1.2(b) (maintaining that the representation of a client does not constitute an endorsement of the client's views or claims).

77. Nevertheless, in ABA Formal Opinion 476, the ABA noted that many courts require further factual enhancement and offered the following guidance on how an attorney should proceed in safeguarding the duty of confidentiality when moving to withdraw on the basis of nonpayment of fees. The attorney could

> (1) initially submit a motion providing no confidential client information apart from a reference to "professional considerations" or the like; (2) upon being informed by the court that further information is necessary, respond, when practicable, by seeking to persuade the court to rule on the motion without requiring the disclosure of confidential client information, asserting all non-frivolous claims of confidentiality and privilege; and if that fails; (3) thereupon under Rule 1.6(b)(5) submit only such information as is reasonably necessary to satisfy the needs of the court and preferably by whatever restricted means of submission, such as *in camera* review under seal, or such other procedures designated to minimize disclosure as the court determines is appropriate. If the court expressly orders the lawyer to make further disclosure, the exception in Rule 1.6(b)(6) for disclosures required to comply with a court order will apply . . . .

ABA Formal Op. 476 (2016).

Duties Owed to the Client After Termination

The lawyer continues to owe duties to the client even after termination. Rule 1.16(d) requires a withdrawing attorney to take reasonable measures "to protect a client's interests." The rule lists four such measures: (1) providing the client with reasonable notice of the withdrawal; (2) giving the client time to hire another attorney; (3) returning papers and property to the client; and (4) refunding advance payments of fees and expenses.

Protecting the client's interests as a fiduciary requires that the client be notified of the intent to withdraw with sufficient time to obtain successor counsel who can continue the representation. Further, the client will need the file and other documents and evidence held by the attorney to successfully proceed with the matter. Recall from *Sallee* above that the attorney was additionally disciplined for refusing to return the entire file, including medical records and brain-tissue slides from the client's daughter's autopsy, which the attorney withheld, claiming that she had no obligation to turn them over until her clients paid her over $80,000 in fees. Most jurisdictions maintain that the entire file presumptively belongs to the client. However, a minority view adopts the "end product" approach whereby the client has a right to the lawyer's end product documents, but "is not entitled to preliminary documents . . . such as internal legal memoranda, preliminary drafts of pleadings, and other preliminary documents."[78]

Whether an attorney can withhold parts of the file as a security for payment of fees — a "retaining lien" — depends on the law of the particular jurisdiction, as indicated in Rule 1.16(d).[79] A number of jurisdictions expressly prohibit retaining liens,[80] while others only allow them if the retention of the papers will not prejudice the client.[81] It is essential that attorneys contemplating a retaining lien carefully consult the applicable law in their jurisdiction.

Further, as noted in *Sather*, attorneys who have obtained an advance fee — even if a flat fee — must refund any unearned portions upon withdrawal from a case. Client receipt of such funds is not solely a matter of obtaining an entitled refund — it also can provide the means for the client to obtain successor counsel and appropriately proceed with the representation.

---

78. SEC v. McNaul, 277 F.R.D. 439, 444-45 (2011).

79. *See* Model Rule 1.16(d) (allowing a lawyer to retain papers after withdrawal "to the extent permitted by other law").

80. *See, e.g.*, Minn. R. Prof'l Conduct 1.16(g) ("A lawyer shall not condition the return of client papers and property on payment of the lawyer's fee or the cost of copying the files or papers.").

81. *See, e.g.*, Iowa State Bar Association, Ethics Op. 07-08 (2007) ("An Attorney may not assert a statutory retaining lien against a client's original documents if, by doing so the client would be otherwise prejudiced.").

Chapter Summary

- Attorney-client relationships can be created either expressly or impliedly; whenever such a relationship exists, attorneys owe the client core duties of loyalty, communication, competence, confidentiality, and conflict avoidance.
- Attorneys owe specific but more limited duties to prospective clients.
- The client has the ultimate authority to determine the objectives of the representation (within the bounds of the law), while the attorney has more control regarding the means by which such objectives are pursued.
- In a civil matter, the client has the ultimate authority as to whether to settle a case; in a criminal matter, the client has the ultimate authority as to the plea to enter, whether to testify, and whether to waive jury trial.
- The attorney for an organization represents the organization and not its constituents, and so the attorney must provide a clarifying entity warning to constituents with interests potentially adverse to the entity. The attorney must protect the entity's interest, including by reporting up when required under the rules.
- Attorneys act as fiduciaries of their clients even when the lawyer's interest and the client's interest diverge; the lawyer must safeguard the client's interests in charging a fee, handling client funds and property, and withdrawing from the case.
- Attorneys must communicate the basis and rate of their fee to the client and are forbidden from charging an unreasonable or fraudulent fee.
- Attorneys have five basic fiduciary duties relating to handling client funds and property: (1) segregation; (2) record keeping; (3) notification; (4) delivery; and (5) accounting.
- Attorneys can only withdraw when required or allowed by the rules and, if a case is before a tribunal, permitted by the court; moreover, the attorney must take measures to protect the client's interests upon withdrawal.

Applying the Rules

1. Matt lives in a small community and is suing a contractor who substantially damaged his home. There are only three attorneys in the community that could competently handle the matter. Otherwise, a person would have to hire an attorney at a substantially higher price from a metropolitan area 50 miles to the west. Matt meets with each of the three attorneys in the community and tells them about his case in detail. Matt believes this will not only help him determine who to hire, but it will preclude those attorneys (having heard Matt's side of the story) from being able to represent the contractor he plans to sue. Under the rules, has Matt succeeded in conflicting out the competent local counsel from representing the contractor?

2. You represent Dave, who is a "high maintenance" client with a short temper and unrealistic expectations. Opposing counsel calls and asks you for a 15-day extension to respond to a motion for summary judgment because his out-of-state daughter had an emergency C-section with a premature baby. Opposing counsel has previously asked for extensions for discovery and pleading, to which you objected at Dave's behest. Both extensions of time were then granted as a matter of course by the judge, who was annoyed to have to rule on motions for modest extensions of time. Dave knows the summary judgment response is due and is anxiously awaiting it. You tell him of opposing counsel's request and he demands that you deny it, threatening to fire you if you do not. How should you proceed?

3. Ella wants to sell off her family farm for commercial or residential development. She asks John to represent her in the transaction. Ella tells John she cannot afford to pay him a cash fee, but she will give him ten acres of the land in payment. John asks Ella what the land is worth, and she tells him she thinks it is worth $3,000 an acre. John agrees to undertake the representation and to accept the ten acres as payment. John writes up an agreement that simply states that John agrees to represent Ella in the development of her land and that Ella agrees to transfer to him ownership of ten acres of the land. Assume that unbeknownst to Ella or John the land is actually worth $50,000 an acre. Has John charged an unreasonable fee? Are there any other Model Rules he needs to consider regarding collecting such a fee?

4. Melody hired Karl to represent her in a personal injury action, from which she recovered $50,000. Karl set up a special needs trust for Melody, with himself as trustee, to ensure that the assets were not depleted quickly and to preserve Melody's ability to remain on public assistance. Melody decided she wanted to obtain access to the trust principal. She talked to an attorney, Mindy. Mindy said she would represent Melody on a contingency fee basis whereby Mindy would get "one-third of whatever is in the trust." Melody agreed and signed a contingency fee agreement to that effect. Mindy called Karl, informed Karl of Melody's desires, and asked him to step aside as trustee. Karl agreed to do so. Mindy created a short document naming herself as the successor trustee. She then prepared documents terminating the trust. Mindy and Melody then went to the bank together and depleted the trust assets, with Mindy receiving the full fee of $16,667 for a couple hours of work. Has Mindy violated the rules?

5. You represent Star Corp and are preparing to close a major deal. The CFO sends you an email asking you to come speak with him. When you arrive, the CFO begins telling you that he is concerned because his malfeasance has resulted in some financial setbacks that have not yet been reflected on Star Corp's financial statements. He is concerned that if these setbacks are accurately reported, it will mess up the deal. What do you tell the CFO? How do you proceed?

Professional Responsibility in Practice

1. Eli comes to you asking you to represent him in slip and fall case against his neighbor, Cyrus, for an incident that occurred ten months ago. You meet with him for a half hour, but decide you do not want to take his case. Draft an appropriate declination letter to Eli.

2. Same facts as above, only this time you decide to take Eli's case and want to charge a one-third contingency fee. Draft a contingency fee agreement that complies with Rule 1.5.

3. Research whether an in-house attorney has a cause of action for wrongful discharge when fired for complying with mandatory rules of professional conduct in the state where you plan to practice or are attending law school.

4. Select a state that has decided to legalize marijuana. Research the ethics opinions in that state to see how that state approaches the problem of compliance with Rule 1.2(d) where state law expressly allows marijuana use but federal law criminalizes it.

4

Competence — The Lawyer's Indispensable Duty

Competence is the lawyer's indispensable duty. Clients come to attorneys to protect client life, liberty, and property interests, yet attorneys who act incompetently can cripple those rights. The very person whom clients pay and trust to vindicate their rights and interests becomes the instrument through which those rights and interests are impaired and perhaps lost entirely. Attorneys have a duty to act with competence — to have or obtain the requisite skill, legal knowledge, and expertise to handle the client's matter, to undertake thorough preparation and perform necessary investigation to obtain the requisite factual knowledge about the case, to act with diligence to advance the client's interests, and to communicate with and counsel the client. Competence, diligence, and communication are core duties essential to protecting client rights and avoiding discipline. Moreover, in criminal cases, the Sixth Amendment guarantees that the accused shall have "the assistance of counsel for his defence." Thus, an attorney who violates duties of competence also undermines her client's constitutional right to effective assistance of counsel.

Attorneys who fulfill the duties of competence, diligence, and communication can literally save their clients' lives, families, and fortunes. Yet, as examples in this chapter will illustrate, an attorney's incompetence can cause irreparable harm to clients: clients have lost custody of children, have gone to prison or have even been executed, have been deported, have had adoptions nullified, and have been evicted from their homes — all due to the incompetence of their own attorneys. In addition, incompetent attorneys

Key Concepts

- Competence requires legal knowledge, skill, thoroughness, and preparation
- The consequences to clients of attorney incompetence
- The lawyer's duty to act with diligence and promptness
- Attorney-client communication as essential to successful representation
- The criminal defendant's right to effective assistance of counsel
- Substance abuse, mental health, and competence

completely undermine their own role in the justice system when their actions divest rather than protect the liberty and property—and in some cases even the life—of their client, the very person who has entrusted those rights to their care.

A. THE COMPETENT ATTORNEY

Clients come to attorneys because clients lack the requisite knowledge, skill, and ability to protect their own legal interests and rights. Attorneys who are incompetent violate their first and basic duty to their clients: to protect their clients' interests. Indeed, incompetent attorneys not only fail to protect client interests, but often impair and destroy client rights.

The whole theory underlying the licensure of attorneys and accompanying unauthorized practice of law rules is that it is essential to the protection of clients and their legal interests to allow only those who have the *specialized knowledge and training* to practice law. If those who are licensed are not willing to become and remain competent in the practice of law, what is the justification for restricting practice to licensed attorneys? As discussed in Chapter 1, attorneys have a social contract with the public, whereby in exchange for an exclusive license they agree to maintain high standards of minimum conduct in order to protect the public and safeguard justice, the profession's public good. The profession must insist on minimum standards of competence to properly protect these interests.

Importantly, the Supreme Court has held that it is not unjust for a client to be bound by his attorney's incompetence: "[The client] voluntarily chose this attorney as his representative in the action, and he cannot now avoid the consequences of the acts or omissions of this freely selected agent. Any other notion would be wholly inconsistent with our system of representative litigation, in which each party is deemed bound by the acts of his lawyer-agent."[1] Thus, the rights of clients can be nullified by their own lawyer's incompetence without full recourse to undo the legal consequences created by that incompetence. Often, and for individual clients generally, the client has no way of measuring or appreciating the incompetence of her counsel precisely because the client lacks the requisite training and skill to protect her own legal rights—which is why the client hired an attorney in the first place. An action for attorney malpractice can sometimes provide monetary compensation to clients harmed by attorney incompetence. But often when legal rights are at stake, money damages cannot provide full compensation for what was lost through attorney incompetence, as will be illustrated repeatedly in this chapter.

Competence—along with the cognate duties of diligence and communication—are placed first in the Model Rules—a reminder of their preeminent importance to protecting your client's rights. Model Rule 1.1 requires attorneys to "provide competent representation to a client," which the rule then explains consists of four basic components: "legal knowledge, skill, thoroughness and preparation."

1. Link v. Wabash Railroad Co., 370 U.S. 626, 633-34 (1962).

1. Legal Knowledge and Skill

Attorneys must obtain the requisite legal knowledge and skill to handle their cases. Comment 1 to Rule 1.1 explains that while expertise in a particular field may be required in some cases, nevertheless, in "many instances, the required proficiency is that of a general practitioner." The comment goes on to explain that generalized legal skills are of primary importance in many types of cases. These skills include "analysis of precedent, the evaluation of evidence, and legal drafting." The comment posits that "[p]erhaps the most fundamental legal skill consists of determining what kind of legal problems a situation may involve"—commonly known to lawyers and law students as "issue-spotting."

Legal knowledge includes not only knowledge of substantive law, but also knowledge of procedural rules and requirements to successfully handle a case. The importance of attorney competence in procedure can hardly be overstated. An attorney who understands procedure can use it skillfully to vindicate client rights, while the attorney who makes procedural missteps can easily forfeit a client's meritorious claims and rights. Notably, an attorney's failure to read, understand, or follow procedural rules does not constitute a basis for obtaining relief from a judgment under Federal Rule of Civil Procedure 60(b).[2] Thus, failure to comply with procedural requirements may lead to a client forfeiting rights and being unable to recover them.

Case Preview

Dahl v. Dahl

Dahl v. Dahl is an appeal from a divorce proceeding where the husband, a cardiologist, divorced his wife, who had been the primary caretaker of their two children and had not worked outside of the home during their 18 years of marriage. Counsel for Ms. Dahl made several major procedural errors. Notably, he failed to file proper expert witness reports as to experts that he had designated to testify in favor of Ms. Dahl relating to child custody. He also failed to make proper pretrial disclosures and provide an exhibit list, and he failed to file or designate for trial the requisite financial declaration to obtain temporary or permanent alimony. Consequently, at trial, the trial court refused to allow Ms. Dahl's experts to testify beyond what was disclosed in their meager reports and excluded from evidence nearly all of Ms. Dahl's trial exhibits. Full custody of the children was awarded to Mr. Dahl, and Ms. Dahl was denied any award of alimony. Ms. Dahl appealed, arguing that a trial in which she was not allowed to introduce most of her exhibits and was not allowed to have child custody experts testify on her behalf was an abuse of the trial court's discretion.

2. Pioneer Inv. Services Co. v. Brunswick Associates Ltd., 507 U.S. 380, 392 (1993) ("[I]nadvertence, ignorance of the rules, or mistakes concerning construing the rules do not usually constitute 'excusable' neglect," under Rule 60(b) allowing for relief from judgment.).

As you read *Dahl v. Dahl*, consider the following:

1. Why is competence so important? What did attorney incompetence cost Ms. Dahl?
2. The Utah Supreme Court indicated that Ms. Dahl could alleviate her losses by suing her attorney for malpractice. Would malpractice fully compensate a client like Ms. Dahl?
3. Is it really fair to bind clients to the mistakes of their "freely selected agent attorney" when an attorney makes egregious procedural missteps?

Dahl v. Dahl

2015 UT 79

Dr. Charles Dahl and Ms. Kim Dahl were married for nearly eighteen years. . . . The divorce proceedings were extremely contentious. The parties fiercely disputed custody of their children, Ms. Dahl's right to temporary and permanent alimony, and the proper distribution of the marital estate. The discovery process was rife with abuses on both sides, which delayed trial. The pretrial disclosure process was similarly fraught and ultimately resulted in the exclusion of most of Ms. Dahl's trial exhibits and expert witnesses. The district court aptly described the pretrial proceedings as a "train wreck."

. . .

B. THE DISTRICT COURT DID NOT ABUSE ITS DISCRETION IN ITS PRETRIAL EVIDENTIARY RULINGS

Ms. Dahl [] argues that the district court abused its discretion [in its evidentiary rulings]. . . . We find no abuse of discretion. Rather, the rulings were appropriate because Ms. Dahl's counsel failed to comply with basic rules of procedure. . . .

2. The District Court Did Not Abuse Its Discretion When It Limited the Number of Exhibits Ms. Dahl Was Allowed to Introduce at Trial

At a June 17, 2009 pretrial conference, the district court ordered the parties to exchange "an actual schedule of the people [they planned] to call and the exhibits [they planned] to use" no later than two weeks before the first day of trial. . . .

The exhibit list submitted by Ms. Dahl's counsel failed to comply with the court's order. Nor did it comport with any reasonable standards of pretrial disclosure. The exhibit list encompassed the entire universe of potential exhibits and was accompanied by a CD containing digital copies of over 8,000 documents. For example, the first exhibit listed was "[a]ny and all documents exchanged by the parties as potential exhibits in this matter on August 31, 2009, to the extent that they are admissible." Other listed exhibits included "[a]ny and all documents maintained in the Court's file"; "[a]ll affidavits filed in this matter"; "[a]ll email communications and other written communications between the parties"; "[a]ny and all admissible information,

received pursuant to Subpoena Duces Tecum or other discovery method in the above-entitled matter"; and "[a]ny rebuttal exhibits." The list was so broad and over-inclusive as to be meaningless. It failed to identify any particular exhibit by an identifying number or a particularized description and made no effort to link the general categories of documents to the electronic documents contained on the CD. In short, the exhibit list failed to identify any single document with enough particularity to allow the court or opposing counsel to identify it as one Ms. Dahl planned to introduce at trial.

At the final pretrial motion hearing on September 15, 2009, the court . . . noted the problems with the exhibit list, stating:

> I thought my direction to you was clear. It's the same direction I give to every litigant who prepares for trial. I tell them to prepare a list of the actual exhibits, one by one that they intend to introduce and you've given me a list that says all the documents maintained, all the affidavits, all the records relied upon, all the marital communications. That's completely unworkable. I'm not going to allow you to simply dump all your discovery on my desk and tell me to sort it out.

The court thereafter struck the exhibit list and ordered counsel to resubmit a list that would identify particular documents that he would use with particular witnesses. In response, Ms. Dahl's counsel filed an amended exhibit list on September 22, 2009, the first day of trial. The amended list, though improved, continued to include designations such as "[a]ny and all documents exchanged by the parties as potential exhibits in this matter on August 31, 2009, to the extent they are admissible." The court again expressed its displeasure at counsel's failure to specifically identify which exhibits he planned to use at trial, citing the need to give all parties fair notice. . . .

On the next trial date, the court noted that counsel for Ms. Dahl had yet to submit an acceptable witness or exhibit list. By October 7, the fifth day of trial, counsel continued to attempt to introduce exhibits that had not previously been disclosed to the court or opposing counsel. The district court properly refused to allow these exhibits. On October 23 and November 4, counsel for Ms. Dahl filed supplemental exhibit lists, which identified particular documents, but did not identify which witness would be used to introduce the documents. Because Ms. Dahl's counsel failed to submit a proper exhibit list, the district court was confronted with the daunting task of determining, on a document-by-document basis during the course of trial, which exhibits had been previously produced. If a document had been previously produced to opposing counsel, the trial court admitted it. If not, the court excluded it.

Ms. Dahl argues that the district court abused its discretion when it excluded *most of her exhibits* based on counsel's failure to submit a proper exhibit list. . . . We disagree. The district court's order clearly directed the parties to designate particular documents to be used with particular witnesses and to exchange those documents with opposing counsel. And even if the district court's order were unclear, counsel was given numerous opportunities to rectify the situation and failed to do so. The district court would have been justified in excluding all of Ms. Dahl's exhibits based on her failure to submit a proper exhibit list prior to the start of trial. And it appropriately exercised its discretion when it excluded all documents except those that the parties stipulated had been previously disclosed during discovery.

3. *The District Court Did Not Abuse Its Discretion When It Limited the Testimony of Ms. Dahl's Expert Witnesses*

Ms. Dahl argues that the district court abused its discretion when it limited the testimony of two of her expert witnesses, Dr. Barden and Dr. Mejia. Ms. Dahl timely designated Drs. Barden and Mejia as experts prior to trial. Although the district court allowed these two experts to testify, it limited the scope of their testimony to the reports and affidavits the experts had filed earlier in the litigation. Ms. Dahl asserts that this limitation was an abuse of discretion. We disagree. . . .

. . . Though counsel for Ms. Dahl filed what were styled as expert witness reports for Drs. Barden and Mejia, neither report complied with the requirements of [Utah Civil Procedure] rule 26.

The expert report for Dr. Barden consisted of a mere four pages, contained no summary of Dr. Barden's qualifications or list of his publications, and identified the proposed subject matter of his testimony only in the most cursory way. . . .

The expert report for Dr. Mejia was similarly deficient. The report was less than two pages and contained only vague descriptions of Dr. Mejia's proposed testimony. The report failed to include a list of Dr. Mejia's publications or of previous cases in which he had testified.

Despite these shortcomings, the district court allowed Drs. Mejia and Barden to testify, but limited their testimony to that consistent with reports they had filed previously in the litigation. Given Ms. Dahl's failure to provide the kind of proper notice of expert testimony contemplated by rule 26, the district court did not abuse its discretion in limiting these experts' testimony in this way.

Pretrial discovery and disclosure are basic skills that we expect all attorneys to possess. Our already overworked district court judges should not be required to provide remedial instructions to counsel on how to properly conduct discovery, designate trial exhibits, or prepare expert reports. Our courts rely heavily on the competence and diligence of counsel. The evidentiary rulings Ms. Dahl complains of were largely the result of her counsel's inability to follow basic rules of procedure and properly manage discovery. Accordingly, we conclude that the district court did not abuse its discretion in its pretrial evidentiary rulings.

. . .

C. THE DISTRICT COURT DID NOT ABUSE ITS DISCRETION IN DENYING MS. DAHL'S REQUESTS FOR BOTH TEMPORARY AND PERMANENT ALIMONY

Ms. Dahl next challenges the district court's denial of her requests for temporary and permanent alimony. . . . We conclude that although Ms. Dahl may have qualified for an award of both temporary and permanent alimony, the district court did not abuse its discretion in refusing to make such an award because Ms. Dahl's counsel repeatedly failed to provide the credible financial documentation necessary for the district court to make an adequate finding as to Ms. Dahl's financial need.

. . . At the hearing on Ms. Dahl's first request for temporary alimony, the commissioner determined that Ms. Dahl's declaration was not sufficiently detailed and did not have enough evidentiary support for him to comply with the rules, statutes, and case law governing alimony awards. . . . Two months later, Ms. Dahl filed an affidavit in support of her request for temporary alimony. The affidavit, however, did not include any verification of the expenses she claimed, nor did it include any verification of her current financial condition or need. Instead, Ms. Dahl attached a 2005 tax return and an appraisal of the marital home in which she was no longer living. The commissioner again found the evidence insufficient to support an alimony award and ordered Ms. Dahl to file a financial declaration that complied with rule 101(d) of the Utah Rules of Civil Procedure.

A third hearing on this issue was held, but Ms. Dahl had not yet complied with the court's prior order that she provide a financial declaration. The commissioner again, relying on the Rules of Civil Procedure, the Utah Code, and relevant case law, declined to award temporary alimony. The matter was then raised in the district court at a hearing just four days later. The district court ordered Ms. Dahl to comply with the commissioner's order for a financial declaration.

Ms. Dahl made a third attempt at documenting her financial need a month and a half later when she filed a "Verified Financial Declaration." In contrast to her first declaration, where she testified to just over $11,000 in monthly expenses, she testified to over $40,000 in monthly expenses . . . . But Ms. Dahl again failed to provide verification of any of these expenses. She provided no proof of income, no bills, no checks, no lease agreement, no bank statements. In short, she provided absolutely no evidence to support the claimed expenses. The commissioner again ruled that Ms. Dahl had failed to provide sufficient evidence to support an alimony award under Utah law. . . . When the district court reviewed and ruled on the commissioner's recommendation, Ms. Dahl had still not complied with the commissioner's order for a financial declaration, and the district court therefore adopted the commissioner's findings. . . .

Nearly a year after the divorce petition had been filed, Ms. Dahl filed another motion for temporary alimony, accompanied by a new affidavit. . . . Again, there was no supporting documentation for this amount. One day prior to the hearing on the motion, Ms. Dahl submitted a notice of errata to her affidavit, which finally, after a year of litigation, included a copy of a rent check, other checks written for unknown purposes, utility bills, and past-due medical bills. These bills totaled $2,651.78.

At the hearing the next day, the commissioner treated this second motion for temporary alimony as a motion to reconsider the court's prior rulings that no temporary alimony was warranted. . . . The district court ultimately adopted the commissioner's recommendation [and] found that "[Ms. Dahl's] [c]ounsel was previously permitted to re-file this Motion several times" but each time had failed to include the necessary supporting documents.

. . . In this case, although Dr. Dahl submitted sufficient evidence to the court to demonstrate his ability to pay alimony, Ms. Dahl's counsel repeatedly failed to comply with the district court's order to supply the court with documentation . . . . Instead of supplying the court with the requested documentation, Ms. Dahl submitted a new declaration, requesting over $40,000 in monthly alimony. . . . And because Ms. Dahl's counsel again provided no evidence to substantiate Ms. Dahl's alleged monthly expenses or earning ability, the district court appropriately denied her request for temporary alimony. . . .

2. The District Court Did Not Abuse Its Discretion in Denying Ms. Dahl's Request for Permanent Alimony

Ms. Dahl next . . . asserts that the district court abused its discretion when it denied her request for permanent alimony. We disagree. . . .

As the party seeking an award of permanent alimony, Ms. Dahl bore the burden of providing the district court with sufficient credible evidence of each factor listed in the Alimony Statute. . . . She provided no financial declaration, no supporting financial documentation, and no expert testimony. . . . We therefore conclude that Ms. Dahl failed to meet her burden of showing her financial need — a necessary prerequisite to an award of permanent alimony.

. . . Any harm Ms. Dahl may have suffered by receiving no permanent alimony was not a result of error on the part of the district court, but instead was due to her counsel's failure to present the evidence necessary to support an award of permanent alimony.[23]

Post-Case Follow-Up

The Utah Supreme Court emphasized that understanding and complying with procedural rules and requirements, including pretrial disclosure of evidence, "are basic skills that we expect all attorneys to possess." Yet, as *Dahl v. Dahl* exemplifies, not all attorneys in fact possess such skills and their clients suffer from such incompetence. Reading, double-checking, and staying current on revisions to and interpretations of procedural rules are all essential to a competent practice. Comment 1 to Rule 1.1 advises lawyers to "maintain the requisite knowledge and skill" for their practice, "to keep abreast of changes in the law and its practice," and to "engage in continuing legal education requirements to which the lawyer is subject."

Dahl v. Dahl: Real Life Applications

1. What, if anything, could Ms. Dahl have done to protect her interests in this case? Could she have fired her attorney during trial once it was clear he had not properly prepared the expert reports or the pretrial disclosures?

2. Madison is an attorney who is filing a claim on behalf of George against the estate of Samuel Zuckerman. Letters testamentary were issued on October 25, 2014. Madison files the claims against the estate on October 15, 2015. Under state law, all claims against the estate are subject to a one-year statute of limitations from the date the letters testamentary are issued. Madison has the executrix served

23. To the extent these deficiencies are due to the negligence of Ms. Dahl's counsel, her remedy lies in a civil action for malpractice. But attorney negligence does not provide a basis for us to sidestep the legal standard that our statutes and case law prescribe for alimony determinations.

on November 5, 2015. Assume that the law of the state requires that service on the executrix must take place to satisfy the statute of limitations. Can Madison obtain relief from the statute by arguing that she misread or misunderstood the statute of limitations and honestly believed that all she had to do was file the complaint within the year? Can George, Madison's client, argue that the statute of limitations should not bar his claim because George relied on his attorney to understand and follow the rules?

2. Inexperienced Lawyers

According to comment 2 to Rule 1.1, "[a] newly admitted lawyer can be as competent as a practitioner with long experience." This is so because, as noted, many legal problems require the same basic legal skills. In deciding whether an attorney can competently undertake a representation, comment 1 identifies several factors for consideration: "the relative complexity and specialized nature of the matter, the lawyer's general experience, the lawyer's training and experience in the field in question, the preparation and study the lawyer is able to give the matter and whether it is feasible to refer the matter to, or associate or consult with, a lawyer of established competence in the field in question." Comment 2 further indicates that for an inexperienced attorney—one undertaking a case in a wholly novel field—the requisite competence can be obtained in one of two ways: (1) through necessary study and preparation; and/or (2) through association with an attorney of established competence.

Case Preview

Attorney Grievance Commission of Maryland v. Kendrick

Karin Kendrick was a close personal friend of Judith Kerr and was appointed a co-personal representative of Kerr's estate, along with Kerr's brother. Although Kendrick apparently sincerely believed that her legal assistance would benefit her friend's estate, Kendrick was not experienced in probate matters. She committed numerous missteps causing the small estate to be open from 1999 until 2007.

As you read through *Kendrick*, consider the following:

1. What could and should Kendrick have done once it became clear that she lacked the knowledge and skill to handle the estate?
2. How important is it for an attorney to engage in candid self-evaluation to recognize and admit her own lack of knowledge or skill? At what point in a case should an attorney stop stubbornly insisting that she can handle a matter when she actually lacks the competence to do so?

Attorney Grievance Commission of Maryland v. Kendrick

943 A.2d 1173 (Md. 2008)

...

Respondent [] excepts to the hearing judge's conclusion that she violated Rule 1.1 (Competence). Respondent claims that her "alleged failure to file [the] Third and Final Administration Account . . . is due to the fact that Respondent . . . has been continually harassed by the Orphans' Court [and its] failure to give Respondent . . . notice and due process." . . .

Respondent's exception does not address the underlying reasoning for the hearing judge's conclusion that she violated Rule 1.1 (Competence), except to complain about her treatment by the Orphans' Court. The hearing judge concluded that Respondent's handling of the Estate violated Rule 1.1 because "despite the eight years of problems that she ha[d] been experiencing with several courts in administering this Estate, [ ] Respondent refuse[d] to admit her ignorance of the probate procedures involved or to seek and accept help from qualified legal professionals in getting her problems solved." The hearing judge found that "[h]er stubbornness over the past eight years to find the guidance necessary to close the Estate amounts to incompetence." The record clearly supports the hearing judge's conclusion. The record shows that Judith Nina Kerr died on February 27, 1999. According to the records of the Register of Wills of Baltimore County, the Estate, valued at approximately $60,000, was not closed until December 20, 2007. Those findings indicate 8 years, 9 months and 23 days had lapsed from the date of Ms. Kerr's death until the closing of her Estate. . . .

Moreover, the record shows that Respondent failed to timely file many of the documents necessary to administer the Estate, leading to her removal as Co-Personal Representative. Pursuant to §7-201, Respondent and/or Mr. Kerr had the duty to file an Inventory with the Register of Wills within three months after their appointments as Co-Personal Representatives. On June 11, 1999, the Orphans' Court issued a Delinquent Notice to Mr. Kerr and Respondent for their failure to file an Inventory and Information Report. Thereafter, a summons and a request for show cause order was issued to the Sheriff of Baltimore County to "cite and summons" Respondent to appear before the Orphans' Court to explain why the Inventory had not been filed as of July 13, 1999. On July 26, 1999, Respondent filed the required Inventory.

On December 10, 1999, the Orphans' Court issued a Delinquent Notice to Mr. Kerr and Respondent for their failure to render and file a First Administration Account for the Estate. Pursuant to §7-305(a)(1), Respondent and Mr. Kerr were required to render an account of the Estate within 9 months of their appointment, on or before December 4, 1999. In response to the notice, Respondent requested two extensions, which were granted; however, a second Delinquent Notice was then issued on February 18, 2000, when Respondent did not comply with the extended deadline. A hearing on the delinquency was then scheduled for March 8, 2000; neither Respondent nor Mr. Kerr appeared for that hearing. On March 9, 2000, the Orphans' Court issued a summons and a request for show cause order was issued to the Sheriff of Baltimore County to "cite and summons" Respondent and Mr. Kerr to appear before the Orphans' Court to explain why the First Administration Account had not been filed as of February 11, 2000. Respondent and Mr. Kerr did not file the "First, Not Final Administration Account" with the Register of Wills until April 10, 2000.

The Orphans' Court's issuance of Delinquent Notices and Summonses continued throughout the administration of the Estate. [The court lists several instances through the issuance of a *sixth* Delinquent Notice for failing to make requisite filings.] . . .

Despite repeated interactions with the Register of Wills and the Orphans' Court regarding Respondent's and Mr. Kerr's tardiness in filing the documents, Respondent and Mr. Kerr did not seek assistance in the administration of the Estate. Consequently, on May 3, 2002, a petition to remove Respondent and Mr. Kerr as Co-Personal Representatives was initiated by the Orphans' Court because of Respondent's and Mr. Kerr's failure to file a Supplemental Inventory, a Supplemental Information Report, and a Third Administration Account. The petition was granted and the Court removed Respondent and Mr. Kerr as Co-Personal Representatives of the Estate on August 28, 2002. The Order mandated that Respondent and Mr. Kerr file the "Third and Final Administration Account" and turn over all assets and financial records in their possession within thirty days of the date of the Order. Despite this significant action, Respondent failed to file the Third and Final Administration Account within the 30 day time-limit prescribed by the order of the Orphans' Court, leading to additional court interactions including the imposition of Civil Contempt by the Orphans' Court on June 2, 2005.

It is clear from the record that Respondent's failure to properly comply with probate law in the administration of the Estate was due to her inexperience and her unwillingness to obtain the help she needed to properly administer the estate. As the hearing judge stated in his analysis, "inexperience does not necessarily amount to a violation of this Rule." We have said, however, that attorneys who undertake legal work in areas unfamiliar to them "must take careful thought as to their competence to practice in 'specialty' areas," like the administration of estates. If an attorney "plunges into a field in which he or she is not competent, and as a consequence makes mistakes that demonstrate incompetence, the Code [of Professional Responsibility] demands that discipline be imposed; that one is simply a general practitioner who knew no better is no defense." *Brown*, 308 Md. at 234-35. . . .

It is clear that Respondent did not employ the requisite knowledge and skill to administer the Estate or to comply with the Orphans' Court's orders. . . .

Post-Case Follow-Up

As indicated in *Kendrick* and Model Rule 1.1 comment 2, "[a] lawyer can provide adequate representation in a wholly novel field through necessary study" or "through association of a lawyer of established competence in the field." Importantly, though, the lawyer cannot charge her client for the extra time taken to educate herself to become competent. For example, in In re Fordham, 668 N.E.2d 816 (Mass. 1996), the Massachusetts Supreme Judicial Court explained:

> It cannot be that an inexperienced lawyer is entitled to charge three or four times as much as an experienced lawyer for the same service. A client should not be expected to pay for the education of a lawyer when he spends excessive amounts of time on tasks which, with reasonable experience, become matters of routine.

Attorney Grievance Commission of Maryland v. Kendrick: *Real Life Applications*

1. Maria is a brand new attorney who decides to start her own practice. A potential client, JaNeal, calls Maria and says that she's been sued in a case. After consulting briefly, JaNeal tells Maria she wants to hire her and to please appear on her behalf in the case. Maria has no idea how to make an appearance. She researches appearances for a few hours, and then drafts an appearance and files it. The appearance she files is compliant with all laws and local rules; however, an experienced attorney normally spends less than five minutes preparing an appearance. Can Maria competently continue with the representation? If so, can she charge JaNeal for the time she actually spent on making an appearance in the case?

2. Robert is a criminal defense attorney who is asked by Eugene to represent him in a civil contract dispute. Robert has not done any civil litigation in the 15 years that he's been practicing law. Eugene does not have much money to spend and does not want Robert to spend too much time on the case. Robert thinks that he remembers civil procedure from law school pretty well. The opposing party files a lengthy motion for summary judgment. Robert decides that since Eugene has denied the allegations in his Answer, summary judgment is not appropriate and—just as when his criminal clients plead not guilty—Eugene will be entitled to a trial based on Eugene's pleading. The court grants summary judgment for the opposing party and against Eugene on all claims, explaining that in civil litigation, the non-movant cannot rest on the allegations of his pleadings but must produce evidence showing there is a genuine issue for trial. What should Robert have done differently? What two basic options did he have?

---

3. Thoroughness and Preparation

Under Model Rule 1.1, competence requires "thoroughness and preparation." Lawyers have a duty to undertake preparations reasonable to the case, including obtaining the requisite factual information regarding a case. As Monroe Freedman and Abbe Smith expound: "Competent representation requires that a lawyer be 'fully informed of all the facts of the matter he is handling.'"[3] Thus, lawyers must thoroughly investigate the facts of a case and make sufficient preparation for

3. Monroe H. Freedman & Abbe Smith, Understanding Lawyers' Ethics 128 (4th ed. 2010) (quoting UpJohn Co. v. United States, 449 U.S. 383, 391 (1981)).

legal proceedings and transactions. Numerous disciplinary proceedings have been brought against lawyers who proverbially dropped the ball and "failed to discover and present readily available evidence supporting" their client's case or "failed to prepare" necessary documentation, briefing, or other materials for court proceedings or transactions.[4]

In some situations, lawyers agree to limit the scope of their representation pursuant to Rule 1.2. Nevertheless, the duty of competence still applies. Thus, in In re Seare, 493 B.R. 198 (Bankr. D. Nev. 2013), the court explained:

> Whether a lawyer fulfilled the duty of competence depends on the client's objectives. The lawyer's duty is to competently attain the client's goals of representation. In the absence of a valid limitation on services, a lawyer *must provide the bundle of services that are reasonably necessary to achieve the client's reasonably anticipated result*, unless and until grounds exist for the lawyer's withdrawal. . . . [T]he duty of competence both informs and survives any and all limitations on the scope of services. The *baseline obligation to inquire into the facts and circumstances of a case and analyze the possible legal issues* is not changed when the scope of services is limited.

A lawyer's failure to thoroughly prepare a matter can have disastrous consequences for the client. Consider what the lack of preparation of pretrial disclosures and expert reports cost Ms. Dahl. Another example occurred in Albrechtsen v. Board of Regents of the University of Wisconsin, 309 F.3d 433 (7th Cir. 2002). Professor Albrechtsen prevailed in a jury trial on a Title VII claim against his employer, the University of Wisconsin. The university filed an appeal to the Seventh Circuit, arguing that there was insufficient evidence to support the jury verdict. Notably, the university had a very difficult hurdle to overcome in order to prevail on its appeal—as it was trying to vacate a jury verdict as a matter of law. Conversely, Albrechtsen's lawyer had a very easy burden on appeal—all he had to do was marshal enough evidence introduced at trial to show that there was a sufficient basis in evidence to support the jury's verdict. Nevertheless, Albrechtsen's lawyer failed to include a statement of facts with citations to the trial transcript in his brief. Instead, "the half-page portion of the brief captioned 'Statement of Facts'" simply referred the Seventh Circuit to examine "the district court's opinion denying the University's motion for summary judgment." The Seventh Circuit explained that this was entirely unacceptable because the summary judgment order (entered before a trial was held) contained no cites to the record at trial or summation of the evidence admitted at trial. Instead, the order simply summarized pretrial discovery showing that there were genuine issues of fact necessitating a trial. The Seventh Circuit concluded, "Albrechtsen has effectively provided no statement of facts at all." Consequently, in ruling on the appeal, the Seventh Circuit said that it would treat Albrechtsen's "silence as assent to the [university's] presentation" of the facts. At oral argument, the appellate court gave Albrechtsen's counsel another opportunity, asking him to identify the evidence admitted at trial that would support the jury verdict. Albrechtsen's lawyer's response was disheartening and betrayed his lack

---

4. People v. Boyle, 942 P.2d 1199 (Colo. 1997).

of preparation: "The entire record." The Seventh Circuit explained: "That will not do . . . . Courts are entitled to assistance from counsel, and an invitation to search without guidance is no more useful than a litigant's request to a district court at the summary judgment stage to paw through the assembled discovery material. Judges are not like pigs, hunting for truffles buried in the record." The Seventh Circuit ruled in favor of the university and overturned Albrechtsen's jury verdict.

Albrechtsen's lawyer did not prepare for the appeal. He should have taken the time to prepare a thorough statement of facts with citations to the trial transcript and other evidence admitted at trial. He did not know the trial record at all—at oral argument he could not pinpoint a single piece of evidence or testimony from trial that would support the verdict and thereby preserve his client's jury victory. Thoroughness indicates that lawyers should not take unwarranted shortcuts. The decision of Albrechtsen's counsel to incorporate the trial court's summary judgment order rather than take the time to read the trial transcript, examine the admitted evidence, and then marshal and present that evidence in a statement of facts (with citations) was a devastating shortcut for Albrechtsen. It cost him a jury verdict and award of nearly $150,000, handing his victory to the opposing party.

4. Competence and Technology

Technological advances have made significant changes to the ways in which lawyers practice law—including in how they communicate with clients and maintain client files. What level of technological competence is required of attorneys? Comment 8 to Model Rule 1.1 explains: "To maintain the requisite knowledge and skill, a lawyer should keep abreast of changes in the law and its practice, including the benefits and risks associated with relevant technology."

A number of jurisdictions have examined whether attorneys should use cloud computing and storage and, correspondingly, what steps attorneys should take to remain competent in the use of such technologies to protect client communications and confidences. The use of cloud computing has become nearly ubiquitous. As the Pennsylvania Bar Association summarized, "[i]f an attorney uses a Smartphone or an iPhone, or uses web-based electronic mail (e-mail) such as Gmail, Yahoo!, Hotmail or AOL Mail, or uses products such as Google Docs, Microsoft Office 365 or Dropbox, the attorney is using 'cloud computing.'"[5] What are the obligations of attorneys who use these now common technologies in their practice? The California bar has opined:

> Many attorneys, as with a large contingent of the general public, do not possess much, if any, technological savvy. Although the Committee does not believe that attorneys must develop a mastery of the security features and deficiencies of each technology

5. Pennsylvania Bar Association Committee on Legal Ethics and Professional Responsibility, Formal Op. 2011-200, *Ethical Obligations for Attorneys Using Cloud Computing/Software as a Service While Fulfilling the Duties of Confidentiality and Preservation of Client Property*, *available at* https://www.pabar.org/members/catalogs/Ethics%20Opinions/formal/F2011-200.pdf.

> available, the duties of confidentiality and competence that attorneys owe to their clients do require a basic understanding of the electronic protections afforded by the technology they use in their practice. If the attorney lacks the necessary competence to assess the security of the technology, he or she *must seek additional information or consult with someone who possesses the necessary knowledge*, such as an information technology consultant.[6]

This approach is entirely consistent with Rule 1.1's basic tenet that attorneys must obtain competence either through necessary study or through association with one who is competent.

Use of Cloud Computing Services

Ohio State Bar Association Informal Advisory Opinion 2013-03

The "cloud" is "merely 'a fancy way of saying stuff's not on your [own] computer.'" More formally, cloud storage is the use of "internet-based computing in which large groups of remote servers are networked so as to allow . . . centralized data storage."

Due to "recent advances in . . . technology, the ways attorneys are able to perform and deliver legal services have drastically changed." The applicable Ohio Rules of Professional Conduct, however, are adaptable to address new technologies. Regarding cloud storage, the key rules are those relating to competent representation, communicating with the client, preserving client confidentiality, safeguarding the client's property and supervising nonlawyers that provide support services. The obligations expressed in these rules operate as they traditionally have for older data storage methods. . . .

This approach—applying existing principles to new technological advances while refraining from mandating specific practices—is a practical one. Because technology changes so quickly, overly-specific rules would become obsolete as soon as they were issued. For example, rules about exactly what security measures are required in order to protect client data stored in the cloud would be superseded quickly by technological advances.

Against that background, there are four main issues to consider in applying the Ohio Rules of Professional Conduct to cloud storage of client data: competently selecting an appropriate vendor; preserving confidentiality and safeguarding the client's data; supervising cloud storage vendors; and communicating with the client.

1. COMPETENTLY SELECTING AN APPROPRIATE VENDOR FOR CLOUD STORAGE

The duty of competence under ORPC 1.1 requires a lawyer to exercise the "legal knowledge, skill, thoroughness, and preparation reasonably necessary for the

6. State Bar of California Standing Committee on Professional Responsibility and Conduct, Formal Op. No. 2010-179, *available at* http://ethics.calbar.ca.gov/LinkClick.aspx?fileticket=wmqECiHp7h4%3D&tabid=836 (emphasis added).

representation." In Ohio Advisory Opinion 2009-6 (Aug. 14, 2009), the Ohio Board of Commissioners on Grievances and Discipline ("Board") opined that a lawyer who selects a vendor for any type of support services that are provided outside the lawyer's firm must exercise "due diligence as to the qualifications and reputation of those to whom services are outsourced," and also as to whether the outside vendor will itself provide the requested services competently and diligently.

Knowing the qualifications, reputation and longevity of your cloud storage vendor is necessary. But in addition, just as you would review and assess the terms of a contract for off-site storage of your clients' paper files in a brick-and-mortar facility, so you must read and understand the agreement you enter into with an online data storage service — sometimes called a "Service Level Agreement." Some commonly-occurring issues include:

- What safeguards does the vendor have to prevent confidentiality breaches?
- Does the agreement create a legally enforceable obligation on the vendor's part to safeguard the confidentiality of the data?
- Do the terms of the agreement purport to give "ownership" of the data to the vendor, or is the data merely subject to the vendor's license?
- How may the vendor respond to government or judicial attempts to obtain disclosure of your client data?
- What is the vendor's policy regarding returning your client data at the termination of its relationship with your firm?
- What plans and procedures does the vendor have in case of natural disaster, electric power interruption or other catastrophic events?
- Where is the server located (particularly if the vendor itself does not actually host the data, and uses a data center located elsewhere)? Is the relationship subject to international law?

2. PRESERVING CONFIDENTIALITY AND SAFEGUARDING CLIENT PROPERTY

Under ORPC 1.6(a), a lawyer "shall not reveal information relating to the representation of a client," with only limited exceptions. . . . [T]he ABA House of Delegates added Model Rule 1.6(c) in August 2012, requiring a lawyer to make "reasonable efforts to prevent the inadvertent or unauthorized disclosure of, or unauthorized access to, information relating to the representation of a client." . . .

[And] in Advisory Opinion 99-2 . . . the Board said that communicating with clients by e-mail was covered by the confidentiality rule . . . . "The duty extends to communications by electronic methods just as it extends to other forms of communication used by an attorney." . . .

. . . [S]toring client data in the cloud involves yielding exclusive control over the information and puts it in the hands of a third party, just as storing a client's paper files off-site does. And similar to storing a client's paper files off-site, cloud storage raises the risk that "a third party could illegally gain access to . . . confidential client data." . . . Therefore, a lawyer's duty under the ORPC to preserve the confidentiality of cloud-stored client data is to exercise competence (1) in selecting an appropriate vendor, (2) in staying abreast of technology issues that have an impact on client data storage and (3) in considering whether any special circumstances call for extra protection for particularly sensitive client information or for refraining from using the cloud to store such particularly sensitive data. . . .

3. SUPERVISING CLOUD VENDORS

. . . [U]nder Rule 5.3(a)-(b), lawyers who contract with a cloud-storage vendor must make reasonable efforts to ensure that the vendor's conduct is compatible with the lawyer's own professional obligations.

While the extent of supervision needed is a matter of professional judgment for the lawyer, the lawyer must exercise due diligence in ascertaining whether the vendor will be capable of conduct consistent with the lawyer's own obligations.

4. COMMUNICATING WITH THE CLIENT

Rule 1.4(a)(2) requires a lawyer to "reasonably consult with the client" about how the client's objectives are to be accomplished. We do not conclude that storing client data in "the cloud" always requires prior client consultation, because we interpret the language "reasonably consult" as indicating that the lawyer must use judgment in order to determine if the circumstances call for consultation. . . . In exercising judgment about whether to consult with the client about storing client data in "the cloud," the lawyer should consider, among other things, the sensitivity of the client's data.

5. ETHICS OPINIONS FROM OTHER JURISDICTIONS REGARDING CLOUD STORAGE

Our conclusion that cloud storage is permissible under the ORPC is echoed by ethics authorities in other jurisdictions. To date, at least 14 states have issued ethics opinions regarding or related to cloud data storage. All have concluded that their respective lawyer conduct rules permit lawyers to store client data in the cloud, with due regard for their state ethics rules, usually their states' versions of ORPC 1.1, 1.6, 1.15 and 5.3. . . .

5. Diligence

Model Rule 1.3 requires lawyers to "act with reasonable diligence and promptness in representing a client." Diligence requires that the lawyer pursue a client's case "despite opposition, obstruction or personal inconvenience to the lawyer, and take whatever lawful and ethical measures are required to vindicate a client's cause or endeavor." *See* Model Rule 1.1 cmt. 1. The very nature of our adversarial system of justice creates a likelihood of unfairness when only one side in a controversy has counsel or only one side has competent and diligent counsel. Attorneys can improve the quality of justice both by representing people regardless of any opposition or personal inconvenience (including taking unpopular cases and performing pro bono representation) and also by fully and diligently pursuing their own client's interests, thus ensuring that their clients are not put at a disadvantage.

As noted in comment 2, in order to be diligent, lawyers must control their workload so that they are able to competently handle each and every case. When an attorney is an associate or other employee whose caseload is assigned by another, this requirement may be more difficult. Subordinate lawyers must communicate with senior and assigning lawyers if their caseload is more than they can realistically handle competently. Similarly, public defenders and other public employee lawyers may have less ability to control their caseload, but they still can take actions to protect their clients' interests, as will be addressed later in this chapter.

As comment 3 cautions, "[p]erhaps no professional shortcoming is more widely resented than procrastination." Why is this so? The comment explains: "A client's interests often can be adversely affected by the passage of time or the change of conditions; in extreme instances, as when a lawyer overlooks a statute of limitations, the client's legal position may be destroyed." Even where procrastination doesn't directly impact a client's rights, "unreasonable delay can cause a client needless anxiety." *See* Model Rule 1.3 cmt. 3. In Shakespeare's famous "To be or not to be" soliloquy, Hamlet lists reasons that would make a person want to commit suicide ("not to be"), and among them is "the law's delay."[7] Legal processes generally take far more time than clients expect even where an attorney acts promptly, with diligence and competence. When attorneys do not act diligently, cases will languish — along with the client.

Case Preview

In re Disciplinary Action Against Howe

Sometimes clients actually want to delay a proceeding. For example, a client may wish to delay proceedings that could lead to time in jail, deportation, or other serious personal consequences. A client may want evidence that is adverse to him to become stale. In the following case, attorney Henry Howe represented the Camachos, a couple who were undocumented immigrants faced with deportation even though they had lived in the United States for over 20 years and had four children who were United States citizens. Howe claimed to have engaged in a dilatory strategy to keep the Camachos in the United States for as long as possible.

As you read *Howe*, consider the following:

1. Was Howe's alleged strategy of delay helpful to his clients?
2. Even if a client wants to delay proceedings, should the lawyer engage in tactics solely for the purpose of delay?

---

7. William Shakespeare, Hamlet, act 3, sc. 1 ("For who would bear the whips and scorns of time, The oppressor's wrong, the proud man's contumely, The pangs of despised love, the law's delay, The insolence of office and the spurns That patient merit of the unworthy takes, When he himself might his quietus make With a bare bodkin?").

In re Disciplinary Action Against Howe

843 N.W.2d 325 (N.D. 2014)

Attorney Henry H. Howe objected to a report of a hearing panel of the Disciplinary Board . . . . We order that Howe be suspended from the practice of law for six months and one day, [and] that he pay $8,871.34 in costs of the disciplinary proceedings . . . .

This proceeding arises from Howe's representation of Elias Angel Camacho-Banda and Margarita Maya-Morales (collectively "Camachos"). The Camachos, undocumented Mexican nationals, have lived in the United States for over twenty years. The Camachos have four United States citizen children and one Mexican citizen child. Subsequent to a February 2007 traffic incident, authorities discovered the Camacho adults and one child did not have legal immigration status. The Camachos were placed in removal proceedings before the Executive Office for Immigration Review, Immigration Court, in Bloomington, Minnesota. The Camachos retained Howe to represent them in the removal proceedings.

During the immigration court's May 16, 2007, master calendar hearing, Howe conceded the Camachos were removable for staying in the United States past the time permitted and stated he would file their applications for cancellation of removal and adjustment of status. To prevail in canceling removal, the Camachos needed to establish removal would result in "exceptional and extremely unusual hardship to the alien's . . . child, who is a citizen of the United States" under 8 U.S.C. §1229b(b)(1)(D). The immigration judge informed Howe he needed significant documentation of hardship, including documentation of one child's alleged learning disability. On May 16, 2007, Howe received an information sheet for gathering "biometrics," which explained the process for collecting fingerprints and personal information as required at immigration proceedings before final status decisions are made. Howe did not file the applications for cancellation of removal until November 21, 2008.

A merits hearing was held on December 1, 2008. Howe had not completed the biometrics process, including failing to obtain the Camachos' fingerprints. When asked why he did not complete the biometrics process, Howe blamed a calendaring error by his paralegal. Howe did not provide the hardship documentation requested by the judge, instead supplying only the children's school records. Further, the Camachos were the only witnesses called. The immigration judge chastised Howe for being unprepared, but allowed him thirty days to augment the Camachos' application for cancellation of removal. In addition to the clarification Howe already received on May 16, 2007, regarding supplemental materials the judge sought, the judge directed Howe to augment the file concerning the Camachos' son's learning disability, including letters from teachers and doctors and information regarding the special educational prospects in Mexico for a child with a learning disability.

The merits hearing was rescheduled for January 13, 2009. The Camachos were not present at the hearing because Howe failed to notify them of the rescheduled hearing. . . . The judge agreed to reschedule the merits hearing from January 13, 2009, to October 21, 2009, warning Howe that if the Camachos again failed to appear, he would issue a removal order in their absence. . . .

Before the rescheduled merits hearing, Howe resubmitted duplicate documents, including country conditions and school records. Howe's submission was rejected for failing to comply with filing requirements. Howe attempted to fix the issues by resending his submission. The court noted that all the documents still were improperly submitted, but that it would nonetheless accept them. On April 23, 2010, Howe submitted additional articles about violence in Mexico, offered to demonstrate hardship. The Camachos' merits hearing was rescheduled to April 8, 2011. Howe obtained letters from the Camacho children's teachers, including a letter from the special education teacher and case manager for the child with the learning disability. Howe argues that while he possessed the letters, in his opinion the letters would not have helped meet the exceptional and extremely unusual hardship standard and possibly could have made things worse.

On April 8, 2011, Howe and the Camachos appeared at the rescheduled merits hearing, but because an interpreter was not available, the judge reserved the case for written submissions and closing arguments to be submitted within two weeks. Howe did not provide additional materials or submit written closing arguments. On November 15, 2011, the judge ordered the Camachos deported to Mexico. Howe was discharged, and the Camachos retained new counsel.

. . .

Rule 1.3, N.D.R. Prof. Conduct, provides that "[a] lawyer shall act with reasonable diligence and promptness in representing a client." Reasonable diligence is defined as: "A fair degree of diligence expected from someone of ordinary prudence under circumstances like those at issue." Black's Law Dictionary 468 (7th ed. 1999). Prompt is defined as: "quick to act or to do what is required[.]" Webster's New World Dictionary 1137 (2nd ed. 1980). "Perhaps no professional shortcoming is more widely resented than procrastination." N.D.R. Prof. Conduct 1.3 cmt. 3.

Howe failed to diligently represent the Camachos in several ways. While Howe paid the biometrics fee and filed the biometrics forms, he did not obtain the Camachos' fingerprints and, therefore, did not complete the biometrics process before the merits hearing. The judge cannot make a decision regarding the Camachos' legal status in the United States until their updated criminal background information is obtained. . . . Even after the judge admonished Howe at the December 1, 2008 hearing to complete biometrics, Howe did not make an appointment for the Camachos to be fingerprinted before the January 13, 2009 merits hearing. Howe blamed a calendaring error to excuse his unpreparedness regarding the biometrics information, but he had more than a month to obtain the fingerprints, or at least make an appointment, before the January 13, 2009 hearing. Howe also failed to timely submit the applications for cancellation of removal. Howe stated on May 16, 2007 that he would file the Camachos' applications for cancellation of removal, yet he waited until November 21, 2008 to file the applications. The result was that the applications were filed just days before the merits hearing on December 1, 2008.

Howe also failed to communicate with his clients concerning important hearing dates, causing them to miss their January 13, 2009 merits hearing. Howe first blamed the communication failure on a change in office personnel. He later testified he spoke with the Camachos concerning the hearing date, but that a miscommunication occurred because the Camachos' daughter who usually translated was not present.

Howe's arguments blaming his paralegal and changes in office personnel are to no avail because he is responsible for ensuring his nonlawyer staff's conduct comports with his professional obligations as an attorney under Rule 5.3(b), N.D.R. Prof. Conduct.

We conclude clear and convincing evidence establishes that Howe did not meet the diligence requirements for the Camachos' case and that he violated Rule 1.3, N.D.R. Prof. Conduct.

. . .

Howe argues in his objection to the hearing panel's recommendations and in his briefing to this Court that his three-part strategy was disregarded, ignored or not understood. Howe's three-part strategy for the Camachos included petitioning for cancellation of removal by showing exceptional and extremely unusual hardship, taking necessary steps to protect the status and assets of the Camacho family and keeping the Camachos in the United States for as long as possible.

Although Rule 3.2, N.D.R. Prof. Conduct, was not included by the disciplinary counsel in its petition for discipline, Howe's arguments implicate Rule 3.2, providing: "A lawyer shall make reasonable efforts to expedite litigation consistent with the interests of the client." "The question is whether a competent lawyer acting in good faith would regard the course of action as having some substantial purpose other than delay." N.D.R. Prof. Conduct 3.2 cmt. 2. Howe's argument that he sought delay at any cost for his clients is legally untenable under Rule 3.2 because a competent and diligent immigration lawyer would not seek delay by purposely failing to timely file documents requested by the judge, and would not refrain from telling clients about hearing dates in the hopes trial would be postponed. A competent and diligent lawyer would not do these things because the judge is not required to show lenience for failure to follow requirements, and lawyers can never predict how a judge will react to such failures. Despite noting Howe's unpreparedness at the December 1, 2008 hearing, the immigration judge allowed thirty extra days to augment the file. Despite Howe failing to tell the Camachos of the rescheduled merits hearing, the immigration judge showed lenience and rescheduled the merits hearing rather than immediately issuing a removal order in their absence. Further, the immigration court showed lenience with Howe's inability or unwillingness to follow document submission requirements. The Camachos are still in the United States and in the appeal process for nothing but the grace of the immigration court judge, rather than due to Howe's alleged strategy.

Howe's arguments on review fail . . . . The numerous egregious risks Howe took during his representation of the Camachos are dispositive. Clear and convincing evidence establishes he violated Rules 1.1, 1.3 and 1.4, N.D.R. Prof. Conduct.

Post-Case Follow-Up

In disciplining Howe under Rule 1.3, the court also invoked Rule 3.2, requiring "reasonable efforts to expedite litigation consistent with the interests of the client." As comment 1 to that rule explains, acting solely to delay proceedings is not permissible under the rule: "Nor will a failure to expedite be reasonable if done for the purpose of frustrating an opposing party's attempt to obtain rightful redress or repose." As the court in *Howe* noted, "[t]he question is whether a competent lawyer acting in good faith would regard the course of action as having some substantial purpose other than delay." Notably, the comment clarifies that such client interests cannot be the realization of "financial or other benefit *from* otherwise improper delay."

In re Disciplinary Action Against Howe: Real Life Applications

1. Janet is representing Devon as a defendant in a personal injury lawsuit. The discovery deadline is March 31. Janet does not know if she will want to do discovery yet or not, but neither she nor her client wants to proceed to trial. Her client, Devon, is hoping to sell some real estate before a potential judgment is entered adverse to him. Thus, Janet files a motion with the court to obtain a 60-day extension of time for the discovery deadline, arguing that she needs more time to conduct discovery, including specific depositions. Over the plaintiff's objection, the court grants the 60-day extension. Janet does not conduct any discovery during the 60 days, but her client is able to sell his real estate and is very pleased with the delay. Has Janet violated the rules?
2. Suppose that you represent Sara in a divorce proceeding from her husband, Ray. Sara indicates to you that she is actually thinking of reconciling and asks you to proceed as slowly as possible while she considers reconciliation. Consequently, you ask the court for several extensions of time on various motions (which are granted), with the primary purpose of delaying the proceedings. Ultimately, however, Sara decides to go through with the divorce. Have you violated the rules?

---

6. Communication

In the animated sitcom "King of the Hill," Peggy Hill, the wife of the protagonist, Hank Hill, asks a neighbor how to improve her marriage, but adds the caveat, "And don't say 'communicate,' because there are some things Hank just will not do." Of course, the joke is that communication is essential to maintaining good relationships with people. And communication is particularly important for successful attorney-client relationships. As Eli Wald has observed:

> Communications between clients and attorneys are the cornerstone of the attorney-client relationship. Because the vast majority of civil and criminal trials settle and plea-bargain, respectively, many clients never actually enter the courtroom, interact with a judge or a jury, or meet the opposing party or its attorney. Consequently, for a good number of Americans, communicating with their own lawyers will constitute most, if not all, of their exposure to law and the legal system. Communications between clients and their own attorneys thus become the main arena in which clients gain any experience with lawyers and the law.[8]

---

8. Eli Wald, *Taking Attorney-Client Communications (and Therefore Clients) Seriously*, 42 U.S.F. L. Rev. 747, 747-48 (2008).

A lawyer's communication with a client is the method whereby a client knows what is going on in her lawsuit—and for many clients a lawsuit implicates intimately important personal interests that weigh heavily and constantly on the client's mind (think of criminal charges, housing, child custody, employment, medical benefits, disability, social security, probate, etc.). Melvin Hirshman, as Bar Counsel for the Maryland Attorney Grievance Commission, urged lawyers to "'step into your client's shoes' and realize how important their legal matter is to them." Hirshman contends that "[e]ven the delivery of bad news is better than no news if that be the case"; rather, "[i]t is the unknown that causes anxiety [] for many clients." Thus, he concludes: "It is not too much to require an attorney to communicate with a client, truthfully and promptly."[9]

In addition to the client's need to hear from the attorney about her case, it is critically important for the attorney to hear from and communicate with the client in order for the attorney to ascertain the client's objectives. Again, Wald observes:

> [T]he attorney-client relationship is an agency relationship in which a lawyer-agent serves the interests of a client-principal. Communications are the mechanism by which the client controls the agency relationship, informs the attorney about his goals and objectives, and provides the lawyer with necessary and relevant information about the representation. Successful representation requires effective communications, without which the attorney-agent cannot know, understand, or represent the client's goals.[10]

The client is also the primary source for obtaining the facts of a case. Lawyers simply must communicate with clients to effectively represent the client and appropriately pursue the client's actual interests and goals. Thus, Model Rule 1.4(b) requires lawyers to "explain a matter to the extent reasonably necessary to permit the client to make informed decisions regarding the representation." How much information does the client need? Comment 5 provides a guideline: the client needs "sufficient information to participate intelligently" in making decisions regarding the representation. Notably, a good attorney-client relationship will likely include far more communication than what is required at a minimum by the rules.

Model Rule 1.4 sets out basic categories of required communication. First, the rule requires that the lawyer "promptly inform the client of any decision or circumstance with respect to which the client's informed consent . . . is required by these Rules." When is the client's informed consent required—thus triggering the communication requirement? Remember that under Rule 1.2(a), there are certain actions that the client has the ultimate authority to decide. In civil cases, the client has ultimate authority to decide whether to settle a matter, and in criminal cases, the client has the ultimate authority regarding entering a plea, waiving a jury trial, and testifying on her own behalf. Thus, in these matters, Rule 1.4 plainly requires the attorney to communicate with the client—and to do so *promptly*. Comment 2 explains that "a lawyer who receives from opposing counsel an offer of settlement in a civil controversy or a proffered plea bargain in a criminal case must promptly

---

9. Melvin Hirshman, *Communication*, 43-Feb. Md. B.J. 61 (2010).
10. Wald, *supra* note 8, at 747, 748.

inform the client of its substance." A lawyer may only forgo telling a client of a plea or settlement offer if "the client has previously indicated that the proposal will be acceptable or unacceptable or has authorized the lawyer to accept or reject the offer." *See* Model Rule 1.4 cmt. 2.

Communicating with the client about matters that are the client's to decide does not mean merely informing the client of his choice without discussing the issue thoroughly. Indeed, the attorney must counsel with the client so that the client can make a truly informed decision. Thus, in communicating settlement and plea offers to a client, the lawyer should consult with the client about the pros, cons, and material consequences of accepting or rejecting such an offer. For example, and as discussed later in this chapter, in the plea bargaining context attorneys should explain to the client material consequences of pleading guilty—including deportation consequences for non-citizen defendants. Similarly, in counseling with a criminal defendant regarding whether to testify on his own behalf, the attorney should explain to the criminal defendant that testifying may allow the prosecution to introduce the prior criminal record of the accused to impeach his credibility. In making these decisions, the client should not act blindly, but should act knowingly, which she can only do with proper counseling from the attorney.

Recognize that if a rule requires informed consent, that triggers the attorney's obligation under Rule 1.4 to promptly communicate the circumstance to the client. The Model Rules require client informed consent in several other instances, notably in waiving conflicts of interest or permitting disclosure of confidential information.

The Model Rules themselves do not define the term "promptly," but as indicated in the *Howe* and *Helmedach* cases in this chapter, jurisdictions take a common parlance approach, construing prompt to mean "quick to act" or "without delay." As *Helmedach* indicates, where a lawyer has ample opportunity to communicate something to a client and fails to do so, the lawyer has not acted promptly.

Rule 1.4 also requires that a lawyer "reasonably consult with the client about the means by which the client's objectives are to be accomplished" and "keep the client reasonably informed about the status of the matter." As comment 3 elucidates, there are times when a lawyer is required to consult with the client prior to acting, but that depends "on both the importance of the action under consideration and the feasibility of consulting with the client." Further, whenever there are material developments in the status of a client's case, the lawyer needs to communicate such developments to the client.

Unfortunately, material developments that a lawyer must communicate to the client can include the lawyer's own mistakes that negatively affect a representation. Some attorneys have gone to extraordinary lengths to hide their own incompetence from their clients. For example, in In re Mays, 495 S.E.2d 30 (Ga. 1998), the attorney allowed the statute of limitations to run, and instead of so informing his client, the attorney lied to his client, telling him about a non-existent settlement offer, and then used his own money to pay a fake settlement. Obviously, such deceit of one's client will only makes matters worse—much worse—for the attorney. Malpractice—or even incompetence under the rules—may warrant slight if any sanction from the bar and perhaps an increase in one's malpractice insurance premiums, but actively defrauding and deceiving one's own client about those same mistakes will likely result in a suspension if not disbarment. So when must an attorney disclose her own mistakes in a representation to her client? The following North Carolina Ethics Opinion discusses that issue.

Disclosing Potential Malpractice to a Client

North Carolina State Bar Ethics Opinion (2015)

INTRODUCTION

Lawyers will, inevitably, make errors, mistakes, and omissions (referred to herein as an "error" or "errors") when representing clients. Such errors may constitute professional malpractice, but are not necessarily professional misconduct. [As] explained in comment [9] to Rule 1.1, Competence:

> An error by a lawyer may constitute professional malpractice under the applicable standard of care and subject the lawyer to civil liability. However, conduct that constitutes a breach of the civil standard of care owed to a client giving rise to liability for professional malpractice does not necessarily constitute a violation of the ethical duty to represent a client competently. A lawyer who makes a good-faith effort to be prepared and to be thorough will not generally be subject to professional discipline, although he or she may be subject to a claim for malpractice. . . .

Although an error during the representation of a client may not constitute professional misconduct, the actions that the lawyer takes following the realization that she has committed an error should be guided by the requirements of the Rules of Professional Conduct. This opinion explains a lawyer's professional responsibilities when the lawyer has committed what she believes may be legal malpractice. . . .

INQUIRY #1

When the lawyer determines that an error that may constitute legal malpractice has occurred, is the lawyer required to disclose the error to the client?

OPINION #1

Disclosure of an error to a client falls within the duty of communication. Rule 1.4(a)(3) requires a lawyer to "keep the client reasonably informed about the status of the matter," while paragraph (b) of the rule requires a lawyer to "explain a matter to the extent reasonably necessary to permit the client to make informed decisions regarding the representation." Comment [3] to the rule explains that paragraph (a)(3) requires that the lawyer keep the client reasonably informed about "significant developments affecting the timing or the substance of the representation." Comment [7] to Rule 1.4 adds that "[a] lawyer may not withhold information to serve the lawyer's own interest or convenience or the interests or convenience of another person."

In the spectrum of possible errors, material errors that prejudice the client's rights or claims are at one end. These include errors that effectively undermine the achievement

of the client's primary objective for the representation, such as failing to file the complaint before the statute of limitations runs. At the other end of the spectrum are minor, harmless errors that do not prejudice the client's rights or interests. These include nonsubstantive typographical errors in a pleading or a contract or missing a deadline that causes nothing more than delay. Between the two ends of the spectrum are a range of errors that may or may not materially prejudice the client's interests.

Whether the lawyer must disclose an error to a client depends upon where the error falls on the spectrum and the circumstances at the time that the error is discovered. The New York State Bar Association, in a formal opinion, described the duty as follows:

> **[W]hether an attorney has an obligation to disclose a mistake to a client will depend on the nature of the lawyer's possible error or omission, whether it is possible to correct it in the present proceeding, the extent of the harm resulting from the possible error or omission, and the likelihood that the lawyer's conduct would be deemed unreasonable and therefore give rise to a colorable malpractice claim.**

N.Y. State Bar Ass'n Comm. Prof'l Ethics, Op. 734 (2000). Under this analysis, it is clear that material errors that prejudice the client's rights or interests as well as errors that clearly give rise to a malpractice claim must always be reported to the client. Conversely, if the error is easily corrected or negligible and will not materially prejudice the client's rights or interests, the error does not have to be disclosed to the client.

Errors that fall between the two extremes of the spectrum must be analyzed under the duty to keep the client reasonably informed about his legal matter. If the error will result in financial loss to the client, substantial delay in achieving the client's objectives for the representation, or material disadvantage to the client's legal position, the error must be disclosed to the client. Similarly, if disclosure of the error is necessary for the client to make an informed decision about the representation or for the lawyer to advise the client of significant changes in strategy, timing, or direction of the representation, the lawyer may not withhold information about the error. Rule 1.4. When a lawyer does not know whether disclosure is required, the lawyer should err on the side of disclosure or should seek the advice of outside counsel, the State Bar's ethics counsel, or the lawyer's malpractice carrier.

Perhaps the most obvious duty to communicate is also the most frequent basis for client complaints — the duty to respond to client requests for information. Model Rule 1.4 states that the lawyer shall "promptly comply with reasonable requests for information." Failure to return phone calls or emails is one of the most common client complaints made to the bar. Martin Cole, who acted as the Director of the Office of Lawyers Professional Responsibility of the Minnesota Bar, called noncommunication and neglect the "hardiest perennials."[11] Noncommunication is a hardy perennial because complaints against attorneys for failing to return calls and emails — like poison ivy or other noxious weeds — come in year after year and seem resilient against warnings and measures undertaken by the bar to improve lawyer communication.

---

11. Perennials are plants that come up year after year without needing to be replanted — and "hardy" perennials will come up despite efforts to kill them.

Martin Cole, The Hardiest Perennials

64 Bench & B. Minn. 12 (2007)

In the October 1971 issue of Bench & Bar of Minnesota, Richey Reavill, the first director of the Office of Lawyers Professional Responsibility, wrote in this column, "As of July 31, the new procedures have been in effect for six months. During that period, almost 45 percent of the complaints which crossed our desk involved neglect of clients' business and the failure to keep the client and others entitled thereto advised as to the status quo. Neglect and failure to communicate seem to go hand in hand, probably because the only response the neglectful lawyer can make to an inquiry is that he has done nothing." . . .

In November 1985, William Wernz, in his first column as director . . . described neglect and noncommunication as a "hardy perennial." He added that "[f]ormer directors Richey Reavill, Paul Sharood, Walt Bachman and Mike Hoover all lamented the number of complaints of attorney neglect and noncommunication with clients. In 1984, as in 1971, 40-45 percent of all complaints alleged such failures."

The Office of Lawyers Professional Responsibility has been in existence for 36 years now, and while some things have changed immensely, others clearly have not. By a wide margin, neglect and noncommunication remain the most common source of client unhappiness and thus of client complaints. A few months ago, in the March 2007 Bench & Bar "Summary of Admonitions," I wrote that, "As in most years, the majority of admonitions last year involved a lack of diligence and/or communication by the attorney." Surely, neglect and noncommunication must be considered the hardiest perennials after so many years without change.

LEARNING FROM HISTORY

After all these years, why is this so? Aren't we supposed to learn from the lessons of history? By now shouldn't we recognize procrastination, lack of diligence, neglect (whatever we call it), when we see it? Do we know it only when we see it in others, while failing to recognize it in ourselves? The applicable Rules of Professional Conduct don't seem especially difficult to understand. . . .

Noncommunication can be . . . tricky to pin down, depending on the circumstances. Not returning one or two phone calls, while a poor business practice, is often forgiven by the client if an apology is proffered. Routinely failing to return phone calls or not replying to correspondence from clients or opposing counsel eventually *will* lead to disciplinary problems. . . .

MINIMIZING THE RISK

Since there isn't a clear line of demarcation announcing when an attorney's conduct goes from "that can happen" to "that simply shouldn't happen," the easiest and best solution is not to put yourself so close to the line that you need to be worried about it. Proper office management skills are attainable even for a busy solo practitioner. An office calendar and "tickler system" for court appearances, meetings and the like are essential. An assistant who may handle some routine inquiries or return some phone calls on the attorney's behalf is certainly permissible and can help

eliminate much client frustration (that said, systematically making it impossible for clients to get beyond support staff or ever talk directly with the lawyer may violate the lawyer's duty to communicate). . . .

As noted, admonitions issued for neglect and/or noncommunication remain common. The annual summary of admonitions published in this column rarely provides details of these admonitions, however. This past year, attorneys were admonished for taking almost one year to complete a QDRO [Qualified Domestic Relations Order] in a marital dissolution matter, taking over two years to complete a generally uncomplicated estate matter, and putting research on an issue concerning the sale of a client's motor home "on the back burner" (the attorney's words) for many months. Attorneys who failed to communicate with their clients for several months at a time, usually despite several calls or letters from the client requesting (eventually begging) for a response, also received admonitions. Admonitions are generally appropriate when the matter is the lawyer's first valid complaint and the ultimate financial harm to the client was minimal. Frustration is a given. . . .

So, one last exhortation: "Don't procrastinate and do communicate!" Do those two things and odds are we'll never meet because of a complaint.

In a similar vein, comment 4 to Rule 1.4 provides a simple rule for complying with client requests for information: promptly respond or acknowledge the communication. The comment says that "when a client makes a reasonable request for information . . . [the rule] requires prompt compliance with the request, or if a prompt response is not feasible, that the lawyer, or a member of the lawyer's staff, acknowledge receipt of the request and advise the client when a response may be expected." Thus, where a lawyer doesn't yet have the requested information or is in the middle of a trial or other time-consuming matter and cannot fully respond to the client request promptly, the lawyer should still acknowledge the client communication and give the client an idea of when the attorney will be able to respond more fully. Respond or acknowledge promptly—it's really that simple.

Case Preview

Utah Bar Journal, Discipline Corner

The following is an excerpt from the *Utah Bar Journal*'s Discipline Corner, which provides a summary of disciplinary proceedings. The excerpt regards attorney Karen Thomas, who failed to communicate (and act diligently and competently) on behalf of her client in securing an adoption.

As you read this excerpt, consider the following:

1. Where did Thomas go wrong? What could and should she have done differently?
2. What impact, including emotional distress, did Thomas cause her client?

Discipline Corner

Utah Bar Journal (Apr. 27, 2007)

On October 30, 2006, the Honorable Sandra N. Peuler, Third Judicial District Court, entered Findings of Fact and Conclusions of Law, and Order of Discipline: Suspension suspending Karen Thomas for six months from the practice of law for violations of Rules 1.1 (Competence), 1.3 (Diligence), 1.4(a) (Communication), 1.5(a) (Fees), 1.16(d) (Declining or Terminating Representation), 3.2 (Expediting Litigation), 8.1(b) (Bar Admission and Disciplinary Matters), and 8.4(a) (Misconduct) of the Rules of Professional Conduct. Ms. Thomas's suspension was effective thirty days from the date of its entry.

Ms. Thomas was hired to finalize an adoption, in which the natural mother had agreed to relinquish her parental rights. The client paid Ms. Thomas for the drafting of the adoption agreement, the finalization of the adoption and the filing fee. The client notified Ms. Thomas of the birth of the baby. The client took the baby home from the hospital. Five weeks after the baby's birth, Ms. Thomas had not arranged for the natural mother to sign the required relinquishment papers in front of a signing judge. The client left numerous messages for Ms. Thomas concerning the status of the relinquishment. Ms. Thomas failed to keep the client informed of the status and failed to promptly comply with the client's requests for information. Ms. Thomas informed her client that the delay was due in part because the signing judge was out of town. The natural mother became frustrated with Ms. Thomas and the delay. The client arranged, on her own, for the natural mother to appear before the judge to sign the relinquishment papers. At the hearing, the natural mother demanded that the baby be returned. The court ordered that the client return the baby within an hour's time. Ms. Thomas informed the client that she would help the client try to get the baby back without charge to the client. Ms. Thomas did not earn the fees she collected from the client. Ms. Thomas collected an excessive fee given the work performed in the adoption.[12]

Post-Case Follow-Up

The Karen Thomas disciplinary matter underscores the importance of these basic core duties that generally go hand in hand: competence, diligence, and communication. Imagine the distress felt by Ms. Thomas's client when she was forced to return a baby she had brought home from the hospital, taken care of and nurtured for over five weeks, and considered her own child. Competently protecting a client's interests is the attorney's indispensable duty.

12. Utah Bar Journal, *Discipline Corner* (Apr. 27, 2007), *available at* http://www.utahbar.org/utah-bar-journal/bar-discipline/discipline-corner-39/.

Thomas Disciplinary Summary: Real Life Applications

1. Shaniqua is representing James in defending against an action to collect a debt James owes. James sells his only major asset—a small commercial building—and obtains $70,000 cash on October 30. The plaintiff in the action checks the title records in mid-November and learns that James sold the building. The plaintiff moves the court for a temporary restraining order (TRO) prohibiting James from disbursing any of the proceeds of the sale and requiring James to make an accounting of the funds at a hearing ten days later, which the court grants the same day. At the hearing, James fails to provide an accounting, and says that all but $15,000 of the sale proceeds have already been spent, transferred, or given away. Further, he indicates that Shaniqua, who was served with the signed TRO ten days previously, had only told him about the TRO the day before the hearing so he had not had adequate time to prepare an accounting and had continued to use the proceeds up until that time. Under the rules, when did Shaniqua need to tell James about the TRO?

2. Larry is an attorney, representing Karen in a contentious divorce. Karen is very worried about how child custody will play out, and so she contacts Larry frequently. Larry is tired of responding to Karen's phone calls. Do the rules require him to do so?

B. INEFFECTIVE ASSISTANCE OF CRIMINAL DEFENSE COUNSEL

When a criminal defense attorney performs poorly, more than the duty of competence is at stake. Incompetent criminal defense attorneys also deprive their clients of their constitutional right to effective assistance of counsel. The Sixth Amendment to the Constitution declares that "[i]n all criminal prosecutions, the accused shall . . . have the Assistance of Counsel for his defence." The Sixth Amendment guarantee was a break from eighteenth-century criminal procedure in England, where a defendant accused of a felony was *prohibited* from having or employing counsel to assist in her defense, and instead was required to "speak for yourself."[13] Yet in the American colonies, the English rule had been rejected even before the federal Constitution's creation. Nearly every colony had provided by law that an accused had a right to have counsel for his defense—and thus that right was an integral part of American conceptions of justice at the time of the creation of the Bill of Rights.

This history underlying the Sixth Amendment was recited by the Supreme Court in Powell v. Alabama, 287 U.S. 45 (1932), wherein the Supreme Court held

---

13. *See* John H. Langbein, *Shaping the Eighteenth-Century Criminal Trial: A View from the Ryder Sources*, 50 U. Chi. L. Rev. 1, 123-30 & nn. 515-16 (1983). In the first half of the eighteenth century, the accused could not have any assistance of counsel, although later in the century, the accused could employ counsel to cross-examine witnesses and address points of law. Nevertheless, defense counsel could only speak as to issues of law (and not fact), and defense "counsel was forbidden to 'address the jury,' that is, to make opening and closing statements." Thus, the accused could not use an attorney "for his 'defense'"—instead the accused had to speak for himself. *See id.*

that states were required by the Due Process Clause of the Fourteenth Amendment to provide effective assistance of counsel to an accused in certain cases. In *Powell*, nine African-American teenagers (commonly referred to as the "Scottsboro boys") had been convicted of gang-raping two Caucasian women on a slow-moving train. The defendants were tried within days of the alleged incident. Immediately before their trials were to begin, the defendants were appointed counsel—characterized by the Supreme Court as being "pro forma [rather] than zealous and active." The trials were completed quickly with all defendants convicted and all but one sentenced to death.[14] The Supreme Court reversed the convictions noting that the appointment of counsel and trials had gone forward not in the "spirit of regulated justice but . . . with the haste of the mob":

> The defendants, young, ignorant, illiterate, surrounded by hostile sentiment, haled back and forth under guard of soldiers, charged with an atrocious crime regarded with especial horror in the community where they were to be tried, were thus put in peril of their lives within a few moments after counsel for the first time charged with any degree of responsibility began to represent them.

According to the State, the appointed counsel "thought there was no defense" and thus "exercised their best judgment in proceeding to trial without preparation." The Court rejected this argument, stating: "Neither [appointed counsel] nor the court could say what a prompt and thorough-going investigation might disclose as to the facts. No attempt was made to investigate. No opportunity to do so was given. Defendants were immediately hurried to trial." Moreover, the Court noted that defendants had not been provided with any counsel "during perhaps the most critical period of the proceedings against these defendants, that is to say, from the time of their arraignment until the beginning of their trial, when consultation, thorough-going investigation and preparation were vitally important"—indeed, the Court emphasized, "they were as much entitled to such aid during that period as at the trial itself." Ultimately, the Court concluded that "in a capital case, where the defendant is unable to employ counsel, and is incapable adequately of making his own defense . . . it is the duty of the court, whether requested or not, to assign counsel for him as a necessary requisite of due process of law; and that duty is not discharged by an assignment at such a time or under such circumstances as to preclude the giving of effective aid in the preparation and trial of the case." The Supreme Court thus indicated the need for *effective* assistance of counsel, which had not been satisfied in *Powell* by a pro forma appointment without real substance. In making its determination, the Court eloquently explained:

> The right to be heard would be, in many cases, of little avail if it did not comprehend the right to be heard by counsel. Even the intelligent and educated layman has small and sometimes no skill in the science of law. If charged with crime, he is incapable, generally, of determining for himself whether the indictment is good or bad. He is unfamiliar with the rules of evidence. Left without the aid of counsel he may be put

---

14. The jury was hung as to life imprisonment or death as the appropriate sentence for Roy Wright, who was 13 years old.

The Scottsboro Boys and the Moral Courage of Judge James E. Horton, Jr.

Attorney Samuel Leibowitz and his clients, the "Scottsboro boys."
AP Photo

On remand after *Powell*, the Scottsboro boys were represented for no fee[15] by Samuel Leibowitz — a renowned Jewish criminal defense attorney from New York, who had obtained 77 acquittals in the course of 78 criminal trials. Haywood Patterson was the first to be retried. The venue was moved from Scottsboro, and Judge James E. Horton, Jr. was assigned to preside. Judge Horton addressed the jury venire: "So far as the law is concerned, it knows neither native nor alien, Jew or Gentile, black or white. This case is no different than any other. We have only our duty to do without fear or favor."[16] Leibowitz masterfully undermined the prosecution's case. He had the Lionel Corporation build a 32-foot replica of the train to show the implausibility of the accusations, including that a gang rape had taken place in a gondola car that was

on trial without a proper charge, and convicted upon incompetent evidence, or evidence irrelevant to the issue or otherwise inadmissible. He lacks both the skill and knowledge adequately to prepare his defense, even though he have a perfect one. He requires the guiding hand of counsel at every step in the proceedings against him. Without it, though he be not guilty, he faces the danger of conviction because he does not know how to establish his innocence. If that be true of men of intelligence, how much more true is it of the ignorant and illiterate, or those of feeble intellect?

In Gideon v. Wainwright, 372 U.S. 335 (1963), the Supreme Court expressly incorporated the Sixth Amendment's guarantee of assistance of counsel as applying to the states through the Fourteenth Amendment, and in Argersinger v. Hamlin, 407 U.S. 25 (1972), the Court extended that right to less serious offenses, holding that "absent a knowing and intelligent waiver, no person may be imprisoned for any offense, whether classified as petty, misdemeanor, or felony, unless he was represented by counsel at his trial."

1. The Constitutional Test for Ineffective Assistance of Counsel

The Supreme Court's recognition and incorporation of the Sixth Amendment's guarantee of assistance of counsel to state prosecutions, as well as federal, did not directly address the problem of incompetent counsel. What should happen if an attorney is appointed, but proceeds incompetently? When, if ever, is an attorney's incompetence so severe that it constitutes a denial of the Sixth Amendment's right to the provision of counsel? Lower courts approached this problem in differing manners until the Supreme Court in *Strickland v. Washington* established a test for determining whether a defendant had been denied his Sixth Amendment right to effective assistance of counsel.

15. J.Y. Smith, *Samuel Leibowitz, Noted Judge Dies*, Wash. Post, Jan. 12, 1978, *available at* https://www.washingtonpost.com/archive/local/1978/01/12/samuel-leibowitz-noted-judge-dies/30cc052b-afa3-4b7c-9326-6838070eb364/?utm_term=.22685be8581f.

16. Regarding the information in this paragraph, see generally Douglas O. Linder, *Without Fear or Favor: Judge James Edwin Horton and the Trial of the "Scottsboro Boys,"* 68 UMKC L. Rev. 549 (2000).

Case Preview

Strickland v. Washington

The facts of *Strickland* are quite unsympathetic. David Leroy Washington was convicted of committing "three groups of crimes, which included three brutal stabbing murders, torture, kidnapping, severe assaults, attempted murders, attempted extortion, and theft." Washington repeatedly went against his attorney's advice by confessing to the murders, pleading guilty to all charges, and waiving his right to a jury trial. Washington's attorney advised Washington to invoke a right to an advisory jury for the sentencing phase, and again, Washington ignored his attorney's advice and waived that right. The attorney then performed a very limited investigation for the sentencing hearing—he talked to Washington's wife and mother over the phone. He also successfully moved to exclude Washington's rap sheet. But defense counsel didn't do further investigation or preparation because of a "sense of hopelessness about overcoming the evidentiary effect of respondent's confessions to the gruesome crimes." The trial court sentenced Washington to death on each of the murders, which convictions and sentences were upheld on direct appeal. Washington then sought state collateral relief and ultimately federal habeas corpus relief, arguing that he was denied effective assistance of counsel at the sentencing hearing based on his attorney's failure to investigate and present mitigating evidence, such as psychiatric, character, and medical evidence.

As you read through *Strickland*, look for the following:

1. What is the Court's two-prong test for determining ineffective assistance of counsel?

filled with chert (small jagged rocks) to within a foot and a half of the roof. He elicited medical testimony that the sperm found vaginally less than two hours after the alleged rape was old and "non-motile" and that the women had no scrapes or bruises (despite the chert). Leibowitz's final witness was Ruby Bates, one of the two women allegedly raped, who recanted her prior accusations and said they had invented the story to avoid vagrancy charges. Nevertheless, the jury convicted Patterson and sentenced him to death. The prosecution had stated in closing argument, "Show them that Alabama justice can't be bought and sold with Jew money from New York." After the verdict, Judge Horton received numerous letters of praise regarding his handling of the case and the result. But then Horton surprised his native Alabama constituency. On June 22, 1933, Judge Horton opened court by granting the defense's motion for a new trial on the basis of insufficiency of the evidence. Horton reviewed all the improbabilities and inconsistencies in the prosecution's case and set aside the verdict and the sentence of death. "Deliberate injustice," he said, "is more fatal to the one who imposes it than to the one on whom it is imposed." Horton lost his judicial seat in the 1934 election.[17]

---

17. *See id.* Patterson and Clarence Norris were retried by a different judge, convicted, and sentenced to death. The U.S. Supreme Court reversed the convictions again, this time based on Alabama's total exclusion of African Americans on juries—an argument Leibowitz had been making and preserving since the first day of jury selection in Patterson's case before Judge Horton. Charges against four of the boys were then dropped, but the others were retried and convicted yet again—each ultimately serving a lengthy prison sentence. *See The Scottsboro Boys: A Chronology*, http://law2.umkc.edu/faculty/projects/ftrials/scottsboro/SB_chron.html.

2. Under the Court's test, how competent must a defense attorney be to satisfy the Sixth Amendment guarantee? How much deference is given to the attorney?
3. In applying the two-prong test, does it matter which prong a court examines first—and why does that matter?
4. When, if ever, is prejudice presumed? How is the test different where the attorney proceeds with a criminal representation under a conflict of interest?
5. Why does Justice Marshall object to the prejudice prong? Is the Sixth Amendment only for the protection of the innocent, or is it also a guarantee for the guilty?

Strickland v. Washington

466 U.S. 668 (1984)

. . .

III

A convicted defendant's claim that counsel's assistance was so defective as to require reversal of a conviction or death sentence has two components. First, the defendant must show that counsel's performance was deficient. This requires showing that counsel made errors so serious that counsel was not functioning as the "counsel" guaranteed the defendant by the Sixth Amendment. Second, the defendant must show that the deficient performance prejudiced the defense. This requires showing that counsel's errors were so serious as to deprive the defendant of a fair trial, a trial whose result is reliable. Unless a defendant makes both showings, it cannot be said that the conviction or death sentence resulted from a breakdown in the adversary process that renders the result unreliable.

A

As all the Federal Courts of Appeals have now held, the proper standard for attorney performance is that of reasonably effective assistance. . . . When a convicted defendant complains of the ineffectiveness of counsel's assistance, the defendant must show that counsel's representation fell below an objective standard of reasonableness.

More specific guidelines are not appropriate. The Sixth Amendment refers simply to "counsel," not specifying particular requirements of effective assistance. It relies instead on the legal profession's maintenance of standards sufficient to justify the law's presumption that counsel will fulfill the role in the adversary process that the Amendment envisions. The proper measure of attorney performance remains simply reasonableness under prevailing professional norms.

Representation of a criminal defendant entails certain basic duties. Counsel's function is to assist the defendant, and hence counsel owes the client a duty of loyalty, a duty to avoid conflicts of interest. From counsel's function as assistant to the defendant derive the overarching duty to advocate the defendant's cause and the more particular duties to consult with the defendant on important decisions and to keep the defendant informed of important developments in the course of the prosecution. Counsel also has a duty to bring to bear such skill and knowledge as will render the trial a reliable adversarial testing process. *See* Powell v. Alabama, 287 U.S., at 68-69.

These basic duties neither exhaustively define the obligations of counsel nor form a checklist for judicial evaluation of attorney performance. In any case presenting an ineffectiveness claim, the performance inquiry must be whether counsel's assistance was reasonable considering all the circumstances. Prevailing norms of practice as reflected in American Bar Association standards and the like, e.g., ABA Standards for Criminal Justice 4-1.1 to 4-8.6 (2d ed. 1980) ("The Defense Function"), are guides to determining what is reasonable, but they are only guides. No particular set of detailed rules for counsel's conduct can satisfactorily take account of the variety of circumstances faced by defense counsel or the range of legitimate decisions regarding how best to represent a criminal defendant. Any such set of rules would interfere with the constitutionally protected independence of counsel and restrict the wide latitude counsel must have in making tactical decisions. Indeed, the existence of detailed guidelines for representation could distract counsel from the overriding mission of vigorous advocacy of the defendant's cause. Moreover, the purpose of the effective assistance guarantee of the Sixth Amendment is not to improve the quality of legal representation, although that is a goal of considerable importance to the legal system. The purpose is simply to ensure that criminal defendants receive a fair trial.

Judicial scrutiny of counsel's performance must be highly deferential. It is all too tempting for a defendant to second-guess counsel's assistance after conviction or adverse sentence, and it is all too easy for a court, examining counsel's defense after it has proved unsuccessful, to conclude that a particular act or omission of counsel was unreasonable. A fair assessment of attorney performance requires that every effort be made to eliminate the distorting effects of hindsight, to reconstruct the circumstances of counsel's challenged conduct, and to evaluate the conduct from counsel's perspective at the time. Because of the difficulties inherent in making the evaluation, a court must indulge a strong presumption that counsel's conduct falls within the wide range of reasonable professional assistance; that is, the defendant must overcome the presumption that, under the circumstances, the challenged action "might be considered sound trial strategy." There are countless ways to provide effective assistance in any given case. Even the best criminal defense attorneys would not defend a particular client in the same way. . . .

Thus, a court deciding an actual ineffectiveness claim must judge the reasonableness of counsel's challenged conduct on the facts of the particular case, viewed as of the time of counsel's conduct. A convicted defendant making a claim of ineffective assistance must identify the acts or omissions of counsel that are alleged not to have been the result of reasonable professional judgment. The court must then determine whether, in light of all the circumstances, the identified acts or omissions were outside the wide range of professionally competent assistance. In making that determination, the court should keep in mind that counsel's function, as elaborated in prevailing professional norms, is to make the adversarial testing process work in the particular case. At the same time, the court should recognize that counsel is strongly presumed to have rendered adequate assistance and made all significant decisions in the exercise of reasonable professional judgment.

These standards require no special amplification in order to define counsel's duty to investigate, the duty at issue in this case. As the Court of Appeals concluded, strategic choices made after thorough investigation of law and facts relevant to plausible options are virtually unchallengeable; and strategic choices made after less than complete investigation are reasonable precisely to the extent that reasonable professional judgments support the limitations on investigation. In other words, counsel has a duty to make reasonable investigations or to make a reasonable decision that makes particular investigations unnecessary. In any ineffectiveness case, a particular decision not to investigate must be directly assessed for reasonableness in all the circumstances, applying a heavy measure of deference to counsel's judgments.

The reasonableness of counsel's actions may be determined or substantially influenced by the defendant's own statements or actions. Counsel's actions are usually based, quite properly, on informed strategic choices made by the defendant and on information supplied by the defendant. In particular, what investigation decisions are reasonable depends critically on such information. For example, when the facts that support a certain potential line of defense are generally known to counsel because of what the defendant has said, the need for further investigation may be considerably diminished or eliminated altogether. And when a defendant has given counsel reason to believe that pursuing certain investigations would be fruitless or even harmful, counsel's failure to pursue those investigations may not later be challenged as unreasonable. In short, inquiry into counsel's conversations with the defendant may be critical to a proper assessment of counsel's investigation decisions, just as it may be critical to a proper assessment of counsel's other litigation decisions.

B

An error by counsel, even if professionally unreasonable, does not warrant setting aside the judgment of a criminal proceeding if the error had no effect on the judgment. The purpose of the Sixth Amendment guarantee of counsel is to ensure that a defendant has the assistance necessary to justify reliance on the outcome of the proceeding. Accordingly, any deficiencies in counsel's performance must be prejudicial to the defense in order to constitute ineffective assistance under the Constitution.

In certain Sixth Amendment contexts, prejudice is presumed. Actual or constructive denial of the assistance of counsel altogether is legally presumed to result in prejudice. So are various kinds of state interference with counsel's assistance. *See* United States v. Cronic, 466 U.S., at 659, and n. 25. Prejudice in these circumstances is so likely that case-by-case inquiry into prejudice is not worth the cost. Moreover, such circumstances involve impairments of the Sixth Amendment right that are easy to identify and, for that reason and because the prosecution is directly responsible, easy for the government to prevent.

One type of actual ineffectiveness claim warrants a similar, though more limited, presumption of prejudice. In Cuyler v. Sullivan, 446 U.S., at 345-350, the Court held that prejudice is presumed when counsel is burdened by an actual conflict of interest. In those circumstances, counsel breaches the duty of loyalty, perhaps the most basic of counsel's duties. Moreover, it is difficult to measure the precise effect on the defense of representation corrupted by conflicting interests. Given the obligation of counsel to avoid conflicts of interest and the ability of trial courts to make early inquiry in certain situations likely to give rise to conflicts, it is reasonable for the criminal justice system to maintain a fairly rigid rule of presumed prejudice for conflicts of interest. Even so, the rule is not quite the per se rule of prejudice that exists for the Sixth Amendment claims mentioned above. Prejudice is presumed only if the defendant demonstrates that counsel "actively represented conflicting interests" and that "an actual conflict of interest adversely affected his lawyer's performance." Cuyler v. Sullivan, *supra*.

Conflict of interest claims aside, actual ineffectiveness claims alleging a deficiency in attorney performance are subject to a general requirement that the defendant affirmatively prove prejudice. The government is not responsible for, and hence not able to prevent, attorney errors that will result in reversal of a conviction or sentence. Attorney errors come in an infinite variety and are as likely to be utterly harmless in a particular case as they are to be prejudicial. . . . Representation is an art, and an act or omission that is unprofessional in one case may be sound or even brilliant in another. Even if a defendant shows that particular errors of counsel were unreasonable, therefore, the defendant must show that they actually had an adverse effect on the defense.

It is not enough for the defendant to show that the errors had some conceivable effect on the outcome of the proceeding. Virtually every act or omission of counsel would meet that test, and not every error that conceivably could have influenced the outcome undermines the reliability of the result of the proceeding. . . .

On the other hand, we believe that a defendant need not show that counsel's deficient conduct more likely than not altered the outcome in the case. . . . [Where there is ineffective assistance of counsel], [t]he result of a proceeding can be rendered unreliable, and hence the proceeding itself unfair, even if the errors of counsel cannot be shown by a preponderance of the evidence to have determined the outcome.

Accordingly, the appropriate test for prejudice [is:] . . . The defendant must show that there is a reasonable probability that, but for counsel's unprofessional errors, the result of the proceeding would have been different. A reasonable probability is a probability sufficient to undermine confidence in the outcome.

. . .

The governing legal standard plays a critical role in defining the question to be asked in assessing the prejudice from counsel's errors. When a defendant challenges a conviction, the question is whether there is a reasonable probability that, absent the errors, the factfinder would have had a reasonable doubt respecting guilt. When a defendant challenges a death sentence such as the one at issue in this case, the question is whether there is a reasonable probability that, absent the errors, the sentencer — including an appellate court, to the extent it independently reweighs the evidence — would have concluded that the balance of aggravating and mitigating circumstances did not warrant death. . . .

IV

A number of practical considerations are important for the application of the standards we have outlined. . . . Although we have discussed the performance component of an ineffectiveness claim prior to the prejudice component, there is no reason for a court deciding an ineffective assistance claim to approach the inquiry in the same order or even to address both components of the inquiry if the defendant makes an insufficient showing on one. In particular, a court need not determine whether counsel's performance was deficient before examining the prejudice suffered by the defendant as a result of the alleged deficiencies. The object of an ineffectiveness claim is not to grade counsel's performance. If it is easier to dispose of an ineffectiveness claim on the ground of lack of sufficient prejudice, which we expect will often be so, that course should be followed. Courts should strive to ensure that ineffectiveness claims not become so burdensome to defense counsel that the entire criminal justice system suffers as a result. . . .

V

. . . Application of the governing principles is not difficult in this case. The facts as described above, make clear that the conduct of respondent's counsel at and before respondent's sentencing proceeding cannot be found unreasonable. They also make clear that, even assuming the challenged conduct of counsel was unreasonable, respondent suffered insufficient prejudice to warrant setting aside his death sentence. . . .

Justice Marshall, dissenting.

The Sixth and Fourteenth Amendments guarantee a person accused of a crime the right to the aid of a lawyer in preparing and presenting his defense. It has long been settled that "the right to counsel is the right to the effective assistance of counsel." The state and lower federal courts have developed standards for distinguishing effective from inadequate assistance. Today, for the first time, this Court attempts to synthesize and clarify those standards. For the most part, the majority's efforts are unhelpful. Neither of its two principal holdings seems to me likely to improve the adjudication of Sixth Amendment claims. . . .

Thurgood Marshall
Library of Congress Prints and Photographs Division Washington, D.C. 20540 USA

I

The opinion of the Court revolves around two holdings. First, the majority ties the constitutional minima of attorney performance to a simple "standard of reasonableness." Second, the majority holds that only an error of counsel that has sufficient impact on a trial to "undermine confidence in the outcome" is grounds for overturning a conviction. I disagree with both of these rulings.

A

My objection to the performance standard adopted by the Court is that it is so malleable that, in practice, it will either have no grip at all or will yield excessive variation in the manner in which the Sixth Amendment is interpreted and applied by different courts. To tell lawyers and the lower courts that counsel for a criminal defendant must behave "reasonably" and must act like "a reasonably competent attorney," is to tell them almost nothing. In essence, the majority has instructed judges called upon to assess claims of ineffective assistance of counsel to advert to their own intuitions regarding what constitutes "professional" representation, and has discouraged them from trying to develop more detailed standards governing the performance of defense counsel. In my view, the Court has thereby not only abdicated its own responsibility to interpret the Constitution, but also impaired the ability of the lower courts to exercise theirs.

. . .

The majority defends its refusal to adopt more specific standards primarily on the ground that "[n]o particular set of detailed rules for counsel's conduct can satisfactorily take account of the variety of circumstances faced by defense counsel or the range of legitimate decisions regarding how best to represent a criminal defendant." I agree that counsel must be afforded "wide latitude" when making "tactical decisions" regarding trial strategy, but many aspects of the job of a criminal defense attorney are more amenable to judicial oversight. For example, much of the work involved in preparing for a trial, applying for bail, conferring with one's client, making timely objections to significant, arguably erroneous rulings of the trial judge, and filing a notice of appeal if there are colorable grounds therefor could profitably be made the subject of uniform standards.

The opinion of the Court of Appeals in this case represents one sound attempt to develop particularized standards designed to ensure that all defendants receive effective legal assistance. By refusing to address the merits of these proposals, and indeed suggesting that no such effort is worthwhile, the opinion of the Court, I fear, will stunt the development of constitutional doctrine in this area.

B

I object to the prejudice standard adopted by the Court for two independent reasons. First, it is often very difficult to tell whether a defendant convicted after a trial in which he was ineffectively represented would have fared better if his lawyer had been competent. Seemingly impregnable cases can sometimes be dismantled by good defense counsel. On the basis of a cold record, it may be impossible for a reviewing court confidently to ascertain how the government's evidence and arguments would have stood up against rebuttal and cross-examination by a shrewd, well-prepared lawyer. The difficulties of estimating prejudice after the fact are exacerbated by the possibility that evidence of injury to the defendant may be missing from the record precisely because of the incompetence of defense counsel. In view of all these impediments to a fair evaluation of the probability that the outcome of a trial was affected by ineffectiveness of counsel, it seems to me senseless to impose on

a defendant whose lawyer has been shown to have been incompetent the burden of demonstrating prejudice.

Second and more fundamentally, the assumption on which the Court's holding rests is that the only purpose of the constitutional guarantee of effective assistance of counsel is to reduce the chance that innocent persons will be convicted. In my view, the guarantee also functions to ensure that convictions are obtained only through fundamentally fair procedures. The majority contends that the Sixth Amendment is not violated when a manifestly guilty defendant is convicted after a trial in which he was represented by a manifestly ineffective attorney. I cannot agree. Every defendant is entitled to a trial in which his interests are vigorously and conscientiously advocated by an able lawyer. A proceeding in which the defendant does not receive meaningful assistance in meeting the forces of the State does not, in my opinion, constitute due process.

In Chapman v. California, 386 U.S. 18, 23 (1967), we acknowledged that certain constitutional rights are "so basic to a fair trial that their infraction can never be treated as harmless error." Among these rights is the right to the assistance of counsel at trial. In my view, the right to effective assistance of counsel is entailed by the right to counsel, and abridgment of the former is equivalent to abridgment of the latter. I would thus hold that a showing that the performance of a defendant's lawyer departed from constitutionally prescribed standards requires a new trial regardless of whether the defendant suffered demonstrable prejudice thereby.

Strickland continues to state the test for determining when an accused has received ineffective assistance of counsel in contravention of the Sixth Amendment. The two-pronged approach requires a defendant to prove (1) deficient performance of counsel and (2) prejudice. As to the first prong, deficient performance of counsel, *Strickland* continues to state the basic standard: "reasonableness under prevailing professional norms." Further, reviewing courts are to engage in a "strong presumption that counsel's conduct falls within the wide range of reasonable professional assistance." *Strickland* also continues to state the basic standard for determining prejudice: "The defendant must show that there is a reasonable probability that, but for counsel's unprofessional errors, the result of the proceeding would have been different."

Strickland v. Washington: Real Life Applications

1. Melinda is charged with shoplifting, a misdemeanor, but a high-level one that carries a potential sentence of incarceration. She is appointed a public defender, Yvonne, to defend her. Yvonne and Melinda meet briefly before the arraignment, where Melinda declares her innocence. She pleads not guilty. Yvonne receives and conveys to Melinda several plea deals, but Melinda refuses all of them, and wants to proceed to trial. Yvonne does very little preparation for trial

and decides not to cross-examine the state's primary witness, Don, an employee at the shop Melinda allegedly stole from who called the police. Melinda is convicted. Is Melinda likely to succeed on an ineffective assistance of counsel claim? What if there is not much evidence of guilt? What if there is substantial evidence of guilt, such as a store security tape clearly showing Melinda taking items and hiding them in her clothes?

2. Sullivan, Carchidi, and DiPasquale are all indicted for the first degree murders of two individuals. DiBona, an attorney, represents all three of them, who are to be tried separately. Sullivan's trial is first. DiBona is concerned that exposing defense witnesses to examination in the first trial could harm the trials of Carchidi and DiPasquale. Consequently, he decides not to use any defense witnesses in Sullivan's case. Sullivan is convicted. In their subsequent trials, where DiBona puts on a full defense with witnesses, Carchidi and DiPasquale are acquitted. Can Sullivan prevail on an ineffective assistance of counsel claim to undo the conviction? What if there is substantial evidence of guilt?

---

2. *Strickland's* First Prong: Deficient Performance

Why should prevailing professional norms define the constitutional standard for effective assistance of counsel? Aren't there some essential components of competent criminal representation that should be constitutionally required, regardless of common practice? In a different context, Judge Learned Hand maintained:

> [I]n most cases reasonable prudence is in fact common prudence; but strictly it is never its measure; a whole calling may have unduly lagged in the adoption of new and available devices. It never may set its own tests, however persuasive be its usages. Courts must in the end say what is required; there are precautions so imperative that even their universal disregard will not excuse their omission.[18]

Are there actions that are "so imperative" in the practice of law that "even their universal disregard will not excuse their omission"? A study of homicide cases in New York City indicated that in over 70 percent of cases, the defense attorneys did not turn in receipts for investigation and did not file any legal motions.[19] If no investigation and no legal motions is a prevailing professional norm, does and should that render such representation compliant with the Constitution? Consider whether it would be a good idea to have the prevailing professional norms found among law enforcement set the standard for the constitutionality of searches and seizures or excessive force under the Fourth Amendment.

---

18. The T.J. Hooper v. Northern Barge Corp., 60 F.2d 737, 740 (2d Cir. 1932).
19. Michael McConville & Chester L. Mirsky, *Criminal Defense of the Poor in New York City*, 15 N.Y.U. Rev. L. & Soc. Change 581 (1987), *cited in* Hazard et al., The Law and Ethics of Lawyering 900.

Failure to Investigate

In *Strickland*, Washington's defense attorney did not investigate in preparation for the sentencing hearing; yet the Court held that his actions did not constitute deficient performance under the first prong of its test. The Court indicated that the attorney's failure to investigate could be sound strategy. But when can failure to investigate a criminal case be a sound strategy? With a possible exception for physical incriminating evidence (e.g., a murder weapon),[20] criminal defense attorneys generally are not required to disclose inculpatory evidence that they find as part of their investigation of a client's case. Thus, if an investigation reveals evidence that is helpful to the client, the criminal defense attorney can use it. If the investigation reveals evidence that is harmful to the client, the criminal defense attorney has no obligation to use it at trial or to disclose it to the prosecution. As criminal defense lawyer William Genego said of the *Strickland* Court:

> The Court was wrong. Having a client examined by a psychiatrist in preparation for a capital sentencing proceeding does not mean that an attorney must introduce the report or the psychiatrist's testimony at the hearing. If a report had been done on Washington and it had been unfavorable, the attorney could have chosen not to introduce the report at the sentencing proceeding. . . . The critical point is that Washington's attorney could not make a reasonable strategic decision about the utility of relying on psychiatric testimony without having his own doctor examine Washington. . . . The Court was similarly misguided about the failure of Washington's attorney to interview character witnesses. In his collateral challenge, Washington introduced fourteen affidavits from friends, neighbors and relatives who said that, had they been asked, they would have testified on his behalf. . . . [Washington's] attorney, however, could not have intelligently speculated about the utility of such evidence . . . [because] the attorney had no idea what the fourteen character witnesses could have said about Washington's request that he be allowed to live.[21]

Subsequently, the Supreme Court in Kimmelman v. Morrison, 477 U.S. 365 (1986), held that conducting no pretrial discovery fell below the standard of reasonable professional assistance under *Strickland*'s first prong. The Court explained, "In this case, [] we deal with a total failure to conduct pre-trial discovery, and one as to which counsel offered only implausible explanations. Counsel's performance at trial, while generally creditable enough, suggests no better explanation for this apparent and pervasive failure to make reasonable investigations or to make a reasonable decision that makes particular investigations unnecessary." Similarly, in Williams v. Taylor, 539 U.S. 362 (2000), the Court found there had been deficient performance of counsel on the basis of failure to investigate, explaining that a "failure to introduce" voluminous evidence in favor of a criminal

---

20. Whether a criminal defense lawyer must turn over physical incriminating evidence to the prosecution or law enforcement is discussed in Chapter 8.

21. William J. Genego, *The Future of Effective Assistance of Counsel: Performance Standards and Competent Representation*, 22 Am. Crim. L. Rev. 181 (1984).

defendant at sentencing "was not justified by a tactical decision to focus on Williams' voluntary confession," but instead "clearly demonstrate[d] that trial counsel did not fulfill their obligation to conduct a thorough investigation of the defendant's background."

Failure to Communicate

As noted in the first part of this chapter, attorneys have duties to communicate with their clients and are required to communicate certain matters over which the client must give informed consent or that fall within the absolute authority of the client to decide. When does an attorney's failure to communicate with her client constitute ineffective assistance of counsel?

In Missouri v. Frye, 566 U.S. 133 (2012), the United States Supreme Court held "as a general rule," that "defense counsel has the duty to communicate formal offers from the prosecution to accept a plea on terms and conditions that may be favorable to the accused." Thus Frye's attorney acted deficiently under *Strickland*'s first prong by failing to communicate a formal plea offer to the accused and allowing the plea offer to expire. The Court relied in part on the ABA rules and standards requiring communication of such offers to criminal defendants.

Case Preview

Helmedach v. Commissioner of Correction

Helmedach deals with a specific application of *Frye* and an interpretation of the duty to communicate found in Rule 1.4. Richard Reeve represented Jennifer Helmedach, who was being tried for felony murder, first degree burglary, and related offenses. During the trial, on the morning that the defense was to begin presenting its case, the prosecution told Reeve that it was offering Helmedach a plea with a ten-year sentence. Reeve did not communicate the plea offer to Helmedach until after she had finished testifying at trial — two and a half days later. When Helmedach learned of the plea offer, she wanted to take it, but the prosecution had withdrawn the plea offer. Helmedach was found guilty at trial and sentenced to 35 years in prison.

As you read *Helmedach*, consider the following:

1. How promptly must defense counsel inform a client of plea offers? What if there is not an express time for expiration of the offer?
2. Did attorney Reeve have a justified trial strategy in delaying communication of the plea offer to Helmedach?
3. Are there other communication obligations found in Rule 1.4, the noncompliance with which might constitute ineffective assistance of counsel in criminal cases?

Helmedach v. Commissioner of Correction

148 A.3d 1105 (Conn. 2016)

. . . [T]he petitioner filed an amended petition for a writ of habeas corpus, alleging ineffective assistance of trial counsel. . . . [T]he habeas court granted the petition . . . and concluded that Reeve's failure to relay the favorable offer to the petitioner in a timely manner before it was withdrawn fell below the objective standard of reasonableness required by attorneys under the state and federal constitutions. . . .

The respondent . . . contends that the habeas court improperly relied on *Missouri v. Frye* in finding that Reeve's performance was deficient, because [*Frye* doesn't address] whether it is reasonable trial strategy for a defense attorney to delay informing the client of a plea offer if valid strategic reasons exist for that decision. . . .

In response, the petitioner argues that Reeve's conduct could not be reasonable trial strategy because, as a matter of law, the decision made by Reeve to delay informing the petitioner of a favorable plea offer is not one that counsel constitutionally is allowed to make because it undermined the petitioner's ability to meaningfully exercise a right that belongs solely to her. Thus, in the petitioner's view, Reeve's conduct cannot be characterized as a matter of trial strategy. . . . We agree with the petitioner that Reeve's decision to delay informing the petitioner about a plea offer was not within the realm of strategic decisions that an attorney is allowed to make.

. . .

"To succeed on a claim of ineffective assistance of counsel, a habeas petitioner must satisfy the two-pronged test articulated in *Strickland v. Washington*. *Strickland* requires that a petitioner satisfy both a performance prong and a prejudice prong. . . .

"The Sixth Amendment guarantees a defendant the right to have counsel present at all critical stages of the criminal proceedings." *Missouri v. Frye, supra*. "[P]lea bargains have become so central to the administration of the criminal justice system that defense counsel have responsibilities in the plea bargain process, responsibilities that must be met to render the adequate assistance of counsel that the Sixth Amendment requires in the criminal process at critical stages. Because ours is for the most part a system of pleas, not a system of trials . . . it is insufficient simply to point to the guarantee of a fair trial as a backstop that inoculates any errors in the pretrial process. . . . In today's criminal justice system, therefore, the negotiation of a plea bargain, rather than the unfolding of a trial, is almost always the critical point for a defendant." . . .

In the present case, the respondent concedes that if indeed Reeve performed deficiently, the habeas court properly determined that the petitioner suffered prejudice on the basis of a reasonable probability that (1) the petitioner would have accepted the ten year plea offer had it been conveyed to her immediately, and (2) the trial court would have accepted the plea agreement and sentenced the petitioner accordingly. Our review and analysis, therefore, is confined to the first prong of *Strickland*, the performance prong. . . .

"Judicial scrutiny of counsel's performance must be highly deferential." *Strickland* . . . . At the same time, however, if the choice at issue implicates a fundamental right of constitutional magnitude, such a choice is "distinguishable from [a] tactical trial [right] that [is] not personal to the defendant and that counsel may choose to [make] as part of trial strategy." . . . But certain decisions regarding the exercise or waiver of basic trial rights are of such moment that they cannot be made for the defendant by a surrogate. A defendant has the ultimate authority to determine whether to plead guilty, waive a jury, testify in his or her own behalf, or take an appeal. Concerning those decisions, an attorney must both consult with the defendant and obtain consent to the recommended course of action.

"A guilty plea . . . is an event of signal significance in a criminal proceeding. By entering a guilty plea, a defendant waives constitutional rights that inhere in a criminal trial, including the right to trial by jury, the protection against self-incrimination, and the right to confront one's accusers. . . . While a guilty plea may be tactically advantageous for the defendant . . . the plea is not simply a strategic choice; it is itself a conviction . . . and the high stakes for the defendant require the utmost solicitude . . . ." Florida v. Nixon, 543 U.S. 175 (2004). . . .

We agree with the petitioner that this court need not consider whether, under the circumstances, Reeve's challenged action might be considered sound trial strategy, because the challenged action does not fall under the umbrella of trial strategy at all. The habeas court found that although Reeve "believed that ten years was a very favorable offer, he was concerned about relaying it to the petitioner immediately prior to her testimony because she was young and flustered, and he believed that this unexpected news would negatively impact her testimony." Such paternalistic decision-making on the part of defense counsel infringed upon the petitioner's basic trial right to plead guilty, which she, alone, had the ultimate authority to determine whether to exercise.[7]

Moreover, defense counsel's decision was not a matter of trial strategy, let alone a reasonable strategic decision, because, pursuant to *Frye*, if defense counsel violates his duty to communicate timely to the accused formal plea offers from the prosecution, he fails to render the effective assistance that the United States constitution requires. The basis for this rule is grounded largely in professional performance standards that govern the practice of law.

In *Frye*, the defendant was charged with a felony arising from driving with a revoked license. The prosecution sent a letter to his defense counsel that offered a choice between two plea bargains, with the offers set to expire on a fixed date. Defense counsel did not inform the defendant of the offers, and after they lapsed, the defendant pleaded guilty but on more severe terms. The court held that, "as a general rule, defense counsel has the duty to communicate formal offers from the prosecution to accept a plea on terms and conditions that may be favorable to the accused. . . . When defense counsel allowed the offer to expire without advising the

7. By not timely informing the petitioner of the ten year plea offer, defense counsel not only deprived the petitioner of critical information that might have resulted in her foregoing the remainder of the trial in favor of pleading guilty, but, by virtue of the point in the trial during which the plea offer was made, deprived her of critical information that may well have factored into how she internally weighed the risks and benefits of testifying in her own defense. The decision made by the petitioner to testify was thus arguably based upon an incomplete calculus. Ultimately, the petitioner was entitled to make both decisions — whether to plead guilty and whether to testify in her own defense — fully informed of the state's very favorable plea offer.

defendant or allowing him to consider it, defense counsel did not render the effective assistance the Constitution requires. Though the standard for counsel's performance is not determined solely by reference to codified standards of professional practice, these standards can be important guides. The American Bar Association recommends defense counsel 'promptly communicate and explain to the defendant all plea offers made by the prosecuting attorney,' ABA Standards for Criminal Justice, Pleas of Guilty 14-3.2(a) (3d ed. 1999) . . . . The standard for prompt communication and consultation is also set out in state bar professional standards for attorneys." *Id.*

The respondent argues that the holding in *Frye* does not apply to the facts of the present appeal because this is not a "lapsed plea" case, i.e., Reeve did not allow the state's ten year plea offer to expire without first advising the petitioner of it. . . .

We agree with the respondent that *Frye* does not necessarily control this case. We decline, however, to read *Frye* as narrowly as urged by the respondent because the respondent's assertion essentially ignores the thorough reasoning that the court provided for the general rule in *Frye* . . . . As previously discussed, the court repeatedly emphasized the requirement for prompt communication between defense counsel and client as set forth in both American Bar Association and state bar professional standards for attorneys. *Id.* Indeed, rule 1.4 of this state's Rules of Professional Conduct provides in relevant part: "(a) A lawyer shall: (1) promptly inform the client of any decision or circumstance with respect to which the client's informed consent . . . is required by these Rules . . . [and] (3) keep the client reasonably informed about the status of the matter . . . . (b) A lawyer shall explain a matter to the extent reasonably necessary to permit the client to make informed decisions regarding the representation." One such circumstance in which an attorney is required to promptly relay information to the client is set forth in rule 1.2(a) of the Rules of Professional Conduct, which provides in relevant part: "In a criminal case, the lawyer shall abide by the client's decision, after consultation with the lawyer, as to a plea to be entered, whether to waive jury trial and whether the client will testify. . . ."

In determining whether Reeve acted promptly, within the confines of *Frye*, when he delayed informing the petitioner of the ten year plea offer until after her trial testimony had concluded, it is necessary to define the meaning of "promptly" as it is used in rule 1.4(a)(1) of our Rules of Professional Conduct. When pressed at oral argument, the respondent conceded that defense attorneys have a duty to communicate plea offers promptly to their clients, but contended that *Frye* does not stand for the proposition that defense attorneys are required to communicate plea offers immediately to their clients . . . . [W]e employ our well established tools of statutory construction to determine the term's meaning. . . .

We first note that rule 1.0 of the Rules of Professional Conduct, entitled "Terminology," does not define "promptly." Absent this definition, in order to assign "promptly" its ordinary definition, "[w]e look to the dictionary definition of the [term] to ascertain [its] commonly approved meaning." The eleventh edition of *Merriam-Webster's Collegiate Dictionary* defines "prompt" as "being ready and quick to act as occasion demands . . . performed readily or immediately." In addition, *Random House Webster's Unabridged Dictionary* defines "prompt" as "done, performed, delivered, etc., at once or without delay." Similarly, although *Black's Law Dictionary* does not offer a definition for the word "prompt" used in the form of an adjective or adverb, it defines the verb form of "prompt" as "[t]o incite, esp. to immediate action." In turn, Black's Law Dictionary defines "immediate" as "[o]ccurring without delay; instant. . . ."

On the basis of these "commonly approved" definitions, an interpretation of the term "promptly" that would allow an attorney to delay informing his client about a plea offer well after counsel had an opportunity to do so, would be unreasonable. Each of these dictionary definitions references either immediacy or a lack of delay, concepts which the petitioner advanced in her construction of the term "promptly." . . .

In applying the common meaning of "promptly" to the facts of the present case, it is clear that Reeve did not act promptly in informing the petitioner of the plea offer. Once Reeve received the extremely advantageous ten year offer from Nicholson on the morning of October 9, he decided to wait to tell the petitioner about the offer until after she had taken the stand in her own defense and gone through her entire trial testimony, which ultimately took two and one-half days to complete. Significantly, the respondent does not claim on appeal that Reeve was prevented by circumstances outside of his control from communicating the plea offer to his client for several days. Because the trial proceeded on October 9, the very same day Reeve received the offer from Nicholson, Reeve obviously was interacting with his client throughout each of the following days and had ample time to communicate the offer and to discuss the risks and benefits of accepting or rejecting it. In making the conscious decision to delay delivering this information to his client, Reeve did not act immediately or without delay within the definition of "promptly." Nicholson's agreement to keep the offer open did not obviate Reeve's duty to promptly inform his client of the offer. Therefore, Reeve failed to comply with our Rules of Professional Conduct and, by extension, failed to fulfill his duty to timely communicate offers from the state in derogation of *Frye*.

Because defense counsel's actions prevented the petitioner from properly exercising her constitutional right to plead guilty and to make a fully informed decision as to whether to testify on her own behalf, we agree with the petitioner that Reeve's decision may not properly be viewed as trial strategy at all, much less a reasonable trial strategy. Nevertheless, even if we were to consider counsel's decision to delay communicating the plea offer as falling within the penumbra of trial strategy, we would find that Reeve's decision was not reasonable under the circumstances.

Post-Case Follow-Up

Helmedach underscores the necessity of prompt communication of plea offers as a constitutional duty and under the Model Rules. Communicating promptly means to do so "without delay"—and even immediately in situations such as in *Helmedach* where the attorney is actively associating with the pertinent client throughout the day and has ample opportunities to communicate the plea.

Helmedach v. Commissioner of Correction: Real Life Applications

1. Beth is charged with residential burglary. She hires a defense attorney, Keith. Keith initially keeps in close contact with Beth and conveys several plea offers to her, which she rejects. As the date for trial becomes imminent, Beth sends Keith numerous letters and leaves him short phone messages (she can make free one-minute phone calls twice a week). Keith fails to respond to Beth's messages and meets her again at a pretrial conference set the week of trial. Beth tells Keith that she needed to talk to him about trial strategy and potential witnesses on her behalf. She tells Keith the names of a couple of friends whom she believes would be willing to act as witnesses. Keith is unable to get ahold of the witnesses prior to trial that week. The state presents overwhelming evidence that Beth committed the burglaries and Beth is convicted. Did Keith violate the Model Rules? Does Beth have a valid claim for ineffective assistance of counsel?

2. Robin represents Wayne in a criminal prosecution for allegedly murdering Lance. Wayne explains to Robin that he shot Lance because he believed that Lance had a gun under his pillow and was about to pull it out and kill him. The police did not find a gun in Lance's apartment in the investigation of the crime. On the eve of trial, Wayne tells Robin that he is planning on testifying in his own behalf and is going to say that he saw Lance pull out a metallic object from under his pillow, which is why he shot him. Robin reminds Wayne that he must testify truthfully, but Wayne insists that it is necessary to his claim of self-defense to say he actually saw a weapon. Robin tells Wayne that he will not let Wayne testify falsely, and thus he will not allow Wayne to testify at all in light of Wayne's proposed testimony. At trial, Wayne tells Robin that he will testify truthfully if Robin will allow him to testify on his own behalf. Robin agrees, and Wayne testifies truthfully and is convicted. Did Robin violate the Model Rules? Does Wayne have a valid claim for ineffective assistance of counsel?

Deportation Consequences of a Plea

As in *Frye*, the Court has indicated that certain practices will typically constitute deficient performance of counsel under the first prong of the *Strickland* test. Notably, in Padilla v. Kentucky, 559 U.S. 356 (2010), the Supreme Court held that it was constitutionally deficient performance of counsel for an attorney to fail to inform a non-citizen criminal defendant of the potential deportation consequences of a guilty plea. Jose Padilla had been a lawful permanent resident of the United States for more than 40 years and had served in the Vietnam War as a member of the U.S. armed forces. He was charged with transporting a large amount of marijuana. His counsel told him that he did not need to worry about deportation because Padilla had been in the United States so long. Relying on this advice, Padilla accepted a deal and pled guilty to a criminal charge that (unbeknownst to him at the time) mandated his deportation. Padilla sought post-conviction relief, arguing that he would have insisted on going to trial rather than pleading guilty had he known that he would be deported as a direct result of his plea. The Supreme Court held as to the first *Strickland* prong that "[t]he weight of prevailing professional norms supports the view that counsel must advise her client regarding the risk of deportation." The Court remanded as to the prejudice prong. The Court also explained that where immigration laws are complex or make deportation consequences unclear or uncertain, "a criminal defense attorney need do no more than advise a noncitizen client that pending criminal charges may carry a risk of adverse immigration consequences."[22]

3. *Strickland's* Second Prong: Prejudice

Strickland's prejudice prong is a serious roadblock to a successful assertion of ineffective assistance of counsel. In cases where there is substantial evidence of guilt, it is nearly impossible to overcome the prejudice prong and show that there is a reasonable probability that but for the errors of counsel the outcome would be different—because in light of the substantial evidence, it appears that the defendant would have been convicted anyway. This hurdle effectively blocks claims despite even substantial errors and incompetence of counsel.

In cases dealing with guilty pleas, the prejudice prong must be considered differently depending on whether the defendant did not accept a favorable plea due to counsel's incompetence (as in *Frye*) or accepted an unfavorable plea due to counsel's incompetence (as in *Padilla*). The Court in *Frye* explained how to determine prejudice in these situations:

> To show prejudice from ineffective assistance of counsel where a plea offer has lapsed or been rejected because of counsel's deficient performance, defendants must demonstrate a reasonable probability they would have accepted the earlier plea offer had they been afforded effective assistance of counsel. Defendants must also demonstrate a reasonable probability the plea would have been entered without the prosecution canceling it or the trial court refusing to accept it, if they had the authority to exercise that discretion under state law....
>
> ... In cases where a defendant complains that ineffective assistance led him to accept a plea offer as opposed to proceeding to trial, the defendant will have to show a reasonable probability that, but for counsel's errors, he would not have pleaded guilty and would have insisted on going to trial.[23]

Thus, in situations like *Padilla* where the accused accepted an unfavorable plea, the defendant has to show that she would not have pled guilty absent her attorney's incompetence but would have proceeded to trial instead; and in situations like *Frye* where the accused failed to accept a favorable plea, the defendant must show both "a reasonable probability [defendant] would have accepted the earlier plea offer" and "that, if the prosecution had the discretion to cancel it or if the trial court had the discretion to refuse to accept it, there is a reasonable probability neither the

22. *Padilla*, 559 U.S. at 369.
23. *Frye*, 566 U.S. at 147-48 (internal citations omitted).

prosecution nor the trial court would have prevented the offer from being accepted or implemented."[24]

There are also situations in which prejudice is presumed and the defendant is relieved of the obligation to prove it to succeed on a claim of ineffective assistance of counsel. As the Supreme Court recognized in United States v. Cronic, 466 U.S. 648 (1984), decided the same day as *Strickland*, there are "circumstances that are so likely to prejudice the accused that the cost of litigating their effect in a particular case is unjustified." Such a presumption was appropriate where it was shown "that [defense] counsel failed to function in any meaningful sense as the Government's adversary." Citing *Powell v. Alabama* as an example, the Court said that it had "uniformly found constitutional error without any showing of prejudice when counsel was either totally absent, or prevented from assisting the accused during a critical stage of the proceeding" or where defense counsel "entirely fail[ed] to subject the prosecution's case to meaningful adversarial testing."[25]

Where a criminal defense counsel's performance is affected by a conflict of interest, the Supreme Court has not required a showing of prejudice. In Cuyler v. Sullivan, 446 U.S. 335 (1980), the Supreme Court held that where a criminal defendant suffers from a conflict of interest (in that case representing three co-defendants), a criminal defendant need only show (1) the existence of an actual conflict of interest; and (2) that the conflict adversely affected counsel's performance.

C. WHEN INCOMPETENCE IS NOT YOUR FAULT

What should an attorney do when incompetence is seemingly forced upon him either through being assigned an unmanageable caseload or being appointed to a representation with insufficient time to prepare? This situation has been a continuous problem, particularly, for many public defenders. In Formal Opinion 06-441, the ABA addressed the problem of unmanageable caseloads for public defenders, reiterating that the duty of competence belongs to all attorneys.

Ethical Obligations of Lawyers Who Represent Indigent Criminal Defendants When Excessive Caseloads Interfere with Competent and Diligent Representation

ABA Formal Opinion 06-441 (2006)

In this opinion, we consider the ethical responsibilities of lawyers, whether employed in the capacity of public defenders or otherwise, who represent indigent persons

24. *Id.*
25. Nevertheless, the Court held that a presumption of prejudice was unwarranted under the facts of *Cronic* itself— even though a young real estate attorney, who had never previously conducted a jury trial, was appointed to represent a defendant charged with mail fraud just 25 days before trial (the government had taken four and a half years for its own investigation and preparation for the trial).

charged with criminal offenses, when the lawyers' workloads prevent them from providing competent and diligent representation to all their clients. Excessive workloads present issues for both those who represent indigent defendants and the lawyers who supervise them.

ETHICAL RESPONSIBILITIES OF A PUBLIC DEFENDER IN REGARD TO INDIVIDUAL WORKLOAD

Persons charged with crimes have a constitutional right to the effective assistance of counsel. Generally, if a person charged with a crime is unable to afford a lawyer, he is constitutionally entitled to have a lawyer appointed to represent him. The states have attempted to satisfy this constitutional mandate through various methods, such as establishment of public defender, court appointment, and contract systems. Because these systems have been created to provide representation for a virtually unlimited number of indigent criminal defendants, the lawyers employed to provide representation generally are limited in their ability to control the number of clients they are assigned. Measures have been adopted in some jurisdictions in attempts to control workloads, including the establishment of procedures for assigning cases to lawyers outside public defenders' offices when the cases could not properly be directed to a public defender, either because of a conflict of interest or for other reasons.

Model Rules of Professional Conduct 1.1, 1.2(a), 1.3, and 1.4 require lawyers to provide competent representation, abide by certain client decisions, exercise diligence, and communicate with the client concerning the subject of representation. These obligations include, but are not limited to, the responsibilities to keep abreast of changes in the law; adequately investigate, analyze, and prepare cases; act promptly on behalf of clients; communicate effectively on behalf of and with clients; control workload so each matter can be handled competently; and, if a lawyer is not experienced with or knowledgeable about a specific area of the law, either associate with counsel who is knowledgeable in the area or educate herself about the area. The Rules provide no exception for lawyers who represent indigent persons charged with crimes.

Comment 2 to Rule 1.3 states that a lawyer's workload "must be controlled so that each matter may be handled competently." The Rules do not prescribe a formula to be used in determining whether a particular workload is excessive. National standards as to numerical caseload limits have been cited by the American Bar Association. Although such standards may be considered, they are not the sole factor in determining if a workload is excessive. Such a determination depends not only on the number of cases, but also on such factors as case complexity, the availability of support services, the lawyer's experience and ability, and the lawyer's nonrepresentational duties. If a lawyer believes that her workload is such that she is unable to meet the basic ethical obligations required of her in the representation of a client, she must not continue the representation of that client or, if representation has not yet begun, she must decline the representation.

A lawyer's primary ethical duty is owed to existing clients. Therefore, a lawyer must decline to accept new cases, rather than withdraw from existing cases, if the acceptance of a new case will result in her workload becoming excessive. When an existing workload does become excessive, the lawyer must reduce it to the extent that what remains to be done can be handled in full compliance with the Rules.

When a lawyer receives appointments directly from the court rather than as a member of a public defender's office or law firm that receives the appointment, she should take appropriate action if she believes that her workload will become, or already is, excessive. Such action may include the following:

- requesting that the court refrain from assigning the lawyer any new cases until such time as the lawyer's existing caseload has been reduced to a level that she is able to accept new cases and provide competent legal representation; and
- if the excessive workload cannot be resolved simply through the court's not assigning new cases, the lawyer should file a motion with the trial court requesting permission to withdraw from a sufficient number of cases to allow the provision of competent and diligent representation to the remaining clients.

If the lawyer has sought court permission to withdraw from the representation and that permission has been denied, the lawyer must take all feasible steps to assure that the client receives competent representation.

When a lawyer receives appointments as a member of a public defender's office or law firm, the appropriate action to be taken by the lawyer to reduce an excessive workload might include, with approval of the lawyer's supervisor:

- transferring non-representational responsibilities within the office, including managerial responsibilities, to others;
- refusing new cases; and
- transferring current case(s) to another lawyer whose workload will allow for the transfer of the case(s).

If the supervisor fails to provide appropriate assistance or relief, the lawyer should continue to advance up the chain of command within the office until either relief is obtained or the lawyer has reached and requested assistance or relief from the head of the public defender's office. . . .

In State v. Miller, 76 A.3d 1250 (N.J. 2013), the New Jersey Supreme Court held that there had not been ineffective assistance when the defendant, Terrence Miller, was represented at trial and convicted of drug-related offenses under the following circumstances:

> On Thursday, December 6, 2007, defendant's new attorney was informed by his supervisors at the Mercer County OPD that he would be transferred from his current assignment in the Mercer County OPD's juvenile unit to a trial team responsible for cases overseen by the trial judge in this case. The attorney was told that day that he would serve as defendant's trial counsel and that defendant's trial was expected to begin on the following Monday, December 10, 2007. It would be his first adult criminal trial in seven years. Defendant's attorney, concerned that he was being assigned a case with an imminent trial date, immediately went to the trial judge's chambers, explained the

reassignment and informally requested that the trial date be adjourned. The trial judge denied his request and advised him that the case would proceed to trial as scheduled.

The attorney spent several hours before Monday preparing, but "[h]e had no contact with defendant in the days leading up to trial." Indeed, the attorney met Miller for the first time on December 10, 2007, when the court held a suppression hearing, with trial proper starting on December 11. After being introduced, "counsel and defendant conferred for approximately twenty-five minutes in a window area of an empty stairwell between two floors of the courthouse." Again, counsel moved for an adjournment, which the court denied despite no opposition from the prosecution. Miller was convicted. On appeal, Miller argued that he had been denied effective assistance of counsel; he also noted that under the circumstances of his representation Miller had not been able to locate and call witnesses that could corroborate Miller's version of the facts, which was essential in both the suppression hearing and the trial. Nevertheless, the New Jersey Supreme Court upheld his conviction, holding that Miller had failed to show that he suffered prejudice under *Strickland.*

Case Preview

Ohio v. Jones

In upholding the conviction in *Miller*, the New Jersey Supreme Court relied in part on the fact that Miller's attorney stated on the record at the beginning of trial that he was prepared to proceed. What if the defense lawyer had stated on the record that he was *not* prepared and couldn't competently go forward? Might the appeal have gone differently? In *Ohio v. Jones*, a criminal defense attorney took that different path.

As you read *Ohio v. Jones*, consider the following:

1. What efforts should a defense attorney take to preserve the right of the criminal defendant to have a fair trial when the state has the burden to prove guilt beyond reasonable doubt (and the defendant has the presumption of innocence on her side)? Is the opportunity to argue ineffective assistance of counsel on appeal an adequate substitute for having competent counsel at trial?
2. What are the costs to the criminal defendant to proceed with a representation when an attorney is simply unprepared and has not been given sufficient time or resources to prepare?

Ohio v. Jones

2008-Ohio-6994 (Ohio Ct. App. 2008)

Appellant, Brian Jones, appeals from the January 7, 2008, judgment entry of the Portage County Municipal Court, Kent Division, in which he was sentenced for contempt.

Appellant, an attorney with the Portage County Public Defender's Office, was appointed on August 15, 2007, to represent Jordan Scott ("defendant Scott") on a charge of misdemeanor assault in State v. Scott. The case was set for trial the following day.

According to appellant's affidavit, on the morning of the trial, he met with six other clients before receiving the Scott file. Appellant then met with defendant Scott for twenty minutes. When the case was called, appellant informed Portage County Municipal Court Judge John J. Plough ("Judge Plough") that he would be filing a jury demand. After Judge Plough stated that the matter was set for trial, appellant indicated that he had been appointed to the case the day before. Appellant voiced concerns that he would not be effective as defendant Scott's counsel and would not feel comfortable representing him. Appellant said that he would need more time to talk to the witnesses. Judge Plough replied that three witnesses were present and the trial would proceed after lunch. Appellant indicated that he needed to speak with other witnesses whom the state had not subpoenaed.

Following the break, the trial court reconvened and proceeded with the Scott case. As appellant attempted to raise a pretrial matter, Judge Plough asked him whether he was ready to start the trial. Appellant replied that he was not and that he did not have an opportunity to interview the witnesses. Judge Plough warned appellant that he would be held in contempt of court if he did not proceed with the trial. Over objection by defense counsel, Judge Plough ordered the trial to commence. Appellee, the state of Ohio, waived its opening statement and appellant informed the trial court that he was not able to participate in the case. Judge Plough threatened appellant that if he did not proceed, he would be taken to jail immediately. . . . Judge Plough wanted appellant to proceed with the trial, and if a conviction resulted, the defendant could file an appeal on the basis of ineffective assistance of counsel. Appellant did not comply. The trial court found appellant in direct criminal contempt and ordered him to be taken into custody.

. . .

In the instant matter, the record reveals that appellant was appointed to represent defendant Scott the day before the case was set for trial. Appellant orally requested a continuance, which was denied by Judge Plough. . . . Here, the facts demonstrate that a continuance was warranted. . . . In addition, the continuance requested by appellant was for legitimate reasons and his conduct did not give rise to the need for one. Again, appellant was permitted merely two hours to familiarize himself with the facts, the witnesses, and his client, before preparing and constructing a defense based upon his findings. The mere fact that defendant Scott was charged with misdemeanor assault does not render the matter simple or inconsequential. Based on the information available to appellant, there may have been any number of potential witnesses and defenses pertinent to the assault charge and it was his obligation to conduct a complete investigation.

Under these circumstances, effective assistance and ethical compliance were impossible as appellant was not permitted sufficient time to conduct a satisfactory investigation as required by Rule 1.1 of the Ohio Rules of Professional Conduct, and the Sixth Amendment of the United States Constitution. It would have been unethical for appellant to proceed with trial as any attempt at rendering effective assistance would have been futile. Appellant properly refused to put his client's constitutional rights at risk by proceeding to trial unprepared.

"The rights of indigent defendants to appointment and effective assistance of counsel are neither lofty philosophical ideals nor rights that only function to give us all faith in the criminal justice system. . . . The rights to appointment of counsel and to effective assistance ultimately impact not only whether people are convicted of crimes based on fair processes but moreover, whether innocent people are convicted of crimes they did not commit. These are both outcomes whose probabilities should be reduced whenever and however feasible." . . .

The rights guaranteed to citizens under the Constitution are clearly defined and include the right to effective and competent assistance of counsel, the right to subpoena witnesses, the right to confront one's accusers and above all a right to a fair trial. Counsel must be given ample opportunity to prepare, investigate and discover the facts of the accusation. Furthermore, counsel must have time to investigate witness testimony, the nature of the allegations, and develop possible defenses in order to properly represent his or her client and provide effective assistance. The right to a speedy trial is a right both constitutional and statutory which inures to the defendant not the court.

By denying appellant's motion for a continuance, Judge Plough improperly placed an administrative objective of controlling the court's docket above its supervisory imperative of facilitating effective, prepared representation and a fair trial. . . .

In his third assignment of error, appellant alleges that [an appellate] court was not the proper forum for curing the types of defects in this matter. [This argument is in response to Judge Plough's suggestion to Jones that any incompetence could be fixed on appeal through a claim of ineffective assistance of counsel.]

Strickland v. Washington (1984), 466 U.S. 668, 687, states:

> . . . "When a convicted defendant complains of the ineffectiveness of counsel's assistance, the defendant must show that counsel's representation fell below an objective standard of reasonableness." *Id.* . . . [Additionally,] "[t]o warrant reversal, '(t)he defendant must show that there is a reasonable probability that, but for counsel's unprofessional errors, the result of the proceeding would have been different. A reasonable probability is a probability sufficient to undermine confidence in the outcome.' "

In the case sub judice, had defendant Scott been convicted, his right to the presumption of innocence would have been unfairly replaced by a burden on appeal to demonstrate a "reasonable probability" that the result of the proceeding would have been different if appellant had been prepared. In denying a continuance, Judge Plough improperly relied on the appellate process to correct the likely deprivation of defendant Scott's constitutional right to effective assistance of counsel. Direct appeal is not a reliable remedy to fix an obvious error, which could have been prevented at inception. The judicial system, the state, the defendant, and the public are always best served when the proceedings and the trial are performed with a "best practices" approach to adhere to constitutional and statutory requirements, especially when the trial record is limited. Also, by the time an appeal would have been perfected, defendant Scott's sentence would have likely been expired. Appellate courts should

not be used to correct errors, especially those involving constitutional rights that a trial court has anticipated and which could have been prevented.

. . .

For the foregoing reasons, . . . [t]he judgment of the Portage County Municipal Court, Kent Division, is reversed with respect to holding appellant in contempt.

Post-Case Follow-Up

Consider what would have happened had Jones proceeded with the trial unprepared and his client had been convicted. What remedy would the client have? Of course, the client could seek to overturn the conviction, claiming ineffective assistance of counsel — but in that situation, the client would have the burden of proof to overcome the "strong presumption" that his attorney acted with reasonable proficiency. Further, the client would have had to prove prejudice — that but for the lack of preparation, there was a reasonable probability that he would not have been convicted. Compare this immense uphill burden for the defendant with what the criminal defendant should have been given: his constitutional right to have competent counsel prepare his case adequately with the presumption of innocence on his side and the burden on the state to prove guilt beyond a reasonable doubt. Jones's contempt preserved these essential constitutional rights of his client, including his right to effective assistance of counsel.

Ohio v. Jones: Real Life Applications

1. A junior public defender is assigned nearly twice as many cases as she can handle. According to ABA Formal Opinion 06-441, what can and should the public defender do?

2. Sandra is an attorney who has just opened her own solo practice. She wants to bring in clientele, so she participates in a Groupon deal of the day. Under the deal, Sandra sells for $50 the first ten hours of legal work on any family law matter. She pledges to complete the work within a month of the purchase of the deal. One hundred people buy the deal on the day it is promoted, meaning that Sandra has to complete 1,000 hours of legal work within the month (there are only 744 hours in the month). What should Sandra do? What should she have done to avoid this problem if she wanted to participate in the Groupon deal of the day?

D. COMPETENCE, MENTAL HEALTH, AND SUBSTANCE ABUSE

In a 2007 article published in the *Professional Lawyer*, J. Nick Badgerow identified an "apocalypse at law," arguing that "four horsemen" are destroying the lives of a sizable contingent of our profession — along with their ability to competently care for their clients' matters. The "four horsemen of the modern bar" Badgerow identified are "drugs, alcohol, gambling, and depression."[26]

Is Badgerow's apocalyptic diagnosis overstated? Probably not. Alcoholism, drug use, depression, and other mental health issues plague the legal profession and lead to incompetent handling of cases and professional discipline.[27] Badgerow reviews case after case where attorneys suffering with these issues have, for example, failed to communicate with clients; failed to perform the requisite legal services for a matter; failed to maintain client files, records, and appropriate accounts; failed to notify clients of receipt of funds; failed to return prepaid unearned fees; misappropriated client funds; and failed to respond to the bar's investigation of their conduct.

Patrick Krill has summarized:

> As it turns out, attorneys who struggle with alcohol dependence—who struggle with the disease of addiction—are substantially more likely to underserve their clients, commit malpractice, face disciplinary action and disbarment, fall victim to mental health problems, and even take their own lives. Notably, at least 25 percent of attorneys who face formal disciplinary charges from their state bar are identified as suffering from addiction or other mental illness, with substance abuse playing at least some role in 60 percent of all disciplinary cases. Furthermore, approximately 60 percent of all malpractice claims and 85 percent of all trust fund violation cases involve substance abuse.[28]

It thus appears that alcoholism and substance abuse create a fairly sure path to the problems with attorney incompetence delineated throughout this chapter (and the resultant harms to clients). Krill subsequently co-authored a study conducted jointly by the ABA Commission on Lawyer Assistance Programs and the Hazelden Betty Ford Foundation, which was published in 2016 in the *Journal of Addiction Medicine*.[29] As summarized by James Podgers, the study revealed two main trends:

> First, the levels of problem drinking and mental health issues in the legal profession appear to be higher than indicated by previous studies. And second, younger lawyers are the segment of the profession most at risk of substance abuse and mental health problems. Previous studies indicated that older lawyers were more at risk for developing problems in both areas.[30]

Indeed, the 2016 study showed that "20.6 percent of the lawyers and judges surveyed reported problematic alcohol use," but "using a variation of the questionnaire

26. J. Nick Badgerow, *Apocalypse at Law: The Four Horsemen of the Modern Bar*, 18 No. 3 PROF. LAW. 2 (2007).
27. As noted in Badgerow's article, gambling is also a significant and problematic addiction among attorneys—in part because attorneys have access to client funds and often addicted gamblers convince themselves to "borrow" them, sure that their luck will turn and they can repay the money with ease. *See id.*
28. Patrick Krill, *If There Is One Bar a Lawyer Cannot Seem to Pass: Alcoholism in the Legal Profession*, THE BRIEF, Vol. 44, no. 1 (2014).
29. *See* Patrick R. Krill, Ryan Johnson & Linda Albert, *The Prevalence of Substance Use and Other Mental Health Concerns Among American Attorneys*, 10 J. ADDICT. MED. 46 (2016).
30. *Younger Lawyers Are Most at Risk for Substance Abuse, and Mental Health Problems, a New Study Reports*, A.B.A. J., Feb. 7, 2016, *available at* http://www.abajournal.com/news/article/younger_lawyers_are_most_at_risk_for_substance_abuse_and_mental_health_prob.

that focuses solely on the frequency of alcohol consumption, [] 36.4 percent of the respondents qualified as problem drinkers."[31] (Keep in mind that for the general adult population, 6.4 percent have an alcohol use disorder.[32]) Further, the study found that "being in the early stages of one's legal career is strongly correlated with a high risk of developing an alcohol use disorder."[33]

Why would substance abuse and mental health problems be more prevalent among younger lawyers? Linda Albert and Patrick Krill surmise:

> Many lawyers find themselves working long hours; getting minimal sleep; not eating well; and distancing themselves from family, friends, and colleagues as they attempt to keep up with the demands of the profession. These patterns are reinforced by organizations that impose heavy workloads on their employees without consideration for the impact upon those employees. Young lawyers are having difficulties finding jobs and paying off student loans and often struggle to maintain adequate social support, while also postponing life events such as marriage and starting a family. It is possible, if not probable, that these circumstances contribute to the higher level of distress symptoms we see among lawyers during their first 15 years of practice.[34]

Do the addictive behaviors destructive of the careers (and lives) of attorneys and the legal rights of their clients begin (or blossom) in law school? The 2016 Survey of Law Student Well-Being (SLSWB) gathered information from law students at 15 U.S. law schools, which resulted in the following statistics as to the law students surveyed:

- 53 percent drank enough to become drunk at least once in the prior 30 days
- 43 percent binge drank at least one time in the prior two weeks
- 22 percent binge drank two or more times in the prior two weeks
- 25 percent used marijuana in the prior year
- 14 percent used marijuana in the prior 30 days
- 6 percent used cocaine in the prior year
- 2 percent used cocaine in the prior 30 days
- 14 percent used prescription drugs without a prescription in the prior year
- 17 percent screened positive for depression (using Patient Health Questionnaire-2)
- 37 percent screened positive for anxiety (using Kessler 6 questionnaire)[35]

Despite these numbers, only 4 percent of surveyed students had actually sought help for drug or alcohol problems. Around 23 percent had sought help for mental illness problems. Why didn't more seek help? The survey asked about deterrents to

---

31. *See id.*
32. *See* Linda Albert & Patrick Krill, *Wellness and the Legal Profession: Implications of the 2016 Landmark Study on the Prevalence of Substance Use and Mental Health Concerns Among U.S. Attorneys*, B. Examiner 50, 54 (2016). The 6.4 percent correlates with the 21 percent of lawyers with problematic drinking. But even as to the questionnaire producing the 36 percent number for problematic drinking by lawyers, the same questionnaire was used to survey problematic drinking among physicians in 2012, with a resultant 15 percent. *See id.* at 52.
33. *See* Krill, Johnson & Albert, *supra* note 29, at 51.
34. *See* Albert & Krill, *supra* note 32, at 54-55.
35. Jerome M. Organ, David B. Jaffe & Katherine M. Bender, *Suffering in Silence: The Survey of Law Student Well-Being and the Reluctance of Law Students to Seek Help for Substance Use and Mental Health Concerns*, 66 J. Legal Educ. No. 1 (2016).

seeking help, and over 60 percent of respondents indicated a concern of a potential threat to bar admission or finding a job (hence the title of the findings from the survey, "Suffering in Silence").[36]

So what can be done? Albert and Krill contend that wellness needs to be taught and emphasized in law school and to legal professionals. They explain: "Wellness concepts include teaching law students and legal professionals about stress management as well as building hardiness and resiliency skills; the importance of physical exercise, good sleep, and quality nutrition; minimizing alcohol use; and incorporating interpersonal connectedness into their lives."[37] Learning to deal with stress in ways other than alcohol and substance abuse is key—and that learning needs to start and be encouraged during law school. Certainly law school is stressful—but law practice is also stressful—thus students who find themselves turning to alcohol and substance abuse or who have mental health issues in law school need to recognize that graduating and moving on to law practice will not solve the problems. Each student should engage in serious self-reflection on whether she is at risk and take appropriate actions, including where appropriate seeking help from health professionals, Lawyer Assistance Programs, or university or law school counselors. Every jurisdiction in the United States has a Lawyers Assistance Program, which offers assistance to both lawyers and law students struggling with substance abuse or other mental or emotional health problems.[38] In many jurisdictions, obtaining help from a Lawyer Assistance Program is confidential. Even if it is not, obtaining help to escape one of the four horsemen is worth the effort.

The Struggle

Above the Law (Aug. 22, 2016)[39]

Hi, my name is [redacted], and I am in recovery from alcoholism and depression. Less than a year ago, I would have never imagined uttering those words. Depression was not even on my radar, and how could I possibly have a drinking problem? At 25 years old, I was in my third year of law school, and successfully interning at two different legal organizations. On the outside, I had my life together. However, on the inside, I was really struggling.

In order to better explain "my law school struggle," I need to briefly explain my past. I grew up in a loving family but also in a family who buried emotions — the "pull yourself up by your own bootstraps" mentality. Growing up, my idea of strength was suffering in silence. It wasn't until a family tragedy occurred right before law school that I even contemplated seeking outside help. However, I quickly

36. *See id.*
37. Albert & Krill, *supra* note 32, at 55.
38. The ABA keeps a directory of Lawyer Assistance Programs for each jurisdiction on its website at http://www.americanbar.org/groups/lawyer_assistance/resources/lap_programs_by_state.html.
39. Anonymous law student story excerpted from Staci Zaretsky, *The Struggle: Will Alcoholism Treatment Affect Your Character and Fitness Review?*, Above the Law, Aug. 22, 2016, *available at* http://abovethelaw.com/2016/08/the-struggle-will-alcoholism-treatment-affect-your-character-and-fitness-review/.

dismissed the idea of mental health therapy, as I was afraid of how that could negatively affect my future legal career. Therefore, I continued to suffer in silence and began law school with unresolved grief and trauma issues. Moreover, while I was a social drinker before law school, my drinking greatly increased during law school, as I was now turning to alcohol as a way to cope with my emotions and the increased stress and pressure I was faced with on a daily basis as a law student.

By my second year of law school, I was suffering from depression and I began abusing alcohol in an attempt to "get happy." However, self-medicating with alcohol only increased my depression and by my third year in law school, I became suicidal and developed signs of alcoholism. While I functioned during the day, my evenings and weekends were spent binge drinking alone in my apartment. I no longer saw the point of living and drank myself into a stupor on multiple occasions. At this point, I knew I needed help but I was too afraid and ashamed to admit it.

Finally, I confided in a mentor who urged me to seek help and I listened. While I was fearful that mental health and addiction treatment could negatively impact my admission to the bar, I knew I had to address these issues before I started my legal career — my life was at risk. Therefore, right before my law school graduation, and to the surprise of my friends and family, I electively entered a thirty-day inpatient treatment program for mental health and alcohol addiction.

Today, I am over nine months sober and I can honestly say my life is now worth living. For the first time in a long time, I am happy and healthy. Unfortunately, I cannot say my journey to health, happiness, and sobriety has been an easy one. It has taken a lot of self-care, mental health therapy, and recovery support to get to this point.

Chapter Summary

- Clients hire attorneys because clients lack the requisite knowledge, skill, and ability to protect their own legal interests and rights; thus attorneys who are incompetent violate their first and basic duty to their clients: to protect their clients' interests.
- Competence requires that an attorney act with the requisite legal knowledge and skill to handle a case; attorneys can obtain competence in a new area of law through necessary study or by associating with an attorney of established competence.
- Competence requires lawyers to thoroughly investigate the facts of a case and make sufficient preparation, including the preparation of appropriate documents and filings, for legal proceedings and transactions.
- Attorneys have a duty to act with reasonable diligence and promptness in representing a client, which requires lawyers to manage their workload and avoid procrastination.
- Communication is essential to a successful attorney-client relationship: the attorney and client must communicate both (1) for the attorney to properly

pursue the client's actual objectives and to determine the factual bases for the claims; and (2) for the client to meaningfully participate in the matter and be informed regarding the status of the case.

- Attorneys must communicate any circumstance regarding which the client must give informed consent, which includes those matters within the sole authority of the client to decide, such as whether to settle a civil matter and, in criminal cases, the plea to be entered, waiver of jury trial, and whether the defendant will testify in her own behalf.
- Attorneys must promptly respond to a client's reasonable request for information, which means the attorney must respond to or at least acknowledge receipt of the communication.
- Criminal defendants have a constitutional right to the effective assistance of counsel. In order to prevail on such a claim, the defendant must show both (1) deficient performance—counsel's conduct fell measurably below that expected of a reasonable attorney gauged by prevailing professional norms; and (2) prejudice—there is a reasonable probability that but for counsel's errors, the result of the proceeding would have been different.
- Alcohol and other substance abuse and mental health problems are particularly prevalent among lawyers and often lead to incompetence, failure to communicate or act with diligence, and other disciplinary problems—all of which inure to the detriment of the client.

Applying the Rules

1. Joel is a solo practitioner who has primarily done criminal defense representation, but wants to change his area of practice. A wealthy neighbor, Sally, asks Joel to draft a will for her. Joel is excited about the opportunity to do something different. However, he knows absolutely nothing about wills or estate planning. Joel wants to have a friend of his, Ralph, assist with the will because Ralph is an established attorney with his own estate planning practice. Does Joel need to tell Sally about his desire to have Ralph assist with the representation? Does Sally need to consent to bringing Ralph into the matter? (Consult comment 6 to Rule 1.1, as well as Rule 1.4.)

2. Mattie is an attorney who has practiced entirely in state court. Mattie decides to file a lawsuit in federal court on behalf of a new client, Landblast, Inc. She reads Rule 8(a) of the Federal Rules of Civil Procedure (FRCP) and sees that it is identical in language to the state civil procedure rule 8(a). In the state where she lives, civil procedure rule 8(a) is construed to only require notice pleading. However, in federal court, and unbeknownst to Mattie, the Supreme Court in the *Twombly* and *Iqbal* cases reinterpreted FRCP 8(a) to require that an attorney plead sufficient facts to plausibly state a claim and held that legal conclusions are not entitled to an assumption of truth. Mattie files a complaint in federal court that contains almost no factual assertions but is just a recital of legal conclusions.

The federal trial court grants the opposing party's FRCP 12(b)(6) motion to dismiss for failure to state a claim upon which relief can be granted, and orders Mattie to file a new amended complaint that complies with federal pleading standards within ten days or the complaint will be dismissed with prejudice. The court's order also directly chastises Mattie for her obvious failure to stay abreast of the Supreme Court's interpretation of Rule 8(a). Has Mattie violated the Model Rules? Must Mattie disclose the court's order to her client or can she just quietly fix it by filing an amended complaint? What does she need to do to ensure that she proceeds in a competent manner?

3. Taylor was in an automobile wreck with Simon. Taylor sued Simon, and Jane undertook the representation of Simon. After lengthy pretrial proceedings, the court ordered that the case be transferred to mandatory arbitration. Jane was aware of this order. Jane did not ever receive notice about the case being scheduled on the arbitration calendar, but four months later, she learned that she had missed the mandatory hearing and the arbitration court had entered a $10,000 default arbitration award against Simon for failure to appear. Jane moved to vacate the award, arguing that she had received no notice of the hearing. The court responded that a postcard notice had been mailed to her, and even if she had not received it she should have checked the mandatory arbitration calendar herself in the intervening four months from the initial order to determine the date of the arbitration hearing. Did Jane have a duty to inquire into the dates if she really did not see the notice (regardless of the reason for her not receiving the notice)?

4. Henry is a bankruptcy attorney who handles a high volume of relatively simple bankruptcy petitions for individuals. Henry delegates most of the work in drafting and handling the bankruptcy petitions to his paralegals. The bankruptcy court determines that the debts of Henry's client, George, are non-dischargeable, and the court issues an order stating that the bankruptcy was neither filed nor handled in a competent manner. George files a grievance with the bar. Can Henry be disciplined for the incompetence of his paralegal's work? What should Henry have done?

5. Tanya is a criminal defense lawyer who has a very heavy caseload and is worn out. She is appointed to represent Trevor in a prosecution for felony murder. At trial, she repeatedly falls asleep during the State's presentation of evidence—and even a few times during the State's cross-examination of her own witnesses. The State presents substantial evidence of guilt, and Trevor is convicted. Does Trevor have a meritorious claim for ineffective assistance of counsel?

Professional Responsibility in Practice

1. You are an associate at the law firm Moore & Less. Three different partners email you an assignment on Monday morning: one needs you to write a summary judgment motion in a large case, one needs you to draft discovery requests and respond to the opposition's discovery requests, and one needs you to prepare pretrial disclosures for an upcoming trial. All three assignments must be completed by the end of the week. You work diligently for a couple days and realize you cannot complete all three assignments by the end of the week, and perhaps cannot complete any one of them. How should you proceed and how soon should you do so? Plan out what you would actually say to a partner under these circumstances.

2. You have a client, Darrin, who calls or emails you daily to discuss the progress of his case. You have taken the case on contingency, so you are not charging Darrin an hourly rate for the time it takes to answer and respond to his inquiries. Darrin's case does not need constant attention—indeed, you have just sent out discovery requests, and it will be 30 days before you receive responses and have any new information to disclose to Darrin. In addition, you have several other matters that need your full attention. Draft an email to your client that will not strain your relationship with him, will fulfill your communication duties to him, and will also allow you to devote your time to your other matters.

3. A number of jurisdictions have adopted ethics opinions about the risks and competent use of cloud computing and other new or emerging technologies. Research whether there are any such opinions in the state in which you now live or intend to practice and write a brief summary of any such opinion.

5

Confidentiality, the Attorney-Client Privilege, and Work-Product Immunity

A. OVERVIEW: UNDERSTANDING CONFIDENTIALITY, THE ATTORNEY-CLIENT PRIVILEGE, AND WORK-PRODUCT IMMUNITY

The attorney-client relationship is a **fiduciary** one that creates obligations of loyalty and secrecy on the part of the lawyer. The attorney must keep her client's information secret, and may not disclose confidences learned during the relationship to the disadvantage of the client. This **confidentiality** obligation is imposed for two primary reasons. First, it furthers the normative goal of protecting the autonomy of the client and her authority to control the purposes and direction of the representation. Second, it serves the utilitarian function of encouraging clients to communicate fully and frankly with their lawyers, even on embarrassing or sensitive topics. The premise here is that lawyers need full and accurate information from their clients in order to render sound legal advice.

There are three sources of the attorney's secrecy obligations — the ethical duty of confidentiality under Model Rules 1.6 and 1.9, the **attorney-client privilege** under the Rules of Evidence, and the common law **work-product immunity** in

Key Concepts

- The ethical obligation to keep client information confidential
- Exceptions to the duty of confidentiality: to defend a claim against the lawyer, or to prevent certain future harms
- Protecting the confidentiality of client communications under the attorney-client evidentiary privilege
- The attorney-client privilege is subject to waivers and exceptions
- Work-product immunity protects from discovery a lawyer's preparations in anticipation of litigation

litigation. You can think of these three secrecy obligations as partially overlapping circles, with the ethical duty of confidentiality being the largest circle, the attorney-client privilege being the second largest circle, and the work-product protection being the smallest circle. See Figure 5.1, Three Circles of Lawyer "Secrets," *infra* at page 295.

The three doctrines can be and often are confused by laymen and by law students; nevertheless, they derive from distinct sources, impose different rights and responsibilities upon attorneys, and carry different exceptions. We will examine each doctrine in turn, and then compare them in the Chapter Summary.

B. THE DUTY OF CONFIDENTIALITY

Confidentiality is part of the professional duty of loyalty (fiduciary duty) that agents owe to their principals. The basic duty of confidentiality is set forth in Model Rule 1.6(a) with exceptions in 1.6(b). The duty of confidentiality prohibits lawyers from voluntarily disclosing information that they learn in the course of representing a client to others (third parties, the media, opposing counsel) unless they have the express or implied permission of their client, or unless an exception applies. Put simply, you cannot blab about non-public aspects of your client's case to other people. Lawyers who breach this confidentiality obligation may be subject to professional discipline and may be sued by their clients in tort for breach of fiduciary duty.

Students often confuse the duty of confidentiality under Rule 1.6 with the attorney-client privilege. But there are important differences. The first is the source of the information. In this regard, the ethical rule of confidentiality is much broader than the rule of privilege.

As you will see below, the privilege protects only information communicated in secret between the client and the attorney. The confidentiality rule, by contrast, protects not only information communicated from the client himself, but also information that the lawyer learns from talking to third-party witnesses, from consulting with experts and consultants, and from preexisting documents that the client provides to the lawyers. Rule 1.6 defines **confidential material** as any "information relating to the representation of a client." Given this very broad definition, even *the fact* of representation may be confidential if the client has not expressly or impliedly authorized it to be revealed. For example, if a famous professional athlete is thinking about getting a divorce and approaches a small law firm that is renowned for litigating high-profile probate matters to discuss his options, that firm could not reveal its representation of the athlete before he makes a final decision to pursue a divorce because this may disadvantage the client.

Given this very broad definition of confidential information, lawyers need to understand that even casual conversations with friends or loved ones about their work on behalf of a client (over dinner or at the gym) may violate the disciplinary rules. Talking about a case in terms of a generalized hypothetical is permissible so long as the listener is not able to ascertain the identity of the client or the particulars of the client's situation. *See* Model Rule 1.6 cmt. [4].

A second important difference between the duty of confidentiality and the rule of privilege is that the privilege is a shield that protects against judicially compelled disclosure (that is, the lawyer or client may refuse to answer or produce documents in response to a subpoena). The ethical rule of confidentiality, by contrast, prohibits at any time the *voluntary* disclosure of client information to third parties (casual friends or acquaintances, opposing counsel, other parties contemplating lawsuits, the media, etc.). The rule of confidentiality cannot be asserted to block disclosure of information that is compelled by a court-sanctioned request for information (subpoena, deposition question, interrogatory); for that you would need to rely on the privilege, which is a rule of evidence, not a rule of professional ethics. In other words, a subpoena can reach information that is confidential, but it cannot reach information that is privileged.

A third respect in which the rules of confidentiality are broader than the rules of privilege is that under the rules of confidentiality a lawyer may not *use* confidential information to the disadvantage of the client, even if that information is never revealed to anyone. *See* Model Rule 1.8(b). Because confidential information is provided to the lawyer in a fiduciary capacity, it is impermissible for the lawyer to use that information to the disadvantage of the principal. For example, if an attorney learns of a business client's intention to relocate its manufacturing facility in the future to a remote part of the state, it would be impermissible for the lawyer to buy a piece of property in that area with the hope of increasing its value in the time period prior to the company's relocation. *See* Model Rule 1.8(b). An exception to this prohibition of "use" of client information is for information that is generally known in the community. *See* RESTATEMENT (THIRD) OF THE LAW GOVERNING LAWYERS §59 and Model Rule 1.9(c). If the same business client had publicly announced its future plans to move the manufacturing plant and this announcement was the subject of newspaper articles in local business journals, it would not be impermissible for the lawyer to speculate on real property in the area of future relocation.

Both the rule of confidentiality and the rule of privilege apply to a lawyer's dealings with **prospective clients**. *See* Model Rules 1.18(b) and 1.9(c). A lawyer who is interviewing a prospective client has a duty not to disclose confidential client information, and not to use it to the prospective client's disadvantage. Both sources of confidentiality survive the death of the client or the termination of the lawyer-client relationship. *See* Rule 1.6 cmt. [20]. So if a client is deceased, the lawyer must obtain any required permissions to waive confidentiality from the client's estate.

Lawyers have a duty to *protect* confidential client information as well as a duty not to disclose it or use it to the client's disadvantage. The duty of confidentiality under Rule 1.6(c) requires lawyers to take "reasonable efforts to prevent the inadvertent or unauthorized disclosure" of client information. So a lawyer cannot carelessly leave her client's file at a coffee shop, cannot talk about the matter with another firm attorney in an audible voice while seated in a crowded subway car, and cannot dispose of client documents in the trash without shredding them. In an era of hacking and surreptitious electronic surveillance, what security protocols will constitute "reasonable efforts" to protect client information is a constantly evolving question.

The exceptions to a lawyer's duty of confidentiality under Rule 1.6 are both numerous and controversial. We will start with the exceptions that are fairly standard from state to state. A lawyer may reveal confidential client information if that disclosure is explicitly or impliedly authorized by the client. *See* Rule 1.6(a). Explicit authorization requires **informed consent** — defined as express agreement after the client has been advised about the risks and available alternatives. *See* Rule 1.0(c). So a politician who is being criticized by his opponent for failing to release his tax returns may authorize his tax lawyer to release those returns and discuss them with the media. But in the absence of such informed consent, the tax attorney would be acting unethically by revealing the politician's tax returns to the media unilaterally, even if he thought it was in the best interests of his client.

Disclosure of confidential client information is "**impliedly authorized**" if it is necessary in order to carry out the purposes of the representation. For example, if a motor vehicle accident victim engages an attorney to sue the driver allegedly responsible for the crash, the attorney may include as factual allegations in the complaint information that the attorney learns from interviewing the client, reviewing her medical records, and consulting her physician. Implicit authorization may be inferred from the circumstances — such as where it is consistent with the goals of the representation. An attorney may write a demand letter to opposing counsel revealing factual information learned from his intake interview with his client and documents provided by the client, if such a demand letter would facilitate a settlement that is desired by the client.

There are four other fairly standard exceptions to client confidentiality that are reflected in Model Rule 1.6(b). A lawyer may reveal confidential client information to the extent the lawyer reasonably believes necessary to secure ethical advice about the lawyer's own responsibilities. *See* Model Rule 1.6(b)(4). For example, a lawyer might consult another lawyer, a retired judge, or a bar ethics committee for advice about complying with the disciplinary rules in the context of a particular legal engagement; in that context, the limited disclosure of client information is permissible to the extent necessary to accurately convey the factual issues involved. Second, a lawyer may reveal client information if reasonably necessary to establish a claim or defense in a controversy between the lawyer and the client, or in a criminal, civil, or disciplinary complaint against the lawyer brought by someone else alleging misconduct by the lawyer in his representation of that client. *See* Model Rule 1.6(f). This is known as the "self-defense" exception. If a lawyer is sued for malpractice, subjected to discipline for alleged ethical misconduct, or has to sue the client for unpaid legal fees, the revelation of confidences is allowed because the lawyer would not be able to assert his claim or defense without revealing client information. Third, a lawyer may reveal client information for the limited purpose of complying with conflict checks when the lawyer changes jobs and moves to a new law firm. *See* Model Rule 1.6(b)(7). In that situation, the lawyer may reveal the names of the clients he previously worked for and the nature of the matters involved in that representation for the purpose of being "screened" from any potential conflicts at the new firm, so long as that limited revelation does not disclose privileged material or in any way disadvantage the prior client. Finally, a lawyer may reveal confidential client information if necessary to "comply with other law or a court order." Rule 1.6(b)(6). As we will see when we study the lawyer's duty with respect to client perjury in Chapter 7, Rule 3.3(b) requires a lawyer to rectify any fraud that the client has perpetrated on an adjudicative tribunal, and this legal obligation trumps the duty of confidentiality under Rule 1.6. *See* Model Rule 3.3(c).

Most states also contain exceptions to their confidentiality rules for disclosures that are necessary to prevent **future harms**. These exceptions are complex and vary considerably from state to state. In fact, there is more variation in these future harm exceptions than in any other area of legal ethics, so students need to be attentive to their local rules. We suggest that students compare Model Rule 1.6(b) with the correlative rule in the state in which they intend to practice.

With respect to future harms, bar committees and state supreme courts drafting the exceptions to Rule 1.6 typically are trying to balance four policies: encouraging frank communications between lawyers and clients; respecting a client's autonomy and his right to control the principal-agent relationship; protecting members of the public from harm; and protecting the integrity of the profession by not allowing legal services to be used for criminal or fraudulent purposes. Proponents of broad exceptions for future harms argue that client candor is not as important as countervailing societal interests in avoiding injury; and anyway, much of what is considered "confidential" under Rule 1.6 comes from non-clients, so disclosure will not impede future candor by clients. Proponents of narrow exceptions for future harms argue that respect for client autonomy and control should outweigh a lawyer's obligations to third parties in all but the most extreme instances.

In order to understand the disagreement among state rulemakers on the issue of future harms, it may be helpful to think of confidentiality exceptions for future harms as running along four possible tracks or axes: (1) is the disclosure mandatory or is it permissive?; (2) is disclosure required/allowed when it is necessary to prevent certain *crimes*, or is it also required/allowed when it is necessary to prevent certain *crimes or frauds*?; (3) is disclosure required/allowed when it is necessary to prevent only serious bodily injury or death to another, or is it also allowed when it is necessary to prevent substantial financial injury to another?; and (4) is disclosure required/allowed only when the *client* is expected to engage in future injurious behavior, or is it also required/allowed when the future harm is likely to be committed by a *third party*?

It is impossible to catalogue here all the state variations with respect to future harm exceptions. In some places revelation may be required, in others it may be permissive, and in still others it may be forbidden. For example, California has a really narrow future harms exception, permitting disclosure only when necessary to prevent a crime involving death or serious bodily injury. *See* CAL. R. PROF'L CONDUCT, R. 3-100(B). New Jersey has an extremely broad exception, *requiring* disclosure when either a client or a third party threatens to commit a crime or a fraud that will result in death, serious bodily injury, substantial financial injury, or fraud on a tribunal. *See* N.J. R. PROF'L CONDUCT 1.6(b).

The ABA Model Rules, as you might expect, take an intermediate approach. Disclosure is permissive, but is not mandatory. While disclosure is allowed to prevent anyone (including a third party) from causing death or serious bodily injury to another person, it is only permitted to prevent a *client* from committing a crime or fraud that is likely to result in substantial financial injury, and even then only if the client has *used the lawyer's services* in furtherance of that crime or fraud. *See* Model Rule 1.6(b)(2). ABA Model Rule 1.6 was amended to add this financial injury component in 2003 in response to the Enron corporate fraud scandal. Thus, an attorney can disclose client confidences to prevent substantial financial injury to others, but only if the client is the perpetrator and only when the client has used the lawyer's services in an attempt to perpetrate that financial fraud.[1]

Imagine a lawyer for a wealthy businessman who is in the process of purchasing a piece of commercial real estate. The lawyer learns in the course of the representation that the client has inflated his assets on a multi-million dollar loan application that is pending with a bank. If the client used the lawyer's services in completing that loan application, the lawyer may reveal the client confidence to the bank in order to prevent substantial financial harm. But if the client completed the bank loan application without the lawyer's assistance, such revelation would not be permitted under ABA Model Rule 1.6(b)(2). However, before the loan closes and the funds are disbursed for the purchase of real estate the lawyer might have to withdraw from representation in order to avoid assisting a crime or fraud. *See* ABA Model Rule 1.2(d). Many lawyers would resolve this dilemma by informing the client that they are ethically required to **withdraw** before the bank closing and purchase, unless the client either remedies his false statements to the bank (by updating or amending his loan application) or gives permission to the lawyer to do so under Rule 1.6(a).

Case Preview

Purcell v. District Attorney for the Suffolk District

After receiving an order to vacate his apartment, Joseph Tyree sought legal advice from a legal services attorney, Jeffrey Purcell. Tyree had recently been discharged from his employment as a maintenance man at the apartment building where he resided. During their consultation, Purcell became suspicious that Tyree intended to burn down the apartment building. Purcell informed the Boston Police Department of his suspicions. The police then searched Tyree's apartment pursuant to a warrant and found incendiary materials, gasoline, and several bottles with wicks attached. The smoke detectors had been disconnected and gasoline had been poured on the floor. Tyree was arrested and charged with attempted arson. Purcell was later subpoenaed to testify at Tyree's trial, but he asserted the attorney-client privilege. The trial judge found that the statements Tyree made to Purcell were not protected by the attorney-client

1. Lawyers for organizational clients have wider latitude in revealing client confidences to prevent future financial harms than lawyers for individual clients. As we saw in Chapter 3, ABA Model Rule 1.13(c) allows a lawyer for an organization who knows that an officer, employee, or other person associated with the organization has engaged in a violation of law that might be imputed to the organization and is likely to result in substantial injury to the organization to report that violation out of the organization after unsuccessfully reporting it up the ladder, irrespective of whether the lawyer's services were used in furtherance of the fraud. *See* Rule 1.13(c) and cmt. [6]. Securities and Exchange Commission regulations mirror Rule 1.13(c) in this regard. *See* 17 C.F.R. §205.3(d)(2).

privilege, and denied Purcell's motion to quash the subpoena. Purcell sought extraordinary relief in a petition before the state supreme court.

As you read *Purcell*, ask yourself the following questions:

1. Was there a way that Attorney Purcell could reasonably have protected the inhabitants of the apartment building without revealing his client's statement and identity?
2. Supposed that Purcell believed he could talk his client out of the attempted arson and assure that incendiary materials were removed from the premises. Would the lawyer still be allowed to reveal the client confidence to authorities?
3. What social value is advanced by making the disclosure for future deadly harms permissive rather than mandatory under Rule 1.6? That is, don't the lives of innocents *always* outweigh the autonomy of clients?

Purcell v. District Attorney for the Suffolk District

676 N.E.2d 436 (Mass. 1997)

. . .

There is no question before this court, directly or indirectly, concerning the ethical propriety of Purcell's disclosure to the police that Tyree might engage in conduct that would be harmful to others. As bar counsel agreed in a memorandum submitted to the single justice, this court's disciplinary rules regulating the practice of law authorized Purcell to reveal to the police "[t]he intention of his client to commit a crime and the information necessary to prevent the crime." S.J.C. Rule 3:07, Canon 4, DR 4-101(C)(3), as appearing in 382 Mass. 778 (1981). The fact that the disciplinary code permitted Purcell to make the disclosure tells us nothing about the admissibility of the information that Purcell disclosed.

. . .

The attorney-client privilege is founded on the necessity that a client be free to reveal information to an attorney, without fear of its disclosure, in order to obtain informed legal advice. It is a principle of long standing. The debate here is whether Tyree is entitled to the protection of the attorney-client privilege in the circumstances.

The district attorney announces the issue in his brief to be whether a crime-fraud exception to the testimonial privilege applies in this case. He asserts that, even if Tyree's communication with Purcell was made as part of his consultation concerning the eviction proceeding, Tyree's communication concerning his contemplated criminal conduct is not protected by the privilege. We shall first consider the case on the assumption that Tyree's statements to Purcell are protected by the attorney-client privilege unless the crime-fraud exception applies.

"It is the purpose of the crime-fraud exception to the attorney-client privilege to assure that the 'seal of secrecy,' . . . between lawyer and client does not extend to communications 'made for the purpose of getting advice for the commission of a fraud' or crime." There is no public interest in the preservation of the secrecy of that kind of communication.

Our cases have not defined a crime-fraud exception to the attorney-client privilege with any precision. In *Matter of John Doe Grand Jury Investigation*, the court stated that there was "no legitimate interest of a client and no public interest would be served by a rule that would preserve the secrecy of" a conversation between attorney and client in a conference related to the possible future defrauding of an insurance company. We cited *Commonwealth v. Dyer*, in which we said that "[t]here is no privilege between attorney and client where the conferences concern the proposed commission of a crime by the client." The cases cited in our *Dyer* opinion and the facts of that case—the attorney was alleged to be part of the conspiracy—demonstrate that the exception asserted concerned conferences in which the attorney's advice was sought in furtherance of a crime or to obtain advice or assistance with respect to criminal activity.

We, therefore, accept the general principle of a crime-fraud exception. The Proposed Massachusetts Rules of Evidence adequately define the crime-fraud exception to the lawyer-client privilege set forth in rule 502(d)(1) as follows: "If the services of the lawyer were sought or obtained to enable or aid anyone to commit or plan to commit what the client knew or reasonably should have known to be a crime or fraud." We need not at this time consider seemingly minor variations of the exception expressed in various sources. The applicability of the exception, like the existence of the privilege, is a question of fact for the judge.

The district attorney rightly grants that he, as the opponent of the application of the testimonial privilege, has the burden of showing that the exception applies. In its *Zolin* opinion, the Supreme Court did not have to decide what level of showing the opponent of the privilege must make to establish that the exception applies. We conclude that facts supporting the applicability of the crime-fraud exception must be proved by a preponderance of the evidence. However, on a showing of a factual basis adequate to support a reasonable belief that an in camera review of the evidence may establish that the exception applies, the judge has discretion to conduct such an in camera review. Once the judge sees the confidential information, the burden of proof normally will be unimportant.

In this case, in deciding whether to conduct a discretionary in camera review of the substance of the conversation concerning arson between Tyree and Purcell, the judge would have evidence tending to show that Tyree discussed a future crime with Purcell and that thereafter Tyree actively prepared to commit that crime. Without this evidence, the crime of arson would appear to have no apparent connection with Tyree's eviction proceeding and Purcell's representation of Tyree. With this evidence, however, a request that a judge inquire in camera into the circumstances of Tyree's apparent threat to burn the apartment building would not be a call for a "fishing expedition," and a judge might be justified in conducting such an inquiry. The evidence in this case, however, was not sufficient to warrant the judge's finding that Tyree consulted Purcell for the purpose of obtaining advice in furtherance of a crime. Therefore, the order denying the motion to quash because the crime-fraud exception applied cannot be upheld.

There is a consideration in this case that does not appear in other cases that we have seen concerning the attorney-client privilege. The testimony that the prosecution seeks from Purcell is available only because Purcell reflectively made a disclosure, relying on this court's disciplinary rule which permitted him to do so. Purcell was under no ethical duty to disclose Tyree's intention to commit a crime. He did so to protect the lives and property of others, a purpose that underlies a lawyer's discretionary right stated in the disciplinary rule. The limited facts in the record strongly suggest that Purcell's disclosures to the police served the beneficial public purpose on which the disciplinary rule was based.

We must be cautious in permitting the use of client communications that a lawyer has revealed only because of a threat to others. Lawyers will be reluctant to come forward if they know that the information that they disclose may lead to adverse consequences to their clients. A practice of the use of such disclosures might prompt a lawyer to warn a client in advance that the disclosure of certain information may not be held confidential, thereby chilling free discourse between lawyer and client and reducing the prospect that the lawyer will learn of a serious threat to the well-being of others. To best promote the purposes of the attorney-client privilege, the crime-fraud exception should apply only if the communication seeks assistance in or furtherance of future criminal conduct. When the opponent of the privilege argues that the communication itself may show that the exception applies and seeks its disclosure in camera, the judge, in the exercise of discretion on the question whether to have an in camera proceeding, should consider if the public interest is served by disclosure, even in camera, of a communication whose existence is known only because the lawyer acted against his client's interests under the authority of a disciplinary rule. The facts of each situation must be considered.

It might seem that this opinion is in a posture to conclude by stating that the order denying the motion to quash any subpoena to testify is vacated and the matter is to be remanded for further proceedings concerning the application of the crime-fraud exception.

However, the district attorney's brief appears to abandon its earlier concession that all communications between Tyree and Purcell should be treated as protected by the attorney-client privilege unless the crime-fraud exception applies. The question whether the attorney-client privilege is involved at all will be open on remand. We, therefore, discuss the issue.

The attorney-client privilege applies only when the client's communication was for the purpose of facilitating the rendition of legal services. See Rule 502(b) of the Proposed Massachusetts Rules of Evidence. The burden of proving that the attorney-client privilege applies to a communication rests on the party asserting the privilege. The motion judge did not pass on the question whether the attorney-client privilege applied to the communication at all but rather went directly to the issue of the crime-fraud exception, although not using that phrase.

A statement of an intention to commit a crime made in the course of seeking legal advice is protected by the privilege, unless the crime-fraud exception applies. That exception applies only if the client or prospective client seeks advice or assistance in furtherance of criminal conduct. It is agreed that Tyree consulted Purcell concerning his impending eviction. Purcell is a member of the bar, and Tyree either was or sought to become Purcell's client. The serious question concerning the application of the privilege is whether Tyree informed Purcell of the fact of his intention to commit arson for the purpose of receiving legal advice or assistance in furtherance of criminal conduct. Purcell's presentation of the circumstances in which Tyree's statements were made is likely to be the only evidence presented.

This is not a case in which our traditional view that testimonial privileges should be construed strictly should be applied. A strict construction of the privilege that would leave a gap between the circumstances in which the crime-fraud exception applies and the circumstances in which a communication is protected by the attorney-client privilege would make no sense. The attorney-client privilege "is founded upon the necessity, in the interest and administration of justice, of the aid of persons having knowledge of the law and skilled in its practice, which assistance can only be safely and readily availed of when free from the consequences or the apprehension of disclosure." Unless the crime-fraud exception applies, the attorney-client privilege should apply to communications concerning possible future, as well as past, criminal conduct, because an informed lawyer may be able to dissuade the client from improper future conduct and, if not, under the ethical rules may elect in the public interest to make a limited disclosure of the client's threatened conduct.

A judgment should be entered in the county court ordering that the order denying the motion to quash any subpoena issued to Purcell to testify at Tyree's trial is vacated and that the matter is remanded for further proceedings consistent with this opinion.

So ordered.

Post-Case Follow-Up

The Massachusetts disciplinary rule was amended in 2015 to create a permissive exception to the duty of confidentiality "to prevent reasonably certain death or substantial bodily harm, or to prevent the wrongful execution or incarceration of another." MASS. R. PROF'L CONDUCT 1.6(b)(1). Note how this future harms exception in Massachusetts is now both *narrower* and *broader* than the future harms exception in effect in Massachusetts at the time of the *Purcell* decision: it is narrower because only certain highly dangerous future acts are included, but it is broader because the attorney may reveal client confidences to the extent reasonably necessary to prevent someone *other than the client* from committing those acts.

Jeffrey W. Purcell

Why were Tyree's threats to burn down the apartment building protected *at all* under the attorney-client privilege in the *Purcell* case? Is it clear that the client's statements to Purcell were part and parcel of a communication made for the purposes of obtaining legal advice? The Supreme Judicial

Court ruled that they were, because a construction of the privilege "that would leave a gap between the circumstances in which the crime-fraud exception applies and the circumstances in which a communication is protected by the attorney-client privilege would make no sense." Is that so obvious? We will return to this question after you read Section C, below.

Purcell v. District Attorney for the Suffolk District: Real Life Applications

1. Suppose that Purcell had represented a client in an employment action against a manufacturing company that had terminated the client from his job as a maintenance man. Imagine further that the client confessed to Purcell that he had unlawfully discharged toxic chemicals into the river behind the company in retribution for his discharge. The river flows into a reservoir that supplies drinking water to the public. May Purcell reveal *that* confidence to authorities? In other words, does the deadly bodily harm have to be imminent under either the 2015 Massachusetts rule or the ABA Model Rule in order for the exception to the confidentiality rule to apply? Although neither rule uses the word "imminent" in its text, the immediacy of the harm may be taken into account by the lawyer in determining whether disclosure "is reasonably necessary to prevent *reasonably certain*" death or substantial bodily harm. *See* Model Rule 1.6 cmt. [6]. Is the harm reasonably certain in the above situation?

Ordinarily, when a client comes to a lawyer and admits that he has done something wrong in the past (robbed a bank, cheated on his taxes, stolen from an employer), the lawyer's role is to help the client to avoid or minimize liability for that past misconduct. No matter how bad the conduct is or how high the stakes are, the lawyer may not favor society's interests over his client's, and must protect the client's confidences. With respect to financial harms, however, section (b)(3) of Rule 1.6 goes one step further than section (b)(2) and permits a lawyer to reveal a client confidence if reasonably necessary "to mitigate or rectify" a past crime or fraud that is reasonably certain to result in substantial financial injury to another and in furtherance of which the client has used the lawyer's services. This allows a lawyer to reveal information needed to rectify certain limited *past* misconduct, not just future misconduct. If the act causing substantial financial injury is past and the client used the lawyer's services to perpetrate that financial fraud, the lawyer may reveal confidences to the extent reasonably necessary to rectify the fraud. Here the rulemakers have valued the integrity of the profession over the client's autonomy because the client has inappropriately used legal services to assist with financial misdealing. The drafters refused to distinguish between past financial frauds and threats of future financial frauds because with financial injury — unlike with purely physical injury — that temporal line is much more difficult to draw; the manager of a company might tell a lie about the financial status of the company in a prospectus or annual report and stakeholders might rely on this fraudulent misstatement days, weeks, or months later. If the lawyer's services were used to assist with that misrepresentation in the prospectus or annual report, Rule 1.6(b)(3) would allow the lawyer to reveal client confidences if necessary to rectify the fraud. This confidentiality exception for limited past crimes or frauds is controversial; over a dozen states have declined to adopt the Model Rule formulation.

Where **confidentiality exceptions** are permissive (as they are in Model Rule 1.6(b)(1) through (7)), the exceptions allow a lawyer to reveal confidential information "to the extent the lawyer reasonably believes necessary" to meet one of the enumerated objectives. So the lawyer cannot disclose client confidences when some other course of conduct would reasonably be expected to meet the same objective; moreover, when the lawyer does reveal client information, the disclosure may be no greater than reasonably necessary to accomplish that objective. In other words, the lawyer cannot use a sledgehammer when a scalpel will suffice. With respect to disclosures reasonably believed necessary to prevent future harms, the lawyer, where feasible, must first make a good faith effort to persuade the client to prevent the harmful conduct, including advising the client of the lawyer's ability to reveal information if the client chooses not to do so. *See* Model Rule 1.6, cmt. [16]. If that fails, the lawyer may disclose only as much information as necessary to prevent the future harm.

Now that you have learned these complex — and in places ambiguous — exceptions to the rule of client confidentiality, how would you advise a new client about your professional obligation of secrecy? Many lawyers begin their discussions with new clients by saying something like "What you share with me is confidential, and I am ethically obliged to keep it secret." While this short introduction may have the advantage of simplicity (and of putting the client at ease), you now know that it is both incomplete and inaccurate. Would it be better to say nothing? We will return to this subject after addressing the attorney-client privilege.

C. THE ATTORNEY-CLIENT PRIVILEGE

1. Introduction

The attorney-client privilege is one of the oldest and broadest evidentiary privileges at common law. A cornerstone of the legal profession, the privilege permits clients to resist being compelled by legal process from disclosing confidential communications with their lawyer for legal services. Thus, a client may refuse a formal request in an interrogatory or a question on cross-examination for his or her confidential communications with counsel.

Evidentiary privileges permit the non-disclosure of otherwise relevant evidence to further important social policies unrelated to the relevancy or significance of the evidence. The attorney-client privilege promotes society's interest in the free flow of communications from the client to the lawyer and generally from the lawyer to the client; a sort of two-way communications street. Clients will hopefully communicate more candidly with their lawyers because the privilege protects their communications. Armed with a better understanding of their client's problem, lawyers can provide more informed representation and better advise their clients to observe the law.

Attorney-Client Privilege Elements Defined

Professor Wigmore's treatise on evidence provides a classic definition of the attorney-client privilege:

> (1) Where legal advice of any kind is sought (2) from a professional legal advisor in his capacity as such, (3) the communications relating to that purpose, (4) made in confidence (5) by the client,[2] (6) are at his instance permanently protected (7) from disclosure by himself or by the legal adviser, (8) except the protection be waived.

Section 68 of the Restatement (Third) of the Law Governing Lawyers (Restatement) similarly provides that the attorney-client privilege protects "(1) a communication (2) made between privileged persons (3) in confidence (4) for the purpose of obtaining or providing legal assistance for the client." The Restatement's more concise formula of the attorney-client privilege is widely accepted by state and federal courts.

Although many states have codified the attorney-client privilege in varying forms, there is no similar codification on the federal level. Instead, Congress enacted the current Rule 501, which broadly states that federal "common law . . . [generally] governs a claim of privilege," underscoring that the attorney-client privilege is a common law rule in federal courts. Federal courts will apply state attorney-client privilege rules, however, when state law provides the rule of decision in a civil action or proceeding, such as in federal cases where jurisdiction is based on diversity of citizenship or a federal cause of action that contains a pendant state law claim.[3]

2. Scope of the Privilege

The Confidential and Privileged Relationship

Privileges do not automatically preclude the disclosure of evidence; the **privilege holder** must make a timely refusal to disclose the evidence. The client is the holder of the attorney-client privilege and ultimately decides whether to assert or waive it. Given their **agency relationship**, the lawyer may sometimes assert or waive the privilege to protect the client's interests.[4] The privilege claimant bears the burden of

---

2. Although not expressly stated in the Wigmore formulation, EVIDENCE IN TRIALS AT COMMON LAW §2292 (McNaughton ed. 1961), the attorney-client privilege also protects lawyer communications to the client providing legal advice. *See* RESTATEMENT (THIRD) OF THE LAW GOVERNING LAWYERS §70, at 537 [hereinafter Restatement].
3. Gray v. Bicknell, 86 F.3d 1472 (8th Cir. 1996). STEVEN I. FRIEDLAND & JACK P. SAHL, EVIDENCE PROBLEMS AND MATERIALS 475 (5th ed. 2015) [hereinafter EVIDENCE PROBLEMS].
4. Drimmer v. Appleton, 628 F. Supp. 1249 (S.D.N.Y. 1986).

proving its applicability. The lawyer should ideally advise the client about the scope of the privilege, including possible exceptions and risks of waiver, during the initial interview or soon thereafter. *See* Rules 1.2 and 1.3.

Communications for the Purpose of Legal Advice

The attorney-client privilege protects the client's oral and written confidential communications to the lawyer in his or her professional capacity for the purpose of obtaining legal services. The client needs only a **reasonable belief** that he is consulting with a licensed lawyer to have otherwise qualified communications protected by the privilege. Once the privilege applies, its protection against compelled disclosure continues even after the client's death.[5]

The privilege also protects the lawyer's oral and written communications to the client providing legal advice or services. For example, a lawyer's email to a client describing the legal strategy for representing him in an automobile accident is a privileged communication. Under the privilege, both the lawyer and the client may refuse to disclose the contents of the lawyer's strategy email and any client response to that email.

Observations are not communications. Evidence that anyone could observe about the client's mental state or appearance during lawyer-client communications is not privileged. Thus, a lawyer's observations that the client looked sad or had a black eye are not privileged and are subject to disclosure.

The privilege protects only client communications with his lawyer that the client intends to be confidential. A client who discloses confidential communications with his lawyer to a friend at dinner, to a third party during an investigation, or in answers to an interrogatory has no reasonable claim that he intended the communications to be confidential. *See* Nguyen v. Excel Corp., 197 F.3d 200 (5th Cir. 1999). In general, the identity of the client, the fact of consultation, the amount of the fee, the general subject matter of consultation, and the client's location are not protected under the evidentiary privilege because this information does not disclose the content of the client's confidential communications.[6] Some courts in criminal cases have used what is referred to as the **"last link doctrine"** to hold that a client's identity is protected by the attorney-client privilege when it connects the client to the offense.[7]

---

5. Swidler & Berlin v. United States, 524 U.S. 399, 410 (1998). *See* Rebecca Blair, *A Novel View of Cravath*, AM. LAW. 15 (Sept. 2016) (reporting that the author of a novel about business giant George Westinghouse's battle with Thomas Edison in the 1880s over the patent for the lightbulb was denied access by Cravath, Swain & Moore to a box of letters from Westinghouse to his lawyer, Paul Cravath, because they are protected by the attorney-client privilege).

6. The attorney-client privilege does prohibit such disclosure to the extent it reveals the content of the client's communications. *See* J. Media Grp. Inc. v. N.J. Dep't of Law & Pub. Safety, No. A-5833-13T4, 2016 BL 259485 (N.J. Super. Ct. App. Div. Aug. 11, 2016) (finding the identities of state employees and their requests for representation and/or indemnification, and any written denial of such requests, are entitled to non-disclosure under state lawyer ethics rule *if not the attorney-client privilege* in the infamous 2013 Bridgegate matter—the linking of the George Washington Bridge lane closures to New Jersey governor Chris Christie's administration) (emphasis added); Ralls v. United States, 52 F.3d 223, 226 (9th Cir. 1995) (involving fee-payer who sought lawyer's advice about fee-payer's involvement in a crime for which the defendant was arrested and holding that fee-payer's identity and fee arrangement were privileged because they were intertwined with confidential communications).

7. Baird v. Koerner, 279 F.2d 623 (9th Cir. 1960). *Cf.* Restatement §69 cmt. g, at 527-28 (reporting the privilege does not prohibit disclosure merely because it might incriminate the client).

The presence of third parties during client-lawyer communications generally defeats a claim that the communications were intended to be confidential. The privilege is not lost, however, by the presence of representatives assisting the lawyer in the delivery of legal services. Representatives may include a secretary, accountant, paralegal, or junior partner who are present during confidential client communications.[8]

The test for determining when the privilege covers a lawyer's representative is whether (1) the lawyer is directing the representative's assistance, and (2) the lawyer is rendering legal advice.[9] Thus, there is no privilege when the client contacts the firm's paralegal to seek her opinion about legal strategy. However, the privilege would apply when the lawyer advises the client about legal strategy in the presence of the paralegal while directing the paralegal to take notes of the meeting.

Sometimes third parties accompanying the client during communications will not defeat the client's claim that he intended the communications to be confidential. For instance, a client who brings an interpreter to facilitate communications will not lose the privilege if the client believes the interpreter will not reveal the communications. Nor will the privilege be lost if the client is a family caretaker who brings a young child or an aged relative to a legal consultation. *See* Stroh v. Gen. Motors Corp., 623 N.Y.S.2d 873 (N.Y. App. Div. 1995).

The privilege does not cover communications between the client and lawyer that do not involve the rendition of legal services. A client who asks his lawyer about whether a private or public high school offers his child the best opportunity to play sports is not a communication seeking legal advice. Similarly, a client request seeking the lawyer's recommendation about whether to invest client funds with one stock broker over another is a request for financial advice. The attorney-client privilege does not cover requests for pure financial or business advice.

Mixed Communications

Client-lawyer communications sometimes involve a mix of legal and non-legal advice, such as business, financial, or personal advice. Whether the privilege protects **mixed communications** from disclosure is a fact-dependent question for the courts. As with all testimonial privileges, courts narrowly construe the attorney-client privilege because it "contravene[s] the fundamental principle that the public has a right to every man's evidence" for a fair and efficient search for the truth.[10] While some courts will protect a communication from disclosure if it has a "legal component," others require a greater degree of legal advice.[11] Most courts hold that if the primary purpose for the communications was to seek legal advice, then the

8. United States v. Evans, 113 F.3d 1457 (7th Cir. 1997).
9. Bloomingburg Jewish Educ. Ctr. v. Vill. of Bloomingburg, New York, 171 F. Supp. 3d 136, 140 (S.D.N.Y. 2016).
10. In re Pacific Pictures Corp., 679 F.3d 1121, 1126 (9th Cir. 2012) (quoting Trammel v. United States, 445 U.S 40, 50 (1980)).
11. *Compare* U.S. Postal Service v. Phelps Dodge Refinance Corp., 852 F. Supp. 156 (E.D.N.Y. 1994), *with* United States v. Mejia, 655 F.3d 126, 132 (2d Cir. 2011) (communications must be solely for obtaining or providing legal advice).

confidential communications are privileged.[12] The privilege claimant must show that the nature of the particular communication involved the lawyer acting in a professional legal capacity, providing advice, and that the client subjectively believed the communication was confidential.[13]

The District of Columbia Circuit Court of Appeals recognized in In re Kellogg Brown & Root, 756 F.3d 754 (D.C. Cir. 2014), that determining the primary purpose for a communication can be a difficult, if not "inherently impossible task" when the primary purpose is motivated by two overlapping purposes, for example, one business and one legal. In *Kellogg*, an employee claimed that KBR had defrauded the U.S. government while administering military contracts in wartime Iraq. The *Kellogg* court held that the primary purpose test is met and the privilege applies if just "one of the significant purposes" of the communication was to obtain or provide legal advice, as was the case here. The appeals court concluded that KBR conducted the internal investigation to comply with regulatory requirements, its own corporate policy, and to obtain or provide legal advice, making the internal investigation documents privileged.

The privilege protects only communications made during the attorney-client relationship or by a prospective client during an initial interview whether or not the lawyer represents the prospective client and whether or not there has been an exchange or an agreement for compensation. The communications can be in electronic form.

No Privilege for Preexisting Client Documents and Underlying Facts

The privilege does not cover a client's statements or documents that were made before the client conferred with or retained the lawyer. For instance, the privilege would not protect a box of letters and tax documents that the client prepared two years before hiring counsel. Depositing this box of preexisting written materials with the lawyer does not alter the fact that these materials were not communications made to the client's lawyer. The client would have to disclose the preexisting materials upon a discovery request but the client's "act of deposit" to the lawyer is a communicative act that would not have to be revealed.

The privilege protects communications, not the underlying facts. For example, the attorney-client privilege protects from disclosure the defendant-client's confidential statement to his lawyer that he was looking at his children in the rear of his car when he struck the plaintiff's vehicle. Although the privilege protects the defendant-client's communication from disclosure, the plaintiff may prove the same fact through non-privileged means. Thus, the plaintiff may offer a bystander's eyewitness testimony that he saw the defendant-client look toward the rear of his car at the time of the collision even if that same fact was independently communicated to a lawyer. The plaintiff may also ask the defendant at trial about whether he was looking in the rear of the car at the time of the accident and the defendant would be required to answer the underlying fact question. The defendant cannot be asked, however, about what he told his attorney as that communication is privileged.

12. In re Kellogg Brown & Root, Inc., 756 F.3d 754, 759-60 (D.C. Cir. 2016).
13. *See* United States v. Chen, 99 F.3d 1495, 1502 (9th Cir. 1996); Restatement §71 cmt. b.

Entity Clients and the Privilege

Although corporations do not have a Fifth Amendment right to refuse to testify, corporations and other legal entities can claim the attorney-client privilege as a basis for refusing to disclose confidential communications between them and their lawyers. *See* Nguyen v. Excel Corp., 197 F.3d 200 (5th Cir. 1999). A common challenge for lawyers in representing entities is determining who is the client or who speaks on behalf of the legal entity. In general, the lawyer is taking direction from the CEO or president concerning the assertion of, or waiver of, the privilege. The leading case on the attorney-client privilege as it applies to corporations is Upjohn Co. v. United States, 449 U.S. 383 (1981).

Case Preview

Upjohn Co. v. United States

Since mid- and lower-level employees may embroil their corporations in legal difficulties, entity lawyers may need to confer with these employees to gather facts to adequately advise their entity-clients. In *Upjohn*, the corporation's general counsel directed all of Upjohn's foreign general and area managers to provide him and outside counsel with information about possible questionable payments to obtain government business. The general counsel also described the investigation as "highly confidential" and directed the managers to discuss the investigation only with Upjohn employees who might be helpful in providing the requested information.

As you read *Upjohn*, consider the following questions:

1. How does the Court describe the underlying policy for the attorney-client privilege?
2. What particular facts concerning the nature of Upjohn general counsel's request for information prompted the Court to note that Upjohn employees knew their responses would be confidential and for the purpose of legal assistance?
3. Why did the appellate court reject the argument that extending the privilege beyond the "control group" was unnecessary?
4. How does the Court address the appellate court's concern that extending the privilege to non–control group employees will place a burden on discovery?

Upjohn Co. v. United States

449 U.S. 383 (1981)

We granted certiorari in this case to address important questions concerning the scope of the attorney-client privilege in the corporate context and the applicability of the work-product doctrine in proceedings to enforce tax summonses. With respect to the privilege question the parties and various *amici* have described our task as

one of choosing between two "tests" which have gained adherents in the courts of appeals. We are acutely aware, however, that we sit to decide concrete cases and not abstract propositions of law. We decline to lay down a broad rule or series of rules to govern all conceivable future questions in this area, even were we able to do so. We can and do, however, conclude that the attorney-client privilege protects the communications involved in this case from compelled disclosure and that the work-product doctrine does apply in tax summons enforcement proceedings.

Petitioner Upjohn Co. manufactures and sells pharmaceuticals here and abroad. In January 1976 independent accountants conducting an audit of one of Upjohn's foreign subsidiaries discovered that the subsidiary made payments to or for the benefit of foreign government officials in order to secure government business. The accountants, so informed petitioner, Mr. Gerard Thomas, Upjohn's Vice President, Secretary, and General Counsel. . . . It was decided that the company would conduct an internal investigation of what were termed "questionable payments." As part of this investigation the attorneys prepared a letter containing a questionnaire which was sent to "All Foreign General and Area Managers" over the Chairman's signature. . . . Managers were instructed to treat the investigation as "highly confidential" and not to discuss it with anyone other than Upjohn employees who might be helpful in providing the requested information. Responses were to be sent directly to Thomas. Thomas and outside counsel also interviewed the recipients of the questionnaire and some 33 other Upjohn officers or employees as part of the investigation.

. . .

. . . On November 23, 1976, the Service issued a summons pursuant to 26 U.S.C. §7602 demanding production of:

> "All files relative to the investigation conducted under the supervision of Gerard Thomas to identify payments to employees of foreign governments and any political contributions made by the Upjohn Company or any of its affiliates since January 1, 1971 and to determine whether any funds of the Upjohn Company had been improperly accounted for on the corporate books during the same period."
>
> "The records should include but not be limited to written questionnaires sent to managers of the Upjohn Company's foreign affiliates, and memorandums or notes of the interviews conducted in the United States and abroad with officers and employees of the Upjohn Company and its subsidiaries."

The company declined to produce the documents specified in the second paragraph on the grounds that they were protected from disclosure by the attorney-client privilege . . . . Federal Rule of Evidence 501 provides that "the privilege of a witness . . . shall be governed by the principles of the common law as they may be interpreted by the courts of the United States in light of reason and experience." The attorney-client privilege is the oldest of the privileges for confidential communications known to the common law. Its purpose is to encourage full and frank communication between attorneys and their clients and thereby promote broader public interests in the observance of law and administration of justice. The privilege recognizes that sound legal advice or advocacy serves public ends and that such advice or advocacy depends upon the lawyer's being fully informed by the client. As we stated last Term: . . . "The lawyer-client privilege rests on the need for the advocate and counselor to know all that relates to the client's reasons for seeking representation if the professional mission is to be carried out." [W]e recognized the purpose of the privilege to be "to encourage clients to make full disclosure to their attorneys." . . . Admittedly complications in the application of the privilege arise when the client is a corporation, which in theory is an artificial creature of the law, and not an individual; but this Court has assumed that the privilege applies when the client is a corporation. . . .

The Court of Appeals, however, considered the application of the privilege in the corporate context to present a "different problem," since the client was an inanimate entity and "only the senior management, guiding and integrating the several operations, . . . can be said to possess an identity analogous to the corporation as a whole." The first case to articulate the so-called "control group test" adopted by the court below, reflected a similar conceptual approach:

> [T]he most satisfactory solution, I think, is that if the employee making the communication, of whatever rank he may be, is in a position to control or even to take a substantial part in a decision about any action which the corporation may take upon the advice of the attorney, . . . then, in effect, *he is (or personifies) the corporation* when he makes his disclosure to the lawyer and the privilege would apply." (Emphasis supplied.)

Such a view, we think, overlooks the fact that the privilege exists to protect not only the giving of professional advice to those who can act on it but also the giving of information to the lawyer to enable him to give sound and informed advice. . . .

Middle-level—and indeed lower-level—employees can, by actions within the scope of their employment, embroil the corporation in serious legal difficulties, and it is only natural that these employees would have the relevant information needed by corporate counsel if he is adequately to advise the client with respect to such actual or potential difficulties.

The control group test adopted by the court below thus frustrates the very purpose of the privilege by discouraging the communication of relevant information by employees of the client to attorneys seeking to render legal advice to the client corporation. The attorney's advice will also frequently be more significant to noncontrol group members than to those who officially sanction the advice, and the control group test makes it more difficult to convey full and frank legal advice to the employees who will put into effect the client corporation's policy.

The narrow scope given the attorney-client privilege by the court below not only makes it difficult for corporate attorneys to formulate sound advice when their client is faced with a specific legal problem but also threatens to limit the valuable efforts of corporate counsel to ensure their client's compliance with the law. In light of the vast and complicated array of regulatory legislation confronting the modern corporation, corporations, unlike most individuals, "constantly go to lawyers to find out how to obey the law," particularly since compliance with the law in this area is hardly an instinctive matter. The test adopted by the court below is difficult to apply in practice, though no abstractly formulated and unvarying "test" will necessarily enable courts to decide questions such as this with mathematical precision. But if the purpose of the attorney-client privilege is to be served, the attorney and client must be able to predict with some degree of certainty whether particular discussions will be protected. An uncertain privilege, or one which purports to be certain but results in widely varying applications by the courts, is little better than no privilege at all. The very terms of the test adopted by the court below suggest the unpredictability of its application. The test restricts the availability of the privilege to those officers who play a "substantial role" in deciding and directing a corporation's legal response.

The communications at issue were made by Upjohn employees to counsel for Upjohn acting as such, at the direction of corporate superiors in order to secure legal advice from counsel. . . . The communications concerned matters within the scope of the employees' corporate duties, and the employees themselves were sufficiently aware that they were being questioned in order that the corporation could obtain legal advice. . . . Pursuant to explicit instructions from the Chairman of the Board, the communications were considered "highly confidential" when made and have been kept confidential by the company. Consistent with the underlying purposes of the attorney-client privilege, these communications must be protected against compelled disclosure.

The Court of Appeals declined to extend the attorney-client privilege beyond the limits of the control group test for fear that doing so would entail severe burdens on discovery and create a broad "zone of silence" over corporate affairs. Application of the attorney-client privilege to communications such as those involved here, however, puts the adversary in no worse position than if the communications had never taken place.

[W]e conclude that the narrow "control group test" . . . sanctioned by the Court of Appeals, in this case cannot, consistent with "the principles of the common law as . . . interpreted . . . in the light of reason and experience," Fed. Rule Evid. 501, govern the development of the law in this area.

Post-Case Follow-Up

The *Upjohn* decision and its rationale have become firmly rooted in federal common law for determining the application and scope of the attorney-client privilege. Many states have also adopted the *Upjohn* decision, recognizing that lawyers need as much information as possible from their entity-clients, which may involve casting a large net to capture facts from a wide range of entity constituents to promote corporate compliance with the law. Some questions about the privilege in the corporate setting remain. For example, when must the lawyer for the corporate entity who is interviewing an entity employee disclose that the employee's interest conflicts with the client-entity's interest and that the employee should retain separate counsel?

Upjohn Co. v. United States: Real Life Applications

1. Imagine the CEO of a local construction company contacts you and your firm to conduct an investigation of the company possibly paying kickbacks to government officials for public contracts. What steps would you take to ensure that

communications with company employees are protected by the attorney-client privilege? In the course of your investigation, you find it necessary to interview a former company employee. He asks whether you are representing him too and, if so, whether his communications to you are protected by the attorney-client privilege. Discuss the former employee's situation with him.

2. Jane Hankins manages a 40-person law firm. She suspects a firm partner, Tom Jones, of mishandling a client's funds. Hankins asks two associates to conduct an internal factual investigation of the matter. The grand jury subpoenas the two associates to learn about their discussions with Hankins. The two associates claim that as lawyers their discussions with Hankins are protected by the attorney-client privilege. The government contends, however, that the privilege is inapplicable because the two associates are merely employees on a fact-finding mission. Hankins asks you, a professional responsibility expert, whether the firm will be successful in claiming the privilege protects her communications with the two associates. Discuss the firm's chances of success.

3. Attorney Irving represents a company and its CEO concerning his executive assistant's recent allegation that she was wrongfully terminated. She alleges that the CEO began sexually harassing her after she confronted the CEO about his financial misrepresentations about the company to lenders. She claims her termination is really a case of sexual discrimination. The executive assistant's lawyers have not yet filed an action in court but are threatening one unless a suitable settlement is offered. Attorney Irving asks for all of the executive assistant's emails on her company laptop for the period of the alleged sexual harassment up to her termination, including emails to the lawyers representing her in this wrongful termination matter. The executive assistant refuses to turn over the laptop and her emails to her lawyers claiming they are protected by the attorney-client privilege. Attorney Irving has concluded based on preliminary investigation that the employee's allegations may have some merit but that there is also evidence supporting the CEO's claim that the executive assistant's work was unsatisfactory.

   Are the former executive assistant's emails privileged? How does the fact that her lawyers have not filed a complaint affect Attorney Irving's strategy in resolving this matter? What other possible ethics issues loom in Attorney Irving's decision to represent the company and the CEO?

Government Lawyers and the Privilege

The attorney-client privilege generally protects communications between government agencies or members of the executive branch and their agency's in-house counsel or the U.S. Department of Justice when the purpose is for legal advice in a civil case. *See* In re County of Erie, 473 F.3d 413 (2d Cir. 2007). Courts differ on whether the privilege protects similar communications in criminal cases.

In In re Grand Jury Investigation, 399 F.3d 527 (2d Cir. 2005), the government sought private communications of Connecticut governor John Rowland and his staff with his office's former chief legal counsel for advice concerning federal grand jury proceedings about possible criminal conduct for the receipt of gifts from persons doing business with the state. The Second Circuit held that it was "crucial" for a government official who faces criminal prosecution to be able to fully consult with counsel to observe the law while working for the public. "Upholding the privilege [in this case promotes the public interest by furthering] a culture in which consultation with government lawyers is accepted . . . [as an] indispensable part of conducting public business."

Other circuit courts considering the same question in grand jury proceedings take a contrary view. For example, the court in In re Grand Jury Subpoena Duces Tecum, 112 F.3d 910, 920 (8th Cir. 1997), concluded that "the general duty of public service calls upon government employees and agencies to favor disclosure over concealment." That same court noted that the "difference between the public and the private interest is perhaps, by itself, reason enough to find *Upjohn* unpersuasive." Unlike private corporations, government entities cannot be held criminally liable. The Eighth Circuit Court also noted a "strong public interest in honest government" and in the revelation of wrongdoing by public officials.[14] Finally, government officials faced with criminal liability can hire their own private lawyers.

The attorney-client privilege covers "communications between the attorney and all agents or employees who are authorized to act or speak" for the government entity concerning the subject matter of the communication.[15] As in the corporate context, the dissemination of legal advice is limited to employees who "need to know" given the scope of their responsibilities, and the privilege belongs to the government client-entity, not to a particular government employee.[16] This means the government entity can waive the privilege over an employee's objection. The government bears the burden of demonstrating all of the requisite elements of the privilege.

Common Interest Doctrine

Sometimes parties need to share or pool confidential information and coordinate strategies in a matter of common legal interest. The **common interest doctrine** involves multiple parties and multiple lawyers — each party having separate counsel — and is distinguishable from the "**joint client**" situation where multiple clients share a lawyer (see the Joint-Clients Exception subsection, *infra* at page 288).

The common interest doctrine treats all lawyers and clients pursuing a common legal interest as a single attorney-client unit where the pooling of information remains privileged or confidential.[17] The common interest doctrine protects

14. In re Grand Jury Subpoena Duces Tecum, 112 F.3d 910, 921 (8th Cir. 1997). *See also* In re Lindsey, 148 F.3d 1100, 1109 (D.C. Cir. 1998) (noting the public interest in honest government and exposing government officials' wrongdoing).
15. Scott Paper Co. v. United States, 943 F. Supp. 489, 499 (E.D. Pa. 1996), *aff'd*, 943 F. Supp. 501 (E.D. Pa. 1996).
16. In re County of Erie, 473 F.3d 413 (2d Cir. 2007).
17. Stephen A. Saltzburg, Michael M. Martin & Daniel J. Capra, 2 Federal Rules of Evidence §501.02[5][e] (11th ed. 2015) [hereinafter Evidence Manual].

attorney-client communications even when common interest members disagree on some matters but still agree to pursue one common legal interest.[18]

For communications to be privileged under the common interest doctrine, all of the usual requirements for the attorney-client privilege must be met. For example, the client's communication must be confidential, and made to a lawyer for the purpose of obtaining legal advice. However, the common interest doctrine provides a safe harbor from the general rules that the privilege does not encompass communications to a third party or communications between the lawyer for one party and the lawyer for another.

Although not uniformly followed, the Restatement notes that the common interest doctrine applies to both litigation and non-litigation situations.[19] The doctrine is sometimes referred to as the "joint defense" or "pooled information" rule.[20] The common interest doctrine promotes the policies of the attorney-client privilege by encouraging full client disclosure for effective representation. The doctrine also promotes cost-efficient representation as common interest members can share information and expenses, such as the cost of empirical studies, experts, or investigators, in pursuit of their common legal matter.

The common interest doctrine protects attorney-client communications when the privilege holder discloses them to another lawyer who represents a person in a matter of common legal interest.[21] Although the common interest doctrine should theoretically apply to (1) communications among group member clients and (2) client communications with another group member's lawyer, the safest policy is for a client's lawyer to communicate with another member's lawyer so there is no question that the communication is advancing the agreed-upon common legal interest.[22] Communications among group member clients with no lawyer present are generally not privileged.[23] One court has also rejected a common interest privilege when one common interest member spoke with another group member's lawyer without ever consulting his own lawyer before or after speaking with the other group member's lawyer.[24] The common interest privilege will not protect the confidentiality of member communications in joint strategy meetings when one member in the meeting decides to use any communication in the meeting against another member in adverse litigation.[25] Nor can one member of a common interest agreement prevent another party to the agreement from revealing work-product materials because that would enlarge work-product protection and be contrary to public policy.[26]

---

18. Eisenberg v. Gagnon, 766 F.2d 770, 787-88 (3d Cir. 1985).
19. Restatement §76, at 584. *But see* Ambac Assurance Corp. v. Countrywide Home Loans, Inc., 57 N.E.3d 30 (N.Y. 2016) (common interest privilege in New York only applies to communications related to pending or anticipated litigation).
20. United States v. Gonzalez, 669 F.3d 974 (9th Cir. 2012).
21. United States v. McPartlin, 595 F.2d 1321 (7th Cir. 1979) (noting common interest doctrine applies even when co-defendants have conflicting defenses but share a common interest in discrediting diary).
22. Evidence Manual, *supra* note 17, §501.02[5][e].
23. United States v. Gotti, 771 F. Supp. 535, 545 (E.D.N.Y. 1991).
24. United States v. Bay State Ambulance & Hosp. Rent. Serv., 874 F.2d 20, 29 (1st Cir. 1989).
25. United States v. Almeida, 341 F.3d 1318, 1326-27 (11th Cir. 2003).
26. In re Grand Jury, 274 F.3d 563, 574-75 (1st Cir. 2001).

The common interest privilege claimant must show (1) that all clients and attorneys with access to the communication had in fact agreed upon a joint approach to the matter communicated; and (2) that the information was imparted with the intent to further the common purpose.[27] The failure to meet the requirements of the "common legal interest" doctrine may result in a court finding that the client waived the attorney-client privilege concerning the subject matter of the communication to the third lawyer. In federal courts, a party cannot seek an immediate interlocutory appeal of a court's rejection of the attorney-client privilege because disclosure is unlikely to deter clients and lawyers from seeking the benefits of full communication in their professional relationship.[28]

Common legal interest agreements should be memorialized in writing. Written agreements provide evidence of the nature and scope of the common legal interest, facilitate the determination of which communications relate to that nature and scope, and permit signatories to waive the use of their common interest communications in future litigation against another common interest member.[29]

EXHIBIT 5.1 Sample Joint Defense and Common Interest Agreement*

THIS JOINT DEFENSE AND COMMON INTEREST AGREEMENT (the "Agreement") is entered into by and among the undersigned Counsel, as of __________, 2010, acting for and on behalf of their respective clients ("the Parties"), each of whom is a defendant in litigation filed by __________ asserting claims of, among other things, __________. The Parties share an interest in the defense of the claims or potential claims of patent infringement concerning the __________ Patent (the "Infringement Claims"), including, without limitation, demonstrating that the __________ Patent is invalid and unenforceable and that the Parties do not infringe any claim of the __________ Patent. Because the undersigned wish to continue to pursue their separate but common interests and to avoid any suggestion of waiver of the confidentiality of privileged communications or documents, they hereby agree as follows:

1. **Definition of Counsel**—For purposes of this Agreement, the term "Counsel" means and includes both outside and in-house Counsel for any Party, and execution of this Agreement by either outside or in-house counsel for a Party binds that Party and all in-house and outside Counsel retained to provide legal services in connection with the Infringement Claims at any time.
2. **Defense Materials**—The Parties and their counsel have concluded that it is in each of their individual and mutual best interests in the defense of the Infringement Claims to share certain information related to that defense with some or all of Counsel and/or the Parties in writing and/or orally. These communications may include but are not limited to written communications, the disclosure of documents, factual and legal

27. In re Teleglobe Communications Corp., 493 F.3d 345 (3d Cir. 2007).
28. Mohawk Indus. v. Carpenter, 558 U.S. 100 (2009).
29. Evidence Manual, *supra* note 17, §501.02[5][e].

analyses, summaries, and memoranda, opinions, legal strategies, interview reports and reports of experts, consultants or investigators, joint meetings between defense counsel, the parties, their representatives and employees, and any meetings with prospective witnesses or consulting experts or litigation support service providers in connection with the litigation in person, by telephone or in any other form, and records or reports of such communications, all of which are included within the term "Defense Materials" used herein. However, nothing in this Agreement shall be construed to affect the separate and independent representation of each client by its respective Counsel.

3. **Common Interest**—The Parties and their counsel agree that all sharing and pooling of information pursuant to this Agreement will be done within the context of and in furtherance of the Parties' common goal and effort in defending against the Infringement Claims.
4. **Privileged Communications**—Some or all of the Defense Materials may be protected from disclosure to adverse or other Parties as a result of the attorney-client privilege, the work product doctrine, or other applicable privileges, protections or immunities. It is the desire, intention, and mutual understanding of the Parties hereto (a) that the sharing of Defense Materials among one another is not intended to, and shall not, waive or diminish in any way the confidentiality of such materials or their continued protection under the attorney-client privilege, the work product doctrine or other applicable privileges, protections or immunities; and (b) that all Defense Materials provided by a Party pursuant to this Agreement that are entitled to protection under the attorney-client privilege, the work product doctrine or other applicable privileges, protections or immunities, shall remain entitled to such protection under the common interest doctrine, and may not be disclosed to persons other than those described in Paragraph 5 without the consent of the providing party. The Parties also intend and understand that any disclosure of Defense Materials pursuant to this Agreement will not constitute a waiver of any available privilege, protection or immunity.
5. **Disclosure of Defense Materials**—Each of the undersigned Counsel has further agreed that he or she will not disclose any exchanged Defense Materials received by him or her from another Party to this Agreement or Counsel for another Party to this Agreement to anyone except (a) in-house counsel, employees or officers of each Party who are responsible for the defense of the Infringement Claims on behalf of their employer; (b) outside Counsel of record for any Party to this Agreement; and (c) paralegals, support staff, or experts who are directly employed by or retained by and assisting outside Counsel in the defense of the Infringement Claims. All persons permitted access to Defense Materials (collectively, "Authorized Persons") shall be specifically advised that the Defense Materials are privileged and subject to the terms of this Agreement.
6. **Limited Use of Defense Materials**—Any shared Defense Materials, and the information contained therein, are to be used by each person or Party receiving them solely in connection with the defense of the Infringement Claims. Neither the Defense Materials nor the information contained therein may be used by any person or Party receiving them for any other purpose whatsoever.
7. **Previously Exchanged Defense Materials**—All Defense Materials exchanged between and among any of the undersigned counsel pursuant to prior oral

agreements or any previous joint defense agreement are now subject to this Agreement. This Agreement specifically preserves the protections afforded to those materials shared between the parties from the time that the commonality of interest came into being until execution of this Agreement under the same terms as contained in this Agreement.

8. **Privilege Not Waived** —The privileges and protections for the Defense Materials to which this Agreement is applicable may not be waived by any Party to this Agreement without the prior written consent of the Party that provided the Defense Materials. Any inadvertent or purposeful disclosure of Defense Materials exchanged pursuant to this Agreement that is made by a Party contrary to the terms of this Agreement shall not constitute a waiver of any privilege or protection. If any Party is required by court order or rule of law to produce or reveal any confidential information, documents or privileged materials which are part of the Parties' efforts pursuant to this Agreement, reasonable notice shall be given to each Party who has executed this Agreement before responding to, or complying with, such requests so that any Party may, at its own cost, have the opportunity to resist the production of such information by timely and appropriate process. In the event the Party from whom disclosure is sought has no objection to the disclosure, such Party shall nevertheless invoke this Agreement during the pendency of any action taken by the objecting Party and shall otherwise make reasonable efforts to prevent disclosure until the final resolution of the objection of the objecting Party.
9. **Withdrawal**—In the event that a Party determines that it no longer has a commonality of interest in the defense of the Infringement Claims, such Party shall withdraw from this Agreement. Each undersigned Counsel has a duty to withdraw from the Agreement when, in good faith, he or she reasonably believes that a commonality of interest no longer exists and to give prompt written notice of such withdrawal to each of the undersigned. Notwithstanding a Party's withdrawal, this Agreement shall remain operative as to: (a) all other remaining Parties to this Agreement; and (b) all previously furnished Defense Materials. Any Party may withdraw from this Agreement on written notice to all of the undersigned Counsel. Any such withdrawal will be solely on a prospective basis and any Defense Materials provided pursuant to this Agreement prior to such withdrawal shall continue to be governed by the terms of this Agreement.
10. **Settlement or Dismissal**—A party who is dismissed or settles all pending claims will be deemed to have withdrawn from the Agreement in accordance with terms of paragraph 9 as of the date of the dismissal or settlement.
11. **Modification**—The provisions of this Agreement may be modified only by written agreement of all affected Parties, and it shall be binding upon all successors and assigns of the Parties.
12. **Additional parties**—The parties recognize that other counsel and their clients may be permitted to join this Agreement at a future time by signing a copy of this Agreement. Any such additions shall be made only with the permission of all then-current signatories to this Agreement.
13. **No endorsement or authorization**—While the undersigned believe that their clients are well served by the sharing of information under this Agreement, they also understand that participation in this Agreement represents neither an endorsement of, nor an authorization to control, the defense strategy or decisions of other participating counsels' clients.

14. **Protective Order obligations**—Nothing in this Agreement shall relieve the Parties or their counsel from any obligation or obligations pursuant to the terms of any protective order or similar order entered by any court regarding the disclosure of dissemination of information pertaining to any Infringement Claims.
15. **Independent work product**—Nothing in this Agreement shall limit the right of any Party to use or disclose any documents or information or work product that have been independently obtained or generated by such Party (i.e. they were not obtained or generated as part of the common defense efforts made pursuant to this Agreement), whether or not such documents, information or work product have been provided to any other Party pursuant to this Agreement.
16. **Effect on Other Agreements**—Nothing in this Agreement shall prevent the Parties from entering into common interest agreements with other parties or among themselves, and this Agreement shall not be deemed to supersede or nullify, in whole or in part, any common interest agreement any Party has entered into prior to the date of its execution of this Agreement.
17. **Scope of Protection**—This Agreement shall be interpreted so as to afford the broadest and greatest protection possible of Defense Materials from disclosure to third parties.
18. **No Attorney-Client Relationship**—Nothing in this Agreement is intended to create any attorney-client relationship for the purposes of conflicts or otherwise. Each undersigned counsel understands that it is his or her sole responsibility to represent his or her or their respective client and that none of the other signatories to this Agreement have in any way assumed any such responsibility. Moreover, the participation in, execution or receipt of any information pursuant to this Agreement shall not disqualify any representative of a signatory (including a law firm) from accepting any other future engagement.
19. **No Admission of Liability**—Nothing in this Agreement is intended as, nor shall be construed or deemed to be, an admission of liability by any Party, or of the existence of facts upon which liability could be based.
20. **Continuing Obligation**—This Agreement shall continue in full force and effect notwithstanding any conclusion or resolution as to any Party of the Infringement Claims.
21. **Confidentiality of Terms**—The contents of this Agreement are confidential and shall not be released to any person or entity not a Party to this Agreement or as necessary to enforce the terms of this Agreement.
22. **Counterparts**—This Agreement may be signed in counterparts. All executed counterparts shall comprise the entire Agreement. This Agreement may be executed by counsel for a Party. Each counsel signing this Agreement represents that he or she has been authorized by his or her client to execute this Agreement on behalf of the client.

IN WITNESS WHEREOF, the Parties have executed this Agreement on the dates indicated below.

By: ______________________	By: ______________________
Counsel for ________________	Counsel for ________________
Dated: ____________________	Dated: ____________________

*This agreement was originally presented as part of a panel titled "Best Practices in Multi-Defendant Litigation," at the Intellectual Property Owners Association (IPO) 2010 Annual Meeting. The following panelists who created the document have granted permission to reprint it: Moderator: "Betty" Ann Morgan, The Morgan Law Firm P.C., Atlanta, GA; William Bergmann, Baker & Hostetler, LLP, Washington, DC; Julianne Hartzell, Marshall, Gerstein & Borun LLP, Chicago, IL; and Preston K. Ratliff, Paul, Hastings, Janofsky & Walker LLP, New York, NY.

Case Preview

Schaeffler v. United States

The appellant, Georg F.W. Schaeffler, is the majority owner of the Schaeffler Group that sought to acquire a minority interest in a German company, Continental AG. The Schaeffler Group found a consortium (Consortium) of banks to loan it 11 billion euros for the acquisition. On July 30, 2008, the Schaeffler Group offered Continental AG shareholders a fixed price for their stock with the offer set to expire on September 16, 2008. The 2008 economic crisis caused a loss of market value for Continental AG. German law governed the acquisition and prevented Schaeffler from retracting its offer, which was oversubscribed. The oversubscription threatened the Schaeffler Group's solvency. The Schaeffler Group and the Consortium refinanced the acquisition debt and restructured the Group, which affected Schaeffler's personal tax liability to the IRS. The Group anticipated IRS scrutiny and hired a tax law firm and Ernst & Young (EY) to advise Schaeffler on federal tax implications and possible future litigation. The Group was unsuccessful in moving to quash an IRS summons for numerous documents created by EY and provided to "outside parties," including the Consortium. The Second Circuit held that the appellant, Schaeffler Group, had not waived the attorney-client privilege when it provided documents to the Consortium because they shared a "common legal interest" in the tax treatment of the refinancing and corporate restructuring caused by the acquisition.

In reading *Schaeffler*, consider the following:

1. What, if any, additional action could the appellant have taken to clarify that it was sharing communications with the Consortium not only for economic and business reasons but also to pursue a common legal strategy?
2. What weight should the court attach to a written agreement titled "Common Legal Interest" between Schaeffler and the Consortium in deciding whether the common interest privilege applies?
3. Given that financial matters often involve tax consequences, does *Schaeffler* open the door to additional common interest privilege claims in financial or corporate litigation?

Schaeffler v. United States

806 F.3d 34 (2d Cir. 2015)

BACKGROUND

a. The Acquisition

. . .

To finance the offer [to purchase an interest in the company, Continental AG], the Schaeffler Group executed an eleven-billion Euro loan agreement with a consortium

of banks. The offer made July 30, 2008 expired on September 16, 2008. The timing of the offer was unlucky, to say the least. On September 14, 2008, two days before the offer expiration date, Lehman Brothers Holding Inc. announced its bankruptcy, the stock market collapsed, and the economic crisis worsened. The market price of Continental AG shares, already declining, fell accordingly. Because German law prohibited the Schaeffler Group from withdrawing its tender offer, far more shareholders than expected or desired accepted the offer, leaving the Schaeffler Group the owner of nearly 89.9% of outstanding Continental AG shares.

These circumstances combined to threaten the Schaeffler Group's solvency and ability to meet its payment obligations to the Consortium. As a result, appellants and the Consortium perceived an urgent need to refinance the acquisition debt and to restructure the Schaeffler Group. Because Mr. Schaeffler is an 80% owner of the ultimate parent of the Schaeffler Group, the tax consequences of his companies' debt refinancing and restructuring substantially affected his personal tax liability to the IRS. Given the complex and novel refinancing and restructuring that ensued, appellants anticipated scrutiny by the IRS. Therefore, they retained Ernst & Young ("EY") and Dentons U.S. LLP ("Dentons") to advise on the federal tax implications of the transactions and possible future litigation with the IRS.

As anticipated, the IRS began an audit of appellants that led to the issuance of the summons at issue in this appeal. The summons sought documents that were (a) created by Ernst & Young and (b) "provided to parties outside" appellants; the summons did not therefore seek documents that were prepared by Dentons, appellant's law firm, or that were prepared by EY and shared only with appellants' counsel. The IRS specifically demanded "all documents . . . including but not limited to legal opinions, analysis and appraisals . . . that relate to [the restructuring]. Appellants produced several thousand documents in response to the information document request from the IRS but sought to quash the demand for legal opinions. For example, appellants sought to withhold memoranda, such as an EY memorandum ("EY Tax Memo") that identified potential U.S. tax consequences of the refinancing and restructuring, identified and analyzed possible IRS challenges to the Schaeffler Group's tax treatment of the transactions, and discussed in detail the relevant statutory provisions, U.S. Treasury regulations, judicial decisions, and IRS rulings.

b. The District Court's Ruling

In denying the petition to quash, the district court held that appellants had waived their attorney-client privilege by sharing the withheld documents with the Consortium. The court noted that "[b]y all accounts, the Schaeffler Group, Ernst & Young, and Dentons worked closely with the Bank Consortium not only in effectuating the refinancing and restructuring but also in analyzing the tax consequences of the [Continental AG] acquisition." The court held that the "common legal interest" or "joint defense privilege" exception to the waiver by third-party disclosure rule did not apply. In the court's view, the Consortium "lack[ed] . . . any common legal stake in Schaeffler's putative litigation with the IRS," because it would not be named as a co-defendant in the anticipated litigation and "only the Consortium's economic interests," as opposed to its legal interests, "were in jeopardy." Therefore, appellants and the Consortium did not have a common legal interest and were not "formulating a common legal strategy." Accordingly, appellants' attorney-client privilege had been waived.

. . .

DISCUSSION

a. Waiver of the Attorney-Client Privilege

We review the district court's finding of waiver of the attorney-client privilege for abuse of discretion. An abuse of discretion occurs when a district court: (i) bases a decision on an error of law or a clearly erroneous factual finding, or (ii) reaches a decision that is outside the range of permissible decisions.

The IRS summons seeks only those documents prepared by EY "that were provided to parties outside the Schaeffler Group." Because there is no evidence indicating disclosure of some or all of the documents beyond the Consortium, we need only determine the effect of disclosure to the Consortium. As noted, the district court held that appellants waived attorney-client privilege by sharing the contested documents with the Consortium because the Consortium's interest was commercial rather than legal.

The purpose of the attorney-client privilege is to enable attorneys to give informed legal advice to clients, which would be undermined if an attorney had to caution a client about revealing relevant circumstances lest the attorney later be compelled to disclose those circumstances. The privilege, and by extension the tax practitioner privilege, protects communications between a client and its attorney that are intended to be, and in fact were, kept confidential. A party that shares otherwise privileged communications with an outsider is deemed to waive the privilege by disabling itself from claiming that the communications were intended to be confidential. Moreover, the purpose of the communications must be solely for the obtaining or providing of legal advice. Communications that are made for purposes of evaluating the commercial wisdom of various options as well as in getting or giving legal advice are not protected.

While the privilege is generally waived by voluntary disclosure of the communication to another party, the privilege is not waived by disclosure of communications to a party that is engaged in a "common legal enterprise" with the holder of the privilege. Under United States v. Schwimmer, 892 F.2d 237 (2d Cir. 1989), such disclosures remain privileged "where a joint defense effort or strategy has been decided upon and undertaken by the parties and their respective counsel . . . in the course of an ongoing common enterprise . . . [and] multiple clients share a common interest about a legal matter." "The need to protect the free flow of information from client to attorney logically exists whenever multiple clients share a common interest about a legal matter."

Parties may share a "common legal interest" even if they are not parties in ongoing litigation. The common-interest-rule serves to "protect the confidentiality of communications passing from one party to the attorney for another party where a joint defense effort or strategy has been decided upon and undertaken by the parties and their respective counsel." "[I]t is therefore unnecessary that there be actual litigation in progress for the common interest rule of the attorney-client privilege to apply[.]" However, "[o]nly those communications made in the course of an ongoing common enterprise and intended to further the enterprise are protected." The dispositive issue is, therefore, whether the Consortium's common interest with appellants was of a sufficient legal character to prevent a waiver by the sharing of those communications. We hold that it was.

The original relationship between the Schaeffler Group and the Consortium arose before the economic crisis and the resultant oversubscription to the Schaeffler Group's tender offer that necessitated the refinancing and restructuring. . . . As a result of the oversubscription, the Schaeffler Group faced a threat of insolvency that would in turn cause a default on the Consortium's eleven-billion Euros loan. The Group and the Consortium could avoid this mutual financial disaster by cooperating in securing a particular tax treatment of a refinancing and restructuring. Securing that treatment would likely involve a legal encounter with the IRS. Both appellants and the Consortium, therefore, had a strong common interest in the outcome of that legal encounter.

On this record, the nature and viability of the refinancing and restructuring had a commercial component and tax law component. . . . [T]he nature and viability of the transaction was driven by U.S. tax law, and both appellants and the Consortium had a common interest in seeing that law applied in a particular way. The documents in question were all directed to the tax issues, a legal problem albeit with commercial consequences, namely the possible insolvency of the Schaeffler Group and its default on the Consortium loan. Appellants' interest was in securing a refinancing. The Consortium's interest was in funding a refinancing that would protect its earlier investment and would itself be repaid, goals dependent on the resolution of legal tax issues. The fact that eleven-billion Euros of sunken investment and any additional sums advanced in the refinancing were at stake does not render those legal issues "commercial," and sharing communications relating to those legal issues is not a waiver of the privilege.

For example, when the possibility of default loomed, the Consortium's counsel became familiar with the Schaeffler Group's organizational structure and advised it during negotiations to restructure the Group and refinance its acquisition. The Consortium needed "access to confidential tax information and analyses" to "assess its credit exposure for potential tax liabilities of Mr. Schaeffler." Together, appellants and the Consortium agreed that Appellants should request an IRS private letter ruling. With regard to issues not resolved by the letter ruling, they agreed to share "certain core tax advice prepared by the U.S. tax advisors." This information was exchanged pursuant to the confidentiality agreement.

The mutual obligations that appellants and the Consortium undertook under the agreement, reflect a common legal strategy. The Consortium agreed, subject to limitations not pertinent here, to permit Mr. Schaeffler to pay up to 885 million Euros in personal tax liabilities before repaying the Schaeffler Group's debt. It further agreed to extend him an additional line of credit to pay tax liabilities up to 250 million Euros. In return, Mr. Schaeffler's right to act unilaterally was restricted. He was required to give notice to the Consortium of any material audit or investigation. The Consortium also retained a right of refusal limiting Mr. Schaeffler's freedom of action with regard to the IRS, *e.g.* paying taxes, suing for a refund, or settling. The communications regarding tax opinions were, therefore, "made in the course of an ongoing common enterprise" and "intended to further the enterprise."

. . . It is true that cases involving criminal prosecutions usually describe the definition of a common defense strategy according to the contours of a particular charging instrument. In the context of civil proceedings, however, these cases emphasized the need of the parties to identify a common legal interest or strategy in obtaining a particular legal goal whether or not litigation is ongoing. . . .

No caselaw in this or another circuit compels us to hold that the Consortium's interest in appellants' obtaining favorable tax treatment for the refinancing and restructuring transaction is not a sufficient common legal interest. In our view, the fact that the Consortium stood to lose a lot of money (along with appellants) if appellants' tax arguments failed is not support for the position that no common legal interest existed. To the contrary, it was the interest in avoiding the losses that established a common legal interest. A financial interest of a party, no matter how large, does not preclude a court from finding a legal interest shared with another party where the legal aspects materially affect the financial interests.

For example, the Consortium's legal interest is underlined by the extent to which the Consortium essentially insured appellants, by extending credit and subordinating its debt, and retained control over Mr. Schaeffler's legal decisions to settle, pay, or sue. . . . See Travelers Cas. & Sur. Co. v. Excess Ins. Co., 197 F.R.D. 601, 607 (S.D. Ohio 2000) (holding that members of a reinsurance group facing similar environmental pollution claims by United States insurance and reinsurance companies "shared [legal] interests sufficiently common or joint to create a need for full and frank communication between and among counsel and their clients").

We, therefore, conclude that appellants did not waive their attorney-client privilege.

. . .

CONCLUSION

[Judgment vacated and remanded] "to determine [consistent with this opinion] whether any remaining documents are protected by the attorney-client privilege or work-product doctrine."

Post-Case Follow-Up

Soon after *Schaeffler*, the New York Court of Appeals issued a significant opinion clarifying the state's approach to the common legal interest doctrine in Ambac Assurance Corp. v. Countrywide Home Loans, Inc., 57 N.E.3d 30 (N.Y. 2016). The *Ambac* court noted that the Restatement and some federal appellate courts had "eliminated the common law requirement that shared communications [had to] relate to pending or anticipated litigation" to remain privileged from disclosure. The court reported nevertheless that a number of jurisdictions have not followed this expansion of the doctrine, including 11 that statutorily restrict the doctrine to communications shared in the context of ongoing litigation. *Id.* at 36 n.2. The *Ambac* court decided to take a "narrow approach" to the common legal interest doctrine by restricting it to only cases where there is pending or anticipated ligation. The *Ambac* court held that a broad construction of the common legal interest doctrine is inconsistent with the trend of liberal discovery rules and would create an obstacle to the truth-finding process by excluding pertinent information. The dissent in *Ambac* was willing to extend the common legal interest doctrine to the instant transactional setting where parties exchanged confidential information for the purpose of obtaining legal and regulatory advice to complete the merger even though there was no anticipated litigation. Ultimately, lawyers must know their jurisdiction's approach to the common legal interest doctrine because jurisdictions differ concerning the doctrine's standards and application.

Schaeffler v. United States: Real Life Applications

1. The Acme Company and Boxcar Company were engaged in merger negotiations. The two firms exchanged documents created by each company's lawyers for their respective CEOs concerning information about their patents, tax issues, and other internal corporate affairs based on a detailed confidentiality agreement. You represent the Hercules Company in a lawsuit against the Boxcar Company. You seek some of the Boxcar documents exchanged with Acme claiming that Boxcar waived the attorney-client privilege. Advise Hercules about the likelihood of the court finding a waiver of the privilege.

2. Nordbank is the administrative agent for five lenders who agreed to loan Hickory Hill, Ltd. up to $200 million to build a condominium complex in Florida. Under the loan agreement, Nordbank is a co-lender and solely responsible for enforcing any rights or remedies in the agreement to protect all of the lenders' interests. The principals of Hickory Hill, Cohen and Smith, executed a Guaranty of Payment, which jointly and severally guaranteed full payment of any unpaid loan balance. The Florida real estate market deteriorated and Nordbank claimed that Hickory Hill defaulted on the loan. Nordbank sued Cohen and Smith for breach of contract and sought immediate repayment of the outstanding loan balance. During the course of discovery, the plaintiff withheld nine documents claiming they are privileged. In these nine documents, Nordbank's lawyer communicated directly with the CEOs of the five non-party co-lenders about the best legal strategy for obtaining relief against Cohen and Smith. The defendants filed a motion to compel the disclosure of the nine documents asserting that they are not privileged under the common legal interest doctrine because the only common interest is a business one. The defendants further asserted that even if the documents involved common legal interests, the communications from Nordbank's lawyer to the non-party lender CEOs waived the privilege because the Nordbank lawyer could only communicate with the other co-lenders' lawyers. Nordbank consults you for your opinion about whether the nine documents are privileged. Discuss your opinion.

---

3. Waivers

A client can waive the protection of the attorney-client privilege in several ways. The client can consent to waive the privilege or authorize agents to relinquish the privilege. For example, the client's lawyer, an agent, generally has implied authority both to waive and to assert the privilege.[30]

The client also permanently waives the privilege by voluntarily disclosing confidential communications to a third party, such as a reporter or a close friend. The client's voluntary disclosure of the communication undermines any claim that the client intended the communications to be confidential.[31]

The client's voluntary disclosure of a *fact* contained in a privileged communication does not necessarily waive the privilege, but it may be used as evidence that the client never intended the communication to be confidential.[32] For example, in a personal injury case a defendant made a privileged communication to his lawyer about the circumstances of an automobile accident, including a statement that "the light was red." At the subsequent trial, opposing counsel asked the client, "Did you see the light was red?"[33] The client replied, "The light was red," but disclosed no other details of his earlier privileged communication. The client's factual reply about the light being red does not constitute a waiver of his privileged communication.[34] Contrast this question with a different one: "Did you tell your lawyer the light was red?" If the client replies: "Yes, I told my lawyer 'the light was red,'" then the client will be deemed to have waived the privilege for that communication with his lawyer.[35]

Protecting the Privilege in Adversarial Proceedings and During Representation

Parties must take effective steps to protect the confidentiality of their communications. For example, the failure to timely object to another party's use of privileged information in a proceeding constitutes a waiver of the attorney-client privilege.[36] Similarly, parties must object to discovery requests for documents containing privileged communications to successfully assert the privilege and prevent disclosure. The lawyer's failure to take steps to protect the confidentiality of client communications exposes the lawyer to malpractice and disciplinary actions for incompetent representation.

Malpractice and disciplinary claims typically result in a general waiver of privilege to all related privileged communications between the claimant and lawyer.[37]

---

30. In re Pacific Pictures Corp., 679 F.3d 1121, 1126 (9th Cir. 2012); Restatement §79 cmt. b.
31. In re Pacific Pictures Corp., 679 F.3d at 1121, 1126-27; Restatement §78, at 596.
32. *See* Restatement §79, at 597-98 (reporting that the public disclosure of facts communicated in confidence to a lawyer does not waive the attorney-client privilege unless the disclosure also reveals that the facts were communicated to the lawyer).
33. *See* Restatement §69 cmt. d, at 526; §79 cmt. e, at 598.
34. *See id.*
35. *See id.*
36. *Id.* §78(3), at 593.
37. In re Lott, 424 F.3d 446, 452-53 (6th Cir. 2005).

It would be unfair to allow the party to pursue claims against the lawyer for inadequate legal assistance while prohibiting the lawyer from using privileged communications necessary to defend his work. However, lawyers should never view allegations of inadequate representation as an unlimited license for them to retaliate against the client by revealing confidences unrelated to the claims of inadequacy. For example, a lawyer who represented a client in a child custody dispute is not permitted to disclose privileged communications about the client's extramarital affairs to retaliate against the client for filing a malpractice action against the lawyer because of his incompetent representation in a subsequent real estate transaction.

Selective Waiver

Most courts, including every federal circuit court that has considered the question except the Eighth Circuit, reject the idea of a "selective" or "limited waiver" where a party voluntarily waives the privilege for communications in one case but later asserts the privilege over the same communications in a different case.[38] For example, a corporate defendant in a lawsuit brought by a government agency might selectively waive the attorney-client privilege regarding a particular communication and then claim it in a different lawsuit brought by a private litigant. Courts believe that "selective waiver" might be used abusively as a tactical maneuver and that permitting selective waivers is not necessary to accomplish the purpose of the privilege, which is to encourage full and candid communications by clients with their lawyers.[39]

Case Preview

In re Pacific Pictures Corp.

DC Comics, a comic book publisher, sued the following parties: the heirs of the creators of Superman, an attorney who was involved in a joint venture with the heirs, and three entities in which that same attorney held a controlling interest (collectively, the "Petitioners"). DC Comics claimed that the attorney had interfered with the publisher's contractual relationships with the heirs. After the instant suit was filed, the U.S. Attorney's Office in another matter issued a grand jury subpoena for documents of the Petitioners. The government promised not to disclose the documents to non-government third parties and the Petitioners complied with the subpoena. D C Comics then sought disclosure of those

DC Comics/Superman
AP Photo/Ed Bailey

38. In re Pacific Pictures Corp., 679 F.3d 1121 (9th Cir. 2012) (noting the ruling in Diversified Industries, Inc. v. Meredith, 572 F.2d 596 (8th Cir. 1978) (en banc)). David M. Greenwald, Robert R. Stauffer & Erin R. Schrantz, 1 Testimonial Privileges §1:102 (3d ed. 2015).
39. In re Pacific Pictures Corp., 679 F.3d at 1121, 1127.

same documents in the instant suit. The magistrate judge found the Petitioners waived the attorney-client privilege when they disclosed the documents to the government in the other matter. Thus, the magistrate ordered the Petitioners to turn over the documents to DC Comics. The Petitioners requested a writ of mandamus, seeking to overturn the district court's order. This case provided the Ninth Circuit Court of Appeals with an opportunity to consider the theory of selective waiver.

In reviewing *In re Pacific Pictures Corp.*, consider the following questions:

1. What facts does the court discuss concerning the lawyer's decision to voluntarily disclose otherwise privileged materials to the government?
2. What is this court's rationale for holding that a client's voluntary disclosure of otherwise privileged materials to selected recipients constitutes a general waiver of the privilege?
3. Why does the court find that selective waiver does not serve the purpose of the attorney-client privilege?
4. Why does the court reject the Petitioners' argument that waiver should not apply to these disclosures because they were made pursuant to a government subpoena?

In re Pacific Pictures Corp.

679 F.3d 1121 (9th Cir. 2012)

We must decide whether a party waives attorney-client privilege forever by voluntarily disclosing privileged documents to the federal government. . . .

Marc Toberoff, a Hollywood producer and a licensed attorney, stepped into the fray around the turn of the millennium. As one of his many businesses, Toberoff pairs intellectual property rights with talent and markets these packages to movie studios. Having set his sights on Superman, Toberoff approached the Heirs with an offer to manage preexisting litigation over the rights Siegel and Shuster had ceded to D.C. Comics. He also claimed that he would arrange for a new Superman film to be produced. To pursue these goals, Toberoff created a joint venture between the Heirs and an entity he owned. Toberoff served as both a business advisor and an attorney for that venture. The ethical and professional concerns raised by Toberoff's actions will likely occur to many readers, but they are not before this court.

While the preexisting litigation was pending, Toberoff hired a new lawyer to work for one of his companies. This attorney remained in Toberoff's employ for only about three months before allegedly absconding with copies of several documents from the Siegel and Shuster files. Unsuccessful in his alleged attempt to use the documents to solicit business from the Heirs, this attorney sent the documents to executives at D.C. Comics. While he did not include his name with the package, he did append a cover letter, written in the form of a timeline, outlining in detail Toberoff's alleged master plan to capture Superman for himself.

. . .

In 2010, D.C. Comics filed this lawsuit against Toberoff, the Heirs, and three entities in which Toberoff owned a controlling interest (collectively, the "Petitioners"), claiming that Toberoff interfered with its contractual relationships with the Heirs. The attorney's cover letter formed the basis of the lawsuit and was incorporated into the complaint. Toberoff has continued to resist the use of any of the documents taken from his offices, including those already disclosed to D.C. Comics and especially the cover letter.

About a month after the suit was filed, Toberoff asked the Office of the United States Attorney for the Central District of California to investigate the theft [of documents from his office]. In response to a request from Toberoff, the U.S. Attorney's Office issued a grand jury subpoena for the documents as well as a letter stating that if Toberoff voluntarily complied with the subpoena the Government would "not provide the . . . documents . . . to non-governmental third parties except as may be required by law or court order." The letter also confirmed that disclosure would indicate that "Toberoff has obtained all relevant permissions and consents needed (if any) to provide the . . . documents . . . to the government." Armed with this letter, Toberoff readily complied with the subpoena, making no attempt to redact anything from the documents.

D.C. Comics immediately requested all documents disclosed to the U.S. Attorney, claiming that the disclosure of these unredacted copies waived any remaining privilege. Examining the weight of authority from other circuits, the magistrate judge agreed that a party may not selectively waive attorney-client privilege. The magistrate judge reasoned that, because a voluntary disclosure of privileged materials breaches confidentiality and is inconsistent with the theory behind the privilege, such disclosure waives that privilege regardless of whether the third party is the government or a civil litigant. Having delivered the documents to the government, the magistrate judge concluded, Petitioners could not rely on the attorney-client privilege to shield them from D.C. Comics.

. . .

III

Under certain circumstances, the attorney-client privilege will protect communications between clients and their attorneys from compelled disclosure in a court of law. . . .

Nonetheless, because, like any other testimonial privilege, this rule "contravene[s] the fundamental principle that the public has a right to every man's evidence," we construe it narrowly to serve its purposes. In particular, we recognize several ways by which parties may waive the privilege. Most pertinent here is that voluntarily disclosing privileged documents to third parties will generally destroy the privilege. The reason behind this rule is that, " '[i]f clients themselves divulge such information to third parties, chances are that they would also have divulged it to their attorneys, even without the protection of the privilege.' " Under such circumstances, there simply is no justification to shut off judicial inquiry into these communications. Petitioners concede that this is the general rule, but they assert a number of reasons why it should not apply to them.

A

Petitioners' primary contention is that because Toberoff disclosed these documents to the government, as opposed to a civil litigant, his actions did not waive the privilege as to the world at large. That is, they urge that we adopt the theory of "selective waiver" initially accepted by the Eight Circuit, Diversified Industries, Inc. v. Meredith, 572 F.2d 596 (8th Cir. 1978) (en banc), but rejected by every other circuit to consider the issue since.

As the magistrate judge noted, we have twice deferred judgment on whether we will accept a theory of selective waiver. But we share the concerns expressed by many of our sister circuits about the cursory analysis behind the *Diversified* rule. The Eighth Circuit — the first court of appeals to consider the issue — adopted what has become a highly controversial rule only because it concluded that "[t]o hold otherwise may have the effect of thwarting the developing procedure of corporations to employ independent outside counsel to investigate and advise them in order to protect stockholders." This apprehension has proven unjustified. Officers of public corporations, it seems, do not require a rule of selective waiver to employ outside consultants or voluntarily to cooperate with the government. More importantly, such reasoning does little, if anything, to serve the public good underpinning the attorney-client privilege. That is, "selective waiver does not serve the purpose of encouraging full disclosure to one's attorney in order to obtain informed legal assistance; it merely encourages voluntary disclosure to government agencies, thereby extending the privilege beyond its intended purpose."

. . .

It is not beyond our power to create such a privilege. But as doing so requires balancing competing societal interests in access to evidence and in promoting certain types of communication, the Supreme Court has warned us not to "exercise this authority expansively." Put simply, "[t]he balancing of conflicting interests of this type is particularly a legislative function."

Since *Diversified*, there have been multiple legislative attempts to adopt a theory of selective waiver. Most have failed. Given that Congress has declined broadly to adopt a new privilege to protect disclosures of attorney-client privileged materials to the government, we will not do so here. *Univ. of Pa.*, 493 U.S. at 189 (requiring federal courts to be particularly cautious when legislators have "considered the relevant competing concerns but [have] not provided the privilege").

. . .

D

Petitioners also argue that they should be treated differently because Toberoff produced these documents subject to a subpoena. Involuntary disclosures do not automatically waive the attorney-client privilege. But without the threat of contempt, the mere existence of a subpoena does not render testimony or the production of documents involuntary. Instead, whether the subpoenaed party "chose not to assert the privilege when it was appropriate to do so is [also] relevant to the waiver analysis."

Toberoff both solicited the subpoena and "chose not to assert the privilege when it was appropriate to do so . . . ." That is, even though the subpoena specifically contemplated that Toberoff may choose to redact privileged materials, he did not. Petitioners assert that the U.S. Attorney would not have been satisfied with redacted

documents, but we will never know because Toberoff never tried. As such, we conclude that the district court properly treated the disclosure of these documents as voluntary. . . .

IV

Because Petitioners have not established error, we need not discuss the other . . . factors. The petition for mandamus is DENIED.

Post-Case Follow-Up

A number of federal and state cases after *In re Pacific Pictures Corp.* have rejected the concept of selective waiver. *E.g.*, Gruss v. Zwirn, 09 Civ. 6441 (PGG) (MHD), 2013 U.S. Dist. LEXIS 100012 (S.D.N.Y. July 10, 2013); Feinstein v. Keenan, No. FSTCV106007235S, 2012 WL 2548331 (Conn. Super. Ct. June 6, 2012). Their reasons for rejection generally track those in *In re Pacific Pictures Corp.*, for example, their concern that selective waiver "has little, if any, relation to fostering frank communication between a client and her attorney"—the public good underlying the privilege. There is also the belief that clients should not be allowed to use selective waiver for their own tactical or strategic benefit to pick and choose among opponents. Finally, there is an appreciation for the general concept that courts should construe privileges narrowly because they exclude information that might assist in the truth-finding process. Thus, these courts hold that when one voluntarily discloses privileged information to third parties, it destroys the privilege.

In one case, the court noted that the attorney-client privilege is not always waived when a party makes an involuntarily disclosure. In Western States Wholesale Natural Gas Antitrust Litigation, MDL No. 1566, Slip Copy (D. Nev. Nov. 16, 2016), the court cited *In re Pacific Pictures Corp.* for the principle that the mere issuance of a subpoena is insufficient to make a disclosure coerced or involuntary; there must also be the threat of contempt. *Western States* acknowledged, however, a contrary California evidence rule that was inapplicable but provides that a subpoena is sufficient to constitute coercion, making the disclosure involuntary and thus not waiving the privilege. It is important

In re Pacific Pictures Corp.: After the Case

Following the Ninth Circuit's *In re Pacific Pictures Corp.* decision rejecting selective waiver, a court granted summary judgment in favor of Toberoff finding that DC Comics' claims of tortious interference with contractual relations were barred by the statute of limitations. DC Comics v. Pac. Pictures Corp., 938 F. Supp. 2d 941 (C.D. Cal. 2013). (This ruling was appealed to the Ninth Circuit by DC Comics, but the parties settled and the case was dismissed.)

The heirs of Joe Shuster, one of the Superman creators, did not fare as well. The district court granted DC Comics' motion for summary judgment regarding the validity of the heirs' copyright termination notice. DC Comics v. Pac. Pictures Corp., No. CV 10-3633 ODW RZX, 2012 WL 4936588, at *9 (C.D. Cal. Oct. 17, 2012), *aff'd*, 545 F. App'x 678 (9th Cir. 2013). The United States Supreme Court refused to hear an appeal of the decision against the heirs. In 1976, Congress changed the copyright law to allow authors and their heirs to terminate previous copyright grants made prior to January 1, 1978. The purpose of the termination provision was to safeguard against unfair copyright transfers made early in an artist's career when the parties had unequal bargaining power. Such was the case with the teenage Superman creators, Jerome Siegel and Joe Shuster, who sold the rights to Superman to DC Comics in 1938 for $130. Due to public pressure, DC Comics provided pensions to the impoverished Siegel and Shuster in 1975. In 1992, Shuster's heirs entered into an agreement with DC Comics to increase the amount of the pension to $25,000 a year. The court held that the 1992 agreement superseded the 1938 copyright transfer, and regranted the copyrights to DC Comics. Thus, the heirs could not avail themselves of the Copyright Act termination provisions, because the transfer occurred after 1978.

to check state evidence rules and cases to see what constitutes a voluntary disclosure and a waiver of the privilege in that jurisdiction.

In re Pacific Pictures Corp.: Real Life Applications

1. The defendants produced documents, including Exhibits 3, 8, 22, 25, and 34, that they wished to claw back under the court's blanket protective order concerning discovery and protection of possible privileged information. The defendants raised a generalized objection that these exhibits were protected by the attorney-client privilege. The plaintiffs filed a motion to compel re-production. Exhibits 3, 8, and 25 were entered as exhibits, formed the basis of questions, and were partially read into the record. The defendants did not object to introduction of Exhibits 22 and 34 and permitted the plaintiffs' counsel to use the exhibits to ask a witness questions. Did the defendants' conduct constitute an inadvertent waiver of the privilege?

2. During discovery, the defendant disclosed two letters written to him by his attorney. The plaintiff argued that this disclosure constituted a voluntary waiver of the defendant's attorney-client privilege and, as a result, the plaintiff asked to review all of the files and records of the defendant's attorney. The defendant maintains the letters were inadvertently disclosed by his paralegals during a large document request. The defendant argues that the privilege is only waived, if at all, regarding these two letters, and not as to other, related documents. Did the production of the two letters during discovery act as a waiver of the attorney-client privilege?

Partial Disclosures and Subject Matter Waivers

A party who voluntarily discloses a privileged communication before a factfinder, for example, in a complaint, in a pretrial proceeding or hearing, or in settlement negotiations, is deemed to have intentionally and completely waived the privilege concerning the subject matter of that particular disclosure.[40] The voluntary disclosure, however, may be misleading because it represents only a fraction of a more extensive communication on the subject matter. A party may seek all portions of

40. Restatement §79 cmt. f.

a single communication and related privileged communications to prevent the opposing party from unfairly distorting the context or meaning of its partial disclosure.[41] In this situation, courts will find a general waiver of the entire subject matter of the communication or related privileged communications "that are reasonably necessary to provide a complete and balanced presentation."[42] The concern regarding fairness and subject matter waiver highlights a familiar refrain: that the "privilege is a shield not a sword," meaning that it is unfair to allow a party to selectively offer only a portion of a privileged communication while withholding less favorable portions.

Courts draw a distinction between testimonial and non-testimonial settings in deciding whether to find **subject matter waiver**. In a testimonial setting, there is a concern that a partial disclosure will mislead the fact-finder and cause an unfair result. In a non-testimonial setting, such as pretrial discovery, there is no factfinder present to be misled and thus no need for the court to find subject matter waiver following a partial disclosure.[43] Nevertheless, a majority of courts will also find broad subject matter waiver of the privilege when a partial disclosure, even one not intended to mislead others, occurs in a non-testimonial setting or in pretrial discovery because courts expect parties who want to assert the privilege to take effective steps to prevent partial disclosure.[44] The prominent case of In re von Bulow, 828 F.2d 94 (2d Cir. 1987), suggests, however, that not all courts automatically find a broad waiver of the privilege in the non-testimonial setting, at least where the client's lawyer makes the partial disclosure.

Claus von Bülow was convicted of assault with intent to murder his wife. The Rhode Island Supreme Court reversed the conviction and he was acquitted upon retrial. Harvard Law professor Alan Dershowitz represented him on appeal. With von Bülow's consent and encouragement, in 1986 Dershowitz published his book, *Reversal of Fortune: Inside the von Bulow Case*, chronicling the case and disclosing some confidential client communications.

The decedent-wife's children from a prior marriage sued von Bülow on behalf of their mother in a civil action, alleging, in part, common law assault, negligence, and fraud. They "moved to compel discovery

In re von Bulow

Claus von Bülow, a Danish-German aristocrat living in London, met Sunny (née Martha Crawford), an American heiress, in the 1960s. The couple got married in 1966, soon after Sunny's divorce from the Austrian prince Alfred von Auersperg, with whom she had two children, Annie Laurie and Alexander.
The von Bülows had a daughter, Cosima, in 1967, and in 1968, Claus left his position with J. Paul Getty and moved to America, to reside in Newport, Rhode Island with his family. In December 1979, Sunny slipped into a coma induced by low blood sugar, but was revived. About a year later, she suffered a brain injury that left her in a persistent vegetative state for nearly 28 years. In the meantime, the von Bülows' marriage experienced difficulties. Based *inter alia* on Annie Laurie and Alexander's suspicions, Claus was investigated as a suspect and later charged with and convicted of two counts of assault with intent to murder Sunny von Bülow by insulin injection. These convictions were reversed on appeal and Claus was acquitted upon retrial. After the acquittal, Alexander

41. *Id.* at 598-99.
42. *Id.* at 598. SEC v. Brady, 238 F.R.D. 429, 441 (N.D. Tex. 2006).
43. Restatement §79 cmt. f, at 599.
44. *Id.*

and Annie Laurie filed a civil action in federal court against Claus on behalf of their mother alleging common law assault, negligence, fraud, and RICO violations and seeking $56 million in damages. The suit was based upon the same facts as the Rhode Island criminal proceedings and ended in an out-of-court settlement in 1988. Claus agreed to divorce Sunny, to renounce all claims to her fortune, to leave the country, and to relinquish all rights to write books or earn money from the case. He returned to England where he worked as an art and theater critic.

Claus von Bülow with Alan Dershowitz, who represented von Bülow on appeal. *AP Photo/Charles Krupa*

of certain discussions between [Claus] and his attorneys based on the alleged waiver of the attorney-client privilege with respect to those communications in the book." The Second Circuit held that von Bülow had waived the privilege "as to the particular matters *actually disclosed* in the book" but that it was an abuse of discretion to broaden the waiver to include those portions of conversations that remained *undisclosed* in the book and any communications on the same or related matters. The court noted that the "fairness doctrine" would warrant a general waiver of the privilege "requir[ing] the production of the remainder" of the communications concerning the book disclosures if they were offered in litigation. The fairness doctrine does not apply, however, "when the privilege-holder or his attorney has made extrajudicial disclosures, and those disclosures have not subsequently been placed at issue during litigation."

Inadvertent Disclosures: Limiting Attorney-Client Privilege and Work-Product Waivers

Litigators fear that the disclosure of confidential communications — no matter how minimal or inadvertent — will constitute a general waiver of all communications or information concerning the subject matter of the disclosure. This fear causes additional litigation expense as lawyers carefully review discovery requests for documents and other information. The fear of subject matter waiver and related costs has exponentially increased with the advent of the electronic age and digital data.[45]

An **inadvertent disclosure** is one where the "disclosing person took precautions reasonable in the circumstances to guard against [the] disclosure" but nevertheless the communication or information was accidently disclosed.[46] The accidental disclosure may not constitute a waiver of the privilege if the client took reasonable precautions to protect the confidential nature of the communications and promptly seeks to "**claw back**" the communication and reestablish its confidentiality.[47] Determining whether reasonable precautions were taken involves looking at the importance of the content of the disclosure; the efficacy of and the

45. Zubulake v. UBS Warburg LLC, 220 F.R.D. 212 (S.D.N.Y. 2003). Judge Scheindlin opined that lawyers are ethically obligated to fully and accurately comply with reasonable discovery requests for electronic communications no matter how onerous, although courts may order the requesting party to pay some of the discovery expense.
46. FRE 502; *see* Restatement §79 cmt. h, at 600.
47. *See* Gray v. Bicknell, 86 F.3d 1472, 1483-84 (8th Cir. 1996) (discussing Hydraflow, Inc. v. Enidine, Inc., 145 F.R.D. 626 (W.D.N.Y. 1993), and its five-step analysis for determining whether inadvertent disclosure constituted waiver and whether the waiver covers related documents).

availability of additional precautions; externally imposed time pressures or the volume of the required disclosure; whether the disclosure was by the client, the lawyer, or some third person; and the degree of disclosure to non-privileged persons.[48]

Federal Rule of Evidence (FRE) 502 recognizes the significant concern that lawyers have in the digital age about complying with discovery requests for large amounts of information while at the same time avoiding any inadvertent disclosure that might waive the attorney-client privilege for a particular subject. FRE 502 provides, in part, that an inadvertent disclosure in federal court will not operate as a waiver in any federal or state court if the privilege holder took reasonable steps to prevent the disclosure and then also to promptly rectify the error.[49] A party's use of advanced analytical software applications and linguistic tools in screening for privilege and work product immunity in some instances may constitute reasonable steps to prevent disclosure.[50]

A party who learns of an inadvertent disclosure should immediately request the document's return and possibly seek a protective order from the court to prevent its further use.[51] FRE 502 also permits federal judges to issue orders that preclude a waiver of the privilege or work-product immunity to assist with discovery as litigants will no longer fear losing protection for confidential information.[52] Litigants can create their own private agreements under FRE 502(e) to limit the waiver of the privilege or work-product immunity, which may be incorporated in the court order.[53]

4. Exceptions

There are several exceptions to the attorney-client privilege. For example, the privilege does not apply to a communication that is relevant to an issue among competing parties claiming inheritance through the same deceased client or a communication concerning the attestation of a document when the lawyer was the attesting witness.[54]

Exceptions are distinguishable from waivers because exceptions involve situations that preclude a finding that the privilege ever arose or existed to protect the communications from disclosure. In contrast, with waivers the elements for a valid privilege arose or existed but the client's subsequent conduct rendered the privilege lost or ineffective.[55] There are three noteworthy exceptions: the crime-fraud exception, the exception for joint clients, and the exception for self-defense.

---

48. Restatement §79 cmt. h, at 600.
49. FRE Advisory Committee Note.
50. *Id.*
51. Evidence Problems, *supra* note 3, at 481.
52. FRE 502(d). FRE 502(d) does not authorize "selective waiver" — where a litigant waives the privilege against one party but claims it against the rest of the world. Christopher B. Mueller & Laird C. Kirkpatrick, 2 Federal Evidence § 5.35 (4th ed. 2013). FRE 502(d) also applies to both intentional and inadvertent disclosures. *Id.*
53. FRE 502(e) (permitting parties to craft their own agreements to facilitate discovery); Evidence Problems, *supra* note 3, at 488.
54. *See* Proposed FRE 503(d)(2) & (4); Restatement §81, at 612-13.
55. Squire, Sanders & Dempsey, L.L.P. v. Givaudan Flavors Corp., 937 N.E.2d 533 (Oh. 2010); *see* In re Lott, 424 F.3d 446 (6th Cir. 2005).

Crime-Fraud Exception

The **crime-fraud exception** to the attorney-client privilege provides that a client's confidential communications with counsel are not protected from disclosure when made for the purpose of furthering a crime or fraud. The purpose of the privilege is to promote the client's full disclosure and observance of the law, not to allow clients to use lawyers for unlawful purposes.

It is the client's, not the lawyer's, intention to commit the crime or fraud, now or in the future, which ultimately determines whether the client's communications are privileged.[56] Even if the intended crime or fraud never takes place, the client's intent alone triggers the crime-fraud exception and requires disclosure; it does not matter whether the lawyer unwittingly participated in the client's scheme.[57] Discerning client intent is a fact-based and sometimes difficult inquiry.

The crime-fraud exception does not apply to client communications concerning the criminal propriety of a proposed course of conduct.[58] The privilege is designed to encourage clients to consult with lawyers about their future conduct to promote compliance with the law. The exception is triggered, however, when the client approaches the lawyer with a preconceived plan that he knows is criminal or fraudulent and uses the lawyer to implement it.[59]

Client disclosure of a past crime or fraud does not trigger the crime-fraud exception.[60] Client communications intended to help the lawyer defend the client's past or current conduct are also privileged. But communications aimed at covering up past or ongoing criminal conduct are not privileged.[61]

The party challenging the applicability of the attorney-client privilege bears the burden of establishing a prima facie case that the client intended his communications to further a crime or fraud. In United States v. Zolin, 491 U.S. 554 (1989), the Supreme Court did not decide the quantum of proof necessary to make the "threshold" or prima facie showing, but it noted "many blatant abuses of privilege which cannot be substantiated by extrinsic [or independent] evidence." Accordingly, the Court held that judges may examine the allegedly privileged statements *in camera* and outside the presence of the party asserting the crime-fraud exception to determine the exception's applicability. The Court also held that "before a district court may engage ***in camera* review**, . . . the party opposing the privilege . . . must present evidence to support a reasonable belief that *in camera* review may yield evidence that establishes the exception's applicability." Although the Court rejected the view that only evidence independent of the alleged privileged communications could be used in making a prima facie showing for the crime-fraud exception, independent evidence remains important. Examples of independent evidence include

---

56. Evidence Manual, *supra* note 17, §501.02[5][l][iii], at 501-64-66; Restatement §82(a), at 613-14. The Restatement also provides that the "crime-fraud exception applies even if the client's purpose was benign at the time of consultation, but later the client used the consultation to commit a crime or fraud." Restatement §82(b) cmt. c. & Reporter's Note at 613-14.

57. Evidence Manual, *supra* note 17, §501.02[5][l][iii].

58. *See* In re Grand Jury Proceedings (Corporation), 87 F.3d 377, 381 (9th Cir. 1996).

59. Evidence Manual, *supra* note 17, §501.02[5][l][iii].

60. *See* In re Grand Jury Proceedings (Corporation), 87 F.3d at 377, 381.

61. *See* In re Sealed Case, 754 F.2d 395, 403 (D.C. Cir. 1985); Evidence Manual, *supra* note 17, §501.02(5)(l)(iii).

a prosecutor's statements or good faith affidavit about testimony already presented to the grand jury or a corporate employee's self-serving testimony that corporate counsel asked him to commit perjury.[62]

Case Preview

In re Grand Jury Investigation

In *In re Grand Jury Investigation*, the appellant corporation operated a call center that marketed surgical devices to medical centers. The FDA believed that the corporation's advertising violated the Food, Drug, and Cosmetics Act by not providing relevant risk information about the devices. The government believed that the corporation's lawyers' responses to FDA letters contained false statements designed to distract the investigators. Under the crime-fraud exception, the grand jury issued subpoenas to three lawyers to produce, among other items, all communications, including documents, notes, and the sources of the information, relating to their FDA correspondence. The lawyers did not fully comply with the subpoena. In a matter of first impression in the circuit, the court held that the district court had committed an error when it ordered the defendants to produce all attorney-client documents without *in camera* review to determine whether they were made in furtherance of a contemplated or ongoing crime or fraud.

In reading *In re Grand Jury Investigation*, consider the following questions:

1. What two-part test did the court use to determine the applicability of the crime-fraud exception?
2. Does the court require an *in camera* review of communications to establish the first part of the crime-fraud exception test?
3. What requirement does the court impose on district courts to comply with the second part of the crime-fraud exception test?

In re Grand Jury Investigation

810 F.3d 1110 (9th Cir. 2016)

I

Appellant Corporation was a call center that marketed a surgical device for medical facilities. In December 2010, the director and health officer for Los Angeles County Public Health sent a letter to the FDA raising concerns that the Corporation's advertisements (large billboards, bus placards, and direct mail) were "inadequately inform[ing] consumers of potential risks" of the surgical device. After the

62. In re Grand Jury Investigation of Schroeder, 842 F.2d 1223 (11th Cir. 1987); White v. American Airlines, 915 F.2d 1414 (10th Cir. 1983).

Corporation received this letter from a local columnist, the company—through counsel—sent its own letter to the FDA disputing many of the letter's assertions and attempting in various ways to dissuade the FDA from investigating.

Despite the attorney's letter, the FDA opened an investigation and sent warning letters to the Corporation and a few medical centers in California. The letters stated that the FDA believed the Corporation's advertising violated the Food, Drug, and Cosmetic Act (FDCA) by not providing "relevant risk information regarding the use of the [device], age and other qualifying requirements for the [surgical] procedure, and the need for ongoing modification of [lifestyle] habits." New counsel for the Corporation responded by letter to the FDA warning letter. A third attorney responded on behalf of the medical centers.

The government alleged that these responses contained false statements designed to obstruct the FDA investigation. Under the crime-fraud exception to attorney-client privilege, grand jury subpoenas were issued to the three lawyers to produce "(1) all communications relating to their correspondence to the FDA, including documents and notes showing the information received and identifying the sources of information for the statements and representations made and (2) retainer agreements and billing records identifying the client(s) who retained and paid for their services in communicating with the FDA on the subject matter of the correspondence." The attorneys provided some information, but they did not fully comply with the subpoenas.

The government filed a motion to compel compliance with the subpoenas. Without reviewing any documents in camera, the district court determined from independent, non-privileged evidence that the government had established a prima facie case that the lawyers' services were obtained "in furtherance of and . . . sufficiently related to ongoing" crimes, i.e., false statements to and obstruction of the FDA. The district court rejected the argument that in camera review of the privileged documents was necessary to determine whether the government established a prima facie case of crime-fraud. The district court granted the government's motion to compel production of all "matters identified in the subpoenas."

II

While the attorney-client privilege is "arguably most fundamental of the common law privileges recognized under Federal Rule of Evidence 501," it is "not absolute." In re Napster, Inc. Copyright Litig., 479 F.3d 1078, 1090 (9th Cir. 2007). Under the crime-fraud exception, communications are not privileged when the client "consults an attorney for advice that will serve him in the commission of a fraud" or crime. *Id.* To invoke the crime-fraud exception, a party must "satisfy a two-part test":

> First, the party must show that "the client was engaged in or planning a criminal or fraudulent scheme when it sought the advice of counsel to further the scheme." Second, it must demonstrate that the attorney-client communications for which production is sought are "sufficiently related to" and were made "*in furtherance of* [the] intended, or present, continuing illegality."

Id.

Appellants first contend that the district court could not find a prima facie case of crime-fraud without examining the privileged documents in camera. The district court correctly rejected this contention. District courts may find a prima facie case of crime-fraud either by examining privileged material in camera or by examining independent, non-privileged evidence.

As *In re Napster* stated, however, the existence of a prima facie case is only step one of the inquiry. In this case, the government relied on independent, non-privileged evidence to establish reasonable cause that the attorneys were enlisted to make false statements to the FDA. No evidence has been presented regarding the second step in the analysis: whether "the attorney-client communications for which production is sought are 'sufficiently related to' and were made 'in furtherance of [the] intended, or present, continuing illegality.'" In re Napster, 479 F.3d at 1090. Thus far, the litigation has not focused on any individual documents. Instead, the district court broadly ordered the attorneys to produce everything identified in the government's subpoenas, without first examining any specific documents in camera to determine whether they contained communications in furtherance of the asserted crime-fraud.

. . .

[W]e agree with the Sixth Circuit. While in camera review is not necessary during step one to establish a prima facie case that "the client was engaged in or planning a criminal or fraudulent scheme when it sought the advice of counsel to further the scheme," a district court must examine the individual documents themselves to determine that the specific attorney-client communications for which production is sought are "sufficiently related to" and were made "in furtherance of the intended, or present, continuing illegality."

For these reasons, we VACATE and REMAND the order compelling production of all subpoenaed documents so the district court may examine the documents in camera to determine the proper scope of the production order, i.e., which documents contained communications in furtherance of the crime-fraud.

Post-Case Follow-Up

In re Grand Jury Investigation followed the U.S. Supreme Court's well-established approach in United States v. Zolin, 491 U.S. 554 (1989), that requires courts to conduct an *in camera* review of specific privileged documents to determine whether they further a crime or fraud and thus are excepted from the attorney-client privilege. *In re Grand Jury Investigation* also represents one approach to an issue left unresolved in *Zolin*: whether a court also has to conduct an *in camera* review of privileged documents to establish the prerequisite finding of a crime or fraud for the application of the crime-fraud exception. The *In re Grand Jury Investigation* approach of not requiring the court to conduct an *in camera* review to establish a crime or fraud seems to strike a reasonable balance between competing interests. It conserves the court's and litigants' time and resources while also protecting the attorney-client privilege by requiring the court, after a prerequisite finding of a crime or fraud, to conduct an *in camera* review of specific communications before ordering their disclosure.

In re Grand Jury Investigation: Real Life Applications

1. Over a year ago, a high-ranking political figure from a poor nation met with Attorney Fonseca in his New York City law office. The politician asked Fonseca how he could "discreetly" bring large sums of money into the United States for the purchase of valuable real estate and manufacturing businesses. The client wanted to avoid publicity and insisted that Fonseca handle everything. The client preferred to transact business on a cash-only basis. Fonseca helped the client with several transactions. The U.S. Attorney has charged Fonseca with money laundering and has asked him for all of his documents regarding this client as well as disclosure of the nature of their communications. The government told Fonseca that if he cooperates, he will not be charged with a crime. Fonseca believes that the documents and communications are protected by the attorney-client privilege, but he wants to know whether he can make the disclosures to avoid criminal charges. He contacts you, a professional responsibility and criminal defense lawyer, for advice. Advise Fonseca.
2. Imagine that the CEO of a small local bank recently retired from his position. The new CEO is a friend of yours and consults you about possible financial improprieties by the former CEO. When you contact the former CEO, he says that he relied on the advice of the bank's lawyer at the time. The former CEO and that lawyer refuse to disclose their communications about the legal propriety of the former CEO's financial dealings, claiming that the dealings are protected by the attorney-client privilege. Are the former CEO and the lawyer correct?

Joint-Clients Exception

The **joint-clients exception** recognizes that sometimes multiple clients with a common legal interest may want the same lawyer to represent them. Joint representation offers the clients and the lawyer potential savings in time and expense. Joint representation also offers the strategic benefit of a unified defense, making it less likely that the opposing party can succeed with a "divide and conquer" approach.

The joint-clients exception provides that a communication to a lawyer that is relevant to a matter of common interest between the joint clients is not privileged when one joint client proceeds against another joint client. To illustrate, clients A and B retain Attorney Jones to defend them in a common matter involving defamation. A's and B's communications to Jones, whether communicated separately or in a joint conference, are privileged from any third-party disclosure request. However, the privilege will not prevent client A from offering her or client B's confidential communications to their joint attorney in a subsequent action by client A against client B.

Self-Defense Exception

The attorney-client privilege does not protect confidential communications related to a client's action against his counsel concerning the quality of his representation.[63] Fairness requires that the lawyer be able to use these communications to defend herself against client allegations of lawyer malpractice, ineffective assistance of counsel, and other misconduct.[64] The lawyer is permitted to disclose only privileged client communications necessary to defend herself against the client's claims of misconduct. The lawyer should not use the **self-defense exception** as an excuse to retaliate against the client by disclosing communications unrelated to the client's claims of misconduct. Some courts permit the lawyer under this exception to use confidential communications to establish a claim for compensation against the client.[65]

D. WORK-PRODUCT IMMUNITY

Work-product immunity prevents the discovery of mental impressions, conclusions, opinions, or legal theories of attorneys or their representatives involved in or preparing for litigation.[66] Work-product immunity at the federal level is found both in **Rule 26(b)(3) of the Federal Rules of Civil Procedure** and in federal common law.[67] Most states have codified the immunity doctrine in statutes or court rules.[68]

Work-product immunity reflects, in part, the belief that even with liberal discovery rules, the truth-seeking process is best advanced by a competitive and confidential development of facts and legal information by opposing parties.[69] The immunity promotes client interests in diligent legal assistance because lawyers know that their work is beyond the reach of opposing parties who may appropriate or "free ride" on their diligent preparations for litigation.[70]

The Restatement (Third) of the Law Governing Lawyers notes that immunity applies when there is a reasonable anticipation of litigation, which requires an objective examination of the facts surrounding the preparation and nature of the materials and the role of the lawyer.[71] The commencement of litigation is not a prerequisite for successfully asserting work-product protection. Litigation includes any adversarial proceeding in which parties contest factual issues or present competing legal arguments, such as criminal and civil trials, proceedings before administrative agencies, claims commissions, and arbitration panels and mediations.[72]

Work-product immunity covers the lawyer's preparation, collection, and assembly of tangible evidence or its intangible equivalents.[73] For example, tangible work product would include the lawyer's photographs of an accident, photographs of the accident that the lawyer collected from a bystander, or pictures the

63. Evidence Manual, *supra* note 17, §501.02[5][l][i].
64. *Id.*
65. *Id.*
66. Evidence Problems, *supra* note 3, at 481.
67. Hickman v. Taylor, 329 U.S. 495 (1947).
68. Restatement §87, at 640.
69. *Id.* at 638.
70. *Id.*
71. *Id.* at 642; Schaeffler v. United States, 806 F.3d 34, 43-45 (9th Cir. 2015).
72. Restatement §87, at 641.
73. In re Cendant Corp. Sec. Litig., 343 F.3d 658 (3d Cir. 2003).

lawyer assembled from a magazine that covered the accident. Other tangible work product can include written notes, for example of witness interviews; financial and other analyses; computer databases; electronic recordings; tapes; surveys; and diagrams.[74] Intangible equivalents of the same work in unwritten, oral, or remembered form are also entitled to work-product protection.[75] For example, the lawyer's unrecorded recollection of a witness's description of an automobile accident would be protected from discovery under work-product immunity.[76]

1. Two Types of Work Product: Ordinary and Opinion

Work product falls into two general categories: ordinary and opinion. **Ordinary work product**, for example, a witness's statement to the lawyer, written or oral, would generally be immune from discovery. The immunity is not absolute, however. The court can compel the lawyer's disclosure of the witness's statement if the inquiring party can show (1) a substantial need for the material in order to prepare for trial, and (2) that the party is unable without undue hardship to obtain the substantial equivalent of the material by other means.[77] For example, a lawyer's notes of the only eyewitness statements about an accident probably warrant disclosure under the "**substantial need-undue hardship**" exception to work-product immunity if the witness died recently. There is a substantial need for the eyewitness's testimony since she saw the accident and any other way of obtaining the information would impose an undue hardship since the eyewitness is dead. The party seeking disclosure should be able to show that she will likely be prejudiced by the absence of discovery of the eyewitness's statements.[78]

Opinion work product includes the lawyer's mental impressions, opinions, and strategy in litigation—often referred to as the "core" work product. For example, the lawyer retains an undisclosed trial consultant to develop a psychological plan for winning the case and attacking the credibility of the opposing party's key witnesses. The consultant will not testify but meets with witnesses and sends the lawyer a document containing a psychological roadmap for winning the case. The lawyer adds some notes reflecting his mental impressions of the roadmap and his thoughts about how to implement the roadmap. The consultant's document, the contents of his discussion with witnesses, and the lawyer's additional notes are considered opinion work product.[79] Opinion work product is extremely difficult to obtain. The inquiring party must show extraordinary circumstances to justify disclosure—a standard that the Restatement notes has never been intelligibly defined.[80]

---

74. *Id.*
75. *Id.*
76. Restatement §87, at 640-41.
77. Baker v. Gen. Motors Corp., 209 F.3d 1051 (8th Cir. 2000).
78. Restatement §88 cmt. b, at 651.
79. In re Cendant Corp. Sec. Litig., 343 F.3d at 658 (holding that it was opinion work product when a trial consultant, here Dr. Phil McGraw who now hosts a television show, prepares a trial plan and talks with witnesses; an attorney's tactical planning is considered opinion work product).
80. Restatement §89 cmt. b, at 656.

2. Waivers and Exceptions to Work-Product Immunity

Parties or their agents can agree to waive work-product immunity.[81] A party who fails to object in a tribunal to another person attempting to offer work-product evidence waives the immunity.[82] Waiver also occurs when the holder of the immunity discloses the work product to third parties and there is a "significant likelihood that an adversary or potential adversary in anticipated litigation will obtain it."[83] A party waives immunity if the material is used to aid or impeach a witness or when the party alleges in a proceeding that the lawyer was ineffective or negligent, or otherwise committed misconduct. Work-product immunity does not protect material if the client uses the work product in furtherance of a crime or fraud that is later accomplished.[84]

Case Preview

Schaeffler v. United States

Recall our discussion of the corporate acquisition in *Schaeffler*, *supra* at page 268. In that case, the Schaeffler Group was unsuccessful in moving to quash an IRS summons for numerous documents created by EY and provided to "outside parties," including the Consortium. In reviewing *Schaeffler v. United States*, consider the kinds of evidence the appellant offered to show that the documents were prepared in anticipation of litigation.

Further, consider the following:

1. What additional kinds of evidence might support such a finding in other cases?
2. Did this case involve ordinary or opinion work product?
3. What is the significance of designating work product as ordinary or opinion?
4. What are the potential costs or disadvantages to the IRS in pursuing its case against Schaeffler given the court's ruling that the EY Tax Memo and other documents are protected by the work-product immunity?

Schaeffler v. United States

806 F.3d 34 (2d Cir. 2015)

BACKGROUND

a.

[The full statement of facts in *Schaeffler v. United States* is provided in this chapter at pages 268-269.]

81. *Id.* §91, at 661-62.
82. *Id.*
83. *Id.*
84. *Id.* §93, at 673.

b. District Court's Ruling

. . .

[T]he district court held that the EY Tax Memo and, presumably, other similar documents were not entitled to work-product protection. After conducting an *in camera* review of the EY Tax Memo, the district court described it as containing: (i) "detailed legal analysis of the federal tax issues implicated," (ii) "assert[ions] that there is no law clearly on point," (iii) "language such as 'although not free from doubt,' 'the better view is that,' 'it may be argued,' and 'it is not inconceivable that the IRS could assert'"; and (iv) "arguments and counter-arguments that could be made by Schaeffler and the IRS with regard to the appropriate tax treatment of [the refinancing and restructuring]."

The district court noted that the EY Tax Memo "does not specifically refer to litigation . . . by discussing what actions peculiar to the litigation process [the parties] might take or what settlement strategies might be considered." The court concluded that appellants would have engaged in the "detailed and complex process of resolving" the unusual tax issues even if they did not anticipate any litigation. It reasoned that "Schaeffler is a rational businessperson" who "would have sought out the type of tax advice provided by Ernst & Young about the transaction had he not been concerned about an audit or litigation with the IRS." Because "any sophisticated businessperson engaging in a complex financial transaction will naturally wish to obtain advice on the relevant tax laws so that the transaction can be structured in such a way as to receive the most favorable tax treatment possible," the court ruled that, "given our assumption that Schaeffler is a rational businessperson who routinely makes efforts to comply with the law, we find that, even had he not anticipated an audit or litigation with the IRS, he still would have had to obtain the type of legal assistance provided by Ernst & Young to carry out the refinancing and restructuring transactions in an appropriate manner."

The court further stated that "petitioners have presented no facts suggesting that Ernst & Young would have acted any differently" or given advice "different in content or form had it known that no audit or litigation would ensue." . . . The court also relied on its view that the language of the EY Tax Memo did not "indicate that the authors are describing any particular anticipated litigation," notwithstanding the document's detailed discussion of legal strategies. Accordingly, the court ruled that the EY Tax Memo and related documents were not protected from disclosure under the work-product doctrine.

. . .

c. Application of Work-Product Doctrine

[W]e address only the district court's view that the EY Tax Memo and related documents were not entitled to work-product protection.

Attorney work product is of course protected from discovery. *See* Hickman v. Taylor, 329 U.S. 495 (1947); *see also* Fed. R. Civ. P. 26(b)(3). The doctrine "is intended to preserve a zone of privacy in which a lawyer can prepare and develop legal theories and strategy with an eye toward litigation, free from unnecessary intrusion by his adversaries." Documents prepared in anticipation of litigation are work product, even when they are also intended to assist in business dealings. We review the district court's ruling on a work-product claim for abuse of discretion.

The district court acknowledged that the EY Tax Memo was prepared at a time when appellants believed litigation was highly probable and contained analyses of the strengths, weaknesses, and likely outcomes of potential legal arguments. Nevertheless, the court found that appellants would have sought and received advice "created in essentially similar form" even if they had not anticipated litigation. On this ground, the court denied work-product protection.

Adlman is the governing precedent. It established a test to determine whether documents should be deemed prepared "in anticipation of litigation" and therefore subject to work-product protection. A document will be protected if, "in light of the nature of the document and the factual situation in the particular case, the document can fairly be said to have been prepared or obtained *because of* the prospect of litigation." Conversely, protection will be withheld from "documents that are prepared in the ordinary course of business or that would have been created in essentially similar form irrespective of the litigation." The district court's application of the "ordinary course of business" or "essentially similar form" example to the documents at issue in this appeal appears to us to virtually swallow the work-product protection *Adlman* extended to documents "prepared or obtained because of the prospect of litigation."

Adlman held that work-product protection would be withheld only from documents that were prepared in the ordinary course of business in a form that would not vary regardless of whether litigation was expected. In the present case, such records would include the supporting records and papers that appellants' external tax return preparers collected and created in the ordinary course of annually completing appellants' federal tax returns.

The tax advice in the EY Tax Memo was quite different. It was specifically aimed at addressing the urgent circumstances arising from the need for a refinancing and restructuring and was necessarily geared to an anticipated audit and subsequent litigation, which was on this record highly likely. *See Adlman*, 134 F.3d at 1195 (predicted litigation was virtually inevitable because of size of transaction and losses).

We also disagree with the district court's characterization of the form of the advice EY would be ethically and legally required to give appellants even in the absence of anticipated litigation. Neither professional standards, tax laws, nor IRS regulations required that appellants' tax advisors provide the kind of highly detailed, litigation-focused analysis and advice included in the EY Tax Memo. The standards relied upon by the district court all target concerns over the "audit lottery," in which aggressive tax advisers might recommend risky tax positions solely because the particular clients were statistically unlikely ever to be audited. That policy concern is simply not implicated here where appellants would not have sought the same level of detail if merely preparing an annual routine tax return with no particular prospect of litigation.

Finally, we address the district court's construct of a hypothetical scenario in which appellants faced exactly the same business and tax issues but did not anticipate litigation. This scenario appears to us to ignore reality. The size of a transaction and the complexity and ambiguity of the appropriate tax treatment are important variables that govern the probability of the IRS's heightened scrutiny and, therefore,

the likelihood of litigation. To hypothesize the same size of the transaction and the same complexity and ambiguity of the tax issues but also a lack of any anticipation of litigation posits a factual situation at odds with reality. . . .

Finally, we note that the district court's holding appears to imply that tax analyses and opinions created to assist in large, complex transactions with uncertain tax consequences can never have work-product protection from IRS subpoenas. This is contrary to *Adlman*, which explicitly embraces the dual-purpose doctrine that a document is eligible for work-product protection "if 'in light of the nature of the document and the factual situation in the particular case, the document can fairly be said to have been prepared or obtained *because of* the prospect of litigation.'"

In our view, the EY Tax Memo contains "legal analysis that falls squarely within [Hickman v. Taylor, 329 U.S. 495 (1947)]'s area of primary concern—analysis that candidly discusses the attorney's litigation strategies [and] appraisal of likelihood of success." They are therefore, protected under the work-product doctrine.

CONCLUSION

[Judgment vacated and remanded] "to determine [consistent with this opinion] whether any remaining documents are protected by the attorney-client privilege or work-product doctrine."

The question in *Schaeffler* about whether the documents were prepared in anticipation of litigation and therefore entitled to work-product immunity is a common one. The standard that is widely cited by courts for answering this question is "whether in light of the nature of the document, and the factual situation in the particular case, the document can fairly be said to have been prepared or obtained because of the prospect of litigation."[85] The *Schaeffler* court focused on the detailed legal advice in the challenged document, including possible legal strategies, and the likelihood of an IRS proceeding. These facts played a key role in the court's finding that the documents were prepared in anticipation of litigation. The *Schaeffler* formula of legal advice, including possible legal strategies and the likelihood of an adversarial proceeding, are important considerations for litigators as they attempt to protect their work and efforts in preparation for litigation. Litigators need to create and preserve evidence to demonstrate compliance with the *Schaeffler* formula. The requirement that work product be in anticipation of litigation is highly fact specific and promises to consume the attention of both litigators and the courts.

85. *Id.* §87 cmt. i, at 649 (citing 8 C. Wright, A. Miller & R. Marcus, Federal Practice and Procedure 343 (2d ed. 1994)).

Schaeffler v. United States: Real Life Applications

1. An elementary teacher is accused of sexually molesting students over several years. Criminal charges are filed against the teacher and several victims sue the principal and school district, claiming that the defendants knew about the alleged abuse but took no action. The school district hired the Smith law firm to investigate the incident. The district's lawyers interviewed 100 people and took only written notes of each interview. The firm summarized its findings in memoranda sent to the district. The Smith firm does not represent the defendants in this litigation. The plaintiffs issue a subpoena for the firm's notes and other internal legal memoranda in its possession concerning its investigation. The Smith firm refuses to produce the documents, relying on the attorney-client privilege and the work-product doctrine. The plaintiffs argue that the law firm was hired to provide only investigative services and not legal advice. How should the judge rule on the Smith claim that (a) the attorney-client privilege protects the documents and (b) that work-product immunity protects the documents?

2. Using the facts above, assume that the district's new litigation firm, Jones and Dower, retains a school-security expert who will testify that the defendant-district's conduct was appropriate in the above sexual molestation case. The security expert submits an expert report. The plaintiffs request the expert's three preliminary drafts of his final expert report. Jones and Dower refuses to comply and claims the preliminary drafts are protected by work-product immunity. How should the court rule on the Jones and Dower claim?

Chapter Summary

FIGURE 5.1 Three Circles of Lawyer "Secrets"

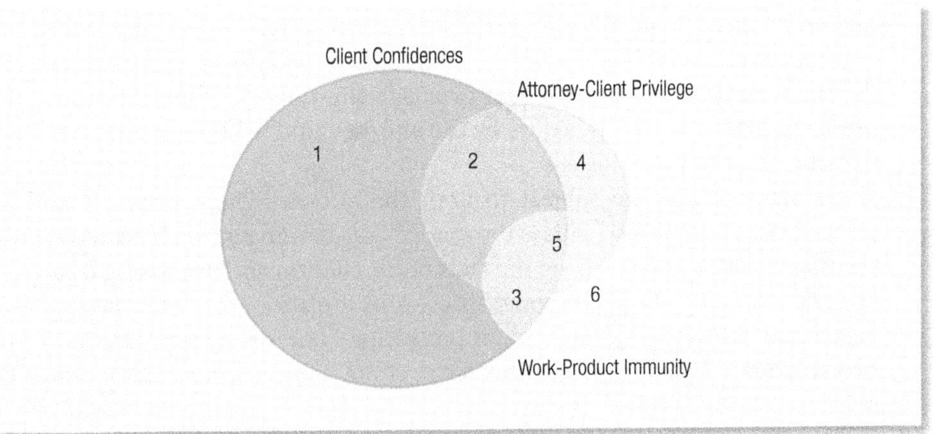

- It may be helpful to think of the three sources of client secrecy as interlocking but not coterminous circles. Look at the diagram above and review the material in this chapter by reference to the number in each section of the circle.

- The largest circle, designated as circle #1, is the protection for client confidences under Model Rule 1.6. This is the largest of the three circles because all information that the lawyer learns while representing a client on any type of matter, regardless of its source, is confidential, unless the client has given express or implied authorization for its disclosure.
- The next circle, #2, is the attorney-client privilege, a creature of evidence law. The attorney-client privilege furthers the policy of encouraging clients to make full and candid disclosures to their lawyers and of encouraging lawyers to provide solid and effective advice to their clients. This circle is smaller than the protection for client confidences circle because the privilege applies only to information communicated directly between the client and the lawyer for the purposes of legal advice — not to preexisting documents, and not to information gathered by the lawyer from third parties. The client holds the attorney-client privilege and ultimately must decide whether to assert it or waive it. There are exceptions to the privilege — most notably for litigation between the client and the attorney (the "self-defense" exception) and the crime-fraud release. Corporations and other legal entities may claim the attorney-client privilege, but the privilege belongs to the corporation and not to its constituents.
- The third circle is the work-product immunity. This provides qualified protection from discovery for documents that contain the mental impressions, opinions, and conclusions of lawyers during litigation. This is the smallest of the three circles because work-product immunity applies only to attorneys and agents involved in *litigation or anticipated litigation*; to documents or tangible things (photographs, charts) prepared by the lawyer or his agents (not documents prepared by the client); and to documents or tangible things that somehow contain or memorialize the mental impressions of the lawyer. There is both "ordinary" and "opinion" work product.
- The section of attorney-client circle privilege that extends beyond the rule of confidentiality (shaded area #4) reflects the fact that a lawyer may engage in a permissive disclosure of confidential information under Rule 1.6, but the information obtained from the client will still remain privileged if subpoenaed in a criminal or civil case. *See Purcell v. District Attorney for the Suffolk District.* Since the client holds the attorney-client privilege and only the client can waive that privilege, a permissive disclosure by the attorney under Rule 1.6 does not waive the attorney-client privilege.
- Some material may be subject to both the attorney-client privilege and the work-product immunity. This is the shaded area designated #5. If a lawyer writes the client a letter summarizing the facts of the client's case, discussing legal strategy and assessing the likelihood of success in litigation, this letter is both privileged and subject to work-product protection. The stronger protection of the two will apply (privilege), and this letter is not subject to discovery unless the privilege is waived by the client.
- Finally, there is attorney work product in litigation that is neither confidential under Rule 1.6 nor privileged under the rules of evidence (shaded area #6). If a lawyer handling a products liability case asks his associate to read and

summarize every products liability decision from the state supreme court in the past 20 years, the associate's memo—if it contains pure legal research and no facts communicated from the client or gathered from third parties—is neither confidential under Rule 1.6 nor privileged under the rules of evidence. Nonetheless, it is the work product of the law firm and it would be protected in discovery during litigation as "opinion" rather than "ordinary" work product.

Applying the Rules

1. Imagine that you work for a law firm that represents one of the nation's largest sports equipment and apparel companies. You have just been asked to work on an endorsement contract under which a major recording artist has tentatively agreed to appear in radio and television commercials endorsing your client's products. The corporation has also agreed to manufacture and market a new sports clothing line bearing the trade name of the recording artist. You are working on all the licensing and trademark agreements. The deal has not yet been made public. You are very excited about this new assignment and confident that it will be challenging and rewarding. Assume that you are out to dinner with your best friend from law school. She asks, "What's new at work?" What can you tell her about your new assignment, if anything?

2. Art Gorski, a non-veteran, represented to federal agencies from 2006 until 2010 that Legion was a Service-Disabled Veteran Owned Small Business Entity (SDVOSB) to obtain government contracts. To be eligible for such contracts, the entity must be at least 51 percent owned by one or more service-disabled veterans and they must control it, making long-term decisions and managing the entity's daily operations. From 2006 until early 2010, veteran A, who is service disabled, owned 55 percent of Legion and Gorski owned 45 percent but controlled the company's daily operations.

   Gorski retained the Gomez law firm on March 1, 2010 to restructure Legion in order to comply with new regulations that became effective on February 8, 2010. The regulations did not change any of the ownership and control requirements pertaining to SDVOSBs. Although the restructuring took place on March 23, 2010, the documents were dated February 1, 2010 by Gomez. It was important that the restructuring occur prior to the new regulations coming into force if Legion was to remain eligible for government contracts as an SDVOSB. The restructuring, however, did not change the fact that veteran A retained majority ownership and that Gorski maintained control of the entity's daily operations. A competitor challenged Legion's status, prompting an agency inquiry. The Gomez firm crafted a response on April 1, 2010, purporting to show that Legion was restructured on February 1, 2010, and still eligible to obtain SDVOSB contracts.

Gorski is indicted for conspiracy to defraud the United States. The U.S. Attorney issues subpoenas to Legion and Gomez for documents from November 2009 to December 2010 concerning Legion's ownership and SDOVSB eligibility and documents concerning their response to the agency inquiry. Legion and Gomez refuse to comply with the subpoena claiming that the items are protected by the attorney-client privilege. The U.S. Attorney consults you and asks several questions.

a) Are there any exceptions to the privilege that might permit disclosure by Gomez?
b) What is the significance, if any, of the fact that the Gomez firm never intended to help Legion evade the law?
c) What standards and processes will the court use to determine whether the crime-fraud exception applies?

3. Plaintiff-surgeon resigned from practice at the Defendant-Benton Hospital (BH). He alleges that the BH participated in race and ethnicity discrimination by entertaining charges of professional misconduct that BH knew were false and harmful to his reputation. The surgeon seeks two chains of emails. The first chain (Jan. 29-30, 2016) was between several hospital employees, including doctors, nurses, the human resources department (HR), and the CEO. This chain discussed the surgeon's alleged misconduct and certain emails in the chain were carbon copied (CC) to BH's in-house counsel.

The second email chain (Mar. 28-26, 2016), between BH's custodian of hospital records and the chief medical officer, concerned the surgeon's request for his personnel record. Assume that BH does not assert work-product immunity for the second email chain but does claim it is protected by the attorney-client privilege. Are either of the email chains protected by the attorney-client privilege? Explain your reasoning.

4. Two investors, Dayton and Smith, jointly retain Attorney Barton to create a partnership to purchase real estate. Following the partnership's first real estate purchase, Smith alleges that the attorney made several mistakes concerning the purchase and the creation of the partnership. Barton has not returned Smith's calls and Smith sues Barton for legal malpractice. Barton hires you to defend him in the malpractice action and asks the following questions:

a) In his defense, can he disclose confidential communications with Dayton and Smith concerning the partnership and real estate purchase?
b) Barton is angry about the malpractice suit. He once represented Smith in a contested divorce in which Smith confidentially informed him of an extramarital affair with a prominent official. Can Barton use this information to help defend himself in Smith's malpractice action?

Professional Responsibility in Practice

1. Imagine that you represent a defendant in a child rape prosecution. The defendant allegedly lured a child into the woods where he sexually assaulted her at knifepoint. The perpetrator allegedly abandoned the attack and ran off when a jogger approached. In the course of your representation, the defendant suddenly and unexpectedly reveals to you that he is responsible for a kidnapping, rape, and murder of another child five years earlier in the same park. You research that event and discover that another defendant was charged and convicted of that crime, and is now serving life in prison. Check the law in the state where you intend to practice. Are you authorized to reveal your client's confession to that crime in order to prevent the continued wrongful incarceration of an innocent man? If so, when and to whom?

2. The state has asked your firm to draft two model statutes, one defining the attorney-client privilege and the other work-product immunity. Draft such statutes.

3. Imagine a husband and wife visit your law office and ask you to draft individual wills for them containing similar provisions, essentially leaving everything to the surviving spouse. Their adult daughter has driven them to the appointment and wishes to sit in on the counseling session. What action would you take to ensure that the attorney-client privilege protects the confidentiality of their communications with you? How would you describe the scope of the attorney-client privilege to the husband and wife?

4. Research the law in your jurisdiction to determine if the common interest privilege protects the confidentiality of group member communications in both litigation and non-litigation matters (e.g., contract negotiations). What is the scope of the common interest doctrine in your jurisdiction? For example, will communications among group members at a joint strategy session without a lawyer present be privileged? Would the common interest doctrine protect a group member's communication with another group member's lawyer?

5. Research and compare a case in your jurisdiction that found material protected by ordinary work-product immunity with a case that found material protected by opinion work-product immunity.

6

Conflicts of Interest

Loyalty and the preservation of client confidences are two fundamental values of the legal profession. As noted in Chapter 3, lawyers are fiduciaries for clients, owing them duties of independent judgment, competence, undivided loyalty, and the protection of client confidences from unauthorized disclosure or misuse.

Sometimes conflicts of interest arise that impair the ability of lawyers to faithfully execute their fiduciary duties. According to §21 of the Restatement (Third) of the Law Governing Lawyers, a conflict of interest exists when there is a substantial risk that the lawyer's ability to perform her fiduciary duties is materially and adversely affected by the lawyer's own competing interests or the lawyer's duties to others. Absent a **conflict of interest waiver**, professional conduct codes and court decisions prohibit lawyers from entering into or continuing with representation that potentially involves a conflict of interest. Lawyers are subject to disqualification, fee disgorgement, professional discipline, and civil liability for failing to avoid this "conflict" prohibition.

Conflicts of interest fall into four general categories: current clients (where the lawyer's responsibilities to multiple current clients clash); former clients (where the lawyer's duties to a current client compromise the lawyer's ongoing duties to a former client); third parties (where another party's interests collide with the lawyer's duty to a current client); and the client's lawyer (where the lawyer's and the

Key Concepts

- Conflicts of interest rules promote fiduciary values
- Four conflict categories—concurrent, former, third-party, and a lawyer's personal-interest
- Concurrent conflicts—directly adverse and a significant risk of material limitation
- Waivable and nonwaivable conflicts
- "Substantial relationship" test applies to former client conflicts
- Imputing a lawyer's conflicts to other firm members
- "Personal and substantial participation" test governs government lawyer-employee conflicts
- Screening to avoid imputation
- Conflict violations—disqualification and other consequences

Client Intake: A Practical Tip

It is important for lawyers during the client intake process and thereafter to learn as much as possible about the client and the client's matter to avoid potential conflicts of interest. Lawyers should pay attention at the intake stage to any personal reactions they develop about the client that might forewarn of a potential personal or other conflict involving the client or client matter. Sometimes one's moral compass for avoiding disloyalty and conflicts of interest is a good, albeit limited, first step in assessing the ethical propriety of providing legal services.

client's interests are at odds). ABA Model Rules 1.7 through 1.12 govern these four conflict categories.

Today's marketplace for the delivery of legal services is undergoing significant change, providing a fertile landscape for conflicts of interest. The changing landscape includes the increasing consolidation of economic enterprises with their network of allied businesses and interlocking boards of directors, the globalization of legal services, and the growth of new technologies that facilitate the easy and rapid development of professional and personal relationships. These developments enhance the potential to enmesh lawyers and lawyers' clients in conflicts of interest. Given these developments and the significant costs associated with conflicts of interest for clients and lawyers, conflicts of interest promise to continue to attract substantial attention in case law and literature.

A. CURRENT-CLIENT CONFLICTS AND CLIENT WAIVERS

1. Directly Adverse and Material Limitation Conflicts

The starting block for understanding conflict analysis is Rule 1.7, *Conflicts of Interest: Current Clients.* Rule 1.7(a) establishes a base line for lawyers to assess the nature of current-client (i.e., **concurrent client**) conflicts, distinguishing "**directly adverse**" conflicts from those less obvious conflicts that involve "**a significant risk that the conflict will materially limit**" the lawyer's representation. These two conflict designations arise in both litigation and non-litigation or transactional settings.

Rule 1.7(b) provides lawyers with a roadmap for obtaining a current-client waiver of a Rule 1.7(a) conflict. Rule 1.7(b)'s waiver provision applies to both "directly adverse" conflicts and to "significant risk of . . . material limit[ation]" conflicts. Rule 1.7(b)'s waiver provision also generally applies to the other conflicts of interest situations (e.g., former client) covered in Rules 1.8 through 1.12.[1] The following four requirements are necessary to constitute a valid waiver under Rule 1.7(b).

First, the lawyer must reasonably believe at the outset of representing a client in a matter that she can independently represent the client in a competent and diligent manner. It is incumbent for lawyers to deliberate on this point. Disciplinary

---

1. Some rules impose additional requirements for a valid conflict of interest waiver beyond those outlined in Rule 1.7(b). For example, Rule 1.8(a) addresses business transactions between a client and lawyer and imposes additional waiver requirements. It requires the client's written consent to the conflict and that the consent be signed by the client after the client has been advised in writing of the desirability of having independent counsel review the client's business transaction with another lawyer.

authorities and the courts in a civil matter will review or "Monday morning quarterback" the lawyer's "reasonableness determination." They will ask whether an objectively reasonable lawyer would have concluded that she could competently and diligently represent a client given her duties to other clients. Second, the representation cannot be prohibited by law, and third, "the representation [must] not involve the assertion of a claim by one client against another client represented by the lawyer in the same litigation or proceeding before a tribunal." Rule 1.7(b)'s fourth waiver requirement, perhaps the most important, mandates that "each affected client give[] informed consent, confirmed in writing." Whether the client gave informed consent and the lawyer was reasonable at the outset in believing she could provide competent and diligent representation are fact-dependent questions that have spawned much debate and litigation.

The following excerpt from Professor W. Bradley Wendel's article, *Conflicts of Interest Under the Revised Model Rules*, discusses Rule 1.7's significance and application to current-client conflict situations. It also highlights the prominent role of informed consent in Rule 1.7(b)'s conflict-waiver process and the rule's parameters.

W. Bradley Wendel, Conflicts of Interest Under the Revised Model Rules

81 Neb. L. Rev. 1363 (2003)

[Concurrent representation conflicts, s]ometimes called "current-client" conflicts, [are] cases [that] involve a lawyer simultaneously representing two or more clients whose interests may be somehow at odds. . . . The key to the analysis here is the concept of independent professional judgment. Under agency law as well as the more specific law governing lawyers, a lawyer is required to be an effective, diligent, loyal representative of the client. The lawyer must be able to give advice about all of the client's options, without holding anything back for fear of interfering with another client's interests. When a lawyer takes on a new client, she must ask whether the duties she is assuming with respect to the new client — competence, diligence, confidentiality, loyalty, and so on — will require her to do something for the new client that will impair her ability to discharge those same duties to existing clients. The essence of a concurrent conflict of interest is therefore the inability of a lawyer to fulfill her professional obligations to one client because of the need to fulfill professional obligations to another client.

. . . A concurrent conflict of interest is defined as the representation of one client *directly adverse* to another client, or a case in which there is a significant risk that the representation of one client will be *materially limited* by the lawyer's obligations to another client. The clearest case of direct adversity is easy to imagine — one client suing another, with the lawyer representing both in the same litigation. As the comments to Rule 1.7 make clear, however, direct adversity conflicts can arise in transactional matters, as where the same lawyer represents both the buyer and seller, or in litigation where the lawyer must cross-examine one client, who appears as a witness, while representing another client at trial. Material limitation conflicts are simply those conflicts that are less severe than direct adversity conflicts, but which nevertheless interfere with the lawyer's ability to exercise independent professional judgment on behalf of all affected clients.

It is important to understand direct adversity and material limitation not as conceptually distinct, but as points along a continuum. Consider, as an example, a well known case that appears in many professional responsibility textbooks. The case involved civil rights litigation against the State of New Hampshire by two classes of plaintiffs, mentally handicapped children who lived in a state institution, and female prison inmates. Both classes were represented by the same legal aid office, but a conflict arose when the State offered to settle the prisoner litigation by constructing a better facility for the female inmates — on the grounds of the school for the handicapped kids! The court handled the conflict for the legal aid lawyers as one of material limitation, but it would not have been wrong to analyze it as a direct adversity conflict. In any event, nothing in the remainder of the analysis turns on whether the conflict is one of direct adversity or material limitation. For this reason, the Ethics 2000 revision of the *Model Rules* rewrote the current-client conflicts rule so that the question is posed as whether a concurrent conflict of interest exists; this term is further defined as either direct adversity or material limitation, and it is clear from the rule that the subsequent analysis of consentability is not affected by what kind of concurrent conflict of interest is present. . . .

The Ethics 2000 version of the *Model Rules* provides a much clearer analysis of the issue of consentability. Under Rule 1.7(b), most concurrent representation is permissible provided that each affected client gives informed consent, confirmed in writing. "Informed consent" is a term of art in the *Model Rules*, drawn from the law of medical malpractice. It means consent by the client after the lawyer has communicated adequate information about the risks of simultaneous representation and the reasonably available alternatives. This information must include "possible effects on loyalty, confidentiality and the attorney-client privilege and the advantages and risks involved." Lawyers often err by disclosing too little, perhaps trying to "finesse" the clients into consenting. In one Nebraska disciplinary proceeding, a lawyer represented a husband and wife jointly in a personal-injury action. A few months later, the wife approached the lawyer to request that he represent her in divorce proceedings. The lawyer requested that the husband (still his client in the personal-injury litigation) consent to him representing the wife in the divorce case, and had him sign a handwritten note, but did not advise the husband of the consequences of his consent. This was a serious error by the lawyer, because without full disclosure of the possible risks to the husband, his consent to the lawyer representing his wife in the divorce proceedings would be ineffective. For example, it is unlikely that the husband, an individual inexperienced in litigation, would have appreciated the potential effect on confidentiality of the multiple representation. In the course of the injury litigation, the lawyer would have access to a great deal of confidential information about the husband, some of which might be useful to the wife in the divorce. Perhaps the lawyer would have to cross-examine the husband at trial if the divorce proceedings went that far, and the lawyer would be in the position of having to attack the credibility of his own client. The husband would likely feel betrayed by this development, because he may assume that his own lawyer would never turn on him in any way. Although in sanctioning the lawyer the court focused on the sexual relationship that later developed between the wife and the lawyer, the lawyer could just as readily have been disciplined for representing the wife in the divorce case without first obtaining informed consent, after full disclosure, from the husband.

Some conflicts are not consentable, even with the most complete disclosure. The *Model Rules* list three categories of non-consentable conflicts:

1. *Representations prohibited by law*, which include cases of former government lawyers who are barred by federal or state statutes from undertaking the representation of particular clients for a given length of time, and representatives of government entities that are prohibited from consenting to conflicts of interest.
2. *Asserting a claim on behalf of one client in litigation in which the same lawyer represents the opponent*. The traditional view, still followed in many jurisdictions, is that a lawyer may never assert a claim against another current client, even if the matters are unrelated and the client is represented by other counsel in the litigation in question. An emerging trend, by contrast, is to permit a lawyer to represent a client in a lawsuit against another client, provided that the lawyer is representing the second client on an unrelated matter. The cases I am aware of that approve of a lawyer suing her own client on behalf of another client all involve large, sophisticated entity clients with diverse operations. It is almost inconceivable that a lawyer could proceed in this kind of case where the clients are individuals.
3. *Other cases in which the lawyer does not reasonably believe that she can provide competent and diligent representation to each affected client*. The key here is to focus on the lawyer's professional duties, and ask whether it is possible for the lawyer to be an effective, vigorous, loyal representative of all clients simultaneously. I sometimes refer to these cases as "zero-sum" conflicts, to capture the idea that there is no way one client can get the best possible result if their lawyer is also trying to get the best possible result for the other client. These cases can arise in business transactions, where there are risks and benefits that have to be allocated among the parties, and there is no win-win solution under which all of the parties come out ahead.

Case Preview

Cinema 5, Ltd. v. Cinerama, Inc.

In *Cinema 5*, the Second Circuit was asked to consider whether the trial judge abused his discretion in disqualifying a plaintiff's lawyer who was suing a defendant who was represented by the plaintiff-lawyer's partner in another law firm in litigation unrelated to the subject matter of the plaintiff's lawsuit. The individual plaintiff-lawyer's conflict of interest was imputed to other members of his firm (see *infra* Section D) warranting their disqualification. In reviewing *Cinema 5*, consider the impact of the decision for large law firms with satellite offices and large corporate clients. The size of these firms and their clients may increase the chance of having a request to represent a client in adverse litigation against another current client in an unrelated matter.

As you read *Cinema 5*, also consider the following questions:

1. Do you think the appellate court reached the right result? What do you think of the appellant's unsuccessful argument that the lawyer's representation of both clients should be permissible because the representation involved issues not "substantially related"?
2. Did this case involve representation that was a "directly adverse" conflict or instead pose a "significant risk of a material limitation" conflict for the firm? Does the conflict designation matter?
3. What did you think of the firm offering to drop one of the two adverse clients? Should law firms be permitted to draft around the *Cinema 5, Ltd.* prohibition by having clients agree in advance to let their lawyers sue them on unrelated matters?

Cinema 5, Ltd. v. Cinerama, Inc.

528 F.2d 1384 (2d Cir. 1976)

Attorney Manly Fleischmann is a partner in Jaeckle, Fleischmann and Mugel of Buffalo and in Webster, Sheffield, Fleischmann, Hitchcock and Brookfield of New York City. He divides his time between the two offices. Cinerama is a distributor of motion pictures and the operator of several large theater chains. In January 1972 the Jaeckle firm was retained to represent Cinerama and several other defendants in an action brought in the United States District Court for the Western District of New York. Plaintiffs in that suit are local upstate theater operators who allege anti-trust violations resulting from discriminatory and monopolistic licensing and distribution of motion pictures in the Rochester area. A similar action involving allegedly illegal distribution in the Buffalo area was commenced in March 1974, and the Jaeckle office represents the interests of Cinerama in this action also. Both suits are presently pending in the Western District.

The instant action, brought in the Southern District of New York in August 1974, alleges a conspiracy among the defendants to acquire control of plaintiff corporation through stock acquisitions, with the intention of creating a monopoly and restraining competition in New York City's first-run motion picture theater market. Judge Brieant found that there was sufficient relationship between the two law firms and the two controversies to inhibit future confidential communications between Cinerama and its attorneys and that disqualification was required to avoid even the appearance of professional impropriety. . . .

Appellant's counsel strongly dispute these findings. They say that they should not be disqualified unless the relationship between the controversies is substantial, and they contend there is nothing substantial in the relationship between an upstate New York conspiracy to deprive local theater operators of access to films and an attempted corporate take-over in New York City.

The "substantial relationship" test is indeed the one that we have customarily applied in determining whether a lawyer may accept employment against a former client. However, in this case, suit is not against a former client, but an existing one. One firm in which attorney Fleischmann is a partner is suing an actively represented client of another firm in which attorney Fleischmann is a partner. The propriety of this conduct must be measured not so much against the similarities in litigation, as against the duty of undivided loyalty which an attorney owes to each of his clients.

A lawyer's duty to his client is that of a fiduciary or trustee. Hafter v. Farkas, 498 F.2d 587, 589 (2d Cir. 1974); Wise, *Legal Ethics* 256 (2d ed.). When Cinerama retained Mr. Fleischmann as its attorney in the Western District litigation, it was entitled to feel that at least until that litigation was at an end, it had his undivided loyalty as its advocate and champion, Grievance Committee v. Rottner, 152 Conn. 59, 65, 203 A.2d 82 (1964), and could rely upon his "undivided allegiance and faithful, devoted service." Because "no man can serve two masters," Matthew 6:24; Woods v. City Nat'l Bank and Trust Co., it had the right to expect also that he would "accept no retainer to do anything that might be adverse to his client's interests." Needless to say, when Mr. Fleischmann and his New York City partners undertook to represent Cinema 5, Ltd., they owed it the same fiduciary duty of undivided loyalty and allegiance.

Ethical Considerations 5-1 and 5-14 of the American Bar Association's Code of Professional Responsibility [principles reflected today in Model Rule 1.7] provide that the professional judgment of a lawyer must be exercised solely for the benefit of his client, free of compromising influences and loyalties, and this precludes his acceptance of employment that will adversely affect his judgment or dilute his loyalty. The Code has been adopted by the New York State Bar Association, and its canons are recognized by both Federal and State Courts as appropriate guidelines for the professional conduct of New York lawyers.

Under the Code, the lawyer who would sue his own client, asserting in justification the lack of "substantial relationship" between the litigation and the work he has undertaken to perform for that client, is leaning on a slender reed indeed. Putting it as mildly as we can, we think it would be questionable conduct for an attorney to participate in any lawsuit against his own client without the knowledge and consent of all concerned. This appears to be the opinion of the foremost writers in the field, *see* Wise, *supra*, at 272; Drinker, *Legal Ethics* 112, 116, and it is the holding of the New York courts. In Matter of Kelly, 23 N.Y.2d 368, 376, 296 N.Y.S.2d 937 (1968), New York's highest court said that "with rare and conditional exceptions, the lawyer may not place himself in a position where a conflicting interest may, even inadvertently, affect, or give the appearance of affecting, the obligations of the professional relationship." Nor is New York alone in this view. In Grievance Committee v. Rottner, *supra,* 152 Conn. at 65, Connecticut's highest court held that the maintenance of public confidence in the bar requires an attorney to decline employment adverse to his client, even though the nature of such employment is wholly unrelated to that of his existing representation.

Whether such adverse representation, without more, requires disqualification in every case, is a matter we need not now decide. We do hold, however, that the "substantial relationship" test does not set a sufficiently high standard by which the necessity for disqualification should be determined. That test may properly be applied only where the representation of a former client has been terminated and the parameters of such relationship have been fixed. Where the relationship is a continuing one, adverse representation is prima facie improper, Matter of Kelly, *supra,* 23 N.Y.2d at 376, and the attorney must be prepared to show, at the very least, that there will be no actual or *apparent* conflict in loyalties or diminution in the vigor of his representation. We think that appellants have failed to meet this heavy burden and that, so long as Mr. Fleischmann and his Buffalo partners continue to represent Cinerama, he and his New York City partners should not represent Cinema 5, Ltd. in this litigation.

Because he is a partner in the Jaeckle firm, Mr. Fleischmann owes the duty of undivided loyalty to that firm's client, Cinerama. Because he is a partner in the Webster firm, he owes the same duty to Cinema 5, Ltd. It can hardly be disputed that there is at least the appearance of impropriety where half his time is spent with partners who are defending Cinerama in multi-million dollar litigation, while the other half is spent with partners who are suing Cinerama in a lawsuit of equal substance.

Because "an attorney must avoid not only the fact, but even the appearance, of representing conflicting interests," Edelman v. Levy, 42 App. Div. 2d 758, 346 N.Y.S.2d 347 (2d Dept. 1973) (mem.), this requires his disqualification. Moreover, because of the peculiarly close relationship existing among legal partners, if Mr. Fleischmann is disqualified, his partners at the Webster firm are disqualified as well. Laskey Bros., Inc. v. Warner Bros. Pictures, Inc., 224 F.2d 824, 826 (2d Cir. 1955) cert. denied, 350 U.S. 932 (1956).

Nothing that we have heretofore said is intended as criticism of the character and professional integrity of Mr. Fleischmann and his partners. We are convinced that the dual representation came about inadvertently and unknowingly, and we are in complete accord with Judge Brieant's finding that there has been no actual wrongdoing. Furthermore, the record shows that after learning of the conflict which had developed, the Jaeckle firm, through Mr. Fleischmann, offered to withdraw its representation of Cinerama in the Western District actions. However, that offer was not accepted, and Mr. Fleischmann continued, albeit reluctantly, to have one foot in each camp.

Under the circumstances, Judge Brieant's order of disqualification cannot be construed as an abuse of his discretion. We therefore affirm.

Post-Case Follow-Up

The *Cinema 5* decision and its prohibition against a lawyer simultaneously representing current clients who are adverse parties in the same or unrelated litigation is widely cited and followed in federal and state courts. The lawyer's loyalty to a client is necessarily called into question when the lawyer simultaneously represents one client suing another current client, or as the court aptly stated: "'No man can serve two masters.' Where the relationship is a continuing one, adverse representation is prima facie improper, and the attorney must be prepared to show, at the very least, that there will be no actual or *apparent* conflict in loyalties or diminution in the vigor of his representation."

Professor Wendel noted in his article earlier in this chapter "an emerging trend" where some courts permit a lawyer on behalf of a current client to sue another current client on an unrelated matter. Thus, a lawyer on behalf of current client #1 could sue current client #2 provided the lawyer's representation of client #2 involves a matter unrelated to client #1's lawsuit. Given the lawyer's division of loyalty in such a scenario, one or both of the clients may question whether the lawyer is pulling punches in favor of the other client. Not surprisingly, the Restatement §128 cmt. c requires the lawyer to obtain the informed consent of both client #1 and client #2 to file the lawsuit.[2] When a lawyer is in doubt about the existence of a potential conflict of interest involving current clients or any other situation, a prudent lawyer should seek the informed consent from each affected client. Of course, as Wendel emphasized, some conflicts are not consentable; thus following Rule 1.7(b)'s waiver roadmap is not a guarantee that a firm will not be subject to a successful disqualification motion or a related malpractice or discipline action.

Cinema 5, Ltd. v. Cinerama, Inc.: Real Life Applications

1. The Tarton Company is a wholly owned subsidiary of CLI. Tarton and CLI share a unity of personnel and are located in the same building in Cleveland, Ohio. Both companies share the same legal department and George Hawk acts as general counsel and statutory agent for both companies. Mr. Hawk currently supervises Tarton's antitrust defense in *Amway v. Tarton* in federal district court.

   Mr. Hawk also supervised Gomez & Baker LLP in its defense of CLI in an antitrust matter in *Moore v. CLI*, in the Sixth Circuit Court of Appeals. The Sixth Circuit case was still pending when Gomez & Baker entered an appearance for Amway. The two cases overlapped for two months. Gomez & Baker's conflicts check revealed that the firm had never represented Tarton, although it had represented Tarton's parent, CLI, in the antitrust case of *Moore v. CLI*. Gomez & Baker never divulged the potential conflict to either party in *Amway v. Tarton*, or to CLI. Hawk consults you about seeking the disqualification of Gomez & Baker in *Amway*. Advise Hawk.

2. Arthur Goldberg meets Stefanie Stark in 2014. They become romantically involved and at Goldberg's request, she gives up her businesses and moves to New Jersey to care for him. Goldberg is a wealthy, longtime client of the Jaffe & Asher (J & A) law firm. At his request, the firm continually represented Stark on a variety of matters. Goldberg died on October 1, 2016 and his will did not leave anything to Stark. The estate's directors retained J & A that same day to deal with any forthcoming litigation.

   Stark retained attorney Rosen on December 1, 2016 to file a palimony suit. On December 2, Rosen provided a draft of the complaint to the estate's directors and agreed not to file it while settlement negotiations were pending. The

2. Restatement (Third) of the Law Governing Lawyers §128 cmt. c(ii) [hereinafter Restatement].

directors shared Rosen's letter with J & A. On December 22, 2016, the firm sent Stark a letter stating, in part:

> [S]ince you have commenced an action against the Goldberg estate, a conflict of interest has arisen in our representation of you and we must withdraw immediately as your lawyers. We ask that you pay in full your current outstanding legal bills in arrears, including for the last two service dates of December 17 and 20, 2016.

Stark consults you, exclaiming: "I've never consented to being dropped like a 'hot potato.' They say 'too bad, you're now a former client.'" Stark plans to file her palimony complaint and wants you to move to disqualify J & A from the representing the estate based on Rule 1.7(a). Discuss with Stark what the chances are for winning the disqualification motion.

Joint Clients and the Attorney-Client Privilege: A Practical Tip

When representing joint clients it is important to remind them that what each client communicates to her lawyer is protected by the attorney-client privilege. However, the privilege will not prevent a joint client from revealing an otherwise privileged communication; a joint client is free to disclose her communication or her fellow joint clients' communications to their lawyer. Also, lawyers for joint clients will want to inform them that the lawyer will not keep one joint client's communication secret from another joint client.

Lawyers sometimes represent multiple clients in a matter. This is called multiple, dual, or joint representation. *Shutterstock.com*

Multiple/Joint Representation Conflicts

Lawyers occasionally represent multiple clients in a matter; this is sometimes called multiple, dual, or **joint representation**. These terms all mean that the lawyer is simultaneously representing more than one client on the same matter. When lawyers undertake joint or multiple representation in civil and criminal matters there is often a risk for a potential conflict of interest. Client matters in all kinds of settings, whether a litigation or a transactional setting, have a life of their own. Even when multiple clients' interests appear aligned at the outset of representation, client needs and other developments may change and affect their objectives. For example, clients may revise settlement claims or liabilities, and there is always the prospect that the discovery of new evidence may create differing interests among multiple or joint clients. Also, it is important to note that when multiple representation fails, the lawyer ordinarily must withdraw from representing all of the multiple clients.[3]

3. Restatement §121 cmt. e(i); Model Rule 1.7 cmt. 29.

EXHIBIT 6.1 Joint Representation Checklist

1. Identify with precision your clients and the matter in which you will be representing them.
2. Identify anyone in the vicinity who is not a client (but who might somehow think they are), and tell them you are not their lawyer, preferably in writing.
3. Evaluate whether any conflict of interest exists in jointly representing these clients in this matter.
4. If there is a conflict, evaluate whether the clients may ethically waive it, watching out for any prohibited joint representations.
   a. If the conflict is one that may be waived, consider whether, under all the circumstances, a waiver is prudent, both for you as the lawyer and for the clients.
   b. If so, work through the consent process to obtain a waiver from the clients.
   c. Memorialize the waiver in writing.
5. Even if there is no conflict of interest, seriously consider discussing with the clients the possibility that a conflict may arise down the road.
6. Regardless of whether there is a conflict of interest, consider whether, under all the circumstances, joint representation is prudent, both for you as the lawyer and for the clients.
7. Discuss with the clients how confidentiality works in a joint representation; obtain their agreement to your sharing confidential and privileged information between or among them; and consider memorializing the agreement in writing.
8. Establish clearly with all clients who is obligated to pay your fees and expenses, including the specifics of any shared obligation, and seriously consider putting [that] in writing.
9. If someone other than the clients is obligated to pay your fees and expenses, confirm with all the clients and this third person that this third person is not your client; that this third person cannot direct or control your work, unless the clients agree; and that you cannot share information about the matter with this third person, unless the clients consent. Consider putting all this in writing.
10. If the ethics rules require that the fee agreement be in writing, put it in a form that complies with the rules.
11. Consider whether you should discuss and reach agreement with the clients on a plan for your continued representation of fewer than all the clients if a conflict of interest does arise later. If this is a good idea under the circumstances, discuss and memorialize the discussion and agreement.
12. Before, during, and after the representation, treat all of the clients equally in all respects, including loyalty, confidentiality, communication, and decision making. . . .
13. Throughout the joint representation, be aware of the possibility of conflicts of interest arising, and carefully monitor developments that may lead to conflicts, including changes in the facts and procedural posture of the matter, the positions of the clients concerning the matter, and relationships among the clients.
14. If a conflict of interest arises in the midst of the representation, evaluate and address it promptly before continuing in the representation.

Reprinted with permission from Lucian T. Pera. Lucian T. Pera, *The Ethics of Joint Representation,* 40 Litig. 1 (2013).

Criminal Cases

Lawyers undertaking joint representation in criminal cases need to be familiar with Rule 44 of the Federal Rules of Criminal Procedure. It recognizes that a defendant who is unable to obtain counsel is entitled to have one appointed at every stage of the proceeding unless the defendant waives the right. The rule is designed to protect defendants from unknowingly waiving their right to separate representation. Rule 44(c) directs the courts to inquire about the propriety of joint representation to safeguard the defendant's constitutional right to effective representation.

> **(c) Inquiry Into Joint Representation.**
>
> **(1) Joint Representation.** Joint representation occurs when:
>
> **(A)** two or more defendants have been charged jointly under Rule 8(b) or have been joined for trial under Rule 13; and
>
> **(B)** the defendants are represented by the same counsel, or counsel who are associated in law practice.
>
> **(2) Court's Responsibilities in Cases of Joint Representation.** The court must promptly inquire about the propriety of joint representation and must personally advise each defendant of the right to the effective assistance of counsel, including separate representation. Unless there is good cause to believe that no conflict of interest is likely to arise, the court must take appropriate measures to protect each defendant's right to counsel.

The Supreme Court addressed joint representation in criminal cases in the prominent case of Holloway v. Arkansas, 435 U.S. 475 (1978). There, the Court reversed a conviction in which a trial judge ignored a defendant's objections to the judge's order of joint representation. The Court stated that a lawyer should "ordinarily decline" multiple representation of clients in a criminal matter given the potential for conflicts of interest and the important interests at stake for defendants. The Court specifically noted that the conflict in *Holloway* may have precluded counsel from pursuing plea negotiations and perhaps having the client testify for the government in return for a lesser sentence. Depending on the criminal matter, other potential conflicts of interest involved in joint representation may include each co-defendant having different levels of criminal responsibility, criminal and family history records, financial support obligations to family and others, and financial ability to pay for representation and damages. In addition, differing interests may arise when one co-defendant asserts the Fifth Amendment and refuses to testify or alternatively when one co-defendant insists on testifying. All of these factors pose a potential conflict of interest. Quoting the ABA, the *Holloway* Court noted that multiple representation should occur only in "unusual situations when, after careful investigation, it is clear no conflict is likely to develop and when the co-defendants give informed consent to the multiple representation." The concerns expressed in *Holloway* about joint representation in criminal litigation represent the prevailing view.[4]

---

4. Similarly, Rule 1.7's comment 23 provides: "The potential for conflict of interest in representing multiple defendants in a criminal case is so grave that ordinarily a lawyer should decline to represent more than one codefendant."

In Cuyler v. Sullivan, 446 U.S. 335 (1980), the Court examined an issue left unresolved in *Holloway* about whether the mere *possibility* of a conflict of interest is enough to conclude that the defendant was deprived of his Sixth Amendment right to effective assistance of counsel and thus calling into question the defendant's conviction. The Court found that it is not; the defendant must establish the existence of an *actual* conflict of interest that had an adverse effect on his lawyer's representation. However, the Court added that once it is established that an actual conflict affected the adequacy of representation, the defendant does not have to show prejudice in order to obtain relief. On this basis, the Court vacated the decision of the court of appeals and remanded the case to afford Sullivan an opportunity to demonstrate that an actual conflict of interest existed.

Although one should approach joint representation in a criminal case as if handling a porcupine, the Supreme Court has recognized the important right of criminal defendants to choose their counsel, and thus trial courts must carefully review motions to disqualify a defendant's choice of joint counsel.[5] For example, in United States v. Turner, 594 F.3d 946 (7th Cir. 2010), the district court disqualified Roosevelt Turner's counsel from representing him in a cocaine-conspiracy case because the attorney was also representing an alleged co-conspirator in sentencing proceedings. Though both defendants waived any conflict of interest, the district court judge found that because the defendants may turn on each other, the conflicts were "absolute," "specific," and that "[t]here's no way that any waiver can overcome these conflicts." The appellate court disagreed, finding the district court's decision to disqualify the attorney was based on the mere possibility that either defendant may turn on the other. Citing Rule 1.7 comment 8, the appellate court considered "the likelihood that a difference in interests will eventuate and, if it does, whether it will materially interfere with the lawyer's independent professional judgment in considering alternatives or foreclose courses of action that reasonably should be pursued on behalf of the client." The court found nothing in the record to suggest that the potential conflict of interest identified by the district court had a serious likelihood of maturing into an actual conflict. Nor was there anything to support a conclusion that the conflict was sufficiently severe to jeopardize Turner's right to effective counsel. The court held that as a general matter, an attorney may represent multiple clients notwithstanding a conflict of interest, if the client gives informed consent.

Civil Cases

Lawyers generally have more leeway to represent persons having similar interests in civil litigation than in criminal cases. Simultaneous representation of parties in civil litigation whose interests may differ is generally permissible if the lawyer

---

5. *See* Richard E. Flamm, Conflicts of Interest in the Practice of Law 689-90 (noting that "'an element of [the Sixth Amendment guarantee is that the defendant has a right] to choose who will defend him,'" and adding this is especially true when the client is paying for counsel (citing United States v. Gonzalez-Lopez, 548 U.S. 140, 144 (2006))). *See also* Wheat v. United States, 486 U.S. 153, 159 (1988) ("the right to select and be represented by one's preferred attorney is comprehended by the Sixth Amendment . . . ," although the case goes on to discuss the limitations of this right).

complies with the waiver provisions in Rule 1.7(b)(1)-(4), in particular, obtaining the informed consent of each party involved in the common representation.[6] "The mere possibility of subsequent harm does not itself require disclosure and consent"; the critical question is what is the likelihood a conflict will eventuate and will it materially interfere with the lawyer's ability to provide independent advice or "foreclose courses of action that reasonably should be" undertaken for the client.[7] The effectiveness of any waiver depends on the client's ability to understand the material risks involved in proceeding with the conflicted representation. The more sophisticated the client the greater the likelihood that the waiver will be upheld, and the waiver is presumptively valid if the client consults independent counsel about the waiver. However, lawyers need to remember that clients can revoke consent at any time. Waivers may need to be updated to reflect new developments in cases or matters that might render the earlier waiver invalid. In general, advance waivers of conflicts of interest are more likely to be upheld when they are more comprehensive in explaining the conflict risks and are more recent in time.

In the non-litigation or transactional setting, a lawyer may also ordinarily represent multiple clients provided their interests are generally aligned or only marginally different. A lawyer may not engage in common or joint representation if the clients' interests are fundamentally antagonistic to each other.[8]

For example, assume four neighbors jointly hired a lawyer to help them limit the size of a home being remodeled on a parcel of land adjacent to each landowner's property. All four joint clients want the size of the remodeled house to be as small as possible, ideally not over 2,500 square feet in living area nor over 35 feet high. They informed the lawyer at a group meeting that limiting the house size is their primary goal. They noted several zoning regulations that permit them to object to the proposed remodeling but are willing to let the project proceed if the new owner limits the house size. One neighbor-client also informed the lawyer that he prefers the remodeled garage to be limited to two bays and three of the four clients prefer the new home to retain its unpaved driveway to fit in with the neighborhood's ambience. The lawyer's joint representation here is permissible because the four clients' interests align on the central purpose for the representation, limiting the house size. The other client preferences about the number of garage bays and an unpaved driveway represent marginal differences of preference. These preferences are not fundamentally antagonistic to the position of another client; for example, no client is saying that another key purpose for retaining the lawyer is to have the driveway paved, while another fundamentally disagrees and insists that it remain unpaved. If the positions are generally aligned and only marginally inconsistent as in this example, then the lawyer may assert the inconsistent marginal positions along with his primary position of limiting the house size, although it may be wise to acknowledge the inconsistent positions in the engagement letter and obtain the four clients' informed consent to the representation.

---

6. Model Rule 1.7 cmt. 23.
7. Model Rule 1.7 cmt. 8.
8. Model Rule 1.7 cmt. 28.

The case of Van Kirk v. Miller, 869 N.E.2d 534 (Ind. Ct. App. 2007), applied the "general alignment of interests" doctrine to the sale of a business. Although some states, like New Jersey, bar lawyers from representing both the buyer and seller in some real estate closings, Indiana took a different approach at least where the parties negotiated the terms of the sale.[9] In *Van Kirk*, Attorney Miller represented Summers who gave Miller permission to contact potential buyers for his B&T Sports Bar. Miller contacted Van Kirk, his client in unrelated matters, and gave Van Kirk Summers's contact information after Van Kirk expressed an interest in the B&T sale. After independently negotiating with Summers and deciding to purchase B&T, Van Kirk decided Miller should represent both him and Summers in the transaction because it would "save money." As Van Kirk admitted in his deposition, he knew that after negotiating with Summers "there would have to be a closing and Mr. Miller . . . [would] handle the written agreements and whatever legal documents needed to be done." Since Miller would be representing both parties, he prepared a conflict of interest waiver that both parties signed.

When Summers called off the closing and sold B&T to someone else, Van Kirk sued Miller for malpractice. Van Kirk also claimed the conflict waiver was invalid because Miller's joint representation of both the seller and buyer constituted a nonconsentable conflict of interests. The appellate court disagreed and ruled the waiver valid. It found the parties' interests were generally aligned; they had a common goal — the finalization of the B&T transaction. Comment 28 to Rule 1.7 provides that dual representation is permissible where the clients' interests are "generally aligned . . . even though there [are] some difference[s]." Further, Summers and Van Kirk independently negotiated the terms of the transaction and contacted Miller to draft an agreement that would finalize the deal. Miller did not sit on both sides of the table during the negotiations. Instead, Miller was simply employed to draft the agreement memorializing the terms that Summers and Van Kirk had independently negotiated.

Sometimes a lawyer may take a position on behalf of one client that is adverse to another client in unrelated matters. This is commonly referred to as a "positional" or an "issue" conflict, which may occur in litigation, transactional, and rulemaking settings. In the litigation context, taking inconsistent positions on issues for different clients may or may not constitute a conflict of interest under Rule 1.7. Comment 24 to Rule 1.7 provides that the "mere fact that advocating a legal

9. The New Jersey Supreme Court has issued a "bright-line rule" prohibiting dual representation of the buyer and seller "in commercial real estate transactions where large sums of money are at stake, where contracts contain complex contingencies, or where options are numerous." Boswell v. Price Meese Shulman & D'Arminio, P.C., No. A-4531-13T2, 2016 N.J. Super. Unpub. LEXIS 1924, at *29 (Super. Ct. App. Div. Aug. 18, 2016). The New Jersey Supreme Court has not issued a blanket prohibition against dual representation of a buyer and seller outside of complex commercial real estate transactions, but its Advisory Committee on numerous occasions has condemned the practice. 13A N.J. Prac., Real Estate Law and Practice §26:9 Conflicts of interest (3d ed. 2013 & Supp. 2016). Some case law deems it inherently improper for a lawyer to represent both buyer and seller. *E.g.*, Iowa Supreme Court Attorney Disciplinary Bd. v. Qualley, 2013 BL 34482, 828 N.W.2d 282 (Iowa 2013). Ethics committees do not agree, however, as to whether a lawyer may represent both a buyer and seller in a real estate transaction. *Compare* North Carolina Ethics Op. 99-8 (1999) (approving dual representation), *with* Florida Ethics Op. 97-2 (1997) (advising against dual representation). According to Restatement §122, cmt. g(iv), a lawyer may not represent both a buyer and seller in negotiating and documenting a complex real estate transaction, where the parties are in sharp disagreement on several key issues or where the parties should receive extensive counseling concerning their rights and possible alternative arrangements.

position on a legal matter [for one client] might create precedent adverse to the interests of a client represented by the lawyer in an unrelated matter does not create a conflict of interest." However, a conflict does exist if advocating for one client's interests presents a significant risk of materially limiting the lawyer's effectiveness in advocating another client's interests in a different matter. Comment 24 identifies factors for deciding whether a significant risk of a material limitation exists, including "where the cases are pending, whether the issue is substantive or procedural, the temporal relationship between the matters, the significance of the issue to the immediate and long-term interests of the clients involved and the clients' reasonable expectation in retaining the lawyer." If these or other factors show a significant risk of a material limitation on the lawyer's effectiveness, then absent informed consent from all of the affected parties, the lawyer needs to refuse one of the representations or withdraw from one or both representations.

Courts have a heightened concern about positional conflicts in criminal litigation given what is at stake: the possible deprivation of life, liberty, and property. In this situation, a conflict of interest exists if the lawyer takes a position for client A that creates precedent that seriously undermines the lawyer's different position for client B. *See* Model Rule 1.7 cmt. 24.

Williams v. State, 805 A.2d 880 (Del. 2002), provides a striking example in a criminal case of the danger of creating adverse precedent. There, the defense lawyer appealed Williams's capital murder case to the Delaware Supreme Court. The lawyer contended on appeal that Williams could argue that the trial court erred in concluding it *had to give great weight* to the jury's 10-2 vote in favor of imposing the death penalty. The lawyer also believed, however, that he may have a conflict in raising this argument for Williams because of another capital murder case that he argued and was still pending on appeal before the Delaware Supreme Court. In the pending case, the lawyer took the exact opposite position and argued that the trial court erred when it *failed to give great weight* to the jury's 2-10 vote rejecting the death penalty.

The lawyer filed a motion to withdraw as counsel for Williams due to a conflict of interest. The Delaware Supreme Court granted the motion to withdraw, finding that the lawyer identified a disqualifying positional conflict of interest. The state supreme court further held that the lawyer could not "effectively argue both sides of the same legal question without compromising the interests of one client or the other."

B. LAWYER PERSONAL-INTEREST CONFLICTS WITH CLIENTS

At the beginning of this chapter we noted four general categories of conflicts of interests. Section A addressed concurrent client conflicts. Section B examines another category of conflicts where the lawyer's personal interests interfere with the lawyer's fiduciary duties to be loyal and competent, and to preserve client confidences. In general, the lawyer's superior training and experience places the lawyer in a unique position to take advantage of the client for the lawyer's own personal interest or aggrandizement. The profession has developed specific rules for certain recurring personal-interest conflict situations. Although not an exclusive list, Rule 1.8(a)-(i) governs lawyer conduct in some very common **personal-interest conflict** situations.

1. Business Transactions and Using Client Information

When a lawyer becomes involved in a business transaction with a client or acquires a pecuniary interest potentially adverse to the client while serving as the client's counsel, there is a risk that the lawyer's self-interest will undermine his duty of loyalty to the client. There are a myriad of circumstances that might violate this rule. Examples of such business transactions include the lawyer who while representing the client on a related matter also sells the client title insurance or financial services, provides a loan to the client, or purchases assets of a client's estate.[10] When the lawyer provides legal services as part of her contribution to a business venture, there is a heightened concern about the client's vulnerability to lawyer overreaching and a potential personal-interest conflict.[11] For example, assume a lawyer's longstanding client wishes to develop her farmland and she has already retained an engineer to help with the project. They both seek the lawyer's help because they lack the money to develop the land and to pay for legal services. The lawyer incorporates the proposed business and convinces the client to convey her land to the corporation. In return for his present and future legal services, the lawyer receives a 20 percent ownership share in the development company with the others each getting 40 percent.[12] Rule 1.8(a) governs the lawyer's conduct in this example and in any other situation where the lawyer "knowing[ly] acquire[s] an ownership, possessory, security or other pecuniary interest adverse to a client." Ultimately, the ethical propriety of the lawyer's conduct here requires his full compliance with all of Rule 1.8(a)'s provisions.

Rule 1.8(a)(1)-(3) provides an important prophylactic process for protecting the client from any overreaching while allowing the lawyer and client to enter into a business transaction. First, the lawyer shall explain the transaction in an understandable manner in writing for the client and the terms must be "fair and reasonable to the client." Second, the lawyer shall advise the client to have independent counsel review the terms of the transaction and give the client an opportunity to obtain such review. Finally, the lawyer shall obtain the informed consent of the client in a writing signed by the client. The lawyer's compliance with these three steps does not guarantee court approval of the lawyer's involvement with a client

10. Model Rule 1.8(a) cmt. 1.
11. *See* Model Rule 1.8(a) cmt. 2 (warning that risk of harm to the client is greatest where the lawyer is expected to represent the client in the transaction or "when the lawyer's financial interest . . . poses a significant risk that the lawyer's representation will be materially limited by the lawyer's financial interest in the transaction").
12. For a case involving somewhat similar facts, see Committee on Professional Ethics v. Mershon, 316 N.W.2d 895 (Iowa 1982) (although the court found that the lawyer had been "forthright and honest" it nevertheless reprimanded the lawyer for violating professional conduct standards that today are in Rule 1.8(a); holding that as a fiduciary the lawyer must ensure that the "client either has independent advice in the matter" or the equivalent from the lawyer, which means more than simply making the client "fully aware of the nature and terms of the transaction").

in a business transaction if the client subsequently challenges the propriety of the business transaction. However, the failure to strictly follow the Rule 1.8(a)(1)-(3) provisions almost certainly guarantees judicial disapproval of the transaction, even if the terms are fair and reasonable. The court may invalidate the transaction and order the lawyer to disgorge any proceeds.

Rule 1.8(a) does not apply to standard commercial business transactions between the lawyer and client. In those transactions, there is less concern for potential overreaching by the lawyer. The lawyer is not providing legal services and is less likely to exploit her fiduciary role as the client's advisor to benefit the lawyer's self-interest. Thus, the lawyer's purchase of a car from the client's auto dealership would not trigger the application of Rule 1.8(a), nor would the creation of a cleaning company by the lawyer and client where each contributes $10,000 startup capital and the lawyer is not providing legal services.

Another potential personal-interest conflict involves lawyers having the opportunity to use client confidential information for the lawyer's own benefit. Consistent with the lawyer's fiduciary duties and absent client consent, Rule 1.8(b) bars lawyers from using confidential information to the client's disadvantage.

Rule 1.8(b) does not prohibit the lawyer from using client confidential information for the lawyer's own personal benefit. But one should check the applicable jurisdiction's agency law to ensure that such use of client information is permitted. Traditional agency principles proscribe agents, in this case lawyers, from personally benefitting from the use of the principal's, here the client's, confidential information, at least without the principal's permission.[13] The lawyer may have to disgorge any personal benefit gained from the use of the client's information under traditional agency law. Thus, if a lawyer obtains confidential information that his client is developing a mall on Whiteacre and the value of the adjacent parcel, Blackacre, is likely to increase, the lawyer may purchase it under professional conduct rules if it will not disadvantage the client. Of course, the lawyer is well advised to ask the client if he has any objections to the lawyer purchasing the adjacent Blackacre, and, although not required, memorializing the client's approval in a follow-up communication. For example, the lawyer may send an email stating: "Thanks for meeting with me today to get your thoughts on the proposed mall development and your approval for my purchase of Blackacre. . . ."

Case Preview

In re Disciplinary Proceedings Against Creedy

In re Disciplinary Proceedings Against Creedy illustrates the ease with which lawyers may find themselves involved in a business transaction with clients. The informality surrounding Creedy's business arrangement with his client is striking—there was no written agreement.

13. RESTATEMENT (THIRD) OF AGENCY §8.05 *Use of Principal's Property; Use of Confidential Information* (2006). "An agent has a duty . . . (2) not to use or communicate confidential information of the principal for the agent's own purposes or those of a third party."

As you review *Creedy*, ask yourself:

1. Would more formality have helped Creedy to appreciate that the business venture with his client was the type of matter covered by Rule 1.8(a)?
2. Would an absolute bar to all lawyer-client business transactions be a better approach for protecting clients from possible lawyer overreaching than Rule 1.8(a)'s current approach?
3. Do you think Creedy's conduct warranted more than a public reprimand? Remember the bar had asked for a four-month suspension.
4. Also, is it fair to punish Creedy for violating Rule 1.8(b)'s ban on using client confidential information when he assisted the government in prosecuting Murphy?
5. Should the lawyer's purpose for violating Rule 1.8(b) matter? Should Creedy's purpose be a mitigating factor concerning possible discipline?

In re Disciplinary Proceedings Against Creedy

854 N.W.2d 676 (Wis. 2014)

Attorney Creedy was admitted to the practice of law in Wisconsin in 1980. . . . He has no previous disciplinary history.

Most of the allegations in the OLR's [Office of Lawyer Regulation's] complaint involve Attorney Creedy's business relationship with a client named Joseph Murphy. Murphy, who is not an attorney, created a company called American Disability Entitlements LLC, intended to represent claimants in Social Security disability matters. Social Security laws and procedures permit nonlawyers to represent such claimants. Murphy learned that if an attorney provides similar services, the attorney can have fees paid directly to the attorney by the Social Security Administration out of any award. Murphy approached Attorney Creedy to see if they could work together representing disability claimants in order to ensure receipt of any fees.

Murphy and Attorney Creedy both represented claimants before the Social Security Administration. They would discuss and mutually agree upon a fair division of fees. They did not have a written agreement.

Murphy was routinely accepting unlawful fee advances, a practice prohibited by applicable Social Security rules and procedures. The parties disputed whether Attorney Creedy knew that Murphy was routinely accepting unlawful fee advances.

Attorney Creedy maintained that he first learned this was occurring in March of 2010, when an attorney representing a claimant advised Attorney Creedy that the claimant had been improperly assessed two fees: one paid by the claimant directly to Murphy, and another later paid to Attorney Creedy by the Social Security Administration. Upon receiving and confirming this information, Attorney Creedy promptly refunded one set of fees to the claimant. He then began dissolving the business arrangement with Murphy.

Meanwhile, law enforcement was investigating Murphy in connection with a variety of matters. Attorney Creedy voluntarily met and provided law enforcement with some information about Murphy.

On June 27, 2013, the OLR filed an eight-count complaint against Attorney Creedy seeking a four-month suspension of his license to practice law. Attorney Creedy filed an answer and the court appointed the referee, who conducted an evidentiary hearing in February 2014.

After the hearing, the parties executed a stipulation whereby the OLR voluntarily dismissed [several] Counts . . . . Attorney Creedy withdrew his answer and pled no contest to the remaining allegations of misconduct . . . .

As relevant to this matter, the referee explicitly stated that he found Attorney Creedy to be both credible and professional. He believed that Attorney Creedy was unaware that Murphy was improperly accepting advance fees until confronted by a claimant's lawyer in March 2010. He deemed Murphy to be a less than credible witness, noting that Murphy is currently serving time for felony convictions related to a variety of fraud-related transactions. Moreover, the referee observed that "it was clear that [Murphy] had personal animosity toward [Attorney] Creedy and went out of his way to express that animosity."

. . .

Count Two of the complaint relates to Attorney Creedy's failure to comply with supreme court rules, specifically in violation of SCR 20:1.8(a), in the manner in which he entered the business arrangement with Murphy to represent Social Security claimants. It is undisputed that Attorney Creedy never disclosed, in writing, the terms upon which the business relationship was based, never advised Murphy in writing of the desirability of seeking the advice of independent legal counsel on the transaction, and never obtained written, informed consent from Murphy to the essential terms of the transaction and to Attorney Creedy's role in the transaction.

The referee noted that it was apparent that Murphy was a sophisticated business person, but this does not excuse failure to comport with the requirements of the rule. Accordingly, the OLR alleged, Attorney Creedy stipulated, and the referee agreed that the record evidence supported a conclusion that Attorney Creedy violated SCR 20:1.8(a).

. . .

In Count Eight, the OLR alleged that Attorney Creedy violated SCR 20:1.8(b) by providing information obtained in the course of his representation of Murphy to the disadvantage of Murphy, without Murphy's consent. It is undisputed that the Green County District Attorney's Office and the Monroe Police Department investigated Murphy. Attorney Creedy met with these entities and provided certain information that was adverse to Murphy, without obtaining Murphy's informed consent. The investigation into Murphy's conduct ultimately led to felony charges and convictions of Murphy. Accordingly, the OLR alleged, Attorney Creedy stipulated, and the referee concluded that by providing information obtained in the course of his representation of Murphy to the Green County District Attorney's Office and the Monroe Police Department to the disadvantage of Murphy, without obtaining Murphy's informed consent, Attorney Creedy violated SCR 20:1.8(b).

Initially the OLR sought a four-month suspension but, following the evidentiary hearing, the parties submitted a joint stipulation agreeing that a public reprimand was sufficient. The referee observed that there was no evidence that any member of the public, other than perhaps Murphy, was harmed by Attorney Creedy's conduct, and characterized any harm to Murphy as de minimus and the proven ethical violations as technical. Indeed, the referee commented that a private reprimand might have been a sufficient sanction. However, he accepted the parties' stipulation and recommends that this court impose a public reprimand.

The only remaining dispute involves whether the court should impose the full costs of this proceeding on Attorney Creedy. The OLR seeks imposition of all costs, which total $17,801.64 as of May 21, 2014. Attorney Creedy filed a timely objection, arguing that no costs should be imposed.

The court's general policy is that upon a finding of misconduct it is appropriate to impose all costs, including the expenses of counsel for the office of lawyer regulation, upon the respondent. In some cases the court may, in the exercise of its discretion, reduce the amount of costs imposed upon a respondent. . . .

The referee carefully considered each of these criteria and recommended, both before and after the filing of Attorney Creedy's objection, that Attorney Creedy should pay one-half of the costs of the proceedings. . . . His statements regarding imposition of costs are telling:

> . . . I have to confess that I find the requested imposition of almost $18,000 in costs to be extraordinarily large. As I wrote in my original Decision, I felt Respondent was "both professional and credible" in his appearance and testimony before me. I thought he acted properly in promptly returning one set of fees to a client as soon as he learned of it and verified it (*Ibid.*, p. 9, 10). I found no evidence that his other two violations harmed either a client or the public.

The referee reminds the court ". . . [t]he violations of the Supreme Court Rules were by no means flagrant." He notes further that Attorney Creedy cooperated fully with the disciplinary process. We agree with the referee's assessment. . . .

IT IS ORDERED that Attorney Carl H. Creedy is publicly reprimanded for professional misconduct [and that he] . . . pay to the Office of Lawyer Regulation one-half the costs of this proceeding.

Post-Case Follow-Up

Creedy underscores the importance of respondent-lawyers having credibility during the disciplinary process. The referee found that Creedy was " 'both professional and credible' in his appearance and testimony. . . ." The court also valued Creedy's quick repayment of the fee owed to a client-claimant who was improperly assessed two fees and Creedy's quick dissolution of his business with his client, Murphy. One important take-away from *Creedy* is that when a lawyer has any question about whether he is involved in a business transaction with a client, the lawyer should follow the guidelines of Rule 1.8(a)(1)-(3). Some law firms require a lawyer who is becoming involved in a business transaction with a client to have the arrangement approved by other members in the law firm and to have another firm lawyer draft any agreements or other documents related to the lawyer-client business transaction. This protocol minimizes the risk of any overreaching by the lawyer directly involved in business transaction with the client.

In re Disciplinary Proceedings Against Creedy: Real Life Applications

1. Gerry Wysocki works in a Midwestern law firm, where he frequently represents farmers in various matters relating to their agricultural businesses. Tom Takala consults with Gerry because he fears that the government will take a substantial part of his land through eminent domain. In explaining his situation, Tom also reveals that his farming business is struggling and that he was thinking of selling other parts of his land to investors willing to take a chance with his business. Because Gerry knows the region's economy rather well, he sees this as a great opportunity to invest some inheritance money. Besides, Gerry thinks that he would be able to build a successful truck stop on Tom's land if Tom's farm fails. Gerry advises Tom on Tom's eminent domain question and then proposes to draft a contract to buy Tom's land that would contain certain clauses regarding Gerry's future participation in Tom's business. How should Gerry proceed to acquire Tom's lands?
2. Attorney helped his client obtain a $200,000 settlement for his client after she was involved in an automobile accident. Following the settlement, the client, who stated she had an alcohol problem, asked the attorney to hold the money on her behalf. He later advised her that she should invest her settlement, with him as an equal partner, in purchasing Coca-Cola collectibles (and other business ventures) to later resell for a profit. Their business was ultimately a bust and she lost a significant portion of her settlement. The attorney argues that upon receiving the settlement, he was no longer acting as her attorney, that he was merely trying to help her financially as a friend. The client contacts you, a local lawyer, and contends that her lawyer acted unethically and seeks your help in recovering her lost money. Discuss her options.

---

2. No Gift Solicitations (or Writing Testimonial Bequests to Yourself)

Lawyers are prohibited from soliciting any substantial gift from a client, unless the gift is from a relative. The rationale for this rule is that given the lawyer's fiduciary and personal relationship with a client, there is a real risk of overreaching and manipulation. The lawyer is free to accept token gifts, for example, a holiday gift basket. If a client insists, however, on giving the lawyer a substantial gift, the lawyer can accept it provided he does not solicit it or prepare an instrument giving him the gift unless it is from a relative. *See* Model Rule 1.8(c). Substantial gifts to lawyers are voidable under the doctrine of undue influence.[14]

In In re Disciplinary Matter Involving Stepovich, 386 P.386 3d 1205 (Alaska 2016), the lawyer, Michael Stepovich, and a client had been friends for several decades. When the client was diagnosed with cancer, he asked Stepovich to draft his will. Although probate was outside Stepovich's normal practice areas, he had helped other friends with "very simple" wills, and agreed to help the client because of their friendship. The will named the client's "good friend, Michael Stepovich," as the sole contingent beneficiary. The client died about six weeks after signing his will, leaving a considerable estate. Because his wife survived, Stepovich received nothing as the contingent beneficiary.

The Alaska Supreme Court emphasized that "[n]aming one[self] as a contingent devisee in a client's will is an obvious conflict of interest that should have been recognized as a problem even absent specific knowledge of Rule 1.8(c)." The court suspended Stepovich for one year and required him to retake and pass the MPRE before reinstatement for failing to follow Rule 1.8(c) and because he had prior history of misconduct.

3. Literary Rights and Financial Assistance

Every state but California has an ethics rule that prohibits lawyers from making or negotiating an agreement for media rights concerning information related to representing a client.[15] The fear is that the lawyer's interest in the media rights will take priority over the client's interests in an efficient, fair, and favorable outcome. The client's desired outcome may not be the best course of conduct for a lawyer interested in maximizing the value of publicity.

One case addressing the impropriety of lawyers acquiring media rights is Harrison v. Mississippi Bar, 637 So. 2d 204 (Miss. 1994). There, the lawyer, Garnett Harrison, faced several allegations of professional misconduct concerning her representation of two clients, including Dorrie Singley. These two cases involved highly charged child custody disputes with allegations of child sexual abuse by the fathers. While still representing the estate of Dorrie Singley, Harrison signed an option contract for $10,000 with a movie production company for the rights to her life story, "The Garnett Harrison Story." The life story was to include a section on her representation of Singley and the founding of Mothers Against Raping Children (MARC). Based on the option contract, Harrison sought and obtained a "permission and release" from Singley's estate. Harrison claimed that she did not intend

14. Model Rule 1.8(c) cmt. 6. *See* Attorney Grievance Comm'n of Maryland v. Lanocha, 896 A.2d 996, 997 n.1 (Md. 2006).

15. Model Rule 1.8(d). *See* ABA/BNA Law. Man. on Prof. Conduct §51:701 (stating the rule does not bar a lawyer from obtaining media rights related to a completed case if the former client provides informed consent) [hereinafter ABA/BNA Man.]. *See also* Burt v. Titlow, 134 S. Ct. 10 (2013) (although a lawyer probably engaged in unethical conduct by having the client sign over the publication rights to her prosecution as part of his fees, Justice Alito held that a violation of the rules of professional conduct, in and of itself, did not constitute a violation of the Sixth Amendment because it did not make the lawyer *per se* ineffective).

to violate Mississippi Rule of Professional Conduct 1.8(d) (which mirrored ABA Model Rule 1.8(d)). Harrison also argued that the Singley story was only a small part of her story and did not harm the client. Nevertheless, the Supreme Court of Mississippi held that "the potential serious injury to the profession is manifest. Realization of personal profit from representation of a client creates an appearance of impropriety which the profession can ill afford. Therefore, disbarment is proper under this Rule."

In general, Rule 1.8(e) prohibits lawyers from providing financial assistance to a client for anticipated or pending litigation. The underlying concern is that if lawyers were permitted to provide such assistance, it may encourage clients to bring lawsuits that otherwise would not be brought, and may give the lawyer too great of a financial stake in the outcome.[16] The lawyer's creditor interest in repayment of his financial assistance or loan may interfere with the lawyer's duty of loyalty and independent judgment to promote the client's best interests.

There are two exceptions to Rule 1.8(e)'s general ban on lawyers providing financial assistance to clients. First, Rule 1.8(e)(1) provides a lawyer "may advance court costs and expenses of litigation" if the repayment is "contingent on the outcome of the matter." The rationale for this exception is that advanced court costs "are virtually indistinguishable from contingent fees," which are permissible, and permitting these advances would help indigent clients access the courts.[17] Under this exception, if lawyers lose, they do not get reimbursed for their expense advances. Second, Rule 1.8(e) authorizes lawyers to simply pay an indigent client's court costs with no expectation of repayment, again to facilitate access to the courts. In essence, the lawyer gifts the litigation expenses, such as filing fees and the cost of medical examinations and expert testimony.

An example of a violation of Rule 1.8(e) was found in Rubio v. BNSF Ry. Co., 548 F. Supp. 2d 1220 (D.N.M. 2008). Before the client's lawsuit was filed in *Rubio*, the client and his attorneys jointly borrowed $86,400 from a bank to subsidize the client's living expenses, in violation of N.M. R. Ann. 16-108(E), which was modeled on ABA Model Rule 1.8(e). The court noted that the purpose for the rule is to prevent a lawyer from acquiring "too great a financial stake in the litigation" as the relationship between a creditor and a debtor is inherently adversarial. The court determined that the attorneys' violation of the rule warranted their disqualification because the loan was not necessary to allow the client access to the courts, there was "no evidence that [the attorneys] co-signed the loan for humanitarian or charitable reasons, 'disqualification' would serve the purposes behind [the rule]," and the loan created a conflict of interest. The court rejected the argument that advances of living expenses should be considered in the same light as contingency fees and indigent expense advances that facilitate access to courts. Some commentators similarly argue that such advances should be permissible because "clients gain financial assistance and more meaningful access to the courts, lawyers can

16. Model Rule 1.8(e) cmt. 10. *See* The Philadelphia Bar Association Prof'l Guidance Committee Op. 2013-8 (2014) (recognizing the ban on living expense advances given Pennsylvania State Bar Opinion 2005-100).
17. Model Rule 1.8(e) cmt. 10.

engage in humanitarian acts, and the public learns that the legal profession seeks to assist all citizens in obtaining justice."[18] At least ten jurisdictions, two because of judicial decisions, permit lawyers to advance some form of living expenses. What do you think?

4. Aggregate Settlements

Lawyers need to be mindful that it is the *client's* and not the lawyer's cause of action or legal matter when providing legal representation in a group setting. The client is the principal in the lawyer-client relationship and "owns" the legal action or matter irrespective of how invested the lawyer-agent becomes in the client's matter. Model Rule 1.8(g) recognizes this fundamental principle and the fact that multiple clients are likely to differ in making or accepting a settlement or in accepting a plea. Thus, Rule 1.8(g) bars lawyers from participating in an aggregate settlement of the claims for or against multiple clients and making an aggregate guilty or nolo contendere agreement unless each client provides informed consent in writing.[19] This rule is consistent with Rule 1.2(a) that similarly recognizes that only a client is authorized to accept a settlement or plea.

In Arce v. Burrow, 958 S.W.2d 239 (Tex. App. 1997) *aff'd and rev'd in part*, 997 S.W.2d 229 (Tex. 1999), Arce and others hired Burrow and others as their attorneys to file individual suits against Phillips 66 in relation to an explosion at a chemical plant that left numerous people dead or injured. The clients agreed to pay the attorneys on a contingency fee basis. The attorneys reached an aggregate settlement with Phillips 66 for the entire lawsuit, allegedly without discussion or individual authority from the clients, save for a 20-minute meeting to discuss settlement arrangements. The clients sued the attorneys for a breach of fiduciary duty and sought fee forfeiture. The court examined the issue of whether the attorneys breached their fiduciary duties to the clients by entering into an aggregate settlement. The attorneys argued that there was no aggregate settlement. The court defined the term "aggregate settlement" as relating to the situation where "an attorney, who represents two or more clients, settles the entire case on behalf of those clients without individual negotiations on behalf of any one client." The court noted that unless there is informed consent, attorneys representing multiple clients have an ethical responsibility, based on their duty of loyalty and good faith to each client, to obtain an individual settlement for each client. Otherwise, mass settlements are unfair to clients and may "result in a benefit to the attorney (speedy resolution and payment of fees) to the detriment of the clients (decreased recovery)." Because of this unfairness, the court concluded the attorneys breached their fiduciary duties to their clients when they entered into aggregate settlements without client consent

18. Jack P. Sahl, *The Cost of Humanitarian Assistance: Ethical Rules and the First Amendment*, 34 ST. MARY'S L.J. 79, 827 (2003). *See* Philip G. Shrag, *The Unethical Ethics Rule: Nine Ways to Fix Model Rule of Professional Conduct 1.8(e)*, 28 GEO. J. LEGAL ETHICS 39, 72 (2014) (the current text of the rule contributes "to homelessness, inadequate medical care, starvation, and in some cases, a denial of access to justice because clients are forced by their poverty to accept inadequate settlements").

19. Model Rule 1.8(g).

and that the aggregate settlements violated the Texas Disciplinary Rules of Professional Conduct. The court remanded the case to the lower court for a determination of the amount of forfeiture.

Unlike the aggregate settlement scenario, in class action representation where a lawyer represents a class of plaintiffs or defendants, the lawyer may not have a full attorney-client relationship with each class member.[20] Upon class certification, the lawyer needs to comply with applicable rules concerning notice and other procedural requirements to protect the entire class.[21]

5. No Prospective Malpractice Limitations

All states have an ethics rule that prohibits lawyers from entering into an agreement to prospectively limit their liability for malpractice.[22] There is one exception to the prohibition in those "rare circumstances" when, under Rule 1.8(h)(1), the client retains independent counsel in making the agreement and, even then, not every state recognizes this exception.[23] Indeed, the potential for overreaching with these malpractice agreements is significant. Lawyers act as trusted fiduciaries for their clients and asking clients to forgo possible malpractice claims against their lawyers is unfair when many clients may not fully appreciate the significance of signing such an agreement. This is especially true at the formation of the professional relationship when there is likely a dearth of information available to the client, for example, information about the risks involved in representation. Also, the malpractice limitation may serve as a disincentive for the lawyer to diligently and competently advance the client's interest. Courts generally frown on any attempt by a lawyer to limit liability. Rule 1.8(h) does not prohibit agreements with clients to arbitrate legal malpractice claims in jurisdictions where such agreements are enforceable and clients appreciate the significance of the agreement.

Rule 1.8(h)(2) prohibits a lawyer from settling a claim or potential claim for malpractice with an unrepresented client or former client unless the client is advised in writing of the benefit of having independent counsel and the client is given an opportunity to seek such independent advice. By way of an example, in In re Carson, 991 P.2d 896 (Kan. 1999), an attorney had a fee dispute with his former client. Carson submitted an agreement to his client without advising her to seek independent counsel concerning a provision that waived malpractice claims against the lawyer. The former client signed the agreement without the benefit of independent counsel. The attorney was charged with a violation of Kansas Rule of Professional Conduct 1.8(h). Carson argued that Rule 1.8(h) could not have applied to him as the agreement was signed by a former client who had not at that time asserted a claim for malpractice against him. The court was unconvinced by the attorney's

20. Model Rule 1.8(g) cmt. 13.

21. *Id.*

22. ABA/BNA Man. §51:1101.

23. *Id.* (reporting the exception as occurring in "rare circumstances").

"technical arguments" and found him in violation of the second part of Rule 1.8(h). It did not matter that no actual claim existed at that time.

6. No Proprietary Interest in Client Matter

Lawyers are prohibited from acquiring a proprietary interest in the subject matter of the client's litigation or other matter under Model Rule 1.8(i). The rule is designed to prevent lawyers from unfairly using their knowledge and fiduciary position to take such an interest. There is also the concern that once the lawyer acquires a proprietary interest, the lawyer's self-interest in protecting that interest may interfere with the lawyer's duty of loyalty to advance the client's interests. There are two exceptions to the Rule 1.8(i) prohibition. First, lawyers can acquire a lien, for example a charging lien[24] or retaining lien,[25] authorized by law to secure his fees or expenses. Second, lawyers are permitted to contract for a contingency fee in a civil case.

In In re Fisher, 202 P.3d 1186 (Colo. 2009), the attorney represented the wife in a marital dissolution case and was charged with several professional conduct rule violations, including what is now Colorado Rule of Professional Conduct 1.8(i), a rule identical to the ABA Model Rule. Fisher was concerned that his client would not pay his professional fees and asked the wife to sign a promissory note in the amount of $3,102, secured by a deed of trust in her marital residence. He explained that it was necessary to ensure payment of his professional fees. The marital residence was subsequently sold and Fisher attempted to have the title company pay all proceeds to him. Fisher argued that this was permissible under Colorado Rule 1.8(i) as his interest in the marital residence constituted a "lien authorized by law" within the meaning of the rule.

The Colorado Supreme Court examined the comments to Colorado Rule 1.8(i) to determine which liens are authorized by law. The comments provided liens "may include liens granted by statute, liens originating in common law, and liens acquired by contract with the client," but ultimately it is "the law of each jurisdiction" that determines which liens are excluded from Rule 1.8(i)'s prohibition. The court concluded that "[a]ttorney's charging liens . . . specifically provided for by statute are excepted" from Rule 1.8(i)'s ban on lawyers obtaining a proprietary interest in the subject matter of the representation. In contrast to charging liens that give lawyers an interest in their clients' judgment for legal services rendered, deeds of trust are

---

24. A charging lien is a lien for services rendered by an attorney "in procuring a judgment, decree, or award for the client" and attaching "to the client's cause of action, verdict and judgment, and the proceeds thereof." R.L. Rossi, 2 Attorneys' Fees §12.13 (3d ed. 2016). Rossi notes that a charging lien is "only applicable to charges rendered for the particular action involved," but does not require possession. *Id.*

25. Atty. Grievance Comm'n of Md. v. Rand, 128 A.3d 107 (Md. 2015) ("A retaining lien permits the attorney to 'secure' his claim for unpaid fees through retention of client property [or funds] in his possession." (citing Charles W. Wolfram, Modern Legal Ethics §9.6.3 Attorney Liens, at 558-59 (1986))). The attorney "holds the property until the client pays the balance of the fees owed or possibly provides some other security." *See* Rossi, *supra* note 24 (adding that the retaining lien may be used to "compel payment of any or all professional charges, whether connected with the action or not").

not authorized by law but rather granted by an individual. Thus, the court held that Fisher violated Rule 1.8(i) by acquiring an interest in the marital residence.

7. Sexual Relations with Clients

Another example of lawyers seeking personal aggrandizement is when they get involved in sexual relations with a client after the commencement of representation. Professional conduct standards prohibit a lawyer from having sexual relations with a client unless the relations existed before the formation of the lawyer-client relationship.[26] There is concern that the lawyer will take advantage of his or her fiduciary position with a client to have such relations, especially with vulnerable clients, and that it will affect the independent judgment of both parties.

In In re Stanton, 376 P.3d 693 (Alaska 2016), the attorney began a sexual relationship with a young woman after he agreed to represent her in a child custody case. Although "sexual relationship" is not defined under Alaska's Professional Conduct Rules, the parties agreed that sexting and physical contact between the lawyer and client constituted a sexual relationship prohibited by Rule 1.8(j). The Alaska Supreme Court noted that "Stanton's pursuit of sexual gratification—either by initiating or answering the client's sexual overtures with genital photos and sexually provocative texts—advanced his personal interests to the detriment of his client." The court further concluded that the "[d]isclosure of the sexual relationship reinforced allegations that his client was a mixed up, troubled young woman who might not be the best parent for a young child. [Stanton's] conflict required him to withdraw and left his client without legal counsel in a contested custody proceeding." The court suspended Stanton from the practice of law in Alaska for three years.[27]

8. Prospective-Client Conflicts and Advance Waivers

Chapter 3 provided a discussion of prospective clients. It is important to understand that such clients pose a risk to lawyers in the conflicts of interest area. The general rule prohibits a lawyer from representing a client with "interests materially adverse to those of a prospective client in the same or substantially related matter if the lawyer received information that might be significantly harmful to the prospective

26. Model Rule 1.8(j). Nearly every state has adopted disciplinary rules regarding sexual relations either under Rule 1.7 or Rule 1.8(j). Ronald J. Mallen, 2 Legal Malpractice §16 (2017). *See* ABA, CPR Policy Implementation Committee (May 2015), *available at* http://www.americanbar.org/content/dam/aba/administrative/professional_responsibility/mrpc_1_8j.authcheckdam.pdf.

27. For another example of a Rule 1.8(j) violation, see In re Albrecht, 845 N.W.2d 184, 192 (Minn. 2014) (disbarring an attorney who had sexual relations with a client over an extended period of time and pressured her for sex whenever she sought legal advice; rejecting the claim there was no client harm because the sex began as consensual and stating the lawyer-client relationship is "'almost always unequal' and can be 'unfairly exploited' in a sexual relationship regardless of how the relationship began" as here when Albrecht sought sex despite the client's objections).

client."[28] Sometimes clients interview several lawyers or law firms before selecting representation that is best suited in terms of expertise and expense to handle their legal needs. This search process is occasionally referred to as a "beauty contest." Lawyers must be concerned about prospective clients laying the groundwork for a subsequent motion to disqualify them by disclosing certain information during the initial interview and before the formation of the lawyer-client relationship.

Some law firms provide prospective clients with written statements warning clients about the risk of disclosing confidential information at the initial consultation. The prospective client may also waive confidentiality for information he provides to the attorney during the initial interview.[29] If the lawyer discovers during the interview a potential conflict of interest, she should inform the prospective client of the conflict and decline to represent the client.[30]

However, a firm may also ask prospective clients to waive their right to file a disqualification motion against the firm should it represent a party in the same or substantially related matter against the prospective clients. The validity of such future conflict of interest waivers ("**advance conflict waivers**") depends on the facts and the extent to which a client meaningfully understood the material risks involved in the waiver. In general, the more detailed the explanation about potential conflicts of interest, the more sophisticated the client, and the more recent the waiver, the more likely a court will find a valid advance waiver. In contrast, vague and broad statements about the firm being permitted to represent adverse interests in anything substantially related to the client's disclosures is generally less likely to be upheld as a valid waiver.[31] The enforceability of advance conflict waivers is greater when a prospective or current client has independent counsel, for example, in-house counsel, reviewing the advance waiver and explaining its material risks to the client. In summary, absent a waiver, lawyers should be careful to limit any discussion with a prospective client that might constitute a basis for disqualifying the firm from representing a current or future client. Of course, advance waivers, like other types of consent to conflicts, may be revoked at any time by the client.

In addition, lawyers must be mindful that certain future conflicts of interest are not consentable under Rule 1.7(b) and an advance waiver would not make them consentable. Therefore, advance waivers are only valid for future conflicts to which a client may consent in accordance with Rule 1.7.[32]

A firm may ask a client to sign a future conflict of interest waiver.
Shutterstock.com

28. Model Rule 1.18(c). *See* Model Rule 1.9(a).
29. Restatement §122 cmt. d.
30. Restatement §122(1).
31. Marian C. Rice, *A Perspective on Waivers*, A.B.A. (May/June 2014), *available at* www.americanbar.org/publications/law_practice_magazine/2014/may-june/ethics.html.
32. See *infra* at pages 303-305 for a discussion of Rule 1.7 and waiver.

9. Advocate-Witness Conflict

Lawyers are prohibited from serving as an advocate in a case in which they are likely to be called as a necessary witness. The concern is that combining the roles of advocate and witness may prejudice the tribunal and the opposing party.[33] The factfinder may be confused about whether the lawyer is testifying to facts from personal knowledge or, as is the case with advocates, commenting and explaining the testimony of others.[34] The jury may overvalue the lawyer's testimony, or poor or weak testimony by an advocate-witness may harm his client's interests.

The dual role as advocate and witness may also create a conflict of interest under Rule 1.7 (current-client conflicts) or Rule 1.9 (former-client conflicts) if the advocate's testimony may reflect adversely on his client.[35] For example, a substantial conflict between the advocate's and his client's testimony would create a Rule 1.7 conflict requiring client consent to continue with representation. The advocate's inability to testify about facts because of his duty to preserve a former client's confidential information would create a Rule 1.9 conflict.[36]

Fognani v. Young, 115 P.3d 1268, 1272 (Colo. 2005), illustrates some of these concerns and discusses Colorado's Rule of Professional Conduct (CRPC) 3.7, its **advocate-witness rule**, which was modeled largely on ABA Model Rule 3.7. The rule states that an attorney "cannot maintain dual roles as advocate and witness in the same matter before the same tribunal." Attorney John D. Fognani, a partner at Fognani Guibord & Homsy, LLP (FGH), was representing his parents in a medical malpractice suit against Dr. Young. Attorney Fognani was named in pretrial disclosures as a fact witness, including with regard to his father's medical condition, the care and treatment he received from Dr. Young, and Dr. Young's alleged apology and admission of fault — "that he was not completely abreast of modern treatment measures that would have averted the injuries." Defendants moved to disqualify Attorney Fognani pursuant to CRPC 3.7.

In examining CRPC 3.7, the Colorado Supreme Court acknowledged the wide discretion that trial courts have to order disqualification. It also noted that motions to disqualify opposing counsel are abused sometimes for dilatory or tactical reasons; thus opposing counsel cannot be disqualified on mere "speculation or conjecture" but only upon facts that show a potential violation of CRPC 3.7.[37]

The court considered the rationales behind the rule, including avoiding jury confusion, and quoted one of its earlier decisions. "[A] lawyer who intermingles the functions of advocate and witness diminishes the effectiveness of both. . . . The client's case is subject to criticism that it is being presented through the testimony of an obviously interested witness who on that account is subject to impeachment,

33. Model Rule 3.7 cmt. 1.
34. Model Rule 3.7 cmt. 2.
35. Model Rule 3.7 cmt. 6.
36. *Id.*
37. Fognani v. Young, 115 P.3d 1268, 1272 (Colo. 2005). The advocate-witness rule's requirements that an advocate be a "necessary witness" with testimony relating to a contested issue help to limit the possible tactical abuse by lawyers who seek to disqualify opposing counsel by calling her as a witness. *See* Model Rule 3.7(a).

and, of equal importance, placed in the unseemly position of arguing his own credibility to the jury."[38]

CRPC 3.7's prohibition applies when the lawyer is "likely to be a necessary witness." The court stated that if the advocate's testimony is merely cumulative of other testimony, then it is not necessary. The court held that "'likely to be a necessary witness' involves a consideration of the nature of the case, with emphasis on the subject of the lawyer's testimony, the weight the testimony might have in resolving disputed issues, and the availability of other witnesses or documentary evidence which might independently establish the relevant issues." The court opined that Fognani's testimony about Dr. Young's declarations of not keeping abreast of modern treatment measures, if proven true, could subject him to liability and thus made Fognani a necessary witness.

The Colorado Supreme Court next considered the three exceptions to the CRPC 3.7 prohibition. The first two exceptions allow a lawyer to testify to an uncontested matter or about the nature and value of legal services rendered in the case. These exceptions are not relevant in the instant case. The third exception allows a lawyer to serve as an advocate and witness if disqualifying the lawyer would work a "substantial hardship on the client." This rule is designed to protect the client; substantial hardship means something more than that the lawyer has invested significant time and expense in the case. The trial court must consider all relevant factors imposing a substantial hardship on the client, for example, "the nature of the case, financial hardship, giving weight to the stage in the proceedings, and the time at which the attorney became aware of the likelihood of his testimony." Weighing these factors, the Colorado Supreme Court concluded that Fognani's disqualification would not impose a substantial hardship on the client.

The court concluded that disqualification pursuant to Rule 3.7 did not necessarily preclude participation in pretrial matters. On this basis, the court limited the scope of Fognani's disqualification to the trial, but allowed the trial court on remand to extend the disqualification to pretrial activity if Fognani's participation would be disclosed to the jury, thereby undermining Rule 3.7.

The Colorado Supreme Court also found that CRPC 3.7(b) did not impose an automatic vicarious disqualification of Fognani's firm, FGH. It remanded the case, however, for a further determination of whether the requirements of CRPC 1.7 had been met and, in particular, whether the plaintiffs consented to be continuously represented by FGH given their son's disqualification.

C. FORMER-CLIENT CONFLICTS OF INTEREST

In an era of increasing lawyer and client mobility and other economic developments, such as the merger of businesses, lawyers may find themselves being asked to represent a current client against a former client. This could create a potential conflict of interest if the lawyer is in a position to use the former client's confidences

38. *Fognani*, 115 P.3d at 1272 (quoting Williams v. Dist. Court, 700 P.2d 549, 553 (Colo. 1985)).

for the current client's benefit. In former-client conflict cases, courts are primarily concerned about protecting the former client's confidences from lawyer misuse. Lawyers are fiduciaries for their clients and have an ongoing duty, even after the conclusion of client representation, to preserve client confidences from intentional and inadvertent disclosure or misuse. If there was no ongoing duty, clients would not be able to trust their lawyers with their confidences.

There is also a concern about loyalty when considering former clients and conflicts of interest. Former clients expect their lawyers not to represent parties with material adverse interests that involve the same or a substantially similar matter that the lawyer worked on for them. Permitting lawyers to represent adverse parties against former clients on substantially similar matters would betray former clients' trust in the loyalty of their lawyers and have a corrosive effect on the public's perception of the profession.

When the current client's matter is substantially related to the former client's matter, the courts will also presume that the lawyer had access to confidential information that can be used to the former client's disadvantage, and may disqualify him from the case.[39] Lawyers may proceed against a former client when the current client's matter is not substantially related to the lawyer's work for the former client.

Sometimes a question arises about whether a client is either a current or a former client. The answer to that question is significant because as discussed earlier in this chapter when considering *Cinema 5*, a lawyer generally cannot sue a current client on behalf of another current client. However, a lawyer can sue a former client on an unrelated matter and does not even have to consult the former client before filing the lawsuit. A lawyer may nevertheless want to consider communicating with the former client about the lawsuit if the former client is not already represented and reassure the former client that the lawyer cannot reveal any prior client confidential information.

When does a current client become a former client for purposes of Rule 1.9? The court in Int'l Bus. Machs. Corp. v. Levin, 579 F.2d 271, 281 (3d Cir. 1978), addressed this question. There, IBM moved to disqualify Carpenter, Bennett & Morrissey (CBM), Levin's counsel in a private antitrust action against IBM, on the ground that CBM represented both IBM and Levin while the case was pending. While CBM did not represent IBM in the antitrust action, CBM had provided occasional legal work for IBM in labor matters prior to the commencement of that action. The Third Circuit Court of Appeals examined, among other issues, whether IBM was a current client of CBM or whether it was a former client.

The trial court found that CBM "had an on-going attorney-client relationship with both IBM and the plaintiffs." The appellate court agreed with this assessment. "Although CBM had no specific assignment . . . from IBM on the day the antitrust complaint was filed and even though CBM performed services for IBM on a fee for service basis rather than pursuant to a retainer arrangement, the pattern of repeated

39. Model Rule 1.9(c). *See T.C. Warner Theaters*, 113 F. Supp. 265 (S.D.N.Y.1953) (Judge Weinfeld is generally credited with establishing the "substantial relationship" test in this landmark case). One way to view Rule 1.9(c) is that the "lawyer's lips are sealed" forever regarding confidential client information, absent a few exceptions, for example, the client consents to disclosure or the applicability of one of the permissive disclosure provisions under Rule 1.6(b)(1)-(7).

retainers, both before and after the filing of the complaint, supports the finding of a continuous relationship." Thus, IBM was a current client and not a former client for purposes of conflict analysis and this warranted disqualification of CBM.[40]

The following two cases, *Gillette Co. v. Provost* and *Damron v. Herzog*, demonstrate how courts apply the substantial relationship test with differing results. They also show the fact-intensive inquiry by courts in applying the substantial relationship test and their concern for protecting both loyalty and confidential information in the former client context.

In Gillette Co. v. Provost, No. 133515 2016 Mass. Super. LEXIS 40 (May 5, 2016), Cekala worked as a patent lawyer for Gillette from 1987 to 1990 and again from 1992 through May 2006. During that period, Cekala "had access to privileged communications and information" concerning Gillette's patents and technologies and developed "detailed knowledge" about Gillette's patents and related licensing agreements.

In 2012, Cekala started working for ShaveLogic on patent matters, and became its general counsel in 2013. ShaveLogic informed investors and prospective business partners that Cekala's "intimate knowledge of Gillette's intellectual property portfolio and patent strategy" gave ShaveLogic "a competitive edge in the market." ShaveLogic hired Cekala "to provide freedom to operate opinions respecting Gillette patents, including patents whose prosecution he oversaw, and to identify potential voids in Gillette's patent portfolio." While employed by ShaveLogic, Cekala also provided similar assistance to other companies that compete with Gillette. Gillette complained that Cekala had represented ShaveLogic in matters that were substantially related to those in which he previously represented Gillette, that he had done so without Gillette's consent, and that as a result Cekala had breached his continuing fiduciary duty to Gillette.

The court granted the defendant's motion to dismiss Gillette's claim and held that Cekala owes a continuing fiduciary duty to Gillette but that the scope of his duty to Gillette today is narrower than the broad duty of undivided loyalty that he owed while employed by Gillette. The court added: "[T]he facts do not plausibly suggest that Cekala has breached any fiduciary duty owed to Gillette under Mass. R. Prof. Conduct 1.9, because they do not suggest that Cekala's current representation of ShaveLogic and alleged assistance to other companies is 'materially adverse' to Gillette's legal interests or that it is 'substantially related' to any work Cekala did [for] Gillette."

The court in Damron v. Herzog, 67 F.3d 211 (9th Cir. 1995), reached a different result than in *Gillette*. The appellate court in *Damron* reversed and remanded for a new trial a former client's malpractice action against Attorney Herzog, who represented Damron in the 1982 sale of his cemetery business. As part of the sale, he drafted a stock purchase agreement that called for payments through 1997. Herzog never represented Damron again but he did represent the purchasers following the sale in various matters, including advising them in 1991 to cease making

40. An "end of engagement" letter is a good practice for firms to follow in memorializing the conclusion of their professional relationships with clients. After such letters, those clients should be treated as former clients for purposes of a conflict of interest review.

payments under the stock purchase agreement. Damron sued Herzog for malpractice, although he did not claim that Herzog used confidential information from his former representation of Damron. The appellate court concluded nevertheless that because the lawsuit involved the same matter that Herzog worked on for Damron, Herzog was presumed to have had access to confidential information when he advised the purchasers who had material and adverse interests to Damron. The court emphasized that it is not the actual misuse but the potential misuse of confidential information that is required for a conflict of interest. Thus, Damron had a potential cause of action against Herzog for breaching his duty to protect his former client's confidences. Also, the court held that Herzog's duty of loyalty to his former client "re-attached" once Herzog became involved in advising the purchasers about the same matter he worked on for Damron. This required him not to betray his former client's trust.

Case Preview

Western Sugar Coop. v. Archer-Daniels-Midland Co.

In the high profile case of *Western Sugar Coop. v. Archer-Daniels-Midland Co.* (*Western Sugar*), the federal trial court considered the possible disqualification of a large law firm, Squire, Patton & Boggs (SPB), on conflict of interest grounds. The SPB firm was the result of a recent mega-merger of two longstanding and nationally prominent law firms: Squire, Sanders and Dempsey and Patton Boggs. SPB's failure to identify potential conflicts of interests stemming from the merger proved costly to both the firm and its former and current clients.

As you examine *Western Sugar*, consider the following questions:

1. How does Patton Boggs's Attorney Smitha Stansbury's post-merger departure affect the outcome of this case? Should it have any effect?
2. What facts in the case support the court's ruling that the Patton Boggs former representation of Ingredion is "substantially related" to its successor firm's, SPB's, representation of Western Sugar?
3. Do you think the court gave sufficient weight to the Patton Boggs lawyers who worked on Ingredion matters before the merger and who declared that they never shared any information post-merger with the Squire Sanders lawyers representing the Western Sugar plaintiffs?
4. What is the significance of the July 2014 meeting when a Patton Boggs lawyer consulted with the plaintiff's expert witness, David Kessler, and the former Squire Sanders attorney, John Burlingame, who is the co-lead attorney for the Western Sugar plaintiffs?
5. Why does the court find a conclusive presumption that SPB possessed confidential information? Is it a fair presumption?
6. Do you agree with the court's view that "[i]t is the possibility of the breach of confidence, not the fact of the breach that triggers disqualification"?

Western Sugar Coop. v. Archer-Daniels-Midland Co.

98 F. Supp. 3d 1074 (C.D. Cal. 2015)

II. PROCEDURAL AND FACTUAL BACKGROUND

The underlying case arises from false advertising claims relating to the marketing of high-fructose corn syrup ("HFCS"), pitting the sugar industry against the corn-refining industry. Plaintiffs are sugar industry manufacturers, trade groups, and associations: Western Sugar Cooperative . . . and the Sugar Association, Inc. (collectively the "Sugar Plaintiffs"). Defendants are manufacturers and trade groups and associations active in the corn and HFCS industry: Archer-Daniels-Midland Company ("ADM"); Ingredion Inc. ("Ingredion"); Tate & Lyle Ingredients Americas, Inc. ("Tate & Lyle"); and The Corn Refiners Association ("CRA") (collectively "Defendants").

Plaintiffs, represented by the legacy law firm of Squire Sanders & Dempsey, LLP ("Squire Sanders"), filed the instant lawsuit on April 22, 2011, and the SAC [Second Amended Complaint] on November 21, 2011. The SAC asserts one cause of action for false advertising under the Lanham Act, alleging that Defendants misled consumers by use of the term "corn sugar."

On September 4, 2012, Defendants ADM, Cargill, Ingredion, and Tate & Lyle each filed a counterclaim against Plaintiff the Sugar Association. Defendants' counterclaim asserts one cause of action for false advertising in violation of the Lanham Act, alleging that the Sugar Association misrepresented HFCS as unhealthy.

A. The Patton Boggs and Squire Sanders Merger

On June 1, 2014, the law firms of Patton Boggs LLP ("Patton Boggs") and Squire Sanders combined to form Squire Patton Boggs ("SPB"). SPB remains the Sugar Plaintiffs' counsel of record. Ingredion and Tate & Lyle each filed motions to disqualify SPB from representing the Sugar Plaintiffs in this action because SPB is now adverse to both Ingredion and Tate & Lyle — long-standing clients of the legacy firm Patton Boggs.

B. Patton Boggs' and SPB's Representation of Tate & Lyle

. . . Tate & Lyle entered into an attorney-client relationship with Patton Boggs in or about February 1998, as documented in a letter dated February 11, 1998, signed by Stuart Pape of Patton Boggs (the "1998 Engagement Letter").

Tate & Lyle has relied on multiple lawyers at Patton Boggs for legal advice on a wide range of matters since 1998 and through the merger in June 2014. . . . Tate & Lyle's counsel declares that Patton Boggs' lawyers advised Tate & Lyle on matters that required a thorough understanding of its business operations, including its operations and processing of ingredients such as HFCS.

1. Tate & Lyle Bring the Conflict to SPB's Attention

In late July 2014, Tate & Lyle's counsel, Heidi Balsley, contacted SPB attorney, who was formerly a Patton Boggs attorney, Dan Waltz, inquiring whether he knew of the pending lawsuit, which he did not. . . . They explained that a paralegal at Patton Boggs had prepared a list of clients with conflicts for considerations as part of the pre-merger conflicts diligence, and Tate & Lyle had been inexplicably omitted from the list. During that call, they asked Tate & Lyle for a conflict waiver.

. . .

2. Tate & Lyle Does Not Agree to Waive the Conflict

[On August 4, 2014], Tate & Lyle [told SPB it] would not waive the conflict [and] requested that SPB withdraw from its representation of the Sugar Plaintiffs.

Thereafter on August 10, 2014, SPB's counsel sent a letter to Tate & Lyle's counsel, enclosing a copy of the 1998 Engagement Letter. The letter states, "the terms of Tate & Lyle's engagement of Patton Boggs . . . provided us with Tate & Lyle's advance consent that we would represent other clients on matters adverse to Tate & Lyle so long as those matters were unrelated to our work for Tate & Lyle." . . .

3. SPB Withdraws from Its Representation of Tate & Lyle

On August 18, 2014, SPB sent a letter to Tate & Lyle's counsel terminating its relationship with Tate & Lyle. [L]awyers at SPB were actively providing services to Tate & Lyle up until SPB's termination on August 18, 2014.

C. Patton Boggs' Representation of Ingredion

Defendant Ingredion provides ingredients to food and beverage companies and refines corn to produce HFCS. Ingredion first retained Patton Boggs in May 2004, and Patton Boggs continued to perform work for Ingredion over the years and last performed work for Ingredion in September 2013. Patton Boggs has provided legal services to Ingredion on at least fifty-six different occasions, and since 2004, Ingredion has paid Patton Boggs over $230,000 in legal fees.

Shortly after Tate & Lyle's counsel raised the conflict, SPB sent Ingredion's counsel a letter dated July 31, 2014, advising it of the merger and that Squire Sanders had been representing the Sugar Plaintiffs and SPB would continue to do so going forward. The letter stated that if Ingredion wanted to have its lawyers from Patton Boggs do any new work, it would be necessary to obtain a waiver from Ingredion due to the conflict presented by SPB's role in the present case.

Ingredion and Tate & Lyle each move to disqualify SPB from representing the Sugar Plaintiffs in this action, contending that the merger resulted in SPB simultaneously representing adverse clients.

III. LEGAL STANDARD

Motions to disqualify counsel are governed by state law. . . . The decision to disqualify counsel is within the trial court's discretion limited by applicable legal principles. Because of the potential for abuse, disqualification motions are subject to strict judicial scrutiny. A court should examine the implications of disqualification, including "a client's right to chosen counsel, an attorney's interest in representing a client, the financial burden on a client to replace disqualified counsel, and the possibility that tactical abuse underlies the disqualification motion."

Motions to disqualify generally arise in one of two contexts: (1) in cases of successive representation, where an attorney seeks to represent a client with interests that are potentially adverse to a former client; and (2) in cases of simultaneous representation, where an attorney seeks to represent in a single action multiple parties with potentially adverse interests. The primary fiduciary duty at stake in each of these contexts differs, and the applicable disqualification standards vary accordingly.

A. *Successive Representation of Adverse Clients*

The rules regarding successive representation of clients with adverse interests focus on an attorney's duty of confidentiality. If an attorney undertakes to represent a client adverse to a former client without obtaining informed consent, the former client may disqualify the attorney by showing a "substantial relationship" between the subjects of the prior and current representations. This protects the enduring duty to preserve client confidences that survives the termination of the attorney's representation. When a substantial relationship between the representations is established, the attorney is automatically disqualified from representing the second client.

In determining whether there is a "substantial relationship," a court should first analyze whether there was a direct relationship with the former client and whether the relationship touched on issues related to the present litigation. The substantial relationship test requires evidence supporting a rational conclusion that "information material to the evaluation, prosecution, settlement or accomplishment of the former representation given its factual and legal issues is material to the evaluation, prosecution, settlement or accomplishment of the current representation given its factual and legal issues."

If the former representation involved a direct relationship with the client and the matters are substantially related, the former client need not prove that the attorney possesses actual confidential information; instead, the attorney is presumed to possess confidential information. The presumption that an attorney has access to confidential information relevant to the subsequent representation and resulting disqualification extends vicariously to the entire firm.

. . .

IV. DISCUSSION

. . .

B. *SPB Is Subject to Disqualification Due to Its Prior Representation of Ingredion in Matters Substantially Related to the Present Action*

1. Ingredion Was a Former Client of SPB

Ingredion first retained Patton Boggs in May 2004, and Patton Boggs has continued to perform work for Ingredion over the years and last performed work for Ingredion in September 2013.

Ingredion contends that it was an existing client at the time of the merger because during the firm's decade-long representation, Ingredion reached out to Patton Boggs on an as-needed basis, but time gaps never resulted in a termination of the attorney-client relationship. Ingredion contends that it was treated as an existing client and was not asked to enter into a new fee agreement when it approached Patton Boggs in February 2009, May 2013, or on other occasions following time gaps. All work was billed to Ingredion's existing account with Patton Boggs.

An engagement letter dated December 14, 2005 (the "2005 Engagement Letter") from Patton Boggs' attorney, Stuart Pape, enclosed Patton Boggs' Standard Terms of Engagement. The Standard Terms of Engagement provides, "[i]t is our policy that the attorney-client relationship will terminate upon our completion of any service that you have retained us to perform." Patton Boggs completed services for Ingredion in September 2013, eight months prior to the merger in June 2014, and under the terms of the 2005 Engagement Letter, its attorney-client relationship with Ingredion ended.

Ingredion contends that it was not rendered a former client by the statements in Patton Boggs' Standard Terms of Engagement because (1) it did not expressly agree to those terms; and (2) the 2005 Engagement Letter that accompanied the Standard Terms of Engagement shows that Ingredion retained Patton Boggs not for a discrete issue or litigation, but to provide ongoing representation in connection with FDA regulation of Ingredion's products.

Ingredion was not required to take any action to show its assent to the Standard Terms of Engagement. The 2005 Engagement Letter from Mr. Pape provides, "[t]his letter supplements and modifies the enclosed terms of engagement. . . . If you agree with these terms and conditions, including those set forth in the [Standard Terms of Engagement], no further action is required. . . ."

The 2005 Engagement Letter also provides that Patton Boggs was retained to "represent [Ingredion] in connection with FDA regulation of the Company's Products." It does not specify that Patton Boggs' representation is ongoing, continuing or open-ended. The Standard Terms of Engagement provides that the attorney-client relationship would end upon completion of Patton Boggs' services and states that should Ingredion continue to retain Patton Boggs, the attorney-client relationship would be re-established at that time. Once Patton Boggs completed its representation of Ingredion in September 2013, the attorney-client relationship terminated.

Accordingly, Ingredion was a former client of Patton Boggs at the time of the June 2014 merger. Whether SPB can represent the Sugar Plaintiffs in this action after previously representing Ingredion depends on whether SPB can do so while maintaining its duty of confidentiality it owes to Ingredion. That, in turn, depends on whether the former and current matters are "substantially related."

2. The Prior and Current Representations Are "Substantially Related"

a. Patton Boggs' Prior Work for Ingredion vs. Its Work in the Present Action

Patton Boggs' attorneys advised Ingredion regarding permissible, common or unusual names for HFCS. Evidence filed *in camera* shows lawyers billed time in 2006 for researching regulations on advertising products with HFCS; reviewing FDA and Department of Agriculture rules and regulations on HFCS, and discussing research and common or unusual names for HFCS with each other and Ingredion.

Patton Boggs' attorneys also advised Ingredion regarding FDA statements and enforcement actions following a letter issued from the FDA dated July 3, 2008, signed by Geraldine June (the "Geraldine June Letter"). The Geraldine June Letter describes aspects of manufacturing HFCS and whether a resulting product could be considered "natural." Ingredion received advice from Patton Boggs regarding interpretation of the Geraldine June Letter, including advice concerning a key aspect of the HFCS manufacturing process and how that might affect whether the resulting HFCS product could be described as "natural." Patton Boggs' lawyers billed time in 2009 for researching and discussing FDA statements and natural claims internally and with Ingredion.

Ingredion contends that in the Geraldine June Letter, the FDA concluded that HFCS qualifies as "natural." Counsel for Ingredion declares that it and other Defendants are relying on the Geraldine June Letter in this action in support of their position that it is not a misrepresentation to claim that HFCS is "natural."

SPB represents Plaintiffs in this lawsuit against Defendants, alleging that they engaged in false advertising of HFCS. Plaintiffs allege that this lawsuit is a response to an educational campaign initiated by Defendant CRA in 2008 that sought to educate the public about HFCS and to address the Sugar Plaintiffs' purported vilification and myths about HFCS with facts and scientific studies. Sugar Plaintiffs allege that Defendant CRA's campaign constitutes false advertising under the Lanham Act, identifying two categories of false and/or misleading representations: the first category is Defendants' use of the term "corn sugar," and the second category is Defendants' statements that HFCS is a "natural" product.

Defendants, including Ingredion, defend that the term "corn sugar" accurately depicts HFCS and that the FDA has confirmed methods of producing HFCS that qualifies as "natural." Ingredion's defense relies, in part, on the Geraldine June Letter. The Geraldine June Letter has been explored in multiple depositions, it is expected to be discussed in motions for summary judgment, and it will likely be addressed at trial.

b. Legal and Factual Similarities

The evaluation of whether the two representations are substantially related centers upon the factual and legal similarities of the representations.

SPB contends that none of the four billing entries from August 2006 relating to HFCS, concern the use of the word "sugar" or any other term at issue in this litigation. SPB further argues that there was no question related to whether the word "sugar" could be used for HFCS in labeling, or any question regarding the relative benefits of sugar versus HFCS, and the inquiry did not relate to advertising.

SPB contends that the Geraldine June Letter is only at issue in this litigation regarding whether Defendants can rely on it as an FDA endorsement of marketing HFCS as "natural." SPB further contends that work performed in August 2009, was performed by attorneys Paul Rubin, who left Patton Boggs in August 2012 (two years before the merger) and Smitha Stansbury, who left SPB in July 2014 (almost two months *after* the merger).

A "substantial relationship" does not necessarily mean an exact match between the facts and issues involved in the two representations. The work Patton Boggs performed for Ingredion in 2006 and 2009 relates to the propriety of characterizing HFCS as "natural" under FDA policy—advice that is germane to issues concerning marketing and advertising HFCS as natural and whether such claims could be false or misleading. Accordingly, the similarities of the legal and factual issues of Patton Boggs' prior representation of Ingredion put Patton Boggs, now SPB, in a position where confidential information material to its current representation of the Sugar Plaintiffs was likely imparted to counsel. Moreover, the fact that former Patton Boggs attorneys Smitha Stansbury and Paul Rubin are no longer at SPB does not change the outcome, particularly since Ms. Stansbury left SPB *after* the merger.

Ingredion has established that there is a "substantial relationship" between the prior and current representations, and the attorneys at Patton Boggs, now SPB, are presumed to possess confidential information. SPB is thus subject to automatic disqualification from this action.

3. SPB's Evidence Does Not Overcome the Presumption

SPB provides declarations from attorneys [who] have worked on the instant lawsuit on behalf of the Sugar Plaintiffs. These attorneys declare that they have never received any information from any lawyer who was with Patton Boggs about either Ingredion or Tate & Lyle, and they have not performed work on any matter for Tate & Lyle after the merger. SPB's counsel declares that the only lawyers who remain at SPB who have worked on Ingredion matters after 2010 are Stuart Pape, Carey Nuttall, and Ann Spiggle. These lawyers declare that they have never provided any information to any lawyer who was at Squire Sanders about Ingredion, and after the firms merged, they did not work on any matter for the Sugar Plaintiffs.

Shortly after the merger in July 2014, Stuart Pape—the Patton Boggs attorney who signed the engagement letters for both Ingredion and Tate & Lyle—consulted with the Sugar Plaintiffs' expert witness, David Kessler, and the former Squire Sanders attorney, John Burlingame, who is co-lead attorney for the Sugar Plaintiffs in this action. This consultation occurred prior to any formal ethical walls being in place. There is a real risk that confidential information was in fact compromised.

In any event, whether the attorneys actually possessed or conveyed confidential information is not the test. Rather, because Ingredion has met its burden showing that a "substantial relationship" exists between the two representations, SPB is *conclusively presumed* to possess confidential information material to the present action. *See Jessen,* 111 Cal. App. 4th at 709 (emphasis in original). The "substantial relationship" test ensures that clients are not forced to reveal the confidences the rule is intended to protect. *Trone*, 621 F.2d at 999 ("It is the possibility of the breach of confidence, not the fact of the breach, that triggers disqualification").

The Court finds that SPB is subject to automatic disqualification because it previously represented Ingredion in matters substantially related to the present action, and SPB is thus presumed to possess client confidences revealed in the prior representations. Evidence showing that the Patton Boggs attorney who signed the engagement letters for Ingredion and Tate & Lyle actually consulted with Sugar Plaintiffs' counsel and expert witness following the merger reinforces the Court's finding.

D. *Other Alternatives to Disqualification*

A disqualification motion may involve considerations such as a client's right to chosen counsel and the possibility that tactical abuse underlies the disqualification motions. The Court balances the need to maintain ethical standards of professional responsibility, preservation of public trust in the scrupulous administration of justice, and the integrity of the bar against a client's right to chosen counsel, and the burden on the client if its counsel were disqualified.

SPB and Plaintiff Sugar Association contend that Ingredion and Tate & Lyle filed their Motions to obtain an improper tactical advantage in this litigation. The merger was highly publicized, and counsel for Sugar Plaintiffs, Mr. Burlingame, opines that the Motions have been filed by Defendants to "gain a tactical advantage both by delaying this [a]ction and by removing The Sugar Association's chosen and experienced counsel." At various depositions, Defendants' counsel never raised the prospect that the merger would create any conflict. Similarly, on June 2, 2014, SPB filed and served a notice, reflecting the firm's name change, and no one called the legacy Squire Sanders lawyers to raise any issue upon the filing. It was not until July 23, 2014 that Tate & Lyle's counsel first raised the conflict.

The Court does not conclude from the evidence provided that the Motions were brought for tactical reasons. The Motions were filed days after Tate & Lyle's counsel met and conferred with SPB's counsel and after it became clear that Tate & Lyle would not consent to the existing conflict. SPB cannot minimize its breach of ethical duties owed to its clients by placing the burden on them to identify and raise the conflicts sooner.

In UMG Recordings v. MySpace, [526 F. Supp. 2d 1046 (C.D. Cal. 2007),] the district court fashioned an alternative remedy to disqualification.... Unlike in *UMG Recordings*, ... SPB's representation of Ingredion regarding the characterization of HFCS as "natural" is an issue that goes to the heart of this lawsuit.

... Also unlike in *UMG Recordings*, where the law firm implemented an ethical wall some seven months *before* the events that led plaintiff to complain of the conflict, here, SPB implemented a formal ethical wall *after* the motions to disqualify were filed, and *after* counsel for the Sugar Plaintiffs met with Mr. Pape, the attorney who engaged both Tate & Lyle and Ingredion.

Additionally, in *UMG Recordings*, the law firm made "crystal clear" that it would not agree to represent the plaintiff UMG unless it agreed to waive any conflict that would prevent the law firm from representing an adverse party in cases concerning infringement of intellectual property rights on the internet. Plaintiff UMG signed the waiver that put it on notice that its law firm might represent a specific party (like the defendant), even if UMG were still an active client of the law firm. Here, the advanced waivers contained in Patton Boggs' Standard Terms of Engagement is a generalized advanced waiver with no specificity and could not have put Ingredion or Tate & Lyle on notice of the conflicts it was agreeing to waive.

The Sugar Plaintiffs have a right to their counsel of choice, and declare that they have relied on SPB as their trusted counsel, who have become "case experts" on "extraordinarily complex issues" central to this litigation. Indeed, disqualification at this late stage would undoubtedly impose hardship on Plaintiffs. The parties have

engaged in extensive discovery and motion practice, and Plaintiffs have incurred over $12 million in fees from Squire Sanders/SPB in this matter, reflecting over 20,000 hours of professional time, demonstrating the depth of the firm's involvement. The Sugar Plaintiffs contend that no replacement firm could master these issues without near-identical effort.

Having considered the competing interests of Plaintiffs' right to chosen counsel and the prejudice they would face if SPB were disqualified against the paramount concern of preserving public trust in the scrupulous administration of justice and the integrity of the bar, the Court finds that no alternative short of disqualification will suffice. While the Court is mindful that this outcome imposes hardship on the Sugar Plaintiffs, "the important right to counsel of one's choice must yield to ethical considerations that affect the fundamental principles of our judicial process."

V. CONCLUSION

The Court hereby GRANTS Tate & Lyle's and Ingredion's Motion to Disqualify Squire Patton Boggs LLP.

Post-Case Follow-Up

The situation presented in *Western Sugar Coop. v. Archer-Daniels-Midland Co.* is certainly not unique. Law firms continue to consider ways to increase market share for the delivery of legal services, for example, through law firm mergers and acquisitions. *Western Sugar* highlights the costly risks involved for clients and lawyers involved in a merger or acquisition where a conflict of interest was not identified. Law firms must remain mindful of how these mergers and acquisitions occur and how they are carried out in order to limit to the greatest extent the possibility of conflicts of interest.

Western Sugar Coop. v. Archer-Daniels-Midland Co.: Real Life Applications

1. Sue Ortiz was terminated by Zena Liu, her employer. Ortiz alleges her termination was in retaliation for filing a workers' compensation action. Ortiz hired attorney Nakisha Williams, who filed an action against Liu seeking damages for Ortiz's wrongful termination. In response, Liu's attorney filed a motion to disqualify both Williams and her law firm because Williams had served as Liu's in-house counsel for 14 years. Liu's counsel alleges that during Williams's 14 years of employment with Liu, Williams had obtained confidential information about Liu's company and that Williams was now directly involved in similar actions. Should Williams be disqualified?

2. Ms. Rodriguez contacted the Justice Project ("JP") seeking legal assistance in her dispute with Mr. Petrof and various collateral matters related to her rental property. Upon visiting JP, Rodriguez spoke to paralegal Keyda Montalban. In

her initial conversation, Rodriguez gave Montalban basic information pertaining to her legal problems concerning accessibility to Rodriguez's apartment. Rodriguez also conveyed relevant financial and background information to determine her eligibility for legal assistance. While employed at JP, Attorney Phillips was responsible for reviewing Montalban's intake file, but the parties dispute the extent of that review function.

With Rodriguez's consent, JP subsequently referred her case to the Legal Assistance Corporation of Central (LACC) for legal assistance, which filed an action against Petrof eight weeks later. Petrof hired the law firm of Kemp and Kemp as defense counsel and it assigned the case to a newly hired lawyer, Attorney Phillips.

Rodriguez filed a motion to disqualify Phillips as the defendant's counsel on conflict of interest grounds because Phillips worked at JP, which had advised Rodriguez about her dispute with Petrof. The judge asks you to draft a memorandum discussing how you would rule on the case. Should Phillips be disqualified? Should the entire firm of Kemp and Kemp be disqualified?

D. IMPUTATION OF CLIENT CONFLICTS

Rule 1.10(a) recognizes a longstanding rule that when one lawyer in a firm is prohibited from representing a client because of a conflict of interest under Rules 1.7 and 1.9, then all other firm members are generally prohibited from undertaking the representation. In short, the individual lawyer's conflict is imputed to each lawyer associated with the "conflicted lawyer's" firm. The rationale for the imputation or vicarious disqualification rule is based on the two fundamental concepts that lawyers owe clients loyalty and that lawyers must protect clients' information.

These principles become at risk when lawyers practice in law firms or any other association where they presumably have access to sensitive client information and files. Firm lawyers also share mutual financial interests, which creates a heightened risk that any confidential information that a firm or firm member has may be accessible to others in the firm and used to a client's disadvantage. Consequently, if one lawyer is disqualified because of a conflict of interest due to his having confidential information, then all firm members must be vicariously disqualified to safeguard the confidential information from misuse. The **imputation doctrine** has generated much debate, with some arguing that it is unfair to think that a firm lawyer with a conflict of interest would not protect client confidences from others in the firm who might use it to the client's disadvantage if there were no imputation rule.

The imputation rule does not apply to "personal" conflict situations where a lawyer's duty of loyalty or protection of client confidential information is not at risk.[41] For example, a lawyer's firmly held political or religious convictions should not generally be imputed to others in the firm. Thus, lawyers in a firm could

---

41. Model Rule 1.10(a)(1) & cmt. 3.

represent an abortion clinic even though a leading partner in the firm is a "right to life" advocate and refuses to assist in the representation of the clinic. However, if the "right to life" partner's interest would materially limit the representation by others in the firm, then that partner's interest would be imputed to them.[42]

The question sometimes arises as to who is a firm member for purposes of the imputation rule. Rule 1.0(c) defines a firm to be "a lawyer or lawyers in a law partnership, professional corporation, sole proprietorship, or other association, authorized to practice law; or lawyers in a legal services organization or the legal department of a corporation or other organization." It does not include lawyers who are acting as co-counsel in a case but who are not in the same firm.[43] In general, a conflict may be imputed to the entire firm from an individual partner, associate, or lawyer serving as "of counsel," and occasionally others, for example, a temporary lawyer,[44] paralegal,[45] or summer intern. The key concern in all of these situations is the risk that a lawyer may have acquired client confidential information and is now in a position to misuse it.

In general, the imputation rule does not apply to office sharing arrangements, but it could. Whether conflicts are imputed among lawyers who share office space depends on the facts and the degree of risk that client confidential information may be improperly shared by them. Important questions to consider in investigating an office sharing arrangement include the following: Are client files and confidential information accessible by others in the office? Do the lawyers sharing space have a protocol in place to protect against inadvertent sharing of client confidences? Do they market themselves as a group and resemble a law firm, thus warranting similar treatment and the application of the imputation rule?[46] The more an office sharing arrangement resembles a classic law firm, the greater the risk of the misuse of client confidences and the more likely the court will impute conflicts to others in the office.

Sometimes law firms are affiliated with other firms even in different jurisdictions, often for cross-referrals of work and other marketing purposes. Firms

---

42. Model Rule 1.10 cmt. 3. Also, Rule 1.8(j)'s prohibition on a lawyer having sexual relations with a client after the commencement of the lawyer-client relationship is not a conflict that is imputed to other firm members. *See* Model Rule 1.8(k).

43. ABA/BNA MAN. §51:2025.

44. ABA Formal Op. 88-356 (1988) considered whether temporary lawyers are "associated" with a firm for purposes of imputing conflicts of interest. "Ultimately, whether a temporary lawyer is treated as being 'associated with the firm' while working on a matter for the firm depends on whether the nature of the relationship is such that the temporary lawyer has access to information relating to the representation of firm clients other than the client on whose matters the lawyer is working and the consequent risk of improper disclosure or misuse of information relating to representation of other clients of the firm."

45. *See, e.g.*, Hodge v. URFA-Sexton, LP, 758 S.E.2d 314 (Ga. 2014). In *Hodge*, the appellant had retained an attorney in a law firm to pursue claims associated with the death of the appellant's sister. A paralegal at the law firm knew the appellant for approximately ten years. Subsequently, the paralegal went to work for the firm that represented appellees. Appellant filed a motion to disqualify appellees' law firm because of the migrating paralegal. The court held that a non-lawyer's conflict of interest can be remedied as in this case by implementing proper screening measures so as to avoid disqualification of an entire law firm.

46. *See* Restatement §123 cmt. e. *See also* Terminology, ANNOTATED MODEL RULES OF PROF'L CONDUCT §1.0 cmt. 2 (acknowledging that whether two or more lawyers constitute a firm depends on the facts); Imputation of Conflicts of Interest: General Rule, ANNOTATED MODEL RULES OF PROF'L CONDUCT §1.10 (citing Monroe v. City of Topeka, 988 P.2d 228 (Kan. 1999), and noting "indicia of lawyers presenting themselves to public as a firm for purposes of imputed disqualification include sharing office space, telephone, facsimile number, and mailing address").

claiming to be affiliated are generally treated as one firm for purposes of conflict of interest analysis and imputation.[47]

Imputation may apply to legal aid societies, depending on the facts, namely whether there is physical or organizational separation of the attorneys.[48] In general, if multiple clients seek representation from a nonprofit legal services agency and their interests conflict, a private lawyer or a lawyer from an autonomous agency must provide the representation.[49] Authority is split concerning the imputation of conflicts of interest in public defender's offices and legal aid offices. Some courts will not automatically disqualify an entire public defender's office based on the disqualification of a single attorney. These courts contend the financial incentives in the organization are absent for lawyers to use confidential information to the disadvantage of another client or to lessen advocacy provided for a client.[50] There is also the concern that automatic disqualification would diminish the pool of defenders.[51] But other courts find a public defender's office is like all other law firms and must be treated as such.[52]

Some jurisdictions had adopted **screening** as an exception to the imputation rule in recognition of the increased mobility of lawyers changing firms. In 2009, the ABA adopted Rule 1.10(a)(2) that similarly permits screening as an exception to the imputation of conflicts under Rules 1.7 and 1.9 in the private law firm market (the ABA already permitted screening in the government sector, as is discussed later in Section E of this chapter). Rule 1.10's screening applies only to lawyers moving between private law firms. It is important when law firms hire lawyers from other firms, called lateral hires, that the hiring firm have a reliable conflicts of interest check system in place to identify potential conflicts of interest. The following examples illustrate how screening under Rule 1.10 applies.

The XYZ law firm laterally hires lawyer A from the Peterson firm, where he and several Peterson colleagues represent client #1. Assume lawyer B is already at the XYZ firm and represents a longtime XYZ client, client #2, who is suing client #1. Lawyer A can make the lateral move or switch sides and move to the XYZ firm, but he will need to be "screened." Lawyer A is presumed to possess confidential information pertaining to client #1's lawsuit with XYZ's client #2 and is thus disqualified under Rule 1.9 (former-client conflict of interest rule) from participating in the suit against his former client #1. Lawyer A's disqualification will be imputed to everyone in the XYZ firm unless that firm institutes a timely screen to ensure that the migrating lawyer A cannot share any of his former client #1 confidences with his new XYZ firm.

It is worth noting several variations of the above migrating lawyer example to better understand the scope of the imputation rule and how it may be applied in other scenarios, appreciating that courts may differ on the application of the imputation rule.

---

47. *See* ABA/BNA Practice Guide 51-2022. *See also* ABA Formal Op. 94-388 (1994) ("As the two firms become more inextricably linked, the need to consider the conflict potential becomes more pronounced." "[W]here two law firms have a relationship in which they have shared profits, it is highly unlikely one could represent a client whose interests are adverse to clients of the other firm without following the procedure proscribed by 1.7(b). . . .").
48. Restatement §123 cmt. d(v).
49. *Id.*
50. ABA/BNA Practice Guide 51-2024.
51. *See* People v. Shari, 204 P.3d 453 (Colo. 2009).
52. *See* Scott v. State, 991 So. 2d 971 (Fla. Dist. Ct. App. 2008); Restatement §123 cmt. d(iv).

I

First, in the original scenario, the Peterson law firm can continue representing client #1 after lawyer A leaves Peterson for XYZ as lawyer A's departure for XYZ does not disqualify Peterson with regard to client #1. (See *Goldberg v. Warner/Chappell Music, Inc., infra.*)

II

Let us vary the original scenario as follows. Suppose that CW, a large law firm based in New York City, is representing client #3 in proceedings against client #1 and retains XYZ's help as local counsel in matters relating to the case. If XYZ is conflicted out (i.e., disqualified) because of its lawyer A's former involvement with client #1, XYZ's conflict of interest is generally not imputed up to CW unless lawyer A actually shared client #1 confidential information with someone at CW. Thus, CW could continue representing client #3 against client #1 provided the CW and XYZ firms are not deemed to be affiliated with each other. In deciding whether firms are affiliated or not, ABA Formal Opinion 94-388 (Dec. 5, 1994) indicated that important considerations including whether the law firms' relationship is "close and regular, continuing and semi-permanent" would be relevant to addressing the issue. However, here it appears that CW retained XYZ as local counsel to handle routine matters, such as serving papers, and would not be affiliated.

III

What if lawyer A in the original scenario had only attended one or two meetings with client #1 as a junior associate and had otherwise not participated in the representation of client #1? The general presumption is that lawyer A acquired confidential information pertaining to client #1 while he worked at Peterson, but he will be allowed to rebut this presumption by showing that he did not in fact acquire any such confidential information. (Silver Chrysler Plymouth, Inc. v. Chrysler Motors Corp., 518 F.2d 751 (2d Cir. 1975); Adams v. Aerojet-General Corp., 104 Cal. Rptr. 2d 116 (Ct. App. 2001).)

Screening under Rule 1.10 does not apply where lawyers A and B already both work in the XYZ law firm and lawyer A wishes to represent a new client, client #3, whose interest conflicts with the interest of a current XYZ firm client represented by lawyer B. Screening lawyer A from lawyer B to allow lawyer A to represent the new client is not permitted here since both lawyers, A and B, already work in the XYZ firm; there is no migrating lawyer in this scenario so screening will not work to allow lawyer A to represent the new client. It is possible, although unlikely, that lawyer A could represent the new client who has a conflict of interest with lawyer B's current client if each affected client consents to the conflicted representation under Rule 1.7(b).[53]

---

53. The provisions of Rule 1.9(a) will apply instead if lawyer B's client becomes a former client of XYZ at some point. Lawyer A thus will not be allowed to represent his new client in the same or a substantially related matter in which his client's interests are materially adverse to the interests of lawyer B's former client unless lawyer B's former client gives written informed consent.

Rule 1.0(k) defines a screen as a complete "isolation of a lawyer from any participation in a matter . . ." in a timely manner "to protect information that the isolated lawyer is obligated to protect under these Rules or by law." The failure to have a timely screen in place, ideally before the lawyer joins his new firm, often results in the disqualification of the migrating lawyer's new firm. An effective screen must be opaque. Ideally, this usually means that the new or migrating lawyer who is presumed to have confidential information that might harm his old firm's former client is physically separated from his new firm's colleagues handling the matter in conflict with his or his old firm's client. The new firm should clearly communicate to its lawyers not to communicate with the migrating lawyer about the case, for example, by denying the lawyer access to email communications among the lawyers and anyone else involved in the case matter against the lawyer's former client. The migrating lawyer should not have any opportunity to share his old client's information with his new firm's lawyers opposing his old client. Remember, under Rule 1.9(c) the migrating lawyer should never use his former client's information to the client's disadvantage by sharing it with his new firm.

In addition, Rule 1.10(a)(2)(i) requires that the disqualified migrating lawyer be apportioned no fee from his new firm's case against his former client. Rule 1.10(a)(2)(ii) further requires that the migrating lawyer promptly provide written notice to any affected former client to enable that client to ascertain whether the lawyer is compliance with the rule, including a description of the screening procedures, a statement by the screened lawyer and the firm of its compliance with the screening rules, and an indication of the ability of the former client to seek review of the procedures. Finally, the firm must also agree to promptly respond to any written questions or concerns about the screening procedures and provide certifications of compliance with the rule at reasonable intervals upon the former client's written request.

Finally, Rule 1.10(d) makes clear that when a lawyer joins a private firm after representing the government, questions about imputation are governed not by Rule 1.10 but by Rule 1.11(b) and (c) (see Section E *infra*).

Case Preview

Goldberg v. Warner/Chappell Music, Inc.

Goldberg is a prominent case in which the court refused to find and impute a conflict of interest to other lawyers in the firm of Mitchell Silberg & Knupp LLP (MSK). It highlights the fact-intensive nature of conflict of interest analysis in disqualification cases and the importance of preserving client confidences as a predicate for granting (or not granting) disqualification.

In reading *Goldberg*, consider the following questions:

1. Did Goldberg have a valid reason for feeling that MSK betrayed its duty of loyalty to her?

2. Is there an appearance of impropriety problem in allowing the firm to represent Goldberg's former employer?
3. What are the benefits and risks of disqualifying lawyers on an "appearance of impropriety" basis?
4. Is the public and profession best served by such a broad and general standard?
5. Finally, would the result in this case be different if Salomon were still at the Mitchell firm? If he were still there, should Salomon's conflict be imputed to all MSK lawyers under Rule 1.10?

Goldberg v. Warner/Chappell Music, Inc.

125 Cal. App. 4th 752 (2005)

[Ilene Goldberg sued the respondents, Warner/Chappell Music, Inc. (Warner), her former employer, and her former supervisor, Edward Pierson, for wrongful termination. She claimed that she was terminated as retaliation for complaining about gender-based discrimination and] "blowing the whistle" on Pierson's illegal conduct, including practicing law without a license.

FACTUAL AND PROCEDURAL BACKGROUND

. . .

Motion to Disqualify

Goldberg formally moved to disqualify [Mitchell Silberberg & Knupp LLP] (MS&K) on December 10, 2003. In her moving papers, she presented evidence that in 1997, while still employed at Warner, she was given a written employment agreement to sign. She asked Salomon, then a partner with MS&K, to advise her with respect to the agreement. She met with Salomon for an hour and a half on May 9, 1997, to go over the terms of the agreement. She purportedly "disclosed confidential information to him including the nature and term of [her] employment agreement, [her] compensation and benefits, disability, termination by [Warner], [her] ability to retain, disclose, and use confidential/privileged information concerning [her] employment relationship with [Warner], scripts and other literary works created by [her], the effect of a change in control of [Warner], expiration of the employment agreement, and [Warner's] obligations under state and federal law." She also had "other conversations and correspondence with [Salomon] relating to his advice about the terms and conditions of [her] employment agreement." On July 29, 1997, she sent him a letter and draft of a proposed employment agreement, and promised to send the final agreement "for [his] files." She asked him to send her a bill for his advice, but he refused to do so.

Subsequently, Goldberg retained MS&K to work on various matters for Warner, and she "did not have an objection to [MS&K's] representation of [Warner] in matters that did not conflict with [MS&K's] prior representation of [her]."

Opposition

Respondents presented evidence in their opposition that in April 1997, one month prior to Goldberg's purported consultation with Salomon, MS&K began legal work on a copyright matter for Warner. A formal retention letter between MS&K and Warner was signed on May 2, 1997.

The executive director of MS&K stated in a declaration that there was no record in any of MS&K's files of Goldberg ever having been a client of the firm, and that the policy of the firm was to execute a formal, written engagement letter before taking on legal representation.

. . .

Salomon stated in a declaration that he practiced law at MS&K from October 1987 through October 2000, when he moved to another firm. He denied that he had been retained by Goldberg to represent her in her contract negotiations with Warner. Instead, Goldberg "told [Salomon] she was going to represent herself in negotiations over the contract, but asked if [Salomon] would talk to her about these agreements generally to get a sense of how [Warner] lawyers dealt with the contract's various provisions." He told Goldberg he "would be glad to talk to her about what she could expect in the course of her negotiations." They primarily discussed "what she might expect with respect to the boilerplate issues." Salomon "never discussed with any other lawyer at [MS&K] what was said in [his] conversation with Ms. Goldberg."

. . .

Trial Court's Ruling

The court denied the motion to disqualify. At the hearing, the court stated that the only potential basis for disqualification was Goldberg's contact with Salomon, not her personal and professional relationships with other MS&K attorneys. The court concluded that there was an attorney-client relationship between Goldberg and Salomon even though Salomon appeared to be helping her "as a friend." The court agreed that if Salomon were still with MS&K, the firm would be disqualified. However, because Salomon had left the firm, there was no need for vicarious disqualification.

In its order, the court specifically found: "The evidence is undisputed that [MS&K] and Salomon never opened a file for Ms. Goldberg. They never billed her. There are no notes or records in their files about the meeting and no documents were prepared. No telephone calls were made. It was simply a meeting late one afternoon where Ms. Goldberg and Mr. Salomon sat down and discussed the meaning of the employment contract she was being offered and what provisions she might request. . . . There is no evidence that Mr. Salomon talked to anyone about this matter when he was with [MS&K]. And more importantly, he had left the firm approximately three years before this matter began. There is no fear of him talking about the case in the lunch room, or having his files seen by other members of the firm, as he is no longer there."

Goldberg filed a petition for writ of mandate for review of the order. By order dated March 24, 2004, the petition was denied, with one dissent. Goldberg noticed an appeal. . . .

DISCUSSION

. . . (2) Rule 3-310(E) of the [California] Rules of Professional Conduct provides that an attorney "shall not, without the informed written consent of the client or former client, accept employment adverse to the client, or former client where, by reason of the representation of the client or former client, the member has obtained confidential information material to the employment." There is no question that an attorney can and should be disqualified for representing a party adverse to a former client where the attorney possesses confidential information that could be helpful to the new client and hurtful to the old. . . .

(3) The courts do not generally inquire into whether the attorney actually possesses confidential information. Instead, the substantial relationship test is applied. "'*When a substantial relationship has been shown to exist between the former representation and the current representation*, and when it appears by virtue of the nature of the former representation or the relationship of the attorney to his former client confidential information material to the current dispute would normally have been imparted to the attorney or to subordinates for whose legal work he was responsible, *the attorney's knowledge of confidential information is presumed*.' "(Rosenfeld Construction Co. v. Superior Court (1991) 235 Cal. App. 3d 566, 574 [286 Cal. Rptr. 609], italics added)

(4) In addition, "[i]t is now firmly established that where the attorney is disqualified from representation due to an ethical conflict, the disqualification extends to the entire firm." (Adams v. Aerojet-General Corp., *supra,* 86 Cal. App. 4th at p. 1333.) "[W]here an attorney is disqualified because he formerly represented and therefore possesses [either actually or presumptively] confidential information regarding the adverse party in the current litigation, vicarious disqualification of the entire firm is compelled as a matter of law. . . .

(5) There is, however, a recognized "limited exception to this conclusive presumption in the rare instance where the lawyer can show that there was no *opportunity* for confidential information to be divulged."

. . .

The court explained why it distinguished the situation before it from the situation where the attorney who sought to undertake adverse representation was still working with the attorneys who had acquired the former client's confidential information: "'No amount of assurances or screening procedures, no "cone of silence," could ever convince the opposing party that the confidences would not be used to its disadvantage. . . . No one could have confidence in the integrity of a legal process in which this is permitted to occur without the parties' consent.' Once an attorney departs the firm, however, a blanket rule to prevent future breaches of confidentiality is not necessary because the departed attorney no longer has presumptive access to the secrets possessed by the former firm. The court need no longer rely on the fiction of imputed knowledge to safeguard client confidentiality. Instead, the court may undertake a dispassionate assessment of whether and to what extent the attorney, during his tenure with the former firm, was reasonably likely to have obtained confidential information material to the current lawsuit."

The court [in *Adams v. Aerojet-General Corp.*] found further support for its decision in the realities of modern law firm practice: "Disqualification based on a conclusive presumption of imputed knowledge derived from a lawyer's past association with a law firm is out of touch with the present day practice of law. Gone are the days when attorneys (like star athletes) typically stay with one organization throughout their entire careers. . . . We have seen the dawn of the era of the 'mega-firm.' Large law firms (like banks) are becoming ever larger, opening branch offices nationwide or internationally, and merging with other large firms. Individual attorneys today can work for a law firm and not even know, let alone have contact with, members of the same firm working in a different department of the same firm across the hall or a different branch across the globe." [*Id.* at 1336.]

From this, the court concluded that "a rule which disqualifies an attorney based on imputed knowledge derived solely from his membership in the former firm and without inquiry into his actual exposure to the former client's secrets sweeps with too broad a brush, is inconsistent with the language and core purpose of rule 3-310(E), and unnecessarily restricts both the client's right to chosen counsel and the attorney's freedom of association. It also clashes with the principle that applying the remedy of disqualification '"when there is no realistic chance that confidences were disclosed [to counsel] would go far beyond the purpose" of the substantial relationship test.'"

We agree with the court in Adams v. Aerojet-General Corp., *supra,* 86 Cal. App. 4th 1324, that at some point, it ceases to make sense to apply a presumption of imputed knowledge as a lawyer moves from firm to firm. Salomon, while at MS&K, gave advice to Goldberg concerning the terms of her contract with Warner. We agree with the trial court that, despite the informality, an attorney-client relationship existed between them. Moreover, if Salomon were still practicing at MS&K, MS&K would likely have to be disqualified from the current litigation because there would be no practical way of ensuring that, despite his best intentions, Salomon would not let slip some confidential information he may not even be aware that he possesses. But Salomon is no longer with MS&K. We need not be concerned that he will inadvertently pass on confidential information to his colleagues in the future because he is no longer there "in the lunch room" as the trial court said. It was appropriate under the circumstances for the trial court to make an assessment of whether Salomon actually passed on confidential information. Since the court found he had not, there was no basis for disqualification.

. . .

(6) If an attorney worked on a matter "substantially related" to the matter in which he or she seeks to represent a party adverse to a former client, the presumption is conclusive that the *attorney* is possessed of confidential information that would impact the present matter. Where tainted attorneys and nontainted attorneys are working together at the same firm, there is not so much a conclusive presumption that confidential information has passed as a pragmatic recognition that the confidential information will work its way to the nontainted attorneys at some point. When, however, the relationship between the tainted attorneys and nontainted attorneys is in the past, there is no need to "rely on the fiction of imputed knowledge to safeguard client confidentiality" and opportunity exists for a "dispassionate

assessment" of whether confidential information was actually exchanged. This is precisely what the trial court did here.

(7) Our conclusion that the trial court analyzed the matter correctly is also in line with the ABA Model Rules of Professional Conduct, which California courts may consult when a matter is not addressed by the California Rules. . . . Model Rule 1.10(b) provides: "When a lawyer has terminated an association with a firm, the firm is not prohibited from thereafter representing a person with interests materially adverse to those of a client represented by the formerly associated lawyer and not currently represented by the firm, unless (1) the matter is the same or substantially related to that in which the formerly associated lawyer represented the client; and (2) any lawyer remaining in the firm has [protected] information . . . that is material to the matter." Courts from other jurisdictions have followed the ABA Model Rule in situations analogous to the present one: where an attorney who presumptively acquired confidential information from a former client leaves the firm, the firm is not automatically disqualified if it chooses to represent a party adverse to the former client. . . . This is further basis to uphold the trial court's determination.

. . .

The order is affirmed.

Post-Case Follow-Up

Goldberg highlights, in part, the risk and relative ease of establishing an attorney-client relationship. MSK and Salomon never opened a client file for Goldberg, made documents for her, telephoned her, created meeting notes for a file, and never billed her, although she requested a bill. "Despite the informality[,]" the appellate court nevertheless agreed with the trial court that an attorney-client relationship existed between Goldberg and Salomon. *Goldberg* is also well known for recognizing an important limitation on the imputation doctrine reflected in ABA Model Rule 1.10(b). It provides that once a tainted lawyer with a potential conflict of interest leaves the firm (Salomon in this case), the risk of his divulging confidential information to others remaining in the firm is reduced. In *Goldberg*, the concern that Salomon may accidently slip and divulge information no longer existed following his departure from the firm. Thus, absent Salomon actually sharing Goldberg's confidential information with another MSK lawyer who may then slip and divulge it to others, there is little need to vicariously disqualify the entire MSK firm.

Goldberg v. Warner/Chappell Music, Inc.: Real Life Applications

1. Plaintiffs, Celebrity Chefs, are suing Kmart for breach of contract, conversion, and trademark infringement. Alleging a conflict of interest, plaintiffs filed a motion to disqualify Kmart's counsel and his firm. The law firm representing Kmart, Seltzer Caplan, had previously represented the plaintiffs in two cases to recover

sponsorship and advertising fees. Plaintiffs allege that during the course of these two representations, Seltzer Caplan learned confidential information about their business and litigation strategies. They argue that because Seltzer Caplan possesses this knowledge, counsel and Seltzer Caplan as a whole must be disqualified.

However, Seltzer Caplan argue that not only is the current case not related to its prior representation of the plaintiffs, but also, the attorneys that worked on those cases did not disclose the confidential information to anyone else in the firm, and they are no longer with Seltzer Caplan. How should the motion be decided?

2. Former employees are suing the defendant, Boston Scientific, for unlawfully firing them when they reported fraudulent billing within the company. Attorney Hasan was employed as in-house counsel for the defendant corporation prior to the initiation of this suit. During her time as in-house counsel, her duties included investigating matters directly related to those at issue here. Two years after leaving the defendant-corporation, Hasan became associated with the plaintiff's law firm, Tank & Blank. Upon learning of her new employment, Boston Scientific moved to disqualify Hasan and to impute her conflict of interest under Rules 1.9 and 1.10 to her new firm, Tank & Blank.

   Tank & Blank argues that even though there was not a proper screen in place, Hassan was de facto screened because she was not in the office very often nor did she disclose any confidential information. Should Hasan be disqualified? Should Hasan's conflict of interest be imputed to Tank & Blank?

3. As an associate at his law firm, Attorney Johnson performed work for Thompson Property Corp., which was in active litigation with Korner Tech over several patents. The lawsuit was still pending between the parties when Johnson left his firm and began working at the ABC law firm, which represented Korner. Though Johnson worked in ABC's Chicago office and the lawyers representing Korner worked in ABC's Tampa office, the law firm nevertheless used a screening protocol to prevent Johnson from disclosing any information he might have about Thompson Corp. Johnson also sent a written notice to Thompson advising the company of his ABC employment and the screening measures taken by ABC. In response, Thompson filed a disqualification motion alleging that because Johnson had performed significant work on the case, screening could not be used to rebut the presumption that he had shared confidential information with the defendant's lawyers (i.e., his colleagues) working on this case or that he will do so in the future. Advise how the court would rule on Johnson's disqualification. Is it likely that the law firm will also be imputed?

E. CONFLICTS OF INTERESTS FOR CURRENT AND FORMER LAWYERS IN GOVERNMENT SERVICE

The conflicts rules governing lawyers who have left private practice to enter government service or have left government service for private practice diverge slightly from the rules governing all other lawyers because they serve some different purposes. Like the rules governing conflicts of interest for lawyers in private practice, protection of former clients' confidential information is paramount. Thus, under Rule 1.11, government lawyers and former government lawyers are subject to the prohibition in Rule 1.9(c) that they shall not reveal their former client's confidential information or use that information to the disadvantage of their former clients.

In the situation of former government lawyers, however, other policy considerations are present. First, government lawyers should not be able to take advantage of their status as government lawyers to improve their opportunities in private practice. At the same time, government agencies need to be able to recruit good lawyers, and overly strict rules would discourage lawyers from entering government service if they could not take advantage of that governmental experience to some degree when they move into private practice. Finally, the public benefits from having lawyers in private practice who served in the government and understand government practice and policy. In theory, these former government lawyers may encourage greater compliance with the law.

As a result, the conflicts rules governing former government lawyers are narrower in some respects and broader in others. Rule 1.11(a) is narrower than Rule 1.9 in that it only limits a former government lawyer from representing a private client "in connection with a matter in which the lawyer *participated personally and substantially*" as a government lawyer, unless the government agency gives informed consent in writing. Thus, a former prosecutor may not turn around and defend a client that he personally prosecuted, but he may defend a client who was prosecuted by the office that he worked in if he did not personally participate in the prosecution.

Further, Rule 1.11 contains a special imputation rule that permits nonconsensual screening: the conflict is not imputed to the firm if the "disqualified lawyer is timely screened" and "written notice is promptly given to the appropriate government agency." Thus, a former prosecutor can join a law firm and the firm can continue to defend clients who are being prosecuted by that office, even a client who its new lawyer personally prosecuted, provided that the former prosecutor is timely screened and the firm provides notice to the prosecutor's office. This imputation rule ensures that a private law firm will not be discouraged from hiring a former government lawyer.

Rule 1.11 is broader than Rule 1.9, however, in that the prohibition extends to *any* representation related to the lawyer's government work even if it is not adverse. Thus, a Securities and Exchange Commission lawyer who personally prosecuted a defendant for securities fraud cannot leave government service and represent plaintiffs in a civil suit against the same defendant. In that way, the former government lawyer is not able to take special advantage of his former role as a governmental lawyer to benefit other clients.

As for current government lawyers, under Rule 1.11(d)(1) they are subject to both Rules 1.7 and 1.9. Thus, consistent with Rule 1.9, a government lawyer may not represent the government adverse to a former client in a matter that is substantially related to the former representation unless the former client gives informed consent in writing. Rule 1.11(d)(2) also contains an additional limitation for government lawyers: they may not participate in any matter in which they personally and substantially participated while in private practice, *whether or not the current matter is adverse* to their former client, unless the government agency gives its informed consent in writing. Finally, a government lawyer's personal conflicts are not imputed to the government agency, but Rule 1.11 comment 2 suggests that it would be "prudent" to screen conflicted lawyers.

F. SPECIFIC CONFLICT RULES: JUDGES, ARBITRATORS, AND OTHERS

Rule 1.12 parallels Rule 1.11 and addresses potential conflicts of interest involving lawyers who are former judges, adjudicative officers, clerks, arbitrators, mediators, and other third-party neutrals. "Adjudicative officers" includes referees, masters, hearing officers, and other officials who play a role in deciding or resolving disputes between parties. Just like Rule 1.11, Rule 1.12 forbids such persons, without written informed consent from all parties, from representing anyone in connection with a matter in which they participated personally and substantially as a judge or other adjudicative officer or law clerk or as an arbitrator, mediator, or other third-party neutral. It also imputes the conflict to the lawyer's law firm, unless the lawyer is screened and apportioned no fee pertaining to the matter and proper written notice is given to the parties and the tribunal. The rule finds its basis in the duty of confidentiality and its keystone is therefore whether the lawyer participated "personally and substantially" in the related matter. A former judge who exercised administrative responsibility in a court does not prevent the former judge from acting as a lawyer in a matter where the judge had previously exercised remote administrative responsibility that did not affect the merits.

In James v. Miss. Bar, 962 So. 2d 528 (Miss. 2007), a former judge sought to represent a party in a divorce case related to a domestic abuse case over which she had previously presided. Similar to ABA Model Rule 1.12(a), Mississippi Rule of Professional Conduct 1.12(a) prohibited a lawyer from representing anyone in connection with a matter in which the lawyer participated personally and substantially as a judge. The court examined whether the former judge had "substantially participated" in the matter, reviewing her interaction with the case and the litigants in her capacity as judge. The court found that she had substantially participated in the domestic abuse case because she had read motions, conducted hearings, heard testimony, and entered orders. Furthermore, the court found that the divorce case in which she was currently involved was connected to the earlier domestic abuse. Although the two cases did not share the same docket numbers, both cases involved the same parties, the same issues, and the same concerns. As a result, the court held that the former judge was precluded from representing either party to the domestic abuse case in the subsequent divorce matter without informed consent in writing from all of the parties.

Chapter Summary

- A lawyer has a fiduciary relationship with a client and owes the client loyalty, competence, and confidentiality. These duties extend to some degree to former clients and prospective clients.
- A conflict of interest exists when there is a significant risk of a material limitation on the ability of the lawyer to exercise independent judgment on behalf of the client or preserve the client's confidential information. When confronted with a conflict of interest, the lawyer should decline or discontinue representation.
- A concurrent conflict of interest exists when the lawyer's independent professional judgment may be compromised because the lawyer represents multiple current clients with potentially differing interests. If the lawyer's independent judgment is compromised, the lawyer must withdraw from representation while preserving the client's confidential information.
- Some concurrent conflicts of interest are waivable when the lawyer reasonably believes that she can provide competent and diligent representation to each client. The lawyer must obtain each client's informed consent in writing, assuming the conflict is waivable, for example, not prohibited by law.
- When lawyers represent a current client against a former client there is a concern about protecting the former client's confidences. Absent both the current and former clients' consent, lawyers are barred from representing a client against a former client in a matter that is substantially related to the lawyer's work for the former client.
- If a lawyer undertakes to represent a client with interests adverse to a former client, without first obtaining the informed consent of both the former and current client, the lawyer risks disqualification if there is a showing of a "substantial relationship" between the subjects of the prior and current representation.
- In general, if a lawyer has a conflict of interest, the conflict will be imputed to all members of the firm. The conflict of interest of a lawyer who moves from one firm to a new firm will not be imputed to a new firm if the lawyer is timely screened from any involvement in the matter and notice is provided to the former firm.
- Where there is no concern about loyalty or protecting confidential information, a conflict of interest based on a lawyer's personal, political, or moral feelings will not be imputed to the entire firm unless the representation by others in the firm would be materially limited. Nor will a lawyer's violation of Rule 1.8(j) involving a sexual relationship with a client be imputed to others in a firm.
- The general rule of imputation also affects non-lawyers of law firms, i.e., paralegals, law clerks, secretaries, and the like.

Applying the Rules

1. Michael Newman retained Jim Jones of the Jones Firm to represent his interests in the formation of the N&F law partnership with John Ferraro, who was separately represented by Rafferty LLP. Attorneys at the Jones Firm drafted the partnership, financing, and security agreements, and other legal documents relating to the N&F partnership formation. Over the next nine years, Jim Jones and the Jones Firm represented both Michael Newman, his wife Lynn Newman, and Michael Newman's interest in the N&F partnership on a wide variety of legal, business, and personal matters.

   Michael and Ferraro decided to renegotiate their partnership. During this process, Michael passed away. Notwithstanding Michael and his wife's relationship with Jim Jones and his firm, Ferraro retained the Jones Firm to represent his interests in an anticipated dispute with the estate of Michael Newman shortly after Michael's death.

   The dispute concerned the partnership agreement that the Jones Firm drafted to protect Michael Newman's interests. It provided that upon dissolution of the partnership for any reason, including the death of Michael Newman, Ferraro was obligated to pay 40 percent of the law firm's gross revenues to Lynn Newman. Lynn Newman is upset about the Jones Firm representing Ferraro and consults you for legal advice. Discuss your advice for Lynn.

2. Natalie and David Parrott are brother and sister. David and Natalie were charged separately with several criminal violations concerning marijuana and weapons in their apartment.

   The state offered a joint plea deal to the Parrotts of ten years' imprisonment with the possibility of probation if they successfully completed a program of shock incarceration. In response, defense counsel wrote a joint letter, advising them both not to take the offer. Defense counsel also acknowledged that the state's case against Natalie was much weaker than its case against David, stating: "I really don't see how the Prosecutor thinks he has any case against Natalie for cultivation. Even the charge of possession against Natalie may be rather weak."

   After the initial plea deal was withdrawn, the prosecution offered Natalie a better deal if she would testify against her brother. The prosecution noted that this new plea deal created a conflict of interest concerning defense counsel's joint representation of David and Natalie. The state said it might move to disqualify defense counsel because "[y]ou would not be able to successfully represent Natalie's interest and her brother's." This plea deal involving Natalie's testimony was also rejected.

   After more negotiations, the prosecution offered 15 years contingent on both Natalie and David entering a plea of guilty but without requiring Natalie's testimony against her brother. The Parrotts' attorney was able to convince his clients to accept the plea deal. David and Natalie are now unhappy with the case outcome and seek your help as a local defense expert. They ask, "What can be done—if anything—to get the plea deal thrown out?" Natalie states, "Due to a conflict of interest, he didn't protect me!" Advise the Parrotts.

3. Company A had a meeting with a large law firm regarding a potential lawsuit against company B and requests information about the firm's services. Expecting to receive an engagement letter from the firm, company A was surprised when the firm decided to represent company B in a lawsuit against company A in a similar, but separate matter. The firm claims it screened the attorneys that met with company A, but company A still moved to disqualify the firm under Rule 1.18 for failing to maintain confidences and sharing privileged information received during their meeting. Company A has provided no concrete evidence on what information was shared and has not shown proof that the firm's representation of company B caused significant harm. Advise how the court should decide the disqualification motion. Does the fact that the firm screened the attorneys that attended the meeting with company A make a difference?

Professional Responsibility in Practice

1. Think of a conflict of interest matter (e.g., involving a politician, businessman, or public servant) that you have recently heard of or read about in the media. What issues did that conflict matter present? How, if at all, were the values of loyalty, independent judgment, and confidentiality involved in the matter? How was the conflict resolved (or not)?

2. Now, find a recent conflict of interest matter in the news that involves a lawyer. How were the lawyer's fiduciary values of loyalty, independent judgment, confidentiality, and competence placed in issue in the matter? Comparing the conflict of interest matters you considered in question 1 above with conflicts of interest problems involving lawyers, what similarities and dissimilarities, if any, do you find in how the conflicts were addressed and resolved? Would you have withdrawn from representation if you were in that lawyer's position? How would you feel if you were the client?

3. Imagine you own a law practice and a prospective client schedules an initial consultation with you regarding her recent termination from employment. What strategies and protocols might you implement in the initial interview and thereafter to uncover any potential conflicts of interest? What are some of the questions you might ask in the initial interview to identify potential conflicts of interest? Prepare a list of five questions to help you identify any potential conflicts of interest issues in handling the unjust dismissal claim.

4. Assume three clients asked you to jointly represent them in the unjust dismissal claim in question 3 above. How would this change your initial interview

discussion and questions concerning possible conflicts of interest? For example, would your explanation about the preservation of their confidences be any different than in question 3? What additional follow-up action might you institute to avoid any future conflicts of interest given your representation of multiple clients?

PART III

Lawyer as Advocate

7 Fairness in Adjudication

An attorney's obligation of loyalty to his client and obligation of candor to the tribunal may collide in the context of litigation. When they do, an attorney's obligations as an officer of the court[1] typically trump her obligations of zealous representation.[2] Lying to the court, assisting or permitting a client or witness to commit perjury, or counseling a client to destroy documents after they have been subpoenaed are perhaps the most obvious examples of behavior that offends a lawyer's obligation to preserve the integrity of judicial proceedings. But there are many others.

A. MERITORIOUS CLAIMS AND EXPEDITING LITIGATION

Model Rule 3.1 prohibits filing claims, defending lawsuits, or advancing issues within litigation that are "frivolous." Whether a claim is **frivolous** is assessed from an objective standard of what a reasonable attorney would have known in the actor's situation, rather than a subjective standard of malice or motive to harass.

A lawyer is permitted to file a civil complaint or answer with a lesser factual foundation than subsequent pleadings, if she believes in good faith that facts will be developed during litigation to support her initial claim or defense. Comment (2) to Rule 3.1 states that "[t]he filing of an action or defense or similar action taken for a client is not frivolous merely because the facts have

Key Concepts

- The attorney's obligation to be honest with the court
- The attorney's responsibility to prevent and remedy perjury
- Why the concealment or destruction of evidence is unlawful
- An attorney's duty to act fairly in dealing with opposing counsel

1. Preamble to the Model Rules of Professional Conduct, [1].
2. As will be discussed *infra*, with respect to frivolous factual and legal contentions, Rule 3.1 partially exempts criminal defense lawyers by providing that "[a] lawyer for the defendant in a criminal proceeding . . . may nevertheless so defend the proceeding as to require that every element of the case be established."

not first been fully substantiated or because the lawyer expects to develop vital evidence only by discovery."

Courts tend to be in a better position than bar disciplinary committees to assess the merits of factual claims. Understanding a legal and factual record well enough to assess whether a complaint, answer, motion, or discovery response is well grounded would impose tremendous information costs on bar counsel. Moreover, litigants have little to gain from referring these cases to bar disciplinary agencies, because even if fines are imposed they will not end up compensating complainants. For both of these reasons Rule 3.1 is infrequently invoked to discipline lawyers. But courts have their own tools to police frivolous pleadings. Rule 11(c) of the Federal Rules of Civil Procedure and its analogue in many states allows a court to sanction a party who signs a written complaint, motion, or other pleading that is not supported by existing law or a good faith argument for an extension of the law, or which is based on factual contentions that have no evidentiary support or are unlikely to derive evidentiary support after reasonable inquiry.[3] Like Rule 3.1, Rule 11 determines the issue of frivolousness by assessing whether an attorney conducted an *objectively reasonable* investigation into the factual and legal predicate for a filing.[4] But unlike Rule 3.1, Rule 11 requires that any factual contentions in a pleading that have not been substantiated be specifically identified as being filed "on information or belief." In order to invoke the sanctions machinery of Rule 11, opposing counsel must serve a separate motion on the offending party requesting sanctions but not file this motion with the court. The attorney accused of misconduct then has a 21-day "safe harbor" to withdraw or correct the challenged pleading before the court is authorized to hold a sanctions hearing.[5]

Case Preview

In re Olsen

The following case excerpt stems from a federal employment claim Olsen filed on behalf of his client, Melissa Mellott, against her former employer, MSN Communications. Olsen sought back pay, equal pay, front pay, and benefits for his client. Maintaining that the suit was frivolous, MSN presented

3. Federal Rule of Civil Procedure 11(b) provides:

> By presenting to the court a pleading, written motion, or other paper—whether by signing, filing, submitting, or later advocating it—an attorney or unrepresented party certifies that to the best of the person's knowledge, information, and belief, formed after an inquiry reasonable under the circumstances:
>
> (1) it is not being presented for any improper purpose, such as to harass, cause unnecessary delay, or needlessly increase the cost of litigation;
>
> (2) the claims, defenses, and other legal contentions are warranted by existing law or by a nonfrivolous argument for extending, modifying, or reversing existing law or for establishing new law;
>
> (3) the factual contentions have evidentiary support or, if specifically so identified, will likely have evidentiary support after a reasonable opportunity for further investigation or discovery; and
>
> (4) the denials of factual contentions are warranted on the evidence or, if specifically so identified, are reasonably based on belief or a lack of information.

4. Business Guides v. Chromatic Communications, 498 U.S. 533, 541 (1991).

5. Fed. R. Civ. P. 11(c)(2); Star Mark Management, Inc. v. Koon Chun Hing Kee Soy & Sauce Factory, Ltd., 682 F.3d 170, 175 (2d Cir. 2012).

documentary evidence (including W-2s) showing that Mellott had been employed for substantial compensation since her termination, that she was fraudulently using someone else's social security number to hide income while collecting unemployment, and that she lied to the district court when she asserted that she had moved to Germany. Olsen filed a memorandum opposing MSN's motion to dismiss the lawsuit as being frivolous, without conducting his own investigation. The Office of Attorney Regulation subsequently filed a suit against Olsen alleging he violated several of Colorado's Rules of Professional Conduct.

As you read *Olsen*, ask yourself the following questions:

1. Was Olsen's professional misstep the filing of the complaint, or the filing of the opposition to the motion to dismiss?
2. Was Olsen guilty of lying in this pleading, or of deliberate indifference to the truth?
3. How could Olsen have prepared his case differently to avoid this sanction?

In re Olsen

326 P.3d 1004 (Colo. 2004)

. . .

II

We affirm the Hearing Board's conclusions that Olsen violated Rules of Professional Conduct 3.1 and 8.4(d), but we reverse its imposition of a six-month suspension with the requirement of reinstatement and instead order that Olsen be, and hereby is, publicly censured for his misconduct. . . .

B. Hearing Board Findings on Rule Violations

. . . [T]he Board concluded that Olsen violated two rules of Professional Conduct. It concluded that he violated Rule 3.1 by advancing three frivolous arguments on behalf of his client in the underlying federal litigation: (i) Mellott's claim for lost wages; (ii) Mellott's theories for why she used multiple SSNs; and (iii) that Mellott had moved to Europe and was unavailable to appear in person for several hearings before the federal magistrate and district court judges. The Board also concluded that Olsen violated Rule 8.4(d) by engaging in protracted and unnecessary litigation that wasted considerable judicial resources and prejudiced the administration of justice. We agree with the Board's conclusions that Olsen violated Rules 3.1 and 8.4(d).

Rule 3.1 states, in pertinent part: "A lawyer shall not bring or defend a proceeding, or assert or controvert an issue therein, unless there is a basis in law and fact for doing so that is not frivolous, which includes a good faith argument for an extension, modification or reversal of existing law." We interpret Rule 3.1 broadly to include all

proceedings in which factual and legal contentions are made, including post-trial and disciplinary proceedings. An objective standard is used to determine whether an attorney's claim is frivolous. See Colo. RPC Preamble cmt. 20 ("[The] Rules . . . establish standards of conduct by lawyers . . . a lawyer's violation of a Rule may be evidence of [a] breach of the applicable standard of conduct."). While an attorney is permitted to rely on factual accounts given by a client, it may not be objectively reasonable to continue to rely exclusively on a client's statement of facts when the attorney is presented with credible contradictory evidence. See Colo. RPC 3.1 cmt. 2 ("What is required of lawyers . . . is that they inform themselves about the facts of their clients' cases . . . and determine that they can make good faith arguments in support of their clients' positions.").

The Board found that Olsen advanced his client's frivolous arguments first in the underlying federal lawsuit, and again in the post-trial proceedings concerning attorney fees and other sanctions. The Board reasoned that "it should have been obvious to [Olsen] that [his client's] shifting narratives were completely contradicted by credible evidence" and also that there was a "dearth of credible evidence indicating that [Olsen] conducted a reasonable investigation of his client's implausible factual assertions."

We agree that Olsen had an ongoing professional duty to independently assess the factual and legal bases for Mellott's claims. At the same time, we recognize that an attorney's role is to advocate for the client. The dissenting Hearing Board member correctly observes that an attorney has a duty of loyalty to the client, along with a duty of candor to the court, and attorneys should generally resolve doubts about the factual underpinnings of a claim in favor of their clients.

Nevertheless, Rule 8.4(d) states, in pertinent part: "It is professional misconduct for a lawyer to . . . engage in conduct that is prejudicial to the administration of justice." The record before us contains ample evidence that Olsen's conduct prejudiced the administration of justice in the underlying federal lawsuit. His unprofessional demeanor in dealing with opposing counsel, Judge Brimmer, and Magistrate Judge Watanabe exceeded the bounds of acceptable litigation strategy and evidenced a disregard for his professional responsibility to the tribunals. As a result of Olsen's pursuit of his client's frivolous arguments, Judge Brimmer and Magistrate Judge Watanabe were each required to expend significant judicial resources scheduling, preparing for, and continuing hearings, and ruling on Olsen's repetitive and often unsupported motions. For these reasons, there is adequate evidence in the record to uphold the Board's conclusion that Olsen violated Rule 8.4(d).

. . .

III

We affirm the Hearing Board's conclusions that Olsen violated Rules of Professional Conduct 3.1 and 8.4(d), but we reverse its imposition of a six-month suspension with the requirement of reinstatement. We hereby censure John R. Olsen for his misconduct.

Post-Case Follow-Up

In the underlying federal litigation in *Olsen*, the district court awarded the defendant $25,000 in attorneys' fees under 28 U.S.C. §1927 (a predecessor to FRCP 11) as a sanction for Olsen's misconduct. Do you think that this case-based sanction influenced the Colorado Supreme Court's decision to reduce the lawyer's discipline from suspension to public censure? Why or why not?

Is public censure of an attorney an effective sanction for ethical misconduct, or is it a mere "slap on the wrist"? Does this depend on how informed and cohesive the legal community is in the particular jurisdiction?

In re Olsen: Real Life Applications

1. Both Rule 3.1 and FRCP 11 allow an attorney to file a factual claim with a tribunal if he reasonably believes that the claim will have evidentiary support after discovery. Does this mean that an attorney may rely solely on his client's factual allegations in drafting and filing a civil complaint, without *any* factual inquiry whatsoever? Suppose that you are a workers' compensation attorney and a new client approaches you claiming to have been injured on the job site. The client has no visible signs of injury. May you file a workers' compensation claim on his behalf without seeking and analyzing documents substantiating both his employment and his injury? Should you?
2. You are an insurance defense attorney. Your client, Providential Insurance Co., represents a chain of "big box" stores. A large percentage of your practice is defending "slip and fall" cases that allegedly occur on store property. May you routinely include a defense of contributory negligence in your answers to complaints without conducting any interviews or analyzing video security footage to determine whether the plaintiff may have been partially responsible for the accident?

As we have just seen, there must be non-frivolous support for an attorney's *factual* claims. But an attorney's *legal* argument may be based on a creative or novel theory that presses for changes in the law. A legal claim or argument is not frivolous within the meaning of Rule 3.1 if it is supported by "a good faith argument for an extension, modification, or reversal of existing law." The comment to this rule recognizes that an action or defense is not frivolous "even though the lawyer believes that the client's position ultimately will not prevail."[6]

6. Model Rule 3.1 cmt. [2].

Rule 3.4(d) imposes obligations on an attorney with respect to discovery requests and responses that parallel Rule 3.1's obligations with respect to pleadings. Again, the emphasis is on candor to the tribunal and avoiding frivolous tactics that abuse the litigation process. Rule 3.4(d) provides that a party shall not "make a frivolous discovery request or fail to make reasonably diligent effort to comply with a legally proper discovery request by an opposing party." Examples of discovery conduct that may violate Rule 3.4(d) include overusing depositions or interrogatories, engaging in questioning techniques that seek embarrassing but irrelevant information, unreasonably delaying document production, and instructing deposition witnesses not to answer clearly pertinent inquiries that call for non-privileged information.

B. OBLIGATION TO BE TRUTHFUL

The attorney's obligation of **candor to the tribunal** may arise in a variety of contexts: for example, when the lawyer makes statements of law to the court during oral argument; when the lawyer cites or fails to cite legal authority in written memoranda or briefs; and when the lawyer calls a witness who makes false statements during testimony. The attorney's ethical obligations are slightly different in each instance. The attorney clearly cannot directly make false statements of her own to the court, nor can she assist her client to make false statements. The attorney's responsibility with respect to a witness who makes false statements is significantly more complex.

With regard to false statement to a tribunal, the responsibilities of an attorney require a delicate balance of three professional obligations: (1) the lawyer must learn as much about the client's case as possible in order to be able to represent the client competently (Rule 1.1); (2) the lawyer must keep confidential any private information divulged by the client, with certain exceptions (Rule 1.6); and (3) the lawyer must not knowingly participate in a fraud on the tribunal (Rule 3.3). This three-way tension is often referred to as the lawyer's "trilemma." Where these tensions collide in the context of litigation, the Model Rules emphasize the attorney's third obligation of candor to the tribunal over the first two, requiring a lawyer to take remedial action to prevent or rectify any fraud on the court.[7] Some states may rank these duties differently, particularly with respect to client perjury where the witness is a criminal defendant, which is discussed later in Chapter 8.

1. Candor to the Court

Rule 3.3(a) provides that a lawyer shall not "knowingly make a false statement of law or fact to a tribunal" or "fail to correct a false statement of material fact or law

7. *See* ABA Formal Op. 87-353 (1987).

previously made to the tribunal by the lawyer." If the judge or magistrate[8] asks a lawyer at a criminal bail hearing "does your client have a job," the lawyer must answer truthfully, and is subject to discipline if she fails to do so. An attorney preparing a brief for appeal may not misstate or overstate testimony from the record below in order to render a legal argument more persuasive.

A lawyer violates Rule 3.3(a) when he makes a statement to the court knowing that it is false; mere suspicion of falsity or recklessness toward the truth will not suffice. Nonetheless, the comment to the rule recognizes that "knowledge that evidence is false . . . can be inferred from the circumstances."[9] While an attorney may resolve doubts or suspicions regarding the truth of statement in favor of the client, a lawyer cannot ignore an obvious falsehood by putting his head in the sand to avoid actual knowledge.

Note that a lawyer's obligations with regard to truthful statements to a tribunal differ depending on their timing. If the lawyer knows that the statement is false at the time he makes it, he may not make the statement to the court, regardless of how significant or trivial the subject. But if a lawyer makes a statement and *subsequently* learns of its falsehood, the attorney has a duty to correct the falsity only if the statement is "**material**." For example, if a lawyer advises the court at a hearing on a motion for a preliminary injunction in a case involving the sale of real property that his client's ownership of real estate is limited to the client's primary residence, he has a duty to correct that statement at a subsequent court hearing with respect that same litigation if he subsequently learns that his client owns a vacation home.[10] But if a lawyer argues to the court at the same motion hearing that his client is 52 years of age when he is actually 53, the lawyer has no duty to subsequently correct that misstatement.

Case Preview

In re Richards

The underlying litigation that lead to this disciplinary action against attorney Robert Richards stems from a case he brought *pro se* against Arthur Adair, represented by George Scarborough. Richards sought to depose a nonparty, Rodeo Nites, but it did not show up for the deposition. Adair and his attorney successfully moved for lost wages and attorneys' fees for their wasted day. Richards filed a motion for a new hearing, believing that Scarborough should not have been able to argue the attorneys' fees and lost wages issue on the same day as his show cause hearing. In his appeal from the district court order, Richards alleged that he objected to Scarborough's motion on that day. He

8. The use of the word "tribunal" in Rule 3.3 means that the obligation of candor applies to all types of adjudicative proceedings, including administrative hearings and arbitrations. *See* Model Rule 1.0(m). For the purposes of discussion in this chapter the authors will use the words tribunal and court interchangeably.
9. Model Rule 3.3 cmt. [8].
10. The duty to take remedial measures may require the lawyer to reveal information that otherwise would be protected by the lawyer's duty of confidentiality under Rule 1.6. *See* Model Rule 3.3 cmt. [10].

presented the transcript from the hearing as evidence, but omitted crucial aspects of the transcript in order to bolster his argument.

As you read *Richards*, ask yourself the following:

1. Why are appellate courts especially vulnerable to misrepresentation or deception by counsel of record?
2. Could Richards have made a non-frivolous argument that his objection was preserved below without using ellipses to redact the lower court transcript?

In re Richards

43 P.2d 1032 (N.M. 1997)

. . .

This matter came before the Court on the recommendation of the disciplinary board that Robert Richards be publicly censured for knowingly making a false statement of material fact in a brief filed in the New Mexico Court of Appeals for the purpose of deceiving the appellate court. This Court, having considered the recommendation and being sufficiently advised, adopts the recommendation and orders that respondent be publicly censured for violation of his duty of candor to the court.

. . .

We agree completely with the Court of Appeals' concluding remarks, that it "expect[s] candor in the memoranda submitted . . ." and that respondent's "memorandum failed to meet that standard."

In his defense, respondent has maintained that the deletion of a portion of the quote did not change the meaning, because he intended to object on two grounds: that Scarborough was representing adverse interests in Adair and Rodeo Nites, and that he had not received notice that Adair's motion would be heard at that hearing. Respondent contended that the trial court cut him off before he could articulate the second basis for his objection. This was not, he argued, fatal to his objection, because Rule 1-046 of the Rules of Civil Procedure for the District Courts provides that, to preserve a question for appeal, it is only necessary that the party makes known to the court the objection to the ruling. From this, respondent argues that his redacted quotation showed that the district court knew that he was objecting to Adair's motion being heard, because she referenced Scarborough's request to have Adair's motion heard and stated she was going to hear it.

Respondent is the only person in the world who knows whether he did intend to object on the additional basis that he had not received proper notice that Adair's motion would be heard. What respondent apparently does not understand is that this point is not determinative of whether he made a material misrepresentation to the Court of Appeals. If respondent had recited the entire discussion he had with Judge Maes, he could have argued to the Court of Appeals (1) that he would have objected on the notice basis had he not been interrupted or (2) that under Rule 1-046, an objection is preserved if the record shows the court understood the basis for the objection, even if it was not articulated by the objecting party. The Court of Appeals, with all relevant information before it, could have decided whether the record supported respondent's version of what objection he was making and whether respondent's interpretation of the requirements for preserving error was correct.

Instead, respondent engaged in a form of advocacy that was deceitful and dishonest. The Court of Appeals was not told that the record failed to reflect an objection on the notice issue, but rather reflected an objection on another topic altogether. Moreover, not only did respondent omit material language, but he also made the affirmative statement that the trial court understood his objection to address the issue of hearing Mr. Adair's motion. As the Court of Appeals noted, respondent achieved this impression by omitting language that showed the objection he actually made.

Certainly a lawyer is expected to make the best argument he or she can to enhance the chance of success. The lawyer's arguments must, however, be based upon the actual state of events, not a distorted version of what occurred. Contrary to respondent's contention, the portion he omitted did change the meaning of the text. If included, there was a very real possibility that the Court of Appeals would find that he had not objected to the motion being heard, but rather had only raised an objection concerning who Scarborough represented. By omitting that portion of the dialogue, respondent attempted to increase the chance that the court would believe he had actually objected to Adair's motion being heard. That is not advocacy; it is deceit.

. . .

We therefore adopt the recommendation of the disciplinary board and find that respondent violated Rule 16-303(A)(1), by knowingly making a false statement of material fact to the Court of Appeals. . . .

Post-Case Follow-Up

Would Richards's conduct have been any less egregious or violative of Rule 3.3 if he had been represented by private counsel in the underlying litigation, and then represented himself *pro se* on appeal?

We tend to think that professional and strategic considerations are distinct, but are they? Where an attorney gains a reputation among judges for playing fast and loose with the facts, could that make her less effective as an advocate?

In re Richards: Real Life Applications

1. You are scheduled to try a motor vehicle accident case, and your primary witness (the plaintiff) inexplicably fails to show up to court. The case is marked "no further continuances," and you know that the judge will be reluctant to grant you an extension. May you tell the judge that your client has had a medical emergency and request a continuance on that basis?

2. You are representing one party to a divorce action in probate court. Your client is seeking alimony from her longtime husband. At the preliminary hearing after the divorce complaint is filed, you lodge an affidavit of financial condition

stating that your client is an unemployed homemaker. After oral argument, the judge orders the husband to make a temporary payment of $1,000 per week to your client pending a final decree of divorce. Following this preliminary hearing, your client obtains a part-time job earning $750 per week. Although your statement to the court was accurate when made, it no longer reflects the financial condition of the client. Do you have an *ethical* duty to inform the court of your client's recent employment, or does that duty, if any, rest on the procedural rules of the probate court?

---

2. Failure to Disclose Adverse Facts in *Ex Parte* Proceeding

Attorneys typically are not required to disclose adverse facts to the court during a trial, because in an adversarial system litigants are expected to present their cases in the best possible light. Adverse facts generally will be disclosed by opposing counsel if it is his tactical advantage to do so. But this presumption breaks down in *ex parte* (one-sided) proceedings, where opposing counsel is not present. Applications for a search warrant or wiretap authorization in criminal cases, and motions for a *lis pendens* or temporary restraining order in civil cases, are examples of ***ex parte* proceedings**. Model Rule 3.3(d) provides that in an *ex parte* proceeding a lawyer must inform the tribunal of "all material facts known to the lawyer that will enable the tribunal to make an informed decision, whether or not the facts are adverse." The principle behind the rule is that hiding material adverse facts from the judge or magistrate in an *ex parte* proceeding would disable the court from making an informed decision.[11]

Suppose that a litigator files a complaint for breach of a real estate contract, and at the time of the filing of the complaint brings a motion for a temporary restraining order asking the court to prevent the defendant and owner of the property from conveying the property to another during the pendency of the proceeding. The plaintiff's theory of breach of contract is that the defendant signed a purchase and sale agreement but then reneged on the sale when he got a higher offer. If the purchase and sale agreement required the plaintiff to secure financing by a specified date and the plaintiff missed that contractual deadline by 24 hours, this would be a "material" adverse fact that the plaintiff's lawyer would be required to bring to the court's attention at the hearing.

A lawyer's duty to reveal material adverse facts at an *ex parte* hearing *includes* facts that are protected by client confidences. Rule 1.6 creates an exception to the obligation of confidentiality for those disclosures that are necessary to comply with law.[12] However, lawyers are not required by Rule 3.3(d) to reveal at *ex parte* hearings information that is protected by the attorney-client privilege.[13]

---

11. Model Rule 3.3(d) cmt. [14].
12. Model Rule 1.6(b)(6) and cmt. [12]. *See* People v. Ritland, 327 P.3d 914 (Colo. 2014) (in *ex parte* petition for adoption of child, lawyer impermissibly misrepresented biological father of child).
13. Restatement (Third) of the Law Governing Lawyers §112 cmt. [b] [hereinafter Restatement].

3. Failure to Disclose Controlling Legal Authority

The duties with respect to factual representations pertain to affirmative misstatements to the tribunal. The *omission* of facts or the failure to reveal facts to the tribunal are not explicitly covered by Rule 3.3(a). Except at an *ex parte* proceeding,[14] a lawyer typically has no affirmative duty to reveal contrary facts to the court unless specifically asked about them, because contrary facts are ordinarily expected to be revealed by opposing counsel to their advantage. However, where the attorney is aware of undisclosed facts that make her factual presentation to the court *fundamentally misleading*, the omission of those facts may rise to the level of "dishonesty, fraud, deceit, or misrepresentation" within the meaning of a separate section of the rules. *See* Model Rule 8.4(c).[15]

With respect to legal argument, however, an attorney has both a duty not to knowingly *misstate* the law and a duty to *reveal* controlling legal authority. Rule 3.3(a)(2) provides that a lawyer has the duty to disclose "legal authority in the controlling jurisdiction known to the lawyer to be directly adverse to the position of the client and not disclosed by opposing counsel." The premise here is that, as an officer of the court, a lawyer has an obligation to assist the court in determining the legal authority properly applicable to the case. Of course, dealing with negative authority is also good lawyering, because usually the opposing counsel or judge is going to uncover it themselves, so it is better tactically to address — and if possible distinguish — negative precedent "up front."

Case Preview

In re Thonert

The following is an excerpt from an Indiana Supreme Court decision upholding discipline on attorney, Richard Thonert. Thonert represented a client charged with operating a motor vehicle while intoxicated. The defendant sought to withdraw his guilty plea and retained Thonert. Thonert failed to inform his client of a directly relevant similar matter in which he represented the defendant and had not prevailed, *Fletcher v. State*. The holding in *Fletcher* was binding precedent on his client's case, but Thonert did not argue for changing or extending the *Fletcher* holding. Instead, both Thonert and the opposing counsel failed to disclose the case to the court on appeal.

As you read *Thonert*, ask yourself the following:

1. Why was it so clear that Thonert had actual knowledge of the adverse legal authority within the meaning of Rule 3.3?

14. See Section B.2, *supra*.

15. *See* In re Cardwell, 50 P.3d 897 (Colo. 2002). *See also* Model Rule 3.3 cmt. [3] ("there are circumstances where failure to make a [factual] disclosure is the equivalent of an affirmative misrepresentation").

2. How does the obligation to disclose adverse legal authority coincide with the right of an attorney under Rule 3.3 to press for changes in the law or the overruling of controlling precedent?

In re Thonert

733 N.E.2d 932 (Ind. 2000)

The respondent in this attorney disciplinary matter is charged with failing to disclose to an appellate tribunal controlling authority known to him, not disclosed by opposing counsel, that was directly adverse to his client's position. He also failed to advise his client of the adverse legal authority when his client was contemplating his legal options.

. . .

The respondent represented the defendant in Fletcher v. State, 649 N.E.2d 1022 (Ind. 1995). In that case, this Court addressed the questions that the respondent raised in his client's case. The ruling in *Fletcher* was adverse to the arguments that the respondent offered on appeal of his client's case. The respondent had served as counsel of record for defendant Fletcher in the appeal before this Court. This Court's ruling in *Fletcher* was issued on May 1, 1995, over one year before the respondent filed his appeal on behalf of the client. In his appellate brief filed on behalf of the client, the respondent failed to cite to *Fletcher* or argue that its holding was not controlling authority in the client's case. The respondent also failed to argue that the holding in *Fletcher* should be changed or extended. . . .

Indiana Professional Conduct Rule 3.3(a)(3) provides that a lawyer shall not knowingly fail to disclose to a tribunal legal authority in the controlling jurisdiction known to the lawyer to be directly adverse to the position of the client and not disclosed by opposing counsel. The concept underlying this requirement of disclosure is that legal argument is a discussion seeking to determine the legal premises properly applicable to the case. *Comment* to Ind. Professional Conduct Rule 3.3. The respondent's intimate familiarity with *Fletcher* is established by his having served as counsel to the defendant. Accordingly, we find that the respondent violated the rule by failing to disclose *Fletcher* to the Court of Appeals in his legal arguments on behalf of the client.

. . .

It is, therefore, ordered that the respondent, Richard J. Thonert, is hereby reprimanded and admonished for his violations of Prof. Cond. R. 3.3(a)(3). . . .

Post-Case Follow-Up

Rule 3.3 allows for discipline of the lawyer only where the adverse legal authority is both known by the attorney and nondisclosed by the opposition. So the provision of this rule does not often present a dilemma for lawyers, because normally an opposing party will disclose authority favorable to her case.

Note how Rule 1.1 and Rule 3.3 work together here. If a lawyer does not conduct adequate research to reveal the controlling legal authority, he may not have actual "knowledge" within the meaning of Rule 3.3 (although knowledge may be inferred from the circumstances under Rule 1.0). But by pleading *negligence*, the attorney may be opening himself up to a charge of incompetence under Rule 1.1.

In re Thonert: Real Life Applications

1. Is *dicta* in an appellate opinion suggesting how a court would likely come out in a factual setting not immediately before the court ever "authority" within the meaning of Rule 3.3(a)(2)? Even if it is "authority," can it ever be "directly" adverse to the position of a client?

2. Suppose that you are an assistant district attorney representing the state on appeal from an assault and battery conviction. The defendant unsuccessfully raised a claim of self-defense at trial. The trial judge refused to allow the defendant to admit evidence of prior violent conduct on the part of the victim that was unknown to the defendant at the time of the fight. Your case is on direct appeal before the state supreme court. You are aware of an opinion from a three-judge panel of the state appeals court in another case holding that prior acts of violence of the victim should be admitted in a case involving self-defense, even if those acts were not known to the defendant. Defense counsel does not cite this opinion in his brief. Do you have an obligation to cite it in your brief, even if you go on to argue that it was erroneously decided? That is, does the word "controlling" in Rule 3.3(a) refer to the word "authority" or to the word "jurisdiction"?

---

4. Client or Other Witness Giving False Testimony in Civil Litigation

Paragraph (a)(3) of Rule 3.3 sets forth an attorney's duties with respect to a client or a witness called by the attorney who gives materially false testimony at an adjudicative proceeding (which includes a deposition, pretrial hearing, trial, or arbitration). In the next chapter, we deal with the responsibilities of defense lawyers in criminal cases. Here we discuss the obligation of lawyers in civil cases when they know that their client or a witness they have called has lied under oath on a material matter. In these situations, the attorney's obligation of candor to the tribunal takes priority over her obligation of confidentiality under Rule 1.6. Even when the witness is the attorney's client, the lawyer who knows that a witness has testified falsely as to a material matter, either on direct or cross-examination, must "take reasonable remedial measures, including, if necessary, disclosure to the tribunal."[16] The comment to

---

16. Model Rule 3.3(a)(3).

the rule suggests that **reasonable remedial measures** include remonstrating with the witness and encouraging the witness to withdraw such testimony, withdrawal from representation upon approval of the court if it will undo the effects of the false testimony, or disclosure to the tribunal of the falsity.[17]

The obligations of an attorney under Model Rule 3.3 differ depending on when the attorney learns of the falsity. If a witness reveals to an attorney his *intention* to commit perjury before testifying, the lawyer is obliged to remonstrate with the witness, attempt to convince him of the dangers and consequences of testifying falsely, and, where the witness is a client, threaten to withdraw from representation if the witness persists in his intention. Usually that will work. But what if it doesn't work, or if the witness surprises the attorney by testifying falsely notwithstanding contrary indications? In those circumstances, the obligation of the attorney to take "remedial measures" depends on the materiality of the evidence. Where the testimony relates to a trivial or inconsequential matter, the attorney may do nothing. Where the testimony relates to a material matter, the attorney must ask the witness to correct his testimony, and if that remonstration fails, disclose the false testimony to the court.[18]

An attorney's duty with respect to false testimony applies in both the trial and pretrial contexts. Nevertheless, the ABA has recognized that the "remedial measures" available to a lawyer may be broader when a witness or client gives false answers in the discovery context—such as with interrogatories or depositions—than when he gives false testimony at trial. In the former situation, it may be sufficient for the attorney to disaffirm the work product, supplement the discovery provided, or notify opposing counsel where the witness persists in giving false evidence.[19]

The requirements of Rule 3.3(a)(3) that we have been discussing apply only if the attorney actually *knows* that her witness's or client's testimony is false. The attorney may suspect or believe that the witness's testimony is false, but in the absence of affirmative knowledge, the lawyer does not need to remonstrate with the witness or inform the court. However, knowledge may be inferred from the circumstances. Comment [9] to Rule 3.3 provides that "although a lawyer should resolve doubts about the veracity of testimony or other evidence in favor of the client, the lawyer cannot ignore an obvious falsehood."[20]

If the attorney suspects but does not know that a witness's testimony will be false before presenting it, the attorney has discretion to refuse to offer the testimony. The attorney may simply refuse to call the person as a witness if he thinks the person is going to lie. But the attorney is not required to do so; the discretion in such instance rests with the attorney. We will soon see that there is an important exception to this rule for criminal cases where the witness is the attorney's client.

---

17. Model Rule 3.3(a)(3) cmt. [10].
18. *See* ABA Formal Op. 87-353 (1987).
19. *See* ABA Formal Op. 93-376 (1993).
20. Model Rule 3.3(a)(3) cmt. [9].

Case Preview

Committee on Professional Ethics v. Crary

Unbeknownst to Sue Evans Curtis and William Crary, Sue's husband hired a private investigator to follow them around and document their love affair. During this period, Mrs. Curtis repeatedly lied to her husband about her whereabouts—occasionally for weeks at a time. When Mrs. Curtis filed for divorce, she employed her paramour as one of the attorneys to represent her in the divorce proceedings. During her deposition, her husband's attorney, armed with all the knowledge of the private investigator, asked Sue Evans Curtis about her alleged trips out of town. Rather than reveal the relationship, she lied under oath while Crary sat idly by allowing her to perjure herself for two days. After the divorce, Curtis and Crary married and a custody battle ensued for her children in which he helped her circumvent the court order awarding custody to her husband. The Iowa State Bar Association filed a complaint with the Grievance Commission of the Iowa Supreme Court against Crary for his unethical conduct with regards to both the perjury incident and the frustration of the custody decree.

As you read this opinion, ask yourself the following:

1. At what point in the proceedings could and should Crary have made different decisions?
2. How does the court dispose of Crary's self-incrimination argument? Is it convincing?

Committee on Professional Ethics v. Crary

245 N.W.2d 298 (Iowa 1976)

II. THE DEPOSITION PERJURY

The charge involving perjury . . . presents two subsidiary problems.

A. The First Problem Is Procedural.

[The court first addressed the interplay between an Iowa statute prohibiting a lawyer from misleading a judge by any artifice or false statement and the Model Code of Professional Responsibility.]

B. The Second Problem Involves the Merits of the Charge Relating to the Perjury

What are the *facts* of the matter? Mr. and Mrs. Curtis were husband and wife, lived together, and had three children. Respondent began to see Mrs. Curtis and stayed with her at various places and slept with her—both before and after Mrs. Curtis commenced her divorce suit against Mr. Curtis.

. . .

Respondent contends . . . that the record contains no express testimony by him or Mrs. Curtis that he put her up to the false stories she related in the deposition. Yet those stories did not come out of thin air; they took some contriving. We doubt that Mrs. Curtis simply developed those stories about Mrs. Needham as the deposition progressed or that she developed them alone.

We think respondent was involved in the whole shameful episode, but we will accept arguendo his contention that he did not contrive the perjury with Mrs. Curtis. Then we have a situation in which respondent as an attorney at a deposition listened, his client started to lie under oath, he knew she was lying, and he just "sat there" and let her lie. More than that, the deposition recessed over Thursday, and respondent did nothing to stop Mrs. Curtis from lying some more. She resumed her lying on Friday and respondent still just sat there.

What is the *law* of this matter? We are not disposed to read §§610.14(3) and 610.24(3) of the Iowa Code in a narrow, technical, or legalistic manner. Assuming respondent did not know in advance that Mrs. Curtis was going to lie, his guilt was in failing to stop her or otherwise to call a halt when she started to lie.

Central to the administration of justice is the fact-finding process. Legislatures and courts can devise the finest rules of law, but if those rules are applied to false "facts," justice miscarries.

The attorney functions at the heart of the fact-finding process, both in trial and in pre- and post-trial proceedings. If he knowingly suffers a witness to lie, he undermines the integrity of the fact-finding system of which he himself is an integral part. Thus the fundamental rule is unquestioned that *an attorney must not knowingly permit a witness to lie*. . . .

But respondent contends he was not required to volunteer to opposing counsel or the court that Mrs. Curtis' testimony was false, since this could have provided evidence for building an adultery case against him. He cites authority that an attorney like others is privileged not to produce evidence which will incriminate him. . . .

Respondent does not seem to grasp the point here. We do not place the decision on respondent's failure to inform opposing counsel or the court of the truth. In the present case no need really existed for this. Opposing counsel was not misled. His subsequent questions revealed he knew the facts; he made Mrs. Curtis' perjury patent. The vice of respondent's conduct was not in failing to reveal the truth but in participating in the corruption of the fact-finding system by knowingly permitting Mrs. Curtis to lie. Indeed if Mr. Curtis had not had private investigators, the falsity of this testimony might never have come to light; Mrs. Curtis' perjury, countenanced by respondent, might have subsequently carried the day in court. Contrast with respondent's conduct the acts of Mr. Gray. When that attorney suspected on Friday that Mrs. Curtis was lying he confronted respondent and upon learning the truth said, "She can't sit there and tell this story." He thereupon recessed the deposition.

Apart from self-incrimination, respondent contends that his duty to protect his client, Mrs. Curtis, conflicted with his duty to the justice system to divulge the falsity, and that he properly placed his duty to his client first. He bases this contention on the attorney-client privilege.

Respondent confuses the duty to divulge the truth after perjury is committed with the duty not to permit a witness to give false testimony in the first place. We will proceed on this contention, however, on respondent's basis, as though respondent's breach was in not divulging the truth to opposing counsel or the court after the false testimony was given. We address respondent's contention as he does under the attorney-client privilege and without reference to any other privilege.

The difficulty with respondent's contention is that it proceeds from a false premise. He cites the article entitled Perjury, The Lawyer's Trilemma, in *Litigation* (Winter 1975 Journ. of A.B.A. Litigation Section). From this article, he concludes that a conflict between two duties exists: one to the client, the other to the justice system.

The flaw in respondent's reasoning is that no duty exists to the client when the client perjures himself to the knowledge of the attorney. Such conduct by the client falls outside the attorney-client relationship. When a prospective client approaches an attorney, he may expect that the attorney will assist him to the best of the attorney's ability. He may not expect, however, that the attorney will tolerate lying or any other species of fraud in the process. . . .

The office of attorney does not permit, much less does it demand of him for any client, violation of law or any manner of fraud or chicane. He must obey his own conscience and not that of his client. Canons of Professional Ethics (A.B.A. 1957).

Correspondingly, the present rules state that "A lawyer shall not . . . engage in conduct involving dishonesty, fraud, deceit, or misrepresentation," "engage in conduct that is prejudicial to the administration of justice," "participate in the creation or preservation of evidence when he knows or it is obvious that the evidence is false," or "counsel or assist his client in conduct that the lawyer knows to be illegal or fraudulent." Iowa Code of Professional Responsibility for Lawyers (1971) DR1-102(A)(4) and (5), DR7-102(A)(6) and (7).

We hold that respondent acted unethically in knowingly permitting Mrs. Curtis to commit perjury on the first day of the deposition and to resume the perjury two days later, and that in so doing he violated §§610.14(3) and 610.24(3) of the Iowa Code.

. . .

Post-Case Follow-Up

Was Crary prohibited by any other ethical rule from agreeing to represent in a divorce proceeding a client with whom he was having a sexual relationship? What about the conflict of interest rules? The attorney-witness rule?

Mr. Crary's client lied in two days of deposition testimony. One typical and acceptable response to client perjury is to remonstrate privately with the client and attempt to convince her to correct the misstatement. Suppose that Crary intended to remonstrate with his client after the first day of deposition was concluded, but before he could do so, opposing counsel approached him with a settlement offer. Would settling the case without correcting the record violate Rule 3.3 or any other rule?

Committee on Professional Ethics v. Crary: Real Life Applications

1. Suppose that you represent a defendant in a motor vehicle tort case. You have examined your client's phone records and compared them to the police report. You know to a substantial degree of certainty that your client was on her cell phone to her boyfriend at the time of the accident. At her deposition in response to questions from opposing counsel, your client denies that she was "using" her cell phone at the time of the crash. What are your options under comment [10] to Rule 3.3?

2. Imagine a similar case as in hypothetical #1, but the client's testimony occurs at trial. Your client has testified in a way that contradicts not only her cell phone records (produced by the plaintiff in discovery) but also her prior statements to you during private meetings. What are your options at trial? Would a motion to withdraw from representation (a so-called noisy withdrawal) be an adequate substitute for affirmatively disclosing the adverse fact to the court? Can such a motion "undo the effect" of the false evidence within the meaning of comment [10]?

Rule 3.4(b) prohibits an attorney from counseling or assisting a witness to testify falsely. This prohibition applies regardless of the materiality of the testimony, consistent with the prohibition in Rule 3.3(a)(3) of knowingly presenting false testimony. An attorney may help prepare a witness to present her testimony in the light most favorable to the attorney's client, by suggesting convincing manners of expression or emphasis. But an attorney may not suggest that a witness knows facts that she does not know, or pressure the witness to testify in a way that is inconsistent with the witness's actual memory or belief.

When does "woodshedding" a witness cross the line?
Library of Congress Prints and Photographs Division Washington, D.C.

Exactly when does rehearsing or "**woodshedding**" a witness cross the line between helping to shape the most accurate and powerful testimony and helping to fashion false or misleading testimony? This question was the subject of the following Ethics Opinion from the District of Columbia Bar.

Case Preview

D.C. Bar Legal Ethics Committee Formal Opinion 79

This opinion issued by the D.C. Legal Ethics Committee addresses three questions raised regarding a lawyer's role in preparing a witness's testimony. The committee, in interpreting the D.C. Code of Professional Responsibility—replaced in 1991 by the D.C. Rules of Professional Conduct—determined that lawyers are allowed to prepare or assist in preparing a witness's testimony so long as he or she did not know or should not have reasonably known that the testimony was false or misleading.

As you read this opinion, ask yourself whether the required mental state for a violation of Rule 3.4(b) hinders or promotes perjured testimony?

Limitations on a Lawyer's Participation in the Preparation of a Witness's Testimony

D.C. Bar Legal Ethics Committee Formal Opinion 79 (1979)

The particular questions put by the inquirer are whether it is ethically proper for a lawyer actually to write the testimony the witness will adopt under oath; whether, if so, the lawyer may engage in "practice cross-examination exercises" intended to prepare the witness for questions that may be asked at the hearing.

In order to present those issues in a more inclusive setting, the questions may usefully be rephrased as follows:

(1) What are the ethical limitations on a lawyer's suggesting the actual language in which a witness's testimony is to be presented, whether in written form or otherwise?

(2) What are the ethical limitations on a lawyer's suggesting that a witness's testimony include information that was not initially furnished to the lawyer by the witness?

(3) What are the ethical limitations on a lawyer's preparing a witness for the presentation of testimony under live examination, whether direct or cross, and whether by practice questioning or otherwise?

A single prohibitory principle governs the answer to all three of these questions: it is, simply, that a lawyer may not prepare, or assist in preparing, testimony that he or she knows, or ought to know, is false or misleading. So long as this prohibition is not transgressed, a lawyer may properly suggest language as well as substance of testimony, and may—indeed should—do whatever is feasible to prepare his or her witnesses for examination.

It follows, therefore—to address the first question here raised—that the fact that the particular words in which testimony, whether written or oral, is cast originated with a lawyer rather than the witness whose testimony it is has no significance so long as the substance of that testimony is not, so far as the lawyer knows or ought to know, false or misleading. If the particular words suggested by the lawyer, even though not literally false, are calculated to convey a misleading impression, this would be equally impermissible from the ethical point of view.

The second question raised by the inquiry—as to the propriety of a lawyer's suggesting the inclusion in a witness's testimony of information not initially secured from the witness—may, again, arise not only with respect to written testimony but with oral testimony as well. In either case, it appears to us that the governing consideration for ethical purposes is whether the substance of the testimony is something the witness can truthfully and properly testify to. If he or she is willing and (as respects his or her state of knowledge) able honestly so to testify, the fact that the inclusion of a particular point of substance was initially suggested by the lawyer rather than the witness seems to us wholly without significance. There are two principal hazards here. One hazard is the possibility of undue suggestion: that is, the risk that the witness may thoughtlessly adopt testimony offered by the lawyer simply because it is so offered, without considering whether it is testimony that he or she may appropriately give under oath. The other hazard is the possibility of a suggestion or implication in the witness's resulting testimony that the witness is testifying on a particular matter of his own knowledge when this is not the fact the cases. . . . [H]owever, there should be no difficulty, for a reasonably skilled and scrupulous lawyer, in avoiding the hazards in question.

We turn, finally, to the extent of a lawyer's proper participation in preparing a witness for giving live testimony—whether the testimony is only to be under cross-examination, as in the particular circumstances giving rise to the present inquiry, or, as more usually the case, direct examination as well. Here again it appears to us that the only touchstones are the truth and genuineness of the testimony to be given. The mere fact of a lawyer's having prepared the witness for the presentation of testimony is simply irrelevant: indeed, a lawyer who did not prepare his or her witness for testimony, having had an opportunity to do so, would not be doing his or her professional job properly.

It matters not at all that the preparation of such testimony takes the form of "practice" examination or cross-examination. What does matter is that whatever the mode of witness preparation chosen, the lawyer does not engage in suppressing, distorting or falsifying the testimony that the witness will give.

D.C. Bar Legal Ethics Committee Formal Opinion 79: Real Life Applications

1. The D.C. Ethics Committee opined that it would not violate the jurisdiction's disciplinary rules for a lawyer to "script" testimony of a witness before her appearance at a tribunal, so long as the attorney was not putting words into the witness's mouth that the attorney knows or should know to be false. But is such formal scripting *wise* as a tactical matter? Imagine what impression such

rigid adherence to a script might leave on the finder of fact, and how it might be exposed on cross-examination. Federal Rule of Evidence 612 allows a court to order opposing counsel to inspect any writing used by a witness to refresh the witness's recollection, either *before* or during testimony.

The Restatement (Third) of the Law Governing Lawyers suggests that the following methods of **witness preparation** are ethically appropriate: explaining the law that applies to the case; telling the witness about likely testimony from others and documents that will be admitted in evidence; suggesting words or phrases that will help make the witness's meaning clearer; and preparing for possibly hostile cross-examination.[21]

C. FAIRNESS TO OPPOSING PARTY AND COUNSEL

1. Obstruction, Alteration, or Destruction of Evidence

Destroying or altering documents after they have been designated by a subpoena or civil discovery request is behavior antithetical to a lawyer's duty of candor and to his obligation as an officer of the court. Model Rule 3.4(a) provides that a lawyer may not "unlawfully obstruct another party's access to evidence or unlawfully alter, destroy, or conceal a document or other material having potential evidentiary value." Because the rule states that a lawyer may not "unlawfully" perform these acts, this is an area of legal ethics in which the attorney must be cognizant of substantive law — including criminal, tort, and procedural law. Whether handling of physical evidence or documents[22] is "unlawful" will depend on the substantive law in your jurisdiction, including the crime of obstruction of justice.

Typically, **obstruction** statutes prohibit destruction or concealment of evidence only if the individual knows or reasonably believes that an official proceeding has been commenced or is about to be instituted. An attorney's professional responsibilities will thus depend on the timing of destruction, whether proceedings are pending or likely to be filed, and the state of mind of the lawyer. In civil cases, if documents are destroyed or altered when a legal proceeding is clearly foreseeable, not only may the attorney face bar disciplinary charges, but the judge also may allow the finder of fact to find an adverse inference against the client in litigation. A lawyer who counsels or assists his client to dispose of potential evidence may end up undermining the client's case if the court gives a **spoliation of evidence**[23] instruction to the jury.

Sometimes lawyers are provided or shown physical evidence by their clients in conjunction with an ongoing proceeding. Imagine that you represent one spouse in a contested divorce and child custody matter. During one of your initial interviews

---

21. Restatement §116.
22. Rule 3.4(a) applies to both documents and physical evidence.
23. *See, e.g.*, Vodusek v. Bayliner Marine Corp., 71 F.3d 148, 155 (4th Cir. 1995).

you ask your client if she uses Facebook. If she answers "yes," may you advise your client to "clean up" her Facebook page by deleting any photographs or messages that might reflect poorly on her as a mother? In Opinion 2014-5, the Philadelphia Bar Association Professional Guidance Committee answered this question in the context of a lawyer representing a client in pending litigation. The committee opined that it was permissible for a lawyer to advise a client to change her privacy settings on Facebook, since that simply restricts permissive access to information rather than conceals it. But a lawyer may only counsel the client to delete material from Facebook if that instruction is accompanied by "appropriate action to preserve" electronic or hard copies of the deleted information in the event that this material is later subject to a subpoena or request for production of documents.

Counseling a client to discard documents does not always run afoul of Rule 3.4(a). The rule speaks to the "potential evidentiary value" of evidence. This language requires the lawyer to assess the probability of future litigation. For example, if a commercial lawyer discovers documents several years old that suggest that a client may be liable to a third party for contract non-performance or breach, but the lawyer does not know whether that party will ever file suit, arguably such documents do need not be preserved. Particularly when an attorney is representing an organizational client, it would be impracticable to require retention of all documents against the mere possibility that an adversary proceeding may be commenced at some future date. One crucial counseling function of a lawyer is to help his clients establish appropriate document retention policies. Document retention policies must both assure compliance with applicable laws while avoiding impracticable accumulation of paper and unnecessary storage costs. It is presumptively lawful to act pursuant to a bona fide document retention program if it is consistently followed.[24]

Much of the legal authority concerning concealment and alteration of physical evidence arises in the context of criminal investigations. We return to this subject in the next chapter.

2. Discovery Obligations

Evasive or incomplete responses to discovery requests appear to be a pervasive problem in the United States.[25] It seems that many litigators adhere to the standard conception of zealous advocacy by exploiting advantages in resources through excessive discovery, narrowly construing discovery demands, and purposefully delaying depositions and production of documents for strategic advantage. Students should appreciate that such discovery abuse can be counterproductive, especially where it provokes a motion for sanctions or equally abusive conduct by opposing counsel. It may also tend to undermine constructive settlement efforts.

---

24. *See* Restatement §118 cmt. (c).

25. Douglas N. Frenkel, Robert L. Nelson & Austin Sarat, *Ethics: Beyond the Rules*, 67 FORDHAM L. REV. 697, 706 (1998) (discussing research by ABA Section on Litigation).

Intentional or even reckless failure to comply with discovery requests may violate Model Rule 3.4(d), which provides that "a lawyer shall not . . . fail to make a reasonably diligent effort to comply with a legally proper discovery request by an opposing party." If opposing counsel makes a discovery request in litigation that is overbroad, burdensome, or seeks protected information, the proper response is to assert these objections affirmatively, rather than merely failing to reply or only partially responding to the request. A lawyer may not knowingly withhold a document that has been requested in discovery unless he does so in a procedurally proper form.[26] In addition, a lawyer responding to discovery requests may not mix together both responsive and non-responsive documents in order to obscure the responsive document's evidentiary value, for such conduct would involve "deceit" within the meaning of Model Rule 8.4(c).

In addition to bar discipline, discovery abuse in civil litigation may lead to imposition of attorneys' fees and punitive damages.[27] Indeed, **discovery abuse** is far more likely to be sanctioned by the courts in the context of ongoing litigation than by bar disciplinary authorities,[28] because judges presiding over the case are thought to be more likely to have a grasp of the complex factual and legal issues involved.

Model Rule 3.2 requires lawyers to make "reasonable efforts to expedite litigation consistent with the interests of the client." That last clause in this sentence is an important limitation on the principle that may swallow the general rule. It recognizes that sometimes the client may *wish* to delay litigation—such as where the client is anticipating persuasive appellate authority in a pending case, is expecting a global settlement of a related matter, or thinks that damages may be impacted by further factual developments. According to the ABA, "[t]he question is whether a competent lawyer acting in good faith would regard the course of action as having some substantial purpose other than delay." Protracting discovery for the sole purposes of running up the attorney's bill would clearly violate the rule. But what about exhausting the resources of your opponent and forcing him into settlement? If that is what the client wishes to do and can afford to pay for it, is it permitted by Rule 3.2? The ABA seems to have punted on this difficult question.

Finally, Model Rule 4.4(b) contains an important provision about a lawyer's responsibility pertaining to **inadvertent discovery**. The rule provides that an attorney who receives a document or electronically stored information relating to the representation of a client and knows or reasonably should know that the document was sent to him inadvertently must promptly notify the sender so that he or she can take protective measures. For example, if opposing counsel attaches the wrong document to an email or includes information in a discovery packet that he obviously did not intend to convey (e.g., a legal memorandum prepared by an associate that is clearly work product), the receiving attorney must notify the sending attorney. The rule does not address the receiving attorney's responsibility with respect to the document (e.g., destruction or return) but rather leaves that issue to the Rules of Civil Procedure, the Rules of Evidence, and the inherent powers of the court.

---

26. Restatement §110 cmt. (e).
27. FED. R. CIV. P. 37.
28. Restatement §110 cmt. (b).

D. TRIAL TACTICS

Several types of obstreperous or disruptive trial tactics may violate attorney disciplinary rules. Here the attorney must be concerned not only with her obligations as a fair adversary, but also with her obligations as an officer of the court.

1. Disruption

While an advocate must be persuasive and should be passionate in representing a client's interests before the court, he must also refrain from "abusive" or "obstreperous" conduct.[29] The Model Rules prohibit conduct during the course of litigation that is "intended to disrupt a tribunal."[30] Examples of **disruptive conduct** may include impugning the integrity of the court,[31] refusing to comply with the court's directives,[32] shouting or using profanity,[33] and assaulting or threatening to assault witnesses, parties, opposing counsel, or court personnel.[34]

A certain amount of contentiousness may be inevitable in the adversarial setting of a courtroom. Lawyers have a professional obligation to protect their client's interests by raising evidentiary objections, and by preserving grounds for appeal where they believe that the court's evidentiary or legal rulings are erroneous. Nevertheless, a court has inherent power to hold a lawyer in contempt where the lawyer persists in a line of inquiry notwithstanding clear instructions from the judge, or exposes the jury to evidence that definitively has been ruled inadmissible.[35] Both the attorney disciplinary rule and a court's inherent contempt power are limited to attorney conduct that actually disrupts the proceedings; as one commentator has argued, tribunals should not confuse an "offense to their sensibilities" with actual obstruction of the judicial process.[36]

2. Civility

While the Model Code expressed a professional norm of "zealous" representation,[37] in the Model Rules this standard conception of a lawyer's role was relegated to

---

29. Model Rule 3.5(d).
30. Model Rule 3.5(d), cmt. [4].
31. In re Romious, 240 P.3d 945 (Kan. 2010) (lawyer called court "kangaroo court" during public proceedings); In re Larvadain, 664 So. 2d 395 (La. 1995) (lawyer attacked integrity of judge by accusing him of being racist).
32. In re Disciplinary Action Against Kirschner, 793 N.W.2d 196, 201 (N.D. 2011) (attorney ignored denial of continuance and did not appear at trial).
33. *See* In re Romious, 240 P.3d at 948 (attorney shouted profanities at court house security officials when he triggered the metal detector).
34. *See* Fla. Bar v. Martocci, 791 So. 2d 1074 (Fla. 2001) (attorney threatened to "beat up" father of party in open court, discipline imposed under "conduct prejudicial to administration of justice" rule).
35. In re Levine, 27 F.3d 594, 595-96 (D.C. Cir. 1994) (lawyer repeatedly asked witness about evidence the court ruled inadmissible).
36. *See* Louis Raveson, *Advocacy and Contempt: Constitutional Limitations on the Judicial Contempt Power*, 65 WASH. L. REV. 477, 514 (1990).
37. MODEL CODE OF PROF'L RESPONSIBILITY EC 7-1 ("A lawyer shall represent a client zealously within the bounds of the law.").

the Preamble[38] and to a comment to Rule 1.3.[39] This change in emphasis signaled recognition by the ABA that the traits of zealousness and civility may sometimes be in tension. In fact, comment [1] to Model Rule 1.3 provides that "[t]he lawyer's duty to act with reasonable diligence does not require the use of offensive tactics or preclude treating all persons involved in the legal process with courtesy and respect." Although there is no express provision in the ABA Model Rules dealing with **civility**, profoundly discourteous or rude behavior in the context of legal practice could be disciplined under the catchall provisions of Rule 8.4(d).[40]

In In re Snyder, 472 U.S. 634 (1985), Chief Justice Burger cautioned lawyers to fulfill their responsibilities toward clients with civility:

> All persons involved in the judicial process—judges, litigants, witnesses, and court officers—owe a duty of courtesy to all other participants. The necessity for civility in the inherently contentious setting of the adversary process suggests that members of the bar cast criticisms of the system in a professional and civil tone.[41]

Notwithstanding that admonition, however, the Court reversed the Eighth Circuit's suspension of a criminal defense attorney for writing an allegedly rude letter to a district court judge's secretary setting forth his decision not to take any more Criminal Justice Act appointments, or to submit any more documentation in support of prior appointments. The Court held that "even assuming that the letter exhibited an unlawyerlike rudeness, a single incident of rudeness or lack of professional courtesy—in this context—does not support a finding of contemptuous or contumacious conduct, or a finding that a lawyer is 'not presently fit to practice law in the federal courts.'"[42]

Chief Justice Warren Burger, proponent of civility
Library of Congress Prints and Photographs Division Washington, D.C.

In response to abusive litigation tactics and what some observers see as the inherent limitations of bar discipline, many states have adopted voluntary and nonbinding "civility" codes.[43] Although the contents of these codes differ, many contain exhortations such as "cooperate in scheduling" and "avoid excessive zeal."[44] A few states also require lawyers to take

38. Model Rules Preamble cmt. [2] ("As an advocate, a lawyer zealously asserts the client's position under the rules of the advocacy system").
39. Model Rule 1.3 cmt. [1] ("A lawyer must also act with commitment and dedication to the interests of the client and with zeal in advocacy upon the client's behalf.").
40. Model Rule 8.4(d) prohibits conduct "prejudicial to the administration of justice." *Cf.* Carroll v. Jacques Admiralty Law Firm, 110 F.3d 290 (5th Cir. 1997) (recognizing inherent authority of federal court to sanction lawyer for profanity and abusiveness toward opposing counsel during deposition).
41. *Id.* at 647.
42. *Id.*
43. Katherine Sylvester, *I'm Rubber, You're Sued: Should Uncivil Lawyers Receive Ethical Sanctions?*, 26 Geo. J. Legal Ethics 1015, 1016 (2013) (distinguishing civility from ethics and discussing the role of voluntary civility codes in regulating attorney conduct).
44. *See, e.g.*, Colorado Bar Association, Principles of Professionalism (2011), http://www.cobar.org/For-Members/Committees/Professionalism-Coordinating-Council/Principles-of-Professionalism (last visited July 11, 2017). For a list of states with civility codes, see http://www.americanbar.org/groups/professional_responsibility/resources/professionalism/professionalism_codes.html.

"civility" oaths upon admission to practice.[45] To date there is little evidence that such oaths or codes have had a substantial influence on lawyer behavior. But even if such empirical evidence is lacking, do you think that the profession may benefit collectively from being perceived as willing and able to reach consensus around civility norms?

E. MAINTAINING THE IMPARTIALITY OF THE TRIBUNAL

Lawyers have a responsibility as officers of the court to avoid conduct that will compromise the fairness and impartiality of the judicial proceedings. This responsibility carries with it an obligation to avoid *ex parte* contact with judges or jurors, to refrain from (and report) any attempts to destroy evidence or improperly influence or intimidate witnesses, and to avoid acting as advocate in cases where the attorney is also likely to be called as a witness.

Under Model Rule 3.5(b), attorneys are prohibited from engaging in ***ex parte* communications** with judges or jurors on the subject of the litigation unless authorized by law. Fairness in adversary proceedings requires that the opposing counsel (or opposing party if self-represented) be present whenever an attorney addresses the court, seated jurors, or prospective jurors. Lawyers and judges often interact socially at bar association events and other professional gatherings. They may also meet each other in the hallways or other common areas of the courthouse. Rule 3.5(d) does not prohibit attorneys from talking to judges or magistrates about matters unrelated to the pending case (e.g., the news, sports, or weather) because those topics are not considered *ex parte* communications; nevertheless, an attorney must scrupulously avoid talking about the matter being litigated, because that could potentially compromise the judge's impartiality.

Paying a bribe or offering a monetary reward to a judge, juror, or fact witness[46] obviously compromises the **impartiality of a tribunal**, and in many instances will constitute a crime under state and federal law. Rule 3.5(a) prohibits a lawyer from "seek[ing] to influence a judge, juror, prospective juror or other official by means prohibited by law." A lawyer has a duty not only to refrain from engaging in such conduct, but also to *report* such conduct if he learns that it has been done by another. Rule 3.3(b) provides that a lawyer representing a client in an adjudicative proceeding "who knows that a person intends to engage, is engaging, or has engaged in criminal or fraudulent conduct relating to the proceeding" must take reasonable remedial measures, including disclosure to the court if necessary. For example, if a relative or friend of the client informs the lawyer that they have offered a bribe to a potential witness or juror, or that they destroyed or altered evidence, the attorney has an obligation to notify the court, even if that notice requires revealing a client confidence under Rule 1.6. If the same person discloses his intent to offer a bribe to a juror or a witness, the lawyer has a duty to do everything in his power to talk the person out of doing so.

---

45. S.C. Code §1976 Ann., App. Ct. Rule 402(h); S.C. App. Ct. R. 402(k); Tex. Gov't Code Ann. §82.037 (West 2015).

46. Expert witnesses may be compensated for their testimony under both state and federal law.

Model Rule 3.5 also limits the situations where an attorney may contact jurors *after* a verdict has been rendered in a case. A lawyer may desire post-verdict contact with jurors because the initial case resulted in a mistrial and the lawyer wants to learn from the first case about what strategies were effective or ineffective before retrying the case in front of another jury. Or, the attorney may seek to contact individual jurors after a verdict because he believes that there might have been impermissible and extraneous matters injected in juror deliberations that could give cause for a motion for new trial. These legitimate objectives, however, are in tension with common law presumptions that jury deliberations are privileged and that verdicts are final. For these reasons, attorneys may not communicate with jurors after a verdict if (1) the communication is prohibited by law or court order; (2) the juror has made known a desire not to be contacted; or (3) the communication involves misrepresentation, coercion, duress, or harassment. Lawyers must be familiar with particular attorney discipline rules and court decisions in the jurisdictions in which they practice, because states differ widely in their allowance of post-verdict contact with jurors. For example, some states prohibit any lawyer initiated contact with jurors unless authorized by the court,[47] and some states require notice to opposing counsel and a waiting period before contact may be made.[48]

Except in narrow situations, under Model Rule 3.7 an attorney may not serve as both an advocate and a witness in the same proceeding. This is known as the **advocate-witness rule**. There are several purported justifications for the rule, none of which are entirely persuasive. The rule may prevent prejudice to the client where the attorney gives factual testimony that differs from that offered by the client or other witnesses. Second, even if an attorney testifies favorably to his client, allowing an attorney to serve as a witness may in some situations prejudice the opposing party, because an attorney may be perceived as having added credibility compared to a lay witness. The jury may be confused as to how to evaluate an attorney's testimony (are they testifying as a fact witness or an expert witness?) and thereby give it inordinate weight. Both of these concerns have led to a presumption that proceedings cannot be fair and impartial where an attorney plays a dual role in the same litigation. But Rule 3.7 contains three notable exceptions: the advocate may serve as a witness in the same proceeding if (1) the testimony relates to an uncontested issue; (2) the testimony relates only to the nature and value of legal services; or (3) disqualification would impose a substantial hardship on the client.

F. PUBLIC COMMENT ON PENDING CIVIL LITIGATION

Disciplinary proceedings against lawyers in civil cases for talking to the media are rare. The likelihood of a lawyer materially prejudicing a civil proceeding by talking to the press is relatively low, because civil cases are less sensational than criminal cases, and because nobody's liberty is at stake. We discuss restrictions on talking

47. *See, e.g.*, Del. Lawyers' R. Prof'l Conduct 3.5(d).
48. Commonwealth v. Moore, 474 Mass. 541 (2016).

to the press in criminal cases in the next chapter, including the Supreme Court's seminal decision in *Gentile v. State Bar of Nevada*.

Rule 3.6(a) prohibits a lawyer participating in the litigation of an ongoing matter from making an "extrajudicial statement" that the lawyer "knows or reasonably should know will be disseminated by means of public communication" and that will have "a substantial likelihood of materially prejudicing an adjudicative proceeding in the matter."[49] Because one of the primary dangers of statements to the press is tainting the jury pool, the likelihood of prejudice from **media statements** is highest in cases that will be tried to a jury, and higher still the closer the matter gets to time of trial. Civil cases that are tried to a judge or arbitrator present the lowest possible risk of prejudice by comments to the media.[50] In addition to complying with Rule 3.6, once a civil trial has started the attorney must also comply with any **gag order** or restriction on media contact that is imposed by the court.[51]

Model Rule 3.6 (b) contains a "safe harbor" provision that allows an attorney to comment on specific subjects, irrespective of how likely they are to prejudice the proceedings. This section provides that "[n]otwithstanding" the prohibitions of Rule 3.6(a), a lawyer may permissibly comment on (1) the claim, offense, or defense involved; (2) information contained in a public record; (3) the fact that an investigation of a matter is in progress; (4) the scheduling or result of any step in litigation; (5) a request for assistance in obtaining evidence; and (6) a warning to the public of any dangers. Lawyers facing media inquiries regarding pending litigation should be mindful of the protection afforded by these six categories of information.

The broadest of these so-called safe harbor provisions is the public records exception. If a lawyer has already made a statement in court or in a written court submission, unless the matter is under seal the information may be repeated to the press. The attorney may also discuss with the press the content of any documents that have been marked in evidence or are otherwise made part of the public record in the case. Rule 3.6 also contains a "**fighting fire with fire**" provision, which allows an attorney to make a public statement that a reasonable lawyer "would believe is required to protect a client from the substantial undue prejudicial effect of recent publicity not initiated by the lawyer or the lawyer's client."

Lawyers may not use spokespeople to undertake conduct that would be impermissible if engaged in by the attorney. Model Rule 5.1(c) states that a lawyer shall be responsible for conduct of another if the lawyer "order[s]" or "ratif[ies]" that conduct, or if the lawyer has direct supervisory authority over a non-lawyer in a law firm and knows about that person's conduct in time to avoid its consequences. *See also* Rule 8.4(a) (which prohibits violating the rules "through the acts of another"). Thus, an attorney violates Rule 3.6 with respect to pretrial publicity if she asks a communications or public relations specialist within the firm to make a prejudicial statement to the media, or if the attorney assists the spokesperson for an organizational client to make such a statement.

49. Model Rule 3.6(a).
50. Model Rule 3.6(a) cmt. [6].
51. *See* Sheppard v. Maxwell, 384 U.S. 333, 363 (1966) ("The courts must take such steps by rule and regulation that will protect their [trial] processes from prejudicial outside interferences.").

Case Preview

Maldonado v. Ford Motor Co.

Justine Maldonado filed suit against Ford Motor Co. alleging that her supervisor, Daniel Bennett, sexually harassed her. Maldonado and her attorney repeatedly publicized Bennett's prior indecent exposure conviction that was subsequently expunged and denied admission as evidence in the harassment suit. Their actions included issuing a press release, meeting with the media to generate news coverage of the expunged conviction, and handing out leaflets containing information about the conviction at "Justice for Justine" rallies. Maldonado's attorney participated in the demonstrations, spoke to a local news station, and accused the judge of being under the influence of Ford Motor Co. This opinion of the Michigan Supreme Court highlights the interaction between Rule 3.6 and the First Amendment.

As you read *Maldonado*, ask yourself:

1. Was Maldonado's attorney at fault for violating Rule 3.6 directly, or by doing so through the actions of another (his client) under Rule 8.4(a)?
2. If the trial judge had not entered an order expressly prohibiting public comment on the indecent exposure conviction, would dismissal of a civil complaint be an available remedy for violation of an attorney disciplinary rule?

Maldonado v. Ford Motor Co.

719 N.W.2d 809 (Mich. 2006)

. . .

III. ANALYSIS

. . .

B. The Trial Court's Authority to Dismiss This Case

. . .

Not only did plaintiff and her counsel disregard Judge Macdonald's order and Judge Giovan's explicit warning to respect the order, counsel violated numerous rules of professional conduct. Plaintiff's counsel's public references to Bennett's excluded conviction violated MRPC 3.6, which was the basis for Judge Giovan's dismissal. Plaintiff's counsel reasonably knew or should have known that their comments would have a substantial likelihood of materially prejudicing the proceedings by improperly influencing prospective jurors regarding Bennett's propensities to commit sexual harassment, especially since trial was approximately two weeks away.

Plaintiff argues that Judge Giovan improperly relied on MRPC 3.6 in dismissing plaintiff's case. She contends that Judge Giovan's dismissal was solely based on plaintiff's comments, and that MRPC 3.6 does not apply to nonlawyers. Plaintiff

correctly argues that the Michigan Rules of Professional Conduct do not apply to nonlawyers, but mistakenly contends that Judge Giovan relied only on her behavior in ordering a dismissal. Plaintiff also erroneously contends that she is free to engage in improper pretrial publicity designed to taint the potential jury pool. The Michigan Court Rules do apply to plaintiff. They authorize the trial court to impose sanctions such as dismissal for party misconduct. MCR 2.504(B)(1). Judge Giovan expressly warned plaintiff that if she continued to disseminate information regarding Bennett's excluded conviction in violation of Judge Macdonald's order, he would dismiss her case. Plaintiff failed to obey this warning and, thus, Judge Giovan properly dismissed her case. In any event, even if plaintiff is not bound by MRPC 3.6, plaintiff's counsel's repeated public references to Bennett's excluded conviction, coupled with Ms. Massie's statement five days before trial that "Metro Detroit" judges were biased in favor of the Ford Motor Company, were substantially likely to materially prejudice the proceedings and improperly influence prospective jurors.

. . .

C. The First Amendment and a Trial Court's Ability to Restrict Speech

. . .

We agree with the majority of the States that the "substantial likelihood of material prejudice" standard [of Rule 3.6] constitutes a constitutionally permissible balance between the First Amendment rights of attorneys in pending cases and the State's interest in fair trials.

When a state regulation implicates First Amendment rights, the Court must balance those interests against the State's legitimate interest in regulating the activity in question. The "substantial likelihood" test . . . is constitutional . . . for it is designed to protect the integrity and fairness of a state's judicial system and it imposes only narrow and necessary limitations on lawyers' speech. The limitations are aimed at two principal evils: (1) comments that are likely to influence the actual outcome of the trial, and (2) *comments that are likely to prejudice the jury venire, even if an untainted panel can ultimately be found.* [*Gentile*, 501 U.S at 1075 (emphasis added).]

The Court noted that "[l]awyers representing clients in pending cases are key participants in the criminal justice system, and the State may demand some adherence to the precepts of that system in regulating their speech as well as their conduct." Id. at 1074, 111 S. Ct. 2720. The Court further observed that "[f]ew, if any, interests under the Constitution are more fundamental than the right to a fair trial by 'impartial' jurors, and an outcome affected by extrajudicial statements would violate that fundamental right." Id. at 1075, 111 S. Ct. 2720.

. . .

More important, however, is that the plaintiff should not be heard to make her argument, which goes like this: "We deny that our behavior was intended to have a substantial likelihood of prejudice. But even if you establish that it was, you cannot dismiss the plaintiff's case until you establish that it has achieved its intended effect."

We believe otherwise. That is not an acceptable standard for preserving the integrity of a court system. The behavior in question has been intentional, premeditated, and intransigent. It was designed to reach the farthest boundaries of the public consciousness. It should be presumed to have had its intended effect.

The Court of Appeals acknowledged that the applicable test under *Gentile* is whether the conduct generated a "substantial likelihood" of prejudice, yet remanded for an evidentiary hearing to determine whether "actual" prejudice occurred.

We hereby affirm the trial court's understanding of *Gentile*. Plaintiff's and her counsel's numerous public references to Bennett's inadmissible, expunged indecent exposure conviction, despite a court order excluding such evidence, were obviously intended to prejudice potential jurors. The trial court thus warned the parties and counsel that all public references to the expunged conviction in violation of the ethical rules would result in dismissal. This limitation on plaintiff's and her counsel's speech only applied to speech that was substantially likely to have a materially prejudicial effect and that, therefore, violated the rules of ethics. It did not prohibit plaintiff and her counsel from speaking about sexual harassment or the general nature of plaintiff's case.

. . .

The Court of Appeals requirement that actual prejudice be shown conflicts not only with the "substantial likelihood" test set forth in *Gentile*, but also with the plain language of MRPC 3.6. Moreover, the Court of Appeals standard has no practical workability. It would be impossible to determine "actual prejudice" to a potential jury pool three years after the incident in question. We decline to order an evidentiary hearing that is no more than a fool's errand.

. . .

V. CONCLUSION

We hold that the trial court's explicit warning prohibiting any references to Bennett's excluded conviction did not violate the First Amendment. Accordingly, we reverse the judgment of the Court of Appeals and reinstate the trial court's order dismissing plaintiff's case.

Post-Case Follow-Up

Rule 3.6 focuses on *pretrial* comments that have potential to prejudice an adversarial proceeding. In addition, disciplinary rules in effect in many jurisdictions prohibit an attorney from knowingly or recklessly making false comments about the qualifications or integrity of a judge — either before or after the proceeding. *See* Model Rule 8.2(a). Under Rule 8.2 it is improper for an attorney participating in litigation to make untruthful comments that call into question the competence of the court. But since criticism of the government is a very core protection of the First Amendment,[52] this method of preserving public confidence in the integrity of the judiciary bumps squarely up against constitutional protections. Because Rule 8.2 prohibits comments that the lawyer knows or should know are untruthful, it puts the risk on

52. Gentile v. State Bar of Nevada, 501 U.S. 1030, 1055 (1991).

lawyers to carefully evaluate the truthfulness of their speech before publicly making any statements that impugn the reputation of judges before whom they appear.[53]

Maldonado v. Ford Motor Co.: Real Life Applications

Imagine a lawyer who makes a statement to the media following a trial that "this was one of the most poorly conducted trials that I have ever participated in; I am confident that the trial judge's ill-conceived and biased evidentiary rulings will be overturned on appeal." Does this statement violate either Rule 3.6 or Rule 8.2? If the trial is over, is there any "substantial likelihood" that this public statement could prejudice the proceeding within the meaning of Rule 3.6? Is the statement about the way the judge conducted the trial a statement of opinion or fact? If the former, is that something that can either be true or false within the meaning of Rule 8.2? If the latter, is it a statement about the judge's "qualifications" or "integrity"?

G. COMMUNICATING WITH REPRESENTED PERSONS

Model Rule 4.2, often called the **"no-contact" rule**, prohibits an attorney from communicating with a person represented by counsel on the subject of that representation without permission of the client's attorney. In substance, when a person is known to be represented in a matter, an attorney must first go through that person's counsel for permission to speak with the client. The purposes of the "no-contact" rule are threefold: (1) to encourage professional courtesy by requiring permission before one lawyer speaks with another lawyer's client; (2) to prevent a lawyer, through overreaching or superior bargaining power, from tricking a represented witness or party into making damaging admissions or concessions; and (3) to discourage uncounseled waivers of the attorney-client privilege.

All 50 states contain a "no-contact" provision in their attorney disciplinary rules, although state rules vary considerably in their terminology and exceptions. The Model Rules provision was amended in 1995 to apply to represented "persons" rather than "parties." Some states still apply their "no-contact" rule only to represented "parties."[54] This is perhaps the most common deviation among states. The potential significance of this distinction will be discussed below.

Where the "no-contact" rule applies to represented parties, an attorney would be subject to discipline if he contacts an opposing party directly to discuss a potential settlement of the case without receiving permission from opposing counsel. Even "cc'ing" the client on a letter to counsel proposing a settlement without the lawyer's permission would violate the rule, because the attorney is "communicating"

---

53. In re Wilkins, 777 N.E.2d 714, 716-17 (Ind. 2002), *modified*, 782 N.E.2d 985 (Ind. 2003) (disciplining lawyer who called the Indiana Court of Appeals' decision "disturbing," accused the judges of making affirmative misstatements of fact, and suggested that they were biased in favor of other party).

54. *See* ARIZ. R. PROF'L CONDUCT 4.2; CAL. R. PROF'L CONDUCT 2-100; CONN. R. PROF'L CONDUCT 4.2.

with the party on the subject of the representation. Note that the rule is not waivable by the client, but only by the attorney. Thus, a prosecutor who is approached by a represented defendant[55] outside of the courtroom must decline to speak to that opposing party without his attorney's permission, or risk being found in violation of the rule.

Even in jurisdictions that apply their "no-contact" rule to represented "parties," the protections of the rule apply outside of the litigation context. Courts and bar disciplinary authorities have declined to limit the rule's application to opposing parties after litigation has been commenced, and have construed the term "party" to apply to clients in a business setting who stand on the opposite side of a transaction.[56] For example, where an attorney is negotiating a commercial lease on behalf of a business tenant and the owner of the premises is known to be represented by counsel, the lawyer may not have communication directly with the owner without that attorney's permission.

Where the jurisdiction applies its "no-contact" rule to a represented "person" an attorney must also be careful not to communicate directly with any *witness* who is represented by counsel. For example, a plaintiff in an employment discrimination suit might seek to take the statement of a former co-worker about the conditions of their employment. If that former co-worker has also retained counsel for purposes of conducting negotiations with the company, the attorney for the plaintiff must seek permission of that lawyer before speaking with the co-worker, even if that former co-worker is not yet a party to any formal litigation and is ostensibly on the "same side." In the same vein, a prosecutor may normally speak to the victim of a crime unencumbered by any proscriptions about obtaining advance permission, but if that victim has retained a lawyer (for example, in order to advise the victim on potential civil recoveries for the same injury), the prosecutor must first go through counsel.

The term "person" in Rule 4.2 includes artificial persons — business entities such as corporations, partnerships, and trusts that are represented by counsel. Those business entities can only act through natural persons, but the question is which of those natural persons — from top management to lower-level employees — are considered "represented" by corporate counsel and thereby shielded from contact under the rule. Here we see that a balance is necessary between protecting attorney-client relationships and providing the public and putative litigants with the ability to gather evidence to investigate wrongdoing. Taking the position that "all employees" are represented by corporate counsel would curtail the informal discovery process and force litigants to conduct expensive depositions. Taking the position that only the senior management of a company is represented by counsel for the purposes of the rule would handicap corporate lawyers from shielding their clients from damaging admissions or revelations of privileged information by lower-level employees. Pay careful attention to how the Massachusetts Supreme Judicial Court resolved these competing tensions in a sex discrimination suit against Harvard University.

55. Where the party is self-represented, communication is permissible.

56. In re Illuzzi, 616 A.2d 233, 236 (Vt. 1992); United States v. Galanis, 685 F. Supp. 901, 902 (S.D.N.Y. 1988).

Case Preview

Messing, Rudavsky & Weliky, P.C. v. President and Fellows of Harvard College

Kathleen Stanford was a sergeant with the Harvard University Police Department who claimed that Harvard and its chief of police discriminated against her because of her gender. During the course of the litigation, a partner with the law firm of Messing, Rudavsky & Weliky (MR&W) contacted five employees of the Harvard Police Department—none of whom were involved in the alleged discrimination—without first seeking permission from Harvard's attorneys. The trial court sanctioned MR&W under Massachusetts Rule of Professional Conduct 4.2, which prohibits a lawyer from communicating directly with any person known to be represented by a lawyer.

As you read *Messing*, ask yourself:

1. How does the "**control group**" test for deciding who is a represented person under Rule 4.2 insufficiently protect organizations from damaging admissions by employees?
2. How does an interpretation of Rule 4.2 that synchronizes the "no-contact" standard with the test for admissions under the Rules of Evidence impede informal discovery? What are the financial consequences of erecting such a barrier in litigation?

Messing, Rudavsky & Weliky, P.C. v. President and Fellows of Harvard College

764 N.E.2d 825 (Mass. 2002)

. . . This appeal raises the issue whether, and to what extent, the rule prohibits an attorney from speaking ex parte to the employees of an organization represented by counsel. . . .

On appeal, MR & W contends that the judge's construction of the rule is overly broad and results from an incorrect interpretation of the rule's commentary.

. . .

The rule has been justified generally as "preserv[ing] the mediating role of counsel on behalf of their clients . . . protect[ing] clients from overreaching by counsel for adverse interests," and "protecting the attorney-client relationship." . . .

When the represented person is an individual, there is no difficulty determining when an attorney has violated the rule; the represented person is easily identifiable. In the case of an organization, however, identifying the protected class is more complicated.

Because an organization acts only through its employees, the rule must extend to some of these employees. However, most courts have rejected the position that the rule automatically prevents an attorney from speaking with all employees of a represented organization.

. . .

According to comment [4] to rule 4.2, an attorney may not speak ex parte to three categories of employees: (1) "persons having managerial responsibility on behalf of the organization with regard to the subject of the representation"; (2) persons "whose act or omission in connection with that matter may be imputed to the organization for purposes of civil or criminal liability"; and (3) persons "whose statement may constitute an admission on the part of the organization." Mass. R. Prof. C. 4.2 comment [4], 426 Mass. 1403 (1998).

. . .

Some jurisdictions have adopted the broad reading of the rule endorsed by the judge in this case. . . . Courts reaching this result do so because, like the Superior Court, they read the word "admission" in the third category of the comment as a reference to Fed. R. Evid. 801(d)(2)(D) and any corresponding State rule of evidence. Id. This rule forbids contact with practically all employees because "virtually every employee may conceivably make admissions binding on his or her employer". . . .

At the other end of the spectrum, a small number of jurisdictions has interpreted the rule narrowly so as to allow an attorney for the opposing party to contact most employees of a represented organization. These courts construe the rule to restrict contact with only those employees in the organization's "control group," defined as those employees in the uppermost echelon of the organization's management. . . .

Other jurisdictions have adopted yet a third test that, while allowing for some ex parte contacts with a represented organization's employees, still maintains some protection of the organization. The Court of Appeals of New York articulated such a rule in Niesig v. Team I, 76 N.Y.2d 363, 559 N.Y.S.2d 493, 558 N.E.2d 1030 (1990), rejecting an approach that ties the rule to Fed. R. Evid. 801(d)(2)(D). Instead, the court defined a represented person to include "employees whose acts or omissions in the matter under inquiry are binding on the corporation . . . or imputed to the corporation for purposes of its liability, or employees implementing the advice of counsel." Id. at 374, 559 N.Y.S.2d 493, 558 N.E.2d 1030.

. . .

We instead interpret the rule to ban contact only with those employees who have the authority to "commit the organization to a position regarding the subject matter of representation." . . . The employees with whom contact is prohibited are those with "speaking authority" for the corporation who "have managing authority sufficient to give them the right to speak for, and bind, the corporation". . . . Employees who can commit the organization are those with authority to make decisions about the course of the litigation, such as when to initiate suit, and when to settle a pending case. . . . We recognize that this test is a retrenchment from the broad prohibition on employee contact endorsed by the comment.

This interpretation, when read in conjunction with the other two categories of the comment, would prohibit ex parte contact only with those employees who exercise managerial responsibility in the matter, who are alleged to have committed the wrongful acts at issue in the litigation, or who have authority on behalf of the corporation to make decisions about the course of the litigation. This result is substantially the same as the *Niesig* test because it "prohibit[s] direct communication . . . 'with those officials . . . who have the legal power to bind the corporation in the matter or who are responsible for implementing the advice of the corporation's lawyer . . . or whose own interests are directly at stake in a representation.'" Niesig v. Team I, *supra* at 374, 559 N.Y.S.2d 493, 558 N.E.2d 1030. . . .

Our test is consistent with the purposes of the rule, which are not to "protect a corporate party from the revelation of prejudicial facts" . . . but to protect the attorney-client relationship and prevent clients from making ill-advised statements without the counsel of their attorney. Prohibiting contact with all employees of a represented organization restricts informal contacts far more than is necessary to achieve these purposes. See Niesig v. Team I, supra at 372-373, 559 N.Y.S.2d 493, 558 N.E.2d 1030. The purposes of the rule are best served when it prohibits communication with those employees closely identified with the organization in the dispute. The interests of the organization are adequately protected by preventing contact with those employees empowered to make litigation decisions, and those employees whose actions or omissions are at issue in the case. We reject the "control group" test, which includes only the most senior management, as insufficient to protect the "principles motivating [Rule 4.2]." See id. at 373, 559 N.Y.S.2d 493, 558 N.E.2d 1030. The test we adopt protects an organizational party against improper advances and influence by an attorney, while still promoting access to relevant facts. See id. at 373-374, 559 N.Y.S.2d 493, 558 N.E.2d 1030. The Superior Court's interpretation of the rule would grant an advantage to corporate litigants over nonorganizational parties. It grants an unwarranted benefit to organizations to require that a party always seek prior judicial approval to conduct informal interviews with witnesses to an event when the opposing party happens to be an organization and the events at issue occurred at the workplace.

. . .

Applying rule 4.2 to the employees interviewed by MR & W. The five Harvard employees interviewed by MR & W do not fall within the third category of the comment as we have construed it. As employees of the HUPD, they are not involved in directing the litigation at bar or authorizing the organization to make binding admissions. In fact, Harvard does not argue that any of the five employees fit within our definition of this category.

The Harvard employees are also not employees "whose act or omission in connection with that matter may be imputed to the organization for purposes of civil or criminal liability." Mass. R. Prof. C. 4.2 comment [4]. Stanford's complaint does not name any of these employees as involved in the alleged discrimination. In fact, in an affidavit she states that the two lieutenants "had no role in making any of the decisions that are the subject of my complaint of discrimination and retaliation," and Harvard does not refute this averment. All five employees were mere witnesses to the events that occurred, not active participants.

We must still determine, however, whether any of the interviewed employees have "managerial responsibility on behalf of the organization with regard to the subject of the representation." Mass. R. Prof. C. 4.2 comment [4]. Although the two patrol officers and the dispatcher were subordinate to Stanford and had no managerial authority, the two lieutenants exercised some supervisory authority over Stanford. However, not all employees with some supervisory power over their coworkers are deemed to have "managerial" responsibility in the sense intended by

the comment. . . . "[S]upervision of a small group of workers would not constitute a managerial position within a corporation". . . . Even if the two lieutenants are deemed to have managerial responsibility, the Massachusetts version of the comment adds the requirement that the managerial responsibility be in "regard to the subject of the representation." Mass. R. Prof. C. 4.2 comment [4]. Thus, the comment includes only those employees who have supervisory authority over the events at issue in the litigation. There is no evidence in the record that the lieutenants' managerial decisions were a subject of the litigation. The affidavits of the two lieutenants indicate that they did not complete any evaluations or offer any opinions of Stanford that Chief Riley considered in reaching his decisions.

5. Conclusion. Because we conclude that rule 4.2 did not prohibit MR & W from contacting and interviewing the five HUPD employees, we vacate the order of the Superior Court judge and remand the case for the entry of an order denying the defendant's motion for sanctions.

Post-Case Follow-Up

The comment to Model Rule 4.2 was amended in 2002 to adopt the *Messing* refinement,[57] limiting the implied representation of corporate employees by corporate counsel to three classes of employees. However, not all states agree with this middle-ground approach to classifying who is represented by corporate counsel for purposes of the "no-contact" rule. As the discussion by the Massachusetts Supreme Judicial Court in *Messing* indicates, some states limit the rule's prohibition to those in the corporate control group (which has the effect of permitting more informal fact investigation) while other states broaden the rule to prevent communication with any employee whose statements might constitute an "admission" at trial — which under the Federal Rules of Evidence constitutes any employee speaking about a subject matter within the scope of her employment — thus preventing informal discovery and requiring resort to depositions.

Messing, Rudavsky & Weliky, P.C. v. President and Fellows of Harvard College: Real Life Applications

1. With little knowledge of a company's business, how is a lawyer supposed to know which employees are considered "represented" by corporate counsel for purposes of the *Messing* test? Suppose that you represent a golfer who was injured when he tripped over an unmarked sprinkler head at a private country club. After filing suit, you wish to conduct informal interviews with the president of the club, the head greenskeeper, an employee of the club who was mowing the grass nearby the accident at the time your client tripped, and your client's caddy.

57. Model Rule 4.2 cmt. [7].

Which individuals may you interview without getting permission from counsel for the country club?

2. You represent one spouse in an increasingly bitter divorce. After a contentious pretrial hearing, your client informs you, "I just want to talk to my husband personally and see if we can work out some of these issues between ourselves." May you counsel your *client* to talk to a represented opposing party without running afoul of Rules 4.2 and 8.4? What values behind the "no-contact" rule are at risk and what values are not at risk in a situation involving party-to-party contact?

3. Suppose that you want to investigate an opposing party in litigation. May you ask a paralegal to send the party a "friend request" on Facebook so that the two of you can peruse the party's personal information, without running afoul of Rule 4.2?

Where corporate employees are concerned, lawyers would be well advised to consult precedent of their individual jurisdiction for an interpretation of Rule 4.2. Most states agree that *former* employees of the corporation are not automatically represented by counsel for the corporation unless they have been expressly retained, because they are no longer part of the relationship sought to be fostered and protected by the rule.[58]

Note that Model Rule 8.4(a) makes it professional misconduct for an attorney to violate a disciplinary rule "through the acts of another." Where an attorney is prevented from contacting a represented person or party under Rule 4.2, the attorney is also prohibited from instructing a paralegal or private investigator to engage in that same contact.

The "no-contact" rule allows an attorney to conduct communications with a represented person without permission of counsel if he is "authorized to do so by law or a court order."[59] What types of *ex parte* communications might be authorized by law? Service of a subpoena to testify at trial or deposition is clearly authorized, because most jurisdictions' rules of procedure allow for in-person service. What else might this include? The "authorized by law" exception has generated heated debate among the criminal justice community about what investigatory steps are allowed by prosecutors with regard to represented targets prior to bringing an indictment. Some of these issues are discussed in the next chapter.

H. COMMUNICATING WITH UNREPRESENTED PERSONS

In representing a client an attorney often comes into contact with persons whose legal rights and obligations may be at issue in the case, but who have not retained their own lawyer. For example, in a motor vehicle accident case involving a multiple car pileup, an attorney for one plaintiff may interview witnesses who also have

58. *Id. See also* ABA Formal Op. 91-359 (1991); Restatement §100 cmt. g.
59. Model Rule 4.2.

potential causes of action against the defendant, but who have not contemplated or commenced litigation. A real estate attorney may negotiate a commercial lease of a business premises directly with an owner who is not represented by counsel. In order to avoid misleading unrepresented persons in these situations, Model Rule 4.3 prohibits a lawyer from stating or implying that a lawyer is disinterested when he is dealing with an unrepresented party. Often times lay witnesses are confused about whom the lawyer represents and what the lawyer's goals are in conducting an interview. Where it is clear to the lawyer that an unrepresented person is confused about the lawyer's role in the matter, the lawyer has an affirmative obligation under Rule 4.3 to correct the misunderstanding. For example, the lawyer representing the plaintiff in our hypothetical motor vehicle accident who is interviewing the driver of another car struck by the defendant, if asked "how much money will I get if you win your case" must explain that the pending proceeding is not a class action, that he represents only one alleged tort victim, and that if the witness seeks to recover on his own he must file his own civil action or speak directly to the defendant's insurance company.

A lawyer must also avoid the conflict of interest that would arise in giving legal advice to someone whose interests are adverse to those of the lawyer's client. Rule 4.3 prohibits the provision of legal advice, other than the "advice to secure counsel," to someone whose interests have a reasonable possibility of being adverse to the interests of the lawyer's client. For example, in the commercial lease example cited above, the owner of the building and the future tenant have interests that may be in conflict. If the building owner does not understand a term of the draft lease and asks the lawyer for the tenant what a particular legal term means and what his legal rights are under that clause of the draft contract, the attorney must explain to the owner that he is not allowed to give him legal advice and that if he wants a legal explanation he needs to engage his own lawyer. In this scenario, the rule recognizes that determining precisely where the lawyer crosses the line between explaining factual terms in a contract and providing "legal advice" to an unrepresented person will depend on "the experience and sophistication of the unrepresented person, as well as the setting in which the behavior and comments occur."[60]

I. TRUTHFULNESS IN STATEMENTS TO OTHERS

Model Rule 4.1 prohibits a lawyer from making a false statement of material fact to a third person during the course of his representation of a client. The rule also requires disclosure of a material fact where necessary to prevent a crime or fraud, *unless* such disclosure is prohibited by Rule 1.6. With respect to omissions and third parties, the duty of confidentiality thus trumps the duty of candor. Compare this to a lawyer's duty of candor to a tribunal in *ex parte* proceedings (Section B.4, *supra*) and with respect to witness perjury (Section B.3, *supra*), where a lawyer's duty as an officer of the court trumps his duty to protect client confidences.

---

60. Model Rule 4.3 cmt. [2].

Note the difference between commissions and omissions in Rule 4.1(a) and (b). A lawyer may not make a false statement of material fact to a third party, period. However, a lawyer's duty to affirmatively correct a false statement made by his client or another is considerably more complicated.

The *commission* component of Rule 4.1(a) would prohibit a personal injury lawyer from advising a prospective witness to a motor vehicle accident that his client lost his job as a result of the accident, if in fact his client was unemployed at the time of the crash. This misstatement is material because it might engender sympathy in the client, increase the witness's view of damages, and cause the witness to be willing to cooperate when otherwise he might not be inclined to do so. On the other hand, Rule 4.1(a) would *not* be violated if that same lawyer misrepresented himself as a relative of the witness in order to get through to the witness on the office switchboard. Such a statement, while false, is irrelevant to the car accident and therefore not material.

Now consider the *omission* component of Rule 4.1(b). A lawyer must disclose a material fact to a third person only if such disclosure (1) is necessary to avoid assisting a criminal or fraudulent act by the client, *and* (2) such disclosure does not violate the rule of client confidences. Here, the protection for client confidences under Rule 1.6 trumps the obligation of truthfulness. For example, a lawyer may discover during his representation of a client in the purchase of real property that his client has substantially misstated his assets on a loan application to a bank. If rectifying this misstatement would require the lawyer to reveal a client confidence (for example, if the lawyer knows this information only as a result of his representation of the client), the lawyer generally may not reveal the information and has not violated Rule 4.1(b). However, if the lawyer assists the client in purchasing the real property *based* on this false mortgage application, he may be assisting in a crime or fraud in violation of Rule 1.2(d). If that is the case, the lawyer must correct the material misstatement if he intends to continue the representation, unless the revelation would violate Rule 1.6. Since the "exceptions" to client confidences in Rule 1.6(b)(1)-(7) are phrased in terms of **permissive disclosures**, exercising discretion to reveal a confidence in one of those enumerated instances would not be "prohibited" by the rule. Thus, with respect to material omissions, the permissive disclosures under Rule 1.6(b) become mandatory disclosures if necessary to avoid assisting in a criminal or fraudulent act by your client. In the case of our supposed bank fraud, the lawyer's options in that situation are either to withdraw from representation; to urge the client to correct the misrepresentation to the bank; to seek the client's permission to breach the client confidence and inform the bank himself; or — and only if the lawyer reasonably believes it is necessary to prevent substantial injury to the financial interests or property of another — to reveal the misstatement to the bank himself. *See* Model Rule 1.6(b)(3).

The Model Rule's prohibition of material misstatements by a lawyer to a third party contains a "puffing" exception. During legal representation a lawyer may engage in negotiations with a third party as to price or value. For example, in the real estate transaction cited above, the client may engage the lawyer to make an offer on his behalf for the purchase of residential real estate. The lawyer may offer $500,000. After a counteroffer of $550,000, the lawyer may meet in the middle and offer $525,000, stating that "this is as high as my client has authorized me to go." If the client has in fact authorized him to purchase the property for as much as $600,000, this is a material misstatement of fact. Nevertheless, it is unlikely to result in bar discipline in most jurisdictions. Comment [2] to Model Rule 4.1 provides that under "generally accepted conventions in negotiations," statements regarding price, value, or settlement intentions are generally considered statements of opinion rather than fact for the purposes of the rule. This "puffing" exception for misstatements to third parties seems to be a pragmatic concession to the limits of attorney regulation with regard to a lawyer's role in negotiations.

With regard to misstatements to others, attorneys must be aware that Model Rule 8.4(c) is broader than Model Rule 4.1 and constrains conduct that would not violate the former rule. Rule 8.4(c) provides that an attorney may not "engage in conduct involving dishonesty, fraud, deceit or misrepresentation." Rule 8.4 is broader than Rule 4.1 because the false statement or misrepresentation does not have to be material and the statement does not have to be in the course of representation of a client. Rule 8.4(c) is thus a broader, potential "catchall" provision that could arguably apply even to an attorney's private affairs. For example, Rule 8.4(c) could be invoked to sanction a lawyer for dishonesty in his personal business dealings or political pursuits.[61]

Should either Rule 4.1 or Rule 8.4 contain an exception allowing attorneys to misrepresent their identity or purpose in order to investigate conduct they believe to be unlawful? Some commentators believe that civil attorneys should be able to engage in or direct "testing" (i.e., undercover investigations) in order to expose unlawful activities. One prominent attorney in Massachusetts thought so, and proceeded to conduct an undercover investigation of alleged judicial misconduct that got him disbarred.

Case Preview

In re Crossen

Attorney Crossen represented one of the family members in a multi-million-dollar shareholder derivative suit involving control of the Demoulas supermarket empire. In an effort to have a Massachusetts superior court judge recused from the case, Crossen took part in an intricate plot designed to uncover evidence of the trial judge's bias. Crossen set up and recorded sham job interviews with the judge's former law clerk in order to coax the clerk into unveiling facts about the judge's deliberative process and alleged bias. Crossen also placed the law clerk under surveillance and threatened to interfere with his state bar application if he did not cooperate. The disciplinary board recommended Crossen be disbarred, and this appeal followed.

61. Finely v. Kentucky Bar Ass'n, 378 S.W.3d 313, 314 (Ky. 2012) (lawyer used his office's Westlaw account to conduct research for personal profit).

Although *Crossen* involved a Massachusetts disciplinary rule that predated the state's adoption of the Model Rules, it is instructive as to the limits of a private attorney's authority to engage in misrepresentation.

As you read *Crossen*, ask yourself:

1. Do you think Crossen's investigatory tactics were influenced by his prior experiences as a prosecutor and Assistant U.S. Attorney? Should they have been?
2. In handing out its sanction of disbarment, the Supreme Judicial Court was influenced by the "unusual scope" of the respondent's misconduct. Do you think the court was motivated by a unique desire to protect the deliberative processes of judges and their law clerks? Would a lawyer's fraud and deceit have warranted such severe discipline if the "victim" had not been the court system itself?

In re Crossen

880 N.E.2d 352 (Mass. 2008)

***(ii) Use of a sham interview.* The board properly determined that Crossen's participation in the New York interview, including the surreptitious tape recording, violated Canon 1, DR 1-102(A)(2) and (4)-(6), and Canon 7, DR 7-102(A)(5) and (7). That the New York interview involved "dishonesty, fraud, deceit, or misrepresentation," Canon 1, DR 1-102(A)(4), and "false" statements and "fraudulent" conduct, Canon 7, DR 7-102(A)(5) and (7), cannot seriously be doubted.**

. . .

The board also correctly concluded that the surreptitious tape recording of the New York interview violated DR 1-102(A)(4) and DR 7-102(A)(5). Crossen is correct that no legal barrier prevented him from secretly tape recording the law clerk's conversation in New York. However, when Crossen orchestrated the surreptitious tape recording in 1997, there was long-standing authority that lawyers violate the ethical rules when they tape record a person without his consent, even if the recording is legal. ABA Formal Op. 337 (1974). In any event, we will not detach the legal act of one-party tape recording in New York from the web of knowing and deliberate misstatements and falsehoods in which it was integrally embedded in this case. . . . The legality of the tape recording does not mask its improper purpose. Where the surreptitious tape recording of the law clerk was in furtherance of an effort to coerce or even manufacture sworn testimony against a judge in a pending matter, Crossen's tape recording of the sham interview not only violated his obligations to eschew misstatement, deceit, and falsehood in his professional dealings, but also manifestly worked to the prejudice of the administration of justice and impugned his own bona fides as an attorney.

. . .

***(iii) Threats and surveillance.* The board concluded that Crossen violated Canon 1, DR 1-102(A)(4)-(6), and Canon 7, DR 7-102(A)(5) and (7), when he threatened that, unless the law clerk stated under oath that Judge Lopez was biased against the Telemachus Demoulas family in the shareholder derivative suit, he, Crossen, would**

disclose the "embarrassing or compromising" statements the law clerk made during the sham job interviews, including the information that the law clerk, in connection with his bar application, had submitted a letter of recommendation from a person whom he did not know. The board also concluded that Crossen violated the same disciplinary rules, with the exception of DR 1-102(A)(5), when he deliberately misrepresented to the law clerk that there existed a tape recording of the Halifax meeting. These conclusions find ample support in the record.

. . .

Again, we consider Crossen's available choices. When the New York interview did not yield the results Crossen sought, Crossen did not lay the matter to rest. He did not confront Curry[62] — whom he was advised by at least three highly regarded cocounsel to view with caution — with exaggerating what the law clerk said in Halifax. Rather, Crossen sought to obtain the results his client wanted by offering the law clerk a stark quid pro quo: an implicit bargain not to make public the law clerk's bar application if the law clerk offered sworn testimony that Judge Lopez had prejudged the Demoulas defendants' case. To further pressure the law clerk, the quid pro quo was presented under a deadline that did not exist. This conduct goes far beyond what a reasonable attorney zealously representing his client would consider either proper investigation of the facts or permissible hard-nosed bargaining. Crossen's most coercive actions occurred *after* the sham interview yielded equivocal results and *after* he was warned about Curry's credibility. . . .

With regard to surveillance, there was substantial evidence for the board to conclude that Crossen intentionally lied to the law clerk when he denied any involvement in or awareness of surveillance of the law clerk in late August. We agree with the board that this misrepresentation is of a piece with his other misstatements and falsehoods in violating DR 1-102(A)(4) and (6).

. . .

b. Investigative techniques. Crossen argues that he had a good faith belief that his conduct was proper, and that his "subjective belief was objectively reasonable, as illustrated by contemporaneous scholarly commentary." He leans particularly on an article coauthored by a former chair of the American Bar Association's Standing Committee on Professional Responsibility. . . . Crossen does not claim that he took guidance from, or even read, the ethics article in the course of the relevant events in this case. More importantly, the ethics article does not discuss, much less endorse, the kind of ruse at issue here. The ethics article's thrust, as Crossen says, is that public and private attorneys who act as investigators and testers conducting undercover investigations or undertaking discrimination testing to gather evidence they otherwise would be unlikely to obtain voluntarily, or who supervise others in such conduct, do not violate rules 4.1(a) and 8.4(c) of the ABA Model Rules of Professional Conduct, which forbid making false statements or material misrepresentations. . . . However, Crossen omits the important caveat of the ethics article's thesis, namely, that it applies only to "elementary, and essential, misrepresentations as to identity

62. Kevin Curry was another attorney representing the Demoulas family who had originally interviewed the law clerk and informed Crossen that the law clerk had heard the judge make prejudicial statements about his client. — EDS.

and purpose made by discrimination undercover investigators and testers". . . . ("Rule 8.4[c], which prohibits conduct involving dishonesty, fraud, deceit or misrepresentation, would not apply to misrepresentations of the *mild sort necessarily* made by discrimination testers and undercover investigators" [emphasis added]). The article makes clear that where the "misrepresentations are of a graver kind, or when a tester/investigator is used by the lawyer specifically for something the lawyer is forbidden to do, or when the lawyer directs a tester/investigator to engage in activities that violate the rights of others," the Model Rules of Professional Conduct are implicated, regardless whether the attorney is private or public counsel. . . . According to the authors of the ethics article, specific conduct that violates Model Rules 4.1(a) and 8.4(c) includes a lawyer acting in his or her capacity as a lawyer who makes "misrepresentations of material fact" . . . as well as a lawyer engaging in conduct or supervising conduct that employs "excessively intrusive investigative techniques," "entrapment," or involves "an actionable invasion of privacy". . . . It is clear from what we have said to this point that Crossen's conduct fails even the ethics article's test.

. . .

We conclude as well that, acting with reason, Crossen should have known that his efforts to intimidate the law clerk with threats of disclosure unless the law clerk produced sworn statements damaging to Judge Lopez was prejudicial to the administration of justice: it was intended or was likely to produce from the law clerk testimony more critical of Judge Lopez than the law clerk otherwise would or could have given.

. . .

6. *Sanction*

. . .

In considering whether the sanction of disbarment is markedly disparate from sanctions in comparable cases, we are immediately struck, as was the special hearing officer, by the sui generis nature of the law clerk episode, ultimately orchestrated and driven by Crossen. Countless bar disciplinary cases concern relatively discrete events of misconduct involving one attorney, and one or a few transactions or clients. We have found none that involves such a large number of attorneys and their agents, or deceit so exquisitely choreographed as to include in one bundle surreptitious tape recording, traveling out of State to avoid the laws of Massachusetts, the masking of multiple identities, the procurement of sham business cards and sham business information, multiple sham interviews, covert surveillance, and multiple threats and attempts at coercion, among other things.

. . .

That there is no blueprint in our prior cases for the facts of this proceeding should come as no surprise, reflecting the unusual scope of the misconduct. The sanction of disbarment we impose is appropriate to ensure that the law clerk episode (or anything like it) remains sui generis.

. . .

7. *Conclusion.* For the reasons stated above, we adopt the recommendation of the board and remand to the county court where a judgment of disbarment shall enter.

Post-Case Follow-Up

If Crossen had truly believed that the judge before whom he appeared was corrupt and unethical, how could he have substantiated that claim in a way that did not violate Rule 8.4? Exactly where and how did he go too far?

Sometimes it is not the conduct that gets you into trouble, but the cover-up. How many lies did Crossen tell after perpetrating the initial ruse?

Food Fight: Inside the Battle for the Market Basket

The *Demoulas v. DeMoulas* case, which was the inter-family dispute undergirding the *Crossen* disciplinary matter, was the subject of an award-winning documentary entitled "Food Fight."

A documentary by Food Fight Films, LLC
http://www.foodfightfilm.com/

In re Crossen: Real Life Applications

1. Suppose that the heirs of a recently deceased widow bring a civil action in state court alleging fraud by the widow's next door neighbor, who happens to be a lawyer. According to the heirs, the lawyer defrauded the elderly and confused woman out of a strip of property between their houses by falsely claiming that she was conveying an easement and not a fee simple. The lawyer subsequently enlarged his estate using the strip of land, to the disadvantage of the neighbor who was deprived of access to a nearby beach. At the time they file the civil fraud suit, the heirs also report the lawyer to the state bar disciplinary authority. If proven, is this conduct a violation of Rule 8.4(c)? Even if it is, is this the type of conduct that you think bar disciplinary agencies should regulate? Why or why not?

2. Imagine that you represent a client who alleges that he was not hired for a position of salesperson at a retail clothing store because of his race. In order to develop evidence of discrimination before filing a lawsuit on his behalf, may you ask paralegals or investigators in your office to go "undercover" to the clothing store and apply for the same job? If your state does not have an "investigatory" exception to Rule 8.4, either expressly in the rule or by judicial construction, would you be comfortable putting your license on the line by engaging in such deception?

Many lawyers use, or direct their subordinates to use, covert investigative techniques designed to gather evidence of wrongdoing. Prosecutors supervise the undercover operations of police officers, which often involve shams. Civil rights lawyers send their agents in to pose as "testers" to ascertain whether a business may be discriminating unlawfully. Do these acts of misidentification in order to gather evidence violate Rule 8.4(c)? This remains an unsettled area of the law. Note that the Supreme Judicial Court in *Crossen* refused to address whether there should be an investigatory exception to the Massachusetts predecessor to Rule 8.4(c), because the court ruled that Crossen's deceit with respect to the law clerk was not the sole basis for discipline, and that Crossen's entire course of conduct was highly prejudicial to the administration of justice. Some courts have ruled that misidentifying yourself and your purpose in order to gather evidence of wrongdoing is not a violation of the rule prohibiting dishonesty and deceit,[63] while others have concluded that it is.[64] Some states have amended their disciplinary codes to expressly allow for an investigatory exception to Rule 8.4, but even those states disagree on whether such an exception should apply only to criminal lawyers working for the government,[65] or also to civil lawyers engaged in covert activity to investigate violations of civil or constitutional rights.[66]

Chapter Summary

- A lawyer may not knowingly make false statements to the court. If a lawyer makes a material false statement to the court and comes to know of its falsity after the statement is made but before the conclusion of the proceedings, the lawyer must correct the false statement.
- A lawyer must disclose adverse legal authority in the controlling jurisdiction to the court, if not disclosed by opposing counsel.
- A lawyer may not counsel or assist a witness to commit perjury, and may not put a witness on the stand in a civil case who he knows will commit perjury. If a witness called by the lawyer surprises the lawyer by testifying falsely on a material matter, the lawyer must take remedial measures.
- During pendency of the litigation, a lawyer may not have any *ex parte* contact with the presiding judge or a juror unless authorized by law.
- A lawyer may not communicate with a person represented by counsel on the subject of that representation without first obtaining permission of the person's lawyer.
- A lawyer may not engage in conduct involving fraud, deceit, or misrepresentation, even in his private dealings.

---

63. Apple Corps Ltd. v. International Collectors Society, 15 F. Supp. 2d 456, 475 (D.N.J. 1998) (lawyers hired private investigators to pose as members of the general public wishing to buy exclusive Beatles stamps from the defendant).
64. In re Gatti, 8 P.3d 966, 974 (Or. 2000) (lawyer claimed to be a chiropractor for the purpose of obtaining information from insurance claims reviewer as to how it was conducting medical screening); In re Pautler, 47 P.3d 1175, 1180 (Colo. 2002) (lawyer presented himself to at-large murder suspect as a public defender for the purpose of apprehending him).
65. Fla. St. Bar Rule 4-8.4(c).
66. Or. R. Prof'l Conduct 8.4(b).

Applying the Rules

1. You represent a UPS driver who claims that he suffered a back injury on the job. In litigation against the company, the plaintiff testified during his deposition that he now walks with a cane and that he is unable to carry on normal day-to-day activities like carrying groceries, picking up his small children, and bending over to tie his shoes. Prior to trial, opposing counsel presents you with photographs allegedly taken by his private investigator showing your client jogging, skiing, and playing golf since the time of the alleged accident. What should you do?

2. You represent one spouse in a divorce contest. You have made a generous settlement offer to opposing counsel, but she has not responded, and she has failed to return several of your phone calls. May you send opposing counsel a registered letter reiterating the offer, and this time copy her client on the letter so that you can be sure the opposing party has been informed?

3. One of your clients is a small automobile repair shop with fewer than ten employees. The owner comes to your office one day and states that she is being investigated by the state attorney general for failing to pay mechanics overtime in violation of the state prevailing wage law. The client delivers to you her laptop computer, which she claims contains all of her payroll records for the past three years. What should you do with the computer?

4. You represent a defendant corporation in a shareholder derivative action. The federal district judge granted summary judgment in favor of your client. Plaintiffs have filed a brief on appeal to the Circuit Court. They have neglected to cite a case from another Circuit that directly supports their position in the litigation. Do you have an obligation to cite this case in your brief, even if it is to distinguish the case or argue that its reasoning is unpersuasive?

Professional Responsibility in Practice

1. Research the law in the jurisdiction in which you intend to practice. Is there any case law or commentary that recognizes an investigative exception to Rule 8.4(c)?

2. Suppose that you represented a plaintiff in an employment discrimination matter. After a two-week jury trial, the jury returned a verdict in favor of the defendant corporation. The day after the verdict, you receive an email from a juror informing you that she was very distraught by the deliberations process and feels like several members of the jury made improper racial comments during deliberations harmful to your client. Research the law of your jurisdiction to determine how, if at all, you may respond to the juror's email or otherwise communicate with the juror.

8

Special Ethical Issues in Criminal Practice

The ethical restraints in litigation we discussed in the last chapter apply to both civil and criminal practitioners. However, there are certain attorney discipline rules that apply only to prosecutors, and others that are more relevant and acute in the context of criminal defense.

A. THE PROSECUTOR

Because she represents the entire community rather than any single client or entity, the prosecutor has unique professional obligations. The source and meaning of such obligations will be discussed below.

1. Who Do You Represent?

Unlike a traditional advocate, a prosecutor does not represent an individual or organizational client, but rather the sovereign at large. This puts the prosecutor in the position of being at the same time both a principal and agent. Unlike a traditional advocate, whose job is to provide his client with informed advice and then to pursue the client's objectives zealously within the bounds of the law, the prosecutor must first make decisions about what is in the

Key Concepts

- Sources of a prosecutor's duty to "seek justice"
- The prosecutor's duty to turn over exculpatory evidence
- The "no-contact" rule and limits on the government's investigation of represented suspects
- The prosecutor and the press—obligations that exceed Rule 3.6
- Dangers for the criminal defense attorney in taking possession of physical evidence
- The criminal defense attorney's "trilemma," and how to handle client perjury

best interests of society before ascertaining a course of action to pursue those goals. Because a prosecutor represents the collective "sovereign," she has no personal client to direct her course of action. She has constituents — the police, the victim(s) of crime, the probation department, members of the public, and even the defendant himself — but none of these constituents can be treated as traditional clients entitled to control the objectives of litigation. As the Supreme Court has recognized, "[the prosecutor] is the representative not of an ordinary party to a controversy, but of a sovereignty whose obligation to govern impartially is as compelling as its obligation to govern at all; and whose interest, therefore, in a criminal prosecution is not that it shall win a case, but that justice shall be done."[1]

The uniqueness of the prosecutor's role — whether it stems from the distinctive nature of the prosecutor's client or the awesome power wielded by the government — has important consequences for a prosecutor's conduct in investigating and prosecuting criminal cases. The ABA has enacted a specific rule of professional conduct applicable only to prosecutors — Model Rule 3.8 — detailing their special responsibilities. Comment [1] to Rule 3.8 is particularly instructive because it describes the prosecutor's role in the following general terms: "A prosecutor has the responsibility of a **minister of justice** and not simply that of an advocate. This responsibility carries with it a specific obligation to see that the defendant is accorded procedural justice [and] that guilt is decided upon the basis of sufficient evidence . . . ." (Emphasis supplied.)

How does a prosecutor go about assessing what constitutes "justice" in any particular case? Professor Fred Zacharias attempts to unpack this "minister of justice" obligation in the following law review article. He suggests that it has both substantive and procedural components. What are they?

Fred Zacharias, Structuring the Ethics of Trial Advocacy

44 Vand. L. Rev. 45 (1991)

II. THE MEANING OF JUSTICE IN THE CONTEXT OF ADVERSARIAL TRIALS

One obvious concern underlying the prosecutor's special ethical duty is to prevent punishment of innocent defendants. At the charging, plea bargaining, and sentencing stages, the heart of the codes' mandate to do justice seems clear: the prosecutor should exercise discretion so as to prosecute only persons she truly considers guilty, and then only in a manner that fits the crime. Many codes reinforce the prosecutor's general obligation with specific rules limiting pretrial conduct along these lines.

Once a case reaches trial, this duty is no longer very meaningful. The prosecutor already has made her good faith determination that the defendant is guilty. Unless some unexpected development makes her reconsider her conclusion, she may pursue a conviction. Thus, in extending the prosecutor's justice obligation to

1. Berger v. United States, 295 U.S. 78, 88 (1935).

the trial stage, the codes almost by definition intend a higher obligation than simply avoiding unjustified prosecutions. The American Bar Association (ABA) proposed specific standards for trial conduct in the 1970s, but these standards were not adopted in the later Model Rules. All modern codes are silent on the meaning of justice at trial.

Reputable scholars have advanced the proposition that the adversary system is ineffective in producing accurate verdicts. Interpreting the codes from that perspective, one might assume that "doing justice" requires prosecutors to temper their zeal. One can hypothesize open-minded prosecutors who present facts neutrally and encourage courts and jurors to emphasize defendants' procedural rights. These idealized government attorneys constantly would reevaluate the strength of their case. They would adjust the content and force of each evidentiary presentation to further the outcome that they believe the jury should reach on the current state of the evidence.

It is beyond the scope of this Article to discuss whether adversarial theory is essentially flawed, whether the image of prosecutorial nonpartisanship is realistic, or whether prosecutors and all other lawyers have uncodified obligations to bring about socially beneficial results. For our purposes, it suffices to recognize that the noncompetitive approach to prosecutorial ethics is inconsistent with the professional codes' underlying theory. The codes are concerned specifically with structuring adversarial practice. They do not exempt prosecutors from the requirements of zealous advocacy. Reading the cursory "do justice" language as a denunciation of competitive fact-finding therefore would create an internal contradiction.

. . .

The Adversary System's General Approach to Lawyer Ethics

. . .

Nevertheless, as David Luban and other commentators have pointed out, law's version of adversary process may not be an effective method for achieving accurate verdicts. The view that a process of contradiction alone exposes truth is counterintuitive and, at least in some circumstances, simply wrong. Proponents of adversaries therefore have looked to alternative justifications to support the system.

One rationale is that adversary process assures procedural fairness, including assertion of all the parties' rights. Aligning attorneys solely with their clients' interests creates an incentive for lawyers to be active and to take full advantage of the law's protections. Ensuring that the parties' views are presented — even if extreme — may make the parties feel as if the legal system has treated them evenhandedly. Not only is that sense of fairness an independent "good," but ultimately, it helps some litigants accept even unfavorable results.

Proponents also argue that the system is an efficient mechanism for resolving disputes. Adversarial process causes lawyers to frame and narrow the issues for the fact finder and creates a system of checks and balances. The attorneys keep an eye on one another and on the judge to make sure that they all perform their assigned roles in proper and ethical fashion.

When the various justifications for the adversary system are considered as a whole, one can see that the "justice" it strives for has several elements. Ascertaining the true facts is not the only or paramount goal. Fairness and respect for client individuality play an equal part, even though full assertion of client rights may interfere with truth-seeking. Efficient fact-finding also is an important objective.

B. How Prosecutors Fit Within the Adversarial Scheme

To the extent that the adversary system works according to theory, government lawyers promote justice by playing the same role at trial as private advocates. They contribute to truth by defending their own factual hypotheses and contesting those of their opponents. Prosecutors help courts assess defendants' rights; the claims of defendants' champions must be contested to determine their validity. Prosecutors also enhance the efficiency aspects of the process by acting adversarially. By challenging defense counsels' positions at every step, prosecutors force defenders to remain vigilant and to frame the issues clearly for proper adjudication.

At one level, the prosecutor thus helps achieve the appropriate systemic results — does adversarial justice — simply by performing as an aggressive advocate. In the context of an adversarial model of adjudication, even prosecutors who develop "conviction psychology" seem justified; ordinarily it is not up to a lawyer to act contrary to her side's interests. Having proceeded to trial, the prosecutor represents the community's interest in conviction. Court-enforced constitutional safeguards (such as the beyond-a-reasonable-doubt standard) arguably suffice to protect the innocent.

The notion that a prosecutor sometimes should refrain from acting as a pure advocate stems from the fact that she has no single client. The prosecutor is simultaneously responsible for the community's protection, victims' desire for vengeance, defendants' entitlement to a fair opportunity for vindication, and the state's need for a criminal justice system that is efficient and appears fair. Described accurately, the prosecutor represents "constituencies" — and several of them at one time.

This multirepresentation is significant for the structure of prosecutorial ethics. Private lawyers confronting ethical dilemmas usually find themselves torn between promoting a single client's goals and safeguarding their own professional or moral self-interest. The disciplinary rules resolve these conflicts largely by casting trial lawyers as agents who must champion client interests, subject only to narrow limits on extreme behavior.

Prosecutors, in contrast, face conflicts among their constituents' interests as well as between constituent and personal interests. Code drafters could have used an agency analysis to shape prosecutorial ethics. The rules simply could state which constituent's interests take precedence in particular situations. The decision not to codify priorities reflects the drafters' sense that prosecutors' multirepresentational role requires an independent framework for governing prosecutorial conduct.

The framework that the drafters have chosen consists primarily of the "do justice" rule. The prosecutor's relative independence provides a theoretical justification for the rule's departure from adversarial norms. As discussed above, drafters committed to the adversary system would not expect the advocate for the prosecution routinely to disavow zeal. But because a prosecutor need not focus exclusively on a single client's interests, her role in promoting the system's goals of procedural fairness and efficient fact-finding becomes more dominant. The code envisions limited circumstances in which she can temper her competitive spirit, yet still contribute to results that the adversary system deems appropriate.

. . .

Moreover, the prosecutor benefits from unique prestige and symbolic power. Because she represents the community, she commonly carries more influence with juries than attorneys allied solely with individual clients. The prosecutor can rely on jurors' natural instincts to be protected against crime. She can draw upon jurors' tendencies to believe that persons a grand jury singles out for prosecution probably are guilty.

Finally, a prosecutor enjoys practical advantages over her adversaries. She benefits from the state's hefty investigative and litigation resources. Through the police and grand jury, she monopolizes the ability to coerce testimony and obtain cooperation in the investigation of crimes. The literature is replete with discussions of ways in which a prosecutor can misuse her singular tools.

The fear of prosecutorial abuses thus explains why code drafters have chosen to adopt a "do justice" obligation. The drafters reasonably expect that, as the symbol of fair criminal justice, prosecutors should not take undue advantage of their built-in resources. Prosecutors who overreach undermine "confidence, not only in [their] profession, but in government and the very ideal of justice itself."

The nature of the prosecutor's unique power also suggests that the duty takes on special meaning at the trial stage. Aspects of prosecutorial power — such as the unusual influence over jurors — come into play solely at trial. Confining the codes' requirements to instituting and maintaining prosecutions in good faith thus would understate the drafters' concerns. The "do justice" rule may not contemplate half-hearted advocacy, but it clearly addresses the use of techniques that tilt trials toward convictions in an unfair way.

To fix the scope of the "do justice" rule, one must consider its theoretical justification and underlying practical concerns in tandem. It would be reading too much into two words — "do justice" — to conclude that the rule embodies a counter-traditional theoretical conception of prosecutors as nonadversarial lawyers. The paradigm of the prosecutor as an unaligned "minister of the system" makes sense in the trial context only if it targets situations in which competitive fact-finding will not produce results that are "acceptable" within the meaning of the adversary system. Yet we have seen that when the adversary system operates in its intended fashion, competition by definition produces appropriate results. The "do justice" rule, therefore, must focus on cases in which the system itself is defective — in which defendants are not tried in accordance with the system's basic, structural elements.

Interpreting prosecutors' obligation to do justice with reference to "adequate adversarial process" rather than "accurate outcomes" helps identify when prosecutors should depart from an advocate's stance: prosecutors must strive for adversarially valid results rather than factually correct results. This systemic approach also defines limits to prosecutors' ethical duty. The codes assign prosecutors a special role within the system because prosecutors are unencumbered by client ties. It follows that the codes accord prosecutors leeway to repair flaws in the process, but impose no general duty to help defendants win.

C. Defining the Prosecutor's Duty to Do Justice at Trial

The key to understanding this adversarial interpretation of justice is to identify the essential elements of adversarial process and isolate ways in which they may fail. When the system breaks down in a significant respect, the codes can no longer expect competition to achieve adversarially appropriate results. If the evidence is in conflict, an ethical prosecutor cannot rationalize a conviction simply on the ground that the trial is fair.

. . .

Consider a case in which a judge deprives one party of an opportunity to present the facts by cowing defense counsel into avoiding relevant lines of questioning. Arguably, the trial does not satisfy the adversary system's design. The premises of a passive tribunal and an equal opportunity to put forth a case may be lacking. The litigant's capacity to obtain a systemically appropriate result is at risk.

. . .

The prosecutor's unique prestige helps justify holding her to a higher ethical responsibility. In the hypothetical scenario, practical considerations might prevent a private attorney from taking advantage of the court's one-sided attitude. The attorney reasonably may fear that the jury will perceive him to be bullying the opponent. In contrast, because a prosecutor starts out with an aura of respectability, she can get away with more. Practical limitations do not restrain her conduct to the same extent.

The prosecutor's resource advantages also weigh in favor of making her rectify the system's failure. By virtue of her access to the grand jury and her relationship with law enforcement agencies, the prosecutor has an institutional identity that helps her deal with the hypothetical judge's conduct. The judge can do without a private attorney's affection and, consequently, may retaliate for the attorney's attempt to challenge him. In contrast, the judge needs the prosecutor's goodwill almost as much as the prosecutor needs his. The court must have the cooperation of the prosecutor's office to manage the criminal justice system; offending one prosecutor may offend them all. Within limits, the nature of the prosecutor's office as the institution in charge of law enforcement resources thus enables individual prosecutors to serve as checks on failures elsewhere in the system.

Hence, viewed from the code drafters' adversarial perspective, "justice" does take on special meaning for government attorneys. The codes impose a different duty to role differentiate than they impose on private lawyers. Once a prosecutor determines the prosecution should proceed, her function is to advocate the defendant's guilt. But when the system breaks down, she at least temporarily must set aside her view that the defendant should be convicted. Her role is not to help him win, yet neither may she passively accept systemically faulty outcomes. As a "minister" of the system, the codes require her to help restore adversarial balance.

. . .

2. Quantum of Proof Necessary for Charging

The invocation of the state's charging power has immeasurable reputational and economic consequences for a defendant, even if he is subsequently acquitted at trial. Zacharias suggests that in making pretrial decisions (e.g., charging, plea bargaining) prosecutors should prosecute only individuals that they truly believe are guilty, and then only in a manner and to a degree that fits the crime.

What quantum of evidence must a prosecutor possess before commencing charges? The non-binding ABA Standards for Criminal Justice suggest that as a "minister of justice" a prosecutor should not commence criminal proceedings unless the state possesses sufficient admissible evidence to prove its case beyond a reasonable doubt (essentially the directed verdict standard).[2] Note, however, that Rule 3.8(a) of the Model Rules of Professional Conduct suggests a lower threshold, that of "**probable cause.**" While the probable cause standard is concededly higher than the standard for filing a civil complaint (*i.e.*, Rule 3.1 prohibits only "frivolous" complaints), it is still remarkably low. It allows for the consideration of hearsay, and it allows a prosecutor to leave questions about the constitutional and legal admissibility of evidence for resolution by the court.

Why do Zacharias and the Criminal Justice Committee of the ABA recommend a higher charging threshold than the attorney discipline rules in effect in most jurisdictions? Or, to phrase the question in the negative, when would it ever be a legitimate exercise of state power for a prosecutor to charge a crime that meets the probable cause threshold, but not the sufficient admissible evidence of guilt threshold?

At the other end of the spectrum, how should a prosecutor conduct himself when objectively there is sufficient admissible evidence to support a finding of guilt, but the prosecutor *personally* believes that the defendant is innocent? ABA Standard 3-4.3 states as an aspirational matter that "[a] prosecutor's office should not file or maintain charges if *it* believes the defendant is innocent, no matter what the state of the evidence." (Emphasis supplied.) But how helpful is this non-binding ABA guideline? "Offices" cannot "believe," only "individuals" can "believe." As a representative of the sovereign, may a prosecutor decline to commence charges when there is sufficient admissible evidence to support a conviction, but the prosecutor herself has lingering personal doubts about the defendant's guilt?

The following story of Daniel Bibb from the Manhattan District Attorney's Office may test the limits of the "do justice" mandate.

Benjamin Weiser, Doubting Case, a Prosecutor Helped the Defense

N.Y. Times, June 23, 2008

The Manhattan district attorney, Robert M. Morgenthau, had a problem. The murder convictions of two men in one of his office's big cases — the 1990 shooting of

2. ABA Standards for Criminal Justice: Prosecution Function, Standard 3-4.3(b) (4th ed. 2015).

a bouncer outside the Palladium nightclub — had been called into question by a stream of new evidence.

So the office decided on a re-examination, led by a 21-year veteran assistant, Daniel L. Bibb.

Mr. Bibb spent nearly two years reinvestigating the killing and reported back: He believed that the two imprisoned men were not guilty, and that their convictions should be dropped. Yet top officials told him, he said, to go into a court hearing and defend the case anyway. He did, and in 2005 he lost.

But in a recent interview, Mr. Bibb made a startling admission: He threw the case. Unwilling to do what his bosses ordered, he said, he deliberately helped the other side win.

He tracked down hard-to-find or reluctant witnesses who pointed to other suspects and prepared them to testify for the defense. He talked strategy with defense lawyers. And when they veered from his coaching, he cornered them in the hallway and corrected them.

"I did the best I could," he said. "To lose."

Today, the two men are free. At the end of the hearing, which stretched over six weeks, his superiors agreed to ask a judge to drop the conviction of one, Olmedo Hidalgo. The judge granted a new trial to the other, David Lemus, who was acquitted in December.

Mr. Bibb, 53, who said it was painful to remain in the office, resigned in 2006 and is trying to build a new career as a defense lawyer in Manhattan — with some difficulty, friends say, in a profession where success can hang on the ability to cut deals with prosecutors.

Mr. Morgenthau's office would not comment on Mr. Bibb's claims. Daniel J. Castleman, chief assistant district attorney, would say only: "Nobody in this office is ever required to prosecute someone they believe is innocent. That was true then, as it is now. That being the case, no useful purpose would be served in engaging in a debate with a former staff member." The office has said it had good reason to believe that the two men were guilty.

Yet whatever the facts of the murder, the dispute offers an unusual glimpse of a prosecutor weighing the demands of conscience against his obligation to his office, and the extraordinary measures he took to settle that conflict in his own mind.

"I was angry," Mr. Bibb said, "that I was being put in a position to defend convictions that I didn't believe in."

The case also reveals a rare public challenge to one of the nation's most powerful district attorneys from within his office. As the hearing unfolded in 2005, Mr. Morgenthau, running for re-election, was sharply criticized by an opponent who said he had prosecuted the wrong men.

By then, the Palladium case had become one of the most troubled in the city's recent history, stirred up every few years by fresh evidence, heralded in newspaper and television reports, that pointed to other suspects.

It is not as if Mr. Morgenthau has refused to admit mistakes. In 2002, in spectacular fashion, his office recommended dismissing the convictions of five men in the attack on a jogger in Central Park, after its reinvestigation showed that another man had acted alone. "It's my decision," Mr. Morgenthau said then. "The buck stops here."

In fact, the prosecutor who led that inquiry, Nancy E. Ryan, was Mr. Bibb's supervisor in the Palladium case — though Mr. Bibb would not detail his conversations with her or other superiors, saying they were privileged.

Defense lawyers confirmed that Mr. Bibb helped them, though he never explicitly stated his intentions. Some praised his efforts to see that justice was done. Others involved in the case suggested he did a disservice to both sides — shirking his duty as an assistant district attorney, and prolonging an injustice by not quitting the case, or the office.

And some blame Mr. Bibb's superiors. Steven M. Cohen, a former federal prosecutor who pushed Mr. Morgenthau's office to reinvestigate, said that while Mr. Bibb should have refused to present the case, his bosses should not have pressed him.

"If Bibb is to be believed, he was essentially asked to choose between his conscience and his job," Mr. Cohen said. "Whether he made the right choice is irrelevant; that he was asked to make that choice is chilling."

At 6-foot-6, Mr. Bibb looks every inch the lawman, with a square jaw, a gravelly voice and a negotiating style that lawyers describe as brutally honest. He joined the district attorney's office right out of Seton Hall Law School in 1982 and went on to handle some of its major murder cases and cold-case investigations.

The Palladium case certainly looked open and shut in 1992, when Mr. Lemus and Mr. Hidalgo were sentenced to 25 years to life. Several bouncers identified them as the men they scuffled with outside the East Village nightclub. Mr. Lemus's ex-girlfriend said he claimed to have shot a bouncer there.

But the next decade brought a string of nagging contradictions. A former member of a Bronx drug gang confessed that he and a friend had done the shooting. That spurred new examinations by the district attorney's office, federal prosecutors, defense lawyers, the police and the press.

When Mr. Morgenthau's office was asked to take another look, Mr. Bibb said, his supervisors gave him carte blanche. "It really was, leave no stone unturned," he said.

Over 21 months, starting in 2003, he and two detectives conducted more than 50 interviews in more than a dozen states, ferreting out witnesses the police had somehow missed or ignored.

Mr. Bibb said he shared his growing doubts with his superiors. And at a meeting in early 2005, he recalled, after defense lawyers won court approval for a hearing into the new evidence, he urged that the convictions be set aside. "I made what I considered to be my strongest pitch," he said.

Instead, he said, he was ordered to go to the hearing, present the government's case and let a judge decide — a strategy that violated his sense of a prosecutor's duty.

"I had always been taught that we made the decisions, that we made the tough calls, that we didn't take things and throw them up against the wall" for a judge or jury to sort out, he said. "If the evidence doesn't convince me, then I'm never going to be able to convince a jury."

Still, Mr. Bibb said, he worried that if he did not take the case, another prosecutor would — and possibly win.

Defense lawyers said he plunged in. In long phone conversations, he helped them sort through the new evidence he had gathered.

"If I make a mistake in my interpretation of what he said, he'll correct me," said Gordon Mehler, who represented Mr. Lemus. "If there's a piece of evidence that bears on another piece of evidence I'm talking about, he'll remind me of it. That's not something that a prosecutor typically does."

As the defense decided which witnesses to call, he again hunted them down—sometimes in prison or witness protection—and, when necessary, persuaded them to testify in State Supreme Court in Manhattan.

"I made sure all of their witnesses were going to testify in a manner that would have the greatest impact, certainly consistent with the truth," Mr. Bibb said. "I wasn't telling anybody to make anything up."

He told them what questions to expect, both from the defense and his own cross-examination—which he admitted felt "a little bit weird." Defense lawyers say they first met some of their witnesses on the day of testimony, outside the courtroom.

During breaks, Mr. Bibb confronted the lawyers when he felt they were not asking the right questions. "Don't you understand?" one lawyer recalled him saying. "I'm your best friend in that courtroom."

Cross-examining the witnesses, Mr. Bibb took pains not to damage their credibility. Facing a former gang member who had pleaded guilty to six murders, he asked only a few perfunctory questions about the man's record.

Daniel J. Horwitz, the other defense lawyer, said the help was invaluable. "Did Dan play a useful role in making sure that justice prevailed in that courtroom? The answer is unequivocally yes."

When the testimony was over, Mr. Bibb said he made one last appeal to his superiors to drop the convictions. They agreed to do so for Mr. Hidalgo, but not for Mr. Lemus—who was still implicated by "strong evidence," the office said at the time.

"I said, 'I'm done,'" Mr. Bibb recalled. "I wanted nothing to do with it."

Another prosecutor made final written arguments, and in October 2005, Justice Roger S. Hayes ordered the new trial for Mr. Lemus. Demoralized by the case, Mr. Bibb resigned a few months later.

A close friend, Robert Mooney, a New York City police detective, said that if not for the Palladium case, Mr. Bibb "would have spent his entire professional life at the prosecutor's office.

"He's brokenhearted that he's not doing this anymore."

In a brief interview after he quit, Mr. Bibb defended Mr. Morgenthau against criticism that the case had been mishandled. "There was never any evil intent on the part of the D.A.'s office," Mr. Bibb said then.

But around the same time, he distanced himself from the office's decisions in remarks to "Dateline NBC." He said that during the hearing, he already believed the two men were not guilty, but proceeded because he had a client to represent: Mr. Morgenthau.

"He was aware of what was going on," Mr. Bibb told the interviewer. "The decision to go to a hearing was not made in my presence."

As for Mr. Bibb's new revelation that he helped the defense, lawyers and others are divided.

Stephen Gillers, a legal ethics professor at the New York University School of Law, said he believed that Mr. Bibb had violated his obligation to his client, and could conceivably face action by a disciplinary panel. "He's entitled to his conscience, but his conscience does not entitle him to subvert his client's case," Mr. Gillers said. "It entitles him to withdraw from the case, or quit if he can't."

On the other hand, he added, Mr. Morgenthau could have defused any conflict by assigning another prosecutor.

John Schwartz, a former detective who worked to exonerate the convicted men, said Mr. Bibb did them no favor by continuing in the case. "He effectively took part in keeping two innocent men in prison an additional year at least, for not going with what he felt was the truth," Mr. Schwartz said.

But Mr. Mehler, the defense lawyer, said Mr. Bibb acted honorably. While lawyers on both sides must advocate for their clients, he said, "a prosecutor has an additional duty to search out the truth.

"I say that he lived up to that."

Today, Mr. Bibb says he does not believe he crossed any line.

"I didn't work for the other side," he said. "I worked for what I thought was the right thing."

After this news story ran, the New York Bar Disciplinary Committee investigated Bibb and concluded that there was "no basis" for any discipline of Bibb pertaining to the Palladium nightclub prosecution.[3] Do you agree?

Professor Stephen Gillers from New York University, quoted in the *Times* story above, argues that Bibb violated a duty of loyalty to his client by actively aiding the defense. Is he correct? The state is not a corporeal client, but it is a client nonetheless. Did Bibb subvert his client's interests? Note that in aiding the defense before and during the hearing on defendants' motion for new trial, Bibb drew the line at refusing to disclose confidential communications between himself and his superiors in the Manhattan District Attorney's Office. Bibb thus appears to have implicitly recognized that the state is a client who can have confidences under Rule 1.6. Why isn't the state also a client who can control the objectives of litigation (Rule 1.2) and demand competent representation toward those objectives (Rule 1.1)? What were Bibb's other alternatives if he doubted the defendants' guilt?

3. Disclosure of Exculpatory Evidence

Failure to disclose **exculpatory evidence** is one of the most frequent contributors to wrongful convictions, along with flawed witness identifications and ineffective assistance of defense counsel. Several high profile cases in recent years have highlighted prosecutorial failures with respect to this disclosure obligation. The conviction of former Senator Ted Stevens from Alaska was reversed after it was revealed that federal prosecutors withheld notes of an interview with a key government witness that undercut that witness's trial testimony. In Texas, Michael Morton was freed from jail after serving 25 years for murdering his wife after it was revealed that the prosecutor failed to disclose notes of an interview with the defendant's child indicating that someone else was in the house at the time of the brutal act. Former

---

3. Benjamin Weiser, *Lawyer Who Threw a City Case Is Vindicated, Not Punished*, N.Y. Times, Mar. 4, 2009, http://www.nytimes.com/2009/03/05/nyregion/05da.html?_r=0.

Durham County North Carolina District Attorney Mike Nifong was disbarred for failing to disclose to the defense exculpatory DNA evidence that showed the presence of multiple unidentified males on a rape kit specimen extracted from an erotic dancer who falsely accused members of the Duke lacrosse team of rape. These stories and others have made the public and the judiciary more highly attuned than ever to prosecutorial misconduct with respect to discovery.

Rules of Criminal Procedure in effect in most jurisdictions require prosecutors after arraignment to disclose police reports, grand jury transcripts, witness statements, and forensic reports, and to make available for inspection by defense counsel any physical exhibits that the government intends to introduce as evidence at trial. *See, e.g.*, FED. R. CRIM. P. 16. Normally, these items — known as "inculpatory" evidence — will link the defendant to the crime in some important respect. Disclosure is required so that the defendant has a fair preview of the government's case.

However, prosecutors also have a duty to disclose to defense counsel any "exculpatory" evidence in their possession — that is, evidence that is helpful to the defendant because it could be used to prove that the defendant did *not* commit the alleged offense, or committed a lesser offense. In other words, prior to the trial a prosecutor must reveal not only the government's case, but must also reveal any evidence that would be helpful to the defendant in building its own case.

This prosecutorial duty to disclose exculpatory evidence dates back at least to the Supreme Court's 1963 decision in *Brady v. Maryland*, excerpted below. It is traditionally justified on two grounds: the imbalance in investigatory resources between the government and the defendant, and the prosecutor's obligation as "minister of justice" to seek the truth rather than to pursue partisan victory. In this regard, the prosecutor's duty of helpful disclosures is one-sided; the defense has no corresponding duty to reveal to the prosecutor evidence in its possession that could help prove the defendant's guilt, and indeed may be committing malpractice if it did so.

Case Preview

Brady v. Maryland

The petitioner in this case, Brady, and his companion, Boblit, were separately convicted of first degree murder and sentenced to death. At his trial, Brady did not deny playing a role in the murder but, seeking to avoid the death penalty, testified that Boblit did the actual killing. While on death row, Brady moved for a new trial after discovering statements made by Boblit — in which Boblit admitted to doing the actual killing — that had previously been withheld by the prosecutor.

As you read the *Brady* decision, ask yourself:

1. Is the withholding of exculpatory evidence really analogous to the knowing presentation of perjured testimony?
2. If so, why does the Court conclude that the Due Process Clause is violated "irrespective of the good faith or bad faith of the prosecution"?
3. What use could Brady have made of Boblit's statement at his sentencing hearing?

Brady v. Maryland

373 U.S. 83 (1963)

We agree with the Court of Appeals that suppression of [Boblit's] confession was a violation of the Due Process Clause of the Fourteenth Amendment. . . .

This ruling is an extension of Mooney v. Holohan, 294 U.S. 103, where the Court ruled on what nondisclosure by a prosecutor violates due process:

> "It is a requirement that cannot be deemed to be satisfied by mere notice and hearing if a state has contrived a conviction through the pretense of a trial which in truth is but used as a means of depriving a defendant of liberty through a deliberate deception of court and jury by the presentation of testimony known to be perjured. Such a contrivance by a state to procure the conviction and imprisonment of a defendant is as inconsistent with the rudimentary demands of justice as is the obtaining of a like result by intimidation."

In Pyle v. Kansas, 317 U.S. 213, 215, we phrased the rule in broader terms:

> "Petitioner's papers are inexpertly drawn, but they do set forth allegations that his imprisonment resulted from perjured testimony, knowingly used by the State authorities to obtain his conviction, and from the deliberate suppression by those same authorities of evidence favorable to him. These allegations sufficiently charge a deprivation of rights guaranteed by the Federal Constitution, and, if proven, would entitle petitioner to release from his present custody. Mooney v. Holohan, 294 U.S. 103."

. . .

We now hold that the suppression by the prosecution of evidence favorable to an accused upon request violates due process where the evidence is material either to guilt or to punishment, irrespective of the good faith or bad faith of the prosecution.

The principle of *Mooney v. Holohan* is not punishment of society for misdeeds of a prosecutor but avoidance of an unfair trial to the accused. Society wins not only when the guilty are convicted but when criminal trials are fair; our system of the administration of justice suffers when any accused is treated unfairly. An inscription on the walls of the Department of Justice states the proposition candidly for the federal domain: "The United States wins its point whenever justice is done its citizens in the courts." A prosecution that withholds evidence on demand of an accused which, if made available, would tend to exculpate him or reduce the penalty helps shape a trial that bears heavily on the defendant. That casts the prosecutor in the role of an architect of a proceeding that does not comport with standards of justice, even though, as in the present case, his action is not "the result of guile," to use the words of the Court of Appeals. 226 Md. at 427.

Affirmed.

Post-Case Follow-Up

Although the Court's decision in *Brady* referenced the prosecutor's constitutional duty to turn over exculpatory evidence "on demand" of defense counsel, subsequent decisions have clarified that this duty is self-executing; that is, it applies whether or not the defendant specifically requested the withheld material. *See, e.g.*, United States v. Agurs, 427 U.S. 97, 107 (1976).

Nine years after the *Brady* decision, the Court expanded the definition of "exculpatory" evidence to include evidence that could be used by the defendant on cross-examination of a government witness to demonstrate bias. Giglio v. United States, 405 U.S. 150, 154-55 (1972). Under *Giglio*, the government must disclose to the defendant any promises, rewards, or inducements made to a government witness in exchange for his testimony.

In *Brady*, the Court ruled that the good faith or bad faith of the prosecutor is irrelevant to the constitutional violation. Three decades later, the Court clarified in *Kyles v. Whitley* that even if the prosecutor does not know about the existence of the exculpatory evidence, so long as that evidence is in possession of a government agent (*e.g.*, police officer, investigator) and material, its nondisclosure offends due process protections for the accused. 514 U.S. 418 (1995). Thus, prosecutors have an affirmative duty to ferret out and turn over exculpatory evidence possessed by anyone "acting on the government's behalf" in the case. *Id.* at 437.

Note that evidence is only exculpatory for due process purposes under *Brady* if it is "material." *Brady*, 373 U.S. at 87. Withheld evidence that would have provided only trivial or cumulative assistance to the accused will not lead to a reversal of the defendant's conviction. In *United States v. Bagley*, the Court defined materiality as "a reasonable probability that, had the evidence been disclosed to the defense, the result of the proceeding would have been different." 473 U.S. 667, 682 (1985). Material evidence is thus evidence that has the capacity to undermine confidence in the outcome of the trial. Scholars have critiqued this materiality standard as unworkable, because it is a retrospective test for a prospective disclosure obligation; that is, in order to determine whether the disclosure of a particular piece of evidence is constitutionally required, the prosecutor must look ahead and forecast its likely impact on a trial that has not yet occurred.[4]

Brady v. Maryland: Real Life Applications

1. Three eye witnesses to the armed robbery of a liquor store are shown a photo array of potential suspects following the incident. Two of the witnesses pick out the accused, but one witness states that he does not see the perpetrator in the photo array. Must the third witness's statement be disclosed to the defense?

2. An alleged get-away driver at a bank robbery is offered a deal by the government. If he testifies against his co-defendant and tells the truth at trial, the charges against him will be reduced to conspiracy and the prosecutor will recommend a suspended sentence on that charge. Must this arrangement be disclosed to the defense prior to trial? Does it matter whether the agreement is reduced to writing?

3. The victim of an alleged sexual assault is taken by ambulance to a nearby hospital. A police officer accompanies her in the ambulance. Dazed and partially

---

4. *See, e.g.*, Daniel S. Medwed, Brady's *Bunch of Flaws*, 67 Wash. & Lee L. Rev. 1522, 1542 (2010).

incoherent, the victim describes her assailant as a light-skinned African-American male wearing a dark sweatshirt. The police officer follows up with the victim the following morning in the hospital and the victim gives a more detailed statement of the attack. In this second statement, which is written down and signed, the victim describes her assailant as "black or Hispanic" and wearing a "dark green hoodie." The prosecutor does not know about the first statement in the ambulance and thus does not disclose it to the defense. Has there been a *Brady* violation?

Like the Due Process Clause, Model Rule 3.8(d) requires a prosecutor to disclose exculpatory evidence; the disciplinary rule provides in part that a prosecutor must "make timely disclosure to the defense of all evidence or information known to the prosecutor that tends to negate the guilt of the accused or mitigates the offense . . . ." Most states have adopted language in their attorney conduct rules that closely tracks this "tends to negate guilt" standard. Prosecutors thus have both a constitutional and an ethical duty to disclose so-called exculpatory evidence to the defense in criminal cases. As the following advisory opinion from the ABA suggests, however, the disclosure obligations of Model Rule 3.8(d) and *Brady* may differ in several important respects.

Prosecutor's Duty to Disclose Evidence and Information Favorable to the Defense

ABA Formal Opinion 09-454 (2009)

THE SCOPE OF THE PRETRIAL DISCLOSURE OBLIGATION

A threshold question is whether the disclosure obligation under Rule 3.8(d) is more extensive than the constitutional obligation of disclosure. A prosecutor's constitutional obligation extends only to favorable information that is "material," *i.e.*, evidence and information likely to lead to an acquittal. . . . The following review of the rule's background and history indicates that Rule 3.8(d) does not implicitly include the materiality limitation recognized in the constitutional case law. The rule requires prosecutors to disclose favorable evidence so that the defense can decide on its utility.

Courts recognize that lawyers who serve as public prosecutors have special obligations as representatives "not of an ordinary party to a controversy, but of a sovereignty whose obligation to govern impartially is as compelling as its obligation to govern at all; and whose interest, therefore, in a criminal prosecution is not that it shall win a case, but that justice shall be done." Similarly, Comment [1] to Model Rule 3.8 states that: "A prosecutor has the responsibility of a minister of justice and not simply that of an advocate. This responsibility carries with it specific obligations to see that the defendant is accorded procedural justice, that guilt is decided upon the basis of sufficient evidence, and that special precautions are taken to prevent and to rectify the conviction of innocent persons."

. . .

Unlike Model Rules that expressly incorporate a legal standard, Rule 3.8(d) establishes an independent one. Courts as well as commentators have recognized that the ethical obligation is more demanding than the constitutional obligation. The ABA Standards for Criminal Justice likewise acknowledge that prosecutors' ethical duty of disclosure extends beyond the constitutional obligation.

In particular, Rule 3.8(d) is more demanding than the constitutional case law, in that it requires the disclosure of evidence or information favorable to the defense without regard to the anticipated impact of the evidence or information on a trial's outcome. The rule thereby requires prosecutors to steer clear of the constitutional line, erring on the side of caution.

Under Rule 3.8(d), evidence or information ordinarily will tend to negate the guilt of the accused if it would be relevant or useful to establishing a defense or negating the prosecution's proof. Evidence and information subject to the rule includes both that which tends to exculpate the accused when viewed independently and that which tends to be exculpatory when viewed in light of other evidence or information known to the prosecutor.

Further, this ethical duty of disclosure is not limited to admissible "evidence," such as physical and documentary evidence, and transcripts of favorable testimony; it also requires disclosure of favorable "information." Though possibly inadmissible itself, favorable information may lead a defendant's lawyer to admissible testimony or other evidence or assist him in other ways, such as in plea negotiations. In determining whether evidence and information will tend to negate the guilt of the accused, the prosecutor must consider not only defenses to the charges that the defendant or defense counsel has expressed an intention to raise but also any other legally cognizable defenses. Nothing in the rule suggests a de minimis exception to the prosecutor's disclosure duty where, for example, the prosecutor believes that the information has only a minimal tendency to negate the defendant's guilt, or that the favorable evidence is highly unreliable.

. . .

THE KNOWLEDGE REQUIREMENT

Rule 3.8(d) requires disclosure only of evidence and information "known to the prosecutor." Knowledge means "actual knowledge," which "may be inferred from [the] circumstances." Although "a lawyer cannot ignore the obvious," Rule 3.8(d) does not establish a duty to undertake an investigation in search of exculpatory evidence.

The knowledge requirement thus limits what might otherwise appear to be an obligation substantially more onerous than prosecutors' legal obligations under other law. Although the rule requires prosecutors to disclose *known* evidence and information that is favorable to the accused, it does not require prosecutors to conduct searches or investigations for favorable evidence that may possibly exist but of which they are unaware. For example, prior to a guilty plea, to enable the defendant to make a well-advised plea at the time of arraignment, a prosecutor must disclose known evidence and information that would be relevant or useful to establishing a defense or negating the prosecution's proof. If the prosecutor has not yet reviewed voluminous files or obtained all police files, however, Rule 3.8 does not require the prosecutor to review or request such files unless the prosecutor actually knows or infers from the circumstances, or it is obvious, that the files contain favorable evidence or information. In the hypothetical, for example, the prosecutor would have to disclose that two eyewitnesses failed to identify the defendant as the assailant and that an informant attributed the assault to someone else, because the prosecutor knew that information from communications with the police. Rule 3.8(d) ordinarily would not require the prosecutor to conduct further inquiry or investigation to discover other evidence or information favorable to the defense unless he was closing his eyes to the existence of such evidence or information.

THE REQUIREMENT OF TIMELY DISCLOSURE

In general, for the disclosure of information to be timely, it must be made early enough that the information can be used effectively. Because the defense can use favorable evidence and information most fully and effectively the sooner it is received, such evidence or information, once known to the prosecutor, must be disclosed under Rule 3.8(d) as soon as reasonably practical.

Evidence and information disclosed under Rule 3.8(d) may be used for various purposes prior to trial, for example, conducting a defense investigation, deciding whether to raise an affirmative defense, or determining defense strategy in general. The obligation of timely disclosure of favorable evidence and information requires disclosure to be made sufficiently in advance of these and similar actions and decisions that the defense can effectively use the evidence and information. Among the most significant purposes for which disclosure must be made under Rule 3.8(d) is to enable defense counsel to advise the defendant regarding whether to plead guilty. Because the defendant's decision may be strongly influenced by defense counsel's evaluation of the strength of the prosecution's case, timely disclosure requires the prosecutor to disclose evidence and information covered by Rule 3.8(d) prior to a guilty plea proceeding, which may occur concurrently with the defendant's arraignment. Defendants first decide whether to plead guilty when they are arraigned on criminal charges, and if they plead not guilty initially, they may enter a guilty plea later. Where early disclosure, or disclosure of too much information, may undermine an ongoing investigation or jeopardize a witness, as may be the case when an informant's identity would be revealed, the prosecutor may seek a protective order.

. . .

THE OBLIGATIONS OF SUPERVISORS AND OTHER PROSECUTORS WHO ARE NOT PERSONALLY RESPONSIBLE FOR A CRIMINAL PROSECUTION

Any supervisory lawyer in the prosecutor's office and those lawyers with managerial responsibility are obligated to ensure that subordinate lawyers comply with all their legal and ethical obligations. Thus, supervisors who directly oversee trial prosecutors must make reasonable efforts to ensure that those under their direct supervision meet their ethical obligations of disclosure, and are subject to discipline for

ordering, ratifying or knowingly failing to correct discovery violations. To promote compliance with Rule 3.8(d) in particular, supervisory lawyers must ensure that subordinate prosecutors are adequately trained regarding this obligation. Internal office procedures must facilitate such compliance.

For example, when responsibility for a single criminal case is distributed among a number of different lawyers with different lawyers having responsibility for investigating the matter, presenting the indictment, and trying the case, supervisory lawyers must establish procedures to ensure that the prosecutor responsible for making disclosure obtains evidence and information that must be disclosed. Internal policy might be designed to ensure that files containing documents favorable to the defense are conveyed to the prosecutor providing discovery to the defense, and that favorable information conveyed orally to a prosecutor is memorialized. Otherwise, the risk would be too high that information learned by the prosecutor conducting the investigation or the grand jury presentation would not be conveyed to the prosecutor in subsequent proceedings, eliminating the possibility of its being disclosed. Similarly, procedures must ensure that if a prosecutor obtains evidence in one case that would negate the defendant's guilt in another case, that prosecutor provides it to the colleague responsible for the other case.

In Formal Opinion 09-454, the ABA Standing Committee on Ethics and Professional Responsibility concluded that Rule 3.8(d) imposes obligations broader than the Due Process Clause in two critical respects: it rejects any consideration of materiality, and it requires prosecutors to disclose exculpatory evidence in advance of a guilty plea.[5] However, in one other critical respect the committee believed that Model Rule 3.8(d) is *narrower* than its constitutional counterpart, because a prosecutor can be subject to bar discipline only if he *knows* of the existence of the exculpatory evidence and fails to disclose it. Under Supreme Court precedent, due process is violated even in the absence of actual knowledge, where the police possess exculpatory information that is never turned over to the prosecutor. This essentially equates to a "knew or should have known" standard.[6]

Not all states agree with the ABA that their state's version of Rule 3.8(d) imposes greater disclosure responsibilities on a prosecutor than the due process requirements of *Brady*. For example, Ohio, Colorado, and Wisconsin[7] have rejected constructions of their attorney disciplinary rules that dispense with a materiality requirement. In Massachusetts and Virginia,[8] however, the pertinent state ethical rule has been interpreted to impose obligations that exceed *Brady*. This difference may be largely a matter of semantics. It is still fairly uncommon for state bar disciplinary committees to discipline prosecutors who violate their *Brady* obligations,

---

5. In United State v. Ruiz, 536 U.S. 622 (2002), the Supreme Court concluded that the primary purpose of the *Brady* doctrine was to protect the defendant's right to a fair trial, and that due process was not violated where the government conditioned a fast-track plea agreement on the defendant's waiver of certain discovery.
6. Kyles v. Whitley, 514 U.S. 418, 437 (1995) (prosecutor has affirmative duty to learn of and turn over exculpatory evidence possessed by anyone "acting on the government's behalf" in the case).
7. Disciplinary Counsel v. Kellogg Martin, 923 N.E.2d 125, 130 (Ohio 2010); In re Attorney C, 47 P.3d 1167, 1173 (Colo. 2002).
8. Mass. R. Prof'l Conduct. 3.8, cmt. [3A]; Va. State Bar Legal Ethics Op. 1862 (2012).

perhaps because they believe reversal of the criminal conviction will impose a sufficient deterrent effect on the government, or perhaps due to separation of powers or institutional competence concerns.[9] If states are not disciplining attorneys for failing to turn over material exculpatory evidence before trial and conviction, they are not likely to discipline prosecutors for failing to turn over less important evidence, or material exculpatory information prior to a guilty plea.

4. Contact with Represented Suspects

Recall that in Chapter 7 we explored the contours of Rule 4.2 (the "no-contact" rule), which prohibits an attorney from communicating with a represented party/person without permission of that person's lawyer. This rule has two important implications for criminal prosecutors because it may inhibit criminal investigations that would otherwise comply with constitutional protections.

In states that prohibit *ex parte* communications with represented "persons," prosecutors must be mindful of police undercover contact with suspects who have "lawyered up" prior to their arrest or indictment. Often times suspects secure counsel as soon as they learn that they are being investigated for a crime. Imagine a murder investigation where the police have focused their suspicions on the victim's former boyfriend. Does the suspect's act of securing counsel prohibit the government from continuing with routine undercover investigations directed toward that individual, such as sending a willing (and perhaps "wired") informant in to discuss the crime, or purchase contraband such as weapons? Rule 4.2 applies only to attorneys, but Rule 5.3 states that an attorney who has direct supervisory authority over a non-lawyer is responsible for the conduct of that non-lawyer if the attorney orders the conduct or ratifies the conduct having knowledge of it. Rule 8.4(a) also makes it professional misconduct for a lawyer to violate the Rules of Professional Conduct "through the acts of another." In the pre-indictment context, police investigatory conduct that might not violate the Fourth Amendment's prohibition of unreasonable searches and seizures or the Fifth Amendment protection against compelled self-incrimination could arguably violate the "no-contact" rule where the suspect has lawyered up and the prosecutor participates in planning or ratifying an undercover operation. In a Formal Opinion, the ABA Committee on Ethics and Professional Responsibility has taken the position that pre-charging undercover contacts with represented persons are not prohibited by Rule 4.2 because these contacts are "authorized by law" within the meaning of the rule, at least where they comport with Fourth and Fifth Amendment guarantees and any applicable statutory constraints on searches and electronic surveillance.[10] Most courts agree. One of the few federal courts that has prohibited pre-charging undercover contact with

---

9. R. Michael Cassidy, Prosecutorial Ethics 64 (2d ed. 2013).

10. ABA Formal Op. 95-396 (1995) (reasoning that undercover investigations by police were accepted practice at time of adoption of Rule 4.2, and that there is a strong public interest in continuing to investigate crime that may outweigh interests served by the "no contact" rule in pre-indictment context, at least where prosecutor does not participate directly in the undercover ruse).

a represented person did so on the ground that the prosecutor engaged in misconduct during the undercover investigation by issuing a fake grand jury subpoena to encourage the target to have a conversation with an undercover informant, and therefore the contact was not deemed "authorized by law."[11]

A second difficult application of the "no-contact" rule pertains to **post-indictment contact** with a represented party who wishes to cooperate with the government without his counsel knowing about it. Cooperating defendants may fear for their safety if persons close to a criminal enterprise were to learn of their informant status. This problem can arise in a jurisdiction that applies its "no-contact" rule to either represented persons or parties. The Sixth Amendment guarantees a criminally accused the right to the assistance of counsel — intentional interference with this right after it has attached (arraignment) may lead to suppression of evidence gained during the communication.[12] But the Sixth Amendment right to counsel is a right that may be *waived by the client*; if the client wishes to talk to the government without his counsel being present, he may voluntarily choose to do so. However, the "no-contact" rule is not a right of the client, it is an ethical rule that requires the *attorney's* permission prior to contact. What should a prosecutor do when a defendant awaiting trial sends a message through the police that he would like to meet with the government to discuss cooperation, but without his attorney's knowledge? This was the dilemma facing the Assistant U.S. Attorney in *Lopez*, below.

Case Preview

United States v. Lopez

Lopez, represented by Tarlow, and Escobedo, represented by Twitty, were both indicted for distribution of cocaine and heroin. Tarlow informed Lopez that it was his general policy not to negotiate pleas with the government in exchange for cooperation. When Twitty began negotiating a plea for Escobedo, Lopez asked to be included in the negotiations. He did not want Tarlow to find out for fear that he would not represent him if the case went to trial. During the course of negotiations, the prosecutor, Lyons, met with Lopez multiple times and did not inform Tarlow. When Tarlow found out from a mutual acquaintance of Lyons, he withdrew from representing Lopez. Represented by new counsel, Lopez successfully moved to dismiss the indictments against him due to prosecutorial misconduct. The district court concluded that Lyons had violated California Rule 2-100, the state equivalent of the Model Rule's "no-contact" provision. This appeal followed.

11. United States v. Hammad, 858 F.2d 834, 840 (2d Cir. 1988). *Cf.* United States v. Carona, 660 F.3d 360 (2d Cir. 2011) (although court will take case-by-case approach in assessing the propriety of pre-indictment contacts, normally undercover operations by police or informants do not violate the "no contact" rule). Such undercover operations have been ruled unethical where, as in *Hammad*, the prosecutor herself engages in fraud or deceit. *See* In re Pautler, 47 P.3d 1175 (Colo. 2002) (prosecutor subject to discipline for impersonating a public defender and engaging in telephone conversation with murder suspect to talk him into surrendering). *See also* Model Rule 8.4(c) (prohibiting conduct by a lawyer that involves "dishonesty, fraud, deceit or misrepresentation").

12. Massiah v. United States, 377 U.S. 201, 206 (1964).

As you read *Lopez*, ask yourself:

1. Why was the prosecutor's conversation with the defendant not "authorized by law," given that the judge had approved the communication beforehand following an *ex parte* hearing?
2. What are some of the reasons that a criminal defendant may not want his counsel to know that he is considering cooperating with the government? Are these legitimate concerns that the judiciary should accommodate?

United States v. Lopez

4 F.3d 1455 (9th Cir. 1993)

. . .

Having retained substitute counsel, Lopez filed a motion to dismiss the indictment on September 27, 1990. Lopez alleged that the government infringed upon his Sixth Amendment rights as well as Rules of Professional Conduct of the State Bar of California Rule 2-100 (1988). Binding pursuant to Local Rule 110-3 in the Northern District of California, Rule 2-100 generally prohibits a lawyer from communicating with another party in the case without the consent of that party's lawyer.

. . .

Rule 2-100 of the Rules of Professional Conduct of the State Bar of California governs communications with a represented party:

> (A) While representing a client, a member shall not communicate directly or indirectly about the subject of the representation with a party the member knows to be represented by another lawyer in the matter, unless the member has the consent of the other lawyer.
>
> . . .
>
> (C) This rule shall not prohibit:
>
> (1) Communications with a public officer, board, committee, or body;
>
> (2) Communications initiated by a party seeking advice or representation from an independent lawyer of the party's choice; or
>
> (3) Communications otherwise authorized by law.

Rule 2-100's prohibition against communicating with represented parties without the consent of their counsel is both widely accepted and of venerable heritage. The California rule tracks the language of Rule 4.2 of the American Bar Association's Model Rules of Professional Conduct, which in turn is nearly identical to its predecessor in the Model Code of Professional Responsibility, Disciplinary Rule 7-104(A)(1). . . .

The rule against communicating with a represented party without the consent of that party's counsel shields a party's substantive interests against encroachment by opposing counsel and safeguards the relationship between the party and her attorney. As Tarlow's withdrawal upon discovering the secret communication between Lopez and the government exemplifies all too well, the trust necessary for a successful attorney-client relationship is eviscerated when the client is lured into clandestine meetings with the lawyer for the opposition. As a result, uncurbed communications with represented parties could have deleterious effects well beyond the context of the individual case, for our adversary system is premised upon functional lawyer-client relationships.

A

The government argues, however, that Rule 2-100 was not intended to apply to prosecutors pursuing criminal investigations. . . . In People v. Sharp, 197 Cal. Rptr. 436 (1983), decided under the predecessor of Rule 2-100, the court noted that:

> [b]ecause the prosecutor's position is unique — he represents authority and the discretion to make decisions affecting the defendant's pending case — his contact carries an implication of leniency for cooperative defendants or harsher treatment for the uncooperative. Such contact intrudes upon the function of defense counsel and impedes his or her ability to negotiate a settlement and properly represent the client, whose interests the rule is designed to protect.

Id. 197 Cal. Rptr. at 439-40. . . .

The cases advanced by the government in support of its position are largely irrelative. [Citations omitted.] In addition, they have noted that during investigation of the case and prior to indictment,

> the contours of the "subject matter of the representation" by [the suspect's] attorneys, concerning which the code bars "communication," [are] less certain and thus even less susceptible to the damage of "artful" legal questions the Code provisions appear designed in part to avoid.

Lemonakis, 485 F.2d at 956; *compare* Rule 2-100 (barring communication "about the subject of the representation").

The government's insistence that there are no salient differences between the pre- and post-indictment contexts for purposes of Rule 2-100 is puzzling. The prosecutor's ethical duty to refrain from contacting represented defendants entifies upon indictment for the same reasons that the Sixth Amendment right to counsel attaches:

> The initiation of judicial criminal proceedings is far from a mere formalism. It is the starting point of our whole system of adversary criminal justice. For it is only then that the government has committed itself to prosecute, and only then that the adverse positions of government and defendant have solidified.
>
> . . .

B

The government next adopts the position that Lyons' conduct falls within the "communications otherwise authorized by law" exception to the rule against attorney communication with represented parties. *See* Rule 2-100(C)(3). The government argues that Lyons' contact with Lopez was authorized by statutes enabling prosecutors to conduct criminal investigations, and that the meetings were authorized by the magistrate judge's approval.

1

The government reasons that federal prosecutors operate pursuant to a "statutory scheme" that permits them to communicate with represented parties in order to detect and prosecute federal offenses. Citing 28 U.S.C. §§509, 515(a) and (c), 516, 533 and 547, the government argues that Justice Department attorneys fall within the "authorized by law" exception to California Rule 2-100 and its counterparts.

The comment to California Rule 2-100 notes that:

> Rule 2-100 is intended to control communications between a member [of the bar] and persons the member knows to be represented by counsel unless a statutory scheme or case law will override the rule. There are a number of *express statutory schemes* which authorize communications between a member and person who would otherwise be subject to this rule . . . . *Other applicable law also includes the authority of government prosecutors and investigators to conduct criminal investigations, as limited by the relevant decisional law.*

(Emphasis supplied). Thus, the "authorized by law" exception to Rule 2-100 requires that a statutory scheme expressly permit contact between an attorney and a represented party. While recognizing the statutory authority of prosecutors to investigate crime, however, Rule 2-100 is intended to allow no more contact between prosecutors and represented defendants than the case law permits. We agree with the district court that the statutes cited by the government are nothing more than general enabling statutes. Nothing in these provisions expressly or impliedly authorizes contact with represented individuals beyond that permitted by case law. As discussed above, "the authority of government prosecutors and investigators to conduct criminal investigations" is "limited by the relevant decisional law" to contacts conducted prior to indictment in a non-custodial setting. Lyons' discussions with Lopez were not so authorized.

2

The government also maintains that by obtaining the prior approval of a magistrate judge, Lyons brought his conversations with Lopez within the realm of the "authorized by law" exception to California Rule 2-100. We agree that in an appropriate case, contact with a represented party could be excepted from the prohibition of Rule 2-100 by court order. *See* Rule 2-100 cmt. (Rule 2-100 forbids communication with represented persons "unless . . . case law will override the rule."). But, as in other areas of the law, judicial approval cannot absolve the government from responsibility for wrongful acts when the government has misled the court in obtaining its sanction. [Citations omitted.] When seeking the authorization of the district court, the prosecutor had an affirmative duty to avoid misleading the court. Rules of Professional Conduct of the State Bar of California Rule 5-200(B) (1988) ("In presenting a matter to a tribunal, a member . . . [s]hall not seek to mislead the judge, judicial officer or jury by an artifice or false statement of fact or law.").

The district court concluded that the magistrate judge approved the meeting between Lyons and Lopez in the mistaken belief, fostered by Lyons, that:

> Tarlow[ ] was being paid by a third party with interests inimical to those of Lopez and that Lopez feared that if Tarlow became aware of his client's interest in cooperating

> with the government, he would pass the information on to others who would harm Lopez and/or his family.

765 F. Supp. at 1452. The district court thus concluded that the magistrate judge's approval could not legally authorize Lyons to meet with Lopez.

The district court found that Lyons materially misled the magistrate judge regarding the facts surrounding Lopez's request to speak directly with the prosecutor. We agree that the magistrate judge apparently did not have a full understanding of the facts surrounding Lopez's request. Without that understanding, she could not have made an informed decision to authorize the communications.

Although it is not necessary to our determination in this case to decide whether the district court erred in its finding that Lyons materially misled the magistrate judge, we suggest that the finding is not sustainable without resolving certain conflicts in the testimony of Twitty, Lyons, and Lopez as to what Lyons knew and when he knew it (the district court, for whatever reason, said it was not necessary to resolve these conflicts). On remand, were the district court to consider lesser sanctions than dismissal of the indictment, resolution of these conflicts would be essential.

C

The government makes several related arguments regarding the effect of Lopez's waiver on its ethical obligations. We note initially that it would be a mistake to speak in terms of a party "waiving" her "rights" under Rule 2-100. The rule against communicating with represented parties is fundamentally concerned with the *duties* of attorneys, not with the *rights* of parties. Lyons' duties as an attorney practicing in the Northern District of California extended beyond his obligation to respect Lopez's rights. Consequently, as the government concedes, ethical obligations are personal, and may not be vicariously waived.

The government also argues, however, that Lopez created a form of "hybrid representation" by waiving his right to counsel for the limited purpose of negotiating with the government, while retaining Tarlow as his counsel for all other purposes. Since Lopez would be unrepresented for purposes of discussions with the government, it would presumably not be a violation of Rule 2-100 for the government to communicate with him directly. We have in the past held, however, that "[i]f the defendant assumes any of the 'core functions' of the lawyer, . . . the hybrid scheme is acceptable only if the defendant has voluntarily waived counsel." United States v. Turnbull, 888 F.2d 636, 638 (9th Cir. 1989) (quoting United States v. Kimmel, 672 F.2d 720, 721 (9th Cir. 1982)), *cert. denied*, 498 U.S. 825 (1990). Representing a client in negotiations with the government is certainly one of the core functions of defense counsel, and there is no question that Lopez did *not* waive his right to counsel. In fact, the magistrate judge, following the hearing with Lopez, clearly communicated to Lyons that while Lopez was waiving his right to have counsel present while inquiring about the possibility of cooperating with the government, he was not waiving his right to counsel. The district court found Lopez did not wish to waive his right to have an attorney present. In *Kimmel*, we explained that:

> [w]hen the accused assumes functions that are at the core of the lawyer's traditional role . . . he will often undermine his own defense. Because he has a constitutional right to have his lawyer perform core functions, he must knowingly and intelligently waive that right.

672 F.2d at 721. While we are not immediately concerned with the constitutional dimensions of Lopez's communications with the government, it is clear that the magistrate judge's intervention could not, as a matter of law, have created a form of "hybrid representation." To the contrary, Lyons was notified by the court that Lopez was still represented by Tarlow, and consequently he could not evade his duty under Rule 2-100 on this basis.

For the same reason, we reject the government's claim that enforcing the ethical prohibition against communication with represented parties would interfere, under these circumstances, with the party's constitutional rights. The government relies on the doctrine established in Faretta v. California, 422 U.S. 806 (1975), that it is unconstitutional to require a criminal defendant to be represented by an attorney. We see no conflict between *Faretta* and Rule 2-100. Of course, Rule 2-100 does not bar communications with persons who have waived their right to counsel, for by its express terms the rule only applies to "communications with a *represented* party." (Emphasis supplied). Because Lopez did not waive his right to counsel, *Faretta* is immaterial.

D

We therefore conclude that the district court was correct in holding that Lyons had an ethical duty to avoid communicating directly with Lopez regarding the criminal prosecution so long as Lopez was represented by Tarlow.

. . .

Post-Case Follow-Up

In an excerpted portion of this opinion, the Ninth Circuit concluded that even if Assistant U.S. Attorney Lyons violated California Disciplinary Rule 2-100 by talking to Lopez without permission of his lawyer, Tarlow, the district court erred in imposing the drastic sanction of dismissal of the indictment. What would have been an appropriate "remedy" for such an ethical violation?

Why was the Ninth Circuit unwilling to conclude that Lopez had waived his right to counsel at the negotiations, and therefore was not "represented" within the meaning of Rule 2-100?

United States v. Lopez: Real Life Applications

1. Sally Smith is arrested for shoplifting. At arraignment she waives her right to an attorney and agrees to proceed *pro se*. After the arraignment Smith approaches the prosecutor in the hallway of the courthouse and wishes to discuss a plea agreement. May the prosecutor speak to Smith outside of court?

2. Joe Jones is arrested for possession with intent to distribute cocaine. He is assigned a public defender at arraignment. While Jones is out on bail, the government receives information that Jones is now selling handguns out of his apartment in addition to cocaine. An informant approaches the police and states that he is willing and able to go undercover to purchase a handgun from Jones. Pursuant to common practice in the jurisdiction, the police seek the prosecutor's permission to "wire" the informant. Is there any advice or direction the prosecutor may give to the police regarding the new operation without violating Rule 4.2?

3. Three suspects are arrested for bank robbery. They are represented by separate defense counsel. One of the defendants sends word to the police through the jail that he would be interested in cooperating and testifying against his confederates, but for security reasons he does not want his attorney to know about his cooperation until a deal is in place. What should the prosecutor do?

Controversy over the "no-contact" rule's application to federal prosecutors and the ways in which it may impose limitations on criminal investigations beyond constitutional protections led to several directives from the Department of Justice in the 1990s trying to limit its reach. For an excellent history of this controversy, see Bruce A. Green, *Whose Rules of Professional Conduct Should Govern Lawyers in Federal Court and How Should the Rules Be Created?*, 64 GEO. WASH. L. REV. 460, 470-79 (1996). This matter was settled in 1998 when Congress enacted the **McDade Amendment**,[13] making it clear that Justice Department prosecutors must abide by the attorney discipline rules in the states in which they practice.

5. Statements to the Media

Prosecutors are in a vital and perhaps unequaled position to keep the public informed about issues of public safety in their communities. Explaining the reasons for prosecutorial decisions is also essential to fulfill the deterrent aims of the criminal law. Yet because prosecutors are in possession of reams of sensitive information about the character and background of the defendant—some of which may not be admissible at trial—the prosecutor is also in a position to potentially taint the jury pool and undermine the presumption of innocence by making pretrial statements that cast the defendant in a highly negative light.

As we saw in Chapter 7, all lawyers participating in adjudication are prohibited under Rule 3.6 from making **public statements** that have a "substantial risk of materially prejudicing an adjudicative proceeding." This standard was upheld against First Amendment attack by the Supreme Court's plurality opinion in Gentile v. State Bar of Nevada, 501 U.S. 1030 (1991).[14] Comment [5] to Rule 3.6

---

13. Pub. L. No. 105-277, §801(a), 112 Stat. 2681, codified as amended at 28 U.S.C. §530B.
14. For a criticism of *Gentile* and its premise that the "substantial risk" standard of Rule 3.6 can be applied equally to prosecutors and defense counsel without offending First Amendment principles, see Margaret Tarkington, *Lost*

sets forth a list of certain subject matters that "are more likely than not" to have a material prejudicial effect on proceedings, in effect creating a presumption that public discussion of those identified topics will violate the rule. Several of those "off-limits" topics are particularly relevant to prosecutors: the defendant's criminal record, any confessions made by the defendant, the results of any scientific tests performed in the case, and information that the lawyer knows is not likely to be admissible in evidence. The theory behind comment [5] is that these facts will likely be the subject of pretrial litigation and ultimately may not be admitted in evidence at trial; once the public (and potential jury pool) hears such damaging information, they may be unable to "unhear" it.

Rule 3.8(f) imposes two additional responsibilities on prosecutors with respect to media comments about pending cases. First, the rule mandates that a prosecutor refrain from making extrajudicial comments that serve no "legitimate law enforcement purpose" and serve only to "heighten[] public condemnation of the accused." Whereas Rule 3.6 looks to the likelihood of *prejudicing the proceeding*, Rule 3.8(f) looks to the likelihood of *disparaging the accused* and holding him up to public opprobrium. Examples may include making a graphic or gory description of a heinous crime scene, displaying shocking or disturbing physical evidence to the media, disclosing criminal associations or uncharged crimes of the defendant, or arranging a "perp walk" for the sole purpose of giving the media footage of the defendant being transported in shackles. Mike Nifong, the prosecutor in the infamous Duke Lacrosse case, was censured by the North Carolina Bar Disciplinary Committee under Rule 3.8(f) for analogizing the alleged gang rape to a "cross burning," and for criticizing the suspects before the media for "refus[ing] to speak to investigators" upon "advice of counsel."[15]

Model Rule 3.8(f) also places an affirmative duty on prosecutors to try to rein in public comments by the police. Police departments often hold press conferences detailing the nature of an arrest and the attendant crime. Normally, an attorney is only responsible for conduct of non-lawyers if the attorney directs, supervises, or ratifies that conduct. But recognizing the synergistic relationship between the prosecutor and the police, Rule 3.8(f) requires prosecutors to "exercise reasonable care" to prevent investigators and other persons assisting or associated with the criminal case from making extrajudicial statements that the prosecutor would be prohibited from making under either Rule 3.6 or Rule 3.8.

B. THE CRIMINAL DEFENSE LAWYER

The common perception of the criminal defense lawyer is the zealous advocate on steroids. If all lawyers are bound to advocate strenuously and competently on behalf of their clients, many believe that the criminal defense lawyer's mission is

in the Compromise: Free Speech, Criminal Justice, and Attorney Pre-Trial Publicity, 66 FLA. L. REV. 1873, 1879 (2014).

15. For a more fulsome discussion of the flaws in the Duke Lacrosse prosecution, see Robert P. Mosteller, *The Duke Lacrosse Case: Innocence, False Identifications, and a Fundamental Failure to "Do Justice,"* 76 FORDHAM L. REV. 1337 (2007).

even more one-sided, because these lawyers are upholding the presumption of innocence and protecting their clients from the coercive power of the state. Where and exactly how a criminal defense lawyer's mission may be different from advocates in civil cases will be explored in the following three sections.

1. Taking Possession of Physical Evidence

Sometimes a defense lawyer will discover or be given a piece of real evidence that has evidentiary value — stolen property, a weapon used in a crime, documents that reveal the client's plan or intentions, or a laptop containing incriminating material. This **real evidence** is not itself a communication between the attorney and the client, but the act of giving it to the attorney (if given for the purposes of providing legal advice and intended to be confidential) may be privileged.

Such real evidence may be damaging to the client if revealed to authorities. So the attorney in this situation is faced with a choice between client loyalty and obligation to the justice system. When should the attorney refuse to accept the real evidence? If he does take possession of it, when does the lawyer have a duty to reveal it to the authorities? Ethicists have grappled with these complex questions for centuries. The answer to them, to the extent that there are clear answers, lies at the intersection of criminal law, criminal procedure, and legal ethics.

We saw in Chapter 7 that Model Rule 3.4 prohibits an attorney from "unlawfully" obstructing another party's access to evidence or "unlawfully" altering, destroying, or concealing evidence. So the rule prohibits only what the law prohibits — and that law may come from various sources: court orders, discovery obligations under the rules of criminal procedure, and the substantive criminal law. "Concealment" of real evidence is impermissible if the lawyer has some legal obligation to disclose the evidence independent of the ethical rule. "Destruction" of the evidence is unlawful if the conduct would violate an **obstruction of justice** statute.

The federal obstruction of justice statutes are particularly broad — they punish alteration, concealment, or destruction of real evidence and inducement of others to do so, where the person's intent is to keep the item from use in an official proceeding (civil, criminal, or agency administrative action).[16] The proceeding does not have to be already initiated so long as it is *foreseeable*.[17]

---

16. The two most commonly invoked federal statutes are the general obstruction of justice prohibition, 18 U.S.C. §1503 (penalizing one who corruptly interferes, obstructs, or impedes the due administration of justice) and the anti-shredding provisions of the Sarbanes-Oxley law, 18 U.S.C §1519 (penalizing whoever knowingly "alters, destroys, mutilates, conceals, covers up, falsifies, or makes a false entry" in any record, document, or tangible object with the intent to impede a federal investigation). Although there are several differences between the elements of these two crimes, for present purposes the most notable is that the former applies both to the destruction of documents and physical objects, while the Supreme Court has interpreted the latter to apply only to documents and electronic records that are capable of storing information. Yates v. United States, 135 S. Ct. 1074, 1081 (2015) (fisherman who directed crew to throw undersize fish overboard before inspector boarded ship could not be convicted under §1519).

17. *See, e.g.*, 18 U.S.C. §1512(c).

A lawyer who is offered physical evidence by a client in a criminal case should not become the repository of the evidence permanently if he knows or should know that the police will be looking for it, for that may constitute "concealment."[18] An attorney may return the evidence to its source unless there is an applicable state or federal statute that requires citizens to turn over to authorities the fruits or instrumentalities of a crime.[19] But an attorney clearly may not return physical evidence to its source with suggestions to destroy or conceal the evidence, because that conduct would constitute "counsel(ing) or assist(ing)" another to obstruct access to evidence in violation of Rule 3.4 (a).

Should an attorney ever refuse to accept real evidence?
Shutterstock.com

Case Preview

"Dead Bodies" Case

The following opinion from the New York State Bar Association, commonly referred to as "The Dead Bodies Case," answers four main questions that arose from actions taken by an attorney in the course of representing a client charged with murder. The client confessed to his attorneys to having committed two prior murders and disclosed the location of those bodies. The client also drew a diagram of their location. One of the attorneys travelled to the location of one of the bodies and, upon discovering the corpse, began to photograph it. While taking pictures, the attorney moved the body slightly to bring it within the range of his camera. At a later date, the attorney destroyed the photographs as well as all record of his conversation with his client concerning the previous murders, including the diagram. Later, while discussing with the prosecutor a possible plea disposition, the lawyer suggested that in exchange for favorable consideration for his client the lawyer might be in position to provide information concerning several unsolved murders. The government refused the plea proposal, trial ensued, and in the context of raising an insanity defense, the client actually testified to having committed the other murders. Public outrage over the lawyer's secret conduct then led the New York Bar Association to take up the controversial subject in a formal ethics opinion.

18. In re Ryder, 263 F. Supp. 360, 361 (E.D Va.), *aff'd*, 381 F.2d 713 (4th Cir. 1967) (lawyer who transferred stolen money and gun from client's safety deposit box to his own safety deposit box violated predecessor to Rule 3.4(a) by assisting his client to conceal evidence, and by unlawfully possessing sawed-off shotgun).

19. Professor Gillers has argued that state laws requiring citizens to turn over fruits or instrumentalities of a crime may be unconstitutional as applied to criminal defense attorneys who receive such evidence from their clients, because they could deprive the defendant of his right to the effective assistance of counsel under the Sixth Amendment. Stephen A. Gillers, *Guns, Fruits, Drugs and Documents: A Criminal Defense Lawyer's Responsibility for Real Evidence*, 63 Stan L. Rev. 813, 827 (2011).

As you read Formal Opinion 479, ask yourself:

1. When and how could the lawyers possibly have made different decisions, given their obligations of client confidentiality under Rule 1.6?
2. Why was the public so outraged by their conduct when it came to light?

Client's Confidences and Secrets; Past Crimes Disclosed to Lawyer; Plea Bargaining

New York State Bar Association Formal Opinion 479 (1978)

QUESTIONS

1. Under the circumstances alleged, would a lawyer be acting improperly in failing to disclose to the authorities his knowledge of the two prior murders and the location of the bodies?

2. Under the circumstances alleged, would a lawyer be acting improperly in withholding and destroying (a) the records of his conversation with the client, (b) the photographs taken by him of the bodies of the victims and (c) the diagram showing the physical location of the bodies?

3. Under the circumstances alleged, would a lawyer be acting improperly in moving parts of one of the bodies prior to taking photographs?

4. Under the circumstances alleged, would a lawyer be acting improperly, in his attempt to negotiate a plea disposition, in suggesting to the District Attorney that he had information concerning two unsolved murders?

OPINION

The questions raised are complex and difficult. Legal issues, upon which we do not pass, may be inextricably interwoven with ethical considerations. Illegal conduct involving moral turpitude is per se unethical. DR1-102(A)(3).

1. The lawyer's failure to disclose his knowledge of the two unrelated homicides was not improper, assuming, as the facts given us indicate, that the information came to the lawyer during the course of his employment. Furthermore, the requirements of Canon 4 that "a lawyer should preserve the confidences and secrets of a client," and of EC 4-1 and DR 4-101(B), would have been violated if such disclosure had been made. . . .

Proper representation of a client calls for full disclosure by the client to his lawyer of all possibly relevant facts, even though such facts may reveal the client's commission of prior crimes. To encourage full disclosure, the client must be assured of confidentiality, a requirement embodied by law in the attorney-client privilege and broadly incorporated into Canon 4 of the Code and the EC's and DR's thereunder.

Frequently clients have a disposition to withhold information from lawyers. If the client suspects that his confidences will not be adequately protected or may in some way be used against him, he will be far more likely to withhold information which he believes may be to his detriment or which he does not want generally known. The client who withholds information from his lawyer runs a substantial risk of not being accorded his full legal rights. At the same time, the lawyer from whom such information is withheld may well be required to assert, in complete good faith and with no violation of EC 7-26 or DR 7-102(A), totally meritless or frivolous claims or defenses to which his client has no legal right. Thus, the interests served by the strict rule of confidentiality are far broader than merely those of the client, but include the interests of the public generally and of effective judicial administration.

Narrow and limited exceptions to the rule of confidentiality have been incorporated in DR 4-101(C) and DR 7-102(B)(1), the most important of which relate to information involving the intention of the client to commit a crime in the future or the perpetration of a fraud during the course of the lawyer's representation of the client, or where the client consents following full disclosure. The future crime exception recognizes both the possible preventability of the crime, as well as the total absence of any societal need to encourage criminal clients to make such disclosures to their lawyers. . . .

Thus, the lawyer was under an injunction not to disclose to the authorities his knowledge of the two prior murders, and was duty bound not to reveal to the authorities the location of the bodies. The lawyer's knowledge with respect to the location of the bodies was obtained solely from the client in confidence and in secret. Without the client's revelation in secret and in confidence, he would not have been in a position to assist the authorities in this regard. Thus, his personal knowledge is a link solidly welded to the chain of privileged communications and, without the client's express permission, must not be disclosed. The relationship between lawyer and client is in many respects like that between priest and penitent. Both lawyer and priest are bound by the bond of silence. . . .

2. A lawyer's obligation to hold a client's confidences and secrets inviolate extends beyond information imparted orally and embraces written material from the client "coming into existence merely as a communication to the attorney." See 8 Wigmore, Evidence §2307 (McNaughton Rev. 1961).

The memorialization by a lawyer of statements, information and documents received from a client, whether by shorthand or longhand notes, dictated and typed memoranda, speedwriting, electronic or magnetic recording, Xerox, Photostat, photograph or other form of recordation or reproduction does not alter the fact that the communication from the client is privileged. Such memorialization may be useful in facilitating the handling of a matter by the lawyer and is part of the lawyer's work product. When the lawyer's purpose is served, the work product may be destroyed without violation of ethical standards.

Similarly, written material prepared by the client for his lawyer is a form of written communication and falls within the attorney-client privilege. Such documents are not instruments or fruits of the crime, which under certain circumstances the lawyer might be obliged to turn over to authorities. See *State v. Olwell*, supra. Accordingly, neither the lawyer nor his client was obliged to reveal an incriminating diagram, whether prepared by the client for his lawyer or by the lawyer on the basis of information gained by him during the course of the client's representation, under EC 7-27 and DR 7-102. Provided it was not contrary to his client's wishes for him to do so, there was no ethical inhibition against its destruction by the lawyer.

3. This Committee does not pass upon the legality of alleged conduct, but if such conduct is illegal, it would of course be unethical, with rare exceptions of inadvertent violations involving no moral turpitude. Thus, any tampering, concealment or destruction of physical evidence in violation of N.Y. Penal Law §215.40 would also be violative of the Code. Even in the absence of any violation of law and in the absence of an intention on the part of the lawyer to tamper, conceal or destroy evidence, there could be an appearance of impropriety in violation of Canon 9 in moving a part of one of the bodies. Such conduct should be avoided to prevent even the appearance that there might have been an intent to tamper with or suppress evidence.

4. There is no ethical impropriety in the lawyer's discussing with the District Attorney the possibility of an appropriate plea disposition, provided that the lawyer had the express consent of his client before making such disclosure. Plea bargaining is an accepted part of our criminal procedures today. A lawyer engaged or attempting to engage in it with his client's consent would be properly serving his client. Thus, the lawyer's suggestion to the District Attorney that he might be in a position to assist the authorities in resolving open cases during such a discussion would appear to involve no violation of proper professional standards. One can conceive of a variety of circumstances in which such a disclosure might be helpful to a client. For example, the disclosure of the client's commission of prior crimes of violence might very well establish the client's need for confinement for medical treatment rather than imprisonment.

Post-Case Follow-Up

Attorney Francis Belge, the attorney who was the subject of this formal opinion, was also criminally charged under two sections of the New York Public Health statute making it a misdemeanor to fail to report the death of someone who died without medical assistance. Although Belge was subsequently exonerated by the trial judge in that criminal matter, the public outcry over the choices he made in the Dead Bodies case undercut his standing in the small-town community and ultimately his law practice. His life was ruined in many ways for "stepping up" to take on a difficult case, and then making a very courageous and unpopular decision within the context of that case.

Defendant Garrow in the Dead Bodies case was actually represented by two attorneys — Francis Belge and Frank Armani. Armani was not present when Belge observed and photographed one of the bodies, so he escaped indictment. In interviews after the Garrow prosecution, both attorneys explained that one of their motivations for checking to see if the bodies were located where the client said they would be was that they thought their client had mental health issues and might be fabricating the other crimes. Is this the sort of "preparation" contemplated by Rule 1.1?

As the New York State Bar Committee acknowledged, where a client informs his attorney of the location of physical evidence but does *not* deliver that evidence to the attorney, the communication is privileged if intended to be confidential.

However, that privilege may be lost if the attorney thereafter acts on this information by moving the evidence, altering it, or destroying it. Because the attorney has compromised the ability of the state to make use of the evidence, some courts have ruled that this form of unethical conduct defeats the privilege.[20]

Compare the Dead Bodies case with *People v. Meredith*, discussed in footnote 20. In the former case, the lawyer left the bodies where he found them and escaped any discipline. In the latter case, the lawyer's investigator moved the victim's discarded wallet but later turned it over to authorities; nonetheless, the defense team was forced to make the government "whole" by testifying at trial as to where the wallet was found. Why should the client — who had not waived the privilege in either instance — be in any worse position in the *Meredith* case than in the Dead Bodies case?

More on the Dead Bodies Case

For a fascinating discussion of the Belge matter, including interviews with the participants, listen to the June 2016 RadioLab podcast *The Buried Bodies Case*, at http://www.radiolab.org/story/the_buried_bodies_case/.

Dead Bodies Case: Real Life Applications

1. Suppose that you represent a local parish. The rector for the parish comes to your office and tells you that the parish recently fired its youth minister after discovering child pornography on the employee's work laptop. The client delivers the laptop to you and asks that you take whatever steps necessary to protect the client from adverse publicity and potential liability with respect to the matter. Although possession of child pornography is a crime, to your knowledge the FBI has not opened an investigation into the youth minister. What should you do with the computer?

2. Imagine that a prominent local businessman comes to you with a problem. He thinks he may have been involved in a hit and run accident the previous night. He didn't stop his car because he was drunk, disoriented, and scared. But this morning he noticed a large dent in his front right fender. He also saw a news report on a local television station saying that a pedestrian was "clinging to life" in a local hospital after being hit by a car matching the general description of his car. Your visitor asks you what should be done with the car. How do you advise him? May it be repaired? May you engage a chemist to test the fender for fibers, blood, or hair? Does that depend on whether such testing would destroy the evidentiary value of the site of impact?

3. Your client is under investigation for murder and conspiracy to commit murder with respect to a drive-by shooting. The client suspects that one of his former friends and associates may be cooperating with the government. He comes to

20. People v. Meredith, 631 P.2d 46, 53 (Cal. 1981) (where the attorney or his agent removes or alters evidence as a result of confidential communication with client, there exists an exception to the attorney-client privilege and the defense lawyer's investigator may be called to testify as to where he found it).

you for advice. During your discussions you ask the client if and when he ever had any communications with the cooperating witness. He tells you that they have texted each other regularly for the past two months, and hands you his cell phone. Should you take possession of the cell phone? If so, what can and should you do with it?

The attorney-client privilege further complicates the attorney's responsibility with respect to real evidence. While a preexisting document or physical object is not subject to the privilege, the fact that a client gives or attempts to give that evidence to his attorney will likely *itself* be considered a communicative act subject to the attorney-client privilege.[21] If the lawyer is forced to deliver the physical evidence to the authorities pursuant to some legal obligation, search warrant, or subpoena, the lawyer may thereafter argue that the state may not use this "act of production" against the client because to do so would whipsaw the attorney between a privileged communication and a legal obligation.[22]

It is thus relatively clear what a lawyer cannot do — destroy likely evidence or counsel his client to do so, or keep the evidence and alter its evidentiary value (e.g., by wiping a gun for fingerprints or deleting the hard drive of a computer). Further, some criminal statutes make it unlawful to even possess certain types of evidence altogether — narcotics, stolen property, firearms — and in those jurisdictions a criminal defense lawyer should not take even temporary possession of such items because then the lawyer would be committing a crime.

Short of those two extremes are actions with respect to physical evidence that pose extremely complex and challenging ethical problems for a criminal defense lawyer. To avoid some of those ambiguities, many lawyers simply refuse to take possession of physical evidence offered to them by a criminal suspect. But there may be cases in which an attorney thinks it is in the best interests of his client to take possession of an item temporarily to have it examined or tested. One state has provided explicit guidance on this question, ruling that it is permissible for an attorney to inspect and test an object of physical evidence and then deliver it to authorities so long as the attorney does not tell the government where he obtained it.[23] Yet another jurisdiction has adopted a third-party intermediary strategy. In the District of Columbia, an attorney who receives incriminating physical evidence may return it to its rightful owner if it is not yet under subpoena and if such return would not compromise client confidences or violate state law. But if returning the evidence to its owner would prejudice the client by implicitly revealing client confidences, or if substantive criminal law requires delivery of the evidence to authorities, the attorney may give the physical evidence to the D.C. Bar Counsel and ask that bar counsel turn it over. *See* D.C. R. PROF'L CONDUCT 3.4(a) cmt. [5].

---

21. State v. Olwell, 394 P.2d 681 (Wash. 1964) (attorney given knife by client could turn it over to government with assurances that prosecution must refrain from telling jury where it came from).

22. *Id. See* Fisher v. United States, 425 U.S. 391, 407 (1976).

23. *Olwell*, 394 P.2d at 684. Professor Gregory Sisk posits that a lawyer may retain the physical evidence long enough to conduct a physical test on it, and then return it to its source, without running afoul of Rule 3.4(a). Gregory Sisk, *The Legal Ethics of Real Evidence*, 89 WASH. L. REV. 819, 881 (2014).

2. Putting Your Client on the Stand

In Chapter 7, we discussed a lawyer's duty of candor to the tribunal and responsibility for remedying perjury. The obligations of a criminal defense lawyer in this regard are more nuanced, because a defendant has a constitutional right to present a defense and to the effective assistance of counsel under the Sixth Amendment. This has sometimes been referred to as the "**lawyer's trilemma**." A lawyer must guard the client's secrets, must act diligently in gathering as much information as will enable him to counsel the accused and competently mount a defense, and must be candid to the court. How can a criminal defense lawyer do all three at the same time, if in gathering information from the accused the lawyer learns that he intends to testify falsely? With regards to civil cases, we saw that when there is a tension between these duties the obligation of candor takes precedence. Should the same be true of a criminal defense attorney? One important difference is that the criminal defendant's Sixth Amendment right to present a defense has been interpreted by the Supreme Court to include the right to take the stand in one's own defense, even against the advice of counsel.[24] In a criminal context where we expect lawyers to take an adversarial stance against the government's attempt to deprive the defendant of liberty and to prefer the client's interests at almost all costs over that of the society, does that justify a different result?

Case Preview

Nix v. Whiteside

Nix v. Whiteside arose from a drug deal gone horribly wrong in which Emanuel Whiteside showed up at Calvin Love's apartment late one night hoping to procure marijuana. An argument broke out between the two and Whiteside, fearing that Love was reaching for a gun, fatally stabbed Love. Whiteside repeatedly told his attorney, Gary L. Robinson, that he had not actually seen the gun, but was convinced Love had one. However, a week before the trial, Whiteside told Robinson for the first time that he had seen something metallic in Love's hand. Robinson immediately saw through Whiteside's attempt to strengthen his self-defense claim, and warned Whiteside that if he insisted on committing perjury, he would withdraw from representation. Whiteside elected not to commit perjury and was convicted of second degree murder. The Supreme Court granted certiorari to decide whether the trial attorney's conduct deprived Whiteside of his Sixth Amendment right to counsel.

As you read *Whiteside*, ask yourself:

1. How did Attorney Robinson "know" that Whiteside intended to commit perjury within the meaning of Rule 3.3?
2. What does the Court identify as the "range of reasonable professional conduct" in response to a criminal defendant's intent to commit perjury?

24. Rock v. Arkansas, 475 U.S. 157 (1986); Harris v. New York, 401 U.S. 222 (1971).

Nix v. Whiteside

475 U.S. 157 (1986) (citations omitted)

I

A

Whiteside gave him a statement that he had stabbed Love as the latter "was pulling a pistol from underneath the pillow on the bed." Upon questioning by Robinson, however, Whiteside indicated that he had not actually seen a gun, but that he was convinced that Love had a gun. No pistol was found on the premises; shortly after the police search following the stabbing, which had revealed no weapon, the victim's family had removed all of the victim's possessions from the apartment. Robinson interviewed Whiteside's companions who were present during the stabbing, and none had seen a gun during the incident. Robinson advised Whiteside that the existence of a gun was not necessary to establish the claim of self-defense, and that only a reasonable belief that the victim had a gun nearby was necessary even though no gun was actually present.

Until shortly before trial, Whiteside consistently stated to Robinson that he had not actually seen a gun, but that he was convinced that Love had a gun in his hand. About a week before trial, during preparation for direct examination, Whiteside for the first time told Robinson and his associate Donna Paulsen that he had seen something "metallic" in Love's hand. When asked about this, Whiteside responded:

> "[I]n Howard Cook's case there was a gun. If I don't say I saw a gun, I'm dead."

Robinson told Whiteside that such testimony would be perjury and repeated that it was not necessary to prove that a gun was available but only that Whiteside reasonably believed that he was in danger. On Whiteside's insisting that he would testify that he saw "something metallic" Robinson told him, according to Robinson's testimony:

> "[W]e could not allow him to [testify falsely] because that would be perjury, and as officers of the court we would be suborning perjury if we allowed him to do it; . . . I advised him that if he did do that it would be my duty to advise the Court of what he was doing and that I felt he was committing perjury; also, that I probably would be allowed to attempt to impeach that particular testimony." App. to Pet. for Cert. A-85.

Robinson also indicated he would seek to withdraw from the representation if Whiteside insisted on committing perjury.

Whiteside testified in his own defense at trial and stated that he "knew" that Love had a gun and that he believed Love was reaching for a gun and he had acted swiftly in self-defense. On cross-examination, he admitted that he had not actually seen a gun in Love's hand. Robinson presented evidence that Love had been seen with a sawed-off shotgun on other occasions, that the police search of the apartment may have been careless, and that the victim's family had removed everything from the apartment shortly after the crime. Robinson presented this evidence to show a basis for Whiteside's asserted fear that Love had a gun.

The jury returned a verdict of second-degree murder, and Whiteside moved for a new trial, claiming that he had been deprived of a fair trial by Robinson's admonitions not to state that he saw a gun or "something metallic." . . .

. . .

B

In *Strickland v. Washington*, we held that to obtain relief by way of federal habeas corpus on a claim of a deprivation of effective assistance of counsel under the Sixth Amendment, the movant must establish both serious attorney error and prejudice. To show such error, it must be established that the assistance rendered by counsel was constitutionally deficient in that "counsel made errors so serious that counsel was not functioning as 'counsel' guaranteed the defendant by the Sixth Amendment." *Strickland*, 466 U.S. at 687. To show prejudice, it must be established that the claimed lapses in counsel's performance rendered the trial unfair so as to "undermine confidence in the outcome" of the trial. Id. at 694. In *Strickland*, we acknowledged that the Sixth Amendment does not require any particular response by counsel to a problem that may arise. Rather, the Sixth Amendment inquiry is into whether the attorney's conduct was "reasonably effective." To counteract the natural tendency to fault an unsuccessful defense, a court reviewing a claim of ineffective assistance must "indulge a strong presumption that counsel's conduct falls within the wide range of reasonable professional assistance." Id. at 689. In giving shape to the perimeters of this range of reasonable professional assistance, *Strickland* mandates that "[p]revailing norms of practice as reflected in American Bar Association Standards and the like, . . . are guides to determining what is reasonable, but they are only guides." Id. at 688.

Under the *Strickland* standard, breach of an ethical standard does not necessarily make out a denial of the Sixth Amendment guarantee of assistance of counsel. When examining attorney conduct, a court must be careful not to narrow the wide range of conduct acceptable under the Sixth Amendment so restrictively as to constitutionalize particular standards of professional conduct and thereby intrude into the state's proper authority to define and apply the standards of professional conduct applicable to those it admits to practice in its courts. In some future case challenging attorney conduct in the course of a state-court trial, we may need to define with greater precision the weight to be given to recognized canons of ethics, the standards established by the state in statutes or professional codes, and the Sixth Amendment, in defining the proper scope and limits on that conduct. Here we need not face that question, since virtually all of the sources speak with one voice.

C

We turn next to the question presented: the definition of the range of "reasonable professional" responses to a criminal defendant client who informs counsel that he will perjure himself on the stand. We must determine whether, in this setting, Robinson's conduct fell within the wide range of professional responses to threatened client perjury acceptable under the Sixth Amendment.

In *Strickland*, we recognized counsel's duty of loyalty and his "overarching duty to advocate the defendant's cause." Ibid. Plainly, that duty is limited to legitimate, lawful conduct compatible with the very nature of a trial as a search for truth. Although counsel must take all reasonable lawful means to attain the objectives of the client, counsel is precluded from taking steps or in any way assisting the client in presenting false evidence or otherwise violating the law. This principle has consistently been recognized in most unequivocal terms by expositors of the norms of professional conduct since the first Canons of Professional Ethics were adopted by the American Bar Association in 1908. . . .

. . .

These principles have been carried through to contemporary codifications of an attorney's professional responsibility. Disciplinary Rule 7-102 of the Model Code of Professional Responsibility (1980), entitled "Representing a Client Within the Bounds of the Law," provides:

> "(A) In his representation of a client, a lawyer shall not:
>
> "(4) Knowingly use perjured testimony or false evidence.
>
> "(7) Counsel or assist his client in conduct that the lawyer knows to be illegal or fraudulent."

This provision has been adopted by Iowa, and is binding on all lawyers who appear in its courts. See Iowa Code of Professional Responsibility for Lawyers (1985). The more recent Model Rules of Professional Conduct (1983) similarly admonish attorneys to obey all laws in the course of representing a client:

> "*RULE 1.2* Scope of Representation
>
> "(d) A lawyer shall not counsel a client to engage, or assist a client, in conduct that the lawyer knows is criminal or fraudulent. . . ."

Both the Model Code of Professional Responsibility and the Model Rules of Professional Conduct also adopt the specific exception from the attorney-client privilege for disclosure of perjury that his client intends to commit or has committed. DR 4-101(C)(3) (intention of client to commit a crime); Rule 3.3 (lawyer has duty to disclose falsity of evidence even if disclosure compromises client confidences). Indeed, both the Model Code and the Model Rules do not merely *authorize* disclosure by counsel of client perjury; they *require* such disclosure. See Rule 3.3(a)(4); DR 7-102(B)(1).

These standards confirm that the legal profession has accepted that an attorney's ethical duty to advance the interests of his client is limited by an equally solemn duty to comply with the law and standards of professional conduct; it specifically ensures that the client may not use false evidence. This special duty of an attorney to prevent and disclose frauds upon the court derives from the recognition that perjury is as much a crime as tampering with witnesses or jurors by way of promises and threats, and undermines the administration of justice. See 1 W. Burdick, Law of Crime §§293, 300, 318-336 (1946).

. . .

It is universally agreed that at a minimum the attorney's first duty when confronted with a proposal for perjurious testimony is to attempt to dissuade the client from the unlawful course of conduct. Model Rules of Professional Conduct, Rule 3.3, Comment; Wolfram, Client Perjury, 50 S. Cal. L. Rev. 809, 846 (1977). A statement directly in point is found in the commentary to the Model Rules of Professional Conduct under the heading "False Evidence":

> "When false evidence is offered by the client, however, a conflict may arise between the lawyer's duty to keep the client's revelations confidential and the duty of candor to the court. Upon ascertaining that material evidence is false, the lawyer *should seek to persuade the client that the evidence should not be offered* or, if it has been offered, that its false character should immediately be disclosed." Model Rules of Professional Conduct, Rule 3.3, Comment (1983) (emphasis added).

The commentary thus also suggests that an attorney's revelation of his client's perjury to the court is a professionally responsible and acceptable response to the conduct of a client who has actually given perjured testimony. Similarly, the Model Rules and the commentary, as well as the Code of Professional Responsibility adopted in Iowa, expressly permit withdrawal from representation as an appropriate response of an attorney when the client threatens to commit perjury. Model Rules of Professional Conduct, Rule 1.16(a)(1), Rule 1.6, Comment (1983); Code of Professional Responsibility, DR 2-110(B), (C) (1980). Withdrawal of counsel when this situation arises at trial gives rise to many difficult questions including possible mistrial and claims of double jeopardy.

The essence of the brief *amicus* of the American Bar Association reviewing practices long accepted by ethical lawyers is that under no circumstance may a lawyer either advocate or passively tolerate a client's giving false testimony. This, of course, is consistent with the governance of trial conduct in what we have long called "a search for truth." The suggestion sometimes made that "a lawyer must believe his client, not judge him" in no sense means a lawyer can honorably be a party to or in any way give aid to presenting known perjury.

D

Considering Robinson's representation of respondent in light of these accepted norms of professional conduct, we discern no failure to adhere to reasonable professional standards that would in any sense make out a deprivation of the Sixth Amendment right to counsel. Whether Robinson's conduct is seen as a successful attempt to dissuade his client from committing the crime of perjury, or whether seen as a "threat" to withdraw from representation and disclose the illegal scheme, Robinson's representation of Whiteside falls well within accepted standards of professional conduct and the range of reasonable professional conduct acceptable under *Strickland*.

...

The Court of Appeals' holding that Robinson's "action deprived [Whiteside] of due process and effective assistance of counsel" is not supported by the record since Robinson's action, at most, deprived Whiteside of his contemplated perjury. Nothing counsel did in any way undermined Whiteside's claim that he believed the victim was reaching for a gun. Similarly, the record gives no support for holding that Robinson's action "also impermissibly compromised [Whiteside's] right to testify in his own defense by conditioning continued representation . . . and confidentiality upon [Whiteside's] *restricted* testimony." The record in fact shows the contrary: (a) that Whiteside did testify, and (b) he was "restricted" or restrained only from testifying falsely and was aided by Robinson in developing the basis for the fear that Love was reaching for a gun. Robinson divulged no client communications until he was compelled to do so in response to Whiteside's post-trial challenge to the quality of his performance. We see this as a case in which the attorney successfully dissuaded the client from committing the crime of perjury.

Paradoxically, even while accepting the conclusion of the Iowa trial court that Whiteside's proposed testimony would have been a criminal act, the Court of Appeals held that Robinson's efforts to persuade Whiteside not to commit that crime were improper, *first*, as forcing an impermissible choice between the right to counsel and the right to testify; and, *second*, as compromising client confidences because of Robinson's threat to disclose the contemplated perjury.

Whatever the scope of a constitutional right to testify, it is elementary that such a right does not extend to testifying *falsely*. In *Harris v. New York*, we assumed the right of an accused to testify "in his own defense, or to refuse to do so" and went on to hold:

> "[T]hat privilege cannot be construed to include the right to commit perjury. . . ."

. . . *Harris* and other cases make it crystal clear that there is no right whatever — constitutional or otherwise — for a defendant to use false evidence.

The paucity of authority on the subject of any such "right" may be explained by the fact that such a notion has never been responsibly advanced; the right to counsel includes no right to have a lawyer who will cooperate with planned perjury. A lawyer who would so cooperate would be at risk of prosecution for suborning perjury, and disciplinary proceedings, including suspension or disbarment.

Robinson's admonitions to his client can in no sense be said to have forced respondent into an *impermissible* choice between his right to counsel and his right to testify as he proposed for there was no permissible choice to testify falsely. For defense counsel to take steps to persuade a criminal defendant to testify truthfully, or to withdraw, deprives the defendant of neither his right to counsel nor the right to testify truthfully. In *United States v. Havens, supra,* we made clear that "when defendants testify, they must testify truthfully or suffer the consequences." *Id.*, 446 U.S. at 626. When an accused proposes to resort to perjury or to produce false evidence, one consequence is the risk of withdrawal of counsel.

On this record, the accused enjoyed continued representation within the bounds of reasonable professional conduct and did in fact exercise his right to testify; at most he was denied the right to have the assistance of counsel in the presentation of false testimony. Similarly, we can discern no breach of professional duty in Robinson's admonition to respondent that he would disclose respondent's perjury to the court. The crime of perjury in this setting is indistinguishable in substance from the crime of threatening or tampering with a witness or a juror. A defendant who informed his counsel that he was arranging to bribe or threaten witnesses or members of the jury would have no "right" to insist on counsel's assistance or silence. Counsel would not be limited to advising against that conduct. An attorney's duty of confidentiality, which totally covers the client's admission of guilt, does not extend to a client's announced plans to engage in future criminal conduct. In short, the responsibility of an ethical lawyer, as an officer of the court and a key component of a system of justice, dedicated to a search for truth, is essentially the same whether the client announces an intention to bribe or threaten witnesses or jurors or to commit or procure perjury. No system of justice worthy of the name can tolerate a lesser standard.

The rule adopted by the Court of Appeals, which seemingly would require an attorney to remain silent while his client committed perjury, is wholly incompatible with the established standards of ethical conduct and the laws of Iowa and contrary to professional standards promulgated by that State. The position advocated by petitioner, on the contrary, is wholly consistent with the Iowa standards of professional conduct and law, with the overwhelming majority of courts, and with codes of professional ethics. Since there has been no breach of any recognized professional duty, it follows that there can be no deprivation of the right to assistance of counsel under the *Strickland* standard.

E

. . .

Whether he was persuaded or compelled to desist from perjury, Whiteside has no valid claim that confidence in the result of his trial has been diminished by his desisting from the contemplated perjury. Even if we were to assume that the jury might have believed his perjury, it does not follow that Whiteside was prejudiced.

In his attempt to evade the prejudice requirement of *Strickland*, Whiteside relies on cases involving conflicting loyalties of counsel. In Cuyler v. Sullivan, 446 U.S. 335 (1980), we held that a defendant could obtain relief without pointing to a specific prejudicial default on the part of his counsel, provided it is established that the attorney was "actively represent[ing] conflicting interests." *Id.* at 350.

Here, there was indeed a "conflict," but of a quite different kind; it was one imposed on the attorney by the client's proposal to commit the crime of fabricating testimony without which, as he put it, "I'm dead." This is not remotely the kind of conflict of interests dealt with in *Cuyler v. Sullivan*. Even in that case we did not suggest that all multiple representations necessarily resulted in an active conflict rendering the representation constitutionally infirm. If a "conflict" between a client's proposal and counsel's ethical obligation gives rise to a presumption that counsel's assistance was prejudicially ineffective, every guilty criminal's conviction would be suspect if the defendant had sought to obtain an acquittal by illegal means. Can anyone doubt what practices and problems would be spawned by such a rule and what volumes of litigation it would generate?

Whiteside's attorney treated Whiteside's proposed perjury in accord with professional standards, and since Whiteside's truthful testimony could not have prejudiced the result of his trial, the Court of Appeals was in error to direct the issuance of a writ of habeas corpus and must be reversed.

Reversed.

Post-Case Follow-Up

In *Whiteside*, the Court ruled that Model Rule 3.3 is constitutional where a criminal defense attorney *threatens* to withdraw or reveal the perjury, and the client does not testify. The Court did not say that this is the *only* course of conduct that would satisfy Sixth Amendment protections. This leaves states free to adopt ethical rules that pose other solutions to the problem of client perjury. Justice Blackmun emphasized this very narrow ground of the Court's ruling in his concurrence: "The only federal issue in this case is whether Robinson's behavior deprived Whiteside of the effective assistance of counsel; it is not whether Robinson's behavior conformed to any particular code of legal ethics . . . . It is for the States to decide how attorneys should conduct themselves in state criminal proceedings, and this Court's responsibility extends only to ensuring that the restrictions a State enacts do not infringe a defendant's federal constitutional rights." *Id.* at 189-90.

Whiteside did not testify at trial that he had seen a gun. Suppose that he had? If his attorney had then revealed the perjury to the court (consistent with Rule 3.3) and Whiteside was convicted, would Whiteside have a stronger claim that his Sixth Amendment right to counsel was violated? Presumably, if threatening to do something is permissible, actually doing the same thing should also be permissible. But the Supreme Court has never directly confronted and answered that question.

The Model Rule's solution to client perjury in Rule 3.3(a)(3) represented a major policy change from prior attorney discipline standards. By contrast, the 1969 Model Code of Professional Responsibility, DR 7-102(A)(4), provided that an attorney "shall not knowingly *use* perjured testimony or false evidence." Unlike the rules, the Code did not require revelation of attorney-client confidences to remedy client perjury; if a client lied on the witness stand notwithstanding the lawyer's remonstrations to the contrary, the attorney would satisfy his ethical obligations if he refrained from *using* that evidence in closing argument. Would the client feel any less betrayed by this approach? Does it not have the same effect of making clear to the judge (and perhaps the jury) that the client lied?

Nix v. Whiteside: Real Life Applications

1. Your client is accused of rape. The alleged attack was committed in a public park between strangers at night. The defendant tells you that he met the victim while strolling through the park, they struck up a conversation, and it led to hand holding, kissing, and then consensual intercourse in a secluded area. You doubt your client's version of events, and you think that a mistaken identification defense is more likely to succeed. The perpetrator used a condom and no male DNA samples were recovered from the victim. What do you do?

2. Your client is accused of armed robbery while masked. He insists he did not commit the crime and offers an alibi for the date and time of the offense. You interview the two alibi witnesses. In your view, they are not credible. Their

stories are full of holes and they have criminal convictions that could be used to impeach them at trial. May you refuse to put these two witnesses on the stand?

3. You are a public defender who is assigned to represent a defendant charged with assault and battery after a barroom brawl. You interview your client on the morning of his arraignment and he tells you that he was drunk and that he punched the victim in the face after the victim insulted his girlfriend. After you receive in discovery the police report and witness statements, you determine that the case against your client is very strong. Your client will not agree to a plea bargain because a criminal conviction will jeopardize his job. Prior to trial, your client tells you for the first time that the victim pushed him, before he struck back in self-defense. What advice do you give to your client, and how do you proceed if he insists on testifying?

There are two significant differences with regard to the ethical obligation of a criminal defense lawyer faced with **perjury by a client** compared to other lawyers. First, lawyers for any other type of client or witness (including a criminal prosecutor) may refuse to put the witness on the stand if they reasonably believe the witness will lie. Under Rule 3.3(a)(3), however, out of respect for a criminal defendant's constitutional right to testify in his own defense, a criminal defense lawyer may not refuse to put the defendant on the witness stand unless she actually *knows* the client will lie. Actual knowledge may be rare as an epistemological matter. In *Nix* the lawyer had actual knowledge, because Whiteside stated that he did not see a gun or any other object on one occasion, and then modified his story to describe seeing something "metallic" because he insisted that if he did not do so he would be "dead." The circumstances would have been different if Whiteside had simply embellished his version of the events over time with new details that had not been disclosed earlier. Although a criminal defense lawyer has an important counseling role to play as a strategic matter in advising his client when implausible testimony will hurt the case, there is nothing wrong with giving the client the benefit of the doubt with respect to the truth of proposed testimony.[25] For this reason, some criminal defense lawyers avoid asking their clients directly if they committed the crime, because full knowledge of the facts may turn out to hamstring the lawyer's options ethically in deciding how to structure a defense. By contrast, civil lawyers typically like to learn as much about factual circumstances of the client's case as possible in order to enable them to mount a case.

Second, with respect to prospective perjury of a criminal defendant, some states require a different solution to the "trilemma" than Model Rule 3.3(a). Massachusetts, Wisconsin, and the District of Columbia,[26] for example, require the criminal defense lawyer who is unable to dissuade his client from committing perjury

---

25. In United States v. Midgett, the Fourth Circuit ruled that the defendant was denied his constitutional right to testify when his lawyer refused to put him on the stand and threatened to withdraw upon a mere belief, "albeit a strong one," that the testimony would be false. 342 F.3d 321, 327 (4th Cir. 2003).

26. Mass. R. Prof'l Conduct 3.3(e); Wis. Stat. §20:3.3(a); D.C. R. Prof'l Conduct 3.3(d). For a list of jurisdictions that follow the narrative approach, see State v. Chambers, 994 A.2d 1248, 1258 n.12 (Conn. 2010).

and unable to withdraw from representation to follow a "narrative" approach: allow the defendant to take the stand, and then ask the defendant to tell the jury what happened in an open-ended, narrative fashion. The attorney may not assist the perjury by structuring the testimony in the form of "question and answer." Nor may the attorney argue the facts gleaned from the narrative in closing argument (which would amount to lack of candor to the tribunal). Chief Justice Burger seemed to reject the wisdom of the narrative approach in footnote 6 of the *Nix* opinion,[27] but as Justice Blackmun's concurring opinion reminds us, states are free to craft their own rules of professional conduct. Comment [7] to Model Rule 3.3 recognizes that some jurisdictions favor the narrative solution, and concedes that this may be an appropriate "remedial measure" in jurisdictions that do so. The benefits of the narrative approach are that the attorney's role in advancing the perjury are minimized, it avoids the instances where the client is deprived of the right to testify because the attorney mistakenly believed that the client would lie, and the attorney is not directly involved in revealing any client confidences. Advocates of the narrative approach also argue that it avoids kicking the problem of client perjury over to the judge: what is a judge supposed to do in a criminal case when an attorney goes to sidebar or chambers and reveals the falsity of the defendant's testimony? Strike the testimony? Declare a mistrial? Even in the rare situation where withdrawal of counsel would not prejudice the client, what would withdrawal accomplish from a systemic point of view — defendant presumably would get a new lawyer and the process would start all over again, although this time the client would likely be slightly less forthcoming with new counsel. In real life, most judges who are informed of a criminal defendant's perjury in states that follow Model Rule 3.3(a)(3) do *nothing* and leave it to the jury to sort out the truth of the evidence after cross-examination. If that is the most likely factual outcome, what has been accomplished by Rule 3.3(a)'s requirement of revelation, other than insulating the lawyer from any possible suggestion of complicity in the lie?

The attorney may not assist the perjury of a criminal defendant by structuring the testimony in the form of "question and answer."
Shutterstock.com

3. Cross-Examining a Truthful Witness

A lawyer's duty of candor to the tribunal precludes him from offering evidence that he knows to be false. Is a criminal defense attorney "offering" evidence when he attempts to impeach a witness on cross-examination who he knows to be telling

27. 475 U.S. at 170 n.6.

the truth (such as with prior convictions, bias, inconsistent statements, problems in perception, etc.)? **Discrediting truthful testimony** may not be the same thing as offering a false fact, but it certainly has a similar effect.

In 1987, Harry Subin and John Mitchell engaged in a vigorous debate on this very issue in the *Georgetown Journal of Legal Ethics*. Subin criticized the arbitrary lines between "presenting" false evidence through your own witnesses (which violates Rule 3.3) and (1) cross-examining a truthful witness to suggest she is fabricating her testimony, or (2) arguing a false inference to the jury from known truthful testimony.[28] Using the example of a rape victim who the defense attorney learns is telling the truth, Subin argues that there is no socially redeeming value in permitting the attorney to discredit her testimony or arguing in closing that the sex was consensual. According to Subin, the criminal defense attorney's sole legitimate role in defending a case where he knows that the victim is telling the truth is to assert all available procedural defenses on behalf of his client, and thereafter act as "monitor" to ensure that the government has satisfied its burden of proof beyond a reasonable doubt. Mitchell's response follows.

John Mitchell, Reasonable Doubts Are Where You Find Them: A Response to Professor Subin's Position on the Criminal Lawyer's "Different Mission"

1 Geo. J. Legal Ethics 339 (1987)

I. INTRODUCTION

In *A Criminal Lawyer's "Different Mission": Reflections on the "Right" to Present a False Case*, Professor Harry L. Subin attempts to draw what he considers to be the line between attorney as advocate, and attorney as officer of the court. Specifically, he "attempts to define the limits on the methods a lawyer should be willing to use when his client's goals are inconsistent with truth." This is no peripheral theme in professional responsibility. Quite the contrary, Professor Subin has chosen a difficult issue which touches upon the very nature of our criminal justice system, the role of the attorney in that system, the relationship of the individual to the state, and the Constitution. Further, Professor Subin takes a tough and controversial stand on this issue and, although I disagree with him, I respect his position.

. . .

. . . While Professor Subin directs his attack on the notion that a criminal defense attorney has a "different mission" than uncovering truth, in my view it is the criminal justice system itself which has a "different mission."

28. Harry I. Subin, *The Criminal Defense Lawyer's Different Mission: Reflections on a Right to Present a False Case*, 1 Geo. J. Legal Ethics 125 (1987).

II. PROFESSOR SUBIN'S ASSUMPTIONS

Professor Subin rests his entire analysis on two basic premises: (1) the principle goal of the criminal justice system is "truth"; and (2) it is contrary to the goal of "truth" to permit a criminal defense attorney to put on a "false defense." In Subin's terms, a false defense is an attempt to "convince the judge or jury that facts established by the state and known to the attorney to be true are not true, or that facts known to the attorney to be false are true." Such a defense is put on by: " . . . (1) cross-examination of truthful government witnesses to undermine their testimony or their credibility; (2) direct presentation of testimony, not in itself false, but used to discredit the truthful evidence adduced by the government, or to accredit a false theory; and, (3) argument to the jury based on any of these acts." I take exception to both of these premises, as set out below.

The Principal Concern of the Criminal Justice System Is Not "Truth"

The idea that the focus of the criminal justice system is not "truth" may initially sound shocking. I have valued truth throughout my life and do not condone lying in our legal system. But the job of our criminal justice system is simply other than determining "truth." Professor Subin himself recognizes that there are rules within the criminal justice system which are barriers to truth, but which are nevertheless supported by strong policy (e.g., privilege, suppression of illegally obtained evidence). Nevertheless, he states early in his article that he "shall argue" that the criminal justice system has the determination of truth as its principle goal. Apparently he means that he shall adopt this fundamental premise by fiat, for nowhere does he articulate an argument for this proposition. I believe there is a good reason for this omission. It is emotionally easy (and perhaps even rhetorically convincing) to proclaim the virtue of "truth" in the abstract; it is more difficult to extol "truth's" virtues when analyzing the American criminal justice system. An analysis of the American criminal justice system in actual operation is appropriate at this point.

A system focused on truth would first collect all information relevant to the inquiry. In our system, the defendant is generally the best source of information in the dispute, but he is not available unless he so chooses. The police may not question him. He may not be called to the stand with his own lawyer beside him and with a judge controlling questioning under the rules of evidence. The prosecutor may not even comment to the jury about the defendant's failure to testify, even though fair inferences may be drawn from the refusal to respond to serious accusations.

A system focused on truth would have the factfinder look at all the information and then decide what it believed had occurred. In our system, the inquiry is dramatically skewed against finding guilt. "Beyond a reasonable doubt" expresses the deep cultural value that "it is better to let ten guilty men go than convict one innocent man." It is a system where, after rendering a verdict of not guilty, jurors routinely approach defense counsel and say, "I thought your guy was guilty, but that prosecutor did not prove it to me beyond a reasonable doubt." What I have just described is not a "truth system" in any sense in which one could reasonably understand that term. Truth may play a role, but it is not a dominant role; there is something else afoot. The criminal defense attorney does not have a "different mission"; the system itself has a "different mission."

Embodying this "different mission" is the concept of "legal guilt" and its distinction from "factual guilt." The latter refers to "did he do it?"; the former to "did the prosecution prove he did it beyond a reasonable doubt?" The criminal justice system focuses exclusively upon "legal guilt." . . .

[T]he criminal justice system protects the individual from the police power of the executive branch of government. Between the individual citizen and the enormous governmental power residing in the executive stands a panel of that individual's peers — a jury. Through them, the executive must pass. Only if it proves its case "beyond a reasonable doubt," thereby establishing legal guilt, may the executive then legitimately intrude into the individual citizen's life. Thus, "factual" guilt or innocence, or what Professor Subin would call "truth," is not the principle issue in the system. Our concern is with the legitimate use of the prosecutor's power as embodied in the concept of "legal guilt."

. . .

A. *Defense Attorney Acting in a Manner Meeting with Subin's Disapproval Is Not Putting on a "False Defense"*

When placed in the "reasonable doubt" context, Professor Subin's implicit distinction between "true" and "false" defenses misportrays both how a defense attorney may actually function in a case, and the very nature of evidence in that case. His categories are too imprecise to capture the subtle middle ground of a pure reasonable doubt defense, in which counsel presents the jury with alternative possibilities that counsel knows are false, without asserting the truth of those alternatives.

For example, imagine I am defending a young woman accused of shoplifting a star one places on top of Christmas trees. I interview the store manager and find that he stopped my client when he saw her walk straight through the store, star in hand, and out the door. When he stopped her and asked why she had taken the star without paying, she made no reply and burst into tears. He was then about to take her inside to the security office when an employee called out, "There's a fire!" The manager rushed inside and dealt with a small blaze in the camera section. Five minutes later he came out to find my client sitting where he had left her. He then took her back to the security room and asked if she would be willing to empty her pockets so that he could see if she had taken anything else. Without a word, she complied. She had a few items not belonging to the store and a ten-dollar bill. The star was priced at $1.79.

In an interview with my client, she admitted trying to steal the star: "It was so pretty, and would have looked so nice on the tree. I would have bought it, but I also wanted to make a special Christmas dinner for Mama and didn't have enough money to do both. I've been saving for that dinner and I know it will make her so happy. But that star . . . . I could just see the look in Mama's eyes if she saw that lovely thing on our tree."

At trial, the manager tells the same story he told me, except he leaves out the part about her waiting during the fire and having a ten-dollar bill. If I bring out these two facts on cross-examination and argue for an acquittal based upon my client "accidentally" walking out of the store with the star, surely Professor Subin will accuse me of raising a "false defense." I have brought out testimony, not itself false, to accredit a false theory and have argued to the jury based on this act. But I am not really arguing a false theory in Professor Subin's sense.

My defense is not that the defendant accidentally walked out, but rather that the prosecution cannot prove the element of intent to permanently deprive beyond a reasonable doubt. Through this theory, I am raising "doubt" in the prosecution's case, and therefore questioning the legitimacy of the government's lawsuit for control over the defendant. In my effort to carry out this legal theory, I will *not assert* that facts known by me to be true are false or those known to be false are true. As a defense attorney, I do not have to prove what *in fact* happened. That is an advantage in the process I would not willingly give up. Under our constitutional system, I do not need to try to convince the factfinder about the truth of any factual propositions. I need only try to convince the factfinder that the prosecution has not met its burden. . . .

. . .

In our shoplifting example, the prosecution will elicit that the defendant burst into tears when stopped by the manager. From this information will run a chain of inferences: defendant burst into tears; people without a guilty conscience would explain their innocence, not cry; defendant has a guilty conscience; her guilty conscience is likely motivated by having committed a theft. Conversely, if the defense brings out that the manager was shaking a lead pipe in his hand when he stopped the defendant, defense counsel is *not asserting* that defendant did not have a guilty conscience when stopped. Counsel is merely *weakening* the persuasiveness of the prosecution's inference by raising the "possibility" that she was crying not from guilt, but from fear. By raising such "possibilities," the defense is making arguments against the ability of the prosecution's inferences to meet their burden of "beyond a reasonable doubt." The defense is not arguing what are true or false facts (i.e., that the tears were from fear as opposed to guilt). Whatever Professor Subin cares to call it, this commentary on the prosecution's case, complete with raising possibilities which weaken the persuasiveness of central inferences in that case, is in no ethical sense a "false case." "False case" is plainly a misnomer. In a system where factual guilt is not at issue, Professor Subin's "falsehoods" are, in fact, "reasonable doubts."

. . .

To illustrate, imagine I am representing a defendant accused of robbery. I have seen the victim at a preliminary hearing, and based upon the circumstances of the identification and my overall impression of the witness, I am certain that he is truthful and accurate. My client has confessed his factual guilt. And therefore I "know" (in Professor Subin's sense) beyond a reasonable doubt that my client has been accurately identified.

In his direct examination, the victim states, "The defendant had this big, silvery automatic pistol right up near my face the whole time he was asking for money." In accordance with Professor Subin's view that defense counsel can "persuade the jury that there are legitimate reasons to doubt the state's evidence," may I raise the general vagarities of eyewitness identification? . . . Perhaps Subin would say I cannot make the misidentification argument. He might argue that the "legitimacy" of reasons to doubt the state's evidence is not to be judged from the perspective of a reasonable juror hearing the prosecution's evidence but from my subjective knowledge. Since I "know" that there was no difficulty with the identification, I cannot put forward a "legitimate" reason to doubt. If this is Professor Subin's meaning, I, as monitor, am left with the following closing argument: "Ladies and gentlemen, thank you for your attention to this case. Remember, the prosecution must prove each element beyond a reasonable doubt. Thank you." . . .

"Legitimate reason" to doubt must refer to a reasonable juror's perception of the state's evidence, not to the defense attorney's private knowledge. Bringing out reasonable doubts in the state's evidence concerning the identification therefore must be legitimate, and yet this would seem to raise a "false defense" (i.e., mistaken identification). Presumably, Subin would permit this defense because of a greater policy than "truth," i.e., the right to have the state prove guilt beyond a reasonable doubt. If this is permissible in Subin's view, it is difficult to understand why it would not be permissible to call an expert on eyewitness identification to testify.

. . .

Another indication that Subin would not adhere to the "stark" definition of lawyer as monitor is that he would allow the defense to demonstrate the inaccuracy of information that may be harmful to its case. Imagine that the robbery victim in my hypothetical testifies that Bloogan's Department Store, directly across the street from where the nighttime robbery occurred, had all of its lights on at the time of the robbery. In fact, I find out in investigation that Bloogan's was closed for remodeling that evening. Subin would undoubtedly allow me to bring this out. What, after all, would a "truth" theory be if I were not permitted to confront "lies" and "misperceptions." If Professor Subin permits me to bring out this "inaccuracy" on cross-examination and/or through other witnesses, he must also allow me to use it in closing or my initial access to this information would be meaningless. In closing, my only real use for this information would be in support of my "false defense" of mistaken identification. The line between advocate and monitor is again blurred.

. . .

B. Bigger Problems: Constitutional Concerns and Jeopardizing an Independent Defense Bar

If Professor Subin's approach is more than a statement of his own private ethics, the vagueness and uncertainty of the line which divides the advocate from the monitor presents a serious problem. First, constitutional concerns additional to those already expressed may arise. Criminal defense representation touches significant interests: 1) protection of the individual from the state; 2) the freedom of the defendant in a nation which values liberty; and 3) significant constitutional rights (fourth, fifth, sixth, eighth, and fourteenth amendments). It is within these areas that the impreciseness in Professor Subin's categories comes to the fore. To the extent defense attorneys are guided by ethical rules which are vague about what conduct is proper, the representation of clients is hampered. Counsel, uncertain as to appropriate behavior, may fall into a "conflict" between pushing the client's interests as far as is legitimate and protecting himself against charges of unethical conduct. Attorneys'

decisions may then tend to fall on the self-protective side, raising constitutional concerns regarding zealous representation.

Second, if Subin's approach were enforced as a rule of professional conduct, the independent defense bar would be seriously jeopardized. Professor Subin may or may not be correct that the public and the bar have a low view of the criminal defense bar. Nonetheless, the independence of that bar has provided all citizens with significant protection against governmental oppression. With Professor Subin's approach, however, if an acquittal were gained by a defense attorney who was a thorn in the government's side, the prosecutor's office might be tempted to file an ethical complaint stating that defense counsel should have known he put on a "false defense." Subin's position now becomes a weapon of repression in the hands of the government. Even if vindication follows upon a disciplinary hearing, time, expense, and public humiliation might ensue. This will deliver a powerful message to defense attorneys. Don't risk fighting, plead your clients guilty.

Mitchell seems to have won this debate with Subin among most practitioners, scholars, and judges. Commentators now agree that it is ethically appropriate — if not required — for a criminal defense attorney to impeach a witness who he knows to be testifying truthfully. Some rest their arguments on the presumption of innocence and the advocate's obligation to hold the government to its extraordinarily high burden of proof in criminal cases.[29] Monroe Freedman has argued that this license stems from the defense lawyer's access to confidential information from the client — which often is the source of the attorney's knowledge of the witness's truthfulness; if a defense lawyer declines to cross-examine a witness based upon what his client has told him, it will dissuade clients in the future from being forthcoming with information.[30] Still others have argued that zealous advocacy on behalf of a client needs to be at its apex in the criminal defense context because we want to curtail the power of the state to punish its citizens.[31] Is Mitchell's position an amalgamation of these arguments, or something distinct? Does it resonate with you?

Clearly siding with Mitchell, Section 4-7.7(b) of the aspirational and non-binding ABA Standards for the Administration of Criminal Justice: Defense Function states that "[d]efense counsel's belief or knowledge that a witness is telling the truth does not preclude vigorous cross-examination, even though defense counsel's cross-examination may cast doubt on the testimony." As ministers of justice, should prosecutors be given the same or less leeway in cross-examining defense witnesses who they believe to be telling the truth?[32]

---

29. David G. Bress, *Professional Ethics in Criminal Trials: A View of Defense Counsel's Responsibility*, 64 MICH. L. REV. 1493, 1494 (1966); Warren E. Burger, *Standards of Conduct for Prosecution and Defense Personnel: A Judge's Viewpoint*, 5 AM. CRIM. L.Q. 11, 14-15 (1966). This position has come to be known as the "Burger-Bress" argument in support of a criminal defense attorney's right to impeach a truthful witness.

30. Monroe H. Freedman, *Professional Responsibility of the Criminal Defense Lawyer: The Three Hardest Questions*, 64 MICH. L. REV. 1469, 1474-75 (1966).

31. *See* David Luban, *The Adversary System Excuse*, *in* THE GOOD LAWYER 83, 92 (David Luban ed., 1984).

32. For a discussion of that question, see R. Michael Cassidy, *Character and Context: What Virtue Theory Can Teach Us About a Prosecutor's Ethical Duty to "Seek Justice,"* 82 NOTRE DAME L. REV. 635, 667 (2006).

Chapter Summary

- The prosecutor has a responsibility as "minister of justice" to make sure that criminal charges are supported by probable cause, that they fairly reflect the gravity of the offense, and that adversarial proceedings are conducted fairly.
- The "no-contact" rule prohibits prosecutors from contacting represented defendants without their lawyer's permission, and thus imposes obligations that exceed Fifth and Sixth Amendment guarantees.
- A prosecutor must disclose to defense counsel all exculpatory evidence in possession of the government, unless relieved of this obligation by an order of the tribunal.
- The prosecutor must avoid media comments about pending cases that heighten public condemnation of the accused and that serve no legitimate law enforcement purpose.
- A criminal defense attorney, unlike a prosecutor, acts properly when she cross-examines a witness who she knows to be telling the truth in order to undermine that witness's credibility.
- A criminal defense attorney who knows that his client intends to commit perjury may not counsel or assist that perjury, and may withdraw from representation if allowed by the court.

Applying the Rules

1. Suppose that you serve as a prosecutor in a local district court, and you are preparing for trial in a domestic assault and battery case. The defendant was arrested after police were called to his marital home to break up a fight. The police took a statement from the victim and took photographs of her injuries. In preparing the case for trial, you call the victim in to your office for an interview. The victim says she does not want to go forward with the case. She says that she lied to the police officers because she was mad at her husband and wanted to get back at him. She denies that the defendant hit her, and instead insists that she received her injuries by falling down the stairs. What do you do with this information? How do you decide whether to proceed with the case?

2. Imagine that you represent the state in a rape prosecution. The defendant is a star professional athlete accused of sexual assaulting a female after escorting her home from a nightclub. The victim has hired a lawyer to commence a civil tort suit against the athlete. May you speak with the alleged rape victim in order to prepare her for the criminal trial without obtaining permission from her counsel in the civil case?

3. Imagine that you are a criminal defense attorney for the same athlete charged with rape in hypothetical #2 above. In interviewing the defendant after his

arraignment, the defendant claims that he was "set up" and that the sex was purely consensual. The athlete tells you that he has security cameras throughout his home and that the video will corroborate his account of the consensual encounter. Should you take any steps to obtain and watch this video?

4. Suppose that you are a public defender assigned to represent a defendant accused of robbing an elderly victim of her purse at knifepoint. When you meet with your client, he confesses to the crime and tells you that he committed the robbery in order to support a drug habit. If you are unsuccessful in obtaining a plea bargain and the case proceeds to trial, should you call your client as a witness? If you decide not to put your client on the witness stand and instead assert a reasonable doubt defense, may you cross-examine the victim to call into question her ability to perceive the perpetrator due to the poor lighting conditions and her fright upon feeling a knife against her back?

Professional Responsibility in Practice

1. Research the law in the jurisdiction in which you intend to practice and determine whether any appellate courts or the state bar have recognized an undercover investigatory exception to Rule 4.2.

2. Imagine that you represent a defendant accused of forcible rape. The government's allegations are that your client forced himself on the victim in his bedroom during a fraternity party. Both the defendant and the victim agree to having consumed large quantities of alcohol during the party. But defendant insists that the sex was consensual. Right before the case is scheduled to go to trial, the defendant tells you for the first time that the victim insisted he use a condom and that she actually unwrapped the condom and put it on the defendant. This is the first time the defendant has revealed this "fact" to you. He did not discuss it with police officers when he was interviewed during the investigation, nor did he reveal it to you during any prior interviews. Play the role of the defense counsel and have a conversation with your client about whether he will testify about the condom.

PART

IV

Delivery of Legal Services and Access to Justice

9

Practicing Law: Issues in Group Lawyering and the Unauthorized Practice of Law

This chapter addresses several issues related to the business and organization of law practice. It begins by examining the ethical responsibilities of lawyers who work in group settings. What are the responsibilities of lawyers with managerial and supervisory authority with respect to those lawyers that they oversee? What are the responsibilities of junior lawyers who are ordered to do something that they believe might violate the rules of professional conduct?

The remainder of the chapter covers several other regulations on law practice including the traditional prohibition on lawyers going into business with non-lawyers and non-lawyers engaging in the practice of law. These rules reflect longstanding concerns about lawyer independence and protecting the public from incompetent services, but they have come under increasing scrutiny as the nature of law practice has changed due to technology and globalization, and countries around the world have liberalized their rules on these issues.

Key Concepts

- The responsibility of lawyers with managerial authority to ensure compliance with ethical obligations
- The independent responsibility of subordinate lawyers to act in compliance with their ethical obligations
- Professional independence of lawyers
- Prohibitions on practicing with non-lawyers
- Agreements restricting lawyer practice
- Prohibitions on practicing law without a license

A. LAW FIRMS AND ASSOCIATIONS

Most lawyers work in a group setting, such as law firms (large and small), non-profit organizations, the corporate counsel division of for-profit businesses, or government law offices. The hierarchical structure of these practices complicates ethical decision making, because lawyers may face institutional pressures or incentives that conflict with their own personal values and professional responsibilities. In the next sections of this chapter, we explore two questions: when supervisory lawyers are responsible for the conduct of junior lawyers within a law practice, and when subordinate lawyers may reasonably rely on ethical judgments made by their superiors.

1. Responsibility of Supervisors

Partners in law firms and other senior lawyers with comparable managerial authority in non–law firm settings are required to make "reasonable efforts" to create procedures and structures to ensure compliance with the applicable disciplinary rules by all lawyers working within that organization. *See* Model Rule 5.1(a). This rule recognizes that the environment in which one practices can have a huge impact on ethical decision making, and it calls upon lawyers with managerial responsibility to take adequate steps to foster a workplace where attention is paid to professionalism. According to comment 2, such steps will include establishing a firm procedure for detecting and resolving conflicts of interest, accounting for client funds and trust property, creating reasonable filing and case tracking systems, and ensuring that inexperienced lawyers are adequately trained and supervised.

Supervisory lawyers may be found to have vicarious responsibility for the actual professional misconduct of junior lawyers in the organization in two instances: when they order or ratify the junior lawyer's conduct, or when they have either general managerial authority over the lawyer or "direct supervisory authority" over the specific legal matter and they learn of the junior lawyer's conduct at a time when its consequences can be avoided and they fail to take reasonable remedial measures. *See* Model Rule 5.1(c). The power to impose vicarious responsibility on senior lawyers under the rules is thus fairly broad — it can sweep in lawyers who have no formal supervisory role or title if they order or ratify the conduct (such as a more senior associate working on the case — *see* Model Rule 5.1(c)(1)), and it can sweep in partners or department heads who are not actively working on the matter in question, but who come to know about the professional misconduct of a junior lawyer in time to prevent or remedy it and fail to do so.

Partners in law firms and managing attorneys in non-partnership settings (government, legal aid, in-house counsel) also have a responsibility to create an environment of professionalism for non-legal staff. Rule 5.3 recognizes that lawyers often rely on non-lawyers to complete their work — such as accountants, investigators, paralegals, and messengers. Rule 5.3 parallels Rule 5.2 in that it requires lawyers with supervisory authority to take efforts to ensure the conduct of non-lawyer assistants is compatible with the professional obligations of the lawyer. A messenger who is sent to deliver privileged and confidential material to a client must have some training on the requirements of confidentiality so he does not leave the file open in a coffee shop. A bookkeeper must be properly trained not to commingle client assets with assets of the firm.[1] Just like with Rule 5.2, a lawyer can have vicarious responsibility for the actual actions of a non-lawyer assistant if she either directs or ratifies the conduct, or is a supervisory lawyer and comes to learn of the conduct in time to avoid or mitigate the consequences but fails to do so. *See* Model Rule 5.3(c). For example, where a lawyer is prohibited from talking to an opposing party without her counsel's permission under the "no contact" rule, *see* Model Rule 4.2, the lawyer violates the rule when he directs an investigator or paralegal to make that very same contact.

2. Responsibility of Junior Lawyers

There is no "Nuremberg" or "following orders" defense to charges of professional misconduct. Model Rule 5.2(a) quite clearly states that "[a] lawyer is bound by the Rules of Professional Conduct notwithstanding that the lawyer acted at the direction of another person." That is, an associate or junior lawyer cannot escape responsibility for violation of the disciplinary rules by arguing that a senior lawyer "made me do it." All lawyers take an oath to uphold the canons of the legal profession, and a junior lawyer cannot escape liability for her own personal actions by relying on a chain of hierarchy within an organization. If a junior lawyer is asked to do something that she knows clearly violates the disciplinary rules, the only acceptable answer is "no."

Rule 5.2(a) creates a limited safe harbor for subordinate lawyers who act "in accordance with a supervisory lawyer's reasonable resolution of an arguable question of professional duty." The comment to the rule recognizes that where a question of professional ethics is a close one, someone has to decide on a course of action, and placing the responsibility on the senior lawyer is consistent with the typical disparity in experience and judgment between the relevant players. But note the limitations of this limited safe harbor — in order for a subordinate lawyer to avoid professional discipline for conduct he is instructed to take by a supervisor, the subordinate lawyer must do *at least enough* factual and legal research to ascertain whether the supervisor's direction is a "reasonable resolution" of an "arguable question." If the ethical question is clear cut, or if it is a gray area and the supervisor's resolution is not "reasonable," the subordinate lawyer cannot rely on the safe harbor of Rule 5.2(a).

Usually, we think of vicarious responsibility as flowing upward: that is, bosses can have responsibility for acts of their subordinates, but usually subordinates do not have responsibility for actions of their bosses (unless they are complicit in those actions). We just saw how this doctrine works with respect to Rule 5.1. Thus, a junior

1. *See* In re Bailey, 821 A.2d 851 (Del. 2003) (managing partner of law firm disciplined under Rule 5.3 for failing to exercise "even a modicum of diligence" to make sure that the firm's bookkeeper paid relevant taxes and did not invade client trust accounts to pay debts of the firm).

lawyer will not normally have responsibility for professional misconduct committed by a partner or senior lawyer in the organization, unless he *participated* in the misconduct. This comports with our sense of moral as well as ethical responsibility—someone who is a position to alleviate or prevent the misconduct has broader responsibilities than a subordinate who does not have the power to control the conduct of others. However, the Model Rules recognize one important exception to this traditional construction of principal/agency relationships. Model Rule 3.3(b) governs a lawyer's obligations of candor to the tribunal, and provides that "[a] lawyer who represents a client in an adjudicative proceeding and who knows that *a person* intends to engage, is engaging, or has engaged in criminal or fraudulent conduct related to the proceeding shall take reasonable remedial measures . . . ." (Emphasis supplied.) The use of the generic term "person" applies to both witnesses, clients, and *lawyers* involved in the case. In the context of litigation, therefore, there may be instances where a junior lawyer needs to speak up or risk being punished for the conduct of a senior lawyer with whom he is litigating the case. For example, if the senior lawyer makes a false statement of material fact to the court and the junior associate knows of its falsity, the associate has violated Rule 3.3(b) by remaining silent.[2]

Case Preview

Davis v. Alabama State Bar

Attorneys Davis and Goldberg were suspended from the practice of law for 60 days for, among other infractions, failing to ensure that lawyers in their firm complied with the Rules of Professional Conduct (Rule 5.1) and failing to ensure that activities of non-lawyer assistants were compatible with professional standards (Rule 5.3). The partners in the firm essentially "churned" civil complaints by taking on an extremely large volume of cases (particularly bankruptcy and social security disability claims) and thereafter neglecting client files. Several of the witnesses against Davis and Goldberg were former associates or secretarial assistants of the firm.

As you read the *Davis* decision, ask yourself:

1. What economic incentives might have led these two small-firm lawyers to establish the following practices at their firm?
   a. Having non-lawyer assistants complete and serve bankruptcy filings;
   b. Requiring associates to open a certain quota of cases per month;
   c. Forbidding associates from returning client phone calls; and
   d. Forbidding associates from interviewing clients before the first scheduled court appearance.

2. For a powerful discussion of the responsibilities of principal and subordinate lawyers in the context of the Berkey-Kodak antitrust litigation, see David Luban, *The Ethics of Wrongful Obedience*, *in* Ethics in Practice: Lawyers' Roles, Responsibilities and Regulation (Deborah L. Rhode ed., 2003).

Davis v. Alabama State Bar

676 So. 2d 306 (Ala. 1996)

. . .

Two attorneys appeal from Alabama State Bar disciplinary proceedings. They challenge the sufficiency of the evidence presented at their disciplinary hearing, claiming that the disciplinary proceeding was nothing more than a "witch-hunt" that they say the Bar conducted because it did not approve of the attorneys' advertising practices. They further challenge the penalties imposed as being too severe.

The Alabama State Bar Disciplinary Board found William Dowsing Davis III and Dan Arthur Goldberg to be violating Rule 1.1, Alabama Rules of Professional Conduct (failure to provide competent representation); Rule 1.4(a) and (b) (failure to keep clients reasonably informed and failure to reasonably explain a matter so as to permit a client to make an informed decision); Rule 5.1 (failure to make reasonable efforts to ensure that the lawyers in their firm conformed to the Rules of Professional Conduct); Rule 5.3(b) (failure to ensure that the activities of a nonlawyer under an attorney's supervision are compatible with professional standards); Rule 5.5(b) (providing assistance to a person engaging in the unauthorized practice of law); Rule 8.4(a) (violation of the Rules of Professional Conduct through the acts of another); Rule 8.4(d) (engaging in conduct prejudicial to the administration of justice); and Rule 8.4(g) (engaging in conduct that adversely reflects on a lawyer's fitness to practice law). Both of the attorneys were suspended from the practice of law for 60 days.

The record before this Court is voluminous. Several former and present attorneys and secretaries of these attorneys' firm testified at the disciplinary hearing. Several clients of the firm also testified.

These two attorneys were the sole partners in the law firm of Davis & Goldberg. The firm spent approximately $500,000 annually on advertising, primarily television advertising, and the advertising attracted a large number of clients. As a result of this large expenditure and the volume of clients produced by the advertising, the attorneys implemented several policies, described below, designed to minimize expenses and maximize profits.

The Bar presented evidence, for example, that Davis and Goldberg allowed nonlawyer secretaries to provide legal services. It was also shown to be common practice at the firm for secretaries to interview clients and prepare legal filings, especially bankruptcy petitions. Evidence also indicated that nonlawyer staff members gave clients legal advice, such as "informing" clients of the differences between Chapter 7 and Chapter 13 bankruptcy. One former associate attorney testified that it was the firm's practice that attorneys would not interview or have any contact with the client before the first scheduled court appearance.

There was further testimony that these two attorneys imposed unmanageable caseloads on associate attorneys, many of whom were inexperienced. Some associate attorneys, for example, maintained caseloads of nearly 600 active cases. Former associates testified that because of the sheer volume of cases, the amount of time that could be spent on each case was so limited as to make it impossible for them to adequately represent their clients. At the hearing before the Disciplinary Board, the attorneys' own expert witness on Social Security law, Charles Tyler Clark, testified that the Social Security caseload, as described by a former associate of the firm, could not have been adequately handled by the one attorney assigned to it.

There was testimony that the firm had an inadequate supply of filing cabinets for case files and that files were simply stacked in various parts of the office, including the employees' break room and the hallway near the bathrooms. The evidence further tended to show that associate attorneys were given the barest of support staffs and that this fact, coupled with the huge volume of cases imposed upon the associates, created a situation in which files were mishandled, resulting in harm to the interests of clients.

The harm resulting from what could be described as a practice of the firm is best illustrated in the testimony of a former client, Brenda Marie Wood. Her husband, Douglas Wayne Wood, suffers from acute peripheral neuropathy and is dying. He was awarded Social Security disability benefits, but did not begin receiving his payments until eight months after he was supposed to. Mr. and Mrs. Wood saw a Davis & Goldberg television commercial that promised that the firm would "cut through the Social Security red tape" and get its clients' Social Security benefits fast. Because of the statement made in the advertisement, Mr. Wood hired the firm of Davis & Goldberg in October 1991 to represent him in his claim for past-due benefits. The firm lost Wood's file three times, and each time Wood was required to fill out a new set of forms. Wood was continuously assured by the firm's staff that his claim had been filed, when in fact it had not been. In February 1992, Wood received a letter from the firm informing him that the deadline for filing the claim had passed, and that it was too late to file his appeal.

The associates employed by Davis & Goldberg were also subjected to policies that interfered with their adequate and professional representation of their clients. These policies included the imposition of time limits or restrictions on the amount of time that they could spend with clients and on cases; the imposition of a quota system that required associates to open a specified number of files in a certain time period; and the imposition of a policy requiring associates not to return the phone calls of existing clients, so that the attorneys could free more time to sign new clients.

The appellants contend that the Bar did not meet its burden of proof as to the allegations against them. The standard of review applicable to an appeal from an order of the Disciplinary Board is "that the order will be affirmed unless it is not supported by clear and convincing evidence or misapplies the law to the facts." . . . We disagree with the attorneys' claims that the evidence was insufficient. In fact, the evidence presented amply showed that the two attorneys, in an effort to turn over a huge volume of cases, neglected their clients and imposed policies on associate attorneys that prevented the attorneys from providing quality and competent legal services. The evidence more than met the clear and convincing standard, and the Board's findings that these lawyers had violated the Rules of Professional Conduct are due to be affirmed.

Even though we affirm the findings that these lawyers had violated the Rules of Professional Conduct, we elect to address their argument that the disciplinary proceeding amounted to a "witch-hunt" conducted because the Bar does not approve of the firm's advertising practices. We reject this contention. Instead, we find that the Disciplinary Board properly fulfilled its role of being a guardian of the image of the legal profession, and, thus, acted as a guardian of the profession itself. We cannot find, as the attorneys ask us to find, that the Bar was conducting a "witch-hunt." In fact, there was evidence that the Bar examined the attorneys' advertising practices; it could have found that their advertisements were misleading, specifically in that the attorneys did not provide the quality legal service advertised. The Disciplinary Board heard evidence that one specific advertisement was misleading as it related to a United States Supreme Court ruling on the availability of Social Security benefits. Even the appellants' expert witness testified that the advertisement could have been misleading under certain circumstances.

This Court recognizes that attorneys have a First Amendment right to engage in various forms of commercial speech. We uphold the discipline imposed upon these attorneys, but we are not upholding it because they advertised; rather, we uphold it because the advertising was misleading in that the attorneys did not provide what they said they would provide. False and misleading advertising by attorneys can, and probably has, greatly harmed the public's perception of the legal profession, at a time when the public's confidence in attorneys has diminished. Indeed, the vast majority of those in the legal profession think advertising is harmful to the image of attorneys.

Justice O'Connor warned in her dissent in *Shapero v. Kentucky Bar Ass'n*, that the advertising practices of some attorneys, similar to those practices followed by these two attorneys, will "undermine professional standards" by giving an attorney "incentives to ignore (or avoid discovering) the complexities that would lead a conscientious attorney to treat some clients' cases as anything but routine." 486 U.S. at 486. . . .

Evidence was presented that these two attorneys placed advertisements that were false and misleading. There can be no constitutional right to advertise in a false and misleading way. The evidence tends to show that these two attorneys' ethical violations were caused by their advertising practices and desire to turn over a huge volume of cases. The harm caused by this practice seems apparent.

Additionally, this Court finds no error or abuse in regard to the sanction the Board imposed, a 60-day suspension of the licenses of Davis and Goldberg. The violations were serious, and we cannot hold that the Board acted improperly in imposing the punishment. Consequently, the orders of the Disciplinary Board are affirmed.

In their application for rehearing, the attorneys argue that in its opinion of December 15, 1995, the Court erred in upholding the disciplinary sanctions based solely on allegations of misleading or false advertising. They are apparently referring to the Board's acquittal as to the charge of violating Rule 7.1, Alabama Rules of Professional Conduct. The Court affirmed the Disciplinary Board's numerous findings of violations of ethical rules, but did not address the Board's acquittal of the alleged violation of Rule 7.1. Instead, the Court addressed the attorneys' contention that the Disciplinary Board had conducted a "witch-hunt" against them because the Board did not approve of their advertising policies.

However, the Disciplinary Board found the attorneys in violation of Rule 8.4(g), which states:

> "It is professional misconduct for a lawyer to:
>
> ". . .
>
> "(g) Engage in any other conduct that adversely reflects on his fitness to practice law."

As we have stated earlier, much evidence was presented at the disciplinary hearing that proved that the attorneys' advertising practices and the procedures and policies adopted by Davis & Goldberg adversely affected the attorneys' ability to practice law in the manner required by the Rules of Professional Conduct. Further, Rule 8.4(g) is broad enough to require that attorney advertisements be honest and accurate and that an attorney's practice of law centered around such heavy advertisement be professional and competent as generally required by the Rules of Profession Conduct.

The evidence presented to the Disciplinary Board showed that Davis & Goldberg advertised that the firm provided legal services of a very high standard, but that the firm's representation of its clients failed to meet the high standard presented in its advertising. This evidence of a failure on the part of Davis & Goldberg to do what was promised in its advertisements, taken with the evidence regarding harmful policies and practices adopted by the firm in response to the fact that a large number of clients were attracted to the firm by its advertising practices, is more than sufficient to support the Board's finding that the attorneys violated Rule 8.4(g).

Post-Case Follow-Up

Many associates of the Davis & Goldberg firm became so dissatisfied with the working conditions that they quit. Thus, the firm was not only churning cases, it was also churning associates.

1. Before they quit, could the associates have insulated themselves from ethical responsibility by following office policies and the demands of the partners? That is, Davis and Goldberg were disciplined for failing adequately to supervise associates in the office. Couldn't the associates also have been disciplined for failure to provide competent representation under Rule 1.1? *See* Model Rule 5.2(a). Why weren't they? Is this a reasonable exercise of the bar disciplinary committee's discretion? Didn't the associates *know* that failure to return client phone calls and failure to interview clients impeded their ability to provide competent representation in individual cases? This wasn't an "arguable question of professional duty," was it? *See* Model Rule 5.2(b).

2. One of the reasons that Davis & Goldberg needed to churn cases was that it spent $500,000 per year on advertising. Keeping labor costs low and minimizing non-advertising expenses was important to maximize the firm's profits. Bar counsel originally charged Davis and Goldberg with false or misleading advertising in violation of Rule 7.1. Does a lawyer who advertises that he will get clients "social security benefits *fast*" engage in false or misleading conduct by his *subsequent* failure to do so? As you see from the opinion above, the hearing officer found that the state had not met its burden of proof on the misleading advertising charge by clear and convincing evidence. We discuss the constitutional limits on regulating lawyer advertising in Chapter 10. The court in *Davis* ruled that the close connection between mass advertising and an unsustainable volume of cases constituted "conduct prejudicial to the administration of justice." Did the Alabama Supreme Court essentially find a Rule 7.1 violation through the back door of Rule 8.4(c)?

3. Is resignation the appropriate step for a lawyer to take when confronted with unprofessional office policies and working conditions? If so, had the associates at Davis & Goldberg been working in a state that recognized the so-called snitch rule,

Model Rule 8.3(a), would they also have had to inform the state bar on their way out the door? Is that a realistic expectation?

Davis v. Alabama State Bar: Real Life Applications

1. You serve as an associate at a large law firm. You are coordinating discovery in a complex commercial antitrust dispute. You uncover a letter in your client's files that is arguably responsive to the request for production of documents, but it is also highly damaging. The letter is from an expert retained by the company to analyze the potential market for one of its new products. The partner who is supervising you on the case brusquely asks you to "withhold it" because the document is a "letter" and not a memorandum or report. How do you engage the partner in a discussion of this discovery issue to assure yourself that you are complying with your professional obligations?
2. You are an associate specializing in patent litigation at a large law firm. The partner for whom you do most of your work calls you late one night to tell you that the son of an important client was arrested for disorderly conduct, being a minor in possession of alcohol, and assault and battery on a police officer. The partner asks you to go to court the following morning and represent the 20-year-old young man at his arraignment — even though you do not have one iota of criminal experience. The partner assures you that "the arraignment will be short and sweet — it's just a formality. Tell the client to plead not guilty and get a new date. We will refer the matter out to a criminal lawyer by the time of the pretrial conference." Can you cover the arraignment without violating Rule 1.1? If so, how do you prepare yourself?
3. You are a partner in a mid-size law firm specializing in commercial real estate matters. Your firm has not historically conducted a formal training program for new associates — relying instead on a "train as you go" model. In working closely with one particular new associate, you notice that the young lawyer does not maintain orderly files, and does not regularly document his communications with clients. None of the clients have yet complained, but you know that the associate's sloppy procedures will eventually reflect poorly on the firm. How do you address these deficiencies in a way that satisfies your obligations under Rule 5.1? Can you wait until the associate's annual performance review?

B. THE LAWYER'S INDEPENDENCE

Since the founding of the United States, an important ideal of lawyer professionalism has been a lawyer's independence.[3] Model Rule 2.1 requires lawyers to "exercise independent professional judgment and render candid advice."

---

3. Rebecca Roiphe traces this ideal of independence to Alexander Hamilton's statements in the Federalist Papers. *See* Rebecca Roiphe, *Redefining Professionalism*, 26 U. Fla. J.L. & Pub. Pol'y 193, 203 (2015).

What does **lawyer independence** mean? There are multiple potential facets to lawyer independence. As Bruce Green states, "[t]he term turns out to be elusive, in part because the various meanings seem to be inconsistent with each other or internally contradictory."[4] Nevertheless, certain meanings of lawyer independence are significant, and as Rebecca Roiphe contends, have "played an important role in American democracy."[5]

First, as noted in Chapters 1 and 2, United States lawyers have largely engaged in "self-regulation," which, as the Preamble to the Model Rules notes, "helps maintain the legal profession's independence from government domination." Indeed, a primary meaning of lawyer independence is independence from government control. This aspect of independence is essential to the lawyer's role in the United States justice system. Lawyers help ensure that government does not overstep its bounds or trample on clients' constitutional and other legal rights. By bringing suits on behalf of aggrieved individuals, lawyers are constantly challenging the legitimacy of government actions—from local and state government action (ranging from the police to governor), to Congress, to federal agencies and officials, including the President. Moreover, every appeal filed by an attorney is also a check on judicial power. Lawyer independence from and probing of government power has been an essential part of the success of our democratic experiment.

Even when government pays for lawyers, the lawyers must retain their independent professional judgment. For example, when Congress created the Legal Services Corporation, there was deep concern that lawyers hired by or accepting LSC funds would not be independent from their government employer in taking on cases for low-income clients. But such fears were unfounded. Lawyers hired by the LSC and accepting LSC funding understood their independence from the government and their loyalty to their clients.[6] In fact, Congress attempted to restrict the ability of LSC lawyers representing welfare recipients from making any arguments challenging the validity of existing welfare law. In Legal Services Corporation v. Velazquez, 531 U.S. 533 (2001), the Supreme Court struck down such restrictions, explaining that the lawyer, even though funded by the government, "is not the government's speaker" but "speaks on behalf of the client in a claim against the government." Further, the Court indicated that a congressional restriction that forbade lawyers from challenging the validity of congressional laws also threatened the judiciary—the "primary mission" of which is to interpret the law and Constitution, "to say what the law is"—but which can only perform that mission when lawyers bring clients' claims or controversies to court. Congress could not "insulate" its laws from judicial review by restricting lawyer advocacy—even when Congress paid for those lawyers.[7] The Court touted the importance of lawyer independence: "An informed, independent judiciary presumes an informed, independent bar." *See id.* at 542-46.

---

4. Bruce Green, *Lawyers' Professional Independence: Overrated or Undervalued*, 46 Akron L. Rev. 599, 601 (2013).
5. *See* Roiphe, *supra* note 3, at 230.
6. *See id.* at 216-21 (describing the history of the LSC, the concerns about its independence, and that ultimately the LSC lawyers showed "fierce and combative independence" from the government).
7. *Velazquez*, 531 U.S. at 546 ("The restriction imposed by the statute here threatens severe impairment of the judicial function . . . [by] sift[ing] out cases presenting constitutional challenges in order to insulate the Government's laws from judicial inquiry.").

John Adams represented British soldiers involved in the Boston Massacre, ensuring a fair process despite his personal alignment with the revolutionary cause.
Library of Congress Prints and Photographs Division, [reproduction number LC-DIG-ppmsca-15705]; LOC.gov.

Going hand in hand with independence from government control is the idea of independence from popular opinion or prejudice. Lawyers recognize an obligation to undertake the representation of unpopular clients and causes[8] — to help in the protection of minority interests from majoritarian tyranny inherent in democracy[9] and to assist in the struggles of the poor and underserved against the wealthy and well-represented. Part of lawyer independence is a recognition that representing a client does not constitute an endorsement of the client's views or actions — it instead provides access to law despite popular suspicions. *See* Model Rule 1.2(b). As noted in Chapter 1, this tradition in the United States dates back to John Adams's representation of British soldiers who were tried for their role in the Boston Massacre.

Lawyer independence from popular opinion and prejudice is a type of individual lawyer independence from pressure by third parties. Model Rule 5.4(c) expresses another aspect of independence from third parties — namely loyalty to the client when a lawyer is paid, recommended, or employed by a third party. According to Rule 5.4(c), lawyers must not allow that third person to "direct or regulate the lawyer's professional judgment in rendering such legal services."

8. *See* Model Rule 6.2 cmt. 1 (noting lawyer responsibility to accept "a fair share of unpopular matters or indigent or unpopular clients").
9. *See* The Federalist No. 10 (James Madison) (expressing concern that "measures are too often decided, not according to the rules of justice and the rights of the minor party, but by the superior force of an interested and overbearing majority").

Finally, independence also denotes the lawyer's independence from her own client. A lawyer is an officer of the court, who has sworn to uphold state and federal constitutions and has independent obligations to the rule of law, to the profession, and to the public good. While representing a client is not an endorsement of that client's views, nevertheless, the lawyer must resist pressure from the client to disregard the lawyer's legal and ethical obligations. Each lawyer is independently obligated to follow the Rules of Professional Conduct and uphold the law. Just as junior lawyers cannot rely on unethical instructions of supervising lawyers, a lawyer cannot advise or assist a client in conduct that is criminal or fraudulent or a violation of the rules — despite a client's wishes for the lawyer to do so. Even as the advocate of the client, the lawyer retains her own essential independence.

1. Independence from Non-Lawyers in Practicing Law

In addition to the conceptions of independence outlined above, the ABA has maintained as an enforceable part of lawyer independence a requirement that, in practicing law, lawyers cannot go into business with non-lawyers. This restriction is reiterated in three basic prohibitions found in Model Rule 5.4: (1) a prohibition on multidisciplinary practice; (2) a prohibition on sharing fees with non-lawyers; and (3) a prohibition on non-lawyer ownership or direction of law firms. Many commentators have decried the ABA's and state bars' insistence on this type of independence, which Green argues "equat[es] professional independence with professional isolation."[10] Historically, the creation of these restrictions was "transparently motivated by the financial self-interest of the bar's leadership" — specifically, to squelch "competition from corporations and, at least implicitly, to protect the profession's native-born, middle- and upper-class elite against competition."[11]

Indeed, Thomas Morgan contends that the prohibitions are outdated, as the practice of law has changed in the past 50 years from being almost exclusively individual lawyer provision of services to "institutional law practice" involving "the multi-person provision of legal services through organizations."[12] He argues that these prohibitions in Rule 5.4 should be liberalized in light of clients' modern needs for lower-cost bundled services and the fact that international firms in the United Kingdom and Australia are allowed to practice with non-lawyers and are competing with U.S. firms. Rather than prohibiting practice with non-lawyers, Morgan argues "the only sensible question is how to embrace it and make it better serve the public interest," including by regulating such businesses "to require competent service, protection of privileged information, and avoidance of conflicts of interest."[13]

As Green quips, the alleged fear driving these prohibitions is that, if allowed, "lawyers are likely to succumb to the improper influence of their nonlawyer[] allies, sell out their clients, divulge client confidences, represent clients ineptly, violate solicitation rules, and disregard their public obligations."[14] Green argues that the

---

10. Bruce A. Green, *The Disciplinary Restrictions on Multidisciplinary Practice, Their Derivation, Their Development, and Some Implications for the Core Values Debate*, 84 Minn. L. Rev. 1115 (2000).

11. *See id.* at 1145, 1157.

12. Thomas D. Morgan, *The Rise of Institutional Law Practice*, 40 Hofstra L. Rev. 1005, 1008 (2012).

13. *See id.* at 1020, 1026.

14. *See* Green, *supra* note 10, at 1117.

prohibitions on non-lawyer alliances trivialize the important meanings of lawyer independence outlined above:

> In much of the bar's rhetoric in other contexts, the threats to the bar's independence come from the executive and legislative branches of government or the general public. In the one ethics rule with "independence" in its title, these threats are not identified; nor are lawyers encouraged to stare them down. Rather, the enemy at the gate of independence is envisioned as . . . accountants! The rule trivializes the ideal of professional independence as it diminishes legal professionals. Surely, the bar could project a loftier ideal of independence and express greater confidence in lawyers' fortitude.[15]

Despite such critics, in all U.S. jurisdictions except Washington, D.C., the prohibitions remain on multidisciplinary practice, fee sharing with non-lawyers, and non-lawyer investment or management of law firms.

Multidisciplinary Practice

Model Rule 5.4(b) prohibits lawyers from "form[ing] a partnership with a non-lawyer if any of the activities of the partnership consist of the practice of law." This rule prohibits **multidisciplinary practices (MDPs)** — that is, businesses that offer bundled services that include the practice of law in addition to other professional services, such as accounting, banking, insurance, public relations, securities dealing, financial planning, etc. Under Model Rule 5.4, lawyers are prohibited from forming MDPs with non-lawyer professionals offering related services. The ABA has considered proposals to change this rule twice since 2000 and rejected it both times, relying on the importance of lawyer independence.[16]

Sharing Fees with Non-Lawyers

With a few narrow exceptions, Rule 5.4(a) prohibits the sharing of legal fees with non-lawyers. The exceptions are limited to (1) paying to the estate or heirs of a deceased lawyer fees owed to that lawyer or money obtained from the sale of that lawyer's law practice; (2) including "nonlawyer employees in a compensation or retirement plan"; and (3) sharing "court-awarded legal fees with a nonprofit organization" that "employed, retained or recommended" the lawyer. The narrowness of these exceptions is blatant. Lawyers generally cannot share fees with non-lawyers — even if the non-lawyer recommended the lawyer or greatly assisted the lawyer in the representation. Non-lawyers include paralegals; secretaries; attorneys who have been suspended or disbarred; attorneys on inactive status; and expert consultants or investigators who assist with the representation. Indeed, although other states disagree, Arizona has included attorneys who are not admitted to practice law in Arizona as "non-lawyers" for this rule — even though the lawyer is admitted in another state.[17]

Model Rule 5.4(a)'s restriction on sharing fees with non-lawyers for *recommending* the lawyer mirrors the restriction in Rule 7.2(b) that prohibits a lawyer

15. Green, *supra* note 4, at 619.
16. *See* Morgan, *supra* note 12, at 1019.
17. *See* Peterson v. Anderson, 745 P.2d 166, 170 (Ariz. 1987) (holding that attorney licensed in Illinois who had not been admitted pro hac vice was "a non-lawyer within the State of Arizona when the fee arrangement was made").

from "giv[ing] anything of value to a person [lawyer or non-lawyer] for recommending the lawyer's services." Rule 7.2(b) makes an exception, allowing lawyers to participate in a non-profit lawyer referral service that has been approved by the state bar or other regulatory agency. Importantly, Rule 7.2(b) also allows lawyers to enter into a **reciprocal referral agreement** with non-lawyer professionals (or other lawyers), whereby the lawyer and the non-lawyer professional refer clients to each other — without paying each other for such referrals. Such a reciprocal referral agreement cannot be exclusive, and the referred client has to be informed "of the existence and nature of the agreement." *See* Model Rule 7.2(b)(4). Thus, despite Rule 5.4, a lawyer can enter into a reciprocal referral agreement with a non-lawyer professional (such as an accountant) as long as no one is being paid for the referral and the other conditions of Rule 7.2(b) are met.

In 2016, Avvo Legal Services, a for-profit corporation with non-lawyer officers and directors,[18] unrolled its online legal services program in 25 states.[19] The program matches lawyers with clients for limited services and charges a "marketing fee." Three bar associations responded by issuing ethics opinions concluding that lawyer participation in such a program violated the rules.[20] Read the following opinion from the Pennsylvania Bar Association and consider the several ways in which the bar association considers the arrangement to be a threat to a lawyer's exercise of independent professional judgment. Is allowing attorneys to practice with non-lawyers more difficult and a greater threat to independent professional judgment than indicated above by the critiques of Green and Morgan? Or could the problems identified by the Pennsylvania Bar Association be alleviated through appropriate amendment of the rules to accommodate non-lawyer involvement and still enforce lawyer obligations regarding confidentiality, handling client property, limiting the scope of representation, etc.?

Ethical Considerations Relating to Participation in Fixed Fee Limited Scope Legal Services Referral Programs

Pennsylvania Bar Association Legal Ethics and Professional Responsibility Formal Opinion 2016-200 (2016)

I. SUMMARY

The Pennsylvania Bar Association Legal Ethics and Professional Responsibility Committee (the "Committee") has reviewed the potential ethics issues arising from lawyers participating in legal services referral programs meeting the following description:

---

18. *See* Avvo, *Leadership Team* (visited Mar. 9, 2017), *available at* https://www.avvo.com/about_avvo/leadership.
19. *See* Samson Habte, *Third Ethics Panel Dings Avvo Flat-Fee Referral Service*, Oct. 5, 2016, ABA/BNA Law. Man. on Prof. Conduct, Current Reports.
20. The opinions do not name Avvo Legal Services, but Josh King, Avvo's chief legal officer, said that it was clear that the opinions were about Avvo Legal Services. *See id.*

> A for-profit business (the "Business"), which is not a law firm or lawyer-owned, assists in pairing up potential clients seeking certain so-called "limited scope" or "unbundled" legal services with lawyers who are willing to provide such services for a flat fee, with the amount of the fee established by the Business. The client remits the full fee, in advance, to the Business. The Business then forwards the fee to the lawyer after confirming, according to its own procedures and standards, that the requested services were performed. The lawyer then separately pays the Business what is described as a "marketing fee" for each assignment completed. The so-called "marketing fee" charged regarding one type of service may represent a different percentage of the legal fee than the marketing fee charged for another type of service; but, in any event, the amount of the "marketing fee" varies directly with the amount of the flat fee for the legal services. In other words, the greater the amount of the flat fee, the greater the amount of the marketing fee, with the marketing fee typically ranging between 20% to 30% of the legal fee.

Based on this description, the Committee concludes that a Pennsylvania lawyer's participation in such a program (. . . a "Flat Fee Limited Scope" or "FFLS" program) would violate the following provisions of the Pennsylvania Rules of Professional Conduct ("RPCs"):

1. RPC 5.4(a), which generally prohibits sharing legal fees with non-lawyers; and
2. RPC 1.15(i), which requires legal fees paid in advance to be deposited in the lawyer's Trust Account.

Participation in such a program also poses a substantial risk that the lawyer could violate the following RPCs:

1. RPC 2.1, which requires a lawyer to exercise independent professional judgment;
2. RPC 5.4(c), which, in pertinent part, prohibits a lawyer from allowing a person who recommends a lawyer to direct or regulate the lawyer's professional judgment;

> [The opinion also lists RPCs 5.3(c)(1) (lawyer responsible for conduct of non-lawyer); RPC 8.4(a) (lawyer cannot violate RPCs through the acts of another); RPC 1.16(d) (lawyer must refund unearned advance payment on termination); RPC 1.2(c) (lawyer can limit scope of representation only if reasonable and client provides informed consent); RPC 1.6(a) (confidentiality of information relating to the representation); RPC 7.7(a) (limiting lawyer referrals); RPC 5.5(a) (assisting unauthorized practice of law).]

II. ETHICAL CONSIDERATIONS RELATING TO FEE SHARING WITH NONLAWYERS AND PAYING FOR RECOMMENDING A LAWYER'S SERVICES

An obvious concern presented by the FFLS programs described above is whether they involve the sharing of legal fees with non-lawyers, which is prohibited under RPC 5.4(a). The Businesses which operate such programs, presumably in recognition of this concern, typically structure payment in such a way that the actual payment of funds by the client is not directly "shared" between the lawyer and the non-lawyer Business. Instead, as described previously, the client pays a flat fee to the Business and, upon the Business supposedly verifying that the lawyer has earned the fee, the

Business remits the full amount of the flat fee to the lawyer, typically by electronic bank transfer to the lawyer's operating account. Then, in an ostensibly separate transaction, the Business collects its marketing fee related to the completed assignment from the lawyer, typically through a pre-authorized, monthly direct debit from the same operating account into which the fees are deposited.

The manner in which the payments are structured is not dispositive of whether the lawyer's payment to the Business constitutes fee sharing. Rather, the manner in which the amount of the "marketing fee" is established, taken in conjunction with what the lawyer is supposedly paying for, leads to the conclusion that the lawyer's payment of such "marketing fees" constitutes impermissible fee sharing with a non-lawyer.

Outright payment of referral fees to a non-lawyer would violate RPC 7.2(c), which prohibits a lawyer from giving "anything of value for recommending the lawyer's services." Comment [6] to RPC 7.2 explains that a "communication contains a recommendation if it endorses or vouches for a lawyer's credentials, abilities, competence, character, or other professional qualities." One FFLS program website lauds all participating lawyers with such terms and descriptions as "highly rated," "top reviewed," "qualified," "experienced," and "licensed to practice anywhere in your state." The individual lawyer profiles prominently feature "star" ratings, on a scale of one to five stars, based on client reviews, as well as the lawyer's score under the program operator's proprietary, "1 to 10" numerical rating system. The profiles also include excerpts from client reviews. Such communications fit the definition of "recommendations" in the Comment to RPC 7.2.

RPC 7.2(c)(1) and (2) [comparable to Model Rule 7.2(b)(1) and (2)] provide two potentially applicable exceptions to RPC 7.2(c)'s general prohibition against giving "anything of value to a person for recommending the lawyer's services." Those exceptions permit payment for the following:

1. the reasonable cost of advertisements or written communications permitted by this Rule; or
2. the usual charges of a lawyer referral service or other legal service organization.

Information published by at least one major operator of a FFLS program asserts that it is not a "lawyer referral service," presumably because the American Bar Association Model Rules of Professional Conduct ("Model Rules"), and many other states' RPCs, limit authorized "lawyer referral services" to not-for-profit organizations or services that are approved by specified regulatory authorities (See Model Rule 7.2(b)(2)). [Pennsylvania does not make the same limitation.] . . .

[In any event], payments to a lawyer referral service remain subject to RPC 5.4(a)'s prohibition against sharing fees with non-lawyers. Ethics opinions that have considered similar compensation arrangements have concluded that marketing, advertising, or referral fees paid to for-profit enterprises that are based upon whether a lawyer received any matters, or how many matters were received, or how much revenue was generated by the matters, constitute impermissible fee sharing under RPC 5.4(a). For example, Ohio Opinion 2016-3, which addresses the same types of FFLS programs discussed in this Opinion, states that "a fee-splitting arrangement that is dependent upon the number of clients obtained or the legal fee earned does not comport with the Rules of Professional Conduct." S.C. Opinion 16-06, which also addressed a FFLS program, reached the same conclusion. . . .

... The proponents of FFLS programs have also claimed that the lawyer's payment of marketing fees which vary based upon (1) the number of matters received, and (2) on the amount of legal fees generated by those matters, is not impermissible fee sharing, because such payments supposedly do not interfere with the lawyer's professional independence. Even if this were accurate, it would not be dispositive of the issue. Moreover, while the premise that the primary policy underlying RPC 5.4(a) is the preservation of the lawyer's professional independence is valid, the assumption that the lawyer's payment to a non-lawyer of marketing fees amounting to 20% to 30% of legal fees earned does not interfere with the lawyer's professional independence is, at a minimum, of questionable validity. As discussed elsewhere in this Opinion, there are a number of aspects of the FFLS programs that pose a substantial risk of interfering with a lawyer's professional independence.

...

III. ETHICAL CONSIDERATIONS RELATING TO HANDLING OF CLIENT FUNDS

As discussed above, the non-lawyer Business collects the client's advance fee payment prior to commencement of the lawyer-client relationship and then retains the advance fee until the Business concludes, to its satisfaction, that the fees have been earned by, and should be remitted to, the lawyer. This poses several ethical issues. Such an arrangement effectively, and exclusively, delegates to a non-lawyer several critical decisions and functions that fall within the exclusive domain of the practice of law. This includes, for example, the decision whether the professional services the client requested of the lawyer have been satisfactorily completed, such that the advance fee has been earned by and is payable to the lawyer. Such delegation violates RPC 2.1, which requires a lawyer to exercise independent professional judgment, and RPC 5.4(c), which prohibits a lawyer from allowing a person who recommends, employs or pays the lawyer to render legal services for another to direct or regulate the lawyer's professional judgment in rendering such legal services.

In at least some circumstances, the Business [] consider[s] the completion of a telephone call between the lawyer and the client on the Business's phone system (which apparently does not monitor content) as alone sufficient to establish that the advance fee has been "earned" and can be remitted to the lawyer's operating account. Clearly, a lawyer would not be permitted to make this determination in such a mechanistic fashion....

Such delegation of responsibility also interferes with the lawyer's independence in carrying out relevant obligations under RPC 1.16(d) .... [O]nce a lawyer-client relationship has been established, it is solely the lawyer's obligation to see to it that, when the representation has been terminated, for whatever reason, any unearned advance fee is returned to the client. Because, under the procedures described above for the FFLS program, the lawyer never possesses or controls the advance fee, the lawyer is unable to ensure that those obligations are fulfilled....

These problems highlight a broader issue with the FFLS programs: The delegation of the possession and distribution of advance fee payments to a non-lawyer violates RPC 1.15(i), which provides:

> A lawyer shall deposit into a Trust Account legal fees and expenses that have been paid in advance, to be withdrawn by the lawyer only as fees are earned or expenses

incurred, unless the client gives informed consent, confirmed in writing, to the handling of fees and expenses in a different manner.

The only way to rectify the issues discussed above would be for the Business to immediately remit advance fee payments to the lawyer, for deposit in the lawyer's Trust Account, as defined in RPC 1.15(a)(11), as soon as a lawyer-client relationship is established. This would not only comply with RPC 1.15(i), but would also allow the lawyer to independently fulfill his or her non-delegable obligations with respect to the disposition of the funds, as required under RPCs 2.1, 5.4(c), and 1.16(d). However, as presently constituted, the FFLS programs do not accommodate this requirement.

IV. ETHICAL CONSIDERATIONS RELATING TO "LIMITED SCOPE" REPRESENTATION

"Limited scope" representation is authorized under RPC 1.2(c) . . . . The two operative requirements for limited scope representation are that (1) the limitation be "reasonable," and (2) "the client gives informed consent." When a prospective client contacts a Business operating a FFLS program seeking legal assistance, the Business, as a non-lawyer, cannot properly assess whether the limited scope legal services the prospective client seeks are appropriate for the client, or that the limitations on the scope of the representation offered through the FFLS program would be "reasonable" within the meaning of RPC 1.2(c), given the prospective client's particular circumstances. The Business cannot secure the prospective client's informed consent to the limitations to the representation, because this is also a nondelegable responsibility of the lawyer who ultimately undertakes the representation.

. . .

In theory, at least, it would be possible for a lawyer who decides to accept a FFLS program referral to fulfill these obligations. . . . [H]owever, given the time and financial constraints imposed by of [*sic*] the FFLS programs, it will be challenging, if not impossible, for a lawyer to make the necessary assessment of the appropriateness and reasonableness of the limited scope assignment, to secure the client's informed consent to such limitations, and to then provide the requested professional services. . . .

The burden on the lawyer to verify the appropriateness of the "limited scope" services to meet the client's needs, as well as the reasonableness of the limitation on the scope of services to be provided, is further heightened by the broad and vague descriptions of limited scope services that are offered on a flat fee basis through a typical FFLS program operator, such as: Document Review; Create a Termination Letter; Create a Business Contract; Create an Operating Agreement; Create a Business Partnership; Create an Asset Purchase Agreement; Create an Estate Plan Bundle; Create a Living Trust Bundle (Couple); Create a Parenting Plan; and Create a Commercial Lease Agreement. Even if the prospective client selects the correct general category of service, the prospective client's perception of what is needed may differ from what is actually required, and the lawyer would have no way of ascertaining the scope and magnitude of the effort required to meet the prospective client's true needs until after speaking with the client, possibly at great length.

This is not to mention that the lawyer must also conduct a proper conflict check which, in most cases, cannot be completed until the lawyer is in direct communication with the prospective client.

. . .

VI. ETHICAL CONSIDERATIONS RELATING TO CONFIDENTIALITY

The structure of the FFLS programs exposes the Business to significant information that would ordinarily be considered confidential under RPC 1.6(a). . . . RPC 1.6(a) prohibits a lawyer from "revealing" confidential information, subject to various exceptions. Under the FFLS program, it is the prospective client who chooses to reveal the information described above to the Business, and that choice is made before the lawyer-client relationship has even been established. Therefore, the client's disclosure of information to the Business prior to formation of a lawyer-client relationship does not directly implicate the lawyer's duty of confidentiality under RPC 1.6(a). The program does, however, place information at risk of disclosure in future litigation, since the communications between the client and the Business would not be protected by the lawyer-client privilege.

With one exception, the FFLS program does not require, or anticipate, further disclosure of potentially confidential information to the Business once the lawyer-client relationship has been established. The one exception is that the Business must be informed, or at least reach the conclusion, that the assignment has been completed, in order to release the advance fee payment to the lawyer. The completion of the assignment, as well as the nature of the work performed is itself "information relating to representation of the client" subject to RPC 1.6(a). No exception to the prohibition against disclosure applies. Disclosure is not "impliedly authorized in order to carry out the representation." Rather, disclosure to the Business is merely the Business's externally-imposed condition to the lawyer's receipt of the client's advance fee payment, which has nothing to do with "carrying out the representation." . . . The lawyer could request the client's informed consent to the disclosure. . . .

. . .

IX. ACCESS TO LEGAL SERVICES

Operators of FFLS programs argue that "unbundling" legal services reduces the cost to clients, thereby making legal services more accessible. Expanding access to legal services is, of course, an important goal that all lawyers, and the organized Bar, should support. However, the manner in which these FFLS programs currently operate raises concerns about whether they advance the goal of expanding access to legal services. Further, compliance with the RPCs should not be considered inconsistent with the goal of facilitating greater access to legal services.

Any lawyer can offer "unbundled" or "limited scope" legal services at, or even below, the rates prescribed by an FFLS program, provided the lawyer can do so in a manner that complies with his or her professional and ethical obligations, including the obligation of competence (see RPC 1.1) and full disclosure of and informed consent to any limitations on the scope of the legal services rendered. If a lawyer cannot fulfill those obligations working outside the scope of an FFLS program, he or she almost

certainly would not be able to do so working within such a program. If anything, services offered through FFLS programs would be expected to be even more costly than they otherwise would have to be, because of the burden of substantial "marketing fees" that vary in direct relation to the revenue derived from such legal services and that bear no relationship to the actual cost of any marketing services provided. . . .

Non-Lawyer Ownership or Direction of Law Firms

Rule 5.4(d) also prohibits lawyers from practicing law "for profit" in a business organization in which "a nonlawyer owns any interest therein," or a non-lawyer is an officer, director, or someone with similar managerial responsibility, or "a nonlawyer has the right to direct or control the professional judgment of a lawyer." For example, even if Avvo directly hired lawyers to provide the limited legal services it offers, those lawyers would be prohibited from engaging in the practice of law because Avvo has non-lawyer officers and directors.

Washington, D.C. has liberalized its version of Rule 5.4 to allow lawyers to practice in a business organization "in which a financial interest is held or managerial authority is exercised by an individual nonlawyer who performs professional services which assist the organization in providing legal services to clients." The D.C. rule requires, among other things, that non-lawyers "having such managerial authority or holding a financial interest undertake to abide by these Rules of Professional Conduct."[21] In a similar vein, as part of Ethics 20/20, the ABA considered, but ultimately rejected, a proposal to amend the Model Rules to allow **Alternative Business Structures (ABS)** with non-lawyer ownership and management. However, the percentage of non-lawyer ownership would be limited, with a recommended 25 percent maximum, so that any ABS would be controlled by lawyers owning a majority interest.[22] Thomas Morgan argues that the current rule, which absolutely prohibits non-lawyer investment in law firms, has negative effects—it "both denies law firms the ability to raise a potentially important form of capital and reduces the incentive a firm can give its members to help build the firm as an effective, ethical institution that would be attractive to outside investors."[23]

2. Restrictions on Lawyer's Practice

Another area where state bars have asserted lawyer independence is in protecting the ability of individual lawyers to freely compete with other lawyers and change

21. *See* D.C. Rule of Prof'l Conduct 5.4(b). The D.C. rule allows non-lawyer ownership or managerial authority but only if the following circumstances are met: (1) the sole purpose of the organization has to be the provision of "legal services to clients"; (2) the non-lawyer managers or interest-holders must "undertake to abide by these Rules of Professional Conduct"; (3) the lawyers with managerial or financial interest in the organization "undertake to be responsible for the nonlawyer participants to the same extent as if nonlawyer participants were lawyers under Rule 5.1"; and (4) these "conditions are set forth in writing." *See id.*
22. *See* Morgan, *supra* note 12, at 1020 and nn.100-08.
23. *See id.* at 1022.

their practice or employment. Thus, Model Rule 5.6 prohibits **covenants not to compete** and other restrictions on an attorney's ability to practice law or compete after terminating employment with a firm or company as a lawyer.

Case Preview

In re Truman

If an associate decides to leave a law firm, can the associate take firm clients with her? Can the law firm restrict the ability of the associate to do so? In *In re Truman*, a law firm attempted do exactly that.

As you read *In re Truman*, consider the following:

1. What is the court's rationale underlying the rule prohibiting restrictions on practice?
2. Did the associate's position in a law firm help him obtain these clients? If so, should the firm be able to restrict the ability of the associate to then take the clients with him?
3. How would it affect client choice of counsel if law firms could restrict the ability of departing lawyers from taking clients?

In re Truman

7 N.E.3d 260 (Ind. 2014)

We find that Respondent, Karl N. Truman, engaged in attorney misconduct by making an employment agreement that restricted the rights of a lawyer to practice after termination of the employment relationship. For this misconduct, we conclude that Respondent should receive a public reprimand. . . .

BACKGROUND

In October 2006, Respondent hired an associate ("Associate") to work in his law firm. As a condition of employment, Associate signed a Confidentiality/Non-Disclosure/Separation Agreement ("the Separation Agreement"). If Associate left the firm, the Separation Agreement provided that only Respondent could notify clients that Associate was leaving, prohibited Associate from soliciting and notifying clients that he was leaving, and prohibited Associate from soliciting and contacting clients after he left. The Separation Agreement also included provisions for dividing fees if Associate left the firm that were structured to create a strong financial disincentive to prevent Associate from continuing to represent clients he had represented while employed by the firm.

In October 2012, Associate informed Respondent that he was leaving the firm. At the time, Associate had substantial responsibility in representing more than a dozen clients ("Associate's Clients"). Respondent insisted on enforcing the terms of the Separation Agreement regarding these clients. Respondent sent notices to Associate's Clients announcing Associate's departure. Not all of the notices explained that these clients could continue to be represented by Associate if they so chose, and the notices did not provide clients with Associate's contact information. The Separation Agreement provided that Respondent would provide Associate's Clients with his contact information only if they requested it, and Respondent provided the information to any such clients who specifically requested it.

Despite the provisions of the Separation Agreement, Associate sent out notices to Associate's Clients that explained that the client could choose to be represented by Respondent or by Associate, and that included Associate's contact information. In response, Respondent filed a complaint against Associate seeking to enforce the Separation Agreement. A settlement was reached through mediation.

Immediately after the Commission began its investigation in this matter, Respondent discontinued his use of the Separation Agreement, and he has not enforced any similar provisions against any other former associates.

. . .

DISCUSSION

Indiana Professional Conduct Rule 5.6(a) is for the protection of both lawyers and clients. Comment [1] to this rule states: "An agreement restricting the right of lawyers to practice after leaving a firm not only limits their professional autonomy but also limits the freedom of clients to choose a lawyer." The Separation Agreement hampered both Associate's right to practice law and Associate's Clients' freedom to choose a lawyer by restricting Associate's ability to communicate with the clients and creating an unwarranted financial disincentive for Associate to continue representing them.

The Ohio Supreme Court recently addressed a similar situation. In that case, an attorney's employment agreement with his associates restrained them from taking clients with them when the associates left the attorney's firm by requiring a departing associate to remit to the attorney 95% of the fees generated in a case involving a former firm client, regardless of the proportion of the work that the attorney and the associate performed on the client's case. The Ohio Supreme Court found that the attorney violated Ohio's Professional Conduct Rules 5.6 and 1.5 (prohibiting excess fees) and approved an agreed public reprimand. *See* Cincinnati Bar Assn. v. Hackett, 950 N.E.2d 969 (2011). A client's "absolute right to discharge an attorney or law firm at any time, with or without cause, subject to the obligation to compensate the attorney or firm for services rendered prior to the discharge[,] . . . would be hollow if the discharged attorney could prevent other attorneys from assuming the client's representation." *Id.* at 970. . . .

The Court concludes that Respondent violated Indiana Professional Conduct Rule 5.6(a) by making an employment agreement that restricted the rights of a lawyer to practice after termination of the employment relationship. For Respondent's professional misconduct, the Court imposes a public reprimand.

Post-Case Follow-Up

Truman represents the majority approach to restrictions on lawyer practice. Nevertheless, a number of jurisdictions do allow a law firm to enter into employment and partnership agreements that impose "reasonable" financial disincentives for terminating employment and taking firm clients. A leading case is Howard v. Babcock, 863 P.2d 150, 156 (Cal. 1993), in which the Supreme Court of California asserted that "a revolution in the practice of law has occurred requiring economic interests of the law firm to be protected as they are in other business enterprises." The court argued:

> It seems to us unreasonable to distinguish lawyers from other professionals such as doctors or accountants, who also owe a high degree of skill and loyalty to their patients and clients. The interest of a patient in a doctor of his or her choice is obviously as significant as the interest of a litigant in a lawyer of his or her choosing. Yet for doctors, reasonable noncompetition agreements binding upon withdrawing partners are permitted.[24]

Quoting Justice Rehnquist, the court noted that "[i]nstitutional loyalty appears to be in decline." Thus, one of the "changes rocking the legal profession is the propensity of withdrawing partners in law firms to 'grab' clients of the firm and set up a competing practice." Seeking "to achieve a balance between the interest of clients in having the attorney of choice, and the interest of law firms in a stable business environment," the court held that "an agreement among partners imposing a reasonable cost on departing partners who compete with the law firm in a limited geographical area is not inconsistent with [the rules] and is not void on its face as against public policy." The court held that its "recognition of a new reality in the practice of law" would not have a "deleterious effect on the current ability of clients to retain loyal, competent counsel of their choice." *See id.* at 157-61.

In re Truman: Real Life Applications

1. Jason is hired as in-house counsel for We Care, Inc. We Care has Jason sign an employment contract that contains the following clause: "During employment and for one year after termination of employment, employee agrees to not accept employment or provide any services to a competitor of We Care, Inc." Two years later Jason receives a more lucrative job offer from The Caring Corp, a competitor of We Care. Can Jason accept the job at The Caring Corp? If the agreement violates the rules, does that make it unenforceable?

2. Maria is a 61-year-old partner at the law firm of Morgan & Taylor, where she has practiced for 32 years. Maria is asked by the other partners to resign. Maria resigns and begins to receive monthly retirement benefits from Morgan & Taylor.

24. *Howard*, 863 P.2d at 160.

Maria would like to continue practicing law and considers taking a position at another firm, Harris & Martinez. Maria is aware that under her partnership agreement with Morgan & Taylor, a person is only eligible for retirement benefits if a person is (1) over 60 years of age; (2) has been associated with Morgan & Taylor for more than 30 years; and (3) has ceased practicing law. Indeed, the agreement states that if a person receiving retirement benefits resumes practicing law, then she must refund any retirement benefits received. Is Morgan & Taylor's restriction on receiving retirement benefits in violation of Rule 5.6?

---

3. Sale of a Law Practice

Traditionally, the sale of a law practice was viewed as unethical—because law was perceived to be a profession involving lawyer loyalty to individual clients rather than a business. In 1990, Model Rule 1.17 was adopted to allow an attorney who is leaving the practice of law (or a certain practice area) to sell his practice. Nevertheless, Rule 1.17 places rigid restrictions on such a sale, only allowing sales under limited and specific conditions. Indeed, comment 1 reiterates the rationale for the traditional prohibition: "The practice of law is a profession, not merely a business" and "[c]lients are not commodities that can be purchased and sold at will."

Under Rule 1.7, a lawyer can only sell a law practice (or an area of practice)—and a lawyer can only buy one—if all of the following conditions are met: (1) the seller must cease practicing law or practicing the specific area of law in that jurisdiction; (2) the seller must be selling the entire law practice or entire area of practice; (3) the seller has to provide a specified notice to clients; and (4) the fees charged to clients cannot be increased because of the sale.

Notably, the first condition is a significant limitation on the right to sell a law practice. Only if a lawyer is planning to stop entirely practicing law or a given area of law can the lawyer sell her practice. There are several situations where this could happen beyond retirement. For example, a lawyer could become a judge or take another public office requiring him to forgo law practice. In addition, a lawyer may move to a different jurisdiction, and the rule allows a lawyer to sell her law practice in the jurisdiction from which she is moving. Further, even in the same jurisdiction, comment 2 clarifies that a lawyer who sells his practice can accept subsequent employment "as a lawyer on the staff of a public agency or a legal services entity that provides legal services to the poor, or as in-house counsel to a business." Further, a lawyer is permitted to sell off just one area of her practice, but the lawyer "must cease accepting any matters in the area of practice that has been sold."[25] The rationale for requiring attorneys to sell the entire practice or area of practice (rather than specific matters separately) is to protect "clients whose matters are less lucrative."[26]

Clients must be given written notice of the sale and be informed of their right "to retain other counsel or take possession of the file" rather than have their matter

---

25. Model Rule 1.17 cmt. 5.
26. Model Rule 1.17 cmt. 6.

undertaken by the purchasing attorney. Further, the notice must tell the client that the client's matter will be undertaken by the purchasing attorney if the client does not take other action within 90 days. If a client cannot be located, the transfer of the case to the purchasing attorney must be done by court order. *See* Model Rule 1.17(c).

C. UNAUTHORIZED PRACTICE OF LAW (UPL)

State law defines the "practice of law" and prohibits individuals who are not licensed from practicing law or holding themselves out as being able to practice law.[27] **UPL** is a crime in many states subjecting the violator to imprisonment and a fine. Depending on the jurisdiction, the prosecutor's office or the state attorney general's office may enforce UPL laws while state and local disciplinary counsel or bar committees may enforce court regulations barring UPL. UPL enforcement is a persistent concern for the profession; state and local bar associations have created committees to promote investigation and litigation of UPL. State supreme courts have established UPL boards to review UPL charges brought by bar counsel and to recommend sanctions for the courts' adoption. The level of UPL enforcement among states varies and depends upon a jurisdiction's resources and other pressing prosecutorial needs. In addition to civil and criminal penalties for UPL violations, a lawyer engaging or assisting another in UPL may face possible disciplinary sanctions. UPL is a concern not just for those who are not licensed to practice law in any jurisdiction but also for those lawyers who practice law in a jurisdiction where they are not licensed.

1. Justifications for the Professional Monopoly

The prohibition on the practice of law by non-lawyers is intended to "protect[] the public against rendition of legal services by unqualified persons."[28] Indeed, incompetent services performed by untrained lay people can and do cause great harm to the public. Immigrants, for example, have frequently been victimized by non-lawyer immigration consultants (sometimes known as "notarios") who charge large fees to process fraudulent or frivolous applications for them.

But many commentators have criticized UPL restrictions as being intended to protect lawyers from competition rather than the public from incompetent services. A broad prohibition on the unauthorized practice of law protects the profession's monopoly on the delivery of legal services by limiting competition and allowing lawyers to charge higher prices to the potential detriment of the public who might benefit from less expensive services offered by alternative service

27. Model Rule 5.5(a) & cmt. [1]-[2].
28. Model Rule 5.5(a) cmt. [2]; Restatement (Third) of the Law Governing Lawyers §2 [hereinafter Restatement].

providers.[29] The Federal Trade Commission has long advocated that "non-attorneys should be permitted to compete with attorneys," particularly in areas "where no specialized legal knowledge and training is demonstrably necessary to protect the interests of consumers."[30] One area of focus for the FTC has been real estate closings: in some states, real estate brokers and title agents may perform the critical tasks at real estate closings; in other states, however, only a lawyer may perform those functions even though no empirical evidence exists suggesting that the use of lawyers in real estate closings protects the public. As Professor Deborah Rhode has argued, in the absence of "evidence of significant injuries resulting from lay assistance, individuals should be entitled to determine the cost and quality of legal services that best meet their needs."[31]

2. Defining the Practice of Law

What constitutes the practice of law is controversial. In 2002, the ABA chartered a task force on the subject, which proposed the following definition: "The practice of law is the application of legal principles and judgment with regard to the circumstances or objectives of a person that requires the knowledge and skill of a person trained in the law."[32] Under this broad standard, a real estate broker consulting with a client about which terms to include in a lease or a sales agreement and a coach advising a player about the terms and benefits of signing a specific agency or endorsement agreement all might constitute the practice of law. The following scenarios also are arguably covered by the ABA's broad standard: a non-lawyer neighbor advising a landowner about the legal meaning of a variance and assisting him in developing evidence and a strategy to obtain the variance; a mailman advising a friend about how to devise his estate and legally challenge an IRS audit; and a legal secretary or second-year law student informing a firm's client who plans to file for a divorce about the consequences of moving out of the marital residence.

The ABA Task Force ultimately abandoned its task of drafting a model definition of the practice of law and recommended that states develop their own definitions. Those definitions have provided little clarity beyond a few basic areas of agreement:

- In most jurisdictions, only lawyers may represent clients in court, draft certain legal documents, and hold themselves out as lawyers.

---

29. Jack P. Sahl, *Cracks in the Profession's Monopoly Armor*, 82 FORDHAM L. REV. 2635, 2636, nn.4-5 (2014) (also citing Thomas D. Morgan, *The Evolving Concept of Professional Responsibility*, 90 HARV. L. REV. 702, 207 (1977) who asserts lawyers draft rules to promote their own interests in a self-regulatory context).

30. *See* Letter from the Fed. Trade Comm'n Office of Policy Planning to the Rules Comm. of the Superior Court 2 (May 17, 2007), *available at* https://www.ftc.gov/sites/default/files/documents/advocacy_documents/ftc-staff-comment-mr.carl-e.testo-counsel-rules-committee-superior-court-concerning-proposed-rules-definition-practice-law/v070006.pdf.

31. Deborah L. Rhode, *Policing the Professional Monopoly: A Constitutional and Empirical Analysis of Unauthorized Practice Prohibitions*, 34 STAN. L. REV. 1, 98-99 (1981).

32. ABA Task Force on the Model Definition of the Practice of Law, Draft Report (Sept. 18, 2002), http://www.americanbar.org/groups/professional_responsibility/task_force_model_definition_practice_law/model_definition_definition.html.

- All jurisdictions recognize the right of an individual to represent himself in litigation and in other non-litigation matters, such as negotiating and preparing a lease or a contract for the sale of personal property, or drafting a will.[33] This personal right, however, does not entitle the individual to assist others with their legal needs. In addition, in most states, a business association cannot proceed *pro se* but instead must be represented by counsel in court proceedings.
- By custom or explicit rule, states generally do not enforce unauthorized practice of law prohibitions against other professionals. For example, Texas specifically excludes licensed real estate agents from its unauthorized practice of law statute.[34]
- Some jurisdictions permit limited practice by non-lawyers in particular contexts. For example, federal regulations permit non-lawyers to represent individuals before certain federal administrative agencies. Patent agents, for example, do not need to be lawyers. In Sperry v. Florida Bar, 373 U.S. 379 (1963), the Supreme Court prohibited Florida from enjoining a non-lawyer agent from preparing and prosecuting patents before the U.S. patent office when both a federal statute and USPTO rules authorized non-lawyers to perform this work. Even though the agents' work constituted the practice of law in Florida, the Supremacy Clause prohibited the state from interfering with the "accomplishment of the federal objectives."
- Several states permit non-lawyers to perform various tasks in order to assist unrepresented litigants in navigating the court system. See Chapter 11.

Beyond that, however, what constitutes the practice of law is a gray area, and most states' definitions sweep just as broadly as the ABA's proposed definition. State definitions of the practice of law are also notoriously circular and vague. For example, the District of Columbia defines the practice of law, in part, to include the "provision of professional legal advice . . . ."[35] The Mississippi Supreme Court has said that "any exercise of intelligent choice in advising another of his legal rights and duties brings the activity within the practice of the legal profession."[36]

A current area of controversy is how UPL regulation applies to LegalZoom, Avvo, and other companies that deliver legal information, legal services, and other products on the Internet. To the extent that these companies provide legal information and legal forms to consumers without advising a particular consumer about his or

Form-alities of the Practice of Law

In *Florida Bar v. Brumbaugh*, discussed on page 492, the Florida Bar sued for an injunction against Marilyn Brumbaugh to prevent her from engaging in the unauthorized practice of law. Fla. Bar v. Brumbaugh, 355 So. 2d 1186 (Fla. 1978). In the late 1970s, Brumbaugh provided typing services for "do-it-yourself" uncontested divorces. *Id.* at 1190. For $50(!), Brumbaugh would prepare "all papers deemed by her to be needed for the pleading, filing, and securing of a dissolution of marriage, as well as detailed instructions as to how the suit should be filed, notice served, hearings set, trial conducted, and the final decree secured." *Id.*

Brumbaugh never held herself out as a lawyer, and her ads were clearly directed to people seeking to obtain a divorce *pro se*. *Id.* In the course of the case, Brumbaugh

33. Restatement §4 cmt. d.
34. Tex. Bus. & Com. Code §83.001.
35. D.C. App. R. 49.
36. Darby v. Miss. State Board of Bar Admissions, 185 So. 2d 684 (Miss. 1966).

was jailed for pleading the Fifth Amendment when she refused to answer the referee's questions. *Id.* Brumbaugh made sure to fly under the radar after the Florida Supreme Court ruled on her case, although she still provided forms, just without any advice. Kevin Spear, *Typist's Trade Is Divorce,* ORLANDO SENTINEL, Mar. 26, 1988, http://articles.orlandosentinel.com/1988-03-26/news/0030020242_1_divorce-papers-do-it-yourself-divorce-divorce-kits. She stated, "I'm paranoid and I think I always will be. I think I have been a threat to the legal system. All they would have to do is catch me giving legal advice, and I'd go back to jail." *Id.*

her problem, they are in the clear. In New York County Lawyers' Ass'n v. Dacey, 234 N.E.2d 459 (N.Y. 1967), the New York Court of Appeals held that a non-lawyer had the right to publish his book *How to Avoid Probate!* because he was providing information about the law and not practicing law. Similarly, in Florida Bar v. Brumbaugh, 355 So. 2d 1186 (Fla. 1978), the Florida Supreme Court held that a non-lawyer "may sell printed material purporting to explain legal practice and procedure to the public in general . . . and sample legal forms." The court further held that she could type out those forms for her clients, though she could "not make inquiries nor answer questions from her clients as to the particular forms which might be necessary, how best to fill out such forms, where to properly file such forms, and how to present necessary evidence at the court hearings."

These modern businesses go far beyond merely providing legal information, however. LegalZoom, for example, uses interactive branching technology to help consumers complete wills, trademarks applications, incorporation papers, and many other legal documents. The company has been operating since 2001 and has served millions of customers notwithstanding a number of UPL lawsuits across the country. In one case, Janson v. LegalZoom, 82 F. Supp. 2d 1053 (W.D. Mo. 2011), a federal district court held that LegalZoom was engaged in the unauthorized practice of law. The court seemed to be particularly troubled by the fact that non-lawyer employees were reviewing the legal documents for completeness, spelling, grammatical errors, consistency, and formatting. But the parties subsequently settled that litigation with LegalZoom making some changes to its business model. Similarly, in Opinion 2016-200 (excerpted above) regarding Avvo's legal services program, the Pennsylvania Bar Association opined that lawyers who participated in the program may be violating Rule 5.5 by assisting non-lawyers in the unauthorized practice of law, inasmuch as the non-lawyer operators of the program make initial "judgments and decisions which are only appropriately made by lawyers."

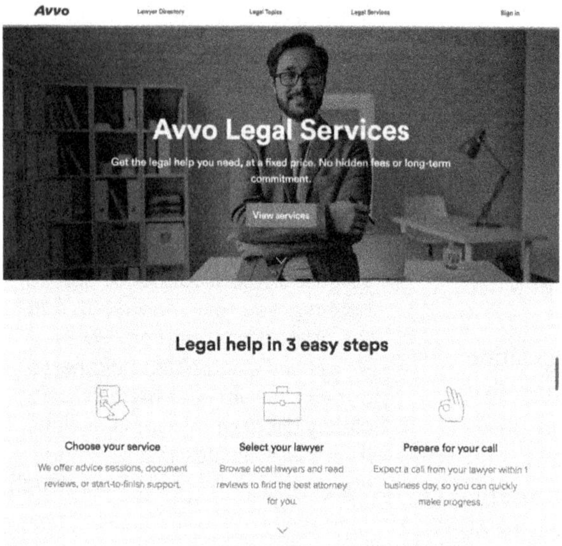

A current area of controversy is how UPL regulation applies to LegalZoom, Avvo, and other companies that deliver legal information, legal services, and other products on the Internet.
avvo.com

In 2015, LegalZoom also settled a dispute with the North Carolina bar in which the bar had said that LegalZoom was engaged in the unauthorized practice of law, and LegalZoom had countered with antitrust claims. Under the settlement, LegalZoom agreed to submit its documents for review by a North Carolina lawyer and inform its customers that their use of LegalZoom's templates are not a substitute for the advice of an attorney. In return, the state bar agreed to support legislation to clarify the definition of "unauthorized practice of law." The parties also agreed to support legislation permitting interactive legal-help websites.[37] On the heels of that settlement, the tide of litigation against LegalZoom seems to have slowed.

D. MULTIJURISDICTIONAL PRACTICE (MJP)

For several decades, lawyers have increasingly practiced in multiple jurisdictions as they try to meet clients' needs across state and national borders. Advances in technology help facilitate MJP as lawyers can more easily communicate and deliver services across territorial boundaries. Is it a problem for a lawyer who is a member of the Pennsylvania Bar to help a client in Florida? Lawyers generally did not worry about this issue until the California Supreme Court gave them a wakeup call.

Case Preview

Birbrower, Montalbano, Condon & Frank v. Superior Court

In 1992 and 1993, two lawyers at Birbrower, a New York law firm, represented ESQ, a California client with its principal place of business in California. No Birbrower lawyer was licensed in California at that time. In 1992, the law firm and ESQ signed a retention agreement in New York obligating the firm to provide legal services, including representing ESQ in the investigation and pursuit of all claims against Tandem Computers Incorporated, a Delaware corporation with its principal place of business in Santa Clara. The dispute involved a software development and marketing contract between ESQ and Tandem. The contract provided that California law would govern the validity of the agreement and related claims. After ESQ settled the case, it sued Birbrower for malpractice and related claims, and the firm filed a counterclaim for unpaid fees. ESQ argued that the fee agreement was unenforceable because Birbrower engaged in unauthorized practice of law in California.

As you read the *Birbrower* decision, ask yourself:

1. What constitutes the practice of law in California?
2. What actions by the Birbrower lawyers constituted the practice of law in California?
3. What purpose does the enforcement of California's UPL statute against the Birbrower lawyers serve?

---

37. Terry Carter, *LegalZoom Resolves $10.5M Antitrust Suit Against North Carolina State Bar*, A.B.A. J. 2015, http://www.abajournal.com/news/article/legalzoom_resolves_10.5m_antitrust_suit_against_north_carolina_state_bar.

Birbrower, Montalbano, Condon & Frank v. Superior Court

949 P.2d 1 (Cal. 1998)

CHIN, J.

. . .

The facts with respect to the unauthorized practice of law question are essentially undisputed. Birbrower is a professional law corporation incorporated in New York, with its principal place of business in New York. During 1992 and 1993, Birbrower attorneys, defendants Kevin F. Hobbs and Thomas A. Condon (Hobbs and Condon), performed substantial work in California relating to the law firm's representation of ESQ. Neither Hobbs nor Condon has ever been licensed to practice law in California. None of Birbrower's attorneys were licensed to practice law in California during Birbrower's ESQ representation.

ESQ is a California corporation with its principal place of business in Santa Clara County. In July 1992, the parties negotiated and executed the fee agreement in New York, providing that Birbrower would perform legal services for ESQ, including "All matters pertaining to the investigation of and prosecution of all claims and causes of action against Tandem Computers Incorporated [Tandem]." The "claims and causes of action" against Tandem, a Delaware corporation with its principal place of business in Santa Clara County, California, related to a software development and marketing contract between Tandem and ESQ dated March 16, 1990 (Tandem Agreement). The Tandem Agreement stated that "The internal laws of the State of California (irrespective of its choice of law principles) shall govern the validity of this Agreement, the construction of its terms, and the interpretation and enforcement of the rights and duties of the parties hereto." Birbrower asserts, and ESQ disputes, that ESQ knew Birbrower was not licensed to practice law in California.

While representing ESQ, Hobbs and Condon traveled to California on several occasions. In August 1992, they met in California with ESQ and its accountants. During these meetings, Hobbs and Condon discussed various matters related to ESQ's dispute with Tandem and strategy for resolving the dispute. They made recommendations and gave advice. During this California trip, Hobbs and Condon also met with Tandem representatives on four or five occasions during a two-day period. At the meetings, Hobbs and Condon spoke on ESQ's behalf. Hobbs demanded that Tandem pay ESQ \$15 million. Condon told Tandem he believed that damages would exceed \$15 million if the parties litigated the dispute.

Around March or April 1993, Hobbs, Condon, and another Birbrower attorney visited California to interview potential arbitrators and to meet again with ESQ and its accountants. Birbrower had previously filed a demand for arbitration against Tandem with the San Francisco offices of the American Arbitration Association (AAA). In August 1993, Hobbs returned to California to assist ESQ in settling the Tandem matter. While in California, Hobbs met with ESQ and its accountants to discuss a proposed settlement agreement Tandem authored. Hobbs also met with Tandem representatives to discuss possible changes in the proposed agreement. Hobbs gave ESQ legal advice during this trip, including his opinion that ESQ should not settle with Tandem on the terms proposed.

ESQ eventually settled the Tandem dispute, and the matter never went to arbitration. But before the settlement, ESQ and Birbrower modified the contingency fee agreement. The modification changed the fee arrangement from contingency to fixed fee, providing that ESQ would pay Birbrower over $1 million. The original contingency fee arrangement had called for Birbrower to receive "one-third (1/3) of all sums received for the benefit of the Clients . . . whether obtained through settlement, motion practice, hearing, arbitration, or trial by way of judgment, award, settlement, or otherwise . . . ."

In January 1994, ESQ sued Birbrower for legal malpractice and related claims in Santa Clara County Superior Court. Birbrower . . . filed a counterclaim, which included a claim for attorney fees for the work it performed in both California and New York . . . . ESQ moved for summary judgment . . . argu[ing] that by practicing law without a license in California and by failing to associate legal counsel while doing so, Birbrower violated section 6125, rendering the fee agreement unenforceable. Based on these undisputed facts, the Santa Clara Superior Court granted ESQ's motion . . . . The court concluded that: (1) Birbrower was "not admitted to the practice of law in California"; (2) Birbrower "did not associate California counsel"; (3) Birbrower "provided legal services in this state"; and (4) "The law is clear that no one may recover compensation for services as an attorney in this state unless he or she was a member of the state bar at the time those services were performed."

Although the trial court's order stated that the fee agreements were unenforceable, at the hearing on the summary adjudication motion, the trial court also observed: "It seems to me that . . . if they aren't allowed to collect their attorney's fees here, I don't think that puts the attorneys in a position from being precluded from collecting all of their attorney's fees, only those fees probably that were generated by virtue of work that they performed in California and not that work that was performed in New York."

. . .

We granted review to determine whether Birbrower's actions and services performed while representing ESQ in California constituted the unauthorized practice of law under section 6125 and, if so, whether a section 6125 violation rendered the fee agreement wholly unenforceable.

II. DISCUSSION

A. The Unauthorized Practice of Law

The California Legislature enacted section 6125 in 1927 as part of the State Bar Act (the Act), a comprehensive scheme regulating the practice of law in the state. Since the Act's passage, the general rule has been that, although persons may represent themselves and their own interests regardless of State Bar membership, no one but an active member of the State Bar may practice law for another person in California. The prohibition against unauthorized law practice is . . . designed to ensure that those performing legal services do so competently.

. . .

Although the Act did not define the term "practice law," case law explained it as "'the doing and performing services in a court of justice in any matter depending therein throughout its various stages and in conformity with the adopted rules of procedure.'" [This court] included in its definition legal advice and legal instrument and contract preparation, whether or not these subjects were rendered in the course of litigation. [This court] later determined that the Legislature "accepted both the definition already judicially supplied for the term and the declaration of the Supreme Court that it had a sufficiently definite meaning to need no further definition. The definition . . . must be regarded as definitely establishing, for the jurisprudence of this state, the meaning of the term 'practice law.'"

In addition to not defining the term "practice law," the Act also did not define the meaning of "in California." In today's legal practice, questions often arise concerning whether the phrase refers to the nature of the legal services, or restricts the Act's application to those out-of-state attorneys who are physically present in the state.

Section 6125 has generated numerous opinions on the meaning of "practice law" but none on the meaning of "in California." In our view, the practice of law "in California" entails sufficient contact with the California client to render the nature of the legal service a clear legal representation. In addition to a quantitative analysis, we must consider the nature of the unlicensed lawyer's activities in the state. Mere fortuitous or attenuated contacts will not sustain a finding that the unlicensed lawyer practiced law "in California." The primary inquiry is whether the unlicensed lawyer engaged in sufficient activities in the state, or created a continuing relationship with the California client that included legal duties and obligations.

Our definition does not necessarily depend on or require the unlicensed lawyer's physical presence in the state. Physical presence here is one factor we may consider in deciding whether the unlicensed lawyer has violated section 6125, but it is by no means exclusive. For example, one may practice law in the state in violation of section 6125 although not physically present here by advising a California client on California law in connection with a California legal dispute by telephone, fax, computer, or other modern technological means. Conversely, although we decline to provide a comprehensive list of what activities constitute sufficient contact with the state, we do reject the notion that a person *automatically* practices law "in California" whenever that person practices California law anywhere, or "virtually" enters the state by telephone, fax, e-mail, or satellite. . . .

This interpretation acknowledges the tension that exists between interjurisdictional practice and the need to have a state-regulated bar. As stated in the American Bar Association Model Code of Professional Responsibility, Ethical Consideration EC 3-9, "Regulation of the practice of law is accomplished principally by the respective states. Authority to engage in the practice of law conferred in any jurisdiction is not per se a grant of the right to practice elsewhere, and it is improper for a lawyer to engage in practice where he is not permitted by law or by court order to do so. However, the demands of business and the mobility of our society pose distinct problems in the regulation of the practice of law by the states. In furtherance of the public interest, the legal profession should discourage regulation that unreasonably imposes territorial limitations upon the right of a lawyer to handle the legal affairs of his client or upon the opportunity of a client to obtain the services of a lawyer of his choice in all matters including the presentation of a contested matter in a tribunal before which the lawyer is not permanently admitted to practice."

. . .

Exceptions to section 6125 do exist, but are generally limited to allowing out-of-state attorneys to make brief appearances before a state court or tribunal. They are narrowly drawn and strictly interpreted . . . .

In addition, with the permission of the California court in which a particular cause is pending, out-of-state counsel may appear before a court as counsel pro hac vice. A court will approve a pro hac vice application only if the out-of-state attorney is a member in good standing of another state bar and is eligible to practice in any United States court or the highest court in another jurisdiction. The out-of-state attorney must also associate an active member of the California Bar as attorney of record and is subject to the Rules of Professional Conduct of the State Bar.

. . .

B. The Present Case

. . . As the Court of Appeal observed, Birbrower engaged in unauthorized law practice *in California* on more than a limited basis, and no firm attorney engaged in that practice was an active member of the California State Bar. As noted, in 1992 and 1993, Birbrower attorneys traveled to California to discuss with ESQ and others various matters pertaining to the dispute between ESQ and Tandem. Hobbs and Condon discussed strategy for resolving the dispute and advised ESQ on this strategy. Furthermore, during California meetings with Tandem representatives in August 1992, Hobbs demanded Tandem pay $15 million, and Condon told Tandem he believed damages in the matter would exceed that amount if the parties proceeded to litigation. Also in California, Hobbs met with ESQ for the stated purpose of helping to reach a settlement agreement and to discuss the agreement that was eventually proposed. Birbrower attorneys also traveled to California to initiate arbitration proceedings before the matter was settled. As the Court of Appeal concluded, " . . . the Birbrower firm's in-state activities clearly constituted the [unauthorized] practice of law" *in California.*

Birbrower contends, however, that section 6125 is not meant to apply to *any* out-of-state *attorneys*. Instead, it argues that the statute is intended solely to prevent nonattorneys from practicing law. This contention is without merit because it contravenes the plain language of the statute. Section 6125 clearly states that *no person* shall practice law in California unless that person is a member of the State Bar. The statute does not differentiate between attorneys or nonattorneys, nor does it excuse a person who is a member of another state bar. . . .

Birbrower next argues that we do not further the statute's intent and purpose — to protect California citizens from incompetent attorneys — by enforcing it against out-of-state attorneys. Birbrower argues that because out-of-state attorneys have been licensed to practice in other jurisdictions, they have already demonstrated sufficient competence to protect California clients. But Birbrower's argument overlooks the obvious fact that other states' laws may differ substantially from California law. Competence in one jurisdiction does not necessarily guarantee competence in another. By applying section 6125 to out-of-state attorneys who engage in the extensive practice of law in California without becoming licensed in our state, we serve the statute's goal of assuring the competence of all attorneys practicing law in this state.

. . .

Assuming that section 6125 does apply to out-of-state attorneys not licensed here, Birbrower alternatively asks us to create an exception to section 6125 for work incidental to private arbitration or other alternative dispute resolution proceedings. Birbrower points to fundamental differences between private arbitration and legal proceedings, including procedural differences relating to discovery, rules of evidence, compulsory process, cross-examination of witnesses, and other areas. As Birbrower observes, in light of these differences, at least one court has decided that an out-of-state attorney could recover fees for services rendered in an arbitration proceeding.

. . .

We decline Birbrower's invitation to craft an arbitration exception to section 6125's prohibition of the unlicensed practice of law in this state. Any exception for arbitration is best left to the Legislature, which has the authority to determine qualifications for admission to the State Bar and to decide what constitutes the practice of law. . . . In the face of the Legislature's silence, we will not create an arbitration exception under the facts presented.

Finally, Birbrower urges us to adopt an exception to section 6125 based on the unique circumstances of this case. Birbrower notes that "Multistate relationships are a common part of today's society and are to be dealt with in commonsense fashion." In many situations, strict adherence to rules prohibiting the unauthorized practice of law by out-of-state attorneys would be "'grossly impractical and inefficient.'"

Although . . . we recognize the need to acknowledge and, in certain cases, to accommodate the multistate nature of law practice, the facts here show that Birbrower's extensive activities within California amounted to considerably more than any of our state's recognized exceptions to section 6125 would allow. Accordingly, we reject Birbrower's suggestion that we except the firm from section 6125's rule under the circumstances here.

C. Compensation for Legal Services

Because Birbrower violated section 6125 when it engaged in the unlawful practice of law in California, the Court of Appeal found its fee agreement with ESQ unenforceable in its entirety. Without crediting Birbrower for some services performed in New York, for which fees were generated under the fee agreement, the court reasoned that the agreement was void and unenforceable because it included payment for services rendered to a California client in the state by an unlicensed out-of-state lawyer. . . . We agree with the Court of Appeal to the extent it barred Birbrower from recovering fees generated under the fee agreement for the unauthorized legal services it performed in California. We disagree with the same court to the extent it implicitly barred Birbrower from recovering fees generated under the fee agreement for the limited legal services the firm performed in New York.

It is a general rule that an attorney is barred from recovering compensation for services rendered in another state where the attorney was not admitted to the bar. The general rule, however, has some recognized exceptions.

[The court found that none of the recognized exceptions applied to Birbrower.]

Birbrower asserts that even if we agree with the Court of Appeal and find that none of the above exceptions allowing fees for unauthorized California services apply to the firm, it should be permitted to recover fees for those limited services it performed exclusively in *New York* under the agreement. In short, Birbrower seeks to recover under its contract for those services it performed for ESQ in New York that did not involve the practice of law in California, including fee contract negotiations and some corporate case research. Birbrower thus alternatively seeks reversal of the Court of Appeal's judgment to the extent it implicitly precluded the firm from seeking fees generated in New York under the fee agreement.

We agree with Birbrower that it may be able to recover fees under the fee agreement for the limited legal services it performed for ESQ in New York to the extent they did not constitute practicing law in California, even though those services were performed for a California client. Because section 6125 applies to the practice of law in California, it does not, in general, regulate law practice in other states. Thus, although the general rule against compensation to out-of-state attorneys precludes Birbrower's recovery under the fee agreement for its actions in California, the severability doctrine may allow it to receive its New York fees generated under the fee agreement, if we conclude the illegal portions of the agreement pertaining to the practice of law in California may be severed from those parts regarding services Birbrower performed in New York.

. . .

In this case, the parties entered into a contingency fee agreement followed by a fixed fee agreement. ESQ was to pay money to Birbrower in exchange for Birbrower's legal services. The object of their agreement may not have been entirely illegal, assuming ESQ was to pay Birbrower compensation based in part on work Birbrower performed in New York that did not amount to the practice of law in California. The illegality arises, instead, out of the amount to be paid to Birbrower, which, if paid fully, would include payment for services rendered in California in violation of section 6125.

Therefore, we conclude the Court of Appeal erred in determining that the fee agreement between the parties was entirely unenforceable because Birbrower violated section 6125's prohibition against the unauthorized practice of law in California. Birbrower's statutory violation may require exclusion of the portion of the fee attributable to the substantial illegal services, but that violation does not necessarily entirely preclude its recovery under the fee agreement for the limited services it performed outside California.

Thus, the portion of the fee agreement between Birbrower and ESQ that includes payment for services rendered in New York may be enforceable to the extent that the illegal compensation can be severed from the rest of the agreement. . . .

Post-Case Follow-Up

The *Birbrower* decision unsettled many lawyers who were already engaged in national and international cross-border practice, particularly given the court's expansive definition of practicing law *in California*. In the wake of the *Birbrower* decision, the ABA appointed the Multijurisdictional Practice (MJP) Commission in 2000 to study and report on the application of ABA ethics rules to multijurisdictional practice. Based on the MJP Commission's recommendations, in 2002 the ABA adopted amendments to Rule 5.5 that most states have adopted in some form.[38]

Rule 5.5(a) reiterates the fundamental principle that lawyers shall not practice law in a jurisdiction or assist another without being admitted to that jurisdiction's bar. Rule 5.5(b) prohibits lawyers from holding themselves out to others as being admitted to practice law or having an office or systemic presence in the jurisdiction for the practice of law. Rule 5.5(c) provides lawyers with four safe harbors to provide legal services on a temporary basis in jurisdictions where they are not admitted if (1) the non-admitted lawyer associates local counsel who actively participates in the matter; (2) the non-admitted lawyer's services are related to a pending or potential proceeding before a tribunal in which the lawyer is authorized or reasonably expects to be authorized to appear; (3) the services are reasonably related to a pending or potential arbitration, mediation, or other alternative dispute resolution proceeding and they arise out of or are reasonably related to the lawyer's practice in the jurisdiction in which he is admitted and do not require pro hac vice admission; and (4) the services are not covered by (c)(3) and (c)(4) but arise out of or are reasonably related to the lawyer's practice in the jurisdiction in which the lawyer is admitted.

Even after the changes to Rule 5.5, the extent to which a lawyer may practice law outside of her home state remains a gray area. Some situations are clear. First, a lawyer admitted in one state may not open an office in another state or engage in regular practice in that state without being admitted to practice law in that state. Second, lawyers in litigation matters can avoid a UPL claim by applying to a tribunal for pro hac vice status, a request to the court for authorization to represent a client in only the instant litigation before it. Once approved, the lawyer may engage in any activity a regularly admitted lawyer to the bar can undertake, for example, deposing witnesses and negotiating and drafting a contract or settlement related to the litigation.

There is no comparable procedure in transactional matters, however, and lawyers in non-litigation matters face uncertainty when they engage in practice across state lines. Under Model Rule 5.5(c)(4), these services are permissible if they are

38. Preface ABA Model Rules of Professional Conduct, ABA Compendium of Professional Responsibility Rules and Standards 7 (2015) (reporting the ABA also amended Rule 8.5). A total of 13 states have adopted a rule identical to Model Rule 5.5 and another 34 have adopted a similar rule or a total of 47 states have embraced or follow the amended version of Rule 5.5. State Implementation of ABA Model Rule 5.5. *See* ABA, CPR Policy Implementation Committee, *Variations of the ABA Model Rules of Professional Conduct, Rule 5.5: Unauthorized Practice of Law; Multijurisdictional Practice of Law* (Feb. 10, 2017), *available at* http://www.americanbar.org/content/dam/aba/administrative/professional_responsibility/mrpc_5_5.authcheckdam.pdf.

"reasonably related" to the lawyer's practice in his state of admission. The Restatement explains that several factors are relevant in determining that issue, including

> whether the lawyer's client is a regular client of the lawyer or, if a new client, is from the lawyer's home state, has extensive contacts with that state, or contacted the lawyer there; whether a multistate transaction has other significant connections with the lawyer's home state; whether significant aspects of the lawyer's activities are conducted in the lawyer's home state; whether a significant aspect of the matter involves the law of the lawyer's home state; and whether either the activities of the client involve multiple jurisdictions or the legal issues involved are primarily either multistate or federal in nature. Because lawyers in a firm often practice collectively, the activities of all lawyers in the representation of a client are relevant. The customary practices of lawyers who engage in interstate law practice is one appropriate measure of the reasonableness of a lawyer's activities out of state.[39]

Birbrower, Montalbano, Condon & Frank v. Superior Court: Real Life Applications

1. A Pennsylvania-licensed lawyer has an office in Philadelphia. New Jersey is right across the river from Philadelphia, and the lawyer periodically gets inquiries from New Jersey clients. May the lawyer see clients from New Jersey in his Philadelphia office and advise them on issues of New Jersey law? May the lawyer open an office in New Jersey to better serve these clients?

2. A lawyer is admitted to practice and has an office in New York, New York and practices in the area of trusts and estates. One of the lawyer's clients retires to Florida and calls the lawyer to request that she revise his will. The client also recommends his lawyer to his new neighbor in Florida, and the lawyer agrees to perform estate planning for the new client. Has the lawyer engaged in the unauthorized practice of law?

Chapter Summary

- Lawyers with managerial authority in a legal organization have a responsibility to create procedures, training programs, and reporting structures that promote compliance with ethical obligations by members of the organization.
- Supervisory lawyers will have vicarious responsibility for ethical missteps of subordinate lawyers if they order or ratify their conduct, or if they become aware of the conduct in time to prevent it and fail to do so.

---

39. Restatement §3 cmt. e.

- Professional independence of lawyers has manifold meanings, including independence from government control, independence from public opinion and prejudice, independence from third-party interference with the attorney-client relationship, and independence from one's own client.
- The Model Rules enforce professional independence from non-lawyers by prohibiting lawyers from going into business with non-lawyers, including prohibiting each of the following: multidisciplinary practice, fee-sharing with non-lawyers, and non-lawyer financial investments or direction of law firms.
- The Model Rules prohibit employment agreements that restrict a lawyer's ability to practice law; however, some jurisdictions allow reasonable restrictions on competition.
- A lawyer who is ceasing to practice law or to practice a particular area of law can sell that entire law practice or area of practice as long as certain conditions are met, including notice to affected clients.
- State law and the Model Rules generally prohibit non-lawyers from practicing law, though state definitions of the practice of law vary widely and are notoriously vague.

Applying the Rules

1. Shana works as a litigation associate at a boutique criminal defense firm. She is tasked with writing an appellate brief for a client convicted of first degree murder. In her draft brief, Shana cites and attempts to distinguish a prior decision of the state supreme court on an issue of law critical to the case. She provides the draft brief to the partner supervising the case. The partner provides her written feedback, suggesting that she delete the paragraph discussing the allegedly controlling precedent and stating that "we will distinguish that case at oral argument if the prosecutor relies on it in her brief." Shana disagrees with this recommendation by the partner. May she sign the brief?

2. You represent a claimant seeking social security benefits. The claimant was previously represented by an authorized non-attorney advocate. Upon completion of the representation, you are paid your fee, but are aware that the non-attorney advocate was not paid. You would like to give the non-attorney advocate the portion of the fee paid to you representing an appropriate amount for the non-attorney's initial work in the matter. Can you give the non-attorney advocate part of the fee? If not, do you have any other options to help the non-attorney receive her appropriate share?

3. Kyle is an attorney who is confused about a difficult area of procedural law. He asks Professor Robertson, his former Civil Procedure and Complex Litigation professor, for some guidance in handling the case. Professor Robertson — whose license is on inactive status in the jurisdiction — gives Kyle some very helpful

suggestions for how to properly move forward. Kyle recovers a substantial fee in the case. Can Kyle give part of it to Professor Robertson? Should Professor Robertson have helped out with the case? What if Kyle had hired Professor Robertson as a consulting expert rather than asking for assistance as a lawyer?

4. Assume that a business, Arrow Legal Services (Arrow), offers a Flat Fee Limited Scope (FFLS) program, like that discussed in Pennsylvania Bar Association Opinion 2016-200. Arrow reviews the Pennsylvania opinion and decides to alter its program. The fee charged to the client is still held by Arrow until completion of the services by the lawyer, but rather than depositing the money into the attorney's own operating account, Arrow deposits the fee into the lawyer's client trust account. Then Arrow deducts the marketing fee from the operating account. The business leaves it up to the lawyer to withdraw the "earned" fee from the client trust account. Has Arrow avoided violating the rules by making this change?

5. A Texas-licensed lawyer moved to Wisconsin and opened a Michigan office but was denied admission to the Wisconsin and Michigan bars. The attorney subsequently was admitted to practice in the U.S. District Court for the Western District of Michigan, where the local rule provides that "[a] person who is duly admitted to practice in a court of record of a state, and who is in active status and in good standing, may apply for admission to the bar of this Court. . . ." The lawyer limited his services to practicing law in federal court. Is he engaged in the unauthorized practice of law?

Professional Responsibility in Practice

1. Research whether the law in the state where you are planning to practice or are attending law school interprets Rule 5.6 to permit reasonable restrictions on lawyer practice and competition.

2. You are an associate in a law firm representing a corporation that is accused of fraud. You are responding to discovery and find a non-privileged document within the scope of the request that strongly indicates that your client is liable. You show the document to a partner who says, "Make that document go away." Consider how you should handle the situation. Draft an appropriate response to the partner.

3. Research the definition of "practice of law" and what activities constitute "unauthorized practice of law" in the jurisdiction where you plan to practice or are attending law school.

10

Marketing Legal Services

Lawyers need clients. Although lawyer marketing is often thought of as limited to personal injury lawyers making flashy television commercials, big firm lawyers also market their services through firm websites, blogs, and golf games with high-ranking corporate officers. In today's competitive legal market, moreover, lawyers in all areas of practice are taking advantage of new methods to market their services; in addition to websites and blogs, many lawyers use LinkedIn, Facebook, and Twitter, and some are even creating apps to attract clients.

The state bars have traditionally shown hostility to marketing, and, in the first half of the twentieth century, lawyer marketing was essentially prohibited. In a series of decisions beginning with Bates v. State Bar of Arizona, 433 U.S. 350 (1977), however, the United States Supreme Court recognized that attorney advertising deserves protection as commercial speech and struck down overly restrictive advertising rules under the First Amendment.

The Model Rules of Professional Conduct today largely reflect the balance struck by the Court: lawyers have the right to market themselves in a truthful, non-deceptive manner, but, in the interest of protecting the public and the reputation of lawyers, states can continue to regulate (and, in some cases, prohibit) marketing that presents a danger of "fraud, undue influence, intimidation, overreaching, and other forms of vexatious conduct."[1] This chapter considers the constitutional doctrine that creates the backdrop for the rules of professional conduct governing lawyer marketing as well as the rules themselves.

Key Concepts

- Rules governing lawyer marketing and their constitutional limits
- **Advertising** treated differently than **solicitation**
- The application of the rules of professional conduct to modern forms of marketing

1. Ohralik v. Ohio State Bar Ass'n, 436 U.S. 447, 462 (1978).

A. ADVERTISING VS. SOLICITATION

Outside of the legal world, solicitation is generally understood as a form of advertising, but the Model Rules distinguish "advertising" from "solicitation" and regulate them differently. Advertising generally refers to marketing that is directed to a broad audience, whereas solicitation is a "targeted communication initiated by the lawyer that is directed to a specific person. . . ." While Rule 7.3 (Solicitation of Clients) prohibits lawyers (with some limited exceptions) from soliciting clients by "in-person, live telephone or real-time electronic contact," lawyers may generally advertise their services, subject to a number of conditions, principally that the advertising cannot be "false or misleading." In considering situations involving lawyer marketing, you first need to decide whether the conduct is prohibited solicitation under Rule 7.3. If it is not, then you need to treat it as advertising and consider whether the marketing is permissible under the advertising rules.

B. REGULATION OF LAWYER ADVERTISING

In deciding how to market their services, lawyers must consult the rules of professional conduct in their jurisdiction. Those rules are shaped by four decades of Supreme Court decisions concerning the constitutionality of regulations governing lawyer marketing. This section considers that constitutional doctrine before turning to the rules governing lawyer advertising.

1. Constitutional Limits on the Bar's Power to Restrict Advertising

The 1908 ABA Canons reflected the organized bar's traditional attitude toward lawyer marketing: "It is unprofessional to solicit professional employment by circulars, advertisements, through touters or by personal communications or interviews not warranted by personal relations. Indirect advertisements for professional employment . . . and all other like self-laudation, offend the traditions and lower the tone of our profession and are reprehensible. . . ."[2] Proponents of restricting lawyer advertising typically argue that law is a "learned profession," not a trade or business, and that marketing demeans the reputation of the profession. In the first half of the twentieth century, lawyer advertising was prohibited.

In Bates v. State Bar of Arizona, 433 U.S. 350 (1977), however, the United States Supreme Court held for the first time that lawyer advertising is constitutionally protected commercial speech. The lawyers in *Bates* operated a low-cost legal clinic that offered routine legal services, such as uncontested divorces, uncontested adoptions, and simple personal bankruptcies. To support their practice, they placed an advertisement in a Phoenix newspaper stating that they offered "legal services at

---

2. MODEL CODE OF PROF'L RESPONSIBILITY CANON 27 (AM. BAR ASS'N 1908) (repealed 1963).

ADVERTISEMENT

DO YOU NEED A LAWYER?

LEGAL SERVICES AT VERY REASONABLE FEES

- **Divorce or legal separation--uncontested (both spouses sign papers)**

  $175.00 plus $20.00 court filing fee

- **Preparation of all court papers and instructions on how to do your own simple uncontested divorce**

  $100.00

- **Adoption--uncontested severance proceeding**

  $225.00 plus approximately $10.00 publication cost

- **Bankruptcy--non-business, no contested proceedings**

  Individual
  $250.00 plus $55.00 court filing fee

  Wife and Husband
  $300.00 plus $110.00 court filing fee

- **Change of Name**

  $95.00 plus $20.00 court filing fee

Information regarding other types of cases furnished on request

Legal Clinic of Bates & O'Steen
617 North 3rd Street
Phoenix, Arizona 85004
Telephone (502) 252-8838

This is the advertisement that led to the United States Supreme Court's seminal decision in Bates v. State Bar of Arizona, 433 U.S. 350 (1977).

very reasonable fees," and listed their fees for certain services. At that time, Arizona prohibited all lawyer advertising.[3] In a 5-4 decision, the Court struck down Arizona's ban as it applied to the lawyers' "truthful advertis[ing] concerning the availability and terms of routine legal services."[4]

In a series of cases following *Bates*, the Court offered further constitutional protection to lawyers using truthful, non-deceptive marketing to promote their qualifications. In each of these cases, the Court held that states' attempt to discipline lawyers for such advertising was unconstitutional under the First Amendment. In In re RMJ, 455 U.S. 191, 205-07 (1982), the Court held that a lawyer may advertise his areas of practice and where he is admitted to practice. In Peel v. Attorney Registration and Disciplinary Commission, 496 U.S. 91, 96, 110-11 (1990), the Court found that a lawyer's letterhead could state that he was a "Certified Civil Trial Specialist" by the National Board of Trial Advocacy. And in Ibanez v. Florida Department of Business and Professional Regulation, 512 U.S. 136, 143-49 (1994), the Court held that the lawyer could promote her practice by stating in her marketing materials that she was a CPA and certified financial planner.

In two other cases, the Supreme Court protected a lawyer's right to target his marketing to a particular group of clients with an identifiable legal problem. In Zauderer v. Office of Disciplinary Counsel, 471 U.S. 626, 630-31, 639-47 (1985), the Court upheld the constitutional right of a lawyer to run a newspaper ad announcing his willingness to represent women who had suffered injuries resulting from their use of a contraceptive known as the Dalkon Shield Intrauterine Device. The advertisement featured a drawing of the device and stated that the Dalkon Shield had generated a large amount of lawsuits and that women should not assume that their claims were time-barred.[5] In Shapero v. Kentucky Bar Ass'n, 486 U.S. 466, 477-78 (1988), the Court went even further in protecting lawyer marketing when it upheld the right of a lawyer to send direct mailings to potential clients who had foreclosure suits filed against them. The letter advised potential clients that "you may be about to lose your home"; "[f]ederal law may allow you to . . . ORDE[R] your creditor to STOP"; "you may call my office . . . for FREE information"; and "[i]t may surprise you what I may be able to do for you."[6] Since the letter did not constitute "face-to-face" communication, the Court treated it as advertising rather than solicitation and applied its commercial speech jurisprudence.[7] The Court held that the state could not categorically prohibit lawyers from soliciting business for pecuniary gain by sending truthful and non-deceptive letters to potential clients known to face particular legal problems.

The Supreme Court's latest opportunity to analyze the constitutionality of restrictions on lawyer marketing came in the 1995 case of *Florida Bar v. Went For It, Inc.*

3. *Bates*, 433 U.S. at 354-55.
4. *Id.* at 384.
5. *Id.* at 630-31.
6. *Id.* at 469.
7. *Id.* at 472-78.

Case Preview

Florida Bar v. Went For It, Inc.

State advertising rules vary widely. In 1990, the Florida Bar, which has been one of the most aggressive regulators of lawyer marketing, issued two novel rules that, in combination, prohibited plaintiffs' lawyers from contacting accident victims or their families for 30 days following the accident. In March 1992, lawyer G. Stewart McHenry, owner of a lawyer referral service called Went For It, Inc., brought suit to challenge the constitutionality of the regulation under the First Amendment.

The case is significant for at least three reasons. First, it serves as an example of the wide variety of ways in which states attempt to regulate lawyer advertising. Second, it illustrates the Court's most recent application of the commercial speech doctrine to lawyer advertising. Third, the majority opinion and dissent lay out some of the core policy arguments advanced on both sides of the lawyer advertising issue.

As you read the case, consider the following questions:

1. Is the direct mail at issue in this case "advertising" or "solicitation" within the meaning of the Model Rules?
2. What test does the Court apply to the advertising rule at issue, and how does the Court apply that test in this case?
3. What were the state interests that the Florida Bar was trying to protect?
4. How does the dissent differ from the majority concerning the policy behind this restriction on lawyer speech?

Florida Bar v. Went For It, Inc.

515 U.S. 618 (1995)

Justice O'Connor delivered the opinion of the Court.

Rules of the Florida Bar prohibit personal injury lawyers from sending targeted direct-mail solicitations to victims and their relatives for 30 days following an accident or disaster. This case asks us to consider whether such Rules violate the First and Fourteenth Amendments of the Constitution. We hold that in the circumstances presented here, they do not.

I

In 1989, the Florida Bar (Bar) completed a 2-year study of the effects of lawyer advertising on public opinion. After conducting hearings, commissioning surveys, and reviewing extensive public commentary, the Bar determined that several changes to its advertising rules were in order. In late 1990, the Florida Supreme Court adopted the Bar's proposed amendments with some modifications. . . . Two of these amendments are at issue in this case. Rule 4-7.4(b)(1) provides that "[a] lawyer shall not send, or knowingly permit to be sent, . . . a written communication to a prospective client

for the purpose of obtaining professional employment if: (A) the written communication concerns an action for personal injury or wrongful death or otherwise relates to an accident or disaster involving the person to whom the communication is addressed or a relative of that person, unless the accident or disaster occurred more than 30 days prior to the mailing of the communication." Rule 4-7.8(a) states that "[a] lawyer shall not accept referrals from a lawyer referral service unless the service: (1) engages in no communication with the public and in no direct contact with prospective clients in a manner that would violate the Rules of Professional Conduct if the communication or contact were made by the lawyer." Together, these Rules create a brief 30-day blackout period after an accident during which lawyers may not, directly or indirectly, single out accident victims or their relatives in order to solicit their business.

In March 1992, G. Stewart McHenry and his wholly owned lawyer referral service, Went For It, Inc., filed this action for declaratory and injunctive relief in the United States District Court for the Middle District of Florida challenging Rules 4-7.4(b)(1) and 4-7.8(a) as violative of the First and Fourteenth Amendments to the Constitution. . . .

The District Court . . . entered summary judgment for the plaintiffs. . . . The Eleventh Circuit affirmed. . . . We granted certiorari . . . and now reverse.

II

A

Constitutional protection for attorney advertising, and for commercial speech generally, is of recent vintage. Until the mid-1970's, we adhered to the broad rule . . . that, while the First Amendment guards against government restriction of speech in most contexts, "the Constitution imposes no such restraint on government as respects purely commercial advertising." In 1976, the Court changed course. In *Virginia Bd. of Pharmacy v. Virginia Citizens Consumer Council, Inc.* . . . we invalidated a state statute barring pharmacists from advertising prescription drug prices. At issue was speech that involved the idea that "'I will sell you the X prescription drug at the Y price.'" Striking the ban as unconstitutional, we rejected the argument that such speech "is so removed from 'any exposition of ideas,' and from 'truth, science, morality, and arts in general, in its diffusion of liberal sentiments on the administration of Government,' that it lacks all protection."

In *Bates v. State Bar of Arizona*, the Court struck a ban on price advertising for what it deemed "routine" legal services. . . . Expressing confidence that legal advertising would only be practicable for such simple, standardized services, the Court rejected the State's proffered justifications for regulation.

Nearly two decades of cases have built upon the foundation laid by *Bates*. It is now well established that lawyer advertising is commercial speech and, as such, is accorded a measure of First Amendment protection. . . . Such First Amendment protection, of course, is not absolute. We have always been careful to distinguish commercial speech from speech at the First Amendment's core. "'[C]ommercial speech [enjoys] a limited measure of protection, commensurate with its subordinate position in the scale of First Amendment values,' and is subject to 'modes of regulation that might be impermissible in the realm of noncommercial expression.'"

Mindful of these concerns, we engage in "intermediate" scrutiny of restrictions on commercial speech, analyzing them under the framework set forth in *Central Hudson Gas & Elec. Corp. v. Public Serv. Comm'n of N.Y.* Under *Central Hudson*, the government may freely regulate commercial speech that concerns unlawful activity or is misleading. Commercial speech that falls into neither of those categories, like the advertising at issue here, may be regulated if the government satisfies a test consisting of three related prongs: First, the government must assert a substantial interest in support of its regulation; second, the government must demonstrate that the restriction on commercial speech directly and materially advances that interest; and third, the regulation must be " 'narrowly drawn.' "

B

The Bar asserts that it has a substantial interest in protecting the privacy and tranquility of personal injury victims and their loved ones against intrusive, unsolicited contact by lawyers. . . . Because direct-mail solicitations in the wake of accidents are perceived by the public as intrusive, the Bar argues, the reputation of the legal profession in the eyes of Floridians has suffered commensurately. The regulation, then, is an effort to protect the flagging reputations of Florida lawyers by preventing them from engaging in conduct that, the Bar maintains, " 'is universally regarded as deplorable and beneath common decency because of its intrusion upon the special vulnerability and private grief of victims or their families.' "

We have little trouble crediting the Bar's interest as substantial. . . .

Under *Central Hudson's* second prong, the State must demonstrate that the challenged regulation "advances the Government's interest 'in a direct and material way.' " . . . That burden, we have explained, " 'is not satisfied by mere speculation or conjecture; rather, a governmental body seeking to sustain a restriction on commercial speech must demonstrate that the harms it recites are real and that its restriction will in fact alleviate them to a material degree.' " In *Edenfield*, the Court invalidated a Florida ban on in-person solicitation by certified public accountants (CPA's). We observed that the State Board of Accountancy had "present[ed] no studies that suggest personal solicitation of prospective business clients by CPA's creates the dangers of fraud, overreaching, or compromised independence that the Board claims to fear." Moreover, "[t]he record [did] not disclose any anecdotal evidence, either from Florida or another State, that validate[d] the Board's suppositions. . . ." Finding nothing in the record to substantiate the State's allegations of harm, we invalidated the regulation.

The direct-mail solicitation regulation before us does not suffer from such infirmities. The Bar submitted a 106-page summary of its 2-year study of lawyer advertising and solicitation to the District Court. That summary contains data—both statistical and anecdotal—supporting the Bar's contentions that the Florida public views direct-mail solicitations in the immediate wake of accidents as an intrusion on privacy that reflects poorly upon the profession. As of June 1989, lawyers mailed 700,000 direct solicitations in Florida annually, 40% of which were aimed at accident victims or their survivors. A survey of Florida adults commissioned by the Bar indicated that Floridians "have negative feelings about those attorneys who use direct mail advertising." Fifty-four percent of the general population surveyed said that contacting persons concerning accidents or similar events is a violation of privacy. A random sampling of persons who received direct-mail advertising from lawyers in 1987 revealed that 45% believed that direct-mail solicitation is "designed to take advantage of gullible or unstable people"; 34% found such tactics "annoying or irritating"; 26% found it "an invasion of your privacy"; and 24% reported that it "made you angry." Significantly, 27% of direct-mail recipients reported that their regard for the legal profession and for the judicial process as a whole was "lower" as a result of receiving the direct mail. . . .

In light of this showing . . . we conclude that the Bar has satisfied the second prong of the *Central Hudson* test.

In reaching a contrary conclusion, the Court of Appeals determined that this case was governed squarely by *Shapero v. Kentucky Bar Assn.* Making no mention of the Bar's study, the court concluded that "'a targeted letter [does not] invade the recipient's privacy any more than does a substantively identical letter mailed at large. The invasion, if any, occurs when the lawyer discovers the recipient's legal affairs, not when he confronts the recipient with the discovery.'" In many cases, the Court of Appeals explained, "this invasion of privacy will involve no more than reading the newspaper."

While some of *Shapero*'s language might be read to support the Court of Appeals' interpretation, *Shapero* differs in several fundamental respects from the case before us. First and foremost, *Shapero*'s treatment of privacy was casual. . . . Second, in contrast to this case, *Shapero* dealt with a broad ban on all direct-mail solicitations, whatever the time frame and whoever the recipient. Finally, the State in *Shapero* assembled no evidence attempting to demonstrate any actual harm caused by targeted direct mail. The Court rejected the State's effort to justify a prophylactic ban on the basis of blanket, untested assertions of undue influence and overreaching. Because the State did not make a privacy-based argument at all, its empirical showing on that issue was similarly infirm. . . .

Here . . . the harm targeted by the Bar cannot be eliminated by a brief journey to the trash can. The purpose of the 30-day targeted direct-mail ban is to forestall the outrage and irritation with the state-licensed legal profession that the practice of direct solicitation only days after accidents has engendered. The Bar is concerned not with citizens' "offense" in the abstract, but with the demonstrable detrimental effects that such "offense" has on the profession it regulates. Moreover, the harm posited by the Bar is as much a function of simple receipt of targeted solicitations within days of accidents as it is a function of the letters' contents. Throwing the letter away shortly after opening it may minimize the latter intrusion, but it does little to combat the former. . . .

Passing to *Central Hudson*'s third prong, we examine the relationship between the Bar's interests and the means chosen to serve them. With respect to this prong, the differences between commercial speech and noncommercial speech are manifest. [T]he "least restrictive means" test has no role in the commercial speech context. "What our decisions require," instead, "is a 'fit' between the legislature's ends and the means chosen to accomplish those ends, a fit that is not necessarily perfect, but reasonable; that represents not necessarily the single best disposition but one whose scope is 'in proportion to the interest served,' that employs not necessarily the least restrictive means but . . . a means narrowly tailored to achieve the desired objective. . . ."

We are not persuaded by respondents' allegations of constitutional infirmity. . . . Rather than drawing difficult lines on the basis that some injuries are "severe" and some situations appropriate (and others, presumably, inappropriate) for grief, anger, or emotion, the Bar has crafted a ban applicable to all postaccident or disaster solicitations for a brief 30-day period. Unlike respondents, we do not see "numerous and obvious less-burdensome alternatives" to Florida's short temporal ban. The Bar's rule is reasonably well tailored to its stated objective of eliminating targeted mailings whose type and timing are a source of distress to Floridians, distress that has caused many of them to lose respect for the legal profession.

III

Speech by professionals obviously has many dimensions. There are circumstances in which we will accord speech by attorneys on public issues and matters of legal representation the strongest protection our Constitution has to offer. This case, however, concerns pure commercial advertising, for which we have always reserved a lesser degree of protection under the First Amendment. Particularly because the standards and conduct of state-licensed lawyers have traditionally been subject to extensive regulation by the States, it is all the more appropriate that we limit our scrutiny of state regulations to a level commensurate with the " 'subordinate position' " of commercial speech in the scale of First Amendment values.

We believe that the Bar's 30-day restriction on targeted direct-mail solicitation of accident victims and their relatives withstands scrutiny under the three-pronged *Central Hudson* test that we have devised for this context. The Bar has substantial interest both in protecting injured Floridians from invasive conduct by lawyers and in preventing the erosion of confidence in the profession that such repeated invasions have engendered. The Bar's proffered study, unrebutted by respondents below, provides evidence indicating that the harms it targets are far from illusory. The palliative devised by the Bar to address these harms is narrow both in scope and in duration. The Constitution, in our view, requires nothing more.

The judgment of the Court of Appeals, accordingly, is Reversed.

Justice KENNEDY, with whom Justice STEVENS, Justice SOUTER, and Justice GINSBURG join, dissenting.

Attorneys who communicate their willingness to assist potential clients are engaged in speech protected by the First and Fourteenth Amendments. That principle has been understood since *Bates*. The Court today undercuts this guarantee in an important class of cases and unsettles leading First Amendment precedents, at the expense of those victims most in need of legal assistance. With all respect for the Court, in my view its solicitude for the privacy of victims and its concern for our profession are misplaced and self-defeating, even upon the Court's own premises.

I take it to be uncontroverted that when an accident results in death or injury, it is often urgent at once to investigate the occurrence, identify witnesses, and preserve evidence. Vital interests in speech and expression are, therefore, at stake when by law an attorney cannot direct a letter to the victim or the family explaining this simple fact and offering competent legal assistance. Meanwhile, represented and better informed parties, or parties who have been solicited in ways more sophisticated and indirect, may be at work. Indeed, these parties, either themselves or by their attorneys, investigators, and adjusters, are free to contact the unrepresented persons to gather evidence or offer settlement. This scheme makes little sense. As is often true when the law makes little sense, it is not first principles but their interpretation and application that have gone awry.

Although I agree with the Court that the case can be resolved by following the three-part inquiry we have identified to assess restrictions on commercial speech, a preliminary observation is in order. Speech has the capacity to convey complex substance, yielding various insights and interpretations depending upon the identity of the listener or the reader and the context of its transmission. It would oversimplify to say that what we consider here is commercial speech and nothing more, for in many instances the banned communications may be vital to the recipients' right to petition the courts for redress of grievances. The complex nature of expression is one reason why even so-called commercial speech has become an essential part of the public discourse the First Amendment secures. If our commercial speech rules are to control this case, then, it is imperative to apply them with exacting care and fidelity to our precedents, for what is at stake is the suppression of information and knowledge that transcends the financial self-interests of the speaker. . . .

[T]he State and the opinion of the Court [emphasize the importance of] protecting the reputation and dignity of the legal profession. The argument is, it seems fair to say, that all are demeaned by the crass behavior of a few. . . . While disrespect will arise from an unethical or improper practice, the majority begs a most critical question by assuming that direct-mail solicitations constitute such a practice. The fact is, however, that direct solicitation may serve vital purposes and promote the administration of justice, and to the extent the bar seeks to protect lawyers' reputations by preventing them from engaging in speech some deem offensive, the State is doing nothing more . . . than manipulating the public's opinion by suppressing speech that informs us how the legal system works. The disrespect argument thus proceeds from the very assumption it tries to prove, which is to say that solicitations within 30 days serve no legitimate purpose. This, of course, is censorship pure and simple; and censorship is antithetical to the first principles of free expression. . . .

Even were the interests asserted substantial, the regulation here fails the second part of the *Central Hudson* test, which requires that the dangers the State seeks to eliminate be real and that a speech restriction or ban advance that asserted state interest in a direct and material way. . . .

It is telling that the essential thrust of all the material adduced to justify the State's interest is devoted to the reputational concerns of the Bar. It is not at all clear that this regulation advances the interest of protecting persons who are suffering trauma and grief, and we are cited to no material in the record for that claim. . . .

Were it appropriate to reach the third part of the *Central Hudson* test, it would be clear that the relationship between the Bar's interests and the means chosen to serve them is not a reasonable fit. The Bar's rule creates a flat ban that prohibits far more speech than necessary to serve the purported state interest. . . .

The accident victims who are prejudiced to vindicate the State's purported desire for more dignity in the legal profession will be the very persons who most need legal advice, for they are the victims who, because they lack education, linguistic ability, or familiarity with the legal system, are unable to seek out legal services. . . .

The reasonableness of the State's chosen methods for redressing perceived evils can be evaluated, in part, by a commonsense consideration of other possible means of regulation that have not been tried. Here, the Court neglects the fact that this problem is largely self-policing: Potential clients will not hire lawyers who offend them. And even if a person enters into a contract with an attorney and later regrets it, Florida, like some other States, allows clients to rescind certain contracts with attorneys within a stated time after they are executed. . . . The State's restriction deprives accident victims of information which may be critical to their right to make a claim for compensation for injuries. The telephone book and general advertisements may serve this purpose in part; but the direct solicitation ban will fall on those who most need legal representation: for those with minor injuries, the victims too ill informed to know an attorney may be interested in their cases; for those with serious injuries, the victims too ill informed to know that time is of the essence if counsel is to assemble evidence and warn them not to enter into settlement negotiations or evidentiary discussions with investigators for opposing parties. . . . The very fact that some 280,000 direct-mail solicitations are sent to accident victims and their survivors in Florida each year is some indication of the efficacy of this device. . . .

It is most ironic that, for the first time since *Bates*, the Court now orders a major retreat from the constitutional guarantees for commercial speech in order to shield its own profession from public criticism. Obscuring the financial aspect of the legal profession from public discussion through direct-mail solicitation, at the expense of the least sophisticated members of society, is not a laudable constitutional goal. There is no authority for the proposition that the Constitution permits the State to promote the public image of the legal profession by suppressing information about the profession's business aspects. If public respect for the profession erodes because solicitation distorts the idea of the law as most lawyers see it, it must be remembered that real progress begins with more rational speech, not less. . . .

Post-Case Follow-Up

In *Went For It*, the Court held that Florida's 30-day blackout period on direct mail solicitation by plaintiffs' attorneys does not violate the First Amendment. Applying its commercial speech doctrine, the Court recognized the Florida Bar's substantial interest in protecting the privacy of personal injury victims and the reputation of Florida lawyers. Moreover, the Court found that the 30-day blackout period "advances the Government's interest in a direct and material way" relying primarily on evidence that the Florida Bar accumulated during a two-year study of lawyer marketing. Finally, the Court held that there is a "fit" between the bar's goals and the means chosen to accomplish its goals. Although the Model Rules do not contain a 30-day blackout period, a few other states — including New York and Louisiana — have adopted similar rules.

Did *Went For It* Go Too Far With It?

Do you think the Court gave undue weight to the report submitted by the Florida Bar? Consider this: less than one-third of the pages in the report mentioned targeted, direct-mail solicitations. Further, the report contained few quotes that supported lawyer advertising or direct-mail solicitations, and the ones it did include were not flattering, for example: "The issue is, don't we all — even attorneys — have the constitutional right to make ourselves look trashy . . . ?" and "The Supreme Court said lawyers can advertise. There's no reason to treat our ads differently than those of the lottery or race tracks or banks." Douglas W. Swalina, Note, *The Florida Bar Went for It, But It Went Too Far*, 26 Stetson L. Rev. 437, 461 n.142 (1996).

The dissent took issue with the report, calling it "noteworthy for its incompetence" and stating that *Central Hudson* required "more than a few pages of self-serving and unsupported statements by the State." Florida Bar v. Went For It, Inc., 515 U.S. 618, 640-41 (1995) (Kennedy, J., dissenting).

Finally, look again at Justice O'Connor's description of the report and the statistics that she quotes — do they really support the majority's conclusion?

The Supreme Court has not revisited the topic of lawyer advertising since *Went For It*, and the Court's decision leaves some significant unanswered questions. In particular, what other types of limited restrictions on lawyer advertising might the Court find constitutional?

Florida Bar v. Went For It, Inc.: Real Life Applications

1. A state bar association is considering a new rule that would prohibit lawyers from sending "written or electronic solicitations to accident victims and their relatives for 60 days following an accident or disaster." You serve on the state's ethics committee. What would you advise the state bar?
2. A state rule provides: "All advertisements shall be predominantly informational. No drawings, animations, dramatizations, music, or lyrics shall be used in connection with televised advertising. No advertisement shall rely in any way on techniques to obtain attention that depend upon absurdity and that demonstrate a clear and intentional lack of relevance to the selection of counsel; included in this category are all advertisements that contain any extreme portrayal of counsel exhibiting characteristics clearly unrelated to legal competence."[8] Is this provision constitutional?

---

2. Rules Governing Advertising

The restrictions on advertising contained in the Model Rules of Professional Conduct reflect the balance struck by the Supreme Court: lawyers have the right to market themselves in a truthful, non-deceptive manner, even if those advertisements strike other lawyers or the public as crass or distasteful. *See* Model Rule 7.2 cmt. 3 ("Questions of effectiveness and taste in advertising are matters of speculation and subjective judgment."). This section discusses the most common pitfalls lawyers face in marketing themselves.

8. N.J. R. Prof. Conduct 7.2(a).

False or Misleading Advertising

The primary rule of thumb is that lawyer marketing may not be "false or misleading." *See* Model Rule 7.1. Thus, lawyers can be disciplined for advertising that is truthful but nevertheless misleading. The advertising rules would be much simpler if regulators stopped there, but the Model Rules (and all state rules) instead contain much more detailed requirements. Many of these rules are simply specific applications of the ban on "false or misleading" advertising.

The prohibition on false advertising is straightforward, but understanding the prohibition on "misleading" communications is more difficult. The comments to Rule 7.1 shed some light on this standard. A truthful statement is misleading "if it omits a fact necessary to make the lawyer's communication considered as a whole not materially misleading." Similarly, a truthful statement is "misleading if there is a substantial likelihood that it will lead a reasonable person to formulate a specific conclusion about the lawyer or the lawyer's services for which there is no reasonable factual foundation."

Deciding whether a particular advertisement is misleading must be done on a case-by-case basis, but there are several recurring situations in which lawyers have run into trouble. First, lawyers who compare themselves to other lawyers need to be very careful. Model Rule 7.1 comment 3 states that "an unsubstantiated comparison of the lawyer's services or fees with the services or fees of other lawyers may be misleading if presented with such specificity as would lead a reasonable person to conclude that the comparison can be substantiated." Thus, a lawyer probably cannot claim that he is "the best trial lawyer in town."[9]

Second, lawyers may not promise future results. Some states have even enacted specific prohibitions against this kind of marketing. In Public Citizen, Inc. v. Louisiana Attorney Disciplinary Board, 632 F.3d 212, 218 (5th Cir. 2011), the Fifth Circuit upheld Louisiana's rule barring communications that "promise results" because "[a] promise that a party will prevail in a future case is necessarily false and deceptive. No attorney can guarantee future results."

A third potential way in which lawyers can violate the prohibition on misleading advertising is by marketing past successes. Although the Model Rules do not specifically ban such advertising, Rule 7.1 comment 3 states: "An advertisement that truthfully reports a lawyer's achievements on behalf of clients or former clients may be misleading if presented so as to lead a reasonable person to form an unjustified expectation that the same results could be obtained for other clients in similar matters without reference to the specific factual and legal circumstances of each client's case." Again, some states have enacted specific bans on such marketing. First Amendment challenges to such bans have led to mixed results. In In re Frank, 440 N.E.2d 676, 676-77 (Ind. 1982), for example, the lawyer obtained the names of individuals who had been charged with drunk driving but had no attorney and sent them letters in which he described "his successful experience in plea bargaining such cases." The court held that his conduct "serves to unduly influence the legally

9. *See* Medina Cty. Bar Ass'n v. Grieselhuber, 678 N.E.2d 535, 537 (1997) (disciplining a lawyer for advertising "We Do It Well" because it was an unverifiable and misleading claim).

unsophisticated persons into believing that [they] could and would get a favorable resolution of their case."[10] More recently, however, in *Rubenstein v. Florida Bar*, a Florida district court struck down a Florida advertising rule that banned lawyers from advertising their past success in indoor or outdoor displays, on television, and in radio commercials. Although the court recognized that the state has substantial interests in regulating lawyer advertising (including protection of the public), the court found that completely banning lawyers from sharing truthful information did not advance those interests.[11] The Fifth Circuit reached the same conclusion concerning a Louisiana rule that "prohibit[ed] communications that contain a reference or testimonial to past successes or results obtained except" when provided in response to a client request.[12]

Fourth, lawyers need to be careful about using nicknames, which states have tried to limit with a number of different justifications. In Florida Bar v. Pape, 918 So. 2d 240 (2005), the Florida Supreme Court held that a lawyer's use of a pit bull logo and the telephone number 1-800-PIT-BULL violated Florida's prohibition on depictions that are "deceptive, misleading, or manipulative." The court said that these "advertising devices would suggest to many persons not only that the lawyers can achieve results but also that they can engage in a combative style of advocacy. The suggestion is inherently deceptive because there is no way to measure whether the attorneys in fact conduct themselves like pit bulls so as to ascertain whether this logo and phone number convey accurate information." Accordingly, the court concluded that the nickname is misleading because it is not objectively verifiable. The court rejected the lawyer's First Amendment challenge to these prohibitions.[13]

The Louisiana Bar has also taken a dim view of nicknames. In its *Handbook on Lawyer Advertising and Solicitation*,[14] the bar has created examples of complying and noncomplying advertisements. As the ad on the following page demonstrates, the Louisiana Bar believes that the nickname "The Golden Retriever" "implies an ability to obtain results" in violation of Rule 7.1.[15]

The Fifth Circuit has upheld Louisiana's ban on communications that "utilize[] a nickname, moniker, motto or trade name that states or implies an ability to obtain results in a matter."[16]

On the other hand, several courts and ethics opinions have concluded that lawyers may tout their selection by ratings services such as Super Lawyers, Best Lawyers in America, and Martindale-Hubbell. For example, Super Lawyers are nominated and voted on by other lawyers. The company also does independent

---

10. 440 N.E.2d 676, 676-77 (Ind. 1982).
11. Rubenstein v. Florida Bar, 72 F. Supp. 3d 1298, 1315-17 (S.D. Fla. 2014). Florida was the only state to ban such advertising.
12. *Public Citizen, Inc.*, 632 F.3d at 217, 221-23.
13. 918 So. 2d 240, 244, 247-49 (2005).
14. Louisiana State Bar Ass'n Rules of Prof'l Conduct Comm., Handbook on Lawyer Advertising and Solicitation (2008), http://files.lsba.org/documents/LawyerAdvertising/LawyerAdHandbook.pdf.
15. *Id.* at 42.
16. *Public Citizen, Inc.*, 632 F.3d 212, 224-27. In contrast, the Second Circuit struck down New York's similar rule. *See* Alexander v. Cahill, 598 F.3d 79, 94-95 (2d Cir. 2010).

Injured in an Accident?

Tired of Being Dogged by Insurance Adjusters?

Others Telling You Your Case is Just Another Dog with Fleas?

Call Me…
"The Golden Retriever" ❶

I'll Run Fast, Sniff Around and Bring Back Gold!! ❷
"No Gold, No Fee Guarantee" ❸

(225) 555-4321
Baton Rouge, Louisiana*

"The Golden Retriever" ❶
D. Elmer Fudd, Attorney At Law
Practice Limited to Personal Injury Matters
Loyal, Honest and Friendly
I'm The Most Ethical Lawyer in Town ❹

*Office Closed During Duck Season

❶ When viewed in conjunction with the balance of the advertisement, the nickname/trade name states or implies an ability to obtain results. Rule 7.2(c)(1)(L).

❷ Promises results. Rule 7.2(c)(1)(E).

❸ Contains Information about fees but fails to disclose whether client will be liable for any costs and/or expenses in addition to any fee. Rule 7.2(c)(6).

❹ Last statement compares the lawyer's services with other lawyers' services with a comparison that cannot be factually substantiated. Rule 7.2(c)(1)(G).

This fake advertisement appears in the Louisiana Bar's *Handbook on Lawyer Advertising and Solicitation* to show lawyers examples of complying and noncomplying advertisements.

research. In the end, only 5 percent of lawyers are selected to be Super Lawyers.[17] The title "Super Lawyer" (like Pit Bull or Golden Retriever) may be misleading in the sense that the lawyer does not actually wear a cape and fly around. Calling oneself a "Super Lawyer" also might tend to imply an ability to obtain results, but authorities considering the title have concluded that it is permissible provided that lawyers who tout this achievement provide sufficient context — "the lawyer's advertising must state accurately the publication by which he or she was ranked, the year of the ranking, and the field of the ranking, if one was specified."[18] In that sense, it is distinguishable from Florida's "Pit Bull" and Louisiana's "Golden Retriever."

17. *Selection Process*, Super Lawyers, http://www.superlawyers.com/about/selection_process.html (last visited Mar. 19, 2017).
18. Alaska Bar Association, Op. 2009-2 (2009).

Specialization

Model Rules 7.4 and 7.5 represent specific applications of Rule 7.1's prohibition on advertising that is false or misleading. Consistent with *Peel*, *R.M.J.*, and *Ibanez*, in which the Supreme Court recognized lawyers' constitutional right to market themselves in truthful, non-deceptive ways, Rule 7.4 permits a lawyer to "communicate the fact that the lawyer does or does not practice in particular fields of law," but lawyers need to be careful if they go beyond that and claim to be an expert or specialist in a particular field. Concerned that the public will misunderstand the basis for such claims, Rule 7.4(d) states that a "lawyer shall not state or imply that a lawyer is certified as a specialist in a particular field of law, unless (1) the lawyer has been certified as a specialist by an organization that has been approved by an appropriate state authority or that has been accredited by the American Bar Association; and (2) the name of the certifying organization is clearly identified in the communication." Some state ethics opinions have concluded that the term "expert" should receive the same treatment as the term "specialist."[19]

Rule 7.4(b) and (c) carves out two specific exceptions: a lawyer who is admitted to the United States Patent and Trademark Bar may state that he is a "Patent Attorney" (7.4(b)) and a lawyer engaged in Admiralty practice may describe herself as a "Proctor in Admiralty" or similar designation (7.4(c)). But under the Model Rules, a lawyer generally may not state that he is a criminal law (or family law or tort law) specialist absent certification by an approved organization.

Trade Names

Rule 7.5 generally proscribes law firm names that are misleading in violation of Rule 7.1. In addition, the rule specifically prohibits law firms from using a "trade name" if it "impl[ies] a connection with a government agency or with a public or charitable legal services organization." For example, a law firm located across from a university may not call itself "University Law Firm" if it has no connection with the university.

Required Disclosures

Finally, the Supreme Court has said that states may require lawyers to provide some additional information in their advertisements "as long as disclosure requirements are reasonably related to the State's interest in preventing deception of consumers."[20] Given this leeway by the Court, states impose a wide variety of requirements. The Model Rules impose two. First, Rule 7.2(c) requires that lawyer advertising "include the name and office address of at least one lawyer or law firm responsible for its content." Second, Rule 7.3(c) provides that "[e]very written, recorded or electronic communication . . . soliciting professional employment from anyone

---

19. *See, e.g.*, Connecticut Bar Association, Op. 05-18 (2005).
20. Zauderer v. Office of Disciplinary Counsel, 471 U.S. 626, 651 (1985).

known to be in need of legal services in a particular matter" must "include the words 'Advertising Material' . . . ."

3. Social Media and Other Forms of Electronic Advertising

In today's competitive market, lawyers are increasingly turning to social media and other electronic forms of marketing. According to the 2016 ABA Legal Technology Survey Report, 76 percent of lawyers use social media for professional purposes, with 73 percent of those lawyers reporting that they do so for career development and networking.[21] Lawyers use websites, blogs, and social media sites such as LinkedIn, Facebook, and Twitter to market themselves and their practices.

In some cases, applying the advertising rules to online marketing is simple: just like traditional advertising, online advertising cannot be false or misleading, and it must also follow the other rules outlined in the previous section. But social media marketing also raises some novel issues, and relatively little authority addresses those issues.

Do the Advertising Rules Apply to Social Media?

A threshold issue is whether a lawyer's web presence constitutes advertising covered by the rules. Comment 1 to Rule 7.1 states that the rule governs "all communications about a lawyer's services." According to a 2010 ABA Ethics Opinion, standard lawyer websites that provide biographical information about lawyers do constitute "communication about the lawyer or the lawyer's services" within the meaning of Rule 7.1 and are therefore subject to the advertising rules.[22] Social media, however, is a gray area. A 2012 California Ethics Opinion is one of the only authorities to analyze this precise issue.

Social Networking

State Bar of California Standing Committee on Professional Responsibility and Conduct Formal Opinion 2012-186 (2012)[23]

Consider the following examples of Attorney's use of personal social media sites for status postings which are visible to all of her "friends," "connections," or "followers" (although not to the public at large):

Example Number 1: "Case finally over. Unanimous verdict! Celebrating tonight."

---

21. Allison Shields, *Social Media*, *in* ABA TECHREPORT 2016 (2016), http://www.americanbar.org/publications/techreport/2016/social_media_blogging.html.

22. *See* ABA Formal Op. 10-457 (2010), http://www.americanbar.org/content/dam/aba/migrated/2011_build/professional_responsibility/ethics_opinion_10_457.authcheckdam.pdf.

23. Available at http://www.calbar.ca.gov/Portals/0/documents/ethics/Opinions/CAL%202012-186%20%2812-21-12%29.pdf The California rules define "communications" subject to the advertising rules as "any message or offer made by or on behalf of a member concerning the availability for professional employment of a member or a law firm directed to any former, present, or prospective client. . . ." CAL. R. PROF'L CONDUCT 1-400(A).

In the Committee's opinion, this statement, standing alone, is not [subject to the advertising rules] because it is not a message or offer "concerning the availability for professional employment," whatever Attorney's subjective motive for sending it. Attorney status postings that simply announce recent victories without an accompanying offer about the availability for professional employment generally will not qualify as a communication.

> Example Number 2: "Another great victory in court today! My client is delighted. Who wants to be next?"

Similarly, the statement "Another great victory in court today!" standing alone is not a communication [subject to the advertising rules] because it is not a message or offer "concerning the availability for professional employment." However, the addition of the text, "[w]ho wants to be next?" [does constitute advertising] because it suggests availability for professional employment. . . .

> Example Number 3: "Won a million dollar verdict. Tell your friends to check out my website."

In the Committee's opinion, this language also qualifies as [an advertisement subject to the rules] because the words "tell your friends to check out my website," in this context, convey a message or offer "concerning the availability for professional employment." It appears that Attorney is asking the reader to tell others to look at her website so that they may consider hiring her. . . .

> Example Number 4: "Won another personal injury case. Call me for a free consultation."

Again, the Committee concludes that this posting is [advertising] due primarily to the second sentence.

[An advertisement] has to include an offer about availability for professional employment so the "free" consultation language at first might indicate the posting is not [an advertisement]. Yet the rule does not limit "communications" to messages seeking financial compensation for services. To the contrary, a communication includes any "message or offer made by or on behalf of a member concerning the availability for professional employment of a member or a law firm." . . . An offer of a free consultation is a step toward securing potential employment, and the offer of a free consultation indicates that the lawyer is available to be hired. On balance, this example in the Committee's opinion constitutes [advertising].

> Example Number 5: "Just published an article on wage and hour breaks. Let me know if you would like a copy."

In this instance, we believe the statement does not concern "availability for professional employment." The attorney is merely relaying information regarding an article that she has published, and is offering to provide copies. . . .

In its opinion, the California Bar's determination of whether a social media item constitutes advertising within the meaning of the rules turns on whether the post includes an offer from the lawyer concerning her availability for professional employment. The Florida Bar has come to the same conclusion: "Pages appearing on networking sites that are used to promote the lawyer or law firm's practice are subject to the lawyer advertising rules."[24]

Unique Dangers of Social Media and Other Forms of Electronic Advertising

If the Internet content is subject to the advertising rules, then the lawyer must, of course, ensure that the content complies with all of the advertising rules that would apply to traditional marketing. But social media and other forms of electronic advertising, such as websites and blogs, also pose some unique dangers.

A central concern is that social media and other forms of electronic advertising often enable third parties to post content on the lawyer's website (or blog or social media posting). Are lawyers responsible for content created by others? In other words, if a third party posts content on a lawyer's Avvo page and that content would violate the rules if the lawyer posted it herself, is the lawyer subject to discipline? In a 2010 ethics opinion, the South Carolina Ethics Advisory Committee concluded that once a lawyer "claims" his website listing, he is "responsible for conforming all information in the . . . listing to the Rules of Professional Conduct. . . . [A] lawyer should monitor a 'claimed' listing to keep all comments in conformity with the Rules. If any part of the listing cannot be conformed to the Rules (e.g., if an improper comment cannot be removed), the lawyer should remove his or her entire listing and discontinue participation in the service."[25] The New York State Bar Association's Social Media Committee reached the same conclusion:

> A lawyer is responsible for all content that the lawyer posts on her social media website or profile. A lawyer also has a duty to periodically monitor her social media profile(s) or blog(s) for comments, endorsements and recommendations to ensure that such third-party posts do not violate ethics rules. If a person who is not an agent of the lawyer unilaterally posts content to the lawyer's social media, profile or blog that violates the ethics rules, the lawyer must remove or hide such content if such removal is within the lawyer's control and, if not within the lawyer's control, she must ask that person to remove it. . . .
>
> A lawyer must ensure the accuracy of third-party legal endorsements, recommendations, or online reviews posted to the lawyer's social media profile. To that end, a lawyer must periodically monitor and review such posts for accuracy and must correct misleading or incorrect information posted by clients or other third-parties.[26]

24. Fla. Bar Comm. on Advertising, The Florida Bar Standing Comm. on Advertising Guidelines for Networking Sites 1 (May 9, 2016). https://webprod.floridabar.org/wp-content/uploads/2017/04/guidelines-social-networking-sites-ada.pdf.

25. S.C. Bar Ethics Advisory Comm., Op. 09-10 (2009), https://www.scbar.org/lawyers/legal-resources-info/ethics-advisory-opinions/eao/ethics-advisory-opinion-09-10/. *But see* Conn. Bar Association Prof'l Ethics Comm., Informal Op. 2012-03 (2012), http://c.ymcdn.com/sites/ctbar.site-ym.com/resource/resmgr/Ethics_Opinions/Informal_Opinion_2012-03.pdf (concluding that lawyers are not responsible for Martindale.com ratings because they "cannot control the content of client reviews" that appear on the website).

26. N.Y. Bar Ass'n Comm. & Fed. Litig. Section, Social Media Ethics Guidelines, Guidelines No. 2.C, 2.D (May 11, 2017) [hereinafter N.Y. Social Media Guidelines], http://www.nysba.org/workarea/DownloadAsset.aspx?id=72708.

In addition, electronic advertising poses other risk management concerns:

- First, lawyers need to be careful about forming inadvertent attorney-client relationships. Although a lawyer may provide legal information on a website, if a lawyer "provide[s] specific legal advice on a social media network... a lawyer's responsive communications may be found to have created an attorney-client relationship."[27]
- Second, lawyers who invite website visitors to contact them may create a prospective client relationship within the meaning of Rule 1.18.[28]

C. REGULATION OF SOLICITATION

Although the Supreme Court recognized in *Bates* that lawyer advertising is constitutionally protected commercial speech, the *Bates* decision did not address the constitutionality of in-person solicitation. The Supreme Court took up that issue the next year in *Ohralik v. Ohio State Bar Association.* This section considers that constitutional doctrine before turning to the rules governing lawyer solicitation.

1. Constitutional Limits on the Bar's Power to Limit Solicitation

Case Preview

Ohralik v. Ohio State Bar Association

Like most state bars, the Ohio Bar prohibited solicitation with some limited exceptions. In February 1974, attorney Albert Ohralik solicited two clients who had been involved in an automobile accident, one in the hospital and one at home after she was released from the hospital. The Ohio Bar subsequently brought disciplinary proceedings against Ohralik and suspended him indefinitely. Relying on *Bates*, Ohralik argued that the application of the solicitation ban against him violated his First Amendment rights. The Supreme Court disagreed and upheld Ohralik's suspension.

As you read the case, consider the following issues:

1. How is the lawyer conduct at issue in *Bates* and *Went For It* different than the lawyer's conduct in this case?
2. What are the Ohio Bar's interests in banning solicitation? How does that state interest justify the outcome in this case?
3. How should the holding and rationale of *Ohralik* apply to solicitation using social media and other electronic means?

---

27. *Id.* at Guideline No. 3.A. *See* Chapter 3.
28. *See* Chapter 3.

Ohralik v. Ohio State Bar Association

436 U.S. 447 (1978)

Mr. Justice Powell delivered the opinion of the Court.

In *Bates v. State Bar of Arizona*, this Court held that truthful advertising of "routine" legal services is protected by the First and Fourteenth Amendments against blanket prohibition by a State. The Court expressly reserved the question of the permissible scope of regulation of "in-person solicitation of clients—at the hospital room or the accident site, or in any other situation that breeds undue influence—by attorneys or their agents or 'runners.'" Today we answer part of the question so reserved, and hold that the State—or the Bar acting with state authorization—constitutionally may discipline a lawyer for soliciting clients in person, for pecuniary gain, under circumstances likely to pose dangers that the State has a right to prevent.

I

Appellant, a member of the Ohio Bar, lives in Montville, Ohio. . . . On February 13, 1974 . . . appellant learned . . . about an automobile accident that had taken place on February 2 in which Carol McClintock, a young woman with whom appellant was casually acquainted, had been injured. Appellant [visited] Ms. McClintock's parents, who . . . explained that their daughter had been driving the family automobile on a local road when she was hit by an uninsured motorist. Both Carol and her passenger, Wanda Lou Holbert, were injured and hospitalized. In response to the McClintocks' expression of apprehension that they might be sued by Holbert, appellant explained that Ohio's guest statute would preclude such a suit. When appellant suggested to the McClintocks that they hire a lawyer, Mrs. McClintock retorted that such a decision would be up to Carol, who was 18 years old and would be the beneficiary of a successful claim.

Appellant proceeded to the hospital, where he found Carol lying in traction in her room. After a brief conversation about her condition, appellant told Carol he would represent her and asked her to sign an agreement. Carol said she would have to discuss the matter with her parents. She did not sign the agreement, but asked appellant to have her parents come to see her. Appellant also attempted to see Wanda Lou Holbert, but learned that she had just been released from the hospital. He then departed for another visit with the McClintocks.

On his way appellant detoured to the scene of the accident, where he took a set of photographs. He also picked up a tape recorder, which he concealed under his raincoat before arriving at the McClintocks' residence. Once there, he . . . discovered that the McClintocks' insurance policy would provide benefits of up to $12,500 each for Carol and Wanda Lou under an uninsured-motorist clause. . . . The McClintocks . . . told appellant that Carol had phoned to say that appellant could "go ahead" with her representation. Two days later appellant returned to Carol's hospital room to have her sign a contract, which provided that he would receive one-third of her recovery.

[Appellant subsequently] visited Wanda Lou at her home, without having been invited. He again concealed his tape recorder and recorded most of the conversation with Wanda Lou. . . . [A]ppellant told Wanda Lou that he was representing Carol and that he had a "little tip" for Wanda Lou: the McClintocks' insurance policy contained an uninsured-motorist clause which might provide her with a recovery of up to $12,500. The young woman, who was 18 years of age and not a high school graduate at the time, replied to appellant's query about whether she was going to file a claim by stating that she really did not understand what was going on. Appellant offered to represent her, also, for a contingent fee of one-third of any recovery, and Wanda Lou stated "O. K."

Wanda's mother attempted to repudiate her daughter's oral assent the following day, when appellant called on the telephone to speak to Wanda. . . . Appellant insisted that Wanda had entered into a binding agreement. A month later Wanda confirmed in writing that she wanted neither to sue nor to be represented by appellant. She requested that appellant notify the insurance company that he was not her lawyer, as the company would not release a check to her until he did so. Carol also eventually discharged appellant. Although another lawyer represented her in concluding a settlement with the insurance company, she paid appellant one-third of her recovery in settlement of his lawsuit against her for breach of contract.

Both Carol McClintock and Wanda Lou Holbert filed complaints against appellant with the Grievance Committee of the Geauga County Bar Association. [After a disciplinary hearing, the Board of Commissioners on Grievances and Discipline of the Supreme Court of Ohio found that appellant had violated Disciplinary Rules (DR) 2-103(A) and 2-104(A) of the Ohio Code of Professional Responsibility.[29] The Supreme Court of Ohio adopted the findings of the board and suspended him indefinitely.]

The decision in *Bates* was handed down after the conclusion of proceedings in the Ohio Supreme Court. We noted probable jurisdiction in this case to consider the scope of protection of a form of commercial speech, and an aspect of the State's authority to regulate and discipline members of the bar, not considered in *Bates*. We now affirm the judgment of the Supreme Court of Ohio.

II

. . .

A

Appellant contends that his solicitation of the two young women as clients is indistinguishable, for purposes of constitutional analysis, from the advertisement in *Bates*. Like that advertisement, his meetings with the prospective clients apprised them of their legal rights and of the availability of a lawyer to pursue their claims.

29. DR 2-103(A) of the Ohio Code (1970), which was in force at that time, provided: "A lawyer shall not recommend employment, as a private practitioner, of himself, his partner, or associate to a non-lawyer who has not sought his advice regarding employment of a lawyer." DR 2-104(A) (1970) provided: "A lawyer who has given unsolicited advice to a layman that he should obtain counsel or take legal action shall not accept employment resulting from that advice, except that: (1) A lawyer may accept employment by a close friend, relative, former client (if the advice is germane to the former employment), or one whom the lawyer reasonably believes to be a client." — Eds.

According to appellant, such conduct is "presumptively an exercise of his free speech rights" which cannot be curtailed in the absence of proof that it actually caused a specific harm that the State has a compelling interest in preventing. But in-person solicitation of professional employment by a lawyer does not stand on a par with truthful advertising about the availability and terms of routine legal services, let alone with forms of speech more traditionally within the concern of the First Amendment.

. . .

B

The state interests implicated in this case are particularly strong. In addition to its general interest in protecting consumers and regulating commercial transactions, the State bears a special responsibility for maintaining standards among members of the licensed professions. "The interest of the States in regulating lawyers is especially great since lawyers are essential to the primary governmental function of administering justice, and have historically been 'officers of the courts.'" While lawyers act in part as "self-employed businessmen," they also act "as trusted agents of their clients, and as assistants to the court in search of a just solution to disputes."

. . .

The substantive evils of solicitation have been stated over the years in sweeping terms: stirring up litigation, assertion of fraudulent claims, debasing the legal profession, and potential harm to the solicited client in the form of overreaching, overcharging, underrepresentation, and misrepresentation. The American Bar Association, as amicus curiae, defends the rule against solicitation primarily on three broad grounds: It is said that the prohibitions embodied in DR 2-103(A) and 2-104(A) serve to reduce the likelihood of overreaching and the exertion of undue influence on lay persons, to protect the privacy of individuals, and to avoid situations where the lawyer's exercise of judgment on behalf of the client will be clouded by his own pecuniary self-interest.

We need not discuss or evaluate each of these interests in detail as appellant has conceded that the State has a legitimate and indeed "compelling" interest in preventing those aspects of solicitation that involve fraud, undue influence, intimidation, overreaching, and other forms of "vexatious conduct. . . ."

III

Appellant's concession that strong state interests justify regulation to prevent the evils he enumerates would end this case but for his insistence that none of those evils was found to be present in his acts of solicitation. He challenges what he characterizes as the "indiscriminate application" of the Rules to him and thus attacks the validity of DR 2-103(A) and DR 2-104(A) not facially, but as applied to his acts of solicitation. And because no allegations or findings were made of the specific wrongs appellant concedes would justify disciplinary action, appellant terms his solicitation "pure," meaning "soliciting and obtaining agreements from Carol McClintock and Wanda Lou Holbert to represent each of them," without more. Appellant therefore argues that we must decide whether a State may discipline him for solicitation per se without offending the First and Fourteenth Amendments.

We agree that the appropriate focus is on appellant's conduct. . . . [But] Appellant's argument misconceives the nature of the State's interest. The Rules prohibiting solicitation are prophylactic measures whose objective is the prevention of harm before it occurs. The Rules were applied in this case to discipline a lawyer for soliciting employment for pecuniary gain under circumstances likely to result in the adverse consequences the State seeks to avert. In such a situation, which is inherently conducive to overreaching and other forms of misconduct, the State has a strong interest in adopting and enforcing rules of conduct designed to protect the public from harmful solicitation by lawyers whom it has licensed.

The State's perception of the potential for harm in circumstances such as those presented in this case is well founded. The detrimental aspects of face-to-face selling even of ordinary consumer products have been recognized and addressed by the Federal Trade Commission, and it hardly need be said that the potential for overreaching is significantly greater when a lawyer, a professional trained in the art of persuasion, personally solicits an unsophisticated, injured, or distressed lay person. Such an individual may place his trust in a lawyer, regardless of the latter's qualifications or the individual's actual need for legal representation, simply in response to persuasion under circumstances conducive to uninformed acquiescence. Although it is argued that personal solicitation is valuable because it may apprise a victim of misfortune of his legal rights, the very plight of that person not only makes him more vulnerable to influence but also may make advice all the more intrusive. Thus, under these adverse conditions the overtures of an uninvited lawyer may distress the solicited individual simply because of their obtrusiveness and the invasion of the individual's privacy, even when no other harm materializes. Under such circumstances, it is not unreasonable for the State to presume that in-person solicitation by lawyers more often than not will be injurious to the person solicited.

The efficacy of the State's effort to prevent such harm to prospective clients would be substantially diminished if, having proved a solicitation in circumstances like those of this case, the State were required in addition to prove actual injury. Unlike the advertising in *Bates*, in-person solicitation is not visible or otherwise open to public scrutiny. Often there is no witness other than the lawyer and the lay person whom he has solicited, rendering it difficult or impossible to obtain reliable proof of what actually took place. This would be especially true if the lay person were so distressed at the time of the solicitation that he could not recall specific details at a later date. If appellant's view were sustained, in-person solicitation would be virtually immune to effective oversight and regulation by the State or by the legal profession, in contravention of the State's strong interest in regulating members of the Bar in an effective, objective, and self-enforcing manner. It therefore is not unreasonable, or violative of the Constitution, for a State to respond with what in effect is a prophylactic rule. . . .

Accordingly, the judgment of the Supreme Court of Ohio is Affirmed.

Post-Case Follow-Up

In *Ohralik*, the Court held that Ohio's ban on solicitation was constitutional as applied to Ohralik's in-person solicitation. The Court recognized that the state has a strong interest in protecting consumers from "fraud, undue influence, intimidation, overreaching and other forms of 'vexatious conduct'" and that the state's absolute ban on in-person solicitation was a necessary "prophylactic measure[]" intended to prevent harm before it occurs.

Ohralik is the only case in which the Court has upheld a categorical ban on lawyer marketing. The question that remains after *Ohralik* is whether a state may ban any other forms of solicitation. As noted earlier, the Supreme Court subsequently found that states may not ban a lawyer's targeted marketing by other means to a particular group of clients with an identifiable legal problem. In Zauderer v. Office of Disciplinary Counsel, 471 U.S. 626 (1985), the Court upheld the constitutional right of a lawyer to run a newspaper advertisement announcing his willingness to represent women who had suffered injuries resulting from their use of a contraceptive known as the Dalkon Shield Intrauterine Device, and in Shapero v. Kentucky Bar Association, 486 U.S. 466 (1988), the Court upheld the right of a lawyer to send direct mailings to potential clients who had foreclosure suits filed against them. Since the letter did not constitute "face-to-face" communication, the Court treated it as advertising rather than solicitation and applied its commercial speech jurisprudence.

On the same day that it handed down *Ohralik*, the Supreme Court also placed another limit on *Ohralik*'s reach when it decided In re Primus, 436 U.S. 412 (1978), in which the Court offered constitutional protection to solicitation in pro bono cases. Edna Smith Primus was a lawyer in Columbia, South Carolina and a cooperating lawyer with the Columbia branch of the American Civil Liberties Union (ACLU). *Id.* at 414. The ACLU learned that pregnant mothers in Aiken County, South Carolina were being sterilized or threatened with sterilization if they wanted to continue receiving Medicaid benefits, and Ms. Primus sent a letter to a prospective litigant communicating the ACLU's offer to represent her for free. *Id.* at 415-16. The South Carolina Supreme Court publicly reprimanded Ms. Primus for soliciting a client in violation of South Carolina's Canon of Ethics. *Id.* at 421. The U.S. Supreme Court reversed, holding that Primus's letter was a form of protected political association under the First Amendment and that she may not be subject to discipline without proof of actual wrongdoing. *Id.* at 434. The Court said that her motivation was to "express personal political beliefs and to advance the civil-liberties objectives of the ACLU." *Id.* at 422. Unlike *Ohralik*, "[t]his was not in-person solicitation for pecuniary gain. [Ms. Primus] was communicating an offer of free assistance by attorneys associated with the ACLU, not an offer predicated on entitlement to a share of any monetary recovery. And her actions were undertaken to express personal political beliefs and to advance the civil liberties objectives of the ACLU, rather than to derive financial gain." *Id.*

Ohralik v. Ohio State Bar Association: Real Life Applications

1. A state bar association is considering bringing a disciplinary case against two different lawyers. Based on *Ohralik* and *Primus*, what would you advise the state bar concerning the constitutionality of bringing these cases?
   a. One lawyer tweeted at an accident victim that he was available to represent her.
   b. The other lawyer went to the hospital of an African-American woman who was shot by the police and asked her if she wanted to bring a civil rights suit against the police.
2. After a gas line exploded in an apartment complex resulting in massive property loss (but no injuries), a law firm set up an RV with the firm's name on it 100 feet from the emergency shelter where the accident victims were staying. What would you advise the state bar about the constitutionality of trying to discipline the firm's lawyers?

---

2. Rules Governing Solicitation

Following *Ohralik*, Model Rule 7.3 states that a "lawyer shall not by in-person, live telephone or real-time electronic contact solicit professional employment when a significant motive for the lawyer's doing so is the lawyer's pecuniary gain." Comment 2 to the rule states that solicitation is dangerous because of the "private importuning of the trained advocate in a direct interpersonal encounter. . . . The situation is fraught with the possibility of undue influence, intimidation, and over-reaching."

The rule does have some narrow exceptions: lawyers may solicit other lawyers as well as those who have a "family, close personal, or prior professional relationship with the lawyer." A lawyer may not solicit even this group, however, if the "target of the solicitation has made known to the lawyer a desire not to be solicited," or "the solicitation involves coercion, duress or harassment."

Remember that even if a lawyer's communication with a prospective client does not constitute solicitation, that communication still must satisfy the advertising rules discussed above.

A lingering area of uncertainty surrounds the ban on "real-time electronic contact." This uncertainty has two components: (1) what exactly is "real-time electronic contact"; and (2) is the categorical ban on "real-time electronic contact" constitutional?

The Model Rules do not define real-time electronic contact. Most authorities agree that "instant messaging and communications transmitted through a chat room" constitute real-time electronic contact, while "[o]rdinary email and web sites" do not.[30] It certainly makes sense to exclude websites and email from the

---

30. N.Y. SOCIAL MEDIA GUIDELINES, *supra* note 26, at Guideline No. 3.B., 10 n.28; *see also* Model Rule 7.3 cmt. 3 ("In particular, communications can be mailed or transmitted by email or other electronic means that do not involve real-time contact and do not violate other laws governing solicitations.").

definition of "real-time electronic contact," since the rationale for banning solicitation is the "possibility of undue influence, intimidation, and over-reaching."[31] These dangers are not present when a consumer visits a law firm's website or receives an email from a lawyer soliciting business because the consumer can simply ignore the email.

Indeed, a state almost certainly could not constitutionally ban email solicitations. Recall that in *Shapero*, the Supreme Court held that a state could not categorically ban lawyers from sending direct mailings to potential clients who had foreclosure suits filed against them. The *Shapero* Court emphasized that the Court's decision in *Ohralik* turned on the fact that, unlike direct mail, face-to-face solicitation is "a practice rife with possibilities for overreaching, invasion of privacy, the exercise of undue influence, and outright fraud" and distinguished it from direct mail.

> Unlike the potential client with a badgering advocate breathing down his neck, the recipient of a letter and the "reader of an advertisement . . . can 'effectively avoid further bombardment of [his] sensibilities simply by averting [his] eyes.'" A letter, like a printed advertisement (but unlike a lawyer), can readily be put in a drawer to be considered later, ignored, or discarded. In short, both types of written solicitation "conve[y] information about legal services [by means] that [are] more conducive to reflection and the exercise of choice on the part of the consumer than is personal solicitation by an attorney."[32]

Shapero v. Kentucky Bar Ass'n, 486 U.S. 466, 475-76 (1988) (citations omitted) (alterations in original).

As for "instant messaging and communications through chat rooms," most authorities conclude that these forms of communication are "real-time electronic contact,"[33] but the Philadelphia Bar Association has taken a different position in a thoughtful opinion.[34] That Opinion reasons: "It seems to us that with the increasing sophistication and ubiquity of social media, it has become readily apparent to everyone that they need not respond instantaneously to electronic overtures, and that everyone realizes that, like targeted mail, e-mails, blogs and chat room comments can be readily ignored, or not, as the recipient wishes."[35] For that reason, the Philadelphia Bar concluded that Rule 7.3 does not bar the use of chat rooms or social media for solicitation purposes "where the prospective clients to whom the lawyer's communication is directed have the ability, readily exercisable, to simply ignore the lawyer's overture, just like they could a piece of directed, targeted mail."[36]

Although the Philadelphia Bar was only expressing its opinion concerning the definition of prohibited "real-time electronic communication," the Opinion's analysis implicitly raises the question of whether it is permissible for states to categorically ban any forms of electronic communication. If the Philadelphia Bar's analysis

---

31. Model Rule 7.3 cmt. 2.
32. Shapero v. Kentucky Bar Ass'n, 486 U.S. 466, 475-76 (1988) (citations omitted) (alterations in original).
33. N.Y. Social Media Guidelines, *supra* note 26, at Guideline No. 3.B.
34. Philadelphia Bar Association Prof'l Guidance Committee, Op. 2010-6 (2010).
35. *Id.* at 6.
36. *Id.*

is correct — that almost all forms of electronic communication can be ignored by the recipient — then *Ohralik*'s rationale for permitting a categorical ban on in-person solicitation should not apply to electronic communication. In other words, an attempt to ban electronic communications with potential clients may be constitutionally suspect.

Chapter Summary

- Advertising generally refers to marketing that is directed to a broad audience, whereas solicitation is a targeted communication initiated by the lawyer that is directed to a specific person.
- In a series of cases, the Supreme Court has recognized that lawyer advertising is protected under the commercial speech doctrine and that lawyers therefore have a constitutional right to advertise in a truthful, non-deceptive manner.
- As *Went For It* demonstrates, however, states may impose limits on lawyer advertising to serve a variety of governmental interests including protecting the public and the reputation of lawyers.
- Under the Model Rules, the primary limit on lawyer advertising is that it may not be false or misleading, but the rules also impose a variety of other requirements.
- In *Ohralik*, the Supreme Court upheld a categorical ban on in-person, face-to-face solicitation for pecuniary gain, finding that such conduct is necessary to protect consumers from "fraud, undue influence, intimidation, overreaching and other forms of vexatious conduct."
- The Model Rules ban solicitation, defined as "in-person, live telephone or real-time electronic contact to solicit professional employment when a significant motive for the lawyer's doing so is the lawyer's pecuniary gain."

Applying the Rules

1. In its opinion above, the California Bar determined that examples 2, 3, and 4 constitute advertising within the meaning of the rules of professional conduct. Do those statements violate the Model Rules?

2. Your law firm has been hired to represent two personal injury lawyers.

    a. The first created a television commercial in which he called himself "The Hammer" and stated that he would "hammer the insurance company."
    b. The second lawyer referred to himself and his partners in the firm's marketing as "The Heavy Hitters."

    The bar has opened an investigation into the propriety of these ads and ordered a hearing. Are the ads permissible under the Model Rules? Would it be constitutional for the bar to discipline the lawyers in these ads?

3. You are a third-year associate in the commercial litigation department at a large law firm and have decided to join LinkedIn to help build your reputation and attract clients. Can you list "Legal Research" under the "Skills and Expertise" section of your LinkedIn page? Can you accept an endorsement for "Legal Research" from a law school classmate? If your law school classmate endorses you for "Tax Advice," what should you do?

4. A lawyer sponsored a poster on the public bus that showed his firm's name and stated: "ACCIDENT VICTIM AWARDED $1,000,000 VERDICT." This statement was true. Is the attorney subject to discipline?

5. A tax lawyer offered an educational seminar on new provisions of the IRS Code that affect small businesses. Fifty small business owners attended. At the end of the seminar, the lawyer announced that the attendees can hire him to help them ensure that their businesses are in compliance with the new provisions. Is the lawyer subject to discipline?

6. A woman tweeted that her car was hit while she was unloading groceries and asked, "Is it smart to post photographs of car accidents online? Can insurance companies use this against you?" An attorney tweeted back: "If you are interested in suing the other driver, I would be happy to represent you." Is the lawyer subject to discipline?

Professional Responsibility in Practice

1. Advertising rules vary greatly from state to state. Look up your state's rules and compare them to the Model Rules.

2. Do you think that any of the Model Rules need to be changed in light of new forms of electronic advertising? What about your state rules?

3. The Association of Professional Responsibility Lawyers (APRL)'s Regulation of Lawyer Advertising Committee has proposed significant changes to the advertising rules: https://aprl.net/wp-content/uploads/2016/07/APRL_2016_Lawyer-Advertising-Supplemental-Report_04-26-16_w-Attach.pdf. Do you agree with APRL's recommendations?

4. Pick an area of law in which you might engage in private practice. Develop a marketing plan for your practice.

15

Access to Justice and Pro Bono Services

We often think of the United States as having the world's greatest justice system; although our system has its flaws, it is, by many measures, a model for the rest of the world. But when it comes to access to justice, we fall far short. The World Justice Project scores the United States 27th out of the 36 countries in our income group under the factor "Civil Justice," and that poor rating is largely due to the United States' score on "accessibility and affordability."[1] Most lawyers charge hundreds of dollars per hour for their services, which prices them far above what millions of low- and moderate-income Americans can afford. Moreover, the Supreme Court has refused to recognize any right to a lawyer in civil cases. Almost 40 years ago, President Jimmy Carter observed, "Ninety percent of our lawyers serve 10 percent of our people."[2] If anything the situation has grown worse. Every year, millions of American face legal crises — mortgage foreclosure proceedings, child custody disputes, debt collection actions, and other serious legal issues — without the help of a lawyer.[3]

Key Concepts

- Parties in civil cases have no right to counsel under federal law, though some states provide lawyers in limited categories of cases
- With no legal right to counsel, low- and moderate-income Americans lack adequate access to representation
- Lawyers, courts, innovators, commentators, and others have proposed a wide range of potential solutions to address the access-to-justice gap

1. World Justice Project, World Justice Project Rule of Law Index 2016, at 153 (2016), http://worldjusticeproject.org/sites/default/files/media/wjp_rule_of_law_index_2016.pdf.
2. Remarks at the 100th Anniversary Luncheon of the Los Angeles Bar Association, 1 Pub. Papers 834, 836 (May 4, 1978); *see* Deborah Rhode, *Access to Justice: Connecting Principles to Practice*, 17 Geo. J. Legal Ethics 369, 371 (2004).
3. Although serious problems exist in our criminal justice system, criminal defendants are guaranteed the right to counsel under the Sixth Amendment, while parties in civil matters enjoy no such protection. For that reason, this chapter will focus on access to justice for parties in civil matters.

Do lawyers bear some responsibility for improving this situation? Professor Deborah Rhode, who has long been a leading voice on access-to-justice issues, articulates two primary reasons why they do:

> [First,] the legal profession has a monopoly on the provision of essential services. Lawyers have special privileges that entail special obligations. In the United States, attorneys have a much more extensive and exclusive right to provide legal assistance than attorneys in other countries. The American bar has closely guarded those prerogatives and its success in restricting lay competition has helped to price services out of the reach of many consumers. . . .
>
> An alternative justification for imposing special obligations on lawyers stems from their special role in our governance structure. As [a New York Committee Report on access to justice] explained, much of what lawyers do
>
>> is about providing justice, [which is] . . . nearer to the heart of our way of life . . . than services provided by other professionals. The legal profession serves as indispensable guardians of our lives, liberties and governing principles. . . . Like no other professionals, lawyers are charged with the responsibility for systemic improvement of not only their own profession, but of the law and society itself.[4]

One way to improve access to justice would be to guarantee individuals the right to a lawyer in at least some category of civil cases, but the courts and legislatures have largely refused to do so. This chapter begins by describing the very limited rights of civil litigants to the assistance of a lawyer. Without a right to counsel, the vast majority of individuals are left to face legal problems on their own. This chapter then turns to the **access-to-justice gap** before discussing some of the potential solutions.

A. "CIVIL GIDEON"

In the famous case of Gideon v. Wainwright, 372 U.S. 335 (1963), the Supreme Court held that indigent defendants in criminal cases have a right to court-appointed counsel under the Sixth Amendment.[5] The Supreme Court has also held that indigent defendants have the right to court-appointed counsel in criminal contempt proceedings (other than summary proceedings).[6] The Court has made clear, however, that the Sixth Amendment does not apply in civil cases. In recent years, advocates of what is commonly referred to as the "**Civil Gideon**" movement, have argued in courts and legislatures for recognition of an expanded right to counsel in civil cases. In the federal courts, the Civil Gideon movement has achieved little success. Although the U.S. Supreme Court recognized a right to counsel for juveniles in delinquency proceedings in the 1967 case of In re Gault, 387 U.S. 1, 41 (1967), the Court has not expanded that right beyond *Gault*. The latest setback came in *Turner v. Rogers*.

---

4. Deborah L. Rhode, *Cultures of Commitment: Pro Bono for Lawyers and Law Students*, 67 FORDHAM L. REV. 2415, 2419 (1999) (footnote omitted).
5. *Id.* at 339-40.
6. United States v. Dixon, 509 U.S. 688, 696 (1993).

Case Preview

Turner v. Rogers

Michael Turner was a father who allegedly owed child support. South Carolina enforces its child support orders by threatening incarceration for civil contempt for those who are able to comply with a child support order but fail to do so. Turner had previously been held in contempt several times and, in some cases, had served time in jail before he paid the amount due. In January 2008, Turner appeared again *pro se* before the South Carolina family court, this time owing $5,728.76 in back child support to his wife, who was also unrepresented. After a very brief hearing, the court sentenced him to 12 months in jail. On appeal, Turner argued that as an indigent person facing potential incarceration, he was entitled to counsel under the Due Process Clause of the Fourteenth Amendment.

As you read *Turner*, consider the following:

1. What do you think about the proceeding at which Turner was found in contempt? How does it compare to your idea of what courtroom proceedings are like? How does it compare to the depiction of legal proceedings in popular media?
2. Why does the Court conclude that Turner was not entitled to counsel?
3. Are the "alternative procedures" required by the Court an adequate replacement for a lawyer?

Turner v. Rogers

564 U.S. 431 (2011)

Justice Breyer delivered the opinion of the Court.

South Carolina's Family Court enforces its child support orders by threatening with incarceration for civil contempt those who are (1) subject to a child support order, (2) able to comply with that order, but (3) fail to do so. We must decide whether the Fourteenth Amendment's Due Process Clause requires the State to provide counsel (at a civil contempt hearing) to an *indigent* person potentially faced with such incarceration. We conclude that where as here the custodial parent (entitled to receive the support) is unrepresented by counsel, the State need not provide counsel to the noncustodial parent (required to provide the support). But we attach an important caveat, namely, that the State must nonetheless have in place alternative procedures that assure a fundamentally fair determination of the critical incarceration-related question, whether the supporting parent is able to comply with the support order.

I

A

South Carolina family courts enforce their child support orders in part through civil contempt proceedings. Each month the family court clerk reviews outstanding

child support orders, identifies those in which the supporting parent has fallen more than five days behind, and sends that parent an order to "show cause" why he should not be held in contempt. The "show cause" order and attached affidavit refer to the relevant child support order, identify the amount of the arrearage, and set a date for a court hearing. At the hearing that parent may demonstrate that he is not in contempt, say, by showing that he is not able to make the required payments. If he fails to make the required showing, the court may hold him in civil contempt. And it may require that he be imprisoned unless and until he purges himself of contempt by making the required child support payments (but not for more than one year regardless).

B

In June 2003 a South Carolina family court entered an order, which (as amended) required petitioner, Michael Turner, to pay $51.73 per week to respondent, Rebecca Rogers, to help support their child. . . . Over the next three years, Turner repeatedly failed to pay the amount due and was held in contempt on five occasions. The first four times he was sentenced to 90 days' imprisonment, but he ultimately paid the amount due (twice without being jailed, twice after spending two or three days in custody). The fifth time he did not pay but completed a 6-month sentence.

After his release in 2006 Turner remained in arrears. On March 27, 2006, the clerk issued a new "show cause" order. And after an initial postponement due to Turner's failure to appear, Turner's civil contempt hearing took place on January 3, 2008. Turner and Rogers were present, each without representation by counsel.

The hearing was brief. The court clerk said that Turner was $5,728.76 behind in his payments. The judge asked Turner if there was "anything you want to say." Turner replied,

> "Well, when I first got out, I got back on dope. I done meth, smoked pot and everything else, and I paid a little bit here and there. And, when I finally did get to working, I broke my back, back in September. I filed for disability and SSI. And, I didn't get straightened out off the dope until I broke my back and laid up for two months. And, now I'm off the dope and everything. I just hope that you give me a chance. I don't know what else to say. I mean, I know I done wrong, and I should have been paying and helping her, and I'm sorry. I mean, dope had a hold to me."

The judge then said, "[o]kay," and asked Rogers if she had anything to say. After a brief discussion of federal benefits, the judge stated,

> "If there's nothing else, this will be the Order of the Court. I find the Defendant in willful contempt. I'm [going to] sentence him to twelve months in the Oconee County Detention Center. He may purge himself of the contempt and avoid the sentence by having a zero balance on or before his release. I've also placed a lien on any SSI or other benefits."

The judge added that Turner would not receive good-time or work credits, but "[i]f you've got a job, I'll make you eligible for work release." When Turner asked why he could not receive good-time or work credits, the judge said, "[b]ecause that's my ruling." *Ibid.*

The court made no express finding concerning Turner's ability to pay his arrearage (though Turner's wife had voluntarily submitted a copy of Turner's application for disability benefits). Nor did the judge ask any followup questions or otherwise address the ability-to-pay issue. After the hearing, the judge filled out a prewritten form titled "Order for Contempt of Court," which included the statement: "Defendant (was) (was not) gainfully employed and/or (had) (did not have) the ability to make these support payments when due." But the judge left this statement as is without indicating whether Turner was able to make support payments.

C

While serving his 12-month sentence, Turner, with the help of *pro bono* counsel, appealed. He claimed that the Federal Constitution entitled him to counsel at his contempt hearing. The South Carolina Supreme Court decided Turner's appeal after he had completed his sentence. And it rejected his "right to counsel" claim. . . .

Turner sought certiorari [and the Supreme Court granted the writ].

. . .

II

[The Court held that the case was not moot even though Turner is no longer incarcerated.]

III

We must decide whether the Due Process Clause grants an indigent defendant, such as Turner, a right to state-appointed counsel at a civil contempt proceeding, which may lead to his incarceration. This Court's precedents provide no definitive answer to that question. This Court has long held that the Sixth Amendment grants an indigent defendant the right to state-appointed counsel in a *criminal* case. Gideon v. Wainwright, 372 U.S. 335 (1963). And we have held that this same rule applies to *criminal contempt* proceedings (other than summary proceedings).

But the Sixth Amendment does not govern civil cases. Civil contempt differs from criminal contempt in that it seeks only to "coerc[e] the defendant to do" what a court had previously ordered him to do. A court may not impose punishment "in a civil contempt proceeding when it is clearly established that the alleged contemnor is unable to comply with the terms of the order." And once a civil contemnor complies with the underlying order, he is purged of the contempt and is free.

Consequently, the Court has made clear (in a case not involving the right to counsel) that, where civil contempt is at issue, the Fourteenth Amendment's Due Process Clause allows a State to provide fewer procedural protections than in a criminal case.

This Court has decided only a handful of cases that more directly concern a right to counsel in civil matters. And the application of those decisions to the present case is not clear. On the one hand, the Court has held that the Fourteenth Amendment requires the State to pay for representation by counsel in a *civil* "juvenile delinquency" proceeding (which could lead to incarceration). In re Gault, 387 U.S. 1 (1967). Moreover, in Vitek v. Jones, 445 U.S. 480 (1980), a plurality of four Members of this Court would have held that the Fourteenth Amendment requires representation by counsel in a proceeding to transfer a prison inmate to a state hospital for the mentally ill. Further, in Lassiter v. Department of Social Servs. of Durham Cty., 452 U.S. 18 (1981), a case that focused upon civil proceedings leading to loss of parental rights, the Court wrote that the "pre-eminent generalization that emerges from this Court's precedents on an indigent's right to appointed counsel is that such a right has been recognized to exist only where the litigant may lose his physical liberty if he loses the litigation." And the Court then drew from these precedents "the presumption that an indigent litigant has a right to appointed counsel only when, if he loses, he may be deprived of his physical liberty."

On the other hand, the Court has held that a criminal offender facing revocation of probation and imprisonment does *not* ordinarily have a right to counsel at a probation revocation hearing. And, at the same time, *Gault, Vitek,* and *Lassiter* are readily distinguishable. The civil juvenile delinquency proceeding at issue in *Gault* was "little different" from, and "comparable in seriousness" to, a criminal prosecution. In *Vitek*, the controlling opinion found *no* right to counsel. And the Court's statements in *Lassiter* constitute part of its rationale for *denying* a right to counsel in that case. We believe those statements are best read as pointing out that the Court previously had found a right to counsel "*only*" in cases involving incarceration, not that a right to counsel exists in *all* such cases. . . .

B

Civil contempt proceedings in child support cases constitute one part of a highly complex system designed to assure a noncustodial parent's regular payment of funds typically necessary for the support of his children. Often the family receives welfare support from a state-administered federal program, and the State then seeks reimbursement from the noncustodial parent. Other times the custodial parent (often the mother, but sometimes the father, a grandparent, or another person with custody) does not receive government benefits and is entitled to receive the support payments herself.

The Federal Government has created an elaborate procedural mechanism designed to help both the government and custodial parents to secure the payments to which they are entitled. These systems often rely upon wage withholding, expedited procedures for modifying and enforcing child support orders, and automated data processing. But sometimes States will use contempt orders to ensure that the custodial parent receives support payments or the government receives reimbursement. Although some experts have criticized this last-mentioned procedure, and the Federal Government believes that "the routine use of contempt for non-payment of child support is likely to be an ineffective strategy," the Government also tells us that "coercive enforcement remedies, such as contempt, have a role to play." South Carolina, which relies heavily on contempt proceedings, agrees that they are an important tool.

We here consider an indigent's right to paid counsel at such a contempt proceeding. It is a civil proceeding. And we consequently determine the "specific dictates of due process" by examining the "distinct factors" that this Court has previously found useful in deciding what specific safeguards the Constitution's Due Process Clause requires in order to make a civil proceeding fundamentally fair. As relevant here those factors include (1) the nature of "the private interest that will be affected," (2) the comparative "risk" of an "erroneous deprivation" of that interest with and without "additional or substitute procedural safeguards," and (3) the nature and magnitude of any countervailing interest in not providing "additional or substitute procedural requirement[s]."

The "private interest that will be affected" argues strongly for the right to counsel that Turner advocates. That interest consists of an indigent defendant's loss of personal liberty through imprisonment. The interest in securing that freedom, the freedom "from bodily restraint," lies "at the core of the liberty protected by the Due Process Clause." And we have made clear that its threatened loss through legal proceedings demands "due process protection."

Given the importance of the interest at stake, it is obviously important to assure accurate decisionmaking in respect to the key "ability to pay" question. Moreover, the fact that ability to comply marks a dividing line between civil and criminal contempt, reinforces the need for accuracy. That is because an incorrect decision (wrongly classifying the contempt proceeding as civil) can increase the risk of wrongful incarceration by depriving the defendant of the procedural protections (including counsel) that the Constitution would demand in a criminal proceeding. And since 70% of child support arrears nationwide are owed by parents with either no reported income or income of $10,000 per year or less, the issue of ability to pay may arise fairly often.

On the other hand, the Due Process Clause does not always require the provision of counsel in civil proceedings where incarceration is threatened. And in determining whether the Clause requires a right to counsel here, we must take account of opposing interests, as well as consider the probable value of "additional or substitute procedural safeguards."

Doing so, we find three related considerations that, when taken together, argue strongly against the Due Process Clause requiring the State to provide indigents with counsel in every proceeding of the kind before us. First, the critical question likely at issue in these cases concerns, as we have said, the defendant's ability to pay. That question is often closely related to the question of the defendant's indigence. But when the right procedures are in place, indigence can be a question that in many — but not all — cases is sufficiently straightforward to warrant determination *prior* to providing a defendant with counsel, even in a criminal case. Federal law, for example, requires a criminal defendant to provide information showing that he is indigent, and therefore entitled to state-funded counsel, *before* he can receive that assistance. Second, sometimes, as here, the person opposing the defendant at the hearing is not the government represented by counsel but the custodial parent *un*represented by counsel. The custodial parent, perhaps a woman with custody of one or more children, may be relatively poor, unemployed, and unable to afford counsel. Yet she may have encouraged the court to enforce its order through contempt. She may be able to provide the court with significant information. A requirement that the State provide counsel to the noncustodial parent in these cases could create an asymmetry of representation that would "alter significantly the nature of the proceeding." Doing so could mean a degree of formality or delay that would unduly slow payment to those immediately in need. And, perhaps more important for present purposes, doing so could make the proceedings *less* fair overall, increasing the risk of a decision that would erroneously deprive a family of the support it is entitled to receive. The needs of such families play an important role in our analysis.

Third, as the Solicitor General points out, there is available a set of "substitute procedural safeguards," which, if employed together, can significantly reduce the risk of an erroneous deprivation of liberty. They can do so, moreover, without incurring some of the drawbacks inherent in recognizing an automatic right to counsel. Those safeguards include (1) notice to the defendant that his "ability to pay" is a critical issue in the contempt proceeding; (2) the use of a form (or the equivalent) to elicit relevant financial information; (3) an opportunity at the hearing for the defendant to respond to statements and questions about his financial status, (*e.g.*, those triggered by his responses on the form); and (4) an express finding by the court that the defendant has the ability to pay. In presenting these alternatives, the Government draws upon considerable experience in helping to manage statutorily mandated federal-state efforts to enforce child support orders. It does not claim that they are the only possible alternatives, and this Court's cases suggest, for example, that sometimes assistance other than purely legal assistance (here, say, that of a neutral social worker) can prove constitutionally sufficient. But the Government does claim that these alternatives can assure the "fundamental fairness" of the proceeding even where the State does not pay for counsel for an indigent defendant.

While recognizing the strength of Turner's arguments, we ultimately believe that the three considerations we have just discussed must carry the day. In our view, a categorical right to counsel in proceedings of the kind before us would carry with it disadvantages (in the form of unfairness and delay) that, in terms of ultimate fairness, would deprive it of significant superiority over the alternatives that we have mentioned. We consequently hold that the Due Process Clause does not *automatically* require the provision of counsel at civil contempt proceedings to an indigent individual who is subject to a child support order, even if that individual faces incarceration (for up to a year). In particular, that Clause does not require the provision of counsel where the opposing parent or other custodian (to whom support funds are owed) is not represented by counsel and the State provides alternative procedural safeguards equivalent to those we have mentioned (adequate notice of the importance of ability to pay, fair opportunity to present, and to dispute, relevant information, and court findings).

We do not address civil contempt proceedings where the underlying child support payment is owed to the State, for example, for reimbursement of welfare funds paid to the parent with custody. Those proceedings more closely resemble debt-collection proceedings. The government is likely to have counsel or some other competent representative. And this kind of proceeding is not before us. Neither do we address what due process requires in an unusually complex case where a defendant "can fairly be represented only by a trained advocate."

IV

The record indicates that Turner received neither counsel nor the benefit of alternative procedures like those we have described. He did not receive clear notice that his ability to pay would constitute the critical question in his civil contempt proceeding. No one provided him with a form (or the equivalent) designed to elicit information about his financial circumstances. The court did not find that Turner was able to pay his arrearage, but instead left the relevant "finding" section of the contempt order blank. The court nonetheless found Turner in contempt and ordered him incarcerated. Under these circumstances Turner's incarceration violated the Due Process Clause.

We vacate the judgment of the South Carolina Supreme Court and remand the case for further proceedings not inconsistent with this opinion.

Justice THOMAS, with whom Justice SCALIA joins, and with whom THE CHIEF JUSTICE and Justice ALITO join as to Parts I-B and II, dissenting.

The Due Process Clause of the Fourteenth Amendment does not provide a right to appointed counsel for indigent defendants facing incarceration in civil contempt proceedings. Therefore, I would affirm. Although the Court agrees that appointed counsel was not required in this case, it nevertheless vacates the judgment of the South Carolina Supreme Court on a different ground, which the parties have never raised. Solely at the invitation of the United States as *amicus curiae*, the majority decides that Turner's contempt proceeding violated due process because it did not include "alternative procedural safeguards." Consistent with this Court's longstanding practice, I would not reach that question. . . .

Post-Case Follow-Up

Although the Supreme Court has declined to recognize a civil right to counsel under federal law, many states mandate or authorize (at the court's discretion) a right to counsel in certain limited circumstances. The most common situations in which states guarantee a right to counsel are proceedings in which parents are accused of abuse or neglect, state-initiated termination of parental rights cases, involuntary commitment proceedings, litigation concerning medical treatment, and guardianship proceedings.[7] In many cases, these rights are provided by statute, though in some cases they are established by court opinions. Again, however, the reach of these laws is quite limited, and most people in most states are not guaranteed counsel in most civil cases.

Turner v. Rogers: Real Life Applications

1. Under a divorce decree, Father was awarded visitation every other weekend. Over several years, Mother denied Father regular visitation, stating that the children were afraid of their father although she could not give any specific

7. For a comprehensive list of state resources, see *Directory of Law Governing Appointment of Counsel in State Civil Proceedings*, ABA COMM. ON LEGAL AID & INDIGENT DEFENDANTS, http://www.americanbar.org/groups/legal_aid_indigent_defendants/initiatives/resource_center_for_access_to_justice/resources---information-on-key-atj-issues/civil_right_to_counsel1.html (last visited Mar. 30, 2017).

reason why. The court held several contempt hearings. Father filed yet another application for contempt after being denied visitation. At the hearing, Father appeared without a lawyer. The court asked Mother if she was prepared to proceed without counsel, even though the hearing could result in jail time, and she agreed. The hearing took about an hour and 20 minutes. Mother offered her own testimony and letters from the minor children detailing how they felt about Father and their visitations with him, as the court would not allow them to testify. The court found that Mother failed to purge her contempt and sentenced her to 30 days in jail. Did the court err in jailing Mother without first providing her with counsel?

2. In her 2003 divorce, Mother was ordered to pay child support. In 2011, the county child support enforcement agency filed a motion for contempt against Mother for failing to pay. Mother appeared at the hearing without counsel. The magistrate said to Mother, "I'm going to deny your request for counsel at this time. There [was] a recent U.S. Supreme Court decision that came down on contempt citations regarding child support, [holding] that obligors that are facing jail time in civil contempts are not entitled to court-appointed counsel." Agency counsel presented evidence that Mother owed over $16,000 in child support. Mother testified that she was not aware of the obligation and that she could not afford the payments since her income consisted of $200 per month in food stamps and she had a medical condition that prevent her from working. The magistrate found Mother in contempt and sentenced her to 30 days in jail. Should Mother appeal?

B. THE JUSTICE GAP

A woman living in poverty receives a notice from her landlord that she is being evicted from her apartment. She cannot afford a lawyer; what should she do? The best option for low-income Americans is to try to obtain the services of a legal services lawyer, funded by the **Legal Services Corporation** (LSC). LSC, a non-profit organization established by Congress in 1974, is the single largest funder of civil legal aid for low-income Americans.[8] LSC does not deliver legal services itself but rather funds legal service providers in every state in the country. Only individuals who live in households with annual incomes below 125 percent of the federal poverty guidelines — $15,075 in household income for a single person and $30,750 for a family of four — are eligible for LSC-funded services.[9]

Unfortunately, LSC funding has not kept up with demand: in 2010, LSC funding was $420 million but that was cut to $365 million in 2014.[10] Even the 2010

8. *About LSC*, LEGAL SERVS. CORP., http://www.lsc.gov/about-lsc (last visited Mar. 30, 2017).
9. Income Level for Individuals Eligible for Assistance, 82 Fed. Reg. 10,442, 10,443 (Feb. 13, 2017) (to be codified at 45 C.F.R. pt. 1611 app. A).
10. Press Release, Legal Services Corporation, House Senate Agreement Cuts LSC Funding (Nov. 15, 2011), http://www.lsc.gov/media-center/press-releases/2011/house-senate-agreement-cuts-lsc-funding; Press Release, Legal

funding level is well below peak LSC funding in the mid-1990s. As a result, LSC-funded offices simply do not have sufficient staffing to meet the needs of individuals with legal problems and have to turn away many people in need. For example, in Massachusetts, 64 percent of eligible low-income people were turned away in 2013.[11]

Legal services offices also fund their budgets with resources derived from some combination of state funding, private fundraising, and grants from **Interest on Lawyer Trust Accounts** (IOLTA). The availability of funding varies dramatically from state to state, prompting an ABA report to observe that when it comes to the availability of legal services "geography is destiny."[12] As a general matter, state government funding has declined. Moreover, IOLTA used to be a significant funding source — $225 million nationwide in 2008 — but has declined significantly — to $75 million in 2014 — as bank interest rates dropped to historic lows.[13] This decline has had real impact on the availability of legal services for the poor. For example, Legal Services of New Jersey, which relies heavily on IOLTA funds, had to cut its staff from 720 employees in 2008 to 330 in 2014.[14]

Where else can our tenant facing eviction go? A variety of public interest organizations provide free legal services in specific locations for particular client groups. In addition to low-income persons, public interest organizations provide services to the elderly, people with disabilities, members of Native American groups, people with HIV/AIDS, homeless people, and veterans. They also provide services on particular legal issues, for example, housing, immigration, or civil rights. Again, the services available to the public vary greatly from state to state.

Law school clinics also provide legal assistance to the poor, but the impact that these clinics can make is

IOLTA Funding and the Fifth Amendment

IOLTA funding has survived several constitutional attacks. In 1998, the Supreme Court held that the interest earned from clients' money in a lawyer's trust account is private property subject to the Fifth Amendment. Phillips v. Wash. Legal Found., 524 U.S. 156 (1998). The Court remanded the case to determine whether that property had been taken for public use without just compensation.

Without a definite answer, litigation continued. Finally, in 2003, the Court settled the issue in Brown v. Legal Found. of Wash., 538 U.S. 216 (2003). The Court found that the use of the interest to benefit those who could not afford lawyers was a public use and a *per se* taking. Nevertheless, it upheld IOLTA funding as constitutional. Since the Fifth Amendment is only violated when there is a taking without just compensation, which is measured by the property owner's loss, the Court concluded that the Fifth Amendment was not violated as the client has lost nothing. Lawyers only deposit client funds into IOLTA accounts when those funds could not earn net interest because the funds are too small and/or they are being held for such a short time that the administrative costs of a separated interest-bearing account would exceed the interest earned by the individual client.

Services Corporation, FY 2015 Spending Bill Increased Funding for LSC by $10 Million (Dec. 19, 2014), http://www.lsc.gov/media-center/press-releases/2014/fy-2015-spending-bill-increased-funding-lsc-10-million.

11. Boston Bar Ass'n, Investing in Justice: A Roadmap to Cost-Effective Funding of Civil Legal Aid in Massachusetts 1 (2014), http://www.bostonbar.org/docs/default-document-library/statewide-task-force-to-expand-civil-legal-aid-in-ma---investing-in-justice.pdf.

12. ABA Comm'n on the Future of Legal Servs., Report on the Future of Legal Services in the United States 13 (2016), http://abafuturesreport.com/2016-fls-report-web.pdf (last visited May 27, 2017). This report contains comprehensive data concerning the access-to-justice gap and analysis of possible solutions.

13. Susanne Cervenka, *Funding Shortfalls Limit Access to Legal Services for Poor*, USA Today, July 29, 2015, http://www.usatoday.com/story/news/nation/2015/07/29/legal-aid-funding-poor-residents/30738877/.

14. *Id.*

limited. To ensure a high-quality educational experience for and careful supervision of law students, the ABA requires clinics to maintain a small faculty-student ratio, thereby limiting the number of cases that law school clinics can take. Although most law school clinics deliver outstanding legal services to their low-income clients, the principal purpose of clinics remains education, not service.

If our tenant were lucky, she might be able to find a lawyer willing to offer her services **pro bono**. Pro bono work by lawyers in private practice is another significant resource for low-income persons, but the good work done by many lawyers does not come anywhere close to solving the problem: "U.S. lawyers would have to increase their pro bono work . . . to over nine hundred hours each to provide some measure of assistance to all households with legal needs."[15]

Although we have assumed so far that our tenant lives in poverty, a middle-income American served with an eviction notice might have almost as much difficulty finding a lawyer. These individuals do not meet the income qualifications for LSC-funded lawyers or most other legal aid providers, yet they often still cannot afford to hire an attorney. As a result, the numbers are startling. According to scholars, "[o]ver four-fifths of the legal needs of the poor and a majority of the needs of middle-income Americans remain unmet."[16] One study concluded that "well over 100 million Americans [are] living with civil justice problems, many involving what the American Bar Association has termed 'basic human needs'" relating to shelter, sustenance, safety, health, and child custody.[17]

As a result, our court system is witnessing an enormous and growing number of unrepresented litigants. One study concluded that more than 80 percent of low-income litigants are unrepresented in cases involving basic life needs (debt collection cases, mortgage foreclosures, child support and custody cases, etc.).[18] Depending on the type of case and particular jurisdiction, the numbers can be even worse. For example, in Utah in 2014, 98 percent of defendants in debt collection cases were unrepresented but 96 percent of the plaintiffs had a lawyer.[19] The large numbers of unrepresented litigants impact the entire justice system.

Access to affordable lawyers remains the biggest issue contributing to the justice gap, but recent research has uncovered another factor: individuals frequently do not recognize that they have a need for legal services, and, even when they do, they often do not seek legal assistance. In *Accessing Justice in the Contemporary USA: Findings from the Community Needs and Services Study*, Professor Rebecca Sandefur found that most individuals do not recognize that their problems have legal solutions, and even when they do, 46 percent said that they are likely to address their problems

---

15. Gillian K. Hadfield, *Innovating to Improve Access: Changing the Way Courts Regulate Legal Markets*, 143 Daedalus 83, 87 (2014).

16. Deborah L. Rhode, *What We Know and Need to Know About the Delivery of Legal Services by Nonlawyers*, 67 S.C. L. Rev. 429, 429 (2016).

17. Rebecca L. Sandefur, *What We Know and Need to Know About the Legal Needs of the Public*, 67 S.C. L. Rev. 433, 446 (2016).

18. Legal Services Corporation, Documenting the Justice Gap (2009), http://www.lsc.gov/sites/default/files/LSC/pdfs/documenting_the_justice_gap_in_america_2009.pdf.

19. Futures Comm'n of the Utah State Bar, Report and Recommendations on the Future of Legal Services in Utah 9 (2015), https://www.utahbar.org/wp-content/uploads/2015/07/2015_Futures_Report_revised.pdf.

themselves, 23 percent get help in whole or part from family and friends, 16 percent do nothing, and only 22 percent report seeking formal help from a lawyer.[20]

C. POSSIBLE SOLUTIONS

1. Simplifying Court Procedures

Our court system is complex and intimidating to those who seek to represent themselves. As one judge testified:

> Most individuals would not attempt to play a sport, play a game, take an exam, or fill out an important application without knowing the rules and instructions. Indeed, we give people clear rules or instructions on how to complete these tasks. But, we . . . do not always provide unrepresented litigants the rules, instructions and necessary tools when they are attempting to navigate the courts. In our adversarial system, the information, rules and forms unrepresented litigants need to be successful on their case are often not available or accessible. We often hide the ball necessary to play the game. It is time to stop hiding the ball, so the game is fair. . . .
>
> In order to achieve a major step forward in access to justice, standardization and simplification of forms and procedures is an effort we must embrace and get done. . . . [J]ustice should not be stymied by obstacles we can remove.[21]

To help unrepresented litigants, our courts need to develop what one commentator has called "The Self-Help Friendly Court."[22] Courts could help unrepresented litigants by simplifying courtroom and other procedures to make them more readily accessible to everybody and by providing standardized and uniform forms that are written in plain language. Judges and court personnel could also be trained in assisting self-represented litigants.

2. Mandatory Pro Bono

The Model Rules do not require that lawyers engage in pro bono work; rather, Rule 6.1 states that a lawyer "*should* aspire to render at least (50) hours of pro bono" service per year. Model Rules of Prof'l Conduct r. 6.1 (emphasis added). For several decades, states have discussed requiring lawyers to perform pro bono work. In 1977,

20. Rebecca L. Sandefur, Accessing Justice in the Contemporary USA: Findings from the Community Needs and Services Study 11-12 (2014), http://www.americanbarfoundation.org/uploads/cms/documents/sandefur_accessing_justice_in_the_contemporary_usa._aug._2014.pdf.

21. *The Chief Judge's 2011 Hearings on Civil Legal Services, First Dep't (Sept. 26, 2011)* 2, 3-4 (written statement of Hon. Fern Fisher, Deputy Chief Administrative Judge for New York City Courts and Director of the New York State Courts Access to Justice Program), https://www.nycourts.gov/accesstojusticecommission/PDF/2011_1stDeptTestifying.pdf.

22. Richard Zorza, The Self-Help Friendly Court: Designed from the Ground Up to Work for People Without Lawyers (2002).

A Robot Lawyer Helps Overturn Parking Tickets

Joshua Browder, creator of the Robot Lawyer app
AP Images

Joshua Browder, a 20-year-old Stanford student, has developed a free artificial intelligence app that helps people in London, New York, San Francisco, Chicago, Denver, and Los Angeles overturn parking tickets. The robot asks the user a series of questions to determine the factual background behind the ticket and then looks for loopholes to overturn the ticket. The current success rate is 60 percent, higher than other apps using actual lawyers. The bot then generates a letter to send to the city and guides the user through the appeal process, all for free.

Browder's app has been expanded beyond parking in some cities, helping with landlord-tenant disputes and unexplained banking charges. He is currently coding the bot to help refugees apply for asylum. Browder has said that his goal is to "level the playing field so anyone can have the same legal access under the law." Arezou Rezvani, *"Robot Lawyer" Makes the Case Against Parking Tickets*, NPR, Jan. 16, 2017, http://www.npr.org/2017/01/16/510096767/robot-lawyer-makes-the-case-against-parking-tickets.

the State Bar of California proposed that practicing lawyers be required to perform 40 hours per year, but the proposal was ultimately rejected. Most recently, the Mississippi Supreme Court proposed mandatory pro bono rules but withdrew the proposal after receiving negative feedback from lawyers. Some states require mandatory *reporting* of pro bono work in the hope of promoting such work but do not require the actual performance of pro bono.

In 2013, New York became the first state to mandate pro bono work, but only for *applicants* to the bar, not members of the bar. To become a member of the bar in New York, applicants must perform 50 hours of pro bono work in law school or some other time before they are admitted. California has since followed suit, and a few other states are considering a similar requirement. Supporters argue that a mandatory pro bono rule for bar applicants will provide at least some help to indigent parties while also allowing future lawyers the opportunity for some practical experience. Critics, on the other hand, argue that it is unfair to impose this requirement on applicants but not on lawyers and, moreover, that compelled assistance from inexperienced lawyers is worse than nothing at all.

3. Technology

Through its adoption of comment 8 to Rule 1.1, the ABA has made clear that a lawyer's duty of competence includes understanding and using technology to benefit clients. Technology also holds great promise for improving access to justice.

Technology is being employed in a variety of ways to improve the delivery of legal services. For example, many legal aid offices and public interest law firms (in addition to private law firms and companies) are using document assembly software to assist clients. These tools are similar to TurboTax: the user is asked a series of questions and the software uses sophisticated branching technology to generate legal documents — for example, wills, leases, or other contracts — based on the user's responses. A lawyer can then review the document and make any necessary changes, but the software saves significant time, allowing the lawyer to operate more efficiently and serve more clients.

In some cases, these resources are available online as part of a unified legal portal that can direct individuals who need legal assistance to the most appropriate form of assistance, whether it be document assembly software, other self-help resources, or the names of attorneys with relevant expertise. An excellent example of such a portal is Illinois Legal Aid Online (www.illinoislegalaid.org) where consumers can find articles, videos, and forms.

Courts are also using technology to improve access to the justice system. For example, some courts are using technology to make services available remotely, such as document filing, document preparation, record searches, and similar services. A particularly powerful example of this is in Arizona where some individuals who live north of the Grand Canyon have to travel up to seven hours to reach their local courthouse on the south side of the Grand Canyon. In order to make the court system more accessible to those residents, the County placed a kiosk in a motor vehicles division building on the north side of the Grand Canyon so that residents who live there can access the courts without having to make that long drive. Residents can use the kiosk for a variety of purposes: for example, they can make appearances in cases that do not involve mandatory jail time. They can also talk with the clerk of the court, ask questions about civil filings, and print court forms.

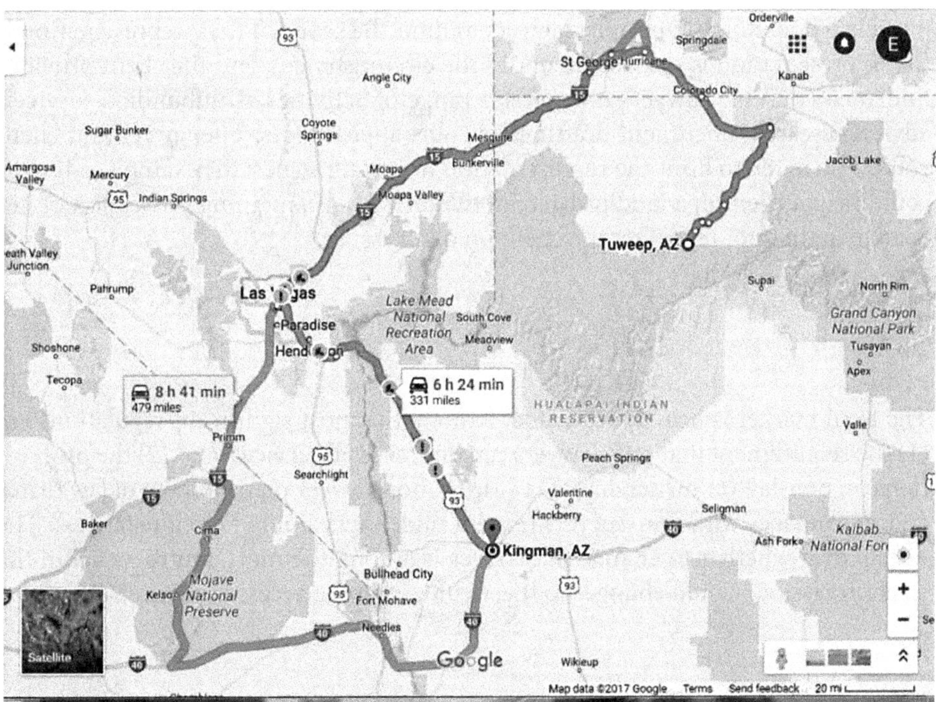

Residents of Tuweep, Arizona have to travel over six hours to the courthouse in Kingman. The self-pay kiosk improves their access to the legal system.
Google Maps

The cost of the kiosk was approximately $7,000, and the only ongoing expense is $75/month for the Internet connection.[23]

Self-help centers are another technological innovation offered at more than 500 courthouses across the country. These self-help centers provide a variety of services including live and/or telephone assistance, referrals, web-based information, and document support.

There are many other examples of technological innovations from across the country and the world. The expansion of these programs and the development of new technological innovations hold great promise in improving access to justice.

4. Unbundled Legal Services

In the traditional attorney-client relationship, the lawyer endeavors to help the client with her legal problem until the issues are fully resolved no matter what is involved or how long the assistance takes. In some cases, however, taking on a complicated and time-consuming pro bono case might seem daunting to a lawyer who otherwise might be interested in helping a client for a low or no fee. Similarly, clients might not be able to afford full-service representation but might have sufficient funds to pay a lawyer to perform certain discrete tasks. One answer to these situations is to allow lawyers to provide **unbundled legal services** — i.e., services limited in their scope. Rule 1.2 permits lawyers to limit the scope of their representation if that representation is reasonable under the circumstances, and the client provides informed consent. Lawyers may offer a range of activities as unbundled services: advice, research, document drafting, or court appearances. The lawyer and client could also agree to limit the representation to certain issues: for example, a lawyer could help a client in a landlord-tenant matter with maintaining possession of her apartment but not represent the client on other issues.

5. Regulatory Changes

The legal market is heavily regulated. Among the most significant regulations are (1) the requirement that only lawyers can deliver legal services; and (2) the prohibitions on non-lawyer ownership of law firms, non-lawyer management of law firms, and sharing fees with non-lawyers (except under very limited circumstances). The debate over whether to change these rules is among the most controversial in the legal profession. Could changes to these rules improve access to justice?

---

23. Stephanie Francis Ward, *Kyle Rimel: Using technology to bring court services to remote areas*, A.B.A. J., Sept. 16, 2015, http://www.abajournal.com/legalrebels/article/kyle_rimel_profile (last visited May 27, 2017).

Non-Lawyers Delivering Legal Services

When you get sick, a doctor is not the only one who can help you. In the health care field, nurse practitioners, physician's assistants, and other professionals are able to supplement the work that doctors do by providing certain basic medical services at a lower price. Similarly, some legal problems may not require a lawyer, and some U.S. jurisdictions have authorized legal service providers other than lawyers to assist individuals in addressing their legal needs.

Federal legislation has long authorized the use of non-lawyers under limited circumstances. For instance:

- Bankruptcy petition preparers who are not lawyers may assist debtors in filling out the paperwork necessary to file for bankruptcy in United States Bankruptcy Court.
- Qualified non-lawyers can represent individuals in immigration proceedings before the Executive Office for Immigration Review.
- The Social Security Administration permits non-lawyers to represent claimants seeking benefits.
- A variety of different professionals, including certified public accountants, are authorized to practice before the IRS.
- Patent agents who are not lawyers may prepare and file patent applications with the Patent and Trademark Office.[24]

States are also experimenting with new forms of legal service providers:

- New York and Arizona permit specially trained and lawyer-supervised college students to be "Court Navigators." Under New York's program, launched in 2014, Court Navigators assist unrepresented litigants in nonpayment proceedings in housing court or consumer debt cases by researching information about the law, collecting necessary documents, and responding to a judge's questions about the case. Under Arizona's program, which began in 2015, Court Navigators help guide self-represented litigants through the court process in family law cases.
- In California and Washington State, non-lawyer "Courthouse Facilitators" provide unrepresented individuals in family law cases with information about court procedures and legal forms.
- Arizona, California, and Nevada authorize specially trained non-lawyer "Document Preparers" to prepare legal documents on specific legal matters.[25]

Many other states are contemplating similar programs.

---

24. ABA Comm'n on the Future of Legal Servs., Report on the Future of Legal Services in the United States 20 (2016), http://abafuturesreport.com/2016-fls-report-web.pdf (last visited May 27, 2017).
25. *Id.* at 19-24.

Case Preview

In the Matter of the Adoption of New APR 28—Limited Practice Rule for Limited License Legal Technicians

The most prominent example of non-lawyers delivering legal services is in Washington State where the Washington Supreme Court has approved the role of **Limited License Legal Technician** (LLLT), which is "the first independent legal paraprofessional in the United States that is licensed to give legal advice."[26]

As you read the Washington Supreme Court's administrative order approving the licensure of Limited License Legal Technicians, consider the following:

1. What are the arguments that the court makes in favor of licensing LLLTs? What are the arguments against them?
2. How will we know if the program is a success? What data would you want to collect to find out?

In the Matter of the Adoption of New APR 28—Limited Practice Rule for Limited License Legal Technicians

Order No. 25700-A-1005 (Wash. June 15, 2012)

The Practice of Law Board having recommended the adoption of New APR 28 — Limited Practice Rule for Limited License Legal Technicians, and the Court having considered the revised rule and comments submitted thereto, and having determined by majority that the rule will aid in the prompt and orderly administration of justice;

Now, therefore, it is hereby

ORDERED.

That we adopt APR 28, the Limited Practice Rule for Limited License Legal Technicians.

It is time. Since this rule was submitted to the Court by the Practice of Law Board in 2008, and revised in 2012, we have reviewed many comments both in support and in opposition to the proposal to establish a limited form of legal practitioner. During this time, we have also witnessed the wide and ever-growing gap in necessary legal and law related services for low and moderate income persons.

. . . The Limited License Legal Technician Rule that we adopt today is narrowly tailored to accomplish its stated objectives, includes appropriate training, financial responsibility, regulatory oversight and accountability systems, and incorporates ethical and other requirements designed to ensure competency within the narrow

26. Paula C. Littlewood, *The Practice of Law in Transition*, NW Law., July-Aug. 2015, at 13, http://nwlawyer.wsba.org/nwlawyer/july-august_2015?pg=15#pg15.

spectrum of the services that Limited License Legal Technicians will be allowed to provide. In adopting this rule we are acutely aware of the unregulated activities of many untrained, unsupervised legal practitioners who daily do harm to "clients" and to the public's interest in having high quality civil legal services provided by qualified practitioners.

The practice of law is a professional calling that requires competence, experience, accountability and oversight. Legal License Legal Technicians are not lawyers. They are prohibited from engaging in most activities that lawyers have been trained to provide. They are, under the rule adopted today, authorized to engage in very discrete, limited scope and limited function activities. Many individuals will need far more help than the limited scope of law related activities that a limited license legal technician will be able to offer. These people must still seek help from an attorney. But there are people who need only limited levels of assistance that can be provided by non-lawyers trained and overseen within the framework of the regulatory system developed by the Practice of Law Board. This assistance should be available and affordable. Our system of justice requires it.

I. THE RULE

[T]he rule establishes a framework for the licensing and regulation of non-attorneys to engage in discrete activities that currently fall within the definition of the "practice of law" and which are currently subject to exclusive regulation and oversight by this Court. The rule itself authorizes no one to practice. It simply establishes the regulatory framework for the consideration of proposals to allow non-attorneys to practice. [T]he rule establishes certification requirements (age, education, experience, pro bono service, examination, etc.), defines the specific types of activities that a limited license legal technician would be authorized to engage in, the circumstances under which the limited license legal technician would be allowed to engage in authorized activities (office location, personal services required, contract for services with appropriate disclosures, prohibitions on serving individuals who require services beyond the scope of authority of the limited license legal technician to perform), a detailed list of prohibitions, and continuing certification and financial responsibility requirements.

In addition to the rule, we are today acting on the Practice of Law Board's proposal to establish a Limited License Legal Technician Board. This Board will have responsibility for considering and making recommendations to the Supreme Court with respect to specific proposals for the authorization of limited license legal technicians to engage in some or all of the activities authorized under the Limited License Legal Technician Rule, and authority to oversee the activities of and discipline certified limited license legal technicians in the same way the Washington State Bar Association does with respect to attorneys. The Board is authorized to recommend that limited license legal technicians be authorized to engage in specific activities within the framework of—and limited to—those set forth in the rule itself. We reserve the responsibility to review and approve any proposal to authorize limited license legal technicians to engage in specific activities within specific substantive areas of legal and law related practice. . . .

Today we adopt that portion of the Practice of Law Board's proposal which authorizes limited license legal technicians who meet the education, application and other requirements of the rule be authorized to provide limited legal and law related services to members of the public as authorized by this rule.

II. THE NEED FOR A LIMITED LICENSE LEGAL TECHNICIAN RULE

Our adversarial civil legal system is complex. It is unaffordable not only to low income people but, as the 2003 Civil Legal Needs Study documented, moderate income people as well (defined as families with incomes between 200% and 400% of the Federal Poverty Level). One example of the need for this rule is in the area of family relations which are governed by a myriad of statutes. Decisions relating to changes in family status (divorce, child residential placement, child support, etc.) fall within the exclusive province of our court system. Legal practice is required to conform to specific statewide and local procedures, and practitioners are required to use standard forms developed at both the statewide and local levels. Every day across this state, thousands of unrepresented (pro se) individuals seek to resolve important legal matters in our courts. Many of these are low income people who seek but cannot obtain help from an overtaxed, underfunded civil legal aid system. Many others are moderate income people for whom existing market rates for legal services are cost-prohibitive and who, unfortunately, must search for alternatives in the unregulated marketplace.

Recognizing the difficulties that a ballooning population of unrepresented litigants has created, court managers, legal aid programs and others have embraced a range of strategies to provide greater levels of assistance to these unrepresented litigants. Innovations include the establishment of courthouse facilitators in most counties, establishment of courthouse-based self-help resource centers in some counties, establishment of neighborhood legal clinics and other volunteer-based advice and consultation programs, and the creation of a statewide legal aid self-help website. As reflected most recently in a study conducted by the Washington Center for Court Research, some of these innovations — most particularly the creation of courthouse facilitators — have provided some level of increased meaningful support for pro se litigants.

But there are significant limitations in these services and large gaps in the type of services for pro se litigants. Courthouse facilitators serve the courts, not individual litigants. They may not provide individualized legal advice to family law litigants. They are not subject to confidentiality requirements essential to the practitioner/client relationship. They are strictly limited to engaging in "basic services". . . . They have no specific educational/certification requirements, and often find themselves providing assistance to two sides in contested cases. Web-based self-help materials are useful to a point, but many litigants require additional one-on-one help to understand their specific legal rights and prerogatives and make decisions that are best for them under the circumstances.

From the perspective of pro se litigants, the gap places many of these litigants at a substantial legal disadvantage and, for increasing numbers, forces them to seek help from unregulated, untrained, unsupervised "practitioners." We have a duty to ensure that the public can access affordable legal and law related services, and that they are not left to fall prey to the perils of the unregulated market place.

III. SPECIFIC CONCERNS AND RESPONSES

A number of specific issues that have been raised both in support of and in opposition to this rule deserve additional discussion and response.

Proponents have suggested that the establishment and licensing of limited license legal technicians should be a primary strategy to close the Justice Gap for low and moderate income people with family related legal problems. While there will be some benefit to pro se litigants in need of limited levels of legal help, we must be careful not to create expectations that adoption of this rule is not intended to achieve.

By design, limited license legal technicians authorized to engage in discrete legal and law related activities will not be able to meet that portion of the public's need for help in family law matters that requires the provision of individualized legal representation in complex, contested family law matters. Such representation requires the informed professional assistance of attorneys who have met the educational and related requirements necessary to practice law in Washington. Limited purpose practitioners, no matter how well trained within a discrete subject matter, will not have the breadth of substantive legal knowledge or requisite practice skills to apply professional judgment in a manner that can be consistently counted upon to meet the public's need for competent and skilled legal representation in complex legal cases.

On the other hand, and depending upon how it is implemented, the authorization for limited license legal technicians to engage in certain limited legal and law related activities holds promise to help reduce the level of unmet need for low and moderate income people who have relatively uncomplicated family related legal problems and for whom some level of individualized advice, support and guidance would facilitate a timely and effective outcome.

Some opposing the rule believe that [allowing] limited licensing legal technicians to engage in certain family related legal and law related activities poses a threat to the practicing family law bar.

First, the basis of any regulatory scheme, including our exercise of the exclusive authority to determine who can practice law in this state and under what circumstances, must start and end with the public interest; and any regulatory scheme must be designed to ensure that those who provide legal and law related services have the education, knowledge, skills and abilities to do so. Protecting the monopoly status of attorneys in any practice area is not a legitimate objective.

It is important to observe that members of the family law bar provide high levels of public and pro bono service. In fact, it is fair to say that the demands of pro bono have fallen disproportionately on members of the family law bar. As pointed out in the comments to the Practice of Law Board's proposal, young lawyers and others have been working for years to develop strategies to provide reduced fee services to moderate income clients who cannot afford market-rate legal help. Over the past year, these efforts have been transformed into the Washington State Bar Association's newly established Moderate Means program, an initiative which holds substantial promise to deliver greater access to legal representation for greater numbers of individuals between 200% and 400% of the federal poverty guideline being provided services at affordable rates.

In considering the impact that the limited licensing of legal technicians might have on the practicing family law bar it is important to push past the rhetoric and focus on what limited license legal technicians will be allowed to do, and what they cannot do under the rule. With limited exception, few private attorneys make a living exclusively providing technical legal help to persons in simple family law matters. Most family law attorneys represent clients on matters that require extended levels of personalized legal counsel, advice and representation — including, where necessary, appearing in court — in cases that involve children and/or property.

Stand-alone limited license legal technicians are just what they are described to be — persons who have been trained and authorized to provide technical help (selecting and completing forms, informing clients of applicable procedures and timelines, reviewing and explaining pleadings, identifying additional documents that may be needed, etc.) to clients with fairly simple legal law matters. Under the rule we adopt today, limited license legal technicians would not be able to represent clients in court or contact and negotiate with opposing parties on a client's behalf. For these reasons, the limited licensing of legal technicians is unlikely to have any appreciable impact on attorney practice.

The Practice of Law Board and other proponents argue that the limited licensing of legal technicians will provide a substantially more affordable product than that which is available from attorneys, and that this will make legal help more accessible to the public. Opponents argue that it will be economically impossible for limited license legal technicians to deliver services at less cost than attorneys and thus, there is no market advantage to be achieved by creating this form of limited practitioner.

No one has a crystal ball. It may be that stand-alone limited license legal technicians will not find the practice lucrative and that the cost of establishing and maintaining a practice under this rule will require them to charge rates close to those of attorneys. On the other hand, it may be that economies can be achieved that will allow these very limited services to be offered at a market rate substantially below those of attorneys. There is simply no way to know the answer to this question without trying it.

That said, if market economies can be achieved, the public will have a source of relatively affordable technical legal help with uncomplicated legal matters. This may reduce some of the demand on our state's civil legal aid and pro bono systems and should lead to an increase in the quality and consistency of paperwork presented by pro se litigants.

Further, it may be that non-profit organizations that provide social services with a family law component (e.g., domestic violence shelters; pro bono programs; specialized legal aid programs) will elect to add limited license legal technicians onto their staffs. The cost would be much less than adding an attorney and could enable these programs to add a dimension to their services that will allow for the limited provision of individualized legal help on many cases — especially those involving domestic violence. Relationships might be extended with traditional legal aid programs or private pro bono attorneys so that there might be sufficient attorney supervision of the activities of the limited license legal technicians to enable them to engage in those activities for which "direct and active" attorney supervision is required under the rule.

Some have suggested that there is no need for this rule at all, and that the WSBA's Moderate Means Program will solve the problem that the limited licensing of legal technicians is intended to address. This is highly unlikely. First, there are large rural areas throughout the state where there are few attorneys. In these areas, many attorneys are barely able to scrape by. Doing reduced fee work through the Moderate Means program (like doing pro bono work) will not be a high priority.

Second, limited licensing of legal technicians *complements*, rather than competes with, the efforts WSBA is undertaking through the Moderate Means program. We know that there is a huge need for representation in contested cases where court appearances are required. We know further that pro se litigants are at a decided disadvantage in such cases, especially when the adverse party is represented. Limited license legal technicians are not permitted to provide this level of assistance; they are limited to performing mostly ministerial technical/legal functions. Given the spectrum of unmet legal needs out there, Moderate Means attorneys will be asked to focus their energy on providing the help that is needed most — representing low and moderate income people who cannot secure necessary representation in contested, often complex legal proceedings.

Opponents of the rule argue that the limited licensing of legal technicians presents a threat to clients and the public. To the contrary, the authorization to establish, regulate and oversee the limited practice of legal technicians within the framework of the rule adopted today will serve the public interest and protect the public. The threat of consumer abuse already exists and is, unfortunately, widespread. There are far too many unlicensed, unregulated and unscrupulous "practitioners" preying on those who need legal help but cannot afford an attorney. Establishing a rule for the application, regulation, oversight and discipline of non-attorney practitioners establishes a regulatory framework that reduces the risk that members of the public will fall victim to those who are currently filling the gap in affordable legal services.

Unlike those operating in the unregulated marketplace, limited license legal technicians will practice within a carefully crafted regulatory framework that incorporates a range of safeguards necessary to protect the public. The educational requirements are rigorous. Unlike attorneys, legal technicians are required to demonstrate financial responsibility in ways established by the Board. There is a testing requirement to demonstrate professional competency to practice, contracting and disclosure requirements are significant, and there will be a robust oversight and disciplinary process. This rule protects the public.

. . .

IV. CONCLUSION

Today's adoption of APR 28 is a good start. The licensing of limited license legal technicians will not close the Justice Gap identified in the 2003 Civil Legal Needs Study. Nor will it solve the access to justice crisis for moderate income individuals

with legal needs. But it is a limited, narrowly tailored strategy designed to expand the provision of legal and law related services to members of the problems.

The Limited License Legal Technician Rule is thoughtful and measured. It offers ample protection for Members of the public who will purchase or receive services from limited license legal technicians. It offers a sound opportunity to determine whether and, if so, to what degree the involvement of effectively trained, licensed and regulated non-attorneys may help expand access to necessary legal help in ways that serve the justice system and protect the public.

Post-Case Follow-Up

Following the Washington Supreme Court's approval of LLLTs to work on family law matters, the LLLT Board went to work setting forth a regulatory framework for LLLTs. In order to practice, LLLTs must have an associate's degree or higher, complete 45 credit hours of core curriculum through a program approved by the ABA or the LLLT Board, pass family law courses offered at the University of Washington School of Law, take part in 3,000 hours of paralegal work, and pass the Practice Area and Professional Responsibility Exams. Once admitted to practice, LLLTs can do most of the work that a lawyer can do except that they cannot represent clients in court or negotiate on behalf of a client, and they can only prepare legal documents that have been approved by the LLLT Board. The board also passed the LLLT Rules of Professional Conduct, similar to those for lawyers, which seek to ensure ethical behavior.

Washington State is considering expanding the licensure of LLLTs to other substantive areas of law, with elder law, landlord-tenant disputes, and immigration under consideration. Several other states, including California, New York, Utah, Colorado, and Oregon, are also exploring the LLLT model.

Limited License Legal Technicians: Real Life Applications

1. If you had a family law issue and lived in Washington State, would you consider hiring an LLLT? What are the pros and cons of using an LLLT as opposed to a lawyer?

2. What good is an LLLT if he can draft documents for you (such as an application for a divorce) but cannot negotiate with opposing counsel?

Alternative Business Structures (ABS)

The Model Rules of Professional Conduct prohibit non-lawyer ownership of law firms, non-lawyer management of law firms, and sharing fees with non-lawyers (except under very limited circumstances). The term **Alternative Business Structures** (ABS) generally refers to business models that deviate from this rule in some way. Only two U.S. jurisdictions permit any form of ABS. First, the District of

Columbia permits non-lawyers to have a financial interest and hold managerial authority in a law firm. Very few ABS firms exist, however, most likely because most attorneys in D.C. hold licenses in other jurisdictions that forbid ABS, and, moreover, D.C. firms that permit ABS could not expand outside of D.C. The only other state that permits ABS is Washington State, where LLLTs may own a minority interest in a law firm.[27]

Outside of the United States, however, many jurisdictions, including Australia, England and Wales, Singapore, Scotland, Italy, Spain, Denmark, Germany, the Netherlands, Poland, Spain, Belgium, New Zealand, and some Canadian provinces permit various forms of ABS.[28] What each jurisdiction allows varies. There are a wide variety of arguments for and against liberalizing the rules concerning ABS, but one relates to the topic of access to justice. Proponents of ABS believe that it will increase access to affordable legal services. As one commentator explained:

> First, [limits on non-lawyer funding] constrain the supply of capital for law firms, thereby increasing the cost which the firms must pay for it. To the extent that this cost of doing business is passed along to consumers, it will increase the price of legal services. Second, bigger firms might be better for access to justice, due to risk-spreading opportunities and economies of scale and scope. Individual clients . . . must currently rely on small partnerships and solo practitioners, and allowing non-lawyer capital and management into the market might facilitate the emergence of large consumer law firms. Large firms would plausibly find it easier than small ones to expand access through flat rate billing, reputational branding, and investment in technology. Finally, insulating lawyers from non-lawyers precludes potentially innovative interprofessional collaborations, which might bring the benefits of legal services to more people even if firms stay small.[29]

To date, however, there is no empirical data about whether the liberal regulatory schemes in jurisdictions that permit ABS actually increase access to justice.

Chapter Summary

- Parties in civil litigation generally have no right to counsel. In its most recent pronouncement on this issue, the Supreme Court ruled in *Turner v. Rogers* that the Due Process Clause does not require the state to provide counsel to an indigent defendant who faces incarceration for civil contempt where the custodial parent was also unrepresented. The majority did hold, however, that the state must provide some basic procedural protections. Some states guarantee lawyers in limited categories of cases by statute or court decision.

---

27. ABA Comm'n on the Future of Legal Servs., Report on the Future of Legal Services in the United States 16 (2016), http://abafuturesreport.com/2016-fls-report-web.pdf (last visited May 27, 2017).

28. *Id.*

29. Noel Semple, Legal Services Regulation at the Crossroads: Justitia's Legions 158 (2015) (emphasis omitted); *see* Gillian K. Hadfield, *The Cost of Law: Promoting Access to Justice Through the (Un)Corporate Practice of Law*, 38 Int'l Rev. L. & Econ. 43 (2014).

- With no legal right to counsel, low- and moderate-income Americans lack adequate access to representation. More than 80 percent of the legal needs of the poor and a majority of the needs of moderate-income Americans go unmet.
- Lawyers, courts, innovators, commentators, and others have proposed a wide range of potential solutions to address the access-to-justice gap. These include simplifying court procedures, allowing greater use of non-lawyers to deliver legal services, technological innovations, loosening of regulatory restrictions, and mandatory pro bono.

Applying the Rules

1. To demonstrate the power of a good legal website, let's pretend that you are a handyman living in Waukegan in Lake County, Illinois. You performed extensive work for a local business that now refuses to pay you the $4,600 they owe you. Go to www.illinoislegalaid.org and find out information about your legal rights and what steps you might take to try to collect what you are owed.

2. Figure out if you or those in your family can afford legal services. Go to the Economic Policy Institute's Family Budget Calculator (http://www.epi.org/resources/budget/) to calculate how much money you need to earn to attain a "modest yet adequate standard of living." If you suddenly face an unexpected legal issue, do you have several hundred (or thousand) dollars left over to hire a lawyer?

Professional Responsibility in Practice

1. As noted earlier, when it comes to access to legal services, "geography is destiny." Find out what resources are available in your state/city/community.

2. Imagine that you have a legal problem (you have received an eviction notice, you plan to get divorced, you have received a complaint in a debt collection action, or some other issue). You plan to solve that problem without a lawyer. How would you proceed? What resources are available in your jurisdiction to help?

3. Visit a local courthouse that hears cases involving low- and moderate-income litigants (small claims court, housing court, etc.). Document what you see. Do the parties have lawyers? How does the judge treat those who do not? How do unrepresented litigants fare?

4. Innovators from all over the world have devised innovations that employ technology to improve the delivery of legal services. Get on the Internet and find one.

5. Beginning with Washington State in 1994, most states launched Access to Justice Commissions to study the justice gap and possible solutions. The final reports of these commissions are a good way to learn about some of the specific barriers to justice in those states. Go to https://public.tableau.com/views/AccesstoJusticeCommissions/Dashboard1?:embed=y&:display_count=yes&:showVizHome=no to find your state's Access to Justice Commission and see what you can learn about the unique issues facing your state.

PART V

The Judiciary

12

Judicial Ethics

Lawyers need to know the laws and rules governing judges for at least three reasons. First, Model Rule of Professional Conduct 8.4(f) provides that a lawyer shall not "knowingly assist a judge or judicial officer in conduct that is a violation of applicable rules of judicial conduct or other law." Thus, lawyers must know the rules governing judges in order to avoid getting in trouble themselves. Second, some lawyers will run for judicial office. Rule 8.2(b) provides that "[a] lawyer who is a candidate for judicial office shall comply with the applicable provisions of the Code of Judicial Conduct." Third, lawyers need to know the circumstances under which they should move to disqualify a judge.

The regulatory structure for judges is similar to the regulatory structure for lawyers. The ABA has issued a Model Code of Judicial Conduct, which states are free to accept, modify, or reject. The Code applies to all individuals who perform "judicial functions" even if they are not full-time judges, and it follows a format similar to the Model Rules of Professional Conduct. The Model Code, which has been largely adopted by the states, was substantially amended in 2007. In contrast to its predecessors, the 2007 Code is similar to a piece of legislation, providing black letter rules for judges to follow that are organized around four canons, or overarching principles. As with the Model Rules, a judge who violates a Code provision is subject to discipline, and most states have commissions comprised

Key Concepts

- The requirement that judges perform their **judicial duties** "impartially, competently, and diligently"
- The requirement that judges' **extrajudicial activities** not interfere with the performance of their judicial duties
- The standards for disqualification under the rules of professional conduct and the United States Constitution
- Understanding and applying the limits on **political activity by judicial candidates** and the First Amendment implications of those limits

of judges and lawyers to enforce the state code. The Code also sets forth the circumstances in which judges should be disqualified.[1]

With its emphasis on judicial independence and integrity, Canon 1 sets the tone for the entire Code: "[a] judge shall uphold and promote the independence, integrity, and impartiality of the judiciary, and shall avoid impropriety and the appearance of impropriety." Among the specific edicts under Canon 1: judges shall "comply with the law";[2] "act at all times in a manner that promotes public confidence in the independence, integrity, and impartiality of the judiciary";[3] "avoid impropriety and the appearance of impropriety";[4] and "not abuse the prestige of judicial office to advance the personal or economic interests of the judge or others."[5]

This chapter explores the specific applications of these concepts in four distinct areas: Section A, judges' performance of their judicial duties, Section B, judges' involvement in extrajudicial activities, Section C, judicial disqualification, and Section D, judicial campaigns and other political activity.

A. PERFORMANCE OF JUDICIAL DUTIES

Canon 2 governs a judge's conduct in performing his judicial duties and requires a judge to "perform the duties of judicial office impartially, competently, and diligently."[6] These judicial duties "take precedence over all of a judge's personal and extrajudicial activities."[7] The rules under Canon 2 serve to ensure the critical principles of independence and impartiality in several ways.

First, Rule 2.2 states the obvious: judges must "uphold and apply the law"; yet on occasion, judges are sanctioned for violating this rule. In *In re Hague*, a Michigan trial judge was suspended for repeatedly refusing to follow the rulings of the Michigan appellate court.[8] More recently, the Alabama Court of the Judiciary suspended Alabama Supreme Court Chief Justice Roy Moore for violating several provisions of the Alabama Code of Judicial Conduct, including Alabama's equivalent to Rule 2.2.[9] After the U.S. Supreme Court had issued its decision in Obergefell v. Hodges, 135 S. Ct. 2584, 2607 (2015), holding that "same-sex couples may exercise the fundamental right to marry in all states," Chief Justice Moore issued an administrative order to Alabama's 68 probate judges that they should continue to follow Alabama state law forbidding same-sex marriage and therefore not issue

1. In addition to the code of judicial ethics, judges are also subject to other federal and state laws. For example, 28 U.S.C. §455 (2012), which contains essentially the same disqualification standard as Rule 2.11 of the Model Code of Judicial Conduct, governs federal judges. In addition, the Due Process Clause of the United States Constitution requires judges to recuse themselves in some extreme cases. *See* Section C, *infra*.
2. Model Code of Judicial Conduct r. 1.1 (Am. Bar. Ass'n 2011) [hereinafter Model Code].
3. *Id.* r. 1.2.
4. *Id.*
5. *Id.* r. 1.3.
6. *Id.* Canon 2.
7. *Id.* r. 2.1.
8. 315 N.W.2d 524 (1982) (suspending the judge for 60 days without pay).
9. *In re Moore*, No. 46 (Ala. Ct. Judiciary Sept. 30, 2016), http://judicial.alabama.gov/judiciary/COJ46Final Judgment_09302016.pdf.

any marriage licenses to same-sex couples.[10] The Alabama Court of the Judiciary concluded that Moore should be disciplined because "the undeniable consequence of [Chief Justice Moore's administrative order] was to order and direct the probate judges to deny marriage licenses in direct defiance of the decision of the United States Supreme Court in *Obergefell*."[11]

Second, to ensure that judges are impartial and independent, the rules constrain the judge in her decision-making process in several ways. First, judges must perform their duties "without bias or prejudice"[12] and free from "external influences."[13] Second, a judge may not engage in *ex parte* communications with a lawyer, except under limited circumstances.[14] Third, judges may not engage in independent investigation (including social media research) concerning the facts of a case.[15] This is a surprisingly easy prohibition to violate in the digital age: a North Carolina judge was publicly reprimanded for Googling one of the parties.[16] With respect to the law, a judge may hire an independent expert, but he must let both the parties know.[17]

Finally, the rules also limit what a judge can say about a case. Rule 2.10 provides that a judge "shall not make any public statement that might reasonably be expected to affect the outcome or impair the fairness of a matter pending or impending."[18] Similarly, judges may not make "pledges, promises or commitments" in connection with a case.[19] The constitutionality of the "pledges and promises" ban, which also applies to judicial candidates, is discussed below in Section D.

B. EXTRAJUDICIAL ACTIVITIES

Off the bench, judges must conduct their activities "to minimize the risk of conflict" with their judicial obligations.[20] Again, the principal guiding factors are the maintenance and appearance of judicial independence and impartiality. Accordingly, Rule 3.1 states rather broad principles: a judge shall not participate in activities that "will interfere with the proper performance of the judge's judicial duties," "will lead to frequent disqualification of the judge," or "would appear to a reasonable person to undermine the judge's independence, integrity, or impartiality."[21] The rules go on to offer several more specific prohibitions.

---

10. *Moore*, No. 46, 9-13.
11. *Id.* at 32. The Alabama Supreme Court upheld the suspension. Moore v. Ala. Judicial Inquiry Comm'n, No. 1160002 (Ala. Apr. 19, 2017), https://www.scribd.com/document/345653431/Alabama-Supreme-Court order-on-Roy-Moore#from_embed.
12. Model Code r. 2.3.
13. *Id.* r. 2.4.
14. *Id.* r. 2.9.
15. *Id.* r. 2.9(c); r. 2.9 cmt. 6.
16. Public Reprimand of B. Carlton Terry, Jr., No. 08-234 (N.C. Jud. Standards Comm'n Apr. 1, 2009), http://www.aoc.state.nc.us/www/public/coa/jsc/publicreprimands/jsc08-234.pdf.
17. Model Code r. 2.9(a)(2).
18. *Id.* r. 2.10(a).
19. *Id.* r. 2.10(b).
20. *Id.* Canon 3.
21. *Id.* r. 3.1.

First, judges can't use the prestige of their office to advance their own or others' interests. Thus, a judge cannot appear before governmental bodies (with some limited exceptions)[22] or testify as a character witness (unless subpoenaed).[23]

Further, because it is important for judges to maintain the public's confidence in the integrity and impartiality of the judiciary, judges "shall not hold membership in any organization that practices invidious discrimination on the basis of race, sex, gender, religion, national origin, ethnicity, or sexual orientation."[24]

Finally, judges may not accept "any gifts, loans, bequests, benefits, or other things of value, if acceptance is prohibited by law or would appear to a reasonable person to undermine the judge's independence, integrity or impartiality."[25] The rule goes on to list a number of items that the judge may accept, including "items with little intrinsic value."[26] In general, judges may also accept reimbursement for expenses in connection with extracurricular activities, such as speeches.[27]

C. JUDICIAL DISQUALIFICATION

Disqualification is perhaps the most difficult doctrinal issue in the field of judicial ethics. This section considers the issue of when judges should be disqualified under the Code of Judicial Conduct, including the possibility that judges' social media use could lead to disqualification, before turning to the exceptional circumstances under which the Due Process Clause of the United States Constitution requires disqualification.

1. Disqualification Under the Code

Rule 2.11 and the federal statute (28 U.S.C. §455) that applies to federal judges both require that judges disqualify themselves "in any proceeding in which the judge's impartiality might reasonably be questioned."[28] Most states have similar provisions for their state judges.[29] This standard goes beyond cases of actual bias and also prohibits judges from sitting in cases involving the appearance of impropriety. A comment to the Code provides: "The test for appearance of impropriety is whether the conduct would create in reasonable minds a perception that the judge violated this Code or engaged in other conduct that reflects adversely on the judge's honesty,

22. Id. r. 3.2.
23. *Id.* r. 3.3.
24. *Id.* r. 3.6(a).
25. *Id.* r. 3.13.
26. *Id.* r. 3.31(b)(1).
27. *Id.* r. 3.14.
28. *Id.* r. 2.11(a). The statute applicable to federal judges, 28 U.S.C. §455, contains an almost identical standard: "Any justice, judge, or magistrate judge of the United States shall disqualify himself in any proceeding in which his impartiality might reasonably be questioned." 28 U.S.C. §455(a) (2012).
29. Richard E. Flamm, Judicial Disqualification: Recusal and Disqualification of Judges §5.2 (2d ed. 2007 & Supp. 2016).

impartiality, temperament, or fitness to serve as a judge."[30] The words "reasonably" in the Code provision and "reasonable" in the comments indicate that this is an objective standard.

Judges also have an affirmative obligation to disclose on the record information that the parties or their lawyers "might reasonably consider relevant" to the disqualification issue, even if the judge believes that disqualification is not warranted.[31] In most circumstances, judges may also ask the parties to waive disqualification.[32]

The Rule provides a non-exclusive list of circumstances requiring disqualification, including when

(1) the judge has a "personal bias or prejudice concerning a party or a party's lawyer" or "personal knowledge" of the facts in dispute;
(2) the judge or a family member is a party, lawyer, or material witness in the proceeding;
(3) the judge or a close family member has an economic interest in the proceeding;
(4) the judge previously served as a lawyer in the matter.

The more difficult question is what circumstances, outside of these enumerated in the rule, require disqualification. Judges' social relationships with litigants, lawyers, or witnesses in pending matters present a particularly knotty issue. Courts have recognized that such a friendship certainly can create an "appearance of partiality."[33] The specific concern is that the personal relationship will cause "a reasonable person knowing all the circumstances [to] believe that the judge will accord different credibility to the testimony or statements of the person known to the judge."[34]

Distinguishing which social relationships are impermissible under the "appearance of impropriety" standard is a challenge, particularly in the context of friendship. For that reason, some commentators have justifiably criticized the standard.[35] The Code does not define the level of friendship with the parties or lawyers that would require a judge to recuse himself. Moreover, judges are certainly permitted—if not encouraged—to maintain a social life and certainly do not have to, as one court put it, "withdraw from society and live an ascetic, antiseptic and socially sterile life."[36] The Code accepts that judges may have a social life by recognizing that judges who accept "ordinary social hospitality" do not run afoul of the prohibition on receiving gifts.[37]

---

30. Model Code r. 1.2 cmt. 5.
31. *Id.* r. 2.11 cmt. 5.
32. *Id.* r. 2.11(c).
33. *See, e.g.*, United States v. Kelly, 888 F.2d 732, 745 (11th Cir. 1989) (holding that trial judge, who was close friends with a key defense witness, improperly failed to disqualify himself under the federal disqualification statute).
34. Leslie W. Abramson, *Appearance of Impropriety: Deciding When a Judge's Impartiality "Might Reasonably Be Questioned,"* 14 Geo. J. Legal Ethics 55, 96 (2000).
35. Jeremy M. Miller, *Judicial Recusal and Disqualification: The Need for a* Per Se *Rule on Friendship (Not Acquaintance)*, 33 Pepp. L. Rev. 575, 577 (2006) (criticizing the "glaring gap in the law on the issue of when a judge must recuse himself or herself because a party or advocate in the case is a friend").
36. United Farm Workers of Am. v. Superior Court, 170 Cal. App. 3d 97, 100 (Ct. App. 1985).
37. Model Code r. 3.13(b)(3).

Because of their shared interests and backgrounds, judges are quite likely to have social relationships with lawyers. There is obviously nothing wrong with such a relationship *per se*, but at some point that relationship becomes disqualifying, perhaps because the relationship is so close or because the judge is interacting with the lawyer while the case is pending. The courts and ethics authorities have struggled to determine what constitutes permissible "ordinary social hospitality," versus an impermissible "appearance of impropriety." Further complicating the matter is Rule 2.7, which imposes on judges a "duty to sit." This rule requires judges to "hear and decide matters assigned to the judge, except when disqualification is required."[38] In other words, judges should not recuse themselves for frivolous reasons, nor should they necessarily err on the side of disqualification in close cases. This issue became the subject of a national debate in 2004 when Justice Antonin Scalia went duck hunting with Vice President Richard Cheney while Cheney was a party to a case pending before the Supreme Court.

Case Preview

Cheney v. United States District Court for the District of Columbia

During President George W. Bush's first term (2000-2004), he appointed Vice President Richard Cheney to chair the National Energy Policy Development Group, the administration's energy task force. As part of this work, Cheney and the other governmental officials on the task force allegedly met behind closed doors with energy industry officials and lobbyists.[39] Two public interest groups with very different political leanings — the Sierra Club and Judicial Watch — filed suit against Cheney seeking records from the task force, arguing that the secretive meetings violated an open government law entitled the Federal Advisory Committee Act (FACA), 5 U.S.C. appx. §§1-16 (2012). The administration maintained that the meetings were not subject to FACA. These meetings were politically significant, particularly during President Bush's 2004 reelection campaign against John Kerry, when Kerry and other critics of the Bush administration argued that these meetings demonstrated that the administration was letting big energy corporations dictate the nation's energy agenda.

On December 15, 2003 (less than a year before the presidential election), the U.S. Supreme Court agreed to hear Vice President Cheney's appeal from a lower court ruling ordering him and other senior officials to produce information about the work of the task force. Three weeks later, in mid-January 2004, Vice President Cheney and Justice Antonin Scalia, who were longtime friends, went duck hunting together at a private camp in southern Louisiana. On February 23, 2004, the Sierra Club moved to disqualify Justice Scalia from hearing the FACA case. Consistent with its historic practice, the motion was referred to Justice Scalia.

38. *Id.* r. 2.7.

39. Bill Mears, *High court hears arguments on Cheney task force*, CNN, June 24, 2004. http://www.cnn.com/2004/LAW/04/27/scotus.cheney/.

Vice President Cheney and Justice Scalia were lifelong friends. The Sierra Club moved to disqualify Justice Scalia from hearing the FACA case.
Albert H. Teich / Shutterstock.com; Collection of the Supreme Court of the United States

As you read Justice Scalia's decision and Lawrence Fox's commentary that follows, consider the following:

1. What are Justice Scalia's most convincing arguments in support of his conclusion that he should not recuse himself? What are Professor Fox's most convincing counter-arguments? Who do you think is right?
2. After reading Justice Scalia's opinion, are you more or less likely to question his impartiality in this case?
3. What is the procedure for handling disqualification motions at the Supreme Court? Can you think of ways to improve the procedure? How is a motion to disqualify a Supreme Court justice different than a motion to disqualify a trial judge?

Cheney v. United States District Court for the District of Columbia

541 U.S. 913 (2004)

Memorandum of Justice Scalia.

. . .

I

The decision whether a judge's impartiality can "'reasonably be questioned'" is to be made in light of the facts as they existed, and not as they were surmised or reported. The facts here were as follows:

For five years or so, I have been going to Louisiana during the Court's long December-January recess, to the duck-hunting camp of a friend whom I met through two hunting companions from Baton Rouge, one a dentist and the other a worker in the field of handicapped rehabilitation. The last three years, I have been accompanied on this trip by a son-in-law who lives near me. Our friend and host, Wallace Carline, has never, as far as I know, had business before this Court. He is not, as some reports have described him, an "energy industry executive" in the sense that summons up boardrooms of ExxonMobil or Con Edison. He runs his own company that provides services and equipment rental to oil rigs in the Gulf of Mexico.

During my December 2002 visit, I learned that Mr. Carline was an admirer of Vice President Cheney. Knowing that the Vice President, with whom I am well acquainted (from our years serving together in the Ford administration), is an enthusiastic duck hunter, I asked whether Mr. Carline would like to invite him to our next year's hunt. The answer was yes; I conveyed the invitation (with my own warm recommendation) in the spring of 2003 and received an acceptance (subject, of course, to any superseding demands on the Vice President's time) in the summer. The Vice President said that if he did go, I would be welcome to fly down to Louisiana with him. (Because of national security requirements, of course, he must fly in a Government plane.) That invitation was later extended — if space was available — to my son-in-law and to a son who was joining the hunt for the first time; they accepted. The trip was set long before the Court granted certiorari in the present case, and indeed before the petition for certiorari had even been filed.

We departed from Andrews Air Force Base at about 10 a.m. on Monday, January 5, flying in a Gulfstream jet owned by the Government. We landed in Patterson, Louisiana, and went by car to a dock where Mr. Carline met us, to take us on the 20-minute boat trip to his hunting camp. We arrived at about 2 p.m., the 5 of us joining about 8 other hunters, making about 13 hunters in all; also present during our time there were about 3 members of Mr. Carline's staff, and, of course, the Vice President's staff and security detail. It was not an intimate setting. The group hunted that afternoon and Tuesday and Wednesday mornings; it fished (in two boats) Tuesday afternoon. All meals were in common. Sleeping was in rooms of two or three, except for the Vice President, who had his own quarters. Hunting was in two- or three-man blinds. As it turned out, I never hunted in the same blind with the Vice President. Nor was I alone with him at any time during the trip, except, perhaps, for instances so brief and unintentional that I would not recall them — walking to or from a boat, perhaps, or going to or from dinner. Of course we said not a word about the present case. The Vice President left the camp Wednesday afternoon, about two days after our arrival. I stayed on to hunt (with my son and son-in-law) until late Friday morning, when the three of us returned to Washington on a commercial flight from New Orleans.

II

Let me respond, at the outset, to Sierra Club's suggestion that I should "resolve any doubts in favor of recusal." That might be sound advice if I were sitting on a Court of Appeals. There, my place would be taken by another judge, and the case would proceed normally. On the Supreme Court, however, the consequence is different: The Court proceeds with eight Justices, raising the possibility that, by reason of a tie vote, it will find itself unable to resolve the significant legal issue presented by the case. Thus, as Justices stated in their 1993 Statement of Recusal Policy: "We do not think it would serve the public interest to go beyond the requirements of the statute, and to recuse ourselves, out of an excess of caution, whenever a relative is a partner in the firm before us or acted as a lawyer at an earlier stage. Even one unnecessary recusal impairs the functioning of the Court." Moreover, granting the motion is (insofar as the outcome of the particular case is concerned) effectively the same as casting a vote against the petitioner. The petitioner needs five votes to overturn the judgment below, and it makes no difference whether the needed fifth vote is missing because it has been cast for the other side, or because it has not been cast at all.

Even so, recusal is the course I must take — and will take — when, on the basis of established principles and practices, I have said or done something which requires that course. I have recused for such a reason this very Term. I believe, however, that established principles and practices do not require (and thus do not permit) recusal in the present case.

A

My recusal is required if, by reason of the actions described above, my "impartiality might reasonably be questioned." 28 U.S.C. §455(a). Why would that result follow from my being in a sizable group of persons, in a hunting camp with the Vice President, where I never hunted with him in the same blind or had other opportunity for private conversation? The only possibility is that it would suggest I am a friend of his. But while friendship is a ground for recusal of a Justice where the personal fortune or the personal freedom of the friend is at issue, it has traditionally *not* been a ground for recusal where *official action* is at issue, no matter how important the official action was to the ambitions or the reputation of the Government officer.

A rule that required Members of this Court to remove themselves from cases in which the official actions of friends were at issue would be utterly disabling. Many Justices have reached this Court precisely because they were friends of the incumbent President or other senior officials — and from the earliest days down to modern times Justices have had close personal relationships with the President and other officers of the Executive. John Quincy Adams hosted dinner parties featuring such luminaries as Chief Justice Marshall, Justices Johnson, Story, and Todd, Attorney General Wirt, and Daniel Webster. Justice Harlan and his wife often "'stopped in'" at the White House to see the Hayes family and pass a Sunday evening in a small group, visiting and singing hymns. Justice Stone tossed around a medicine ball with members of the Hoover administration mornings outside the White House. Justice Douglas was a regular at President Franklin Roosevelt's poker parties; Chief Justice Vinson played poker with President Truman. A no-friends rule would have disqualified much of the Court in *Youngstown Sheet & Tube Co. v. Sawyer*, the case that challenged President Truman's seizure of the steel mills. Most of the Justices knew Truman well, and four had been appointed by him. A no-friends rule would surely have required Justice Holmes's recusal in *Northern Securities Co. v. United States*, the case that challenged President Theodore Roosevelt's trust-busting initiative.

It is said, however, that this case is different because the federal officer (Vice President Cheney) is actually a *named party*. That is by no means a rarity. At the beginning of the current Term, there were before the Court (excluding habeas actions) no fewer than 83 cases in which high-level federal Executive officers were named in their official capacity—more than 1 in every 10 federal civil cases then pending. That an officer is named has traditionally made no difference to the proposition that friendship is not considered to affect impartiality in official-action suits. Regardless of whom they name, such suits, when the officer is the plaintiff, seek relief not for him personally but for the Government; and, when the officer is the defendant, seek relief not against him personally, but against the Government. That is why federal law provides for *automatic substitution* of the new officer when the originally named officer has been replaced....

Richard Cheney's name appears in this suit only because he was the head of a Government committee that allegedly did not comply with the Federal Advisory Committee Act (FACA), and because he may, by reason of his office, have custody of some or all of the Government documents that the plaintiffs seek. If some other person were to become head of that committee or to obtain custody of those documents, the plaintiffs would name that person and Cheney would be dismissed. Unlike the defendant in *United States v. Nixon* or *Clinton v. Jones*, Cheney is represented here, not by his personal attorney, but by the United States Department of Justice in the person of the Solicitor General. And the courts at all levels have referred to his arguments as (what they are) the arguments of "the government."

The recusal motion, however, asserts the following:

> "Critical to the issue of Justice Scalia's recusal is understanding that this is not a run-of-the-mill legal dispute about an administrative decision.... Because his own conduct is central to this case, the Vice President's 'reputation and his integrity are on the line.' (Chicago Tribune.)"

I think not. Certainly as far as the legal issues immediately presented to me are concerned, this *is* "a run-of-the-mill legal dispute about an administrative decision." I am asked to determine what powers the District Court possessed under FACA, and whether the Court of Appeals should have asserted mandamus or appellate jurisdiction over the District Court. Nothing this Court says on those subjects will have any bearing upon the reputation and integrity of Richard Cheney. Moreover, even if this Court affirms the decision below and allows discovery to proceed in the District Court, the issue that would ultimately present itself *still* would have no bearing upon the reputation and integrity of Richard Cheney. That issue would be, quite simply, whether some private individuals were *de facto* members of the National Energy Policy Development Group (NEPDG). It matters not whether they were caused to be so by Cheney or someone else, or whether Cheney was even aware of their *de facto* status; if they *were de facto* members, then (according to D.C. Circuit law) the records and minutes of NEPDG must be made public.

The recusal motion asserts, however, that Richard Cheney's "'reputation and his integrity are on the line'" because "respondents have alleged, *inter alia*, that the Vice President, as the head of the Task Force and its subgroups, was responsible for the involvement of energy industry executives in the operations of the Task Force, as a result of which the Task Force and its subgroups became subject to FACA."

As far as Sierra Club's *complaint* is concerned, it simply is not true that Vice President Cheney is singled out as having caused the involvement of energy executives.

But even if the allegation had been made, it would be irrelevant to the case. FACA assertedly requires disclosure if there were private members of the task force, *no matter who* they were — "energy industry executives" or Ralph Nader; and *no matter who* was responsible for their membership — the Vice President or no one in particular. I do not see how the Vice President's "'reputation and . . . integrity are on the line'" any more than the agency head's reputation and integrity are on the line in virtually all official-action suits, which accuse his agency of acting (to quote the Administrative Procedure Act) "arbitrar[ily], capricious[ly], [with] an abuse of discretion, or otherwise not in accordance with law." Beyond that always-present accusation, there is nothing illegal or immoral about making "energy industry executives" members of a task force on energy; some people probably think it would be a good idea. If, in doing so, or in allowing it to happen, the Vice President went beyond his assigned powers, that is no worse than what every agency head has done when his action is judicially set aside.

To be sure, there could be political consequences from disclosure of the fact (if it be so) that the Vice President favored business interests, and especially a sector of business with which he was formerly connected. But political consequences are not my concern, and the possibility of them does not convert an official suit into a private one. That possibility exists to a greater or lesser degree in virtually all suits involving agency action. To expect judges to take account of political consequences — and to assess the high or low degree of them — is to ask judges to do precisely what they should not do. It seems to me quite wrong (and quite impossible) to make recusal depend upon what degree of political damage a particular case can be expected to inflict.

In sum, I see nothing about this case which takes it out of the category of normal official-action litigation, where my friendship, or the appearance of my friendship, with one of the named officers does not require recusal.

B

The recusal motion claims that "the fact that Justice Scalia and his daughter [*sic*] were the Vice President's guest on Air Force Two on the flight down to Louisiana" means that I "accepted a sizable gift from a party in a pending case," a gift "measured in the thousands of dollars." Let me speak first to the value, though that is not the principal point. Our flight down cost the Government nothing, since space-available was the condition of our invitation. And, though our flight down on the Vice President's plane was indeed free, since we were not returning with him we purchased (because they were least expensive) round-trip tickets that cost precisely what we would have paid if we had gone both down and back on commercial flights. In other words, none of us saved a cent by flying on the Vice President's plane. The purpose of going with him was not saving money, but avoiding some inconvenience to ourselves (being taken by car from New Orleans to Morgan City) and considerable inconvenience to our friends, who would have had to meet our plane in New Orleans, and schedule separate boat trips to the hunting camp, for us and for the Vice President's party. . . .

The principal point, however, is that social courtesies, provided at Government expense by officials whose only business before the Court is business in their official capacity, have not hitherto been thought prohibited. Members of Congress and others are frequently invited to accompany Executive Branch officials on Government planes, where space is available. That this is not the sort of gift thought likely to affect a judge's impartiality is suggested by the fact that the Ethics in Government Act of 1978, which requires annual reporting of transportation provided or reimbursed, excludes from this requirement transportation provided by the United States. I daresay that, at a hypothetical charity auction, much more would be bid for dinner for two at the White House than for a one-way flight to Louisiana on the Vice President's jet. Justices accept the former with regularity. While this matter was pending, Justices and their spouses were invited (*all* of them, I believe) to a December 11, 2003, Christmas reception at the residence of the Vice President — which included an opportunity for a photograph with the Vice President and Mrs. Cheney. Several of the Justices attended, and in doing so they were fully in accord with the proprieties.

III

When I learned that Sierra Club had filed a recusal motion in this case, I assumed that the motion would be replete with citations of legal authority, and would provide some instances of cases in which, because of activity similar to what occurred here, Justices have recused themselves or at least have been asked to do so. In fact, however, the motion cites only two Supreme Court cases assertedly relevant to the issue here discussed, and nine Court of Appeals cases. Not a single one of these even involves an official-action suit. And the motion gives not a single instance in which, under even remotely similar circumstances, a Justice has recused or been asked to recuse. Instead, the argument section of the motion consists almost entirely of references to, and quotations from, newspaper editorials. The core of Sierra Club's argument is as follows:

> "Sierra Club makes this motion because . . . damage [to the integrity of the system] is being done right now. As of today, 8 of the 10 newspapers with the largest circulation in the United States, 14 of the largest 20, and 20 of the 30 largest have called on Justice Scalia to step aside. . . . Of equal import, there is no counterbalance or controversy: not a single newspaper has argued against recusal. Because the American public, as reflected in the nation's newspaper editorials, has unanimously concluded that there is an appearance of favoritism, any objective observer would be compelled to conclude that Justice Scalia's impartiality has been questioned. These facts more than satisfy Section 455(a), which mandates recusal merely when a Justice's impartiality 'might reasonably be questioned.'"

The implications of this argument are staggering. I must recuse because a significant portion of the press, which is deemed to be the American public, demands it.

The motion attaches as exhibits the press editorials on which it relies. Many of them do not even have the facts right. The length of our hunting trip together was said to be several days (San Francisco Chronicle), four days (Boston Globe), or nine days (San Antonio Express-News). We spent about 48 hours together at the hunting camp. It was asserted that the Vice President and I "spent time alone in the rushes," "huddled together in a Louisiana marsh," where we had "plenty of time . . . to talk privately" (Los Angeles Times); that we "spent . . . quality time bonding [together] in a duck blind" (Atlanta Journal-Constitution); and that "[t]here is simply no reason to think these two did not discuss the pending case" (Buffalo News). As I have described, the Vice President and I were never in the same blind, and never discussed the case. (Washington officials know the rules, and know that discussing with judges pending cases — their own or anyone else's — is forbidden.) The Palm Beach Post stated that our "transportation [was] provided, appropriately, by an oil services company," and Newsday that a "private jet . . . whisked Scalia to Louisiana." The Vice President and I flew in a Government plane. The Cincinnati Enquirer said that "Scalia was Cheney's guest at a private duck-hunting camp in Louisiana." Cheney and I were Wallace Carline's guests. Various newspapers described Mr. Carline as "an energy company official" (Atlanta Journal-Constitution), an "oil industrialist" (Cincinnati Enquirer), an "oil company executive" (Contra Costa Times), an "oilman" (Minneapolis Star Tribune), and an "energy industry executive" (Washington Post). All of these descriptions are misleading. . . .

Such a blast of largely inaccurate and uninformed opinion cannot determine the recusal question. It is well established that the recusal inquiry must be "made from the perspective of a *reasonable* observer who is *informed of all the surrounding facts and circumstances.*"

IV

While Sierra Club was apparently unable to summon forth a single example of a Justice's recusal (or even motion for a Justice's recusal) under circumstances similar to those here, I have been able to accomplish the seemingly more difficult task of finding a couple of examples establishing the negative: that recusal or motion for recusal did *not* occur under circumstances similar to those here.

Justice White and Robert Kennedy

The first example pertains to a Justice with whom I have sat, and who retired from the Court only 11 years ago, Byron R. White. Justice White was close friends with Attorney General Robert Kennedy from the days when White had served as Kennedy's Deputy Attorney General. In January 1963, the Justice went on a skiing vacation in Colorado with Robert Kennedy and his family, Secretary of Defense Robert McNamara and his family, and other members of the Kennedy family. . . . At the time of this skiing vacation there were pending before the Court at least two cases in which Robert Kennedy, in his official capacity as Attorney General, was a party. In the first of these, moreover, the press might have said, as plausibly as it has said here, that the reputation and integrity of the Attorney General were at issue. There the Department of Justice had decreed deportation of a resident alien on grounds that he had been a member of the Communist Party. (The Court found that the evidence adduced by the Department was inadequate.)

Besides these cases naming Kennedy, another case pending at the time of the skiing vacation was argued to the Court *by Kennedy* about two weeks later. That case was important to the Kennedy administration. . . . When the decision was announced, it was front-page news. Attorney General Kennedy argued for affirmance of a three-judge District Court's ruling that the Georgia Democratic Party's county-unit voting system violated the one-person, one-vote principle. This was Kennedy's only argument before the Court, and it certainly put "on the line" his reputation as a lawyer, as well as an important policy of his brother's administration.

Justice Jackson and Franklin Roosevelt

The second example pertains to a Justice who was one of the most distinguished occupants of the seat to which I was appointed, Robert Jackson. Justice Jackson took the recusal obligation particularly seriously. Nonetheless, he saw nothing wrong with maintaining a close personal relationship, and engaging in " 'quite frequen[t]' " socializing with the President whose administration's acts came before him regularly.

In April 1942, the two "spent a weekend on a very delightful house party down at General Watson's in Charlottesville, Virginia. I had been invited to ride down with the President and to ride back with him." Pending at the time, and argued the next month, was one of the most important cases concerning the scope of permissible federal action under the Commerce Clause, Wickard v. Filburn, 317 U.S. 111 (1942). Justice Jackson wrote the opinion for the Court. Roosevelt's Secretary of Agriculture, rather than Roosevelt himself, was the named federal officer in the case, but there is no doubt that it was important to the President.

I see nothing wrong about Justice White's and Justice Jackson's socializing — including vacationing and accepting rides — with their friends. Nor, seemingly, did anyone else at the time. (The Denver Post, which has been critical of me, reported the White-Kennedy-McNamara skiing vacation with nothing but enthusiasm.) If friendship is basis for recusal (as it assuredly is when friends are sued personally) then activity which suggests close friendship must be avoided. But if friendship is *no* basis for recusal (as it is not in official-capacity suits) social contacts that do no more than evidence that friendship suggest no impropriety whatever. . . .

V

Since I do not believe my impartiality can reasonably be questioned, I do not think it would be proper for me to recuse. That alone is conclusive; but another consideration moves me in the same direction: Recusal would in my judgment harm the Court. If I were to withdraw from this case, it would be because some of the press has argued that the Vice President would suffer political damage *if* he should lose this appeal, and *if*, on remand, discovery should establish that energy industry representatives were *de facto* members of NEPDG — and because some of the press has elevated that possible political damage to the status of an impending stain on the reputation and integrity of the Vice President. But since political damage often comes from the Government's losing official-action suits; and since political damage can readily be characterized as a stain on reputation and integrity; recusing in the face of such charges would give elements of the press a veto over participation of any Justices who had social contacts with, or were even known to be friends of, a named official. That is intolerable.

My recusal would also encourage so-called investigative journalists to suggest improprieties, and demand recusals, for other inappropriate (and increasingly silly) reasons. The Los Angeles Times has already suggested that it was improper for me to sit on a case argued by a law school dean whose school I had visited several weeks before — visited not at his invitation, but at his predecessor's. The same paper has asserted that it was improper for me to speak at a dinner honoring Cardinal Bevilacqua given by the Urban Family Council of Philadelphia because (according to the Times's false report) that organization was engaged in litigation seeking to prevent same-sex civil unions, and I had before me a case presenting the question (whether same-sex civil unions were lawful? — no) whether homosexual sodomy could constitutionally be *criminalized*. While the political branches can perhaps survive the constant baseless allegations of impropriety that have become the staple of Washington reportage, this Court cannot. The people must have confidence in the integrity of the Justices, and that cannot exist in a system that assumes them to be corruptible by the slightest friendship or favor, and in an atmosphere where the press will be eager to find foot-faults.

. . .

As I noted at the outset, one of the private respondents in this case has not called for my recusal, and has expressed confidence that I will rule impartially, as indeed I will. Counsel for the other private respondent seek to impose, it seems to me, a standard regarding friendship, the appearance of friendship, and the acceptance of social favors, that is more stringent than what they themselves observe. Two days before the brief in opposition to the petition in this case was filed, lead counsel for Sierra Club, a friend, wrote me a warm note inviting me to come to Stanford Law School to speak to one of his classes. (Judges teaching classes at law schools normally have their transportation and expenses paid.) I saw nothing amiss in that friendly letter and invitation. I surely would have thought otherwise if I had applied the standards urged in the present motion.

There are, I am sure, those who believe that my friendship with persons in the current administration might cause me to favor the Government in cases brought against it. That is not the issue here. Nor is the issue whether personal friendship with the Vice President might cause me to favor the Government in cases in which *he* is named. None of those suspicions regarding my impartiality (erroneous suspicions, I hasten to protest) bears upon recusal here. The question, simply put, is whether someone who thought I could decide this case impartially despite my friendship with the Vice President would reasonably believe that I *cannot* decide it impartially because I went hunting with that friend and accepted an invitation to fly there with him on a Government plane. If it is reasonable to think that a Supreme Court Justice can be bought so cheap, the Nation is in deeper trouble than I had imagined.

As the newspaper editorials appended to the motion make clear, I have received a good deal of embarrassing criticism and adverse publicity in connection with the matters at issue here — even to the point of becoming (as the motion cruelly but accurately states) "fodder for late-night comedians." If I could have done so in good conscience, I would have been pleased to demonstrate my integrity, and immediately silence the criticism, by getting off the case. Since I believe there is no basis for recusal, I cannot. The motion is *Denied.*

Lawrence J. Fox, I Did Not Sleep with That Vice President

15 No. 2 Prof. Law. 1 (2004)

. . . Why is the Scalia memorandum extraordinary? First, there is the question of its length. . . . Me thinks the gentleman doth protest too much.

The tone of the memorandum does not help. Justice Scalia is known for his rapier pen. He often demonstrates how clever he is in terms that must leave the litigants with whom he doesn't agree and his fellow Justices in similar circumstances quivering at the poverty of their own cognitive powers. But with his own integrity on the line, one would have hoped—as it turns out, against hope—that Justice Scalia would have adopted a less belligerent, cynical and dismissive voice in defending his willingness to sit on this important case. Instead we get a strident brief, dripping with annoyed sarcasm that anyone would question his rectitude and, as it turns out, one that raises far more questions than it answers, one that highlights the infirmities of the good Justice's self-assured stance.

Make no mistake about it. Justice Scalia thinks he is a trial lawyer. Right from the beginning he goes for our sympathy vote. How else can one explain Justice Scalia's remarkable narrative, which begins by telling us the totally irrelevant fact that the Justice was introduced to the man who hosted this exclusive soirée by a dentist and, drum roll please, a worker in handicapped rehabilitation? With that as a starting point, one cannot help but feeling all warm and fuzzy about the down to earth altruistic folk who brought the Justice and the veep together.

Next, Justice Scalia addresses the issue of his host, Wallace Carline, a magnanimous gentleman, who has been inviting Justice Scalia to Louisiana for years. On this occasion Mr. Carline agreed, at Justice Scalia's request, to invite the Vice-President, an avid duck hunter, as well, an invitation the host permitted Justice Scalia to extend personally.

Justice Scalia tells us a lot more about what the host is not, than what he is. But this must be very important because twice in the memorandum Justice Scalia addresses the issue of how his host makes his less than modest living.

The host is not:

"an energy industry executive,"
"an oil company executive,"
"an oil man,"
"an energy company official," or
"an oil industrialist. . . ."

In fact his host, far from being an oil industrialist—drum roll please—"runs his own company that provides services and equipment rental to"—pause—"*oil* rigs." (Emphasis added). Certainly doesn't sound like an "oil industrialist" to me. In fact—how could anyone make such a mistake? He was in point of fact an "oil rig and oil equipment industrialist." The gauze is lifted from our eyes.

What Justice Scalia apparently wanted to make clear was that his host was not an "ExxonMobil" or "Con Ed" executive; he apparently was not a Halliburton executive either, though the host's wholly-owned company does sound an awful lot like a competitor of Halliburton. I guess Justice Scalia is asserting that these oil field supply folks, unlike the BP Unocal gang, are totally indifferent to the administration's energy policy, not caring one way or the other whether the Bush-Cheney administration allows offshore or North Slope drilling for petroleum.

Justice Scalia then tells us — a real confidence builder here — that the trip was set even before certiorari was granted, and was completed long before the case is to be argued. Justice Scalia does not, however, cite any authority for the remarkable proposition that it would be okay to preside over a case involving a litigant with whom you spent the weekend before oral argument, but not okay to arrange for the same thing after certiorari is granted.

Only then does Justice Scalia address the trip on Air Force Two, the Vice President's personal jet that whisked Scalia and party to Louisiana. One of the most interesting aspects of this disquisition is what Scalia does not address. While later we learn who was with whom during the duck hunt, in the section of the opinion dealing with the sumptuous air travel arrangements, that subject is studiously not discussed. From the opinion, all one learns is that the complement included the Vice President and his staff and security detail, Justice Scalia and his son and son-in-law, quite a cozy group for a multiple-hour plane ride on a Gulfstream jet. Perhaps the cabin was too noisy for any conversation, unlike a duck blind. We will never know, though somehow we doubt it. In any event, we receive no assurance that the justice was sequestered from the litigant.

But if we were concerned about this omission our fears are quickly put to rest by Justice Scalia's assertion that, when he rode on Air Force Two, the trip cost the taxpayers nothing; the plane was flying there anyway and Justice Scalia received nothing of value when his son, son-in-law and he were offered these otherwise vacant seats on Air Force Two. This is because — damnit — they were only able to hitch a one-way ride with the Vice President. This meant — groan — the Scalia party had to buy one-way tickets back. But since one-way tickets, in addition to being a clear sign that the flyers are terrorists, are so much more expensive than round-trip tickets, the Scalia group bought round-trip tickets and, in violation of the airline's rules, tore up the other half. So the out-of-pocket expense for the Scalia party was the same as it would have been if the Vice President had never offered this little perquisite. In Justice Scalia's flamboyant rhetoric, "none of us saved a cent." End of discussion.

Well, not quite. Not many have flown on private jets. The author was lucky enough to do it once. And let me tell you there is real value to flying in the rarefied world of the dedicated private Gulfstream. The plane leaves when you want. It makes no stops. There is no racing through a hub to change planes. The space is luxurious. The food custom prepared. I can still taste the smoked salmon sandwiches served on monogrammed china aboard the Merrill Lynch Gulfstream. And you land not in New Orleans — how inconvenient — but at a private airport in Morgan City right next to your duck-hunting destination.

Justice Scalia grudgingly recognizes that even if he did not save any money, there was some very small value in what he received. But he wants us to put that value into perspective. He observes that at a charity auction one would bid far more for a dinner at the White House — something typically provided to Supreme Court justices — than for a trip on Air Force Two.

Does Justice Scalia think for one minute that this astonishing assertion proves that a trip on Air Force Two is not valuable? I have no idea what people would bid for seats at a Christmas dinner at the White House, but it would certainly be in the thousands. That certainly leaves lots of room to value the Air Force Two trip at a very high number as well — even if it could be snared at a lower dollar figure than dinner at the White House. . . .

Finally, Justice Scalia addresses the duck hunting itself. We are told there were 13 hunters in all, a group Justice Scalia characterizes as "not intimate," even "sizable," perhaps because he found the flight down so much more *intime*. We learn they took meals together. One day they went fishing — in two boats. And though Justice Scalia studiously fails to tell us whether he was in the Vice President's fishing boat, we know in our hearts that is where he fished because when it came to the duck hunting, Justice Scalia makes it quite clear that Mr. Cheney and he never shared a duck blind, as it sadly turns out. Finally, lest you were worried about the Vice President having a Clinton problem, we are told that, although virtually everyone shared sleeping rooms, this sharing did not include the Vice President, who was not forced to sleep with Justice Scalia, his son or his son-in-law.

I make light of Justice Scalia's exegesis of the facts. I might even be accused of adopting a Scalia-like tone. But the fact that Justice Scalia spends all this time arguing the facts is really quite informative. Taking the time to share them with us, Justice Scalia must feel that they are critical, if not dispositive to dismissing any allegations that he should recuse himself. But what is he really saying?

If I had been introduced to my host by an oil man, not someone — tears now — who works with the handicapped, then I would have been forced to recuse.

If the host was an oil man and not an oil rig man, then I would have been forced to recuse.

If certiorari had been granted before the trip was set, then I would have been forced to recuse.

If I took a round trip on Air Force Two — and saved the cost of a round-trip ticket — then I would have been forced to recuse.

If I had been in the same duck blind — like he was in the same small plane and same small fishing boat — I would have been forced to recuse.

If I had shared a room with the Vice President, I would have been forced to recuse.

Why *is* Justice Scalia telling us all this? In my view, it demonstrates the weakness of his position. Should any motion to recuse turn on the facts to which Justice Scalia so tenaciously clings? The fact is Justice Scalia spent this huge amount of time with a litigant with a present matter before the court. No amount of tap dancing about who introduced who to whom, whether the host was an oil man or an oil rig man, or whether they were in the same duck blind changes the substance of what occurred. Justice Scalia engaged in conduct vis-à-vis the Vice President that required him to recuse himself. From the point of view of the adverse litigants this situation is intolerable. . . .

It is true that different standards might apply in personal versus official capacity lawsuits. The Social Security Administrator might well be indifferent to the fact that he or she is sued hundreds of times a month. And the idea that a judge played golf with that administrator while hearing some poor soul's social security appeal might not raise serious questions of judicial ethics. But to analogize such an unremarkable prosaic circumstance to *this* lawsuit against *this* vice president is surely to exalt form above substance.

It is also certainly true, as Justice Scalia repeatedly observes, that the Vice President has been sued in his official capacity. But the concept of official capacity-private capacity cannot be an on-off switch for deciding when a justice must recuse himself. Some official capacity lawsuits are far more personal than lawsuits that are classified as personal. Despite Justice Scalia's naked assertion to the contrary, this lawsuit raises an issue that has garnered significant attention for years — the highly charged question of who was sitting down in secret with the former CEO of Halliburton to decide our country's energy policy. Who were these oil industrialists? Oil men? Energy industry executives? It is an issue on which the Vice President has literally staked his reputation, one that might even affect the Vice President's re-nomination or re-election. And to assert that the Vice President does not have a deep, abiding and personal interest in whether he is going to be forced to share this information with an inquisitive world is to ignore the dozens of editorials that have been written on the topic.

And that is something we know Justice Scalia did not do. Indeed, he proclaims that the unanimous view of these editorial writers, whose facts he so carefully has checked, is not going to persuade him to recuse himself. That lesson is one conclusion of the Justice with which I agree. Just because 20 newspapers say a judge should recuse himself is no reason to do it. But that 20 newspapers thought this case was so important that they commented on the recusal issue demonstrates in a dramatic way that Justice Scalia's attempts to assure his participation in this case on the basis that this case is just like any garden variety run-of-the-mill Social Security appeal does not pass the straight face test.

But I have spent too much time addressing Justice Scalia on his own terms (this is all about the Vice President and me) and not nearly enough confronting the very serious ethical lapse his failure to recuse creates. Imagine you are a lawyer. You are handling a major case for a distraught client. The case will be tried next month to a judge. Your client, on your advice, takes a weekend of rest and relaxation at the Homestead. The client enters the elegant dining room with his wife and, as they are escorted to their table, they notice the judge, the adversary and the adversary's wife hoisting martini glasses filled with a silver liquid, laughing boisterously. As your client passes their way, there is an embarrassed silence followed by the judge's halting comment, "Great to see you, Mr. Jones. Just down here for some trout fishing. Of course, we haven't discussed that little matter."

How does that client feel? How do you feel? What has this done to the system of justice? Can the client ever be convinced that the judge will still be impartial? Should there be a need to convince the client of that fact? Even if you know the judge will be impartial, the appearance of bias is both profound and destructive. There is no place for judges fraternizing with litigants who have matters before them. And that is precisely what Justice Scalia brazenly and insensitively did and yet, when called on it, instead of curing the problem by graciously acknowledging the conflict of interest, he launches a rhetorical broadside that only fans the flames.

This Homestead scenario also highlights how useless is Justice Scalia's reliance on the matter being one in which Cheney is sued in his official capacity. If at our dining room scene our dismayed client had also been told, "Don't worry. The case I'm deciding next week is against my olive-loving friend in his official capacity," do you suppose the client would feel relieved, any lingering concerns evaporating once those words were uttered by the convivial judge? You see the problems with the personal-official distinction, are that (a) the offended party, a layman, will not understand the distinction and (b) even if he did, in the eyes of the offended party the betrayal looks identical. While the judge may think it is perfectly alright to go duck hunting with a litigant whose case is pending before him (so long as he does not occupy the same duck blind) because the matter involves the litigant in the litigant's official capacity, that fact is of no consequence to the litigant who was not invited to join the hunting party.

What does all of this teach us? I think there are two lessons here. First, Supreme Court practice apparently provides that the Justice who is the subject of a recusal motion decides whether the motion should be granted. Thus, we are the recipients of Justice Scalia's twenty-page pronuncimento. How much better would it be if every justice but the justice who is the object of attention were to decide this matter? These other justices are fully cognizant of the special considerations that must inform a Supreme Court motion to recuse, given the fact if one Justice steps down there is no one to take her place. Moreover, they are objective in a way that any judge who is the subject of such a motion cannot be. You can be sure that if the present eight Justices, without Scalia participating, had decided this motion, the world would have been treated, in the best sense of that word, to a far shorter and more persuasive opinion — even if the Court decided to deny the motion — than the one Scalia handed down. And the world would also have far more confidence that the result that was reached was a fair one.

Second, we could not find a better poster child than Justice Scalia's conduct and his defense for the importance of maintaining an appearance standard, if not the current appearance of impropriety standard, in our canons of judicial conduct. Since Justice Scalia may be completely unaffected by his sojourn with Dick Cheney, some of us might agree with Justice Scalia's assertion that if a Justice of the Supreme Court could be corrupted by this little fishing adventure then the nation is in real trouble. On the other hand, the appearance that Justice Scalia would be biased as a result of his Louisiana sojourn is something our canons of judicial ethics cannot condone or ignore. . . .

In the world of judging, appearances count and anyone who thinks that a requirement that judges be unfettered, honest and erudite in all things is enough, if what the judges appear to be doing goes unregulated, is failing to recognize how fragile is the trust the American public is currently willing to repose in our judiciary. . . .

What is it then that we don't want our judges to appear to be doing, even if they are not in fact doing it? We don't want them to engage in conduct that might lead the public to question their impartiality. We don't want them to engage in conduct that might lead the public to question their independence. We don't want them to engage in conduct that might lead the public to question their honesty. And we don't want them to engage in conduct that might lead the public to question their competence. . . .

Justice Scalia's adventure with Vice President Cheney not only reflected an appearance of impropriety, but also reflected an appearance that Justice Scalia was not impartial. . . .

For so many of us, the Supreme Court is the most important symbol of both the separation of powers and the rule of law. Maintaining the Court's dignity is critical to both of its symbolic roles. Gentle reader, please read Justice Scalia's 21-page tirade again. Has Justice Scalia enhanced the dignity of the Court by providing us with this? Do we feel better about the Court knowing that this Justice did not recuse himself because he did not sleep with Vice President Cheney? I don't think so and I'll bet you don't either.

Post-Case Follow-Up

Justice Scalia declined to recuse himself because he did not believe that his duck hunting trip with the Vice President created a situation where his "impartiality might be reasonably questioned."

In its subsequent decision on the merits, the Supreme Court, with Justice Scalia joining the seven-justice majority, declined to force Vice President Cheney to disclose the requested information under FACA and sent the case back to the D.C. Circuit.[40] The D.C. Circuit subsequently dismissed the case.[41] The Bush administration's allegedly cozy relationship with big corporations and special interests continued to be a major issue in the 2004 presidential campaign, which ultimately saw President Bush win reelection for a second term.

The entire incident brought renewed attention to the issue of judicial recusal. First, Justice Scalia's opinion provided little in the way of clarity concerning the recusal standard. It remains difficult to distinguish which social relationships are impermissible under the "appearance of impropriety" standard.

Second, the case brought scrutiny to the procedures the Supreme Court and other courts use for deciding recusal motions. For example, at the Supreme Court level, some, like Professor Fox, have called for recusal motions to be referred to the entire Court rather than to the justice who is the subject of the motion, while others have called for allowing retired justices or court of appeals judges to sit in place of disqualified justices.

Cheney v. United States District Court: Real Life Applications

1. Arizona trial judge Mary H. Murguia was presiding over a highly controversial case. Plaintiffs had filed suit against infamous Maricopa County Sheriff Joseph M. Arpaio and the county, alleging that defendants were engaging in racial profiling and unlawful detention of persons of Hispanic appearance and descent.

40. Cheney v. United States District Court for the District of Columbia, 542 U.S. 367 (2004).
41. In re Cheney, 406 F.3d 723 (D.C. Cir. 2005).

Judge Murguia's identical twin sister was the president and CEO of the National Council of La Raza, the largest Latino civil rights organization in the United States. Defendants moved to recuse Judge Murguia based on this relationship. How should she rule?

2. Given the important political cases that come before the Supreme Court, it is not surprising that calls for justices to recuse themselves remain a hot topic, particularly in politically charged cases. No formal motions were made in any of the following cases. Do you think any of these justices should have recused themselves? What are the best arguments for and against recusal?
    a. When the constitutionality of the Affordable Care Act (ACA) was pending before the Supreme Court, activists on both sides of the issue argued that justices who were likely to vote against their position should recuse themselves.
        i. Opponents of the ACA said that Justice Elena Kagan should recuse herself because she had been solicitor general in President Barack Obama's administration when the health care law was moving through Congress.
        ii. Those who supported the ACA said that Justice Thomas should recuse himself because of the political advocacy work that his wife had done to fight the law. Virginia Thomas was the founder and head of a non-profit group named Liberty Central, which described itself as opposed to the leftist "tyranny" of President Obama and dedicated to "protecting the [nation's] core founding principles." Mrs. Thomas was a vocal critic of the ACA and gave public speeches describing "Obamacare" as a "disaster" for small businesses and arguing that it was unconstitutional.[42]
    b. After the Supreme Court decided Citizens United v. FEC, 558 U.S. 310 (2010), in which the Court struck down limits on political expenditures by non-profit organizations, Common Cause, a liberal advocacy group, asked the Justice Department to investigate whether Justices Scalia and Thomas should have recused themselves in that case because they had allegedly attended political retreats organized by the conservative businessman Charles Koch, who opposed limits on campaign spending.
    c. Opponents of gay marriage said that Justices Elena Kagan and Ruth Bader Ginsburg should recuse themselves in Obergefell v. Hodges, 135 S. Ct. 2584 (2015), in which the Supreme Court considered (and ultimately struck down) state laws banning same-sex marriage because both justices had previously officiated same-sex marriages.

---

2. Judges' Use of Social Media

While Justice Scalia's duck hunting involved traditional, in-person friendship, social media poses a new challenge for judges. Should judges participate in social

42. George Zornick, *The Nation: Clarence Thomas v. Legal Ethics*, National Public Radio, Nov. 15, 2011. http://www.npr.org/2011/11/15/142339329/the-nation-clarence-thomas-vs-legal-ethics.

media at all? When judges do participate in social media, under what circumstances should their social media "friendships" disqualify them?

The American Bar Association and several jurisdictions have issued ethics opinions addressing these issues. All of the ethics opinions endorse judges using social media, albeit in a "judicious" way. As the ABA opinion concluded, such use "can benefit judges in both their personal and professional lives" and also keep them from being "thought of as isolated or out of touch."[43]

The more difficult question is whether judges' social media connections with lawyers and litigants who may appear before them create an "appearance of impropriety" requiring disqualification; on this issue, the ethics opinions are divided.

Some states, such as Florida, adhere to a restrictive view, and forbid a judge from "friending" lawyers who may appear before the judge. The Florida Committee reasoned that when a judge "friends" a lawyer, he is selecting a special class of accepted individuals while rejecting others. That preference is then publicly communicated through social networking, which conveys the impression that the lawyer is in a special position to influence the judge.[44] On the other hand, states in the more permissive camp generally allow judges to be "friends" with lawyers who may appear before them. For example, the Kentucky Ethics Committee concluded that a judge does not violate the Judicial Code simply by connecting with a lawyer on social media.[45] Similarly, the New York Committee concluded that social network connections are allowed, but judges must consider whether the circumstances of each case would indicate a "close social relationship" and require disclosure, recusal, or both.[46] The ABA's opinion strikes somewhat of a middle ground, declining to offer any *per se* rule. Instead, the ABA mentioned that state committees "have expressed a wide range of views" on the issue and noted that "designation as [a social media] connection does not, in and of itself, indicate the degree or intensity of a judge's relationship with a person." The opinion concluded that "context is significant."[47]

3. Constitutional Dimensions of Disqualification

Although "most matters relating to judicial disqualification [do] not rise to a constitutional level,"[48] in extreme cases — when, using an objective standard, there is a "serious risk of actual bias" — the Supreme Court has held that the Due Process Clause requires a judge to recuse himself.[49]

In three cases, the Court found constitutional violations where the judge had a direct pecuniary stake in the outcome of the case. First, in *Tumey v. Ohio*, the Court struck down an Ohio statute that permitted local mayors to sit as judges and

43. ABA Formal Op. 462 at 1, 4 (2013).
44. *See, e.g.*, Fla. Judicial Ethics Advisory Comm., Op. 2009-20 (2009), http://www.jud6.org/LegalCommunity/LegalPractice/opinions/jeacopinions/2009/2009-20.html.
45. Ethics Comm. of Ky. Judiciary Formal Op. JE-119 at 2 (2010).
46. N.Y. Advisory Comm. on Judicial Ethics, Op. 08-176 (2009).
47. ABA Formal Op. 462 at 2, 3 (2013).
48. FTC v. Cement Inst., 333 U.S. 683, 702 (1948).
49. Caperton v. A.T. Massey Coal Co., 556 U.S. 868, 884 (2009).

be paid out of the fines collected from those convicted of violating Ohio's Prohibition Act. The mayors only received compensation if they convicted the defendants. The Court said the scheme was impermissible under the Fourteenth Amendment because it gave the mayor "a direct, personal, pecuniary interest in convicting the defendant who came before him for trial."[50] Forty-five years later, in *Ward v. Village of Monroeville*, the Court considered another Ohio statute that incentivized the presiding mayor to convict defendants. In *Ward*, the fines did not go to the mayor personally, but went instead into his town's coffers and made up a "substantial portion" of the municipality's budget. The Court said that this scheme was impermissible because it created a "possible temptation" for the mayor to "maintain the high level of contribution from the mayor's court."[51] Finally, in *Aetna Life Insurance Co. v. Lavoie*, the Court found that it was impermissible for an Alabama Supreme Court justice to hear a case involving allegations of bad faith against an insurance company, where he was a plaintiff in a lawsuit involving a "very similar bad-faith-refusal-to-pay" in another Alabama court. As in *Tumey* and *Ward*, the Court held that the judge had a "direct, personal, substantial and pecuniary" interest in the case and that his participation therefore violated due process.[52]

More recently, in *Caperton v. A.T. Massey Coal Co.*, the Supreme Court addressed for the first time the circumstances under which the Due Process Clause requires a judge to recuse himself as a result of campaign contributions received from one of the parties. The facts of *Caperton* are so compelling that they inspired John Grisham to write a novel. (See the sidebar.) The *Caperton* plaintiffs, who operated a coal company, sued the much larger Massey Coal Company for anti-competitive behavior and won a $50 million verdict at trial, which Massey appealed to the Supreme Court of Appeals of West Virginia. While the appeal was pending, Don Blankenship, Massey's chairman, decided to support a conservative candidate, Brent Benjamin, to unseat one of the court's more liberal members, Justice Warren McGraw, in the belief that Benjamin would be more likely to overturn the verdict than McGraw. He contributed the statutory maximum $1,000 to Benjamin's campaign committee, donated almost $2.5 million to his political action committee, and made more than $500,000 in individual expenditures for direct mailings soliciting donations and for television and newspaper advertisements. The $3 million that Blankenship spent was more than the total amount spent by all other Benjamin supporters and three times the amount spent by Benjamin's own campaign committee. Benjamin won the seat.

When the appeal came before the West Virginia Supreme Court, Caperton moved on three separate occasions to disqualify Justice Benjamin because of Blankenship's support for his campaign, but Justice Benjamin denied each motion, concluding that he had no direct pecuniary interest in the case: he did not stand to gain anything from the outcome. The court reversed the jury verdict in a 3-2 decision (with Justice Benjamin in the majority), and Caperton filed a petition for certiorari in the U.S. Supreme Court.

50. 273 U.S. 510, 523-24 (1927).
51. 409 U.S. 57, 58-60 (1972).
52. 475 U.S. 813, 822-25 (1986).

The Supreme Court agreed to hear the case and reversed in a controversial 5-4 decision. Writing for the majority, Justice Kennedy concluded:

> Not every campaign contribution by a litigant or attorney creates a probability of bias that requires a judge's recusal, but this is an exceptional case. We conclude that there is a serious risk of actual bias — based on objective and reasonable perceptions — when a person with a personal stake in a particular case had a significant and disproportionate influence in placing the judge on the case by raising funds or directing the judge's election campaign when the case was pending or imminent. The inquiry centers on the contribution's relative size in comparison to the total amount of money contributed to the campaign, the total amount spent in the election, and the apparent effect such contribution had on the outcome of the election.

In reaching this conclusion, the Court stressed the size of Blankenship's campaign contributions, particularly "in comparison to the total amount contributed to the campaign . . . [and] spent in the election." The Court also emphasized that this case was unusual, repeatedly describing it as "extraordinary," "extreme," and "rare."[53] In his dissent, Chief Justice Roberts criticized the Court for providing "no guidance to judges and litigants about when recusal will be constitutionally required" and listed 40 "fundamental questions" that the Court's decision failed to address. He also predicted that the uncertainty of the standard would "inevitably lead to an increase in allegations that judges are biased."[54]

The Supreme Court's most recent decision addressing the application of the Due Process Clause to recusal issues is *Williams v. Pennsylvania*. In *Williams*, Ronald Castille had been the District Attorney of Philadelphia at the time the decision was made to seek the death penalty against defendant Terrance Williams. As the head of the office, Castille reviewed the trial prosecutor's memorandum in support of seeking the death penalty and wrote a note at the bottom of the document, "Approved to proceed on the death penalty." Thirty years later, Castille sat as Chief Justice of the Pennsylvania Supreme Court when the Commonwealth's appeal of Williams's habeas petition came before the court. Williams moved to recuse Castille based on a provision in the Pennsylvania Code of

Straight Out of (or Is That Into?) a Grisham Novel?

If you think that the facts of the *Caperton* case seem fantastic enough to be the subject of a legal thriller, you would be right. The events surrounding the case inspired bestselling author John Grisham to write *The Appeal*. In *The Appeal*, the plaintiff sues a chemical company for allowing pollutants to seep into the town's water supply, killing her husband and son. The jury awards $41 million in damages. The billionaire majority stockholder of the defendant company then vows to do "whatever it takes" to preserve his company, appealing the judgment to the Mississippi Supreme Court. He then recruits an inexperienced, naïve candidate for the Mississippi Supreme Court to unseat a justice up for reelection who is known to be plaintiff-friendly, and pumps millions of dollars into the campaign. The billionaire's candidate wins and immediately starts overturning judgments on appeal. We won't spoil the end for you — you'll have to read *The Appeal* yourself to find out whether the candidate overturns the judgment against the corporation that helped him get elected.

One other note: Grisham, a notoriously fast writer, was able to write his book and get it published before the U.S. Supreme Court managed to issue its decision in *Caperton*.

53. 556 U.S. 868, 872-75, 884-87, 890 (2009).
54. *Id.* at 890-91, 893-98 (Roberts, J. dissenting).

Judicial Conduct (similar to the Model Code) that disqualifies judges from any proceeding in which "they served as a lawyer in the matter in controversy." Chief Justice Castille declined to recuse himself without any explanation. The Pennsylvania Supreme Court, with Chief Justice Castille joining the majority opinion, vacated the trial court's order staying Williams's execution and ordering a new sentencing hearing.

The U.S. Supreme Court reversed, finding that Chief Justice Castille's participation in the appeal violated due process. The Court held: "[w]here a judge has had an earlier significant, personal involvement as a prosecutor in a critical decision in the defendant's case, the risk of actual bias in the judicial proceeding rises to an unconstitutional level." Writing for the 5-3 majority, Justice Kennedy stated:

> When a judge has served as an advocate for the State in the very case the court is now asked to adjudicate, a serious question arises as to whether the judge, even with the most diligent effort, could set aside any personal interest in the outcome. There is, furthermore, a risk that the judge "would be so psychologically wedded" to his or her previous position as a prosecutor that the judge "would consciously or unconsciously avoid the appearance of having erred or changed position." In addition, the judge's "own personal knowledge and impression" of the case, acquired through his or her role in the prosecution, may carry far more weight with the judge than the parties' arguments to the court.[55]

D. JUDICIAL CAMPAIGNS AND OTHER POLITICAL ACTIVITY

Although federal judges are appointed, judges in many states are elected. Thirty-eight states have some form of judicial election for their highest state court; 32 of the 41 states that have intermediate appellate courts elect those judges; and 39 states hold elections for their trial courts.[56] The form of election varies — some are partisan, some are nonpartisan, and in some cases, judges face uncontested retention elections after their initial appointment. If judges in these states hope to get elected, they must raise funds and campaign for office. Their actions on the campaign trail raise a number of ethical issues.

1. Fundraising

Judges have to raise money for their campaigns, and those campaigns have become expensive — a 2014 study calculated that $275 million had been spent on judicial elections since the year 2000.[57] Another study concluded that spending in judicial

55. 136 S. Ct. 1899, 1903-10 (2016) (citations omitted).

56. For an interactive map showing judicial selection methods by court level and phase of selection (first full term, interim selection, and additional terms), see *Judicial Selection: An Interactive Map*, N.Y.U. Sch. of Law Brennan Ctr. for Justice, http://judicialselectionmap.brennancenter.org/?court=Supreme (last updated May 8, 2015).

57. Bert Brandenburg, *Justice for Sale*, Politico, Sept. 1, 2014, http://www.politico.com/magazine/story/2014/09/elected-judges-110397#.VN-7o2TuU3Q.

elections in the period 2000-2009 was double what it was in 1990-1999.[58] Moreover, the amount of money spent on campaigns correlates to success at the ballot box. In one study, 90 percent of the contested seats were won by the candidate who spent the most money.[59]

The existence of money in judicial elections poses a threat to the public's confidence in the independence and impartiality of the judiciary. Is it reasonable for citizens to infer that judges will favor litigants and/or lawyers who contributed money to them? Even if judges are not actually biased by contributions, will the public perceive that a problem exists? In public opinion surveys, the large majority of citizens (87 percent in one survey) express concern that money in judicial elections is impacting the judges' decision making.[60]

The Model Code of Judicial Conduct provides that a judge should recuse herself where "[t]he judge knows or learns by means of a timely motion that a party, a party's lawyer, or the law firm of a party's lawyer has within the previous [insert number] year[s] made aggregate contributions to the judge's campaign in an amount that [is greater than $[insert amount] for an individual or $[insert amount] for an entity] [is reasonable and appropriate for an individual or an entity]."[61] Thus, the Model Code leaves it up to each state to decide whether to select an express dollar limit or instead use a "reasonable and appropriate" standard. In addition to the Code of Judicial Conduct, as we saw in *Caperton*, in extreme cases, the Due Process Clause requires judges who receive substantial donations from parties to recuse themselves.

Rule 4.1 also prohibits candidates from personally soliciting campaign contributions as opposed to through a committee. In its most recent decision addressing speech by judicial candidates, Williams-Yulee v. Florida Bar, 135 S. Ct. 1656 (2015), the Supreme Court upheld this restriction. In that case, Lanell Williams-Yulee sent a letter to local voters announcing her candidacy for county court judge in Hillsborough County, Florida and asking for a contribution. The Florida Bar filed a complaint against her for violating Florida's ban on personal solicitation of funds, a restriction that Williams-Yulee claimed was a violation of her First Amendment rights. The Supreme Court held that this was a "rare case" in which the restriction was narrowly tailored to serve the state's interest in protecting the integrity of the judiciary and maintaining the public's confidence in an impartial judiciary: "[s]imply put, Florida and most other States have concluded that the public may lack confidence in a judge's ability to administer justice without fear or favor if he comes to office by asking for favors."[62]

---

58. *Money & Elections*, Justice at Stake, http://www.justiceatstake.org/issues/state_court_issues/money-and-elections/ (last accessed Mar. 22, 2017).
59. Scott Greytak et al., Bankrolling the Bench: The New Politics of Judicial Elections 2013-14, at 1 (Oct. 2015), http://newpoliticsreport.org/app/uploads/JAS-NPJE-2013-14.pdf. *But see* Ronald D. Rotunda, *Judicial Elections, Campaign Financing, and Free Speech*, 2 Election L.J. 79 (2003); Ronald D. Rotunda, *A Preliminary Empirical Inquiry into the Connection Between Judicial Decision Making and Campaign Contributions to Judicial Candidates*, 14 Prof. Law. 16, 16, Winter 2003, in which Professor Rotunda concluded that there was no such correlation.
60. Brandenburg, *supra* note 57.
61. Model Code r. 2.11(a)(4).
62. 135 S. Ct. at 1656, 1663-66.

President Andrew Jackson championed electing judges to give ordinary people more power over the justice system. Since she retired from the bench, Justice Sandra Day O'Connor has been a strong advocate of depoliticizing the selection of judges. Her judicial selection plan can be found here: http://iaals.du.edu/sites/default/files/documents/publications/oconnor_plan.pdf.
Ritchie, A. H. & Carter, D. M. (ca. 1860) Andrew Jackson / painted by D.M. Carter ; engraved by A.H. Ritchie, ca. 1860. New York: Ritchie & Co. [Photograph] Retrieved from the Library of Congress, https://www.loc.gov/item/96521663/; Library of Congress Prints and Photographs Division Washington, D.C.

2. Other Political Activity

Even without the need to raise money, when judges and judicial candidates engage in political activity, that conduct poses a significant threat to judges' impartiality, or at least to the appearance of impartiality. The public expects judges to make decisions based upon the facts and law in particular cases and not for political reasons. When judges engage in political activity, however, it could cause them to base their decisions on the political impact of those decisions, or at least give the public that impression. For that reason, Canon 4 provides that "[a] judge or candidate for judicial office shall not engage in political or campaign activity that is inconsistent with the independence, integrity, or impartiality of the judiciary." To that end, Rule 4.1 imposes broad restrictions on political activity by judges and judicial candidates. For example, judges and judicial candidates cannot act as leaders for a political organization,[63] make speeches for a political organization, publicly

63. The Terminology section of the Code defines "political organization" as "a political party or other group sponsored by or affiliated with a political party or candidate, the principal purpose of which is to further the election or appointment of candidates for political office."

endorse political candidates for any office, or solicit funds or make contributions to a political organization or political candidate.

Judicial campaigns pose yet another quandary: judicial candidates need to be able to communicate their views to the public so that voters can make an informed decision about how to vote. At the same time, it is important that judges have an open mind once they reach the bench and actually hear cases, and it is equally important that the public perceives them to have an open mind. Statements that judges made on the campaign trail could lead litigants and the public to believe that the judge has already made up her mind about an issue. Thus, states have an interest in limiting judicial campaign speech, but any restrictions on judicial candidates' political speech pose significant First Amendment concerns.

Case Preview

Republican Party of Minnesota v. White

For more than 30 years, Minnesota, like most states, followed an ABA Model Code provision, known as the "announce" clause, that states that a "candidate for a judicial office, including an incumbent judge," shall not "announce his or her views on disputed legal or political issues."[64] In 1996, Gregory Wersal ran for associate justice of the Minnesota Supreme Court, and, during his campaign, criticized several Minnesota Supreme Court decisions on crime, welfare, and abortion. The Minnesota Office of Lawyers Professional Responsibility brought disciplinary proceedings against him for violating the announce clause. Those charges were subsequently dismissed, but Wersal nevertheless withdrew from the election. In 1998, Wersal ran again and sought an advisory opinion from the Lawyers Board about whether it planned to enforce the announce clause. After the Lawyers Board stated that it could not answer his question because he had not submitted a list of the announcements he wished to make, he filed suit arguing that the announce clause violated his First Amendment rights.

As you read the case, consider the following issues:

1. What is the Minnesota Office of Lawyers Professional Responsibility's interest in enforcing the announce clause?
2. How is Minnesota's "announce" clause different than the "promises and pledges" clause? Is this difference significant?
3. How does Justice Scalia's majority opinion define "impartiality" and what is the significance of that understanding for the Court's conclusion?

64. Model Code Canon 7(b)(1)(c) (1972) (repealed 1990).

Republican Party of Minnesota v. White

536 U.S. 765 (2002)

Justice SCALIA delivered the opinion of the Court.

The question presented in this case is whether the First Amendment permits the Minnesota Supreme Court to prohibit candidates for judicial election in that State from announcing their views on disputed legal and political issues.

I

Since Minnesota's admission to the Union in 1858, the State's Constitution has provided for the selection of all state judges by popular election. . . . Since 1974, they have been subject to a legal restriction which states that a "candidate for a judicial office, including an incumbent judge," shall not "announce his or her views on disputed legal or political issues." Minn. Code of Judicial Conduct, Canon 5(A)(3)(d)(i) (2000). This prohibition . . . is known as the "announce clause. . . ."

In 1996, one of the petitioners, Gregory Wersal, ran for associate justice of the Minnesota Supreme Court. In the course of the campaign, he distributed literature criticizing several Minnesota Supreme Court decisions on issues such as crime, welfare, and abortion. A complaint against Wersal challenging, among other things, the propriety of this literature was filed with the Office of Lawyers Professional Responsibility. . . . The Lawyers Board dismissed the complaint; with regard to the charges that his campaign materials violated the announce clause, it expressed doubt whether the clause could constitutionally be enforced. Nonetheless, fearing that further ethical complaints would jeopardize his ability to practice law, Wersal withdrew from the election. In 1998, Wersal ran again for the same office. Early in that race, he sought an advisory opinion from the Lawyers Board with regard to whether it planned to enforce the announce clause. The Lawyers Board responded equivocally, stating that, although it had significant doubts about the constitutionality of the provision, it was unable to answer his question because he had not submitted a list of the announcements he wished to make.

Shortly thereafter, Wersal filed this lawsuit in Federal District Court against respondents, seeking, *inter alia*, a declaration that the announce clause violates the First Amendment and an injunction against its enforcement. . . .

Other plaintiffs in the suit, including the Minnesota Republican Party, alleged that, because the clause kept Wersal from announcing his views, they were unable to learn those views and support or oppose his candidacy accordingly. . . .

II

Before considering the constitutionality of the announce clause, we must be clear about its meaning. Its text says that a candidate for judicial office shall not "announce his or her views on disputed legal or political issues."

We know that "announc[ing] . . . views" on an issue covers much more than *promising* to decide an issue a particular way. The prohibition extends to the candidate's mere statement of his current position, even if he does not bind himself to maintain that position after election. All the parties agree this is the case, because the Minnesota Code contains a so-called "pledges or promises" clause, which *separately* prohibits judicial candidates from making "pledges or promises of conduct in office other than the faithful and impartial performance of the duties of the office," — a prohibition that is not challenged here and on which we express no view.

There are, however, some limitations that the Minnesota Supreme Court has placed upon the scope of the announce clause that are not (to put it politely) immediately apparent from its text. The statements that formed the basis of the complaint against Wersal in 1996 included criticism of past decisions of the Minnesota Supreme Court. One piece of campaign literature stated that "[t]he Minnesota Supreme Court has issued decisions which are marked by their disregard for the Legislature and a lack of common sense." It went on to criticize a decision excluding from evidence confessions by criminal defendants that were not tape-recorded, asking "[s]hould we conclude that because the Supreme Court does not trust police, it allows confessed criminals to go free?" It criticized a decision striking down a state law restricting welfare benefits, asserting that "[i]t's the Legislature which should set our spending policies." And it criticized a decision requiring public financing of abortions for poor women as "unprecedented" and a "pro-abortion stance." Although one would think that all of these statements touched on disputed legal or political issues, they did not (or at least do not now) fall within the scope of the announce clause. The Judicial Board issued an opinion stating that judicial candidates may criticize past decisions, and the Lawyers Board refused to discipline Wersal for the foregoing statements because, in part, it thought they did not violate the announce clause. . . .

There are yet further limitations upon the apparent plain meaning of the announce clause: In light of the constitutional concerns, the District Court construed the clause to reach only disputed issues that are likely to come before the candidate if he is elected judge. The Eighth Circuit accepted this limiting interpretation by the District Court, and in addition construed the clause to allow general discussions of case law and judicial philosophy. The Supreme Court of Minnesota adopted these interpretations as well when it ordered enforcement of the announce clause in accordance with the Eighth Circuit's opinion.

It seems to us, however, that — like the text of the announce clause itself — these limitations upon the text of the announce clause are not all that they appear to be. First, respondents acknowledged at oral argument that statements critical of past judicial decisions are *not* permissible if the candidate also states that he is against *stare decisis*. Thus, candidates must choose between stating their views critical of past decisions and stating their views in opposition to *stare decisis*. Or, to look at it more concretely, they may state their view that prior decisions were erroneous only if they do not assert that they, if elected, have any power to eliminate erroneous decisions. Second, limiting the scope of the clause to issues likely to come before a court is not much of a limitation at all. One would hardly expect the "disputed legal or political issues" raised in the course of a state judicial election to include such matters as whether the Federal Government should end the embargo of Cuba. Quite obviously, they will be those legal or political disputes that are the proper (or by past decisions have been made the improper) business of the state courts. And within that relevant category, "[t]here is almost no legal or political issue that is unlikely to come before a judge of an American court, state or federal, of general jurisdiction." Third, construing the clause to allow "general" discussions of case law and judicial philosophy turns out to be of little help in an election campaign. At oral argument, respondents gave, as an example of this exception, that a candidate is free to assert that he is a " 'strict constructionist.' " But that, like most other philosophical generalities, has little meaningful content for the electorate unless it is exemplified by application to a particular issue of construction likely to come before a court — for example, whether a particular statute runs afoul of any provision of the Constitution. Respondents conceded that the announce clause would prohibit the candidate from exemplifying his philosophy in this fashion. Without such application to real-life issues, all candidates can claim to be "strict constructionists" with equal (and unhelpful) plausibility.

In any event, it is clear that the announce clause prohibits a judicial candidate from stating his views on any specific nonfanciful legal question within the province of the court for which he is running, except in the context of discussing past decisions — and in the latter context as well, if he expresses the view that he is not bound by *stare decisis*.

Respondents contend that this still leaves plenty of topics for discussion on the campaign trail. These include a candidate's "character," "education," "work habits," and "how [he] would handle administrative duties if elected." Indeed, the Judicial Board has printed a list of preapproved questions which judicial candidates are allowed to answer. These include how the candidate feels about cameras in the courtroom, how he would go about reducing the caseload, how the costs of judicial administration can be reduced, and how he proposes to ensure that minorities and women are treated more fairly by the court system. Whether this list of preapproved subjects, and other topics not prohibited by the announce clause, adequately fulfill the First Amendment's guarantee of freedom of speech is the question to which we now turn.

III

. . .

The Court of Appeals concluded that respondents had established two interests as sufficiently compelling to justify the announce clause: preserving the impartiality of the state judiciary and preserving the appearance of the impartiality of the state judiciary. Respondents reassert these two interests before us, arguing that the first is compelling because it protects the due process rights of litigants, and that the second is compelling because it preserves public confidence in the judiciary. Respondents are rather vague, however, about what they mean by "impartiality. . . ."

A

One meaning of "impartiality" in the judicial context — and of course its root meaning — is the lack of bias for or against either *party* to the proceeding. Impartiality in this sense assures equal application of the law. That is, it guarantees a party that the judge who hears his case will apply the law to him in the same way he applies it to any other party. This is the traditional sense in which the term is used. . . .

We think it plain that the announce clause is not narrowly tailored to serve impartiality (or the appearance of impartiality) in this sense. Indeed, the clause is barely tailored to serve that interest *at all*, inasmuch as it does not restrict speech for or against particular *parties*, but rather speech for or against particular *issues*. To be sure, when a case arises that turns on a legal issue on which the judge (as a candidate) had taken a particular stand, the party taking the opposite stand is likely to lose.

But not because of any bias against that party, or favoritism toward the other party. *Any* party taking that position is just as likely to lose. The judge is applying the law (as he sees it) evenhandedly.

B

It is perhaps possible to use the term "impartiality" in the judicial context (though this is certainly not a common usage) to mean lack of preconception in favor of or against a particular *legal view*. This sort of impartiality would be concerned, not with guaranteeing litigants equal application of the law, but rather with guaranteeing them an equal chance to persuade the court on the legal points in their case. Impartiality in this sense may well be an interest served by the announce clause, but it is not a *compelling* state interest, as strict scrutiny requires. A judge's lack of predisposition regarding the relevant legal issues in a case has never been thought a necessary component of equal justice, and with good reason. For one thing, it is virtually impossible to find a judge who does not have preconceptions about the law.... Indeed, even if it were possible to select judges who did not have preconceived views on legal issues, it would hardly be desirable to do so. "Proof that a Justice's mind at the time he joined the Court was a complete *tabula rasa* in the area of constitutional adjudication would be evidence of lack of qualification, not lack of bias." The Minnesota Constitution positively forbids the selection to courts of general jurisdiction of judges who are impartial in the sense of having no views on the law. Minn. Const., Art. VI, §5 ("Judges of the supreme court, the court of appeals and the district court shall be learned in the law"). And since avoiding judicial preconceptions on legal issues is neither possible nor desirable, pretending otherwise by attempting to preserve the "appearance" of that type of impartiality can hardly be a compelling state interest either.

C

A third possible meaning of "impartiality" (again not a common one) might be described as open-mindedness. This quality in a judge demands, not that he have no preconceptions on legal issues, but that he be willing to consider views that oppose his preconceptions, and remain open to persuasion, when the issues arise in a pending case. This sort of impartiality seeks to guarantee each litigant, not an *equal* chance to win the legal points in the case, but at least *some* chance of doing so. It may well be that impartiality in this sense, and the appearance of it, are desirable in the judiciary, but we need not pursue that inquiry, since we do not believe the Minnesota Supreme Court adopted the announce clause for that purpose.

Respondents argue that the announce clause serves the interest in openmindedness, or at least in the appearance of openmindedness, because it relieves a judge from pressure to rule a certain way in order to maintain consistency with statements the judge has previously made. The problem is, however, that statements in election campaigns are such an infinitesimal portion of the public commitments to legal positions that judges (or judges-to-be) undertake, that this object of the prohibition is implausible. Before they arrive on the bench (whether by election or otherwise) judges have often committed themselves on legal issues that they must later rule upon. More common still is a judge's confronting a legal issue on which he has expressed an opinion while on the bench. Most frequently, of course, that prior expression will have occurred in ruling on an earlier case. But judges often state their views on disputed legal issues outside the context of adjudication — in classes that they conduct, and in books and speeches. Like the ABA Codes of Judicial Conduct, the Minnesota Code not only permits but encourages this. See Minn. Code of Judicial Conduct, Canon 4(B) (2002) ("A judge may write, lecture, teach, speak and participate in other extra-judicial activities concerning the law . . ."); Minn. Code of Judicial Conduct, Canon 4(B), Comment. (2002) ("To the extent that time permits, a judge is encouraged to do so . . ."). That is quite incompatible with the notion that the need for open-mindedness (or for the appearance of open-mindedness) lies behind the prohibition at issue here.

The short of the matter is this: In Minnesota, a candidate for judicial office may not say "I think it is constitutional for the legislature to prohibit same-sex marriages." He may say the very same thing, however, up until the very day before he declares himself a candidate, and may say it repeatedly (until litigation is pending) after he is elected. As a means of pursuing the objective of openmindedness that respondents now articulate, the announce clause is so woefully underinclusive as to render belief in that purpose a challenge to the credulous. . . .

IV

To sustain the announce clause, the Eighth Circuit relied heavily on the fact that a pervasive practice of prohibiting judicial candidates from discussing disputed legal and political issues developed during the last half of the 20th century. It is true that a "universal and long-established" tradition of prohibiting certain conduct creates "a strong presumption" that the prohibition is constitutional. . . . The practice of prohibiting speech by judicial candidates on disputed issues, however, is neither long nor universal.

. . .

The first code regulating judicial conduct was adopted by the ABA in 1924. It contained a provision akin to the announce clause: "A candidate for judicial position . . . should not announce in advance his conclusions of law on disputed issues to secure class support. . . ." ABA Canon of Judicial Ethics 30 (1924). The States were slow to adopt the canons, however. "By the end of World War II, the canons . . . were binding by the bar associations or supreme courts of only eleven states." Even today, although a majority of States have adopted either the announce clause or its 1990 ABA successor, adoption is not unanimous. Of the 31 States that select some or all of their appellate and general-jurisdiction judges by election, 4 have adopted no candidate-speech restriction comparable to the announce clause, and 1 prohibits only the discussion of "pending litigation." This practice, relatively new to judicial elections and still not universally adopted, does not compare well with the traditions deemed worthy of our attention in prior cases.

. . .

There is an obvious tension between the article of Minnesota's popularly approved Constitution which provides that judges shall be elected, and the Minnesota Supreme Court's announce clause which places most subjects of interest to the voters off limits. (The candidate-speech restrictions of all the other States that have them are also the product of judicial fiat.) The disparity is perhaps unsurprising, since the ABA, which originated the announce clause, has long been an opponent of judicial elections. That opposition may be well taken (it certainly had the support of the Founders of the Federal Government), but the First Amendment does not permit it to achieve its goal by leaving the principle of elections in place while preventing candidates from discussing what the elections are about. "[T]he greater power to dispense with elections altogether does not include the lesser power to conduct elections under conditions of state-imposed voter ignorance. If the State chooses to tap the energy and the legitimizing power of the democratic process, it must accord the participants in that process . . . the First Amendment rights that attach to their roles."

The Minnesota Supreme Court's canon of judicial conduct prohibiting candidates for judicial election from announcing their views on disputed legal and political issues violates the First Amendment. Accordingly, we reverse the grant of summary judgment to respondents and remand the case for proceedings consistent with this opinion.

[Justice O'Connor wrote a concurring opinion to emphasize the following point: "Minnesota has chosen to select its judges through contested popular elections instead of through an appointment system or a combined appointment and retention election system along the lines of the Missouri Plan. In doing so the State has voluntarily taken on the risks to judicial bias described above. As a result, the State's claim that it needs to significantly restrict judges' speech in order to protect judicial impartiality is particularly troubling. If the State has a problem with judicial impartiality, it is largely one the State brought upon itself by continuing the practice of popularly electing judges."]

[In his dissenting opinion, joined by three other justices, Justice Stevens reasoned as follows: "By recognizing a conflict between the demands of electoral politics and the distinct characteristics of the judiciary, we do not have to put States to an all or nothing choice of abandoning judicial elections or having elections in which anything goes. As a practical matter, we cannot know for sure whether an elected judge's decisions are based on his interpretation of the law or political expediency. . . . But we do know that a judicial candidate, who announces his views in the context of a campaign, is effectively telling the electorate: 'Vote for me because I believe X, and I will judge cases accordingly.' Once elected, he may feel free to disregard his campaign statements, but that does not change the fact that the judge announced his position on an issue likely to come before him *as a reason to vote for him.* Minnesota has a compelling interest in sanctioning such statements."]

[In her dissenting opinion, Justice Ginsburg emphasized the interrelationship between the "pledges and promises" clause and the "announce" clause. "Uncoupled

from the Announce Clause, the ban on pledges or promises is easily circumvented. By prefacing a campaign commitment with the caveat, 'although I cannot promise anything,' or by simply avoiding the language of promises or pledges altogether, a candidate could declare with impunity how she would decide specific issues. . . . By targeting statements that do not technically constitute pledges or promises but nevertheless 'publicly mak[e] known how [the candidate] would decide' legal issues, the Announce Clause prevents this end run around the letter and spirit of its companion provision. No less than the pledges or promises clause itself, the Announce Clause is an indispensable part of Minnesota's effort to maintain the health of its judiciary, and is therefore constitutional for the same reasons."]

Post-Case Follow-Up

In *White*, the Court held that Minnesota's "announce" clause (which mirrored the ABA Model Code's language) was unconstitutional. The Court found that the ban on judicial candidates announcing their views on disputed legal or political issues was not narrowly tailored to serve the state's stated goal of ensuring the judiciary's impartiality.

The *White* decision had a real impact on judicial elections. At a minimum, it enabled judicial candidates to speak more freely about contested political issues. Some have argued that the *White* decision marked a significant shift in the tone and intensity of judicial elections since it allows judicial candidates to engage in aggressive campaigning on issues, though the research on *White*'s impact is mixed.[65]

Following *White*, the drafters of the Model Code of Judicial Conduct removed the "announce" clause, but retained the ban on pledges and promises. Thus, a judicial candidate shall not "in connection with cases, controversies, or issues that are likely to come before the court, make pledges, promises, or commitments that are inconsistent with the impartial performance of the adjudicative duties of judicial office."[66] As a result, it is permissible for a judicial candidate to announce that he disagrees with *Roe v. Wade* and favors laws restricting a woman's ability to get an abortion, but it is unlawful for a candidate to state that if he is elected, he promises to uphold any restriction on abortions. The comments to Rule 4.1 state that whether a statement is a "pledge, promise, or commitment is not dependent upon, or limited to, the use of any specific words or phrases; instead, the totality of the statement must be examined to determine if a reasonable person would believe that the candidate for judicial office has specifically undertaken to reach a particular result."

---

65. *See* David M. O'Brien, *State Court Elections and Judicial Independence*, 31 J.L. & Pol. 417 (2016).
66. Model Code r. 4.1(a)(13).

Republican Party of Minnesota v. White: Real Life Applications

1. The *White* majority did not address the constitutionality of the "pledges and promises" clause of the Minnesota rules (which is substantially similar to Rule 4.1 of the current Model Code). What are the arguments for and against the constitutionality of this provision?
2. Willie Singletary was a candidate for traffic court judge in Philadelphia. While campaigning for the primary election, he spoke to a gathering of a motorcycle club. During the meeting, he asked attendees to donate to his campaign and stated, "You're going to need me in traffic court, am I right about that? . . . Now you all want me to get there, you're all going to want my hook-up, right?" Is Judge Singletary subject to discipline?
3. As noted earlier, Model Rule 4.1 prohibits judges from "act[ing] as a leader in, or hold[ing] an office in, a political organization," "mak[ing] speeches on behalf of a political organization," "mak[ing] a contribution to a political organization or a candidate," and "publicly endors[ing] . . . a candidate for any public office." Are these restrictions on political activity a good idea? Are they constitutional?
4. Some states hold nonpartisan elections. Are these restrictions a good idea? Are they constitutional?
5. Other states pose restrictions on judicial candidates' ability to associate themselves with political parties. Are these restrictions a good idea? Are they constitutional?
   a. Kentucky used to prohibit judicial candidates from disclosing their party affiliation "in any form of advertising, or when speaking to a gathering" except in answer to a question by a voter one on one or in "very small private informal" settings.
   b. Ohio permits judicial candidates to run in partisan primaries but does not allow them to list their party affiliation on the general election ballot.[67]

Chapter Summary

- The guiding principles behind the Model Code of Judicial Conduct are ensuring that judges act with independence, integrity, and impartiality, and promoting the appearance of the same.
- On the bench, judges must perform their duties impartially, competently, and diligently. For example, judges must "uphold and apply the law" and avoid bias,

67. Ohio Rev. Code Ann. §3505.04 (LexisNexis 2013 & Supp. 2016).

prejudice, and other external influences in their decision making. Judges must also limit their public statements about pending cases.

- Off the bench, judges must minimize activities that conflict with their judicial obligations. For example, judges may not use the prestige of their office to advance their own or others' interests or hold membership in discriminatory organizations.
- Judges should be disqualified "in any proceeding in which the judge's impartiality might reasonably be questioned." This standard is vague and can be difficult to apply, particularly with respect to judges' social relationships with lawyers and parties who appear before the judge. Justice Scalia declined to recuse himself after he went duck hunting with Vice President Cheney while a case in which Cheney was a named defendant was pending before the Supreme Court.
- The Model Code and the states impose a wide variety of restrictions on political activity by judges and judicial candidates. In *White*, the Supreme Court held that Minnesota's "announce" clause (which mirrored the ABA Model Code's language) was unconstitutional. The Court did not address the "pledges and promises" clause or a host of other restrictions on political activity by judicial candidates.

Applying the Rules

1. In 1978, Judge George C. Paine II, Chief Judge of the United States Bankruptcy Court for the Middle District of Tennessee, became a member of the Belle Meade Country Club, which had no female or African-American members. In 1990, Judge Paine wrote a strong letter to the Club's board of directors stating that he thought it "long overdue that the Club have Jewish and black associate and resident members" and that it was "patently preposterous that there are not persons in these racial and religious groups who would not be excellent participating members of the Club." Despite Judge Paine's letter, the club continued to lack female and minority members. Is Judge Paine subject to discipline?

2. James Singleton is a candidate for trial court judge in a state election. To support his campaign, he creates a Facebook page. His college roommate and best friend Michael Schwartz is running for Congress and has set up a Facebook page to support his congressional campaign. Can James "like" Michael's page?

3. After President George W. Bush nominated Harriet Miers to the U.S. Supreme Court, Texas Supreme Court Justice Nathan Hecht, a longtime friend, gave over 100 interviews about her:

   - He shared information about Miers's background and experience.
   - He described Miers's views on religion and abortion.
   - He shared his positive view of her nomination, describing the appointment as "great," "solid," and "strong."

- He describing her in various interviews as being "remarkable," "charming," "gracious," "solid," "strong," "sterling," and "stellar."
- He said that after the American public had a chance to review her record, they were "going to herald this nomination as a good one" and that her detractors were "going to be happy as clams" after they learned more about her.
- He predicted that during the confirmation process, Senators would be "convinced that this is the right person for the job." . . .
- He described their close personal relationship acknowledging his "admiration" for her.

Is Justice Hecht subject to discipline for these comments?

4. Attorney Sandra Perlman represented defendant Lawrence Braynen in a criminal case pending before Judge Cheryl Aleman. Perlman was one of 34 members serving on the steering committee for a judicial candidate that opposed Judge Aleman in the recent election. Perlman moved to recuse Judge Aleman. Should Judge Aleman grant the motion?

Professional Responsibility in Practice

1. The Code of Judicial Conduct varies greatly from state to state. Look up your state's Code and compare it to the Model Code.

2. The 1972 Code of Judicial Conduct effectively prohibited broadcast media in the courtroom, but since 1982, the Code has not contained such a prohibition, and it is up to each court to consider the issue. In Chandler v. Florida, 449 U.S. 560 (1981), the Supreme Court held that there was no constitutional prohibition on a state permitting radio, television, or photographic coverage of a criminal trial. Some courts now permit video cameras in the courtroom while others (including the U.S. Supreme Court) do not. Should courts permit live coverage of court proceedings?

3. Research how judges are selected in your state. How does it compare to other states? What do you think are the pros and cons of your state's process?

4. Retired Justice Sandra Day O'Connor has long championed changes to how states select judges. Evaluate the pros and cons of Justice O'Connor's plan: http://iaals.du.edu/sites/default/files/documents/publications/oconnor_plan.pdf.

Glossary

access-to-justice gap The gap between the legal needs of low- and moderate-income Americans and the resources available to meet those needs. (Ch. Eleven)

accounting Lawyer's fiduciary duty to provide a full accounting of any funds or property, if a client or a third person claiming an interest in property or funds held by the attorney makes a request. (Ch. Three)

advance conflict waivers Document that asks prospective clients to waive their right to file a disqualification motion against the firm should it represent a party in the same or substantially related matter against the prospective clients. (Ch. Six)

advertising Marketing that is directed to a broad audience. (Ch. Ten)

advocate-witness rule An attorney cannot maintain dual roles as advocate and witness in the same matter before the same tribunal. (Chs. Six, Seven)

agency relationship Relationship between parties whereby one agrees to act on behalf of another. (Ch. Five)

aggravating factors After the establishment of misconduct, these factors establish the severity of sanctions needed. (Ch. Two)

alternative business structures Proposed structures that allow for nonlawyer ownership and/or management of a business or firm. Also known as alternative legal practice structures. (Chs. Nine, Eleven)

alternative discipline program (ADP) Occurs before disciplinary counsel files formal charges, and depending on the jurisdiction, might include arbitration, mediation, law office management assistance, lawyer assistance programs, psychological counseling and continuing legal education. (Ch. Two)

attorney-client privilege Client's privilege to refuse disclosure of confidential communications between the client and the attorney. (Ch. Five)

autonomous self-interest Ideology that views clients as individualistic and atomistic entities whose goal is to pursue and maximize their self-interest without regard to others. (Ch. One)

candor to the tribunal The attorney's obligation to be truthful to the court. (Ch. Seven)

churning Unnecessarily overstaffing a case or performing duplicative or unnecessary work to drive up a bill. A form of fraudulent billing. (Ch. Three)

Civil Gideon A movement to recognize an individual's right to counsel in civil cases. (Ch. Eleven)

civility Obligation to act with courtesy and respect. (Ch. Seven)

clawback To get something back. (Ch. Five)

common interest doctrine When multiple parties and multiple lawyers share or pool confidential information and coordinate strategies in a matter of common legal interest. (Ch. Five)

communication The method of conveying information so that the attorney accurately ascertains the client's objectives, and the client thereafter is kept apprised of what is going on in the matter or transaction. (Ch. Four)

competence For attorneys, consists of four components: legal knowledge, skill, thoroughness, and preparation. (Ch. Four)

concurrent client Another term for current client. (Ch. Six)

confidential material Any information relating to the representation of a client. (Ch. Five)

confidentiality The state of keeping or being kept secret or private. (Ch. Five)

confidentiality exceptions Exceptions that allow a lawyer to reveal confidential information to the extent the lawyer reasonably believes necessary for particular purposes. (Ch. Five)

conflict of interest Exists when there is a substantial risk that the lawyer's ability to perform her fiduciary duties is affected by the lawyer's own competing interests or the lawyer's duties to others. (Ch. Six)

conflict of interest waiver Legal document stating that a conflict of interest may be present in a situation, all parties are aware, and steps are being taken to keep things fair and reasonable. (Ch. Six)

conflict shopping When someone arranges to have initial consultations with several attorneys with the purpose of disclosing information and subsequently arguing that the opposing side is conflicted out from using any of those attorneys. (Ch. Three)

continuing legal education Professional education for attorneys that takes place after their initial admission to the bar. (Ch. Two)

control group test One possible test used to determine whether the attorney-client privilege protects communications made by corporate employees to the company's lawyer. (*See* Model Rule 4.2) (Chs. Five, Seven)

covenants not to compete An agreement in which one party agrees not to work for the other party's direct competition in a specified area for a certain amount of time. (Ch. Nine)

crime-fraud exception Provides that a client's confidential communications with counsel are not protected by the attorney-client privilege from compelled disclosure when made for the purpose of furthering a crime or fraud. (Ch. Five)

deficient performance Defined by *Strickland* as "unreasonableness" under prevailing professional norms. Reviewing courts engage in a "strong presumption that counsel's conduct falls within the wide range of reasonable professional assistance." (Ch. Four)

delivery Lawyer's fiduciary duty to promptly deliver any funds or property to the client (or third person with the ownership interest.) (Ch. Three)

diligence Requires that the lawyer pursue a client's case "despite opposition, obstruction or personal inconvenience to the lawyer, and take whatever lawful and ethical measures are required to vindicate a client's cause or endeavor." (*See* Model Rule 1.1, Comment 1) (Ch. Four)

disbarment A permanent separation from the bar, with no chance of reinstatement in some jurisdictions. (Ch. Two)

discovery abuse The misuse of the discovery process by making unnecessary requests for information, by responding to opponent's discovery requests in an improper manner, or by conducting discovery for an improper purpose. (Ch. Seven)

double bill Charging for the same hour of work more than once. (Ch. Three)

entity theory of organizational representation When a lawyer represents an organization, the client is the organization itself and not any of the organization's individual constituents (such as officers, directors, employees or shareholders). (Ch. Three)

entity warning Requirement under Model Rule 1.13(f) that an organization's attorney should clarify her role and "explain the identity of the client" to an organization's constituents "when the lawyer knows or reasonably should know that the organization's interests are adverse to those of the constituents with whom the lawyer is dealing." (Ch. Three)

ex parte communications Any communication between a judge or juror and a party to a legal proceeding or his counsel outside of the presence of the opposing party or the opposing party's attorney. (Ch. Seven)

ex parte proceedings One-sided proceedings, where opposing counsel is not present. (Ch. Seven)

exculpatory evidence Evidence that is favorable to the defendant in a criminal case in that it tends to negate guilt. (Ch. Eight)

extrajudicial duties Activities of a judge off of the bench. Should be conducted in such a manner that minimizes the risk of conflict with their judicial obligations. (Ch. Twelve)

fiduciary A relationship of trust that creates obligations of loyalty, care, and secrecy on the part of the lawyer. (Ch. Five)

frivolous Groundless. In the context of litigation, whether a pleading is frivolous will be assessed from an objective standard of what a reasonable attorney would have known in the actor's situation, rather than a subjective standard of malice or motive to harass. (Ch. Seven)

future harms Potential harms. In the context of professional responsibility, most states also contain exceptions to their confidentiality rules for disclosures that are necessary to prevent these. (Ch. Five)

gag order Restriction on media contact that is imposed by the court. (Ch. Seven)

good character and fitness Requirement for admission to the bar. Concerned with the present ability and disposition of the applicant to practice competently and honestly. (Ch. Two)

implied attorney-client relationship When an attorney-client relationship is created without an express agreement. (Ch. Three)

impliedly authorized Authorization for a lawyer to do what is reasonably necessary in order to effectively perform his explicit duties. (Ch. Five)

imputation doctrine Where one lawyer is disqualified because of a conflict of interest due to his having confidential information, then all firm members must be vicariously disqualified to safeguard the confidential information from misuse. (Ch. Six)

***in camera* review** A legal proceeding where a judge privately examines documents or a witness in chambers. (Ch. Five)

inadvertent disclosure Occurs when the disclosing person took precautions reasonable in the circumstances to guard against a disclosure but the communication or information was still accidently revealed. (Ch. Five)

ineffective assistance of counsel Denial of an accused's Sixth Amendment right to counsel. The two-pronged approach to determine ineffective assistance is defined by *Strickland v. Washington*, requiring a defendant to prove (1) deficient performance of counsel and (2) prejudice. (Ch. Four)

informed consent Express agreement after the client has been advised about the risks and available alternatives. (Ch. Five)

interest on lawyer trust accounts (IOLTA) Interest received on client funds held in trust accounts in situations when it is impractical for the attorney to establish a separate account for each client. (Ch. Eleven)

integrated state bar association State bar association where the high court requires bar membership to practice law. (Ch. Two)

joint client A situation where multiple clients share a lawyer. (Ch. Five)

joint representation When a lawyer represents more than one client in the same matter. (Ch. Six)

joint-clients exception Provides that a communication to a lawyer that is relevant to a matter of common interest between joint clients is not privileged when one joint client proceeds against another joint client. (Ch. Five)

judicial duties Duties of judicial office that must be performed impartially, competently, and diligently. (Ch. Twelve)

last link doctrine Holding of courts that a client's identity is protected by the attorney-client privilege when it connects the client to the offense. (Ch. Five)

lawyer independence Requirement of Model Rule 2.1. Multiple facets include independence from government control, need for independent professional judgment, independence from popular opinion and prejudice, and independence from clients. (Ch. Nine)

lawyer's trilemma Situation where lawyer considers whether to put his client on the witness stand. A lawyer must simultaneously act diligently in gathering as much information as will enable him to counsel the client, guard the client's secrets, and be candid to the court. (Ch. Eight)

legal malpractice Negligence, breach of fiduciary duty, or breach of contract by an attorney that causes harm to his or her client. To establish legal malpractice the following must be shown: (1) the existence of an attorney-client relationship that establishes a duty on the part of the attorney, (2) a negligent act or omission constituting a breach of that duty, (3) the proximate cause (or legal cause) of the injury, and (4) the actual damages suffered by the plaintiff. (Ch. Two)

Legal Services Corporation (LSC) A non-profit organization established by Congress in 1974, which is the single largest funder of civil legal aid for low-income Americans. (Ch. Eleven)

limited liability companies (LLC) Form of business enterprise, recognized in all states, offering the pass-through tax status of a partnership and the limited liability of a corporation. (Ch. Two)

limited liability partnership (LLP) Form of partnership in which a partner has no personal liability for the misconduct of another partner (and, in 49 jurisdictions, no personal liability for contractual obligations of the partnership). (Ch. Two)

Limited License Legal Technicians (LLLTs) Independent legal paraprofessionals licensed to give legal advice in Washington State. (Ch. Eleven)

material Important; affecting the merits of a case. (Ch. Seven)

McDade Amendment Federal law that makes it clear that Justice Department prosecutors must abide by the attorney discipline rules in the states in which they practice. (Ch. Eight)

minister of justice Designation of the special role of a prosecutor, as described in Model Rule 3.8. (Ch. Eight)

mitigating factors After the establishment of misconduct, these factors help determine whether a lesser sanction is appropriate. (Ch. Two)

mixed communications Mix of legal and non-legal advice, such as business, financial, or personal advice. (Ch. Five)

moral dialogue Discussion with the client to determine the client's actual desires and moral ends. (Ch. One)

multidisciplinary practices (MDPs) Businesses that offer "bundled services" that include the practice of law in addition to other professional services. Under Model Rule 5.4, lawyers are prohibited from forming MDPs with nonlawyer professionals offering related services. (Ch. Nine)

no contact rule Prohibits an attorney from communicating with a person represented by counsel on the subject of that representation without permission of the client's attorney. (*See* Model Rule 4.2) (Ch. Seven)

non-integrated state bar association State bar association where bar membership is voluntary. (Ch. Two)

notification Lawyer's fiduciary duty to promptly notify a client (or third party with an ownership interest) when funds or other property in which the client has an interest are received. (Ch. Three)

obstruction Any attempt to hinder or interfere with the administration of justice. (Chs. Seven, Eight)

opinion work product Work product that includes the lawyer's mental impressions, opinions, and strategy in litigation, also referred to as the "core" work-product. The inquiring party must show extraordinary circumstances to justify disclosure. (Ch. Five)

ordinary work product Work product that is the result of gathering basic facts or conducting interviews with witnesses. This is generally immune from discovery except upon establishment of a substantial need for the material and the inability to obtain the substantial equivalent of the material without substantial hardship. (Ch. Five)

perjury The offense of willfully telling an untruth in a court after having taken an oath or affirmation. (Ch. Eight)

permissive disclosures The "exceptions" to client confidences in Rule 1.6(b) 1-7 where attorneys may exercise discretion to reveal a confidence in one of those enumerated instances. (Ch. Seven)

personal-interest conflict Where the lawyer's personal interests interfere with the lawyer's fiduciary duties to be loyal and competent, and to preserve client confidences. (Ch. Six)

political activity by judicial candidates Fundraising, campaigning, and other political activity by judges and candidates who seek judicial office. (Ch. Twelve)

post-indictment contact Pertains to a prosecutor's communication with a represented party after arraignment. (Ch. Eight)

predominant effects Standard that the jurisdiction where the predominant effect of the conduct will occur determines which jurisdiction's rule applies to conduct. (Ch. Two)

prejudice The second prong of the test for showing ineffective assistance of counsel, as defined by *Strickland*, that "the defendant must show that there is a reasonable probability that, but for counsel's unprofessional errors, the result of the proceeding would have been different." (Ch. Four)

privilege holder The one with the ability to assert a privilege. The client is the holder of the attorney-client privilege and ultimately decides whether to assert or waive it. (Ch. Five)

pro bono Legal work performed voluntarily and without payment. (Ch. Eleven)

pro hac vice admission Practice where a lawyer who has not been admitted to practice in a certain jurisdiction is allowed to participate in a case in that jurisdiction. (Ch. Two)

probable cause Sufficient reason based upon known facts to believe a crime has been committed. (Ch. Eight)

professional liability insurance Insures the firm or individual lawyers for errors and omissions or negligent mistakes. Also called "errors and omissions" ("E & O") policies. (Ch. Two)

prospective clients Rule 1.18 defines prospective clients as "a person who consults with a lawyer about the possibility of forming a client-lawyer relationship." Lawyers owe specific limited duties to prospective clients. (Chs Three, Five)

real evidence Physical evidence. (Ch. Eight)

reasonable belief What an ordinary person of average intelligence and sound mind would believe. (Ch. Five)

reciprocal discipline Practice of courts of commonly imposing the same disciplinary sanction both in terms of length of time and severity as to that which was issued by another jurisdiction. A lawyer disciplined for misconduct in one state is subject to reciprocal discipline in every other jurisdiction in which he or she is admitted to practice. (Ch. Two)

reciprocal referral agreement Agreement whereby a lawyer and nonlawyer professional refer clients to each other—without paying each other for such referrals. (Ch. Nine)

record keeping Requirement that attorneys keep complete records of trust account funds and other property. (Ch. Three)

relational self-interest Ideology that understands clients as attempting to pursue and maximize their self-interest in relation to others. (Ch. One)

role morality Occurs when a lawyer acts as an agent for the client's purposes. (Ch. One)

sanctions Penalties or other means of enforcement used to provide incentives for obedience. For lawyers, can include disbarment, suspension, public reprimand, private reprimand, and financial restitution. (Ch. Two)

screening Segregating lawyers or administrative staff who may have a conflict of interest in regards to current clients of the law firm or former clients of the lawyer or administrative staff. (Ch. Six)

segregation Requirement that client money must be placed in a client trust account, separate from lawyer's funds. The lawyer is absolutely forbidden from commingling her own funds with those of the client. (Ch. Three)

self-defense exception The lawyer is permitted to disclose only privileged client communications necessary to defend herself against the client's claims of misconduct. (Ch. Five)

solicitation Targeted marketing communication initiated by a lawyer that is directed to a specific person. (Ch. Ten)

spoliation of evidence Intentional or reckless destruction of, or tampering with, evidence that is relevant to a legal proceeding. (Ch. Seven)

subject matter waiver A party may seek all portions of a single communication and related privileged communications to prevent the opposing party from unfairly distorting the context or meaning of its partial disclosure. (Ch. Five)

substantial need-undue hardship When demonstrated, provides limited circumstances when an opposing party may discover or compel disclosure of work product. (Ch. Five)

tripartite relationship The relationship between the insured, the insurer, and the attorney hired by the insurer. (Ch. Three)

unauthorized practice of law Engaging in the practice of law by persons or entities not authorized to practice law. (Ch. Nine)

withdraw To cease representing a client. (Ch. Five)

woodshedding Rehearsing a witness in advance of their testimony by telling them exactly how to answer questions. (Ch. Seven)

work-product immunity A rule that an opposing party generally may not discover or compel disclosure of written or oral materials prepared by or for an attorney in the course of litigation. (Ch. Five)

Table of Cases

Principal Cases Indicated by Italics

Table of Rules

FEDERAL RULES OF CIVIL PROCEDURE

FEDERAL RULES OF CRIMINAL PROCEDURE

FEDERAL RULES OF EVIDENCE

RESTATEMENT THIRD OF THE LAW GOVERNING LAWYERS

FEDERAL STATUTES AND ADMINISTRATIVE REGULATIONS

Section **Page(s)**

Index

Y

Z